More Java 17

An In-Depth Exploration of the Java Language and Its Features

Third Edition

Kishori Sharan

Peter Späth

Apress®

More Java 17: An In-Depth Exploration of the Java Language and Its Features

Kishori Sharan
Montgomery, AL, USA

Peter Späth
Leipzig, Sachsen, Germany

ISBN-13 (pbk): 978-1-4842-7134-6
https://doi.org/10.1007/978-1-4842-7135-3

ISBN-13 (electronic): 978-1-4842-7135-3

Managing Director, Apress Media LLC: Welmoed Spahr
Acquisitions Editor: Steve Anglin
Development Editor: Matthew Moodie
Coordinating Editor: Mark Powers

Cover designed by eStudioCalamar

Cover image by Ben Kolde on Unsplash (www.unsplash.com)

Distributed to the book trade worldwide by Apress Media, LLC, 1 New York Plaza, New York, NY 10004, U.S.A. Phone 1-800-SPRINGER, fax (201) 348-4505, e-mail orders-ny@springer-sbm.com, or visit www.springeronline.com. Apress Media, LLC is a California LLC and the sole member (owner) is Springer Science + Business Media Finance Inc (SSBM Finance Inc). SSBM Finance Inc is a **Delaware** corporation.

For information on translations, please e-mail booktranslations@springernature.com; for reprint, paperback, or audio rights, please e-mail bookpermissions@springernature.com.

Apress titles may be purchased in bulk for academic, corporate, or promotional use. eBook versions and licenses are also available for most titles. For more information, reference our Print and eBook Bulk Sales web page at http://www.apress.com/bulk-sales.

Any source code or other supplementary material referenced by the author in this book is available to readers on GitHub via the book's product page, located at www.apress.com/9781484271346. For more detailed information, please visit http://www.apress.com/source-code.

Printed on acid-free paper

To Paulina

Table of Contents

About the Authors

Kishori Sharan works as a senior software engineer lead at IndraSoft, Inc. He earned a master of science degree in computer information systems from Troy University, Alabama. He is a Sun-certified Java 2 programmer and has over 20 years of experience in developing enterprise applications and providing training to professional developers using the Java platform.

Peter Späth graduated in 2002 as a physicist and soon afterward became an IT consultant, mainly for Java-related projects. In 2016, he decided to concentrate on writing books on various aspects, but with the main focus set on software development. With two books about graphics and sound processing, three books for Android app development, and several books about Java and Jakarta EE development, the author continues his effort in writing software development–related literature.

About the Technical Reviewers

Massimo Nardone has more than 25 years of experience in security, web/mobile development, cloud, and IT architecture. His true IT passions are security and Android. He has been programming and teaching how to program with Android, Perl, PHP, Java, VB, Python, C/C++, and MySQL for more than 20 years. He holds a master of science degree in computing science from the University of Salerno, Italy.

He has worked as a CISO, CSO, security executive, IoT executive, project manager, software engineer, research engineer, chief security architect, PCI/SCADA auditor, and senior lead IT security/cloud/SCADA architect for many years. His technical skills include security, Android, cloud, Java, MySQL, Drupal, Cobol, Perl, web and mobile development, MongoDB, D3, Joomla, Couchbase, C/C++, WebGL, Python, Pro Rails, Django CMS, Jekyll, Scratch, and more.

He worked as a visiting lecturer and supervisor for exercises at the Networking Laboratory of the Helsinki University of Technology (Aalto University). He holds four international patents (PKI, SIP, SAML, and Proxy areas). He is currently working for Cognizant as head of cyber security and CISO to help both internally and externally with clients in areas of information and cyber security, like strategy, planning, processes, policies, procedures, governance, awareness, and so forth. In June 2017, he became a permanent member of the ISACA Finland Board.

Massimo has reviewed more than 45 IT books for different publishing companies and is the co-author of *Pro Spring Security: Securing Spring Framework 5 and Boot 2-based Java Applications* (Apress, 2019), *Beginning EJB in Java EE 8* (Apress, 2018), *Pro JPA 2 in Java EE 8* (Apress, 2018), and *Pro Android Games* (Apress, 2015).

Satej Kumar Sahu works in the role of Senior Enterprise Architect at Honeywell. He is passionate about technology, people, and nature. He believes through technology and conscientious decision making, each of us has the power to make this world a better place. In his free time, he can be found reading books, playing basketball, and having fun with friends and family.

Introduction

How This Book Came About

My first encounter with the Java programming language was during a one-week Java training session in 1997. I did not get a chance to use Java in a project until 1999. I read two Java books and took a Java 2 programmer certification examination. I did very well on the test, scoring 95%. The three questions that I missed on the test made me realize that the books that I had read did not adequately cover details of all the topics. I made up my mind to write a book on the Java programming language. So I formulated a plan to cover most of the topics that a Java developer needs to use Java effectively in a project, as well as to become certified. I initially planned to cover all essential topics in Java in 700–800 pages.

As I progressed, I realized that a book covering most of the Java topics in detail could not be written in 700–800 pages. One chapter alone that covered data types, operators, and statements spanned 90 pages. I was then faced with the question, "Should I shorten the content of the book or include all the details that I think a Java developer needs?" I opted for including all the details in the book, rather than shortening its content to maintain the original number of pages. It has never been my intent to make lots of money from this book. I was never in a hurry to finish this book because that rush could have compromised the quality and coverage. In short, I wrote this book to help the Java community understand and use the Java programming language effectively, without having to read many books on the same subject. I wrote this book with the plan that it would be a comprehensive one-stop reference for everyone who wants to learn and grasp the intricacies of the Java programming language.

One of my high-school teachers used to tell us that if one wanted to understand a building, one must first understand the bricks, steel, and mortar that make up the building. The same logic applies to most of the things that we want to understand in our lives. It certainly applies to an understanding of the Java programming language. If you want to master the Java programming language, you must start by understanding its basic building blocks. I have used this approach throughout this book, endeavoring to build upon each topic by describing the basics first. In the book, you will rarely find a topic described without first learning about its background. Wherever possible, I tried to correlate the programming practices with activities in daily life. Most of the books about the Java programming language available on the market either do not include any pictures at all or have only a few. I believe in the adage "A picture is worth a thousand words." To a reader, a picture makes a topic easier to understand and remember. I have included plenty of illustrations in the book to aid readers in understanding and visualizing the concepts. Developers who have little or no programming experience have difficulty in putting things together to make it a complete program. Keeping them in mind, I have included over 390 complete Java programs that are ready to be compiled and run.

I spent countless hours doing research when writing this book. My main sources were the Java Language Specification, whitepapers and articles on Java topics, and Java Specification Requests (JSRs). I also spent quite a bit of time reading the Java source code to learn more about some of the Java topics. Sometimes, it took a few months of researching a topic before I could write the first sentence on it. Finally, it was always fun to play with Java programs, sometimes for hours, to add them to the book.

Introduction to the Second Edition

I am pleased to present the second edition of the *Java Language Features* book. It is the second book in the three-volume "Beginning Java 9" series. It was not possible to include all JDK9 changes in one volume. I have included JDK9-specific changes at appropriate places in the three volumes, including this one. If you are interested in learning only JDK9-specific topics, I suggest you read my *Java 9 Revealed* book (ISBN 9781484225912). There are several changes in this edition, as follows:

- I added the following five chapters to this edition: Implementing Services, The Module API, Breaking Module Encapsulation, Reactive Streams, and Stack Walking.

- Implementing services in Java is not new to JDK9. I felt this book was missing a chapter on this topic. A chapter covers in detail how to define services and service interfaces and how to implement service interfaces using JDK9-specific and pre-JDK9 constructs. This chapter shows you how to use them and provides statements in a module declaration.

- Another chapter covers the Module API in detail, which gives you programmatic access to modules. This chapter also touches on some of the advanced topics, such as module layers. The first volume of this series covered basics on modules, such as how to declare modules and module dependence.

- The following chapter covers how to break module encapsulation using command-line options. When you migrate to JDK9, there will be cases requiring you to read the module's internal APIs or export non-exported packages. You can achieve these tasks using command-line options covered in this chapter.

- Reactive Streams is an initiative for providing a standard for asynchronous stream processing with non-blocking backpressure. It is aimed at solving the problems processing a stream of items, including how to pass a stream of items from a publisher to a subscriber without requiring the publisher to block or the subscriber to have an unbounded buffer. One more chapter covers the Reactive Streams API, which was added in JDK9.

- A new chapter covers the Stack-Walking API, which was added in JDK9. This API lets you inspect the stack frames of threads and get the class reference of the caller class of a method. Inspecting a thread's stack and getting the caller's class name were possible before JDK9. The new Stack-Walking API lets you achieve this easily and efficiently.

- I received several emails from the readers about the fact that the books in this series do not include questions and exercises, which are needed mainly for students and beginners. Students use this series in their Java classes, and many beginners use it to learn Java. Due to this popular demand, I spent over 60 hours preparing questions and exercises at the end of each chapter. My friend Preethi offered her help and provided the solutions.

Apart from these additions, I updated all the chapters that were part of the first edition. I edited the contents to make them flow better, changed or added new examples, and updated the contents to include JDK9-specific features.

It is my sincere hope that this edition will help you learn Java better.

Introduction to the Third Edition

The third edition is the second author Peter Späth's work. Pleasantly taking over much of Kishori Sharan's efforts, the original text was substantially shortened by omitting a couple of chapters, and instead adding API-related topics from the book *Java APIs, Extensions and Libraries*, again from Kishori Sharan. In addition, all topics covered were hovered to Java 17, in order to maximize the benefit for the reader facing contemporary Java projects and wishing to use the new features included with the JRE 17.

Caution   Oracle changed the licensing with JDK8. You must enter a paid program if you plan to use Oracle's JRE or JDK for commercial projects. If you want to avoid this, consider using OpenJDK.

Structure of the Book

This book contains 14 chapters. The first seven chapters contain language-level topics of Java such as annotations, reflection, generics, lambda expressions, streams, etc. The chapters introduce Java topics in increasing order of complexity. The subsequent six chapters introduce some of the more important Java APIs and modules, like network programming, remote method invocation, scripting, and more. The last chapter, "Miscellanea," gives the rationale for chapters omitted in this edition compared to the previous one.

In the appendix, solution hints to the exercises are provided.

Audience

This book is designed to be useful to anyone who wants to learn the Java programming language. If you are a beginner, with little or no programming background in Java, you are advised to read one of the beginning-level Java books from Apress, and also the online Java documentation including the Java tutorial will help. This book contains topics of various degrees of complexity. As a beginner, if you find yourself overwhelmed while reading a section in a chapter, you can skip to the next section or the next chapter and revisit it later when you gain more experience.

If you are a Java developer with an intermediate or advanced level of experience, you can jump to a chapter or to a section in a chapter directly. If a section covers an unfamiliar topic, you need to visit that topic before continuing the current one.

If you are reading this book to get a certification in the Java programming language, you need to read almost all of the chapters, paying attention to all of the detailed descriptions and rules. Most of the certification programs test your fundamental knowledge of the language, not the advanced knowledge. You need to read only those topics that are part of your certification test. Compiling and running the Java programs included with the book will help you prepare for your certification.

If you are a student who is attending a class on the Java programming language, you should read the chapters of this book selectively. Some topics, such as lambda expressions, collections, and streams, are used extensively in developing Java applications, whereas other topics are infrequently used. You need to read only those chapters that are covered in your class syllabus. I am sure that you, as a Java student, do not need to read the entire book page by page.

How to Use This Book

This book is the beginning, not the end, of learning the Java programming language. If you are reading this book, it means you are heading in the right direction to learn the Java programming language, which will enable you to excel in your academic and professional career. However, there is always a higher goal for you to achieve, and you must constantly work hard to achieve it. The following quotations from some great thinkers may help you understand the importance of working hard and constantly looking for knowledge with both your eyes and mind open.

> *The learning and knowledge that we have, is, at the most, but little compared with that of which we are ignorant.*
>
> —Plato

> *True knowledge exists in knowing that you know nothing. And in knowing that you know nothing, that makes you the smartest of all.*
>
> —Socrates

Readers are advised to use the API documentation for the Java programming language as much as possible while reading this book. The Java API documentation includes a complete list of everything available in the Java class library. You can download (or view) the Java API documentation from the official website of Oracle Corporation at www.oracle.com.

While you read this book, you need to practice writing Java programs. You can also practice by tweaking the programs provided in the book. It does not help much in your learning process if you just read this book and do not practice writing your own programs. Remember that "practice makes perfect," which is also true in learning how to program in Java.

Source Code and Errata

Source code for this book can be accessed by clicking the **Download Source Code** button located at www.apress.com/9781484271346.

CHAPTER 1

Annotations

In this chapter, you will learn:

- What annotations are
- How to declare annotations
- How to use annotations
- What meta-annotations are and how to use them
- Commonly used annotations that are used to deprecate APIs, to suppress named compile-time warnings, override methods, and declare functional interfaces
- How to access annotations at runtime
- How to process annotations in source code

All example programs in this chapter are a member of a `jdojo.annotation` module, as declared in Listing 1-1.

Listing 1-1. The Declaration of a jdojo.annotation Module

```
// module-info.java
module jdojo.annotation {
    exports com.jdojo.annotation;
}
```

What Are Annotations?

Before I define annotations and discuss their importance in programming, let's look at a simple example. Suppose you have an `Employee` class, which has a method called

© Kishori Sharan, Peter Späth 2021
K. Sharan and P. Späth, *More Java 17*, https://doi.org/10.1007/978-1-4842-7135-3_1

setSalary() that sets the salary of an employee. The method accepts a parameter of the type double. The following snippet of code shows a trivial implementation for the Employee class:

```
public class Employee {
    public void setSalary(double salary) {
        System.out.println("Employee.setSalary():" +
            salary);
    }
}
```

A Manager class inherits from the Employee class. You want to set the salary for managers differently. You decide to override the setSalary() method in the Manager class. The code for the Manager class is as follows:

```
public class Manager extends Employee {
    // Override setSalary() in the Employee class
    public void setSalary(int salary) {
        System.out.println("Manager.setSalary():" +
            salary);
    }
}
```

There is a mistake in the Manager class, when you attempt to override the setSalary() method. You'll correct the mistake shortly. You have used the int data type as the parameter type for the incorrectly overridden method. It is time to set the salary for a manager. The following code is used to accomplish this:

```
Employee ken = new Manager();
int salary = 200;
ken.setSalary(salary);
Employee.setSalary():200.0
```

This snippet of code was expected to call the setSalary() method of the Manager class, but the output does not show the expected result.

What went wrong in your code? The intention of defining the setSalary() method in the Manager class was to override the setSalary() method of the Employee class, not to overload it. You made a mistake. You used the type int as the parameter type in the setSalary() method, instead of the type double in the Manager class. You put comments indicating your intention to override the method in the Manager class. However, comments do not stop you from making logical mistakes. You might spend, as every programmer does, hours and hours debugging errors resulting from this kind of logical mistake. Who can help you in such situations? Annotations might help you in a few situations like this.

Let's rewrite your Manager class using an annotation. You do not need to know anything about annotations at this point. All you are going to do is add one word to your program. The following code is the modified version of the Manager class:

```
public class Manager extends Employee {
    @Override
    public void setSalary(int salary) {
        System.out.println("Manager.setSalary():" +
            salary);
    }
}
```

All you have added is an @Override annotation to the Manager class and removed the "dumb" comments. Trying to compile the revised Manager class results in a compile-time error that points to the use of the @Override annotation for the setSalary() method of the Manager class:

```
Manager.java:2: error: method does not override or
          implement a method from a supertype
        @Override
        ^
1 error
```

The use of the @Override annotation did the trick. The @Override annotation is used with a non-static method to indicate the programmer's intention to override the method in the superclass. At the source code level, it serves the purpose of documentation. When the compiler comes across the @Override annotation, it makes sure that the method really overrides the method in the superclass. If the method annotated does not override a method in the superclass, the compiler generates an error. In your case, the setSalary(int salary) method in the Manager class does not override any method in the superclass Employee. This is the reason that you got the error. You may realize that using an annotation is as simple as documenting the source code. However, they have compiler support. You can use them to instruct the compiler to enforce some rules. Annotations provide benefits much more than you have seen in this example. Let's go back to the compile-time error. You can fix the error by doing one of the following two things:

- You can remove the @Override annotation from the setSalary(int salary) method in the Manager class. It will make the method an overloaded method, not a method that overrides its superclass method.

- You can change the method signature from setSalary(int salary) to setSalary(double salary).

Since you want to override the setSalary() method in the Manager class, use the second option and modify the Manager class as follows:

```
public class Manager extends Employee {
    @Override
    public void setSalary(double salary) {
        System.out.println("Manager.setSalary():" +
            salary);
    }
}
```

Now the following code will work as expected:

```
Employee ken = new Manager();
int salary = 200;
ken.setSalary(salary);
Manager.setSalary():200.0
```

Note that the @Override annotation in the setSalary() method of the Manager class saves you debugging time. Suppose you change the method signature in the Employee class. If the changes in the Employee class make this method no longer overridden in the Manager class, you will get the same error when you compile the Manager class again. Are you starting to understand the power of annotations? With this background in mind, let's start digging deep into annotations.

According to the Merriam-Webster dictionary, the meaning of annotation is

A note added by way of comment or explanation.

This is exactly what an annotation is in Java. It lets you associate (or annotate) metadata (or notes) to the program elements in a Java program. The program elements may be a module, a package, a class, an interface, a field of a class, a local variable, a method, a parameter of a method, an enum, an annotation, a type parameter in a generic type/method declaration, a type use, etc. In other words, you can annotate any declaration or type use in a Java program. An annotation is used as a "modifier" in a declaration of a program element like any other modifiers (public, private, final, static, etc.). Unlike a modifier, an annotation does not modify the meaning of the program elements. It acts like a decoration or a note for the program element that it annotates.

An annotation differs from regular documentation in many ways. A regular documentation is only for humans to read, and it is "dumb." It has no intelligence associated with it. If you misspell a word, or state something in the documentation and do just the opposite in the code, you are on your own. It is very difficult and impractical to read the elements of documentation programmatically at runtime. Java lets you generate Javadocs from your documentation and that's it for regular documentation. This does not mean that you do not need to document your programs. You do need regular documentation. At the same time, you need a way to enforce your intent using a documentation-like mechanism. Your documentation should be available to the compiler and the runtime. An annotation serves this purpose. It is human readable, which serves as documentation. It is compiler readable, which lets the compiler verify the intention of the programmer; for example, the compiler makes sure that the programmer has really overridden the method if it comes across an @Override annotation for a method. Annotations are also available at runtime so that a program can read and use it for any purpose it wants. For example, a tool can read annotations and generate boilerplate code. If you have worked with Enterprise JavaBeans (EJB), you know the pain of keeping all the interfaces and classes in sync and adding entries to XML configuration files. EJB 3.0 uses annotations to generate the boilerplate code, which makes EJB development painless for programmers. Another example of an annotation being used in a framework/tool is JUnit version 4.0. JUnit is a unit test framework for Java programs. It uses annotations to mark methods that are test cases. Before that, you had to follow a naming convention for the test case methods. Annotations have a variety of uses, which are documentation, verification, and enforcement by the compiler, the runtime validation, code generation by frameworks/tools, etc.

To make an annotation available to the compiler and the runtime, an annotation has to follow rules. In fact, an annotation is another type like a class and an interface. As you have to declare a class type or an interface type before you can use it, you must also declare an annotation type.

An annotation does not change the semantics (or meaning) of the program element that it annotates. In that sense, an annotation is like a comment, which does not affect the way the annotated program element works. For example, the @Override annotation for the setSalary() method did not change the way the method works. You (or a tool/framework) can change the behavior of a program based on an annotation. In such cases, you use the annotation rather than the annotation doing anything on its own. The point is that an annotation by itself is always passive.

Declaring an Annotation Type

Declaring an annotation type is similar to declaring an interface type, except for some restrictions. According to Java specification, an annotation type declaration is a special kind of interface type declaration. You use the interface keyword, which is preceded by the @ sign (at sign) to declare an annotation type. The following is the general syntax for declaring an annotation type:

```
[modifiers] @ interface <annotation-type-name> {
    // Annotation type body goes here
}
```

[modifiers] for an annotation declaration is the same as for an interface declaration. For example, you can declare an annotation type at the public or package level. The @ sign and the interface keyword may be separated by whitespace, or they can be placed together. By convention, they are placed together as @interface. The interface keyword is followed by an annotation type name. It should be a valid Java identifier. The annotation type body is placed within braces.

Suppose you want to annotate your program elements with the version information, so you can prepare a report about new program elements added in a specific release of your product. To use a custom annotation type (as opposed to a built-in annotation, such as @Override), you must declare it first. You want to include the major and the minor versions of the release in the version information. Listing 1-2 contains the complete code for your first annotation declaration.

Listing 1-2. The Declaration of an Annotation Type Named Version

```
// Version.java
package com.jdojo.annotation;
public @interface Version {
    int major();
    int minor();
}
```

Compare the declaration of the Version annotation with the declaration of an interface. It differs from an interface definition only in one aspect: it uses the @ sign before its name. You have declared two abstract methods in the Version annotation type: major() and minor(). Abstract methods in an annotation type are known as its elements. You can think about it in another way: an annotation can declare zero or more elements, and they are declared as abstract methods. The abstract method names are the names of the elements of the annotation type. You have declared two elements, major and minor, for the Version annotation type. The data types of both elements are int.

Note   Although you can declare static and default methods in interface types, they are not allowed in annotation types. Static and default methods are meant to contain some logic. Annotations are meant to represent just the values for elements in the annotation type. This is the reason that static and default methods are not allowed in annotation types.

You need to compile the annotation type. When the Version.java file is compiled, it will produce a Version.class file. The simple name of your annotation type is Version, and its fully qualified name is com.jdojo.annotation.Version. Using the simple name of an annotation type follows the rules of any other types (e.g., classes, interfaces, etc.). You will need to import an annotation type the same way you import any other types.

How do you use an annotation type? You might be thinking that you will declare a new class that will implement the Version annotation type, and you will create an object of that class. You might be relieved to know that you do not need to take any additional steps to use the Version annotation type. An annotation type is ready to be used as soon as it is declared and compiled. To create an instance of an annotation type and use it to annotate a program element, you need to use the following syntax:

```
@annotationType(name1=value1, name2=value2, name3=value3...)
```

The annotation type is preceded by an @ sign. It is followed by a list of comma-separated name=value pairs enclosed in parentheses. The name in a name=value pair is the name of the element declared in the annotation type, and the value is the user-supplied value for that element. The name=value pairs do not have to appear in the same order as they are declared in the annotation type, although by convention name=value pairs are used in the same order as the declaration of the elements in the annotation type.

Let's use an instance of the Version type, which has the major element value as 1 and the minor element value as 0. The following is an instance of your Version annotation type:

```
@Version(major=1, minor=0)
```

You can rewrite this annotation as @Version(minor=0, major=1) without changing its meaning. You can also use the annotation type's fully qualified name as

```
@com.jdojo.annotation.Version(major=0, minor=1)
```

You use as many instances of the Version annotation type in your program as you want. For example, you have a VersionTest class, which has been in your application since release 1.0. You have added some methods and instance variables in release 1.1. You can use your Version annotation to document additions to the VersionTest class in different releases. You can annotate your class declaration as

```
@Version(major=1, minor=0)
public class VersionTest {
    // Code goes here
}
```

An annotation is added in the same way you add a modifier for a program element. You can mix the annotation for a program element with its other modifiers. You can place annotations in the same line as other modifiers or in a separate line. It is a personal choice whether you use a separate line to place the annotations or you mix them with other modifiers. By convention, annotations for a program element are placed before all other modifiers. Let's follow this convention and place the annotation in a separate line by itself, as shown. Both of the following declarations are technically the same:

```
// Style #1
@Version(major=1, minor=0) public class VersionTest {
    // Code goes here
}
```

```
// Style #2
public @Version(major=1, minor=0)
class VersionTest {
    // Code goes here
}
```

Listing 1-3 shows the sample code for the VersionTest class.

Listing 1-3. A VersionTest Class with Annotated Elements

```
// VersionTest.java
package com.jdojo.annotation;
// Annotation for class VersionTest
@Version(major=1, minor=0)
public class VersionTest {
    // Annotation for instance variable xyz
    @Version(major=1, minor=1)
    private int xyz = 110;
    // Annotation for constructor VersionTest()
    @Version(major=1, minor=0)
    public VersionTest() {
    }
    // Annotation for constructor VersionTest(int xyz)
    @Version(major=1, minor=1)
    public VersionTest(int xyz) {
        this.xyz = xyz;
    }

    // Annotation for the printData() method
    @Version(major=1, minor=0)
    public void printData() {
    }
    // Annotation for the setXyz() method
    @Version(major=1, minor=1)
    public void setXyz(int xyz) {
        // Annotation for local variable newValue
```

```
        @Version(major=1, minor=2)
        int newValue = xyz;
        this.xyz = xyz;
    }
}
```

In Listing 1-3, you use the @Version annotation to annotate the class declaration, class field, local variables, constructors, and methods. There is nothing extraordinary in the code for the VersionTest class. You just added the @Version annotation to various elements of the class. The VersionTest class would work the same, even if you remove all @Version annotations. It is to be emphasized that using annotations in your program does not change the behavior of the program at all. The real benefit of annotations comes from reading it at compile time and runtime.

What do you do next with the Version annotation type? You have declared it as a type. You have used it in your VersionTest class. Your next step is to read it at runtime. Let's defer this step for now; I cover it in detail in a later section. I discuss more on annotation type declarations first.

Restrictions on Annotation Types

An annotation type is a special type of interface with some restrictions. I cover some of the restrictions in the sections to follow.

Restriction #1

An annotation type cannot inherit from another annotation type. That is, you cannot use the extends clause in an annotation type declaration. The following declaration will not compile because you have used the extends clause to declare the WrongVersion annotation type:

```
// Won't compile
public @interface WrongVersion extends BasicVersion {
    int extended();
}
```

Every annotation type implicitly inherits from the java.lang.annotation. Annotation interface, which is declared as follows:

```
package java.lang.annotation;
public interface Annotation {
    boolean equals(Object obj);
    int hashCode();
    String toString();
    Class<? extends Annotation> annotationType();
}
```

This implies that all of the four methods declared in the Annotation interface are available in all annotation types.

Caution   You declare elements for an annotation type using abstract method declarations. The methods declared in the Annotation interface do not declare elements in an annotation type. Your Version annotation type has only two elements, major and minor, which are declared in the Version type itself. You cannot use the annotation type Version as @Version(major=1, minor=2, toString="Hello"). The Version annotation type does not declare toString as an element. It inherits the toString() method from the Annotation interface.

The first three methods in the Annotation interface are the methods from the Object class. The annotationType() method returns the class reference of the annotation type to which the annotation instance belongs. The Java creates a proxy class dynamically at runtime, which implements the annotation type. When you obtain an instance of an annotation type, that instance class is the dynamically generated proxy class, whose reference you can get using the getClass() method on the annotation instance. If you get an instance of the Version annotation type at runtime, its getClass() method will return the class reference of the dynamically generated proxy class, whereas its annotationType() method will return the class reference of the com.jdojo.annotation.Version annotation type.

Restriction #2

Method declarations in an annotation type cannot specify any parameters. A method declares an element for the annotation type. An element in an annotation type lets you associate a data value to an annotation's instance. A method declaration in an annotation is not called to perform any kind of processing. Think of an element as an instance variable in a class having two methods, a setter and a getter, for that instance variable. For an annotation, the Java runtime creates a proxy class that implements the annotation type (which is an interface). Each annotation instance is an object of that proxy class. The method you declare in your annotation type becomes the getter method for the value of that element you specify in the annotation. See, for example, the int major(); and int minor(); method declarations in Listing 1-2. The Java runtime will take care of setting the specified value for the annotation elements. Since the goal of declaring a method in an annotation type is to work with a data element, you do not need to (and are not allowed to) specify any parameters in a method declaration. The following declaration of an annotation type would not compile because it declares a concatenate() method, which accepts two parameters:

```
// Won't compile
public @interface WrongVersion {
    // Cannot have parameters
    String concatenate(int major, int minor);
}
```

Restriction #3

Method declarations in an annotation type cannot have a throws clause. A method in an annotation type is defined to represent a data element. Throwing an exception to represent a data value does not make sense. The following declaration of an annotation type would not compile because the major() method has a throws clause:

```
// Won't compile
public @interface WrongVersion {
    int major() throws Exception; // Cannot have a
                                  // throws clause
    int minor(); // OK
}
```

Restriction #4

The return type of a method declared in an annotation type must be one of the following types:

- Any primitive type: byte, short, int, long, float, double, boolean, and char

- java.lang.String

- java.lang.Class

- An enum type

- An annotation type

- An array of any of the previously mentioned types, for example, String[], int[], etc. The return type cannot be a nested array. For example, you cannot have a return type of String[][] or int[][].

Note   The reason behind these data type restrictions is that all values for allowed data types must be represented in the source code, which the compiler should be able to represent for compile-time analysis.

The return type of Class needs a little explanation. Instead of the Class type, you can use a generic return type that will return a user-defined class type. Suppose you have a Test class and you want to declare the return type of a method in an annotation type of type Test. You can declare the annotation method as shown:

```
public @interface GoodOne {
    Class element1();
      // <- Any Class type
    Class<Test> element2();
      // <- Only Test class type
    Class<? extends Test> element3();
      // <- Test or its subclass type
}
```

Restriction #5

An annotation type cannot declare a method, which would be equivalent to overriding a method in the Object class or the Annotation interface.

Restriction #6

An annotation type cannot be generic.

Default Value of an Annotation Element

The syntax for an annotation type declaration lets you specify a default value for its elements. You are not required to, but you can, specify a value for an annotation element that has a default value specified in its declaration. The default value for an element can be specified using the following general syntax:

```
[modifiers] @interface <annotation-type-name> {
    <data-type> <element-name>() default <default-value>;
}
```

The keyword `default` is used to specify the default value. The default value of the type must be compatible with the data type for the element.

Suppose you have a product that is not frequently released, so it is less likely that it will have a minor version other than zero. You can simplify your `Version` annotation type by specifying a default value for its minor element as zero, as shown:

```
public @interface Version {
    int major();
    int minor() default 0; // Set zero as default value
                           // for minor
}
```

Once you set the default value for an element, you do not have to pass its value when you use an annotation of this type. Java will use the default value for the missing element:

```
@Version(major=1)          // minor is zero, which is
                           // its default value
@Version(major=2)          // minor is zero, which is
                           // its default value
@Version(major=2, minor=1) // minor is 1, which is the
                           // specified value
```

All default values must be compile-time constants. How do you specify the default value for an array type? You need to use the array initializer syntax. The following snippet of code shows how to specify default values for an array and other data types:

```
// Shows how to assign default values to elements of
// different types
public @interface DefaultTest {
    double d() default 12.89;
    int num() default 12;
    int[] x() default {1, 2};
    String s() default "Hello";
    String[] s2() default {"abc", "xyz"};
    Class c() default Exception.class;
    Class[] c2() default {Exception.class,
        java.io.IOException.class};
}
```

The default value for an element is not compiled with the annotation. It is read from the annotation type definition when a program attempts to read the value of an element at runtime. For example, when you use @Version(major=2), this annotation instance is compiled as is. It does not add the minor element with its default value as zero. In other words, this annotation is not modified to @Version(major=2, minor=0) at the time of compilation. However, when you read the value of the minor element for this annotation at runtime, Java will detect that the value for the minor element was not specified. It will consult the Version annotation type definition for its default value. The implication of this mechanism is that if you change the default value of an element, the changed default value will be read whenever a program attempts to read it, even if the annotated program was compiled before you changed the default value.

Annotation Type and Its Instances

I use the terms "annotation type" and "annotation" frequently. An annotation type is a type like an interface. Theoretically, you can use an annotation type wherever you can use an interface type. Practically, we limit its use only to annotate program elements. You can declare a variable of an annotation type as shown:

```
Version v = null; // Here, Version is an annotation type
```

Like an interface, you can also implement an annotation type in a class. However, you are never supposed to do that, as it will defeat the purpose of having an annotation type as a new construct. You should always implement an interface in a class, not an annotation type. Technically, the code in Listing 1-4 for the DoNotUseIt class is valid. This is just for the purposes of demonstration. Do not implement an annotation in a class even if it works.

Listing 1-4. A Class Implementing an Annotation Type

```java
// DoNotUseIt.java
package com.jdojo.annotation;
import java.lang.annotation.Annotation;
public class DoNotUseIt implements Version {
    // Implemented method from the Version annotation
    // type
    @Override
    public int major() {
        return 0;
    }
    // Implemented method from the Version annotation
    // type
    @Override
    public int minor() {
        return 0;
    }
    // Implemented method from the Annotation annotation
    // type, which is the supertype of the Version
    // annotation type
    @Override
    public Class<? extends Annotation> annotationType() {
        return null;
    }
}
```

The Java runtime implements the annotation type to a proxy class. It provides you with an object of a class that implements your annotation type for each annotation you use in your program. You must distinguish between an annotation type and instances (or objects) of that annotation type. In your example, Version is an annotation type. Whenever you use it as @Version(major=2, minor=4), you are creating an instance of the Version annotation type. An instance of an annotation type is simply referred to as an annotation. For example, we say that @Version(major=2, minor=4) is an annotation or an instance of the Version annotation type. An annotation should be easy to use in a program. The syntax @Version(...) is shorthand for creating a class, creating an object of that class, and setting the values for its elements. I cover how to get to the object of an annotation type at runtime later in this chapter.

Using Annotations

In this section, I discuss the details of using different types of elements while declaring annotation types. Keep in mind that the supplied value for elements of an annotation must be a compile-time constant expression, and you cannot use null as the value for any type of elements in an annotation.

Primitive Types

The data type of an element in an annotation type could be any of the primitive data types: byte, short, int, long, float, double, boolean, and char. The Version annotation type declares two elements, major and minor, and both are of int data type. The following code snippet declares an annotation type called PrimitiveAnnTest:

```
public @interface PrimitiveAnnTest {
    byte a();
    short b();
    int c();
    long d();
    float e();
    double f();
    boolean g();
    char h();
}
```

You can use an instance of the PrimitiveAnnTest type as

```
@PrimitiveAnnTest(a=1, b=2, c=3, d=4, e=12.34F, f=1.89, g=true, h='Y')
```

You can use a compile-time constant expression to specify the value for an element of an annotation. The following two instances of the Version annotation are valid and have the same values for their elements:

```
@Version(major=2+1, minor=(int)13.2)
@Version(major=3, minor=13)
```

String Types

You can use an element of the String type in an annotation type. Listing 1-5 contains the code for an annotation type called Name. It has two elements, first and last, which are of the String type.

Listing 1-5. Name Annotation Type, Which Has Two Elements, first and last, of the String Type

```java
// Name.java
package com.jdojo.annotation;
public @interface Name {
    String first();
    String last();
}
```

The following snippet of code shows how to use the Name annotation type in a program:

```java
@Name(first="John", last="Jacobs")
public class NameTest {
    @Name(first="Wally", last="Inman")
    public void aMethod() {
        // More code goes here...
    }
}
```

It is valid to use the string concatenation operator (+) in the value expression for an element of a String type. The following two annotations are equivalent:

```java
@Name(first="Jo" + "hn", last="Ja" + "cobs")
@Name(first="John", last="Jacobs")
```

Typically, you will use string concatenation in an annotation when you want to use a compile-time constant such as a `final class` variable as part of the value for an annotation element. In the following annotation, `Test` is a class that defines a compile-time constant `String` class variable named `UNKNOWN`:

```
@Name(first="Mr. " + Test.UNKNWON, last=Test.UNKNOWN)
```

The following use of the @Name annotation is not valid because the expression `new String("John")` is not a compile-time constant expression:

```
@Name(first=new String("John"), last="Jacobs")
```

Class Types

The benefits of using the `Class` type as an element in an annotation type are not obvious. Typically, it is used where a tool/framework reads the annotations with elements of a class type and performs some specialized processing on the element's value or generates code. Let's go through a simple example of using a class type element. Suppose you are writing a test runner tool for running test cases for a Java program. Your annotation will be used in writing test cases. If your test case must throw an exception when it is invoked by the test runner, you need to use an annotation to indicate that. Let's create a `DefaultException` class, as shown in Listing 1-6.

Listing 1-6. A DefaultException Class That Is Inherited from the Throwable Exception Class

```
// DefaultException.java
package com.jdojo.annotation;
public class DefaultException
        extends java.lang.Throwable {
    public DefaultException() {
    }
    public DefaultException(String msg) {
        super(msg);
    }
}
```

Listing 1-7 shows the code for a `TestCase` annotation type.

Listing 1-7. A TestCase Annotation Type Whose Instances Are Used to Annotate Test Case Methods

```java
// TestCase.java
package com.jdojo.annotation;

import java.lang.annotation.ElementType;
import java.lang.annotation.Retention;
import java.lang.annotation.RetentionPolicy;
import java.lang.annotation.Target;

@Retention(RetentionPolicy.RUNTIME)
@Target(ElementType.METHOD)
public @interface TestCase {
    Class<? extends Throwable> willThrow() default
        DefaultException.class;
}
```

The return type of the `willThrow` element is defined as the wildcard of the `Throwable` class, so that the user will specify only the `Throwable` class or its subclasses as the element's value. You could have used the `Class<?>` type as the type of your willThrow element. However, that would have allowed the users of this annotation type to pass any class type as its value. Note that you have used two annotations, `@Retention` and `@Target`, for the `TestCase` annotation type. The `@Retention` annotation type specified that the `@TestCase` annotation would be available at runtime. It is necessary to use the retention policy of `RUNTIME` for your `TestCase` annotation type because it is meant for the test runner tool to read it at runtime. The `@Target` annotation states that the `TestCase` annotation can be used only to annotate methods. I cover the `@Retention` and `@Target` annotation types in detail in later sections when I discuss meta-annotations. Listing 1-8 shows the use of your `TestCase` annotation type.

Listing 1-8. A Test Case That Uses the TestCase Annotations

```java
// PolicyTestCases.java
package com.jdojo.annotation;
import java.io.IOException;
public class PolicyTestCases {
    // Must throw IOException
```

```
@TestCase(willThrow=IOException.class)
public static void testCase1(){
    // Code goes here
}
// We are not expecting any exception
@TestCase()
public static void testCase2(){
    // Code goes here
}
}
```

The testCase1() method specifies, using the @TestCase annotation, that it will throw an IOException. The test runner tool will make sure that when it invokes this method, the method does throw an IOException. Otherwise, it will fail the test case. The testCase2() method does not specify that it will throw an exception. If it throws an exception when the test is run, the tool should fail this test case.

Enum Type

An annotation can have elements of an enum type. Suppose you want to declare an annotation type called Review that can describe the code review status of a program element. Let's assume that it has a status element and it can have one of the four values: PENDING, FAILED, PASSED, and PASSEDWITHCHANGES. You can declare an enum as an annotation type member. Listing 1-9 shows the code for a Review annotation type.

Listing 1-9. An Annotation Type That Uses an enum Type Element

```
// Review.java
package com.jdojo.annotation;
public @interface Review {
    ReviewStatus status() default ReviewStatus.PENDING;
    String comments() default "";
    // ReviewStatus enum is a member of the Review
    // annotation type
    public enum ReviewStatus {PENDING, FAILED, PASSED,
        PASSEDWITHCHANGES};
}
```

Note   The enum type used as the type of an annotation element need not be declared as a nested enum type of the annotation type, as you did in this example. The enum type can also be declared outside the annotation type.

The Review annotation type declares a ReviewStatus enum type, and the four review statuses are the elements of the enum. It has two elements, status and comments. The type of the status element is the enum type ReviewStatus. The default value for the status element is ReviewStatus.PENDING. You have an empty string as the default value for the comments element.

Here are some of the instances of the Review annotation type. You will need to import the com.jdojo.annotation.Review.ReviewStatus enum in your program to use the simple name of the ReviewStatus enum type:

```
import com.jdojo.annotation.Review.ReviewStatus;
...
// Have default for status and comments. Maybe the code
// is new.
@Review()
// Leave status as Pending, but add some comments
@Review(comments=
    "Have scheduled code review on December 1, 2017")
// Fail the review with comments
@Review(status=ReviewStatus.FAILED,
    comments="Need to handle errors")
// Pass the review without comments
@Review(status=ReviewStatus.PASSED)
```

Here is the sample code that annotates a Test class indicating that it passed the code review:

```
import com.jdojo.annotation.Review.ReviewStatus;
import com.jdojo.annotation.Review;
@Review(status=ReviewStatus.PASSED)
public class Test {
    // Code goes here
}
```

Annotation Type

An annotation type can be used anywhere a type can be used in a Java program. For example, you can use an annotation type as the return type for a method. You can also use an annotation type as the type of an element inside another annotation type's declaration. Suppose you want to have a new annotation type called `Description`, which will include the name of the author, version, and comments for a program element. You can reuse your `Name` and `Version` annotation types as its `name` and `version` elements type. Listing 1-10 shows the code for the `Description` annotation type.

Listing 1-10. An Annotation Type Using Other Annotation Types As Its Elements

```
// Description.java
package com.jdojo.annotation;
public @interface Description {
    Name name();
    Version version();
    String comments() default "";
}
```

To provide a value for an element of an annotation type, you need to use the syntax that creates an annotation type instance. For example, `@Version(major=1, minor=2)` creates an instance of the `Version` annotation. Note the nesting of an annotation inside another annotation in the following snippet of code:

```
@Description(name=@Name(first="John", last="Jacobs"),
    version=@Version(major=1, minor=2),
    comments="Just a test class")
public class Test {
    // Code goes here
}
```

Array Type Annotation Element

An annotation can have elements of an array type. The array type could be one of the following types:

- A primitive type
- `java.lang.String` type
- `java.lang.Class` type
- An enum type
- An annotation type

You need to specify the value for an array element inside braces. Elements of the array are separated by a comma. Suppose you want to annotate your program elements with a short description of a list of things that you need to work on. Listing 1-11 creates a ToDo annotation type for this purpose.

Listing 1-11. ToDo Annotation Type with a String Array As Its Sole Element

```java
// ToDo.java
package com.jdojo.annotation;

public @interface ToDo {
    String[] items();
}
```

The following snippet of code shows how to use a @ToDo annotation:

```java
@ToDo(items={"Add readFile method", "Add error handling"})
public class Test {
    // Code goes here
}
```

If you have only one element in the array, you can omit the braces.

The following two annotation instances of the ToDo annotation type are equivalent:

```java
@ToDo(items={"Add error handling"})
@ToDo(items="Add error handling")
```

> **Note**   If you do not have valid values to pass to an element of an array type, you can use an empty array. For example, @ToDo(items={}) is a valid annotation where the items element has been assigned an empty array.

No Null Value in an Annotation

You cannot use a null reference as a value for an element in an annotation. Note that it is allowed to use an empty string for the String type element and an empty array for an array type element. Using the following annotations will result in compile-time errors:

```
@ToDo(items=null)
@Name(first=null, last="Jacobs")
```

Shorthand Annotation Syntax

The shorthand annotation syntax is a little easier to use in a few circumstances. Suppose you have an annotation type Enabled with an element having a default value, as shown:

```
public @interface Enabled {
    boolean status() default true;
}
```

If you want to annotate a program element with the Enabled annotation type using the default value for its element, you can use the @Enabled() syntax. You do not need to specify the values for the status element because it has a default value. You can use a shorthand in this situation, which allows you to omit the parentheses. You can just use @Enabled instead of using @Enabled(). The Enabled annotation can be used in either of the following two forms:

```
@Enabled
public class Test {
    // Code goes here
}
```

```
@Enabled()
public class Test {
    // Code goes here
}
```

An annotation type with only one element also has a shorthand syntax.

You can use this shorthand if you adhere to a naming rule for the sole element in the annotation type. The name of the element must be value. If an annotation type has only one element that is named value, you can omit the name from the name=value pair from your annotation. The following snippet of code declares a Company annotation type, which has only one element named value:

```
public @interface Company {
    String value(); // the element name is value
}
```

You can omit the name from the name=value pair when you use the Company annotation, as shown here. If you want to use the element name with the Company annotation, you can always do so as

```
@Company(value="Abc Inc.")
@Company("Abc Inc.")
public class Test {
    // Code goes here
}
```

You can use this shorthand of omitting the name of the element from annotations, even if the element data type is an array. Consider the following annotation type called Reviewers:

```
public @interface Reviewers {
    String[] value(); // the element name is value
}
```

Since the `Reviewers` annotation type has only one element, which is named value, you can omit the element name when you are using it:

```
// No need to specify name of the element
@Reviewers({"John Jacobs", "Wally Inman"})
public class Test {
    // Code goes here
}
```

You can also omit the braces if you specify only one element in the array for the value element of the `Reviewers` annotation type:

```
@Reviewers("John Jacobs")
public class Test {
    // Code goes here
}
```

You just saw several examples using the name of the element as a value. Here is the general rule of omitting the name of the element in an annotation: if you supply only one value when using an annotation, the name of the element is assumed value. This means that you are not required to have only one element in the annotation type, which is named value, to omit its name in the annotations. If you have an annotation type, which has an element named value (with or without a default value) and all other elements have default values, you can still omit the name of the element in annotation instances of this type. Here are some examples to illustrate this rule:

```
public @interface A {
    String value();
    int id() default 10;
}
// Same as @A(value="Hello", id=10)
@A("Hello")
public class Test {
    // Code goes here
}
// Won't compile. Must use only one value to omit the
// element name
@A("Hello", id=16)
```

27

```
public class WontCompile {
    // Code goes here
}
// OK. Must use name=value pair when passing more than
// one value
@A(value="Hello", id=16)
public class Test {
    // Code goes here
}
```

Marker Annotation Types

A marker annotation type does not declare any elements, not even one with a default value. Typically, a marker annotation is used by annotation processing tools, which generate some kind of boilerplate code based on the marker annotation type:

```
public @interface Marker {
    // No element declarations
}
@Marker
public class Test {
    // Code goes here
}
```

An example would be a @Monitor annotation for methods to be monitored by some performance monitoring tool:

```
public class Calculator {
    ...
    @Monitor
    public void calc() {
        ...
    }
}
```

The tool would automatically add code for measuring elapse times, call frequency, and the like.

Meta-Annotation Types

Meta-annotation types are used to annotate other annotation type declarations. The following are meta-annotation types:

- `Target`
- `Retention`
- `Inherited`
- `Documented`
- `Repeatable`

Meta-annotation types are part of the Java class library. They are declared in the `java.lang.annotation` package. I discuss meta-annotation types in detail in subsequent sections.

Note   The `java.lang.annotation` package contains a `Native` annotation type, which is not a meta-annotation. It is used to annotate fields indicating that the field may be referenced from native code. It is a marker annotation. Typically, it is used by tools that generate some code based on this annotation.

The Target Annotation Type

As a first member of the set of meta-annotations, the `Target` annotation type is used to specify the context in which an annotation type can be used. It has only one element named value, which is an array of the `java.lang.annotation.ElementType` enum type. Table 1-1 lists all constants in the `ElementType` enum.

Table 1-1. *List of Constants in the java.lang.annotation.ElementType Enum*

Constant Name	Description
ANNOTATION_TYPE	Used to annotate another annotation type declaration. This makes the annotation type a meta-annotation.
CONSTRUCTOR	Used to annotate constructors.
FIELD	Used to annotate fields and enum constants.
LOCAL_VARIABLE	Used to annotate local variables.
METHOD	Used to annotate methods.
MODULE	Used to annotate modules. It was added in Java 9.
PACKAGE	Used to annotate package declarations.
PARAMETER	Used to annotate parameters.
TYPE	Used to annotate class, interface (including annotation type), or enum declarations.
TYPE_PARAMETER	Used to annotate type parameters in generic classes, interfaces, methods, etc. It was added in Java 8.
TYPE_USE	Used to annotate all uses of types. It was added in Java 8. The annotation can also be used where an annotation with ElementType.TYPE and ElementType.TYPE_PARAMETER can be used. It can also be used before constructors, in which case it represents the objects created by the constructor.

The following declaration of the Version annotation type annotates the annotation type declaration with the Target meta-annotation, which specifies that the Version annotation type can be used with program elements of only three types: any type (class, interface, enum, and annotation types), constructors, and method.

```
// Version.java
package com.jdojo.annotation;
import java.lang.annotation.Target;
import java.lang.annotation.ElementType;
@Target({ElementType.TYPE, ElementType.CONSTRUCTOR,
    ElementType.METHOD})
```

```
public @interface Version {
    int major();
    int minor();
}
```

The Version annotation type cannot be used on any program elements other than the three types specified in its Target annotation. Its following use is incorrect because it is being used on an instance variable (a field):

```
public class WontCompile {
    // A compile-time error. Version annotation cannot
    // be used on a field.
    @Version(major = 1, minor = 1)
    int id = 110;
}
```

The following uses of the Version annotation are valid:

```
// OK. A class type declaration
@Version(major = 1, minor = 0)
public class VersionTest {
    // OK. A constructor declaration
    @Version(major = 1, minor = 0)
    public VersionTest() {
        // Code goes here
    }
    // OK. A method declaration
    @Version(major = 1, minor = 1)
    public void doSomething() {
        // Code goes here
    }
}
```

Prior to Java 8, annotations were allowed on formal parameters of methods and declarations of packages, classes, methods, fields, and local variables. Java 8 added support for using annotations on any use of a type and on type parameter declarations. The phrase "any use of a type" needs a little explanation. A type is used in many contexts, for example, after the extends clause as a supertype, in an object creation expression after the new operator, in a cast, in a throws clause, etc. From Java 8, annotations may appear before the simple name of the types wherever a type is used. Note that the simple name of the type may be used only as a name, not as a type, for example, in an import statement. Consider the declarations of the Fatal and NonZero annotation types shown in Listings 1-12 and 1-13.

Listing 1-12. A Fatal Annotation Type That Can Be Used with Any Type Use

```java
// Fatal.java
package com.jdojo.annotation;
import java.lang.annotation.ElementType;
import java.lang.annotation.Target;
@Target({ElementType.TYPE_USE})
public @interface Fatal {
}
```

Listing 1-13. A NonZero Annotation Type That Can Be Used with Any Type Use

```java
// NonZero.java
package com.jdojo.annotation;
import java.lang.annotation.ElementType;
import java.lang.annotation.Target;
@Target({ElementType.TYPE_USE})
public @interface NonZero {
}
```

The Fatal and NonZero annotation types can be used wherever a type is used. Their uses in the following contexts are valid:

```java
public class Test {
    public void processData() throws @Fatal Exception {

        double value = getValue();
        int roundedValue = (@NonZero int) value;
        Test t = new @Fatal Test();
        // More code goes here
    }
```

```
public double getValue() {
    double value = 189.98;
    // More code goes here
    return value;
  }
}
```

Note   If you do not annotate an annotation type with the `Target` annotation type, the annotation type can be used everywhere, except in a type parameter declaration.

The Retention Annotation Type

You can use annotations for different purposes. You may want to use them solely for documentation purposes, to be processed by the compiler, and/or to use them at runtime. An annotation can be retained at three levels:

- Source code only

- Class file only (the default)

- Class file and runtime

The `Retention` meta-annotation type is used to specify how an annotation instance of an annotation type should be retained by Java. This is also known as the retention policy of an annotation type. If an annotation type has a "source code only" retention policy, instances of its type are removed when compiled into a class file. If the retention policy is "class file only," annotation instances are retained in the class file, but they cannot be read at runtime. If the retention policy is "class file and runtime" (simply known as runtime), the annotation instances are retained in the class file, and they are available for reading at runtime.

The Retention meta-annotation type declares one element, named value, which is of the `java.lang.annotation.RetentionPolicy` enum type. The `RetentionPolicy` enum has three constants, `SOURCE`, `CLASS`, and `RUNTIME`, which are used to specify the retention policy of source only, class only, and class-and-runtime, respectively. The following code uses the Retention meta-annotation on the Version annotation type. It specifies that the Version annotations should be available at runtime. Note the use of two meta-annotations on the Version annotation type: Target and Retention.

```
// Version.java
package com.jdojo.annotation;

import java.lang.annotation.Target;
import java.lang.annotation.ElementType;
import java.lang.annotation.Retention;
import java.lang.annotation.RetentionPolicy;

@Target({ElementType.TYPE, ElementType.CONSTRUCTOR,
    ElementType.METHOD})
@Retention(RetentionPolicy.RUNTIME)
public @interface Version {
    int major();
    int minor();
}
```

Note   If you do not use the Retention meta-annotation on an annotation type, its retention policy defaults to class file only. This implies that you will not be able to read those annotations at runtime. You will make this common mistake in the beginning. You would try to read annotations, and the runtime will not return any values. Make sure that your annotation type has been annotated with the Retention meta-annotation with the retention policy of RetentionPolicy.RUNTIME before you attempt to read them at runtime. An annotation on a local variable declaration is never available in the class file or at runtime irrespective of the retention policy of the annotation type. The reason for this restriction is that the Java runtime does not let you access the local variables using reflection at runtime; unless you have access to the local variables at runtime, you cannot read annotations for them.

The Inherited Annotation Type

The Inherited annotation type is a marker meta-annotation type. If an annotation type is annotated with an Inherited meta-annotation, its instances are inherited by a subclass declaration. It has no effect if an annotation type is used to annotate any program elements other than a class declaration. Let's consider two annotation type declarations: Ann2 and Ann3. Note that Ann2 is not annotated with an Inherited meta-annotation, whereas Ann3 is.

```
public @interface Ann2 {
    int id();
}
@Inherited
public @interface Ann3 {
    int id();
}
```

Let's declare two classes, A and B, as follows. Note that class B inherits class A:

```
@Ann2(id=505)
@Ann3(id=707)
public class A {
    // Code for class A goes here
}
// Class B inherits Ann3(id=707) annotation from the
// class A
public class B extends A {
    // Code for class B goes here
}
```

In this snippet of code, class B inherits the @Ann3(id=707) annotation from class A because the Ann3 annotation type has been annotated with an Inherited meta-annotation. Class B does not inherit the @Ann2(id=505) annotation because the Ann2 annotation type is not annotated with an Inherited meta-annotation.

The Documented Annotation Type

The Documented annotation type is a marker meta-annotation type. If an annotation type is annotated with a Documented annotation, the Javadoc tool will generate documentation for all of its instances. Listing 1-14 has the code for the final version of the Version annotation type, which has been annotated with a Documented meta-annotation.

Listing 1-14. The Final Version of the Version Annotation Type

```java
// Version.java
package com.jdojo.annotation;

import java.lang.annotation.Documented;
import java.lang.annotation.Target;
import java.lang.annotation.ElementType;
import java.lang.annotation.Retention;
import java.lang.annotation.RetentionPolicy;

@Target({ElementType.TYPE, ElementType.CONSTRUCTOR,
    ElementType.METHOD, ElementType.MODULE,
    ElementType.PACKAGE, ElementType.LOCAL_VARIABLE,
    ElementType.TYPE_USE})
@Retention(RetentionPolicy.RUNTIME)
@Documented
public @interface Version {
    int major();
    int minor();
}
```

Suppose you annotate a Test class with your Version annotation type as follows:

```java
package com.jdojo.annotation;
@Version(major=1, minor=0)
public class Test {
    // Code for Test class goes here
}
```

When you generate documentation for the Test class using the Javadoc tool, the Version annotation on the Test class declaration is also generated as part of the documentation. If you remove the Documented annotation from the Version annotation type declaration, the Test class documentation would not contain information about its Version annotation.

The Repeatable Annotation Type

An annotation type declaration must be annotated with a @Repeatable annotation if its repeated use is to be allowed. The Repeatable annotation type has only one element named value whose type is a class type of another annotation type. Creating a repeatable annotation type is a two-step process:

- Declare an annotation type (say T) and annotate it with the Repeatable meta-annotation. Specify the value for the annotation as another annotation that is known as containing an annotation for the repeatable annotation type being declared.

- Declare the containing annotation type with one element that is an array of the repeatable annotation.

Listings 1-15 and 1-16 contain declarations for the ChangeLog and ChangeLogs annotation types. ChangeLog is annotated with the @Repeatable(ChangeLogs.class) annotation, which means that it is a repeatable annotation type and its containing annotation type is ChangeLogs.

Listing 1-15. A Repeatable Annotation Type That Uses the ChangeLogs As the Containing Annotation Type

```
// ChangeLog.java
package com.jdojo.annotation;
import java.lang.annotation.Repeatable;
import java.lang.annotation.Retention;
import java.lang.annotation.RetentionPolicy;
@Retention(RetentionPolicy.RUNTIME)
@Repeatable(ChangeLogs.class)
```

```
public @interface ChangeLog {
    String date();
    String comments();
}
```

Listing 1-16. A Containing Annotation Type for the ChangeLog Repeatable Annotation Type

```
// ChangeLogs.java
package com.jdojo.annotation;
import java.lang.annotation.Retention;
import java.lang.annotation.RetentionPolicy;
@Retention(RetentionPolicy.RUNTIME)
public @interface ChangeLogs {
    ChangeLog[] value();
}
```

You can use the ChangeLog annotation to log change history for the Test class, as shown:

```
@ChangeLog(date="08/28/2017",
    comments="Declared the class")
@ChangeLog(date="09/21/2017",
    comments="Added the process() method")
public class Test {
    public static void process() {
        // Code goes here
    }
}
```

Commonly Used Standard Annotations

The Java API defines many standard annotation types. This section discusses four of the most commonly used standard annotations. They are defined in the java.lang package. They are

- Deprecated
- Override

- SuppressWarnings

- FunctionalInterface

Deprecating APIs

Deprecating APIs in Java is a way to provide information about the lifecycle of the APIs. You can deprecate modules, packages, types, constructors, methods, fields, parameters, and local variables. When you deprecate an API, you are telling its users

- Not to use the API because it is dangerous

- To migrate away from the API because a better replacement for the API exists

- To migrate away from the API because the API will be removed in a future release

The JDK contains two constructs that are used to deprecate APIs:

- The @deprecated Javadoc tag

- The java.lang.Deprecated annotation type

The @deprecated Javadoc tag lets you specify the details about the deprecation with a rich set of text formatting features of HTML. The java.lang.Deprecated annotation type can be used on the API elements, which are deprecated.

The Deprecated annotation type is retained at runtime.

The @deprecated tag and the @Deprecated annotation are supposed to be used together. Both should be present or both absent. The @Deprecation annotation does not let you specify a description of the deprecation, so you must use the @deprecated tag to provide the description.

Note   Using a @deprecated tag, but not a @Deprecated annotation, on an API element generates a compiler warning.

Listing 1-17 contains the declaration for a class named FileCopier. Suppose this class is shipped as part of a library.

Listing 1-17. A FileCopier Utility Class

```java
// FileCopier.java
package com.jdojo.deprecation;
import java.io.File;
/**
* The class consists of static methods that can be used
* to copy files and directories.
*
* @deprecated Deprecated since 1.4. Not safe to use. Use
* the <code>java.nio.file.Files</code> class instead. This
* class will be removed in a future release of this library.
*
* @since 1.2
*/

@Deprecated
public class FileCopier {
    // No direct instantiation supported
    private FileCopier() {
    }
    /**
     * Copies the contents of src to dst.
     * @param src The source file
     * @param dst The destination file
     * @return true if the copy is successfully,
     * false otherwise.
     */
    public static boolean copy(File src, File dst) {
        // More code goes here
        return true;
    }
    // More code goes here
}
```

The `FileCopier` class is deprecated using the `@Deprecated` annotation. Its Javadoc uses the `@deprecated` tag to give the deprecation details such as when it was deprecated, its replacement, and its removal notice. Before JDK9, the `@Deprecated` annotation type did not contain any elements, so you had to provide all details about the deprecation using the `@deprecated` tag in the Javadoc for the deprecated API. Note that the `@since` tag used in the Javadoc indicates that the `FileCopier` class has existed since version 1.2 of this library, whereas the `@deprecated` tag indicates that the class has been deprecated since version 1.4 of the library.

The Javadoc tool moves the contents of the @deprecated tag to the top in the generated Javadoc to draw the reader's attention. The compiler generates a warning when non-deprecated code uses a deprecated API. Annotating an API with `@Deprecated` does not generate a warning; however, using an API that has been annotated with a `@Deprecated` annotation does. If you used the `FileCopier` class outside the class itself, you will receive a compile-time warning about using the deprecated class.

Suppose you compiled your code and deployed it to production. If you upgraded the JDK version or libraries/frameworks that contain new, deprecated APIs that your old application uses, you do not receive any warnings, and you would miss a chance to migrate away from the deprecated APIs. You must recompile your code to receive warnings. There was no tool to scan and analyze the compiled code (e.g., JAR files) and report the use of deprecated APIs. Even worse is the case when a deprecated API is removed from the newer version, and your old, compiled code receives unexpected runtime errors. Developers were also confused when they looked at a deprecated element Javadoc—there was no way to express when the API was deprecated and whether the deprecated API will be removed in a future release. Prior to JDK9, all you could do was specify these pieces of information in text as part of the @deprecated tag. For this reason, there are two additional elements enhancing the `@Deprecated` annotation (since JDK9): `since` and `forRemoval`. They are declared as follows:

- String since() default "";

- boolean forRemoval() default false;

Both new elements have default values specified, so the existing uses of the annotation do not break. The `since` element specifies the version in which the annotated API element became deprecated. It is a string and you are expected to follow the same version naming convention as the JDK version scheme, for example, "9" for JDK9. It defaults to the empty string. Note that JDK9 did not add an element to the @Deprecated annotation type to specify a description of the deprecation. This was done for two reasons:

- The annotation is retained at runtime. Adding descriptive text to the annotation would add to the runtime memory.

- The descriptive text cannot be just plain text. For example, it needs to provide a link to the replacement of the deprecated API. The existing @deprecated Javadoc tag already provides this feature.

The forRemoval element indicates that the annotated API element is subject to removal in a future release, and you should migrate away from the API. It defaults to false.

Note   The @since Javadoc tag on an element indicates when the API element was added, whereas the since element of the @Deprecated annotation indicates when the API element was deprecated. In JDK9, reasonable efforts have been made to backfill these two elements' values in most, if not all, use-sites of the @Deprecated annotations in the Java SE APIs.

The addition of the forRemoval element in the @Deprecation annotation type has added five more use cases. When an API is deprecated with forRemoval set to false, such a deprecation is known as an ordinary deprecation, and the warnings issued in such cases are called ordinary deprecation warnings. When an API is deprecated with forRemoval set to true, such a deprecation is known as a terminal deprecation, and the warnings issued in such cases are called terminal deprecation warnings or removal warnings. Table 1-2 shows the matrix of deprecation warnings (issued in JDK9).

Table 1-2. *Matrix of Deprecation Warnings*

API Use-Site	API Declaration Site, Not Deprecated	API Declaration Site, Terminally Deprecated	API Declaration Site, Ordinarily Deprecated
Not Deprecated	No Warning	Ordinary Deprecation Warning	Removal Deprecation Warning
Ordinarily Deprecated	No Warning	No Warning	Removal Deprecation Warning
Terminally Deprecated	No Warning	No Warning	Removal Deprecation Warning

The warning issued in one case, where both the API and its use-site are terminally deprecated, needs a little explanation. Both API and the code that uses it have been deprecated, and both will be removed in the future, so what is the point of getting a warning in such a case? This is done to cover cases where the terminally deprecated API and its use-site are in two different codebases and are maintained independently. If the use-site codebase outlives the API codebase, the use-site will get an unexpected runtime error because the API it uses no longer exists. Issuing a warning at the use-site will give its maintainers a chance to plan for alternatives in case the terminally deprecated API goes away before the code at use-sites.

If you use @SuppressWarnings("deprecation"), the compiler suppresses only ordinary deprecation warnings. To suppress removal warnings, you need to use @SuppressWarnings("removal"). If you want to suppress both ordinary and removal deprecation warnings, you need to use @SuppressWarnings({"deprecation", "removal"}).

As an example, I show you all use cases of deprecating APIs, using the deprecated API with and without suppressing warnings with a simple example. In the example, I deprecate only methods and use them to generate compile-time warnings. You are, however, not limited to deprecating only methods. Comments on the methods should help you understand the expected behavior. Listing 1-18 contains the code for a class named Box. The class contains three methods—one in each category of deprecation—not deprecated, ordinarily deprecated, and terminally deprecated. I have kept the class simple, so you can focus on the deprecation being used. Compiling the Box class will not generate any deprecation warnings because the class does not use any deprecated API; rather, it contains the deprecated APIs.

Listing 1-18. A Box Class with Three Types of Methods: Not Deprecated, Ordinarily Deprecated, and Terminally Deprecated

```java
// Box.java
package com.jdojo.annotation;
/**
* This class is used to demonstrate how to deprecate APIs.
*/
public class Box {
    /**
     * Not deprecated
     */
    public static void notDeprecated() {
        System.out.println("notDeprecated...");
    }
    /**
     * Deprecated ordinarily.
     * @deprecated  Do not use it.
     */
    @Deprecated(since="2")
    public static void deprecatedOrdinarily() {
        System.out.println("deprecatedOrdinarily...");
    }
    /**
     * Deprecated terminally.
     * @deprecated  It will be removed in a future release.
     * Migrate your code now.
     */
    @Deprecated(since="2", forRemoval=true)
    public static void deprecatedTerminally() {
        System.out.println("deprecatedTerminally...");
    }
}
```

Listing 1-19 contains the code for a BoxTest class. The class uses all methods of the Box class. A few methods in the BoxTest class have been deprecated ordinarily and terminally. The first nine methods correspond to nine use cases in Table 1-2, which will generate four deprecation warnings—one ordinary warning and three terminal warnings. Methods named like m4X(), where X is a digit, show you how to suppress ordinary and terminal deprecation warnings.

Listing 1-19. A BoxTest Class That Uses Deprecated APIs and Suppresses Deprecation Warnings

```java
// BoxTest.java
package com.jdojo.annotation;

public class BoxTest {
    /**
     * API: Not deprecated
     * Use-site: Not deprecated
     * Deprecation warning: No warning
     */
    public static void m11() {
        Box.notDeprecated();
    }
    /**
    * API: Ordinarily deprecated
    * Use-site: Not deprecated
    * Deprecation warning: No warning
    */
    public static void m12() {
        Box.deprecatedOrdinarily();
    }
    /**
     * API: Terminally deprecated
     * Use-site: Not deprecated
     * Deprecation warning: Removal warning
     */
    public static void m13() {
        Box.deprecatedTerminally();
    }
```

```java
/**
 * API: Not deprecated
 * Use-site: Ordinarily deprecated
 * Deprecation warning: No warning
 * @deprecated Dangerous to use.
 */
@Deprecated(since="1.1")
public static void m21() {
    Box.notDeprecated();
}
/**
 * API: Ordinarily deprecated
 * Use-site: Ordinarily deprecated
 * Deprecation warning: No warning
 * @deprecated Dangerous to use.
 */
@Deprecated(since="1.1")
public static void m22() {
    Box.deprecatedOrdinarily();
}

/**
 * API: Terminally deprecated
 * Use-site: Ordinarily deprecated
 * Deprecation warning: Removal warning
 * @deprecated Dangerous to use.
 */
@Deprecated(since="1.1")
public static void m23() {
    Box.deprecatedTerminally();
}
/**
 * API: Not deprecated
 * Use-site: Terminally deprecated
 * Deprecation warning: No warning
 * @deprecated Going away.
```

```
 */
@Deprecated(since="1.1", forRemoval=true)
public static void m31() {
    Box.notDeprecated();
}
/**
* API: Ordinarily deprecated
* Use-site: Terminally deprecated
* Deprecation warning: No warning
* @deprecated Going away.
*/
@Deprecated(since="1.1", forRemoval=true)
public static void m32() {
    Box.deprecatedOrdinarily();
}
/**
 * API: Terminally deprecated
 * Use-site: Terminally deprecated
 * Deprecation warning: Removal warning
 * @deprecated Going away.
*/
@Deprecated(since="1.1", forRemoval=true)
public static void m33() {
    Box.deprecatedTerminally();
}
/**
 * API: Ordinarily and Terminally deprecated
 * Use-site: Not deprecated
 * Deprecation warning: Ordinary and removal warnings
*/
public static void m41() {
    Box.deprecatedOrdinarily();
    Box.deprecatedTerminally();
}
```

```
/**
 * API: Ordinarily and Terminally deprecated
 * Use-site: Not deprecated
 * Deprecation warning: Ordinary warnings
 */
@SuppressWarnings("deprecation")
public static void m42() {
    Box.deprecatedOrdinarily();
    Box.deprecatedTerminally();
}
/**
 * API: Ordinarily and Terminally deprecated
 * Use-site: Not deprecated
 * Deprecation warning: Removal warnings
 */
@SuppressWarnings("removal")
public static void m43() {
    Box.deprecatedOrdinarily();
    Box.deprecatedTerminally();
}
/**
 * API: Ordinarily and Terminally deprecated
 * Use-site: Not deprecated
 * Deprecation warning: Removal warnings
 */
@SuppressWarnings({"deprecation", "removal"})
public static void m44() {
    Box.deprecatedOrdinarily();
    Box.deprecatedTerminally();
}
}
```

You need to compile the BoxTest class using the -Xlint:deprecation compiler flag, so the compiler emits deprecation warnings:

```
C:\Java9LanguageFeatures>javac -Xlint:deprecation ^
    -d build\modules\jdojo.annotation ^
src\jdojo.annotation\classes\com\jdojo\annotation\
    BoxTest.java
src\jdojo.annotation\classes\com\jdojo\annotation\
    BoxTest.java:20: warning: [deprecation]
deprecatedOrdinarily() in Box has been deprecated
        Box.deprecatedOrdinarily();
          ^
src\jdojo.annotation\classes\com\jdojo\annotation\
    BoxTest.java:29: warning: [removal]
deprecatedTerminally() in Box has been deprecated
    and marked for removal
        Box.deprecatedTerminally();
          ^
src\jdojo.annotation\classes\com\jdojo\annotation\
    BoxTest.java:62: warning: [removal]
deprecatedTerminally() in Box has been deprecated
    and marked for removal
        Box.deprecatedTerminally();
          ^
src\jdojo.annotation\classes\com\jdojo\annotation\
    BoxTest.java:95: warning: [removal]
deprecatedTerminally() in Box has been deprecated
    and marked for removal
        Box.deprecatedTerminally();
          ^
src\jdojo.annotation\classes\com\jdojo\annotation\
    BoxTest.java:104: warning: [deprecation]
deprecatedOrdinarily() in Box has been deprecated
        Box.deprecatedOrdinarily();
          ^
src\jdojo.annotation\classes\com\jdojo\annotation\
    BoxTest.java:105: warning: [removal]
```

49

```
deprecatedTerminally() in Box has been deprecated
    and marked for removal
        Box.deprecatedTerminally();
        ^
src\jdojo.annotation\classes\com\jdojo\annotation\
    BoxTest.java:116: warning: [removal]
deprecatedTerminally() in Box has been deprecated
    and marked for removal
        Box.deprecatedTerminally();
        ^
src\jdojo.annotation\classes\com\jdojo\annotation\
    BoxTest.java:126: warning: [deprecation]
deprecatedOrdinarily() in Box has been deprecated
        Box.deprecatedOrdinarily();
        ^
8 warnings
```

(No line break and no spaces after "annotation\" in the command.)

Recall that deprecation warnings are compile-time warnings. You will not get any warnings if compiled code for your deployed application starts using an ordinarily deprecated API or generates a runtime error because an API that was once valid had been terminally deprecated and removed. JDK9 and later improve this situation by providing a static analysis tool called `jdeprscan` that scans compiled code to give you the list of deprecated APIs being used. Currently, the tool reports the use of only deprecated JDK APIs. If your compiled code uses deprecated APIs from other libraries, say, Spring or Hibernate, or your own libraries, this tool will not report those uses.

The `jdeprscan` tool is in the `JDK_HOME\bin` directory. The general syntax to use the tool is as follows:

```
jdeprscan [options] {dir|jar|class}
```

Here, [`options`] is a list of zero or more options. You can specify a list of space-separated directories, JARs, fully qualified class names, or class file paths as arguments to scan. The available options are as follows:

- `-l, -list`

- `-class-path <CLASSPATH>`

- -for-removal

- -release <6|7|8|9|...|17>

- -v, -verbose

- -version

- -full-version

- -h, -help

The -list option lists the set of deprecated APIs in Java SE. No arguments specifying the location of compiled classes should be specified when this option is used.

The -class-path specifies the class path to be used to find dependent classes during the scan.

The -for-removal option restricts the scan or list to only those APIs that have been deprecated for removal.

The -release option specifies the Java SE release that provides the set of deprecated APIs during scanning. For example, to list all deprecated APIs in JDK15, you will use the tool as follows: jdeprscan -list -release 15.

The -verbose option prints additional messages during the scanning process.

The -version and -full-version options print the abbreviated and full versions of the jdeprscan tool, respectively.

The -help option prints a detailed help message about the jdeprscan tool.

Listing 1-20 contains the code for a JDeprScanTest class. The code is trivial. It is intended to just compile, not run. Running it will not produce any interesting output. It creates two threads. One thread is stopped using the stop() method of the Thread class, and another thread is destroyed using the destroy() method of the Thread class. The stop() and destroy() methods have been ordinarily deprecated since JDK 1.2 and JDK 1.5, respectively. JDK9 has terminally deprecated the destroy() method, whereas it continued to keep the stop() method ordinarily deprecated. I use this class in the following examples.

Listing 1-20. A JDeprScanTest Class That Uses the Ordinarily Deprecated Method stop() and the Terminally Deprecated Method destroy() of the Thread Class

```java
// JDeprScanTest.java
package com.jdojo.annotation;
public class JDeprScanTest {
    public static void main(String[] args) {
        Thread t = new Thread(() ->
            System.out.println("Test"));
        t.start();
        t.stop();
        Thread t2 = new Thread(() ->
            System.out.println("Test"));
        t2.start();
        t2.destroy();
    }
}
```

The following command prints the list of all deprecated APIs in JDK16. The command takes a few seconds to start printing the results because it scans the entire JDK:

```
C:\Java9LanguageFeatures>jdeprscan --list --release 16
@Deprecated(since="16", forRemoval=true)
    javax.management.relation.RoleStatus()
@Deprecated(since="9") interface
    java.beans.AppletInitializer
...
```

The following command prints all terminally deprecated APIs in JDK16. That is, it prints all deprecated APIs that have been marked for removal in a future release:

```
C:\Java9LanguageFeatures>jdeprscan --list --for-removal ^
    --release 16
@Deprecated(since="16", forRemoval=true)
    javax.management.relation.RoleStatus()
...
```

The following command prints the list of all APIs deprecated in JDK8:

```
C:\ Java9LanguageFeatures >jdeprscan --list --release 8
@Deprecated class javax.swing.text.TableView.TableCell
...
```

The following command prints the list of deprecated APIs in JDK16 used by the java.lang.Thread class:

```
C:\Java9LanguageFeatures>jdeprscan --release 16 ^
    java.lang.Thread
class java/lang/Thread uses deprecated method
    java/lang/Thread::resume()V (forRemoval=true)
```

Note that the previous command does not print the list of deprecated APIs in the Thread class. Rather, it prints the list of APIs in the Thread class that uses those deprecated APIs.

The following command lists all uses of deprecated JDK APIs in some directory:

```
C:\Java9LanguageFeatures>jdeprscan --release 16 ^
    path/to/folder
class com/test/Jdk17 uses deprecated method
    java/lang/Integer::<init>(I)V (forRemoval=true)
```

The jdeprscan tool is a static analysis tool, so it will skip dynamic uses of deprecated APIs. For example, you can call a deprecated method using reflection, which this tool will miss during scanning. You can also call deprecated methods in providers loaded by a ServiceLoader, which will be missed by this tool.

Until JDK9, the compiler generated a warning if you imported deprecated constructs using import statements, even if you used a @SuppressWarnings annotation on all use-sites of the deprecated imported constructs. This was an annoyance if you were trying to get rid of all deprecation warnings in your code. You just could not get rid of them because you cannot annotate import statements. JDK9 improved on this by omitting the deprecation warnings on import statements.

Suppressing Named Compile-Time Warnings

The SuppressWarnings annotation type is used to suppress named compile-time warnings. It declares one element named value whose data type is an array of String. Let's consider the code for the SuppressWarningsTest class, which uses the raw type for the ArrayList<T> in the test() method. The compiler generates an unchecked named warning when you use a raw type. See Listing 1-21.

Listing 1-21. A Class That Will Generate Warnings When Compiled

```
// SuppressWarningsTest.java
package com.jdojo.annotation;
import java.util.ArrayList;
public class SuppressWarningsTest {
    public void test() {
        ArrayList list = new ArrayList();
        list.add("Hello"); // The compiler issues an
                           // unchecked warning
    }
}
```

Compile the SuppressWarningsTest class with an option to generate an unchecked warning using the command:

```
javac -Xlint:unchecked SuppressWarningsTest.java
com\jdojo\annotation\SuppressWarningsTest.java:10:
    warning: [unchecked] unchecked call to add(E) as a
    member of the raw type ArrayList
             list.add("Hello");
                 ^
  where E is a type-variable
    E extends Object declared in class ArrayList
1 warning
```

As a developer, sometimes you are aware of such compiler warnings, and you want to suppress them when your code is compiled. You can do so by using a @SuppressWarnings annotation on your program element by supplying a list of the names of the warnings to be suppressed. For example, if you use it on a class declaration, all specified warnings will be suppressed from all methods inside that class declaration. It is recommended that you use this annotation on the innermost program element on which you want to suppress the warnings.

Listing 1-22 uses a @SuppressWarnings annotation on the test() method. It specifies two named warnings: "unchecked" and "deprecation." The test() method does not contain code that will generate a "deprecated" warning. It was included here to show you that you could suppress multiple named warnings using a SuppressWarnings annotation. If you recompile the SuppressWarningsTest class with the same options shown previously, it will not generate any compiler warnings.

Listing 1-22. The Modified Version of the SuppressWarningsTest Class

```
// SuppressWarningsTest.java
package com.jdojo.annotation;
import java.util.ArrayList;
public class SuppressWarningsTest {
    @SuppressWarnings({"unchecked", "deprecation"})
    public void test() {
        ArrayList list = new ArrayList();
        list.add("Hello"); // The compiler does not
                           // issue an unchecked warning
    }
}
```

Overriding Methods

The java.lang.Override annotation type is a marker annotation type. It can only be used on methods. It indicates that a method annotated with this annotation overrides a method declared in its supertype. This is very helpful for developers to avoid typos that lead to logical errors in the program. If you mean to override a method in a supertype, it is recommended to annotate the overridden method with an @Override annotation. The compiler will make sure that the annotated method really overrides a method in the supertype. If the annotated method does not override a method in the supertype, the compiler will generate an error.

Consider two classes, A and B. Class B inherits from class A. The m1() method in class B overrides the m1() method in its superclass A. The annotation @Override on the m1() method in class B just makes a statement about this intention. The compiler verifies this statement and finds it to be true in this case:

```
public class A {
    public void m1() {
    }
}
public class B extends A {
    @Override
    public void m1() {
    }
}
```

Let's consider class C:

```
// Won't compile because m2() does not override any method
public class C extends A {
    @Override
    public void m2() {
    }
}
```

The method m2() in class C has an @Override annotation. However, there is no m2() method in its superclass A. The method m2() is a new method in class C. The compiler finds out that method m2() in class C does not override any superclass method, even though its developer has indicated so. The compiler generates an error in this case.

Declaring Functional Interfaces

An interface with one abstract method declaration is known as a functional interface. Previously, a functional interface was known as a SAM (Single Abstract Method) type. The compiler verifies that all interfaces annotated with a @FunctionalInterface really contain one and only one abstract method. A compile-time error is generated if the interfaces annotated with this annotation are not functional. It is also a compile-time error to use this annotation on classes, annotation types, and enums. The FunctionalInterface annotation type is a marker annotation.

The following declaration of the Runner interface uses a @FunctionalInterface annotation. The interface declaration will compile fine:

```
@FunctionalInterface
public interface Runner {
    void run();
}
```

The following declaration of the Job interface uses a @FunctionalInterface annotation, which will generate a compile-time error because the Job interface declares two abstract methods, and therefore it is not a functional interface:

```
@FunctionalInterface
public interface Job {
    void run();
    void abort();
}
```

The following declaration of the Test class uses a @FunctionalInterface annotation, which will generate a compile-time error because a @FunctionalInterface annotation can only be used on interfaces:

```
@FunctionalInterface
public class Test {
    public void test() {
        // Code goes here
    }
}
```

Note   An interface with only one abstract method is always a functional interface whether it is annotated with a @FunctionalInterface annotation or not. The use of the annotation instructs the compiler to verify the fact that the interface is really a functional interface.

Annotating Packages

Annotating program elements such as classes and fields are intuitive, as you annotate them when they are declared. How do you annotate a package? A package declaration appears in a compilation unit as part of top-level type declarations. Further, the same package declaration occurs multiple times in different compilation units. The question arises: How and where do you annotate a package declaration?

You need to create a file, which should be named `package-info.java`, and place the annotated package declaration in it. Listing 1-23 shows the contents of the `package-info.java` file. When you compile the `package-info.java` file, a class file will be created.

Listing 1-23. Contents of a package-info.java File

```
// package-info.java
@Version(major=1, minor=0)
package com.jdojo.annotation;
```

You may need some `import` statements to import annotation types, or you can use the fully qualified names of the annotation types in the `package-info.java` file. Even though the `import` statements appear after the package declaration, it should be okay to use the imported types. You can have contents like the following in a `package-info.java` file:

```
// package-info.java
@com.jdojo.myannotations.Author("John Jacobs")
@Reviewer("Wally Inman")
package com.jdojo.annotation;
import com.jdojo.myannotations.Reviewer;
```

Annotating Modules

You can use annotations on `module` declarations. For this aim, the `java.lang.annotation.ElementType` enum has a value called `MODULE`. If you use `MODULE` as a target type on an annotation declaration, it allows the annotation type to be used on modules. The two annotations `java.lang.Deprecated` and `java.lang.SuppressWarnings` can be used on module declarations as follows:

```
@Deprecated(since="1.2", forRemoval=true)
@SuppressWarnings("unchecked")
module com.jdojo.myModule {
    // Module statements go here
}
```

When a module is deprecated, the use of that module in `requires`, but not in `exports` or opens statements, causes a warning to be issued. This rule is based on the fact that if module M is deprecated, a "requires M" statement will be used by the module's users who need to get the deprecation warnings. Other statements such as `exports` and opens are within the module that is deprecated. A deprecated module does not cause warnings to be issued for uses of types within the module. Similarly, if a warning is suppressed in a module declaration, the suppression applies to elements within the module declaration and not to types contained in that module.

Note   You cannot annotate individual module statements. For example, you cannot annotate an `exports` statement with a @Deprecated annotation indicating that the exported package will be removed in a future release. During the early design phase, it was considered and rejected on the ground that this feature will take a considerable amount of time that is not needed at this time. This could be added in the future, if needed.

Accessing Annotations at Runtime

Accessing annotations on a program element is easy. Annotations on a program element are Java objects. All you need to know is how to get the reference of objects of an annotation type at runtime. Program elements that let you access their annotations implement the `java.lang.reflect.AnnotatedElement` interface. There are several methods in the `AnnotatedElement` interface that let you access annotations of a program element. The methods in this interface let you retrieve all annotations on a program element, all declared annotations on a program element, and annotations of a specified type on a program element. I show some examples of using those methods shortly. The following classes implement the `AnnotatedElement` interface:

- `java.lang.Class`
- `java.lang.reflect.Executable`

- `java.lang.reflect.Constructor`

- `java.lang.reflect.Field`

- `java.lang.reflect.Method`

- `java.lang.reflect.Module`

- `java.lang.reflect.Parameter`

- `java.lang.Package`

- `java.lang.reflect.AccessibleObject`

Methods of the `AnnotatedElement` interface are used to access annotations on these types of objects.

Caution   It is very important to note that an annotation type must be annotated with the `Retention` meta-annotation with the retention policy of `runtime` to access it at runtime. If a program element has multiple annotations, you would be able to access only annotations, which have `runtime` as their retention policy.

Suppose you have a `Test` class and you want to print all its annotations. The following snippet of code will print all annotations on the class declaration of the `Test` class:

```
// Get the class object reference
Class<Test> cls = Test.class;
// Get all annotations on the class declaration
Annotation[] allAnns = cls.getAnnotations();
System.out.println("Annotation count: " + allAnns.length);
// Print all annotations
for (Annotation ann : allAnns) {
    System.out.println(ann.toString());
}
```

The `toString()` method of the Annotation interface returns the string representation of an annotation. Suppose you want to print the `Version` annotation on the `Test` class. You can do so as follows:

```
Class<Test> cls = Test.class;
// Get the instance of the Version annotation of Test
// class
Version v = cls.getAnnotation(Version.class);
if (v == null) {
    System.out.println(
        "Version annotation is not present.");
} else {
    int major = v.major();
    int minor = v.minor();
    System.out.println("Version: major=" + major +
        ", minor=" + minor);
}
```

This snippet of code shows that you can use the `major()` and `minor()` methods to read the value of the `major` and `minor` elements of the `Version` annotation. It also shows that you can declare a variable of an annotation type (e.g., `Version v`), which can refer to an instance of that annotation type. The instances of an annotation type are created by the Java runtime. You never create an instance of an annotation type using the `new` operator.

You will use the `Version` and `Deprecated` annotation types to annotate your program elements and access those annotations at runtime. You will also annotate a package declaration and a method declaration. You will use the code for the `Version` annotation type, as listed in Listing 1-24. Note that it uses the `@Retention(RetentionPolicy.RUNTIME)` annotation, which is needed to read its instances at runtime.

Listing 1-24. A Version Annotation Type

```
// Version.java
package com.jdojo.annotation;

import java.lang.annotation.Documented;
import java.lang.annotation.Target;
import java.lang.annotation.ElementType;
import java.lang.annotation.Retention;
import java.lang.annotation.RetentionPolicy;
```

```
@Target({ElementType.TYPE, ElementType.CONSTRUCTOR,
    ElementType.METHOD, ElementType.MODULE,
    ElementType.PACKAGE})
@Retention(RetentionPolicy.RUNTIME)
@Documented
public @interface Version {
    int major();
    int minor();
}
```

Listing 1-25 shows the code that you need to save in a `package-info.java` file and compile it along with other programs. It annotates the `com.jdojo.annotation` package. Listing 1-26 contains the code for a class for demonstration purposes that has some annotations.

Listing 1-25. Contents of the package-info.java File

```
// package-info.java
@Version(major=1, minor=0)
package com.jdojo.annotation;
```

Listing 1-26. AccessAnnotation Class Has Some Annotations, Which Will Be Accessed at Runtime

```
// AccessAnnotation.java
package com.jdojo.annotation;
@Version(major=1, minor=0)
public class AccessAnnotation {
    @Version(major=1, minor=1)
    public void testMethod1() {
        // Code goes here
    }
    @Version(major=1, minor=2)
    @Deprecated
    public void testMethod2() {
        // Code goes here
    }
}
```

Listing 1-27 is the program that demonstrates how to access annotations at runtime. Its output shows that you are able to read all annotations used in the `AccessAnnotation` class successfully. The `printAnnotations()` method accesses the annotations. It accepts a parameter of the `AnnotatedElement` type and prints all annotations of its parameter. If the annotation is of the `Version` annotation type, it prints the values for its major and minor versions.

Listing 1-27. Using the AccessAnnotationTest Class to Access Annotations

```java
// AccessAnnotationTest.java
package com.jdojo.annotation;
import java.lang.annotation.Annotation;
import java.lang.reflect.AnnotatedElement;
import java.lang.reflect.Method;

public class AccessAnnotationTest {
    public static void main(String[] args) {
        // Read annotations on the class declaration
        Class<AccessAnnotation> cls =
            AccessAnnotation.class;
        System.out.println("Annotations for class: " +
            cls.getName());
        printAnnotations(cls);
        // Read annotations on the package declaration
        Package p = cls.getPackage();
        System.out.println("Annotations for package: " +
            p.getName());
        printAnnotations(p);
        // Read annotations on the methods declarations
        System.out.println("Method annotations:");
        Method[] methodList = cls.getDeclaredMethods();
        for (Method m : methodList) {
            System.out.println("Annotations for method: " +
                m.getName());
            printAnnotations(m);
        }
    }
```

```
    public static void printAnnotations(
            AnnotatedElement programElement) {
        Annotation[] annList = programElement.
            getAnnotations();
        for (Annotation ann : annList) {
            System.out.println(ann);
            if (ann instanceof Version) {
                Version v = (Version) ann;
                int major = v.major();
                int minor = v.minor();
                System.out.println(
                    "Found Version annotation: "
                        + "major=" + major +
                        ", minor=" + minor);
            }
        }
        System.out.println();
    }
}
Annotations for class:
    com.jdojo.annotation.AccessAnnotation
@com.jdojo.annotation.Version(major=1, minor=0)
Found Version annotation: major=1, minor=0
Annotations for package: com.jdojo.annotation
@com.jdojo.annotation.Version(major=1, minor=0)
Found Version annotation: major=1, minor=0
Method annotations:
Annotations for method: testMethod1
@com.jdojo.annotation.Version(major=1, minor=1)
Found Version annotation: major=1, minor=1
Annotations for method: testMethod2
@com.jdojo.annotation.Version(major=1, minor=2)
Found Version annotation: major=1, minor=2
@java.lang.Deprecated(forRemoval=false, since="")
```

Accessing instances of a repeatable annotation is a little different. Recall that a repeatable annotation has a companion containing an annotation type. For example, you declared a ChangeLogs annotation type that is a containing annotation type for the ChangeLog repeatable annotation type. You can access repeated annotations using either the annotation type or the containing annotation type. Use the getAnnotationsByType() method, passing it the class reference of the repeatable annotation type to get the instances of the repeatable annotation in an array. Use the getAnnotation() method, passing it the class reference of the containing annotation type to get the instances of the repeatable annotation as an instance of its containing annotation type.

Listing 1-28 contains the code for a RepeatableAnnTest class. The class declaration has been annotated with the ChangeLog annotation twice. The main() method accesses the repeated annotations on the class declaration using both of these methods.

Listing 1-28. Accessing Instances of Repeatable Annotations at Runtime

```
// RepeatableAnnTest.java
package com.jdojo.annotation;
@ChangeLog(date = "09/18/2017",
    comments = "Declared the class")
@ChangeLog(date = "10/22/2017",
    comments = "Added the main() method")
public class RepeatableAnnTest {
    public static void main(String[] args) {
        Class<RepeatableAnnTest> mainClass =
            RepeatableAnnTest.class;
        Class<ChangeLog> annClass = ChangeLog.class;
        // Access annotations using the ChangeLog type
        System.out.println("Using the ChangeLog type...");
        ChangeLog[] annList = mainClass.
            getAnnotationsByType(ChangeLog.class);
        for (ChangeLog log : annList) {
            System.out.println("Date=" + log.date() +
            ", Comments=" + log.comments());
        }
        // Access annotations using the ChangeLogs
        // containing annotation type
```

```
        System.out.println(
            "\nUsing the ChangeLogs type...");
        Class<ChangeLogs> containingAnnClass =
            ChangeLogs.class;
        ChangeLogs logs = mainClass.getAnnotation(
            containingAnnClass);
        for (ChangeLog log : logs.value()) {
            System.out.println("Date=" + log.date() +
                ", Comments=" + log.comments());
        }
    }
}
Using the ChangeLog type...
Date=09/18/2017, Comments=Declared the class
Date=10/22/2017, Comments=Added the main() method

Using the ChangeLogs type...
Date=09/18/2017, Comments=Declared the class
Date=10/22/2017, Comments=Added the main() method
```

Evolving Annotation Types

An annotation type can evolve without breaking the existing code that uses it. If you add a new element to an annotation type, you need to supply its default value. All existing instances of the annotation will use the default value for the new elements. If you add a new element to an existing annotation type without specifying a default value for the element, the code that uses the annotation will break.

Annotation Processing at Source Code Level

This section is for experienced programmers. You may skip this section if you are learning Java for the first time. We discuss in detail how to develop annotation processors to process an annotation at the source code level when you compile Java programs.

Note   The University of Washington developed a *Checker Framework* that contains a lot of annotations to be used in programs. It also ships with many annotation processors. You can download the Checker Framework from `https://checkerframework.org/`. It contains a tutorial for using different types of processors and a tutorial on how to create your own processor.

Java lets you process annotations at runtime as well as at compile time. You have already seen how to process annotations at runtime. Now, I discuss, in brief, how to process annotations at compile time (or at the source code level).

Why would you want to process annotations at compile time? Processing annotations at compile time opens up a wide variety of possibilities that can help Java programmers during development of applications. It also helps developers of Java tools immensely. For example, boilerplate code and configuration files can be generated based on annotations in the source code; custom annotation-based rules can be validated at compile time, etc.

Annotation processing at compile time is a two-step process. First, you need to write a custom annotation processor. Second, you need to use the `javac` command-line utility tool. You need to specify the module path for your custom annotation processor to the `javac` compiler using the `-processor-modulepath` option. The following command compiles the Java source file, `MySourceFile.java`:

```
javac --processor-module-path <path> MySourceFile.java
```

Using the `-proc` option, the `javac` command lets you specify if you want to process the annotation and/or compile the source files. You can use the `-proc` option as `-proc:none` or `-proc:only`. The `-proc:none` option does not perform annotation processing. It only compiles source files. The `-proc:only` option performs only annotation processing and skips the source file compilation. If the `-proc:none` and the `-processor` options are specified in the same command, the `-processor` option is ignored. The following command processes annotations in the source file `MySourceFile.java` using custom processors: `MyProcessor1` and `MyProcessor2`. It does not compile the source code in the `MySourceFile.java` file:

```
javac -proc:only --processor-module-path <path> ^
    MySourceFile.java
```

To see the compile-time annotation processing in action, you must write an annotation processor using the classes in the `javax.annotation.processing` package, which is in the `java.compiler` module.

While writing a custom annotation processor, you often need to access the elements from the source code, for example, the name of a class and its modifiers, the name of a method and its return type, etc. You need to use classes in the `javax.lang.model` package and its subpackages to work with the elements of the source code. In your example, you will write an annotation processor for your `@Version` annotation. It will validate all `@Version` annotations that are used in the source code to make sure the `major` and `minor` values for a `Version` are always zero or greater than zero. For example, if `@Version(major=-1, minor=0)` is used in source code, your annotation processor will print an error message because the major value for the version is negative.

An annotation processor is an object of a class, which implements the `Processor` interface. The `AbstractProcessor` class is an abstract annotation processor, which provides a default implementation for all methods of the `Processor` interface, except an implementation for the `process()` method. The default implementation is fine in most circumstances. To create your own processor, you need to inherit your processor class from the `AbstractProcessor` class and provide an implementation for the `process()` method. If the `AbstractProcessor` class does not suit your need, you can create your own processor class, which implements the `Processor` interface. Let's call your processor class `VersionProcessor`, which inherits from the `AbstractProcessor` class, as shown:

```
public class VersionProcessor extends AbstractProcessor {
    // Code goes here
}
```

The annotation processor object is instantiated by the compiler using a no-args constructor. You must have a no-args constructor for your processor class, so that the compiler can instantiate it. The default constructor for your `VersionProcessor` class will meet this requirement.

The next step is to add two pieces of information to the processor class. The first one is about what kind of annotation processing is supported by this processor. You can specify the supported annotation type using the `@SupportedAnnotationTypes` annotation at the class level. The following snippet of code shows that the `VersionProcessor` supports processing of the `com.jdojo.annotation.Version` annotation type:

```
@SupportedAnnotationTypes({"com.jdojo.annotation.Version"})
public class VersionProcessor extends AbstractProcessor {
    // Code goes here
}
```

You can use an asterisk (*) by itself or as part of the annotation name of the supported annotation types. The asterisk works as a wildcard. For example, "com. jdojo.*" means any annotation types whose names start with "com.jdojo." An asterisk only ("*") means all annotation types. Note that when an asterisk is used as part of the name, the name must be of the form PartialName.*. For example, "com*" and "com.*jdojo" are invalid uses of an asterisk in the supported annotation types. You can pass multiple supported annotation types using the SupportedAnnotationTypes annotation. The following snippet of code shows that the processor supports processing for the com.jdojo.Ann1 annotation and any annotations whose name begins with com.jdojo.annotation:

```
@SupportedAnnotationTypes({"com.jdojo.Ann1",
    "com.jdojo.annotation.*"})
```

You need to specify the latest source code version that is supported by your processor using a @SupportedSourceVersion annotation. The following snippet of code specifies the source code version 17 as the supported source code version for the VersionProcessor class:

```
@SupportedAnnotationTypes({"com.jdojo.annotation.Version"})
@SupportedSourceVersion(SourceVersion.RELEASE_17)
public class VersionProcessor extends AbstractProcessor {
    // Code goes here
}
```

The next step is to provide the implementation for the process() method in the processor class. Annotation processing is performed in rounds. An instance of the RoundEnvironment interface represents a round. The javac compiler calls the process() method of your processor by passing all annotations that the processor declares to support and a RoundEnvironment object. The return type of the process() method is boolean. If it returns true, the annotations passed to it are considered to be claimed by the processor. The claimed annotations are not passed to other processors. If it returns false, the annotations passed to it are considered as not claimed, and other processors will be asked to process them. The following snippet of code shows the skeleton of the process() method:

```
public boolean process(Set<? extends TypeElement>
        annotations, RoundEnvironment roundEnv) {
    // The processor code goes here
}
```

The code you write inside the process() method depends on your requirements. In your case, you want to look at the major and minor values for each @Version annotation in the source code. If either of them is less than zero, you want to print an error message. To process each Version annotation, you will iterate through all Version annotation instances passed to the process() method as follows:

```
for (TypeElement currentAnnotation : annotations) {
    // Code to validate each Version annotation goes here
}
```

You can get the fully qualified name of an annotation using the getQualifiedName() method of the TypeElement interface:

```
Name qualifiedName = currentAnnotation.getQualifiedName();
// Check if it is a Version annotation
if (qualifiedName.contentEquals(
        "com.jdojo.annotation.Version")) {
    // Get Version annotation values to validate
}
```

Once you are sure that you have a Version annotation, you need to get all its instances from the source code. To get information from the source code, you need to use the RoundEnvironment object. The following snippet of code will get all elements of the source code (e.g., classes, methods, constructors, etc.) that are annotated with a Version annotation:

```
Set<? extends Element> annotatedElements =
    roundEnv.getElementsAnnotatedWith(currentAnnotation);
```

At this point, you need to iterate through all elements that are annotated with a Version annotation; get the instance of the Version annotation present on them; and validate the values of the major and minor elements. You can perform this logic as follows:

```
for (Element element : annotatedElements) {
    Version v = element.getAnnotation(Version.class);
    int major = v.major();
    int minor = v.minor();
    if (major < 0 || minor < 0) {
        // Print the error message here
    }
}
```

You can print the error message using the printMessage() method of the Messager. The processingEnv is an instance variable defined in the AbstractProcessor class that you can use inside your processor to get the Messager object reference, as shown next. If you pass the source code element's reference to the printMessage() method, your message will be formatted to include the source code file name and the line number in the source code for that element. The first argument to the printMessage() method indicates the type of the message. You can use Kind.NOTE and Kind.WARNING as the first argument to print a note and warning, respectively.

```
String errorMsg = "Version cannot be negative. major=" +
    major + " minor=" + minor;
Messager messager = this.processingEnv.getMessager();
messager.printMessage(Kind.ERROR, errorMsg, element);
```

Finally, you need to return true or false from the process() method. If a processor returns true, it means it claimed all the annotations that were passed to it. Otherwise, those annotations are considered unclaimed, and they will be passed to other processors. Typically, your annotation processors should be packaged in a separate module. Listing 1-29 contains the declaration for a jdojo.annotation.processor module, which contains the annotation processor named VersionProcessor for the Version annotation type, as shown in Listing 1-30.

Listing 1-29. The Declaration for a jdojo.annotation.processor Module

```java
// module-info.java
module jdojo.annotation.processor {
    exports com.jdojo.annotation.processor;
    requires jdojo.annotation;
    requires java.compiler;
    provides javax.annotation.processing.Processor
        with
        com.jdojo.annotation.processor.VersionProcessor;
}
```

The module reads the `jdojo.annotation` module because it uses the `Version` annotation type in the `VersionProcessor` class. It reads the `java.compiler` module to use annotation processor–related types. Notice the use of the provides statement in the module's declaration. Java will load all annotation processors on the processor module path mentioned in the `with` clause of the provides statement. The statement specifies that the `VersionProcessor` class provides an implementation for the `Processor` service interface. Refer to Chapter 7 for more details on the `provides` statement and implementing services.

Listing 1-30. An Annotation Processor to Process Version Annotations

```java
// VersionProcessor.java
package com.jdojo.annotation.processor;

import java.util.Set;
import javax.annotation.processing.AbstractProcessor;
import javax.annotation.processing.Messager;
import javax.annotation.processing.RoundEnvironment;
import javax.annotation.processing.SupportedAnnotationTypes;
import javax.annotation.processing.SupportedSourceVersion;
import javax.lang.model.SourceVersion;
import javax.lang.model.element.Element;
import javax.lang.model.element.Name;
import javax.lang.model.element.TypeElement;
import javax.tools.Diagnostic.Kind;
```

```java
@SupportedAnnotationTypes({
    "com.jdojo.annotation.Version"})
@SupportedSourceVersion(SourceVersion.RELEASE_17)
public class VersionProcessor extends AbstractProcessor {
    // A no-args constructor is required for an
    // annotation processor
    public VersionProcessor() {
    }
    @Override
    public boolean process(Set<? extends TypeElement>
        annotations, RoundEnvironment roundEnv) {
        // Process all annotations
        for (TypeElement currentAnnotation: annotations) {
            Name qualifiedName = currentAnnotation.
                getQualifiedName();
            // check if it is a Version annotation
            if (qualifiedName.contentEquals(
                    "com.jdojo.annotation.Version" )) {
                // Look at all elements that have Version
                // annotations
                Set<? extends Element> annotatedElements;
                annotatedElements = roundEnv.
                    getElementsAnnotatedWith(
                    currentAnnotation);
                for (Element element: annotatedElements) {
                    Version v = element.getAnnotation(
                        Version.class);
                    int major = v.major();
                    int minor = v.minor();
                    if (major < 0 || minor < 0) {
                        // Print the error message
                        String errorMsg =
                            "Version cannot be negative." +
                            " major=" + major +
                            " minor=" + minor;
```

```
                    Messager messager = this.
                        processingEnv.getMessager();
                    messager.printMessage(Kind.ERROR,
                        errorMsg, element);
                }
            }
        }
    }
    return true;
    }
}
```

Now you have an annotation processor. It is time to see it in action. You need to have a source code that uses invalid values for the major and minor elements in the Version annotation. You will place the source code in a module named jdojo.annotation. test, as shown in Listing 1-31. The VersionProcessorTest class in Listing 1-32 uses the Version annotation three times. It uses negative values for major and minor elements for the class itself and for the method m2(). The processor should catch these two errors when you compile the source code for the VersionProcessorTest class.

Listing 1-31. The Declaration of a jdojo.annotation.test Module

```
// module-info.java
module jdojo.annotation.test {
    exports com.jdojo.annotation.test;
    requires jdojo.annotation;
}
```

Listing 1-32. A Test Class to Test VersionProcessor

```
// VersionProcessorTest.java
package com.jdojo.annotation.test;
@Version(major = -1, minor = 2)
public class VersionProcessorTest {
    @Version(major = 1, minor = 1)
    public void m1() {
    }
```

```
    @Version(major = -2, minor = 1)
    public void m2() {
    }
}
```

To see the processor in action, you need to run the following command. You need to specify the path for the `VersionProcessor` class's module using the `-processor-module-path` option. The modules that the annotation processor depends on should also be specified in the processor module path. When the command is run, the compiler will automatically discover the `VersionProcessor` as an annotation processor, and it will pass all `@Version` instances to this processor. The output displays two errors with the source file name and the line number at which errors were found in the source file:

```
C:\Java9LanguageFeatures>javac --module-path ^
    dist\jdojo.annotation.jar ^
    --processor-module-path ^
    dist\jdojo.annotation.processor.jar;
    dist\jdojo.annotation.jar ^
    -d build\modules\jdojo.annotation.test
src\jdojo.annotation.test\classes\module-info.java
src\jdojo.annotation.test\classes\com\jdojo\annotation\
    test\VersionProcessorTest.java
src\jdojo.annotation.test\classes\com\jdojo\annotation\
    test\VersionProcessorTest.java:7:
error: Version cannot be negative. major=-1 minor=2
public class VersionProcessorTest {
    ^
src\jdojo.annotation.test\classes\com\jdojo\annotation\
    test\VersionProcessorTest.java:13:
error: Version cannot be negative. major=-2 minor=1
    public void m2() {
        ^
2 errors
```

(No line break and no spaces after "dist\jdojo.annotation.processor.jar;".)

Summary

Annotations are types in Java. They are used to associate information to the declarations of program elements or type uses in a Java program. Using annotations does not change the semantics of the program.

Annotations can be available in the source code only, in the class files, or at runtime. Their availability is controlled by the retention policy that is specified when the annotation types are declared.

There are two types of annotations: regular annotations or simple annotations and meta-annotations. Annotations are used to annotate program elements, whereas meta-annotations are used to annotate other annotations. When you declare an annotation, you can specify its targets that are the types of program elements that it can annotate. It is possible for annotations to be repeated on the same element.

The Java library contains many annotation types that you can use in your Java programs—Deprecated, Override, SuppressWarnings, FunctionalInterface, etc. are a few of the commonly used annotation types. They have compiler support, which means that the compiler generates errors if the program elements annotated with these annotations do not adhere to specific rules.

Java lets you write annotation processors that can be plugged into the Java compiler to process annotations when Java programs are compiled. You can write processors to enforce custom rules based on annotations.

Deprecation in Java is a way to provide information about the lifecycle of the API. Deprecating an API tells its users to migrate away because the API is dangerous to use, a better replacement exists, or it will be removed in a future release. Using deprecated APIs generates compile-time deprecation warnings. The @deprecated Javadoc tag and the @Deprecated annotation are used together to deprecate API elements such as modules, packages, types, constructors, methods, fields, parameters, and local variables. This annotation is retained at runtime.

The Deprecated annotation type contains since and forRemoval as elements. The since element defaults to an empty string. Its value denotes the version of the API in which the API element was deprecated. The forRemoval element's type is boolean, and it defaults to false. Its value of true denotes that the API element will be removed in a future release.

The compiler (starting at JDK9) generates two types of deprecation warnings depending on the value of the `forRemoval` element of the `@Deprecated` annotation: ordinary deprecation warnings when `forRemoval=false` and removal warnings for `forRemoval=true`.

You need to use `@SuppressWarnings("deprecation")` to suppress ordinary warnings, `@SuppressWarnings("removal")` to suppress removal warnings, and `@SuppressWarnings({"deprecation", "removal"})` to suppress both types of warnings. Just importing a deprecated construct, and not actually using it, does not generate deprecation warnings.

Exercises

Exercise 1

What are annotations? How do you declare them?

Exercise 2

What are meta-annotations?

Exercise 3

What is the difference between an annotation type and annotation instances?

Exercise 4

Can you inherit an annotation type from another annotation type?

Exercise 5

What are marker annotations? Describe their use. Name two marker annotations available in Java SE API.

Exercise 6

Name the annotation type whose instances are used to annotate an overridden method. What is the fully qualified name of this annotation type?

Exercise 7

What are the allowed return types for methods in an annotation type declaration?

Exercise 8

Declare an annotation type named `Table`. It contains one `String` element named name. The sole element does not have any default value. This annotation must be used only on classes. Its instances should be available at runtime.

Exercise 9

What is wrong with the following annotation type declaration?

```
public @interface Version extends BasicVersion {
    int extended();
}
```

Exercise 10

What is wrong with the following annotation type declaration?

```
public @interface Author {
    void name(String firstName, String lastName);
}
```

Briefly describe the use of the following built-in meta-annotations: Target, Retention, Inherited, Documented, Repeatable, and Native.

Exercise 11

Declare an annotation type named ModuleOwner, which contains one element name, which is of the String type. The instances of the ModuleOwner type should be retained only in the source code, and they should be used only on module declarations.

Exercise 12

Declare a repeatable annotation type named Author. It contains two elements of String type: firstName and lastName. This annotation can be used on types, methods, and constructors. Its instances should be available at runtime. Name the containing annotation type for the Author annotation type as Authors.

Exercise 13

What annotation type do you use to deprecate your APIs? Describe all the elements of such an annotation type.

Exercise 14

What annotation type do you use to annotate a functional interface?

Exercise 15

How do you annotate a package?

Exercise 16

Create an annotation type named Owner. It should have one element, name, of the String type. Its instances should be retained at runtime. It should be repeatable. It should be used only on types, methods, constructors, and modules. Create a module

named jdojo.annotation.test and create a class named Test in the com.jdojo.
annotation.exercises package. Add a constructor and a method to the class. Annotate
the class, its module, constructor, and method with the Owner annotation type. Add a
main() method to the Test class and write code to access and print the details of these
instances of the Owner annotation.

Exercise 17

Consider the following declaration of an annotation type named Status:

```
public @interface Status {
    boolean approved() default false;
    String approvedBy();
}
```

Later, you need to add another element to the Status annotation type.

Modify the declaration of the annotation to include a new element named
approvedOn, which is of the String type. The new element will contain a date in ISO
format whose default value may be set to "1900-01-01".

Exercise 18

Consider the declaration of the following annotation type named LuckyNumber:

```
public @interface LuckyNumber {
    int[] value() default {19};
}
```

Which of the following uses of the LuckyNumber annotation type is/are invalid?
Explain your answer.

    a) @LuckyNumber

    b) @LuckyNumber({})

    c) @LuckyNumber(10)

    d) LuckyNumber({8, 10, 19, 28, 29, 26})

    e) LuckyNumber(value={8, 10, 19, 28, 29, 26})

    f) @LuckyNumber(null)

Exercise 19

Given a LuckyNumber annotation type, is the following variable declaration valid?

```
LuckNumber myLuckNumber = null;
```

Exercise 20

Consider the following declaration for a jdojo.annotation.exercises module:

```
module jdojo.annotation.exercises {
    exports com.jdojo.annotation.exercises;
}
```

The module exists since version 1.0. The module has been deprecated and will be removed in the next version. Annotate the module declaration to reflect these pieces of information.

CHAPTER 2

Reflection

In this chapter, you will learn:

- What reflection is

- What a class loader is and about the built-in class loaders

- How to use reflection to get information about classes, constructors, methods, etc. at runtime

- How to access fields of an object and a class using reflection

- How to create objects of a class using reflection

- How to invoke methods of a class using reflection

- How to create arrays using reflection

Most example programs in this chapter are a member of a `jdojo.reflection` module, as declared in Listing 2-1. I use more modules in this chapter, which I show later.

Listing 2-1. The Declaration of a jdojo.reflection Module

```
// module-info.java
module jdojo.reflection {
    exports com.jdojo.reflection;
}
```

What Is Reflection?

Reflection is the ability of a program to query and modify its state "as data" during the execution of the program. The ability of a program to query or obtain information about itself is known as introspection. The ability of a program to modify its execution state,

© Kishori Sharan, Peter Späth 2021
K. Sharan and P. Späth, *More Java 17*, https://doi.org/10.1007/978-1-4842-7135-3_2

modify its own interpretation or its meaning, or add new behaviors to the program as it is executing is called intercession. Reflection is further divided into two categories:

- Structural reflection

- Behavioral reflection

The ability of a program to query about the implementation of its data and code is called structural introspection, whereas its ability to modify or create new data structure and code is called structural intercession.

The ability of a program to obtain information about its runtime environment is called behavioral introspection, whereas its ability to modify the runtime environment is called behavioral intercession.

Providing the ability to a program to query or modify its state requires a mechanism for encoding the execution state as data. In other words, the program should be able to represent its execution state as data elements (as objects in object-oriented languages such as Java) so that it can be queried and modified. The process of encoding the execution state into data is called reification. A programming language is called reflective if it provides the programs with reflection capability.

Reflection in Java

The support for reflection in Java is mostly limited to introspection. It supports intercession in a very limited form. The introspection features provided by Java let you obtain class information about an object at runtime. Java also lets you obtain information about the fields, methods, modifiers, and the superclass of a class at runtime.

The intercession features provided by Java let you create an instance of a class whose name is not known until runtime, invoke methods on such instances, and get/set its fields. However, Java does not allow you to change the data structure at runtime. For example, you cannot add a new field or a method to an object at runtime. All fields of an object are always determined during the startup of a program. Examples of behavioral intercession are the ability to change the method execution at runtime or add a new method to a class at runtime. Java does not provide any of these intercession features. That is, you cannot change a class's method code at runtime to change its execution behavior; neither can you add a new method to a class at runtime.

Java provides reification by providing an object representation for a class and its methods, constructors, fields, etc. at runtime. In most cases, Java does not support reification for generic types. Java 5 added support for generic types. Refer to Chapter 3 for more details on generic types. A program can work on the reified objects in order to get information about the runtime execution. For example, you have been using the object of the `java.lang.Class` class to get the information about the class of an object. A Class object is the reification of the bytecode for the class of an object. When you want to gather information about the class of an object, you do not have to worry about the bytecode of the class from which the object was instantiated. Rather, Java provides the reification of the bytecode as an object of the `Class` class.

The reflection facility in Java is provided through the reflection API. Most of the reflection API classes and interfaces are in the `java.lang.reflect` package. The `Class` class, which is central to the reflection in Java, is in the `java.lang` package. Some of the frequently used classes in reflection are listed in Table 2-1.

Table 2-1. *Commonly Used Classes in Reflection*

Class Name	Description
Class	An object of this class represents a single class loaded by a class loader in the JVM.
Field	An object of this class represents a single field of a class or an interface. The field represented by this object may be a static field or an instance field.
Constructor	An object of this class represents a single constructor of a class.
Method	An object of this class represents a method of a class or an interface. The method represented by this object may be a class method or an instance method.
Modifier	This class has static methods that are used to decode the access modifiers for a class and its members.
Parameter	An object of this class represents a method's parameter.
Array	This class provides static methods that are used to create arrays at runtime.

Some of the things you can do using the reflection features in Java are as follows:

- If you have an object reference, you can determine the class name of the object.

- If you have a class name, you can know its full description, for example, its package name, its access modifiers, etc.

- If you have a class name, you can determine the methods defined in the class, their return type, access modifiers, parameter type, parameter names, etc. The support for parameter names was added in Java 8.

- If you have a class name, you can determine all field descriptions of the class.

- If you have a class name, you can determine all constructors defined in the class.

- If you have a class name, you can create an object of the class using one of its constructors.

- If you have an object reference, you can invoke its method knowing just the method's name and method's parameter types.

- You can get or set the state of an object at runtime.

- You can create an array of a type dynamically at runtime and manipulate its elements.

Loading a Class

The Class<T> class is central to reflection in Java. The Class<T> class is a generic class. It takes a type parameter, which is the type of the class represented by the Class object. For example, Class<String> represents the class object for the String class. Class<?> represents a class type whose class is unknown.

The Class class lets you discover everything about a class at runtime. An object of the Class class represents a class in a program at runtime. When you create an object in your program, Java loads the class's bytecode and creates an object of the Class class to represent the bytecode. Java uses that Class object to create any object of that class.

No matter how many objects of a class you create in your program, Java creates only one Class object for each class loaded by a class loader in a JVM from one module. Each class from a module is also loaded only once by a particular class loader. In a JVM, a class is uniquely identified by its fully qualified name, its class loader, and its module. If two different class loaders load the same class, the two loaded classes are considered two different classes, and their objects are not compatible with each other.

You can get the reference to the Class object of a class in one of the followings ways:

- Using class literal

- Using the getClass() method of the Object class

- Using the forName() static method of the Class class

Using Class Literals

A class literal is the class name or interface name followed by a dot and the word "class." For example, if you have a class Test, its class literal is Test.class, and you can write

```
Class<Test> testClass = Test.class;
```

Note that the class literal is always used with a class name, not with an object reference. The following statement to get the class reference is invalid:

```
Test t = new Test();
Class<Test> testClass = t.class;    // A compile-time error.
                                    // Must use Test.class
```

You can also get the class object for primitive data types and the keyword void using class literals as boolean.class, byte.class, char.class, short.class, int.class, long.class, float.class, double.class, and void.class. Each wrapper class for these primitive data types has a static field named TYPE, which has the reference to the class object of the primitive data type it represents. Therefore, int.class and Integer.TYPE refer to the same class object, and the expression int.class == Integer.TYPE evaluates to true. Table 2-2 shows the class literals for all primitive data types and the void keyword.

Table 2-2. *Class Literals for Primitive Data Types and the void Keyword*

Data Type	Primitive Class Literal	Wrapper Class static Field
boolean	boolean.class	Boolean.TYPE
Byte	byte.class	Byte.TYPE
Char	char.class	Character.TYPE
Short	short.class	Short.TYPE
Int	int.class	Integer.TYPE
Long	long.class	Long.TYPE
Float	float.class	Float.TYPE
Double	double.class	Double.TYPE
Void	void.class	Void.TYPE

Using the `Object::getClass()` Method

The Object class contains a getClass() method, which returns the reference to the Class object of the class of the object. This method is available in every class in Java because every class in Java, explicitly or implicitly, inherits the Object class. The method is declared final, so no descendant class can override it. For example, if you have testRef as a reference to an object of class Test, you can get the reference to the Class object of the Test class as follows:

```
Test testRef = new Test();
Class<?> testClass = testRef.getClass();
```

Using the `Class::forName()` Method

The Class class has a forName() static method, which loads a class and returns the reference to its Class object. It is an overloaded method. Its declarations are as follows:

- Class<?> forName(String className) throws
  ClassNotFoundException

- `Class<?> forName(String className, boolean initialize, ClassLoader loader) throws ClassNotFoundException`

- `Class<?> forName(Module module, String className)`

The `forName(String className)` method takes the fully qualified name of the class to be loaded. It loads the class, initializes it, and returns the reference to its `Class` object. If the class is already loaded, it simply returns the reference to the `Class` object of that class.

The `forName(String className, boolean initialize, ClassLoader loader)` method gives you options to initialize or not to initialize the class when it is loaded, and which class loader should load the class. The first two versions of the method throw a `ClassNotFoundException` if the class could not be loaded.

The `forName(Module module, String className)` method loads the class with the specified className in the specified module without initializing the loaded class. If the class is not found, the method returns `null`.

To load a class named `pkg1.Test`, you would write

```
Class testClass = Class.forName("pkg1.Test");
```

To get a `Class` object reference using the `forName()` method, you do not have to know the name of the class until runtime. The `forName(String className)` method initializes the class if it is not already initialized, whereas the use of a class literal does not initialize the class. When a class is initialized, all its static initializers are executed, and all static fields are initialized. Listing 2-2 lists a `Bulb` class with only one static initializer, which prints a message on the console. Listing 2-3 uses various methods to load and initialize the `Bulb` class.

Listing 2-2. A Bulb Class to Demonstrate Initialization of a Class

```java
// Bulb.java
package com.jdojo.reflection;
public class Bulb {
    static {
        // This will execute when this class is loaded
        // and initialized
        System.out.println("Loading class Bulb...");
    }
}
```

Listing 2-3. Testing Class Loading and Initialization

```java
// BulbTest.java
package com.jdojo.reflection;
public class BulbTest {
    public static void main(String[] args) {
        /* Uncomment only one of the following statements
           at a time. Observe the output to see the
           difference in the way the Bulb class is loaded
           and initialized.
         */
        BulbTest.createObject();
        // BulbTest.forNameVersion1();
        // BulbTest.forNameVersion2();
        // BulbTest.forNameVersion3();
        // BulbTest.classLiteral();
    }

    public static void classLiteral() {
        // Will load the class, but won't initialize it.
        Class<Bulb> c = Bulb.class;
    }
    public static void forNameVersion1() {
        try {
            String className = "com.jdojo.reflection.Bulb";
            // Will load and initialize the class
            Class c = Class.forName(className);
        } catch (ClassNotFoundException e) {
            System.out.println(e.getMessage());
        }
    }
    public static void forNameVersion2() {
        try {
            String className = "com.jdojo.reflection.Bulb";
            boolean initialize = false;
            // Get the classloader for the current class
```

```
        ClassLoader cLoader = BulbTest.class.
            getClassLoader();
        // Will load, but not initialize the class,
        // because we have set the initialize variable
        // to false
        Class c = Class.forName(className, initialize,
            cLoader);
    } catch (ClassNotFoundException e) {
        System.out.println(e.getMessage());
    }
}
public static void forNameVersion3() {
    String className = "com.jdojo.reflection.Bulb";
    // Get the module reference for the current class
    Module m = BulbTest.class.getModule();
    // Will load, but not initialize, the class
    Class c = Class.forName(m, className);
    if(c == null) {
        System.out.println(
            "The bulb class was not loaded.");
    } else {
        System.out.println(
            "The bulb class was loaded.");
    }
}

public static void createObject() {
    // Will load and initialize the Bulb class
    new Bulb();
}
}
Loading class Bulb...
```

Class Loaders

At runtime, every type is loaded by a class loader, which is represented by an instance of the java.lang. ClassLoader class. You can get the reference of the class loader of a type by using the getClassLoader() method of the Class class. The following snippet of code shows how to get the class loader of the Bulb class:

```
Class<Bulb> cls = Bulb.class;
ClassLoader loader = cls.getClassLoader();
```

The Java runtime uses three class loaders to load classes as shown in Figure 2-1. The direction of the arrows indicates the delegation direction. These class loaders load classes from different locations and of different types. You can add more class loaders, which would be a subclass of the ClassLoader class. Using custom class loaders, you can load classes from custom locations, partition user code, and unload classes. For most applications, the built-in class loaders are sufficient.

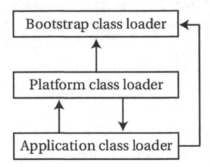

Figure 2-1. *Class loader hierarchy*

Note   Since JDK9, the application class loader can delegate to the platform class loader as well as the bootstrap class loader; the platform class loader can delegate to the application class loader.

The bootstrap class loader is implemented in the library code and in the virtual machine. Classes under its custody return null if you call getClassLoader(), as in Object.class.getClassLoader() == null. Not all Java SE Platform and JDK modules are loaded by the bootstrap class loader. To name a few, modules loaded by the bootstrap class loader are java.base, java.logging, java.prefs, and java.desktop.

Other Java SE Platform and JDK modules are loaded by the platform class loader and the application class loader, which are described next. Use the -Xbootclasspath/a option to specify additional boot class paths. Its value is stored in the system property jdk.boot. class.path.append.

The platform class loader may be used to implement a class loading extension mechanism (the JDK8 extension mechanism for loading classes is no longer supported). The ClassLoader class contains a new static method named getPlatformClassLoader(), which returns the reference of the platform class loader. Table 2-3 lists the modules loaded by the platform class loader.

Table 2-3. *The JDK Modules Loaded by the Platform Class Loader*

java.compiler	java.net.http	java.scripting
java.security.jgss	java.smartcardio	java.sql
java.sql.rowset	java.transaction.xa	java.xml.crypto
jdk.accessibility	jdk.charsets	jdk.crypto.cryptoki
jdk.crypto.ec	jdk.dynalink	jdk.httpserver
jdk.jsobject	jdk.localedata	jdk.naming.dns
jdk.security.auth	jdk.security.jgss	jdk.xml.dom
jdk.zipfs		

The platform class loader serves another purpose. Classes loaded by the bootstrap class loader are granted all permissions by default. However, several classes did not need all permissions. Such classes are loaded by the platform class loader.

The application class loader loads the application modules found on the module path and a few JDK modules that provide tools or export tool APIs, as listed in Table 2-4. You can still use the static method named getSystemClassLoader() of the ClassLoader class to get the reference of the application class loader.

Table 2-4. *The JDK Modules Loaded by the Application Class Loader*

jdk.compiler	jdk.internal.opt	jdk.jartool
jdk.javadoc	jdk.jdeps	jdk.jlink
jdk.unsupported.desktop		

Note   Before JDK9, the extension class loader and the application class loader were an instance of the `java.net.URLClassLoader` class. In JDK9 and later, the platform class loader (the erstwhile extension class loader) and the application class loader are an instance of an internal JDK class. If your code relied on the methods specific to the `URLClassLoader` class, your pre-JDK9 code may break in JDK9 or later.

The JDK modules not listed in Tables 2-3 and 2-4 are loaded by the bootstrap class loader. Listing 2-4 shows you how to print module names and their class loader names. A partial output is shown. The output depends on the modules resolved by the runtime. To print all JDK modules and their class loaders, you should add a "requires java.se.ee" in your module declaration before running this class. I discuss module layers in Chapter 7.

Listing 2-4. Listing the Names of Loaded Modules by Class Loader

```
// ModulesByClassLoader.java
package com.jdojo.reflection;
public class ModulesByClassLoader {
    public static void main(String[] args) {
        // Get the boot layer
        ModuleLayer layer = ModuleLayer.boot();
        // Print all module's names and their class loader
        // names in the boot layer
        for (Module m : layer.modules()) {
            ClassLoader loader = m.getClassLoader();
            String moduleName = m.getName();
            String loaderName = loader == null ?
                "bootstrap" : loader.getName();
            System.out.printf("%s: %s%n", loaderName,
                moduleName);
        }
    }
}
```

```
bootstrap: java.base
platform: java.net.http
bootstrap: java.security.sasl
app: jdk.internal.opt
...
```

The three built-in class loaders work in tandem to load classes. When the application class loader needs to load a class, it searches modules defined to all class loaders. If a suitable module is defined to one of these class loaders, that class loader loads the class, implying that the application class loader can now delegate to the bootstrap class loader and the platform class loader. If a class is not found in a named module defined to these class loaders, the application class loader delegates to its parent, which is the platform class loader. If a class is still not loaded, the application class loader searches the class path. If it finds the class on the class path, it loads the class as a member of its unnamed module. If it does not find the class on the class path, a `ClassNotFoundException` is thrown.

When the platform class loader needs to load a class, it searches modules defined to all class loaders. If a suitable module is defined to one of these class loaders, that class loader loads the class, implying that the platform class loader can delegate to the bootstrap class loader as well as the application class loader. If a class is not found in a named module defined to these class loaders, the platform class loader delegates to its parent, which is the bootstrap class loader.

When the bootstrap class loader needs to load a class, it searches its own list of named modules. If a class is not found, it searches the list of files and directories specified through the command-line option: `Xbootclasspath/a`. If it finds a class on the bootstrap class path, it loads the class as a member of its unnamed module. If a class is still not found, a `ClassNotFoundException` is thrown.

Reflecting on Classes

This section demonstrates the features of Java reflection that enable you to get the description of a class, such as its package name, access modifiers, etc. You will use a `Person` class, as listed in Listing 2-5, to demonstrate the reflection features. It is a simple class with two instance fields, two constructors, and some methods. It implements two interfaces.

Listing 2-5. A Person Class Used to Demonstrate Reflection

```java
// Person.java
package com.jdojo.reflection;
import java.io.Serializable;
public class Person implements Cloneable, Serializable {
    private int id = -1;
    private String name = "Unknown";
    public Person() {
    }
    public Person(int id, String name) {
        this.id = id;
        this.name = name;
    }
    public int getId() {
        return id;
    }
    public String getName() {
        return name;
    }
    public void setName(String name) {
        this.name = name;
    }

    @Override
    public Person clone() {
        try {
            return (Person) super.clone();
        } catch (CloneNotSupportedException e) {
            throw new RuntimeException(e.getMessage());
        }
    }
    @Override
    public String toString() {
        return "Person: id=" + this.id + ", name=" +
            this.name;
    }
}
```

Listing 2-6 illustrates how to get the description of a class. It lists the class access modifiers, the class name, its superclass name, and all interfaces implemented by the class.

Listing 2-6. Reflecting on a Class

```java
// ClassReflection.java
package com.jdojo.reflection;
import java.lang.reflect.Modifier;
import java.lang.reflect.TypeVariable;
public class ClassReflection {
    public static void main(String[] args) {
        // Print the declaration of the Person class
        String clsDecl = getClassDescription(Person.class);
        System.out.println(clsDecl);
        // Print the declaration of the Class class
        clsDecl = getClassDescription(Class.class);
        System.out.println(clsDecl);
        // Print the declaration of the Runnable interface
        clsDecl = getClassDescription(Runnable.class);
        System.out.println(clsDecl);
        // Print the declaration of the class representing
        // the int data type
        clsDecl = getClassDescription(int.class);
        System.out.println(clsDecl);
    }
    public static
    String getClassDescription(Class<?> cls) {
        StringBuilder classDesc = new StringBuilder();
        // Prepare the modifiers and construct keyword
        // (class, enum, interface etc.)
        int modifierBits = 0;
        String keyword = " ";
```

```
            // Add keyword @interface, interface or class
        if (cls.isPrimitive()) {
            // We do not want to add anything
        } else if (cls.isInterface()) {
            modifierBits = cls.getModifiers() & Modifier.
                interfaceModifiers();
            // An annotation is an interface
            if (cls.isAnnotation()) {
                keyword = "@interface";
            } else {
                keyword = "interface";
            }
        } else if (cls.isEnum()) {
            modifierBits = cls.getModifiers() &
                Modifier.classModifiers();
            keyword = "enum";
        } else {
            modifierBits = cls.getModifiers() &
                Modifier.classModifiers();
            keyword = "class";
        }
        // Convert modifiers to their string representation
        String modifiers = Modifier.toString(modifierBits);
        // Append modifiers
        classDesc.append(modifiers);
        // Append the construct keyword
        classDesc.append(" ");
        classDesc.append(keyword);
        // Append simple name
        String simpleName = cls.getSimpleName();
        classDesc.append(" ");
        classDesc.append(simpleName);
        // Append generic parameters
        String genericParms = getGenericTypeParams(cls);
        classDesc.append(genericParms);
```

```java
        // Append super class
        Class superClass = cls.getSuperclass();
        if (superClass != null) {
            String superClassSimpleName = superClass.
                getSimpleName();
            classDesc.append(" extends ");
            classDesc.append(superClassSimpleName);
        }
        // Append Interfaces
        String interfaces = ClassReflection.
            getClassInterfaces(cls);
        if (interfaces != null) {
            classDesc.append(" implements ");
            classDesc.append(interfaces);
        }
        return classDesc.toString().trim();
    }
    public static String getClassInterfaces(Class<?> cls) {
        // Get a comma-separated list of interfaces
        // implemented by the class
        Class<?>[] interfaces = cls.getInterfaces();
        if (interfaces.length == 0) {
            return null;
        }
        String[] names = new String[interfaces.length];
        for (int i = 0; i < interfaces.length; i++) {
            names[i] = interfaces[i].getSimpleName();
        }
        String interfacesList = String.join(", ", names);
        return interfacesList;
    }
    public static
    String getGenericTypeParams(Class<?> cls) {
        StringBuilder sb = new StringBuilder();
        TypeVariable<?>[] typeParms = cls.
            getTypeParameters();
```

```
        if (typeParms.length == 0) {
            return "";
        }
        String[] paramNames = new String[typeParms.
            length];
        for (int i = 0; i < typeParms.length; i++) {
            paramNames[i] = typeParms[i].getTypeName();
        }
        sb.append('<');
        String parmsList = String.join(",", paramNames);
        sb.append(parmsList);
        sb.append('>');
        return sb.toString();
    }
}
```

```
public class Person extends Object implements Cloneable,
    Serializable
public final class Class<T> extends Object implements
    Serializable, GenericDeclaration,
Type, AnnotatedElement
public abstract interface Runnable
int
```

The getName() method of the Class class returns the fully qualified name of the class. To get the simple class name, use the getSimpleName() method of the Class class, like so:

```
String simpleName = c.getSimpleName();
```

The modifiers of a class are the keywords that appear before the keyword class in the class declaration. In the following example, public and abstract are the modifiers for the MyClass class:

```
public abstract class MyClass {
    // Code goes here
}
```

The getModifiers() method of the Class class returns all modifiers for the class. Note that the getModifiers() method returns an integer. To get the textual form of the modifiers, you need to call the toString(int modifiers) static method of the Modifier class, passing the modifiers value in an integer form. Assuming cls is the reference of a Class object, you get the modifiers of the class as shown:

```
// You need to AND the returned value from the
// getModifiers() method with appropriate value returned
// from xxxModifiers() method of the Modifiers class
int mod = cls.getModifiers() & Modifier.classModifiers(); String modStr =
Modifier.toString(mod);
```

It is straightforward to get the name of the superclass of a class. Use the getSuperclass() method of the Class class to get the reference of the superclass. Note that every class in Java has a superclass except the Object class. If the getSuperclass() method is invoked on the Object class, it returns null:

```
Class superClass = cls.getSuperclass();
if (superClass != null) {
    String superClassName = superClass.getSimpleName();
}
```

Note   The getSuperclass() method of the Class class returns null when it represents the Object class, a class for an interface such as List.class, and a class for a primitive type such as int.class, void.class, etc.

To get the names of all interfaces implemented by a class, you use the getInterfaces() method of the Class class. It returns an array of Class objects. Each element in the array represents an interface implemented by the class:

```
// Get all interfaces implemented by cls
Class<?>[] interfaces = cls.getInterfaces();
```

The getClassDescription() method of the ClassReflection class puts all parts of a class declaration into a string and returns that string. The main() method of this class demonstrates how to use this class.

A method called toGenericString() of the Class class returns a string describing the class. The string contains the modifiers and type parameters for the class. The call Person. class.toGenericString() will return public class com.jdojo.reflection.Person.

Reflecting on Fields

A field of a class is represented by an object of the java.lang.reflect.Field class. The following four methods in the Class class can be used to get information about the fields of a class:

- Field[] getFields()

- Field[] getDeclaredFields()

- Field getField(String name)

- Field getDeclaredField(String name)

The getFields() method returns all the accessible public fields of the class or interface. The accessible public fields include public fields declared in the class or inherited from its superclass. The getDeclaredFields() method returns all the fields that appear in the declaration of the class. It does not include inherited fields. The other two methods, getField() and getDeclaredField(), are used to get the Field object if you know the name of the field. Let's consider the following declarations of classes A and B and an interface IConstants:

```
interface IConstants {
    int DAYS_IN_WEEK = 7;
}
class A implements IConstants {
    private int aPrivate;
    public int aPublic;
    protected int aProtected;
}
class B extends A {
    private int bPrivate;
    public int bPublic;
    protected int bProtected;
}
```

If bClass is the reference of the Class object for class B, the expression bClass.getFields() will return the following three fields that are accessible and public:

- public int B.bPublic

- public int A.aPublic

- public static final int IConstants.DAYS_IN_WEEK

The bClass.getDeclaredFields() method will return the three fields that are declared in class B:

- private int B.bPrivate

- public int B.bPublic

- protected int B.bProtected

To get all the fields of a class and its superclass, you must get the reference of the superclass using the getSuperclass() method and use the combinations of these methods. Listing 2-7 illustrates how to get the information about the fields of a class. Note that you do not get anything when you call the getFields() method on the Class object of the Person class because the Person class does not contain any public fields.

Listing 2-7. Reflecting on Fields of a Class

```
// FieldReflection.java
package com.jdojo.reflection;
import java.lang.reflect.Field;
import java.lang.reflect.Modifier;
import java.util.ArrayList;
public class FieldReflection {
    public static void main(String[] args) {
        Class<Person> cls = Person.class;
        // Print declared fields
        ArrayList<String> fieldsDescription =
            getDeclaredFieldsList(cls);
        System.out.println("Declared Fields for " +
            cls.getName());
        for (String desc : fieldsDescription) {
            System.out.println(desc);
        }
```

```java
        // Get the accessible public fields
        fieldsDescription = getFieldsList(cls);
        System.out.println("\nAccessible Fields for " +
            cls.getName());
        for (String desc : fieldsDescription) {
            System.out.println(desc);
        }
    }
    public static
    ArrayList<String> getFieldsList(Class c) {
        Field[] fields = c.getFields();
        ArrayList<String> fieldsList =
            getFieldsDescription(fields);
        return fieldsList;
    }
    public static
    ArrayList<String> getDeclaredFieldsList(Class c) {
        Field[] fields = c.getDeclaredFields();
        ArrayList<String> fieldsList =
            getFieldsDescription(fields);
        return fieldsList;
    }

    public static ArrayList<String>
    getFieldsDescription(Field[] fields) {
        ArrayList<String> fieldList = new ArrayList<>();
        for (Field f : fields) {
            // Get the modifiers for the field
            int mod = f.getModifiers() &
                Modifier.fieldModifiers();
            String modifiers = Modifier.toString(mod);
            // Get the simple name of the field type
            Class<?> type = f.getType();
            String typeName = type.getSimpleName();
            // Get the name of the field
            String fieldName = f.getName();
```

```
            fieldList.add(modifiers + " " + typeName +
                " " + fieldName);
        }
        return fieldList;
    }
}
```

```
Declared Fields for com.jdojo.reflection.Person
private int id
private String name
Accessible Fields for com.jdojo.reflection.Person
```

Note   You cannot use this technique to describe the length field of an array
object. Each array type has a corresponding class. When you try to get the fields of
an array class using the getFields() method, you get an array of Field objects
of zero length. The array length is not part of the array's class definition. Rather, it
is stored as part of the array object in the object header.

Reflecting on Executables

An instance of the Method class represents a method. An instance of the Constructor
class represents a constructor. Structurally, methods and constructors have a few things
in common. Both use modifiers, parameters, and a throws clause. Both can be executed.
These classes inherit from a common abstract superclass, Executable. Methods to
retrieve information common to both are methods of the Executable class.

A parameter in an Executable is represented by an object of the Parameter class.
The getParameters() method in the Executable class returns all parameters of an
Executable as Parameter[]. By default, the formal parameter names are not stored in
the class files to keep the file size smaller. The getName() method of the Parameter class
returns synthesized parameter names like arg0, arg1, etc. unless the actual parameter
names are retained. If you want to retain the actual parameter names in class files, you
need to compile the source code using the -parameters option with the javac compiler.

The getExceptionTypes() method of the Executable class returns an array of Class objects, which describes the exceptions thrown by the Executable. If no exceptions are listed in the throws clause, it returns an array of length zero.

The getModifiers() method of the Executable class returns the modifiers as an int.

The getTypeParameters() method of the Executable class returns an array of TypeVariable that represents the type parameters for generic methods/constructors. The examples in this chapter do not include the generic type variable declarations in methods/constructors.

Listing 2-8 contains a utility class that consists of static methods to get information about an Executable such as the list of modifiers, parameters, and exceptions. I use this class when I discuss methods and constructors in the subsequent sections.

Listing 2-8. A Utility Class to Get Information for an Executable

```java
// ExecutableUtil.java
package com.jdojo.reflection;

import java.lang.reflect.Constructor;
import java.lang.reflect.Executable;
import java.lang.reflect.Method;
import java.lang.reflect.Modifier;
import java.lang.reflect.Parameter;
import java.util.ArrayList;

public class ExecutableUtil {
    public static
    ArrayList<String> getParameters(Executable exec) {
        Parameter[] parms = exec.getParameters();
        ArrayList<String> parmList = new ArrayList<>();
        for (int i = 0; i < parms.length; i++) {
            // Get modifiers, type, and name of the
            // parameter
            int mod = parms[i].getModifiers() &
                Modifier.parameterModifiers();
            String modifiers = Modifier.toString(mod);
            String parmType = parms[i].getType().
                getSimpleName();
```

```
        String parmName = parms[i].getName();
        String temp = modifiers + " " + parmType +
            " " + parmName;
        // Trim it as it may have leading spaces when
        // modifiers are absent
        parmList.add(temp.trim());
    }

    return parmList;
}
public static
ArrayList<String> getExceptionList(Executable exec) {
    ArrayList<String> exceptionList =
        new ArrayList<>();
    for (Class<?> c : exec.getExceptionTypes()) {
        exceptionList.add(c.getSimpleName());
    }

    return exceptionList;
}
public static String
getThrowsClause(Executable exec) {
    ArrayList<String> exceptionList =
        getExceptionList(exec);
    String exceptions = ExecutableUtil.
        arrayListToString(exceptionList, ",");
    String throwsClause = "";

    if (exceptionList.size() > 0) {
        throwsClause = "throws " + exceptions;
    }
    return throwsClause;
}
public static String getModifiers(Executable exec) {
    // Get the modifiers for the class
    int mod = exec.getModifiers();
```

```
        if (exec instanceof Method) {
            mod = mod & Modifier.methodModifiers();
        } else if (exec instanceof Constructor) {
            mod = mod & Modifier.constructorModifiers();
        }
        return Modifier.toString(mod);
    }
    public static String
    arrayListToString(ArrayList<String> list,
                      String saparator) {
        String[] tempArray = new String[list.size()];
        tempArray = list.toArray(tempArray);
        String str = String.join(saparator, tempArray);
        return str;
    }
}
```

Reflecting on Methods

The following four methods in the Class class can be used to get information about the methods of a class:

- Method[] getMethods()

- Method[] getDeclaredMethods()

- Method getMethod(String name, Class... parameterTypes)

- Method getDeclaredMethod(String name, Class...
  parameterTypes)

The getMethods() method returns all the accessible public methods of the class. The accessible public methods include any public method declared in the class or inherited from the superclass. The getDeclaredMethods() method returns all the methods declared only in the class. It does not return any methods that are inherited from the superclass. The other two methods, getMethod() and getDeclaredMethod(), are used to get the Method object if you know the name of the method and its parameter types.

The getReturnType() method of the Method class returns the Class object, which contains information about the return type of the method.

Listing 2-9 illustrates how to get information about the methods of a class. You can uncomment the code in the main() method to print all methods in the Person class—declared in the Person class and inherited from the Object class.

Listing 2-9. Reflecting on Methods of a Class

```java
// MethodReflection.java
package com.jdojo.reflection;
import java.lang.reflect.Method;
import java.util.ArrayList;
public class MethodReflection {
    public static void main(String[] args) {
        Class<Person> cls = Person.class;
        // Get the declared methods
        ArrayList<String> methodsDescription =
            getDeclaredMethodsList(cls);
        System.out.println("Declared Methods for " +
            cls.getName());
        for (String desc : methodsDescription) {
            System.out.println(desc);
        }
        /* Uncomment the following code to print all
           methods in the Person class
        // Get the accessible public methods
        methodsDescription = getMethodsList(cls);
        System.out.println("\nMethods for " + cls.getName());
        for (String desc : methodsDescription) {
            System.out.println(desc);
        }
         */
    }
    public static ArrayList<String>
    getMethodsList(Class c) {
        Method[] methods = c.getMethods();
```

```
        ArrayList<String> methodsList =
            getMethodsDescription(methods);
        return methodsList;
    }
    public static ArrayList<String>
    getDeclaredMethodsList(Class c) {
        Method[] methods = c.getDeclaredMethods();
        ArrayList<String> methodsList =
            getMethodsDescription(methods);
        return methodsList;
    }
    public static ArrayList<String>
    getMethodsDescription(Method[] methods) {
        ArrayList<String> methodList = new ArrayList<>();

        for (Method m : methods) {
            String modifiers = ExecutableUtil.
                getModifiers(m);
            // Get the method return type
            Class returnType = m.getReturnType();
            String returnTypeName =
                returnType.getSimpleName();
            // Get the name of the method
            String methodName = m.getName();
            // Get the parameters of the method
            ArrayList<String> paramsList =
                ExecutableUtil.getParameters(m);
            String params = ExecutableUtil.
                arrayListToString(paramsList, ",");
            // Get the Exceptions thrown by method
            String throwsClause = ExecutableUtil.
                getThrowsClause(m);
            methodList.add(modifiers + " " +
                returnTypeName + " " + methodName +
                    "(" + params + ") " + throwsClause);
        }
```

```
        return methodList;
    }
}
```

```
Declared Methods for com.jdojo.reflection.Person
public String toString()
public Object clone()
public String getName()
public int getId()
public void setName(String arg0)
```

Reflecting on Constructors

Getting information about constructors of a class is similar to getting information about methods of a class. The following four methods in the Class class are used to get information about the constructors represented by a Class object:

- Constructor[] getConstructors()

- Constructor[] getDeclaredConstructors()

- Constructor<T> getConstructor(Class... parameterTypes)

- Constructor<T> getDeclaredConstructor(Class... parameterTypes)

The getConstructors() method returns all public constructors. The getDeclaredConstructors() method returns all declared constructors. The other two methods, getConstructor() and getDeclaredConstructor(), are used to get the Constructor object if you know the parameter types of the constructor. Listing 2-10 illustrates how to get information for the constructors represented by a Class object.

Listing 2-10. Reflecting on Constructors of a Class

```
// ConstructorReflection.java
package com.jdojo.reflection;
import java.lang.reflect.Constructor;
import java.util.ArrayList;
```

```java
public class ConstructorReflection {
    public static void main(String[] args) {
        Class<Person> cls = Person.class;
        // Get the declared constructors
        System.out.println("Constructors for " +
            cls.getName());
        Constructor[] constructors = cls.getConstructors();
        ArrayList<String> constructDescList =
            getConstructorsDescription(constructors);
        for (String desc : constructDescList) {
            System.out.println(desc);
        }
    }
    public static
    ArrayList<String> getConstructorsDescription(
            Constructor[] constructors) {
        ArrayList<String> constructorList =
            new ArrayList<>();
        for (Constructor constructor : constructors) {
            String modifiers = ExecutableUtil.
                getModifiers(constructor);
            // Get the name of the constructor
            String constructorName = constructor.getName();
            // Get the parameters of the constructor
            ArrayList<String> paramsList = ExecutableUtil.
                getParameters(constructor);
            String params = ExecutableUtil.
                arrayListToString(paramsList, ",");
            // Get the Exceptions thrown by the constructor
            String throwsClause = ExecutableUtil.
                getThrowsClause(constructor);
            constructorList.add(modifiers + " " +
                constructorName + "(" + params + ") " +
                throwsClause);
        }
```

```
        return constructorList;
    }
}
```

```
Constructors for com.jdojo.reflection.Person
public com.jdojo.reflection.Person()
public com.jdojo.reflection.Person(int arg0,String arg1)
```

Creating Objects

Java lets you use reflection to create objects of a class. The class name need not be known until runtime. You can create the object by invoking one of the constructors of the class using reflection. You can also access the values of fields of objects, set their values, and invoke their methods. If you know the class name and have access to the class code at compile time, do not use reflection to create its object; rather, use the new operator in your code to create objects of the class. Typically, frameworks and libraries use reflection to create objects.

You can create an object of a class using reflection. You need to get the reference of the constructor before you can create an object. The previous section showed you how to get the reference of a specific constructor of a class. Use the newInstance() method of the Constructor class to create an object. You can pass the actual parameter to the constructor to the newInstance() method, which is declared as follows:

```
public T newInstance(Object... initargs) throws
  InstantiationException,
  IllegalAccessException,
  IllegalArgumentException,
  InvocationTargetException
```

Here, initargs are the actual parameters for the constructor. You will not pass any parameters for the no-args constructor.

The following snippet of code gets the reference of the no-args constructor of the Person class and invokes it. I have omitted the exception handling for brevity:

```
Class<Person> cls = Person.class;
// Get the reference of the Person() constructor
Constructor<Person> noArgsCons = cls.getConstructor();
Person p = noArgsCons.newInstance();
```

Listing 2-11 contains the complete code to illustrate how to use the Person(int, String) constructor of the Person class to create a Person object using reflection. Note that the Constructor<T> class is a generic type. Its type parameter is the class type that declares the constructor, for example, the Constructor<Person> type represents a constructor for the Person class.

Listing 2-11. Using a Specific Constructor to Create a New Object

```java
// InvokeConstructorTest.java
package com.jdojo.reflection;
import java.lang.reflect.Constructor;
import java.lang.reflect.InvocationTargetException;
public class InvokeConstructorTest {
    public static void main(String[] args) {
        Class<Person> personClass = Person.class;

        try {
            // Get the constructor "Person(int, String)"
            Constructor<Person> cons = personClass.
                getConstructor(int.class, String.class);
            // Invoke the constructor with values for id
            // and name
            Person chris = cons.newInstance(1994, "Chris");
            System.out.println(chris);
        } catch (NoSuchMethodException | SecurityException
                | InstantiationException
                | IllegalAccessException
                | IllegalArgumentException
                | InvocationTargetException e) {
            System.out.println(e.getMessage());
        }
    }
}

Person: id=1994, name=Chris
```

Invoking Methods

You can invoke methods of an object using reflection. You need to get the reference to the method that you want to invoke. Suppose you want to invoke the setName() method of the Person class. You can get the reference to the setName() method as follows:

```
Class<Person> personClass = Person.class;
Method setName = personClass.getMethod("setName",
    String.class);
```

To invoke this method, call the invoke() method on the method's reference, which is declared as follows:

```
public Object invoke(Object obj, Object... args)
    throws IllegalAccessException,
        IllegalArgumentException,
        InvocationTargetException
```

The first parameter of the invoke() method is the object on which you want to invoke the method. If the Method object represents a static method, the first argument is ignored or it may be null. The second parameter is a varargs parameter in which you pass all the actual parameters in the same order as declared in the method's declaration.

Since the setName() method of the Person class takes a String argument, you need to pass a String object as the second argument to the invoke() method. Listing 2-12 illustrates how to invoke a method on a Person object using reflection.

Listing 2-12. Invoking a Method on an Object Reference Using Reflection

```
// InvokeMethodTest.java
package com.jdojo.reflection;
import java.lang.reflect.InvocationTargetException;
import java.lang.reflect.Method;

public class InvokeMethodTest {
    public static void main(String[] args) {
        Class<Person> personClass = Person.class;
        try {
            // Create an object of Person class
            Person p = personClass.newInstance();
```

```
            // Print the details of the Person object
            System.out.println(p);
            // Get the reference of the setName() method
            Method setName = personClass.getMethod(
                "setName", String.class);
            // Invoke the setName() method on p passing
            // passing "Ann" as the actual parameter
            setName.invoke(p, "Ann");
            // Print the details of the Person object
            System.out.println(p);
        } catch (InstantiationException
                | IllegalAccessException
                | NoSuchMethodException
                | SecurityException
                | IllegalArgumentException
                | InvocationTargetException e) {
            System.out.println(e.getMessage());
        }
    }
}
```

```
Person: id=-1, name=Unknown
Person: id=-1, name=Ann
```

Accessing Fields

You can read or set the value of a field of an object using reflection. First, you need to get the reference of the field you want to work with. To read the field's value, you need to call the getXxx() method on the field, where Xxx is the data type of the field. For example, to read a boolean field value, you would call the getBoolean() method, and to read an int field, you would call the getInt() method. To set the value of a field, you call the corresponding setXxx() method. The following are the declarations of the getInt() and setInt() methods where the first argument, obj, is the object's reference whose field is being read or written:

- int getInt(Object obj) throws IllegalArgumentException, IllegalAccessException

- void setInt(Object obj, int newValue) throws IllegalArgumentException, IllegalAccessException

---

Note   static and instance fields are accessed the same way. In the case of static fields, the first argument to the `get()` and `set()` methods is the reference of the class/interface.

Note that you can access fields only that have been declared as accessible, such as a public field. In the `Person` class, all fields are declared private. Therefore, you cannot access any of these fields using normal Java programming language rules. To access a field that is not normally accessible, for example, if it is declared private, refer to the "Deep Reflection" section later in this chapter. You will use the `PublicPerson` class listed in Listing 2-13 to learn the technique to access the fields.

Listing 2-13. A PublicPerson Class with a Public Name Field

```
// PublicPerson.java
package com.jdojo.reflection;
public class PublicPerson {
    private int id = -1;
    public String name = "Unknown";
    public PublicPerson() {
    }
    @Override
    public String toString() {
        return "Person: id=" + this.id + ", name=" +
            this.name;
    }
}
```

Listing 2-14 demonstrates how to get the reference of a field of an object and how to read and set its value.

Listing 2-14. Accessing Fields Using Reflection

```java
// FieldAccessTest.java
package com.jdojo.reflection;
import java.lang.reflect.Field;
public class FieldAccessTest {
    public static void main(String[] args) {
        Class<PublicPerson> ppClass = PublicPerson.class;
        try {
            // Create an object of the PublicPerson class
            PublicPerson p = ppClass.newInstance();
            // Get the reference of the name field
            Field name = ppClass.getField("name");
            // Get and print the current value of the
            // name field
            String nameValue = (String) name.get(p);
            System.out.println("Current name is " +
                nameValue);

            // Set the value of name to Ann
            name.set(p, "Ann");
            // Get and print the new value of name field
            nameValue = (String) name.get(p);
            System.out.println("New name is " + nameValue);
        } catch (InstantiationException
                | IllegalAccessException
                | NoSuchFieldException
                | SecurityException
                | IllegalArgumentException e) {
            System.out.println(e.getMessage());
        }
    }
}

Current name is Unknown
New name is Ann
```

Deep Reflection

There are two things you can do using reflection:

- Describe an entity

- Access the members of an entity

Describing an entity means knowing the entity's details. For example, describing a class means knowing its name, modifiers, packages, modules, fields, methods, and constructors. Accessing the members of an entity means reading and writing fields and invoking methods and constructors. Describing an entity does not pose any issues of access control. If you have access to a class file, you should be able to know the details of the entity represented in that class file. However, accessing members of an entity is controlled by the Java language access control. For example, if you declare a field of a class as private, the field should be accessible only within the class. Code outside the class should not be able to access the private field of the class. However, this is half-true. The Java language access control rules are applied when you access members statically. The access control rules can be suppressed when you access members using reflection.

The following snippet of code accesses the private name field of the Person class. This code will compile only within the Person class:

```
Person john = new Person();
String name = john.name;   // Accessing the private field
                           // name statically
```

Java has been allowing access to rather inaccessible members such as a private field of a class outside the class using reflection. This is called deep reflection. Reflective access to inaccessible members made it possible to have many great frameworks in Java such as Hibernate and Spring. These frameworks perform most of their work using deep reflection. You can access the private name field of the Person class outside the Person class using deep reflection.

So far in this chapter, I kept the examples simple and stayed away from violating the Java language access control. I accessed only public fields, methods, and constructors; the accessed members and the accessing code were in the same module. Before JDK9, accessing inaccessible members was easy. All you had to do was call the setAccessible(true) method on the inaccessible Field, Method, and Constructor

117

objects before accessing them. The introduction of the module system in JDK9 has made deep reflection a bit complicated. In this section and its subsections, I walk you through rules and examples for deep reflection in JDK9 and later.

Note   If a security manager is present, the code performing deep reflection must have a ReflectPermission("suppressAccessChecks") permission.

To perform deep reflection, you need to get the reference of the desired field, method, and constructor using the getDeclaredXxx() method of the Class object, where Xxx can be Field, Method, or Constructor. Note that using the getXxx() method to get the reference of an inaccessible field, method, or constructor will throw an IllegalAccessException. The Field, Method, and Constructor classes have the AccessibleObject class as their superclass. The AccessibleObject class contains the following methods to let you work with the accessible flag:

- void setAccessible(boolean flag)

- static void setAccessible(AccessibleObject[] array, boolean flag)

- boolean trySetAccessible()

- boolean canAccess(Object obj)

The setAccessible(boolean flag) method sets the accessible flag for a member (Field, Method, and Constructor) to true or false. If you are trying to access an inaccessible member, you need to call setAccessible(true) on the member object before accessing the member. The method throws an InaccessibleObjectException if the accessible flag cannot be set. The static setAccessible(AccessibleObject[] array, boolean flag) is a convenience method to set the accessible flag for all AccessibleObject in the specified array.

The trySetAccessible() method attempts to set the accessible flag to true on the object on which it is called. It returns true if the accessible flag was set to true and false otherwise. Compare this method with the setAccessible(true) method. This method does not throw a runtime exception on failure, whereas the setAccessible(true) does.

The canAccess(Object obj) method returns true if the caller can access the member for the specified obj object. Otherwise, it returns false. If the member is a static member or a constructor, the obj must be null.

I discuss accessing rather inaccessible members within a module, across modules, in unnamed modules, and of JDK modules in the next sections.

Deep Reflection Within a Module

Let's start with an example. You want to access the private name field of a Person object. First, you get the reference of the name field in a Field object and try reading its current value. Listing 2-15 contains the code for the IllegalAccess1 class.

Listing 2-15. Accessing the Private Name Field of the Person Class

```
// IllegalAccess1.java
package com.jdojo.reflection;
import java.lang.reflect.Constructor;
import java.lang.reflect.Field;

public class IllegalAccess1 {
    public static void main(String[] args)
            throws Exception {
        // Get the class reference for the Person class
        String className = "com.jdojo.reflection.Person";
        Class<?> cls = Class.forName(className);
        // Create a Person object
        Constructor<?> cons = cls.getConstructor();
        Object person = cons.newInstance();
        // Get the reference of the name field
        Field nameField = cls.getDeclaredField("name");
        // Try accessing the name field by reading its
        // value
        String name = (String) nameField.get(person);
        // Print the person and its name separately
        System.out.println(person);
        System.out.println("name=" + name);
    }
}
```

```
Exception in thread "main" java.lang.
    IllegalAccessException: class com.jdojo.reflection.
IllegalAccess1 (in module jdojo.reflection) cannot access
    a member of class com.jdojo.
reflection.Person (in module jdojo.reflection) with
    modifiers "private"
        at java.base/jdk.internal.reflect.Reflection.
            newIllegalAccessException(Reflection.java:361)
        at java.base/java.lang.reflect.AccessibleObject.
            checkAccess(AccessibleObject.java:589)
        at java.base/java.lang.reflect.Field.checkAccess(
            Field.java:1075)
        at java.base/java.lang.reflect.Field.get(
            Field.java:416)
        at jdojo.reflection/com.jdojo.reflection.
            IllegalAccess1.main(IllegalAccess1.java:21)
```

In Listing 2-15, I added the Exception class in the throws clause of the main() method to keep the logic simple inside the method. I keep doing this for all examples in this section, so you can focus on the illegal access rules rather than on exception handling. The IllegalAccess1 and the Person class are in the same jdojo.reflection module. You were able to create a Person object successfully because you used the public no-args constructor of the Person class. The name field in the Person class is declared as private, and accessing it from another class failed. Fixing this error is simple—you set the accessible flag to the Field object using the setAccessible(true) or the trySetAccessible() method. Listing 2-16 contains the complete code.

Listing 2-16. Accessing the Private Name Field of the Person Class After Making It Accessible

```
// IllegalAccess2.java
package com.jdojo.reflection;
import java.lang.reflect.Constructor;
import java.lang.reflect.Field;
```

```
public class IllegalAccess2 {
    public static void main(String[] args)
            throws Exception {
        // Get the class reference for the Person class
        String className = "com.jdojo.reflection.Person";
        Class<?> cls = Class.forName(className);
        // Create a Person object
        Constructor<?> cons = cls.getConstructor();
        Object person = cons.newInstance();
        // Get the reference of the name field
        Field nameField = cls.getDeclaredField("name");
        // Try making the name field accessible before
        // accessing it
        boolean accessEnabled = nameField.
            trySetAccessible();
        if (accessEnabled) {
            // Try accessing the name field by reading
            // its value
            String name = (String) nameField.get(person);
            // Print the person and its name separately
            System.out.println(person);
            System.out.println("name=" + name);
        } else {
            System.out.println("The Person.name field " +
                "is not accessible.");
        }
    }
}
```

```
Person: id=-1, name=Unknown
name=Unknown
```

So far, everything looks fine. You might think that if you cannot access the private member of a class, you can always use reflection to access them. However, this is not always true. Access to otherwise inaccessible members of a class is handled through the Java security manager. By default, when you run your application on your computer, the security manager is not installed for your application. The absence of the security manager for your application lets you access all fields, methods, and constructors of a class in the same module after you set the accessible flag to true as you did in the previous example. However, if a security manager is installed for your application, whether you can access an inaccessible class member depends on the permission granted to your application to access such members. You can check if the security manager is installed for your application or not by using the following piece of code:

```
SecurityManager smgr = System.getSecurityManager();
if (smgr == null) {
    System.out.println(
        "Security manager is not installed.");
}
```

You can install a default security manager by passing the -Djava.security.manager option on the command line when you run the Java application. The security manager uses a Java security policy file to enforce the rules specified in that policy file. The Java security policy file is specified using the -Djava.security.policy command-line option. If you want to run the IllegalAccess2 class with a Java security manager with the Java policy file stored in the C:\Java17LanguageFeatures\conf\myjava.policy file, you would use the following command:

```
C:\Java17LanguageFeatures>java -Djava.security.manager
-Djava.security.policy=conf\myjava.policy --module-path
    build\modules\jdojo.reflection
--module jdojo.reflection/com.jdojo.reflection.
    IllegalAccess2
Exception in thread "main" java.security.
    AccessControlException: access denied
("java.lang.reflect.ReflectPermission"
    "suppressAccessChecks")
        at java.base/java.security.AccessControlContext.
            checkPermission
            (AccessControlContext.java:472)
        at java.base/java.security.AccessController.
            checkPermission
            (AccessController.java:895)
```

```
    at java.base/java.lang.SecurityManager.
       checkPermission(SecurityManager.java:558)
    at java.base/java.lang.reflect.AccessibleObject.
       checkPermission
       (AccessibleObject.java:85)
    at java.base/java.lang.reflect.AccessibleObject.
       trySetAccessible
       (AccessibleObject.java:245)
    at jdojo.reflection/com.jdojo.reflection.
       IllegalAccess2.main
       (IllegalAccess2.java:26)
```

The myjava.policy file is empty when this command was run, which means that the application did not have permission to suppress the Java language access control.

If you want to allow your program to access an inaccessible field of a class using reflection, the contents of the myjava.policy file would look as shown in Listing 2-17.

Listing 2-17. Contents of the conf\myjava.policy File

```
grant {
    // Grant permission to all programs to access
    // inaccessible members
    permission java.lang.reflect.ReflectPermission
        "suppressAccessChecks";
};
```

Let's rerun the IllegalAccess2 class with a security manager and the Java policy as shown in Listing 2-17:

```
C:\Java17LanguageFeatures>java -Djava.security.manager ^
-Djava.security.policy=conf\myjava.policy ^
--module-path build\modules\jdojo.reflection ^
--module ^
jdojo.reflection/com.jdojo.reflection.IllegalAccess2

Person: id=-1, name=Unknown
name=Unknown
```

This time, you were able to access the private name field of the Person class when you granted the appropriate security permission. The rules for accessing the inaccessible members have just begun. You saw the rules for deep reflection within a module, when the code gaining illegal access and the code being illegally accessed were in the same module. The next section describes the illegal access behavior across modules.

Deep Reflection Across Modules

Let's set up a new module named jdojo.reflection.model, as shown in Listing 2-18, and a simple class in it called Phone, as shown in Listing 2-19. The module declaration contains no module statements. The Phone class contains a number instance variable, two constructors, and a getter and a setter for the number instance variable. The toString() method returns the phone number.

Listing 2-18. The Declaration of a jdojo.reflection.model Module

```
// module-info.java
module jdojo.reflection.model {
    // No module statements at this time
}
```

Listing 2-19. A Phone Class

```
// Phone.java
package com.jdojo.reflection.model;
public class Phone {
    private String number = "9999999999";

    public Phone() {
    }
    public Phone(String number) {
        this.number = number;
    }
    public String getNumber() {
        return number;
    }
```

```
    public void setNumber(String number) {
        this.number = number;
    }
    @Override
    public String toString() {
        return this.number;
    }
}
```

Let's create a class called IllegalAccess3 in the jdojo.reflection module.
The class will try to create an object of the Phone class in the jdojo.reflection.model
module and read the object's private field, number. The IllegalAccess3 class in
Listing 2-20 contains the complete code. It is very similar to the IllegalAccess2 class.
The only difference is that you are accessing the Phone class and its private instance
variable across the module's boundary.

Listing 2-20. Accessing the Private Number Field of the Phone Class

```
// IllegalAccess3.java
package com.jdojo.reflection;
import java.lang.reflect.Constructor;
import java.lang.reflect.Field;
public class IllegalAccess3 {
    public static void main(String[] args)
            throws Exception {
        // Get the class reference for the Phone class
        String className =
            "com.jdojo.reflection.model.Phone";
        Class<?> cls = Class.forName(className);
        // Create a Phone object
        Constructor<?> cons = cls.getConstructor();
        Object phone = cons.newInstance();
        // Get the reference of the number field
        Field numberField = cls.getDeclaredField("number");
        // try making the number field accessible before
```

```
        // accessing it
        boolean accessEnabled = numberField.
            trySetAccessible();
        if (accessEnabled) {
            // Try accessing the number field by reading
            // its value
            String number = (String) numberField.
                get(phone);
            // Print the phone number
            System.out.println("number=" + number);
        } else {
            System.out.println("The Phone.number field " +
                "is not accessible.");
        }
    }
}
```

Let's run the IllegalAccess3 class using the following command:

```
C:\Java17LanguageFeatures>java ^
--module-path build\modules\jdojo.reflection;build\modules\
    jdojo.reflection.model ^
--module ^
    jdojo.reflection/com.jdojo.reflection.IllegalAccess3
Exception in thread "main"
    java.lang.ClassNotFoundException:
    com.jdojo.reflection.model.Phone
        at java.base/jdk.internal.loader.
            BuiltinClassLoader.loadClass(BuiltinClassLoader.
            java:582)
        at java.base/jdk.internal.loader.ClassLoaders$
            AppClassLoader.loadClass(ClassLoaders.
            java:185)
        at java.base/java.lang.ClassLoader.loadClass
            (ClassLoader.java:496)
        at java.base/java.lang.Class.forName0
            (Native Method)
```

126

```
    at java.base/java.lang.Class.forName
        (Class.java:292)
    at jdoj9o.reflection/com.jdojo.reflection.
        IllegalAccess3.main(IllegalAccess3.java:11)
```

(No line break and no spaces after "modules\".)

Can you guess what is wrong with the command? The error is indicating that the runtime did not find the Phone class. You were able to compile the IllegalAccess3 class because the class does not use the Phone class reference in the source code. It attempts to use the Phone class using reflection at runtime. You have included the jdojo.reflection.model module in the module path. However, including a module in the module path does not resolve the module. The jdojo.reflection module does not read the jdojo.reflection.model module, so running the IllegalAccess3 did not resolve the jdojo.reflection.model module, and this is why the runtime did not find the Phone class. You need to resolve the module manually by using the –addmodules command-line option:

```
C:\Java17LanguageFeatures>java ^
--module-path build\modules\jdojo.reflection;build\modules\
    jdojo.reflection.model ^
--add-modules jdojo.reflection.model ^
--module ^
    jdojo.reflection/com.jdojo.reflection.IllegalAccess3
Exception in thread "main" java.lang.
    IllegalAccessException: class com.jdojo.reflection.
IllegalAccess3 (in module jdojo.reflection) cannot access
    class com.jdojo.reflection.model.Phone (in module
    jdojo.reflection.model) because module jdojo.
    reflection.model does not export com.jdojo.reflection.
    model to module jdojo.reflection
        at java.base/jdk.internal.reflect.Reflection.
            newIllegalAccessException
            (Reflection.java:361)
        at java.base/java.lang.reflect.AccessibleObject.
            checkAccess
            (AccessibleObject.java:589)
```

```
   at java.base/java.lang.reflect.Constructor.
      newInstance
      (Constructor.java:479)
   at jdojo.reflection/com.jdojo.reflection.
      IllegalAccess3.main
      (IllegalAccess3.java:15)
```

(No line break and no spaces after "modules\".)

This time, the runtime was able to find the Phone class, but it complained about accessing the Phone class in the jdojo.reflection.model module from another module, jdojo.reflection. The error is stating that the jdojo.reflection.model module does not export the com.jdojo.reflection.model package, so the Phone class is in the com.jdojo.reflection.model package and is not accessible outside the jdojo.reflection.model module. Listing 2-21 contains the modified version of the jdojo.reflection.model module. Now it exports the com.jdojo.reflection.model package.

Listing 2-21. The Modified Declaration of a jdojo.reflection.model Module

```
// module-info.java
module jdojo.reflection.model {
    exports com.jdojo.reflection.model;
}
```

Let's rerun the IllegalAccess3 class using the previous command:

```
C:\Java17LanguageFeatures>java ^
--module-path ^
    build\modules\jdojo.reflection;
    build\modules\jdojo.reflection.model
--add-modules jdojo.reflection.model ^
--module ^
    jdojo.reflection/com.jdojo.reflection.IllegalAccess3

The Phone.number field is not accessible.
```

(No line break and no spaces after "reflection;".)

This time, you were able to instantiate the Phone class, but you would not access its private number field. Notice that the jdojo.reflection module does not read the jdojo.reflection.model module. Still the IllegalClass3 class is able to access the Phone class and instantiate it using reflection. If you write the following snippet of code in the IllegalAccess3 class, it would not compile:

```
Phone phone = new Phone();
```

When module M accesses the types in module N using reflection, a read from module M to module N is granted implicitly. Such a read must be specified explicitly using a requires statement when such access is needed statically (without reflection). This is what the previous command did when creating an object of the Phone class.

If you used the setAccessible(true) in the IllegalAccess3 class to make the number field accessible, the previous command would have produced an error message similar to the following:

```
Exception in thread "main" java.lang.reflect.
InaccessibleObjectException: Unable to make field private
java.lang.String com.jdojo.reflection.model.Phone.number
accessible: module jdojo.reflection.model does not "opens
com.jdojo.reflection.model" to module jdojo.reflection
...
```

This error message is loud and clear. It is stating that the runtime could not make the private number field accessible because the jdojo.reflection.model module does not open the com.jdojo.reflection.model package to the jdojo.reflection module. Here comes the concept of opening a module's package and opening an entire module.

Exporting a package of a module grants access to the public types in the package and the accessible public members of those types to another module. Exporting a package grants the access at compile time and at runtime. You can use reflection to access the same accessible public members that you can access without reflection. That is, Java language access control is always enforced for exported packages of a module.

If you want to allow deep reflection on types of a package in a module by code in other modules at runtime, you need to open the package of the module using the opens statement. The syntax for the opens statement is as follows:

```
opens <package-name> [to <module-name>,<module-name>...];
```

The syntax allows you to open a package to all other modules or a set of specific modules. In the following declaration, module M opens its package p to modules S and T:

```
module M {
    opens p to S, T;
}
```

In the following declaration, module N opens its package q to all other modules:

```
module N {
    opens q;
}
```

It is possible that a module exports and opens the same package. It is needed if other modules need to access the types in the package statically at compile time and runtime and using deep reflection at runtime. The following module declaration exports and opens the same package p to all other modules:

```
module J {
    exports p;
    opens p;
}
```

An opens statement in a module declaration allows you to open one package to all other modules or selective modules. If you want to open all packages of a module to all other modules, you can declare the module itself as an open module. You can declare an open module by using the open modifier in the module declaration. The following declares an open module named K:

```
open module K {
    // Other module statements go here
}
```

An open module cannot contain an opens statement. This is because an open module means it has opened all its packages to all other modules for deep reflection. The following declaration of module L is invalid because it declares the module as open and, at the same time, contains an opens statement:

```
open module L {
    opens p; // A compile-time error
    // Other module statements go here
}
```

It is fine to export packages in an open module. The following declaration of module D is valid:

```
open module D {
    exports p;
    // Other module statements go here
}
```

So, now you know what to do with the jdojo.reflection.model module for the jdojo.reflection module to perform deep reflection on the Phone class. You need to do either of the following:

- Open the com.jdojo.reflection.model package of the jdojo.reflection.model module to all other modules or at least to the jdojo.reflection module.

- Declare the jdojo.reflection.model module as an open module.

Listings 2-22 and 2-23 contain the modified module declaration of the jdojo.reflection.model module. You will need to use one of them, not both. For this example, you do not need to export the package in the module's declaration because you are not accessing the Phone class at compile time in the jdojo.reflection module.

Listing 2-22. The Modified Declaration of a model Module, Which Opens the com.jdojo.reflection.model Package to All Other Modules

```
// module-info.java
module jdojo.reflection.model {
    exports com.jdojo.reflection.model;
    opens com.jdojo.reflection.model;
}
```

Listing 2-23. The Modified Declaration of a model Module, Which Declares It As an Open Module

```
// module-info.java
open module jdojo.reflection.model {
    exports com.jdojo.reflection.model;
}
```

Let's rerun the IllegalAccess3 class using the previous command with the com.jdojo.reflection.model package open. This time, you will receive the desired output:

```
C:\Java17LanguageFeatures>java ^
--module-path build\modules\jdojo.reflection;
    build\modules\jdojo.reflection.model ^
--add-modules jdojo.reflection.model ^
--module ^
    jdojo.reflection/com.jdojo.reflection.IllegalAccess3
```

```
number=9999999999
```

(No line break and no spaces after "reflection;".)

Deep Reflection and Unnamed Modules

All packages in an unnamed module are open to all other modules. Therefore, you can always perform deep reflection on types in unnamed modules.

Deep Reflection on JDK Modules

Prior to JDK9, deep reflection was allowed on members of all types—JDK internals and your types. One of the main goals of JDK9 is strong encapsulation, and you should not be able to access rather inaccessible members of an object using deep reflection. Since JDK9, deep reflection on JDK modules is only possible from the unnamed module. If applications are modularized, deep reflection on JDK modules is illegal. The weakened restrictions for unnamed modules are for backward compatibility only; modern applications should never access JDK internals like private fields.

Let's walk through an example of this. The java.lang.Long class is immutable. It contains a private field named value to hold the long value that this object represents. Listing 2-24 shows you how to access and modify the private value field of the Long class using deep reflection, which is not possible using the Long class statically.

Listing 2-24. Accessing and Modifying the Private Value Field of the java.lang. Long Class Using Deep Reflection

```java
// IllegalAccessJDKType.java
package com.jdojo.reflection;
import java.lang.reflect.Field;
public class IllegalAccessJDKType {
    public static void main(String[] args)
            throws Exception {
        // Create a Long object
        Long num = 1969L;
        System.out.println("#1: num = " + num);
        // Get the class reference for the Long class
        String className = "java.lang.Long";
        Class<?> cls = Class.forName(className);
        // Get the value field reference
        Field valueField = cls.getDeclaredField("value");
        // try making the value field accessible before
        // accessing it
        boolean accessEnabled = valueField.
            trySetAccessible();
        if (accessEnabled) {
            // Get and print the current value of the
            // Long.value private field of the num object
            // that you created in the beginning of this
            // method
            Long value = (Long) valueField.get(num);
            System.out.println("#2: num = " + value);
            // Change the value of the Long.value field
            valueField.set(num, 1968L);
            value = (Long) valueField.get(num);
            System.out.println("#3: num = " + value);
```

```
        } else {
            System.out.println("The Long.value field is " +
                "not accessible.");
        }
    }
}
```

In the beginning of the main() method, you create a Long object, called num, and set its value to 1969L:

```
Long num = 1969L;
System.out.println("#1: num = " + num);
```

Later, you get the reference of the Class object for the Long class and get the reference of the private value field and try to make it accessible. If you were able to make the field accessible, you read its current value, which would be 1969L. Now you change its value to 1968L and read it back in your program.

The IllegalAccessJDKType class is a member of the jdojo.reflection module. Let's run it using the following command:

```
C:\Java17LanguageFeatures>java ^
--module-path build\modules\jdojo.reflection ^
--module ^
jdojo.reflection/com.jdojo.reflection.IllegalAccessJDKType
```

```
#1: num = 1969
The Long.value field is not accessible.
```

You were not able to make the private value field of the Long class accessible because the IllegalAccessJDKType class is part of a named module, and code in named modules is not allowed to have illegal access to the members of the JDK internal types. The following command reruns the class from the class path (effectively unmodularizing it and implicitly using the unnamed module), and you get the desired output. Notice the one-time warnings even though you have accessed the private field three times:

```
C:\Java17LanguageFeatures>java ^
--class-path build\modules\jdojo.reflection ^
com.jdojo.reflection.IllegalAccessJDKType
```

```
#1: num = 1969
WARNING: An illegal reflective access operation has
    occurred
WARNING: Illegal reflective access by com.jdojo.reflection.
    IllegalAccessJDKType
(file:/C:/Java17LanguageFeatures/build/modules/
    jdojo.reflection/) to field java.lang.Long.value
WARNING: Please consider reporting this to the maintainers
of com.jdojo.reflection.IllegalAccessJDKType
WARNING: Use --illegal-access=warn to enable warnings of
    further illegal reflective access operations
WARNING: All illegal access operations will be denied in a
future release
#2: num = 1969
#3: num = 1968
```

Reflecting on Arrays

Java provides special APIs to work with arrays. The Class class lets you find out if a Class reference represents an array by using its isArray() method. You can also create an array and read and modify its element's values using reflection. The java.lang. reflect.Array class is used to dynamically create an array and manipulate its elements. As stated before, you cannot reflect on the length field of an array using a normal reflection procedure. However, the Array class provides the getLength() method to get the length value of an array. Note that all methods in the Array class are static, and most of them have the first argument as the array object's reference on which they operate.

To create an array, use the newInstance() static method of the Array class. The method is overloaded and has two versions:

- Object newInstance(Class<?> componentType, int arrayLength)

- Object newInstance(Class<?> componentType, int... dimensions)

One version of the method creates an array of the specified component type and the array length. The other version creates an array of the specified component type and dimensions. Note that the return type of the newInstance() method is Object. You need to use an appropriate cast to convert it to the actual array type.

135

If you want to create an array of int of length 5, you would write

```
int[] ids = (int[]) Array.newInstance(int.class, 5);
```

This statement has the same effect as the following statement:

```
int[] ids = new int[5];
```

If you want to create an array of int of dimension 5x8, you would write

```
int[][] matrix = (int[][]) Array.newInstance(
int.class, 5, 8);
```

Listing 2-25 illustrates how to create an array dynamically and manipulate its elements.

Listing 2-25. Reflecting on Arrays

```java
// ArrayReflection.java
package com.jdojo.reflection;
import java.lang.reflect.Array;
public class ArrayReflection {
    public static void main(String[] args) {
        try {
            // Create the array of int of length 2
            Object arrayObject = Array.newInstance(
                int.class, 2);
            // Print the values in array element. Default
            // values will be zero
            int n1 = Array.getInt(arrayObject, 0);
            int n2 = Array.getInt(arrayObject, 1);
            System.out.println("n1 = " + n1 +
                ", n2 = " + n2);
            // Set the values to both elements
            Array.set(arrayObject, 0, 101);
            Array.set(arrayObject, 1, 102);
            // Print the values in array element again
            n1 = Array.getInt(arrayObject, 0);
            n2 = Array.getInt(arrayObject, 1);
```

```
        System.out.println("n1 = " + n1 +
            ", n2 = " + n2);
    } catch (NegativeArraySizeException
            | IllegalArgumentException
            | ArrayIndexOutOfBoundsException e) {
        System.out.println(e.getMessage());
    }
}
}
```

```
n1 = 0, n2 = 0
n1 = 101, n2 = 102
```

Java does not support a truly multidimensional array. Rather, it supports an array of arrays. The Class class contains a method called getComponentType(), which returns the Class object for an array's element type. Listing 2-26 illustrates how to get the dimension of an array.

Listing 2-26. Getting the Dimension of an Array

```
// ArrayDimension.java
package com.jdojo.reflection;
public class ArrayDimension {
    public static void main(String[] args) {
        int[][][] intArray = new int[6][3][4];
        System.out.println("int[][][] dimension is " +
            getArrayDimension(intArray));
    }
    public static int getArrayDimension(Object array) {
        int dimension = 0;
        Class c = array.getClass();
        // Perform a check that the object is really
        // an array
        if (!c.isArray()) {
            throw new IllegalArgumentException(
                "Object is not an array.");
        }
```

```
        while (c.isArray()) {
            dimension++;
            c = c.getComponentType();
        }

        return dimension;
    }
}
int[][][] dimension is 3
```

Expanding an Array

After you create an array, you cannot change its length. You can create an array of a bigger size and copy the old array elements to the new one at runtime. The Java collection classes such as ArrayList apply this technique to let you add elements to the collection without worrying about its length. You can use the combination of the getComponentType() method of the Class class and the newInstance() method of the Array class to create a new array of a given type. You can use the arraycopy() static method of the System class to copy the old array elements to the new array. Listing 2-27 illustrates how to create an array of a particular type using reflection. All runtime checks have been left out for clarity.

Listing 2-27. Expanding an Array Using Reflection

```java
// ExpandingArray.java
package com.jdojo.reflection;
import java.lang.reflect.Array;
import java.util.Arrays;
public class ExpandingArray {
    public static void main(String[] args) {
        // Create an array of length 2
        int[] ids = {101, 102};
        System.out.println("Old array length: " +
            ids.length);
        System.out.println("Old array elements: " +
            Arrays.toString(ids));
```

```
    // Expand the array by 1
    ids = (int[]) expandBy(ids, 1);
    // Set the third element to 103
    ids[2] = 103; // This is newly added element
    System.out.println("New array length: " +
        ids.length);
    System.out.println("New array elements: " +
        Arrays.toString(ids));
}
public static Object
expandBy(Object oldArray, int increment) {
    // Get the length of old array using reflection
    int oldLength = Array.getLength(oldArray);
    int newLength = oldLength + increment;
    // Get the class of the old array
    Class<?> cls = oldArray.getClass();
    // Create a new array of the new length
    Object newArray = Array.newInstance(
        cls.getComponentType(), newLength);
    // Copy the old array elements to new array
    System.arraycopy(oldArray, 0, newArray,
        0, oldLength);
    return newArray;
    }
}
Old array length: 2
Old array elements: [101, 102]
New array length: 3
New array elements: [101, 102, 103]
```

Who Should Use Reflection?

If you have used any integrated development environment (IDE) to develop a GUI application using drag-and-drop features, you have already used an application that uses reflection in one form or another. All GUI tools that let you set the properties of a control, say a button, at design time use reflection to get the list of the properties for that control. Other tools such as class browsers and debuggers also use reflection. As an application programmer, you will not use reflection much unless you are developing advanced applications that use dynamism provided by the reflection API. It should be noted that using too much reflection slows down the performance of your application.

Summary

Reflection is the ability of a program to query and modify its state "as data" during the execution of the program. Java represents the bytecode of a class as an object of the Class class to facilitate reflection. The class fields, constructors, and methods can be accessed as an object of the Field, Constructor, and Method classes, respectively. Using a Field object, you can access and change the value of the field. Using a Method object, you can invoke the method. Using a Constructor object, you can invoke a given constructor of a class. Using the Array class, you can also create arrays of a specified type and dimension using reflection and manipulate the elements of the arrays.

Java has been allowing access to rather inaccessible members such as a private field of a class outside the class using reflection. This is called deep reflection. Before you can access the inaccessible member, you need to call the setAccessible(true) on that member, which could be a Field, a Method, or a Constructor. The setAccessible() method throws a runtime exception if the accessibility cannot be enabled. JDK9 added a trySetAccessible() method for the same purpose, which does not throw a runtime exception. Rather, it returns true if accessibility is enabled and false otherwise.

Deep reflection in JDK9 and later across modules is prohibited by default. If a module wants to allow deep reflection on types in a given package, the module must open that package to at least the module that will use deep reflection. You can open a package using the opens statement in a module declaration. You can declare a module as an open module, which opens all packages in the module for deep reflection. If a named module M uses reflection to access types in another module N, the module M implicitly reads module N. All packages in an unnamed module open for deep reflection.

JDK9 and later allow deep reflection on JDK internal types by code only from the unnamed module or unmodularized applications.

Exercises

Exercise 1

What is reflection?

Exercise 2

Name two Java packages that contain the reflection-related classes and interfaces.

Exercise 3

What does an instance of the `Class` class represent?

Exercise 4

List three ways to get the reference of an instance of the Class class.

Exercise 5

When do you use the `forName()` method of the `Class` class to get an instance of the Class class?

Exercise 6

Name three built-in class loaders. How do you get references of these class loaders?

Exercise 7

If you get a reference of the `Class` class, how do you know if this reference represents an interface?

Exercise 8

What do instances of the `Field`, `Constructor`, and `Method` classes represent?

Exercise 9

What is the difference between using the `getFields()` and `getDeclaredFields()` methods of the `Class` class?

Exercise 10

You need to use `setAccessible(true)` or `trySetAccessible()` method of the `AccessibleObject` class to make a `Field`, `Constructor`, and `Method` object accessible even if they are inaccessible (e.g., they are declared private). What is the difference between these two methods?

Exercise 11

Assume that you have two modules named R and S. Module R contains a public `p.Test` class with a public method `m()`. The code in module S needs to use the class `p.Test` to declare variables and create its objects. Module S also needs to use reflection to access the public method `m()` of the `p.Test` class in module R. What is the minimum you need to do while declaring module R, so module S can perform these tasks?

Exercise 12

What is opening a package in a module? What is an open module?

Exercise 13

What is the difference between exporting and opening a package of a module? Give an example when you will need to export and open the same package of a module.

Exercise 14

Consider the declarations of a module named jdojo.reflection.exercise.model and a MagicNumber class in that module as follows:

```java
// module-info.java
module jdojo.reflection.exercises.model {
    /* Add your module statements here */
}
// MagicNumber.java
package com.jdojo.reflection.exercises.model;
public class MagicNumber {
    private int number;
    public int getNumber() {
        return number;
    }
    public void setNumber(int number) {
        this.number = number;
    }
}
```

Modify the module declaration so that code in other modules can perform deep reflection on the objects of the MagicNumber class. Create a class named MagicNumberTest in a module named jdojo.reflection.exercises. The code in the MagicNumberTest class should use reflection to create an object of the MagicNumber class, set its private number field directly, and read the current value of the number field using the getNumber() method.

Exercise 15

Can you access private members of JDK classes in Java 9 or later? If your answer is yes, describe the rules and restrictions for such access.

Exercise 16

Assume there are two modules, P and Q. Module P is an open module. Module Q wants to perform deep reflection on types in module P. Is module Q required to read module P in its module's declaration?

Exercise 17

Assume there are two modules, M and N. Module M does not open any of its packages to any modules, but it exports a `com.jdojo.m` to all other modules. Can module N use reflection to access publically accessible members of the `com.jdojo.m` package of module M?

CHAPTER 3

Generics

In this chapter, you will learn:

- What generics are
- How to define generic types, methods, and constructors
- How to define bounds for type parameters
- How to use wildcards as the actual type parameters
- How the compiler infers the actual type parameters for generic type uses
- Generics and their limitations in array creations
- How the incorrect use of generics may lead to heap pollution

All example programs in this chapter are a member of a `jdojo.generics` module, as declared in Listing 3-1.

Listing 3-1. The Declaration of a jdojo.generics Module

```
// module-info.java
module jdojo.generics {
    exports com.jdojo.generics;
}
```

What Are Generics?

Generics let you write true polymorphic code that works with any type.

Let's discuss a simple example before I define what generics are and what they do for you. Suppose you want to create a new class whose sole job is to store a reference to any type, where "any type" means any reference type. Let's call this class `ObjectWrapper`, as shown in Listing 3-2.

© Kishori Sharan, Peter Späth 2021
K. Sharan and P. Späth, *More Java 17*, https://doi.org/10.1007/978-1-4842-7135-3_3

Listing 3-2. A Wrapper Class to Store a Reference of Any Type

```java
// ObjectWrapper.java
package com.jdojo.generics;
public class ObjectWrapper {
    private Object ref;

    public ObjectWrapper(Object ref) {
        this.ref = ref;
    }
    public Object get() {
        return ref;
    }
    public void set(Object ref) {
        this.ref = ref;
    }
}
```

As a Java developer, you would agree that you write this kind of code when you do not know the type of the objects that you have to deal with. The ObjectWrapper class can store a reference of any type in Java, such as String, Integer, Person, etc. How do you use the ObjectWrapper class? The following is one of the ways to use it to work with the String type:

```java
ObjectWrapper stringWrapper = new ObjectWrapper("Hello");
stringWrapper.set("Another string");
String myString = (String) stringWrapper.get();
```

There's one problem in this snippet of code. Even though you knew that you stored (and wanted to) a string in the stringWrapper object, you had to cast the return value of the get() method to a String type in (String) stringWrapper.get(). Consider writing the following snippet of code:

```java
ObjectWrapper stringWrapper = new ObjectWrapper("Hello");
stringWrapper.set(new Integer(101));
String myString =(String) stringWrapper.get();
```

This snippet of code compiles fine. However, the third statement throws a ClassCastException at runtime because you stored an Integer in the second statement and attempted to cast an Integer to a String in the third statement. First, it allowed you to store an Integer in stringWrapper. Second, it did not complain about the code in the third statement because it had no knowledge of your intent that you only wanted to use a String with stringWrapper.

Java has made some progress with the way it helps developers write type-safe programs. Wouldn't it be nice if the ObjectWrapper class allowed you to specify that you want to use this class only for a specific type, say, String this time and Integer the next? Your wish is fulfilled by generics in Java. They let you specify a type parameter with a type (class or interface). Such a type is called a generic type (more specifically generic class or generic interface). The type parameter value could be specified when you declare a variable of the generic type and create an object of your generic type. You have seen specifying parameters for a method. This time, I am talking about specifying parameters for types such as classes or interfaces.

Note   A type with type parameters in its declaration is called a generic type.

Let's rewrite the ObjectWrapper class to use generics naming the new class simply Wrapper. The formal parameters of a generic type are specified in the generic type's declaration. Parameter names are valid Java identifiers and are specified in angle brackets (< >) after the name of the parameterized type. You will use T as the type parameter name for the Wrapper class:

```
public class Wrapper<T> {
}
```

It is an unwritten convention that type parameter names are one character and to use T to indicate that the parameter is a type, E to indicate that the parameter is an element, K to indicate that the parameter is a key, N to indicate the parameter is a number, and V to indicate that the parameter is a value. In the previous example, you could have used any name for the type parameter, like so:

```
public class Wrapper<Hello> {
}
public class Wrapper<MyType> {
}
```

Multiple type parameters are separated by a comma. The following declaration for MyClass takes four type parameters named T, U, V, and W:

```
public class MyClass<T, U, V, W> {
}
```

You will be using your type parameter named T inside the class code in instance variable declarations, constructors, the get() method, and the set() method. Right now, T means any type for you, which will be known when you use this class. Listing 3-3 contains the complete code for the Wrapper class.

Listing 3-3. Using a Type Parameter to Define a Generic Class

```
// Wrapper.java
package com.jdojo.generics;
public class Wrapper<T> {
    private T ref;
    public Wrapper(T ref) {
        this.ref = ref;
    }
    public T get() {
        return ref;
    }
    public void set(T ref) {
        this.ref = ref;
    }
}
```

Are you confused about using T in Listing 3-3? Here, T means any class type or interface type. It could be String, Object, com.jdojo.generics.Person, etc. If you replace T with Object everywhere in this program and remove <T> from the class name, it is the same code that you had for the ObjectWrapper class.

How do you use the Wrapper class? Since its class name is not just Wrapper, rather it is Wrapper<T>, you may specify (but do not have to) the value for T. To store a String reference in the Wrapper object, you create it as follows:

```
Wrapper<String> greetingWrapper =
    new Wrapper<String>("Hello");
```

How do you use the set() and get() methods of the Wrapper class? Since you have specified the type parameter for class Wrapper<T> to be String, the set() and get() methods will work only with String types. This is because you used T as an argument type in the set() method and T as the return type in the get() method declarations. Imagine replacing T in the class definition with String, and you should have no problem understanding the following code:

```
greetingWrapper.set("Hi");
    // <- OK to pass a String
String greeting = greetingWrapper.get();
    // <- No need to cast
```

This time, you did not have to cast the return value of the get() method. The compiler knows that greetingWrapper has been declared of type Wrapper<String>, so its get() method returns a String. Let's try to store an Integer object in greetingWrapper:

```
// A compile-time error. You can use greetingWrapper
// only to store a String.
greetingWrapper.set(new Integer(101));
```

The statement will generate the following compile-time error:

```
error: incompatible types: Integer cannot be converted to
    String
        greetingWrapper.set(new Integer(101));
```

You cannot pass an Integer to the set() method. The compiler will generate an error. If you want to use the Wrapper class to store an Integer, your code will be as follows:

```
Wrapper<Integer> idWrapper =
    new Wrapper<Integer>(new Integer(101));
idWrapper.set(new Integer(897));
    // <- OK to pass an Integer
Integer id = idWrapper.get();
// A compile-time error. You can use idWrapper only
// with an Integer.
idWrapper.set("hello");
```

Assuming that a `Person` class exists that contains a constructor with two parameters, you store a `Person` object in `Wrapper` as follows:

```
Wrapper<Person> personWrapper = new Wrapper<Person>(
    new Person(1, "Chris"));
personWrapper.set(new Person(2, "Laynie"));
Person laynie = personWrapper.get();
```

The parameter that is specified in the type declaration is called a formal type parameter; for example, `T` is a formal type parameter in the `Wrapper<T>` class declaration. When you replace the formal type parameter with the actual type (e.g., in `Wrapper<String>` you replace the formal type parameter `T` with `String`), it is called a parameterized type. A reference type in Java, which accepts one or more type parameters, is called a generic type. A generic type is mostly implemented in the compiler. The JVM has no knowledge of generic types. All actual type parameters are erased at compile time using a process known as erasure. Compile-time type-safety is the benefit that you get when you use a parameterized generic type in your code without the need to use casts.

Polymorphism is about writing code in terms of a type that also works with many other types. In any introductory level book about Java, you learn how to write polymorphic code using inheritance and interfaces. Inheritance in Java offers inclusion polymorphism where you write code in terms of the base type, and the code also works with all subtypes of that base type. In this case, you are forced to have all other types fall under a single inheritance hierarchy. That is, all types for which the polymorphic code works must inherit from the single base type. Interfaces in Java lift this restriction and let you write code in terms of an interface. The code works with all types that implement the interface. This time, all types for which the code works do not have to fall under one type hierarchy. Still, you had one constraint that all those types must implement the same interface. Generics in Java take you a step closer to writing "true" polymorphic code. The code written using generics works for any type. Generics in Java do have some restrictions as to what you can do with the generic type in your code. Showing you what you can do with generics in Java and elaborating on the restrictions are the topics of discussion in this chapter.

Supertype-Subtype Relationship

Let's play a trick. The following code creates two parameterized instances of the Wrapper<T> class, one for the String type and one for the Object type:

```
Wrapper<String> stringWrapper =
    new Wrapper<String>("Hello");
stringWrapper.set("a string");
Wrapper<Object> objectWrapper =
    new Wrapper<Object>(new Object());
objectWrapper.set(new Object());
// Use a String object with objectWrapper
objectWrapper.set("a string"); // OK
```

It is fine to store a String object in objectWrapper. After all, if you intended to store an Object in objectWrapper, a String is also an Object. Is the following assignment allowed?

```
objectWrapper = stringWrapper;
```

No, this assignment is not allowed. That is, a Wrapper<String> is not assignment compatible to a Wrapper<Object>. To understand why this assignment is not allowed, let's assume for a moment that it was allowed and you could write code like the following:

```
// Now objectWrapper points to stringWrapper
objectWrapper = stringWrapper;
// We could store an Object in stringWrapper using
// objectWrapper
objectWrapper.set(new Object());
// The following statement will throw a runtime
// ClassCastException
String s = stringWrapper.get();
```

Do you see the danger of allowing an assignment like objectWrapper=stringWrapper? The compiler cannot make sure that stringWrapper will store only a reference of String type if this assignment was allowed.

Remember that a String is an Object because String is a subclass of Object. However, a Wrapper<String> is not a Wrapper<Object>. The normal supertype/subtype rules do not apply to parameterized types. Don't worry about memorizing this rule if you do not understand it. If you attempt such assignments, the compiler will tell you that you can't.

Raw Types

The implementation of generic types in Java is backward compatible. If an existing non-generic class is rewritten to take advantage of generics, the existing code that uses the non-generic version of the class should keep working. The code may use (though it is not recommended) a non-generic version of a generic class by just omitting references to the generic type parameters. The non-generic version of a generic type is called a raw type. Using raw types is discouraged. If you use raw types in your code, the compiler will generate unchecked warnings, as shown in the following snippet of code:

```
// Use the Wrapper<T> generic type as a raw type Wrapper
Wrapper rawType = new Wrapper("Hello"); // An unchecked
                                         // warning
// Using the Wrapper<T> generic type as a parameterized
// type Wrapper<String>
Wrapper<String> genericType = new Wrapper<String>("Hello");
// Assigning the raw type to the parameterized type
genericType = rawType; // An unchecked warning
// Assigning the parameterized type to the raw type
rawType = genericType;
```

The compiler generates the following warnings when this snippet of code is compiled:

```
warning: [unchecked] unchecked call to Wrapper(T) as a
    member of the raw type Wrapper
        Wrapper rawType = new Wrapper("Hello");
                      ^
  where T is a type-variable:
    T extends Object declared in class Wrapper
```

```
warning: [unchecked] unchecked conversion
        genericType = rawType;
                      ^
    required: Wrapper<String>
    found:    Wrapper
2 warnings
```

Unbounded Wildcards

Let's start with an example. It will help you understand the need for as well as the use of wildcards in generic types. Let's build a utility class for the Wrapper class and call it WrapperUtil. Add a static utility method called printDetails() to this class, which will take an object of the Wrapper<T> class. How should you define the argument of this method? The following is the first attempt:

```
public class WrapperUtil {
    public static
    void printDetails(Wrapper<Object> wrapper){
        // More code goes here
    }
}
```

Since your printDetails() method is supposed to print details about a Wrapper<T> of any type, Object as the type parameter seems to be more suitable. Let's use your new printDetails() method, as shown:

```
Wrapper<Object> objectWrapper =
    new Wrapper<Object>(new Object());
WrapperUtil.printDetails(objectWrapper); // OK
Wrapper<String> stringWrapper =
    new Wrapper<String>("Hello");
WrapperUtil.printDetails(stringWrapper); // A compile-time
                                         // error
```

The compile-time error is as follows:

```
error: method printDetails in class WrapperUtil cannot be
    applied to given types;
        WrapperUtil.printDetails(stringWrapper);
                    ^
  required: Wrapper<Object>
  found: Wrapper<String>
  reason: argument mismatch; Wrapper<String> cannot be
    converted to Wrapper<Object>
1 error
```

You are able to call the printDetails() method with the Wrapper<Object> type, but not with the Wrapper<String> type because they are not assignment compatible, which is contradictory to what your intuition tells you. To understand it fully, you need to know about the wildcard type in generics. A wildcard type is denoted by a question mark, as in <?>. For a generic type, a wildcard type is what an Object type is for a raw type. You can assign a generic of known type to a generic of wildcard type. Here is the sample code:

```
// Wrapper of String type
Wrapper<String> stringWrapper = new Wrapper<String>("Hi");
// You can assign a Wrapper<String> to Wrapper<?> type
Wrapper<?> wildCardWrapper = stringWrapper;
```

The question mark in a wildcard generic type (e.g., <?>) denotes an unknown type. When you declare a parameterized type using a wildcard (means unknown) as a parameter type, it means that it does not know about its type:

```
// wildCardWrapper has unknown type
Wrapper<?> wildCardWrapper;
// Better to name it as an unknownWrapper
Wrapper<?> unknownWrapper;
```

Can you create a Wrapper<T> object of an unknown type? Let's assume that John cooks something for you. He packs the food in a packet and hands it over to you. You hand over the packet to Donna. Donna asks you what is inside the packet. Your answer is that you do not know. Can John answer the same way you did? No. He must know what he cooked because he was the person who cooked the food. Even if you did not know what was inside the packet, you had no problem in carrying it and giving it to Donna. What would be your answer if Donna asked you to give her the vegetables from the packet? You would say that you do not know if vegetables are inside the packet.

Here are the rules for using a wildcard (unknown) generic type. Since it does not know its type, you cannot use it to create an object of its unknown type. The following code is illegal:

```
// Cannot use <?> with new operator. It is a compile-time
// error.
new Wrapper<?>("");
error: unexpected type
        new Wrapper<?>("");
              ^
  required: class or interface without bounds
  found:    ?
1 error
```

As you were holding the packet of unknown food type (John knew the type of food when he cooked it), a wildcard generic type can refer to a known generic type object, as shown:

```
Wrapper<?> unknownWrapper = new Wrapper<String>("Hello");
```

There is a complicated list of rules as to what a wildcard generic type reference can do with the object. However, there is a simple rule of thumb to remember. The purpose of using generics is to have compile-time type-safety. As long as the compiler is satisfied that the operation will not produce any surprising results at runtime, it allows the operation on the wildcard generic type reference.

Let's apply the rule of thumb to your unknownWrapper reference variable. One thing that this unknownWrapper variable is sure about is that it refers to an object of the Wrapper<T> class of a known type. However, it does not know what that known type is. Can you use the following get() method? The following statement generates a compile-time error:

```
String str = unknownWrapper.get();
error: incompatible types: CAP#1 cannot be converted
    to String
        String str = unknownWrapper.get();
                                      ^
  where CAP#1 is a fresh type-variable:
    CAP#1 extends Object from capture of ?
1 error
```

The compiler knows that the get() method of the Wrapper<T> class returns an object of type T. However, for the unknownWrapper variable, type T is unknown. Therefore, the compiler cannot ensure that the method call, unknownWrapper.get(), will return a String and its assignment to str variable is fine at runtime. All you have to do is convince the compiler that the assignment will not throw a ClassCastException at runtime. Will the following line of code compile?

```
Object obj = unknownWrapper.get(); // OK
```

This code will compile because the compiler is convinced that this statement will not throw a ClassCastException at runtime. It knows that the get() method returns an object of a type, which is not known to the unknownWrapper variable. No matter what type of object the get() method returns, it will always be assignment compatible with the Object type. After all, all reference types in Java are subtypes of the Object type. Will the following snippet of code compile?

```
unknownWrapper.set("Hello");        // A compile-time error
unknownWrapper.set(new Integer());  // A compile-time error
unknownWrapper.set(new Object());   // A compile-time error
unknownWrapper.set(null);           // OK
```

Were you surprised by errors in this snippet of code? You will find out that it is not as surprising as it seems. The set(T a) method accepts the generic type argument. This type, T, is not known to unknownWrapper, and therefore the compiler cannot make sure that the unknown type is a String type, an Integer type, or an Object type. This is why the first three calls to set() are rejected by the compiler. Why is the fourth call to the set() method correct? A null is assignment compatible to any reference type in Java. The compiler thought that no matter what type T would be in the set(T a) method for the object to which unknownWrapper reference variable is pointing to, a null can always be safe to use. The following is your printDetails() method's code. If you pass a null Wrapper object to this method, it will throw a NullPointerException:

```
public class WrapperUtil {
    public static void printDetails(Wrapper<?> wrapper) {
        // Can assign get() return value to an Object
        Object value = wrapper.get();
        String className = null;
        if (value != null) {
            className = value.getClass().getName();
        }
        System.out.println("Class: " + className);
        System.out.println("Value: " + value);
    }
}
```

Note   Using only a question mark as a parameter type (<?>) is known as an unbounded wildcard. It places no bounds as to what type it can refer. You can also place an upper bound or a lower bound with a wildcard. I discuss bounded wildcards in the next two sections.

Upper-Bounded Wildcards

Suppose you want to add a method to your WrapperUtil class. The method should accept two numbers that are wrapped in your Wrapper objects, and it will return their sum. The wrapped objects may be an Integer, Long, Byte, Short, Double, or Float. Your first attempt is to write the sum() method as shown:

```
public static double sum(Wrapper<?> n1, Wrapper<?> n2) {
    //Code goes here
}
```

There are some obvious problems with this method signature. The parameters n1 and n2 could be of any parameterized type of Wrapper<T> class. For example, the following call would be a valid call for the sum() method:

```
// Try adding an Integer and a String
sum(new Wrapper<Integer>(new Integer(125)),
    new Wrapper<String>("Hello"));
```

Computing the sum of an Integer and a String does not make sense. However, the code will compile, and you should be ready to get some runtime exceptions depending on the implementation of the sum() method. You must restrict this kind of code from compiling. It should accept two Wrapper objects of type Number or its subclasses, not just anything. Therefore, you know the upper bound of the type of the actual parameter that the Wrapper object should have. The upper bound is the Number type. If you pass any other type, which is a subclass of the Number type, it is fine. However, anything that is not a Number type or its subclass type should be rejected at compile time. You express the upper bound of a wildcard as

```
<? extends T>
```

Here, T is a type. <? extends T> means anything that is of type T or its subclass is acceptable. Using your upper bound as Number, you can define your method as

```
public static double sum(Wrapper<? extends Number> n1,
        Wrapper<? extends Number> n2) {
    Number num1 = n1.get();
    Number num2 = n2.get();
    double sum = num1.doubleValue() + num2.doubleValue();
    return sum;
}
```

The following snippet of code inside the method compiles fine:

```
Number num1 = n1.get();
Number num2 = n2.get();
```

No matter what you pass for n1 and n2, they will always be assignment compatible with Number because the compiler will make sure that the parameters passed to the sum() method follow the rules specified in its declaration of <? extends Number>. The attempt to compute the sum of an Integer and a String will be rejected by the compiler. Consider the following snippet of code:

```
Wrapper<Integer> intWrapper =
    new Wrapper<Integer>(new Integer(10));
Wrapper<? extends Number> numberWrapper = intWrapper;
    // <- OK
numberWrapper.set(new Integer(1220));
    // <- A compile-time error
numberWrapper.set(new Double(12.20));
    // <- A compile-time error
```

Can you figure out the problem with this snippet of code? The type of numberWrapper is <? extends Number>, which means it can refer to (or it is assignment compatible with) anything that is a subtype of the Number class. Since Integer is a subclass of Number, the assignment of intWrapper to numberWrapper is allowed. When you try to use the set() method on numberWrapper, the compiler starts complaining because it cannot make sure at compile time that numberWrapper is a type of Integer or Double, which are subtypes of a Number. Be careful with this kind of compile-time error when working with generics. On the surface, it might look obvious to you, and you would think that code should compile and run fine. Unless the compiler ensures that the operation is type-safe, it will not allow you to proceed. After all, compile-time and runtime type-safety is the primary goal of generics!

Lower-Bounded Wildcards

Specifying a lower-bounded wildcard is the opposite of specifying an upper-bounded wildcard. The syntax for using a lower-bounded wildcard is <? super T>, which means "anything that is a supertype of T." Let's add another method to the WrapperUtil class. You will call the new method copy(), and it will copy the value from a source wrapper object to a destination wrapper object. Here is the first attempt. The <T> is the formal type parameter for the copy() method. It specifies that the source and dest parameters must be of the same type. I explain generic methods in detail in the next section.

```
public class WrapperUtil {
    public static <T> void
    copy(Wrapper<T> source, Wrapper<T> dest) {
        T value = source.get();
        dest.set(value);
    }
}
```

Copying the content of a Wrapper<String> to a Wrapper<Object> using your copy() method will not work:

```
Wrapper<Object> objectWrapper =
    new Wrapper<Object>(new Object());
Wrapper<String> stringWrapper =
    new Wrapper<String>("Hello");
WrapperUtil.copy(stringWrapper, objectWrapper);
    // <- A compile-time error
```

This code will generate a compile-time error because the copy() method requires the source and the dest arguments be of the same type. However, for all practical purposes, a String is always an Object. Here, you need to use a lower-bounded wildcard, as shown:

```
public class WrapperUtil {
    // New definition of the copy() method
    public static <T> void
    copy(Wrapper<T> source, Wrapper<? super T> dest){
        T value = source.get();
        dest.set(value);
    }
}
```

Now you are saying that the dest argument of the copy() method could be either T, same as source, or any of its supertype. You can use the copy() method to copy the contents of a Wrapper<String> to a Wrapper<Object> as follows:

```
Wrapper<Object> objectWrapper =
    new Wrapper<Object>(new Object());
Wrapper<String> stringWrapper =
    new Wrapper<String>("Hello");
WrapperUtil.copy(stringWrapper, objectWrapper);
    // <- OK with the new copy() method
```

Since Object is the supertype of String, the new copy() method will work. However, you cannot use it to copy from an Object type wrapper to a String type wrapper, because "an Object is a String" is not always true. Listing 3-4 shows the complete code for the WrapperUtil class.

Listing 3-4. A WrapperUtil Utility Class That Works with Wrapper Objects

```
// WrapperUtil.java
package com.jdojo.generics;
public class WrapperUtil {
    public static void printDetails(Wrapper<?> wrapper) {
        // Can assign get() return value to Object
        Object value = wrapper.get();
        String className = null;
        if (value != null) {
            className = value.getClass().getName();
        }
        System.out.println("Class: " + className);
        System.out.println("Value: " + value);
    }
    public static double sum(Wrapper<? extends Number> n1,
            Wrapper<? extends Number> n2) {
        Number num1 = n1.get();
        Number num2 = n2.get();
        double sum = num1.doubleValue() +
            num2.doubleValue();
        return sum;
    }
```

```
    public static <T> void copy(Wrapper<T> source,
            Wrapper<? super T> dest) {
        T value = source.get();
        dest.set(value);
    }
}
```

Listing 3-5 shows you how to use the Wrapper and WrapperUtil classes.

Listing 3-5. Using the WrapperUtil Class

```
// WrapperUtilTest.java
package com.jdojo.generics;

public class WrapperUtilTest {
    public static void main(String[] args) {
        Wrapper<Integer> n1 = new Wrapper<>(10);
        Wrapper<Double> n2 = new Wrapper<>(15.75);
        // Print the details
        WrapperUtil.printDetails(n1);
        WrapperUtil.printDetails(n2);
        // Add numeric values in two WrapperUtil
        double sum = WrapperUtil.sum(n1, n2);
        System.out.println("sum: " + sum);
        // Copy the value of a Wrapper<Double> to a
        // Wrapper<Number>
        Wrapper<Number> holder = new Wrapper<>(45);
        System.out.println("Original holder: " +
            holder.get());
        WrapperUtil.copy(n2, holder);
        System.out.println("After copy holder: " +
            holder.get());
    }
}
```

```
Class: java.lang.Integer
Value: 10
Class: java.lang.Double
Value: 15.75
sum: 25.75
Original holder: 45
After copy holder: 15.75
```

Generic Methods and Constructors

You can define type parameters in a method declaration. They are specified in angle brackets before the return type of the method. The type that contains the generic method declaration does not have to be a generic type, so you can have generic methods in a non-generic type. It is also possible for a type and its methods to define different type parameters.

Note   Type parameters defined for a generic type are not available in static methods of that type. Therefore, if a static method needs to be generic, it must define its own type parameters. If a method needs to be generic, define just that method as generic rather than defining the entire type as generic.

The following snippet of code defines a generic type Test with its type parameter named T. It also defines a generic instance method m1() that defines its own generic type parameter named V. The method also uses the type parameter T, which is defined by its class. Note the use of <V> before the return type void of the m1() method. It defines a new generic type named V for the method.

```
public class Test<T> {
    public <V> void m1(Wrapper<V> a, Wrapper<V> b, T c) {
        // Do something
    }
}
```

Can you think of the implication of defining and using the generic type parameter V for the m1() method? Look at its use in defining the first and second parameters of the method as Wrapper<V>. It forces the first and the second parameters to be of the same type. The third argument must be of the same type T, which is the type of the class instantiation.

How do you specify the generic type for a method when you want to call the method? Usually, you do not need to specify the actual type parameter when you call the method. The compiler figures it out for you using the value you pass to the method. However, if you ever need to pass the actual type parameter for the method's formal type parameter, you must specify it in angle brackets (< >) between the dot and the method name in the method call, as shown:

```
Test<String> t = new Test<String>();
Wrapper<Integer> iw1 =
    new Wrapper<Integer>(new Integer(201));
Wrapper<Integer> iw2 =
    new Wrapper<Integer>(new Integer(202));
// Specify that Integer is the actual type for the type
// parameter for m1()
t.<Integer>m1(iw1, iw2, "hello");
// Let the compiler figure out the actual type parameters
// using types for iw1 and iw2
t.m1(iw1, iw2, "hello"); // OK
```

Listing 3-4 demonstrated how to declare a generic static method. You cannot refer to the type parameters of the containing class inside the static method. A static method can refer only to its own declared type parameters.

Here is the copy of your copy() static method from the WrapperUtil class. It defines a type parameter T, which is used to constrain the type of arguments source and dest:

```
public static <T> void copy(Wrapper<T> source,
        Wrapper<? super T> dest) {
    T value = source.get();
    dest.set(value);
}
```

The compiler will figure out the actual type parameter for a method whether the method is non-static or static. However, if you want to specify the actual type parameter for a static method call, you can do so as follows:

```
WrapperUtil.<Integer>copy(iw1, iw2);
```

You can also define type parameters for constructors the same way as you do for methods. The following snippet of code defines a type parameter U for the constructor of class Test. It places a constraint that the constructor's type parameter U must be the same or a subtype of the actual type of its class type parameter T:

```
public class Test<T> {
    public <U extends T> Test(U k) {
        // Do something
    }
}
```

The compiler will figure out the actual type parameter passed to a constructor by examining the arguments you pass to the constructor. If you want to specify the actual type parameter value for the constructor, you can specify it in angle brackets between the new operator and the name of the constructor, as shown in the following snippet of code:

```
// Specify the actual type parameter for the constructor
// as Double
Test<Number> t1 = new <Double>Test<Number>(
    new Double(12.89));
// Let the compiler figure out that we are using Integer
// as the actual type parameter for the constructor
Test<Number> t2 = new Test<Number>(new Integer(123));
```

Type Inference in Generic Object Creation

In many cases, the compiler can infer the value for the type parameter in an object creation expression when you create an object of a generic type. Note that the type inference support in the object creation expression is limited to the situations where the type is obvious. Consider the following statement:

```
List<String> list = new ArrayList<String>();
```

With the declaration of list as List<String>, it is obvious that you want to create an ArrayList with the type parameter as <String>. In this case, you can specify empty angle brackets, <> (known as the diamond operator or simply the diamond), as the type parameter for ArrayList. You can rewrite this statement as shown:

```
List<String> list = new ArrayList<>();
```

Note that if you do not specify a type parameter for a generic type in an object creation expression, the type is the raw type, and the compiler generates unchecked warnings. For example, the following statement will compile with an unchecked warning:

```
// Using ArrayList as a raw type, not a generic type
List<String> list = new ArrayList(); // Generates an
                                      // unchecked warning
warning: [unchecked] unchecked conversion
        List<String> list = new ArrayList();
                                ^
  required: List<String>
  found:    ArrayList
1 warning
```

Sometimes, the compiler cannot correctly infer the parameter type of a type in an object creation expression. In those cases, you need to specify the parameter type instead of using the diamond operator (<>). Otherwise, the compiler will infer a wrong type, which will generate an error.

When the diamond operator is used in an object creation expression, the compiler uses a four-step process to infer the parameter type for the parameterized type. Let's consider a typical object creation expression:

```
T1<T2> var = new T3<>(constructor-arguments);
```

1. First, it tries to infer the type parameter from the static type of the constructor arguments. Note that constructor arguments may be empty, for example, new ArrayList<>(). If the type parameter is inferred in this step, the process continues to the next step.

2. It uses the left side of the assignment operator to infer the type. In the previous statement, it will infer T2 as the type if the constructor arguments are empty. Note that an object creation expression may not be part of an assignment statement. In such cases, it will use the next step.

3. If the object creation expression is used as an actual parameter for a method call, the compiler tries to infer the type by looking at the type of the formal parameter for the method being called.

4. If all else fails and it cannot infer the type using these steps, it infers Object as the type parameter.

Let's discuss a few examples that involve all steps in the type inference process. Create the two lists, list1 of List<String> type and list2 of List<Integer> type:

```
import java.util.Arrays;
import java.util.List;
// More code goes here...
List<String> list1 = Arrays.asList("A", "B");
List<Integer> list2 = Arrays.asList(9, 19, 1969);
```

Consider the following statement that uses the diamond operator:

```
List<String> list3 = new ArrayList<>(list1);
    // <- Inferred type is String
```

The compiler used the constructor argument list1 to infer the type. The static type of list1 is List<String>, so the type String was inferred by the compiler. The previous statement compiles fine. The compiler did not use the left side of the assignment operator, List<String> list3, during the inference process. You may not trust this argument. Consider the following statement to prove this:

```
List<String> list4 = new ArrayList<>(list2);
    // <- A compile-time error
```

```
required: List<String>
found:    ArrayList<Integer>
1 error
```

Do you believe it now? The constructor argument is `list2` whose static type is `List<Integer>`. The compiler inferred the type as `Integer` and replaced `ArrayList<>` with `ArrayList<Integer>`. The type of variable `list4` is `List<String>`, which is not assignment compatible with the `ArrayList<Integer>`, which resulted in the compile-time error.

Consider the following statement:

```
List<String> list5 = new ArrayList<>();
    // <- Inferred type is String
```

This time, there is no constructor argument. The compiler uses the second step to look at the left side of the assignment operator to infer the type. On the left side, it finds `List<String>`, and it correctly infers the type as `String`. Consider a `process()` method that is declared as follows:

```
public static void process(List<String> list) {
    // Code goes here
}
```

The following statement makes a call to the `process()` method, and the inferred type parameter is `String`:

```
// The inferred type is String
process(new ArrayList<>());
```

The compiler looks at the type of the formal parameter of the `process()` method, finds `List<String>`, and infers the type as `String`.

Note Using the diamond operator saves some typing. Use it when the type inference is obvious. However, it is better, for readability, to specify the type, instead of the diamond operator, in a complex object creation expression. Always choose readability over brevity.

JDK9 added support for the diamond operator in anonymous classes if the inferred types are denotable. You cannot use the diamond operator with anonymous classes—even in JDK9 or later—if the inferred types are non-denotable. The Java compiler uses types that cannot be written in Java programs. Types that can be written in Java programs are known as denotable types. Types that the compiler knows but cannot be written in Java programs are known as non-denotable types. For example, `String` is a denotable type because you can use it in programs to denote a type; however, `Serializable & CharSequence` is not a denotable type, even though it is a valid type for the compiler. It is an intersection type that represents a type that implements both interfaces, `Serializable` and `CharSequence`. Intersection types are allowed in generic type definitions, but you cannot declare a variable using this intersection type:

```
// Not allowed in Java code. Cannot declare a variable
// of an intersection type.
Serializable & CharSequence var;
// Allowed in Java code
class Magic<T extends Serializable & CharSequence> {
    // More code goes here
}
```

Java contains a generic `Callable<V>` interface in the `java.util.concurrent` package. It is declared as follows:

```
public interface Callable<V> {
    V call() throws Exception;
}
```

In JDK9 and later, the compiler will infer the type parameter for the anonymous class as `Integer` in the following snippet of code:

```
// A compile-time error in JDK8, but allowed in JDK9.
Callable<Integer> c = new Callable<>() {
    @Override
    public Integer call() {
        return 100;
    }
};
```

169

No Generic Exception Classes

Exceptions are thrown at runtime. The compiler cannot ensure the type-safety of exceptions at runtime if you use a generic exception class in a catch clause, because the erasure process erases the mention of any type parameter during compilation. This is the reason that it is a compile-time error to attempt to define a generic class, which is a direct or indirect subclass of `java.lang.Throwable`.

No Generic Anonymous Classes

An anonymous class is a one-time class. You need a class name to specify the actual type parameter. An anonymous class does not have a name. Therefore, you cannot have a generic anonymous class. However, you can have generic methods inside an anonymous class. Your anonymous class can inherit a generic class. An anonymous class can implement generic interfaces. Any class, except an exception type, enums, and anonymous inner classes, can have type parameters.

Generics and Arrays

Let's look at the following code for a class called `GenericArrayTest`:

```
public class GenericArrayTest<T> {
    private T[] elements;
    public GenericArrayTest(int howMany) {
        elements = new T[howMany]; // A compile-time error
    }
    // More code goes here
}
```

The `GenericArrayTest` class declares a type parameter T. In the constructor, it attempts to create an array of the generic type. You cannot compile the previous code. The compiler will complain about the following statement:

```
elements = new T[howMany]; // A compile-time error
```

Recall that all references to the generic type parameter are erased from the code when a generic class or code using it is compiled. An array needs to know its type when it is created, so that it can perform a check at runtime when an element is stored in it to make sure that the element is assignment compatible with the array type. An array's type information will not be available at runtime if you use a type parameter to create the array. This is the reason that the statement is not allowed.

You cannot create an array of a generic type because the compiler cannot ensure the type-safety of the assignment to the array element. You cannot write the following code:

```
Wrapper<String>[] gsArray = null;
// Cannot create an array of generic type
gsArray = new Wrapper<String>[10]; // A compile-time error
```

It is allowed to create an array of unbounded wildcard generic types, as shown:

```
Wrapper<?>[] anotherArray = new Wrapper<?>[10]; // Ok
```

Suppose you want to use an array of a generic type. You can do so by using the newInstance() method of the java.lang.reflect.Array class as follows. You will have to deal with the unchecked warnings at compile time because of the cast used in the array creation statement. The following snippet of code shows that you can still bypass the compile-time type-safety check when you try to sneak in an Object into an array of Wrapper<String>. However, this is the consequence you have to live with when using generics, which does not carry its type information at runtime. Java generics are as skin-deep as you can imagine.

```
Wrapper<String>[] a = (Wrapper<String>[]) Array.
    newInstance(Wrapper.class, 10);
Object[] objArray = (Object[]) a;
objArray[0] = new Object();
    // <- Will throw a java.lang.
    // ArrayStoreExceptionxception
a[0] = new Wrapper<String>("Hello");
    // <- OK. Checked by compiler
```

Runtime Class Type of Generic Objects

What is the class type of the object for a parameterized type? Consider the program in Listing 3-6.

Listing 3-6. All Objects of a Parameterized Type Share the Same Class at Runtime

```java
// GenericsRuntimeClassTest.java
package com.jdojo.generics;
public class GenericsRuntimeClassTest {
    public static void main(String[] args) {
        Wrapper<String> a =
            new Wrapper<String>("Hello");
        Wrapper<Integer> b =
            new Wrapper<Integer>(new Integer(123));

        Class aClass = a.getClass();
        Class bClass = b.getClass();
        System.out.println("Class for a: " +
            aClass.getName());
        System.out.println("Class for b: " +
            bClass.getName());
        System.out.println("aClass == bClass: " +
            (aClass == bClass));
    }
}
```

```
Class for a: com.jdojo.generics.Wrapper
Class for b: com.jdojo.generics.Wrapper
aClass == bClass: true
```

The program creates objects of the Wrapper<String> and Wrapper<Integer>. It prints the class names for both objects, and they are the same. The output shows that all parameterized objects of the same generic type share the same class object at runtime. As mentioned earlier, the type information you supply to the generic type is removed from the code during compilation. The compiler changes the Wrapper<String> a; statement to Wrapper a;. For the JVM, it's business as usual (before generics)!

Heap Pollution

Representing a type at runtime is called *reification.* A type that can be represented at runtime is called a *reifiable* type. A type that is not completely represented at runtime is called a *non-reifiable* type. Most generic types are non-reifiable because generics are implemented using erasure, which removes the type's parameter information at compile time. For example, when you write Wrapper<String>, the compiler removes the type parameter <String>, and the runtime sees only Wrapper instead of Wrapper<String>.

Heap pollution is a situation that occurs when a variable of a parameterized type refers to an object not of the same parameterized type. The compiler issues an unchecked warning if it detects possible heap pollution. If your program compiles without any unchecked warnings, heap pollution will not occur. Consider the following snippet of code:

```
Wrapper nWrapper = new Wrapper<Integer>(101);     // #1
// Unchecked warning at compile-time and heap pollution
// at runtime
Wrapper<String> sWrapper = nWrapper; // #2
String str = sWrapper.get();              // #3
                                          // ClassCastException
```

The first statement (labeled #1) compiles fine. The second statement (labeled #2) generates an unchecked warning because the compiler cannot determine if nWrapper is of the type Wrapper<String>. Since parameter type information is erased at compile time, the runtime has no way of detecting this type mismatch. The heap pollution in the second statement makes it possible to get a ClassCastException in the third statement (labeled #3) at runtime. If the second statement was not allowed, the third statement will not cause a ClassCastException.

Heap pollution may also occur because of an unchecked cast operation. Consider the following snippet of code:

```
Wrapper<? extends Number> nW = new Wrapper<Long>(1L); // #1
// Unchecked cast and unchecked warning occurs when the
// following statement #2 is compiled. Heap pollution
// occurs, when it is executed.
Wrapper<Short> sw = (Wrapper<Short>) nW; // #2
short s = sw.get();                        // #3
                                           // ClassCastException
```

The statement labeled #2 uses an unchecked cast. The compiler issues an unchecked warning. At runtime, it leads to heap pollution. As a result, the statement labeled #3 generates a runtime ClassCastException.

Varargs Methods and Heap Pollution Warnings

Java implements the varargs parameter of a varargs method by converting the varargs parameter into an array. If a varargs method uses a generic type varargs parameter, Java cannot guarantee the type-safety. A non-reifiable generic type varargs parameter may possibly lead to heap pollution. Consider the following snippet of code that declares a process() method with a parameterized type parameter. The comments in the method's body indicate the heap pollution and other types of problems:

```
public static void process(Wrapper<Long>...nums) {
    Object[] obj = nums;                // Heap pollution
    obj[0] = new Wrapper<>("Hello");    // An array
                                        // corruption
    Long lv = nums[0].get();            // A ClassCastException
    // Other code goes here
}
```

Note   You need to use the -Xlint:unchecked,varargs option with the javac compiler to see the unchecked and varargs warnings.

When the process() method is compiled, the compiler removes the type information <Long> from its parameterized type parameter and changes its signature to process(Wrapper[] nums). When you compile the declaration of the process() method, you get the following unchecked warning:

```
warning: [unchecked] Possible heap pollution from
    parameterized vararg type Wrapper<Long>
        public static void process(Wrapper<Long>...nums) {
                                   ^

1 warning
```

Consider the following snippet of code that calls the process() method:

```
Wrapper<Long> v1 = new Wrapper<>(10L);
Wrapper<Long> v2 = new Wrapper<>(11L);
process(v1, v2); // An unchecked warning
```

When this snippet of code is compiled, it generates the following compiler unchecked warning:

```
warning: [unchecked] unchecked generic array creation for
    varargs parameter of type
Wrapper<Long>[]
            process(v1, v2);
                  ^
```

```
1 warning
```

Warnings are generated at the method declaration as well as at the location of the method call. If you create such a method, it is your responsibility to ensure that heap pollution does not occur inside your method's body.

If you create a varargs method with a non-reifiable type parameter, you can suppress the unchecked warnings at the location of the method's declaration as well as the method's call by using the @SafeVarargs annotation. By using @SafeVarargs, you are asserting that your varargs method with non-reifiable type parameter is safe to use. The following snippet of code uses the @SafeVarargs annotation with the process() method:

```
@SafeVarargs
public static void process(Wrapper<Long>...nums) {
    Object[] obj = nums;
        // <- Heap pollution
    obj[0] = new Wrapper<String>("Hello");
        // <- An array corruption
    Long lv = nums[0].get();
        // <- A ClassCastException
        // Other code goes here
}
```

When you compile this declaration of the process() method, you do not get an unchecked warning. However, you get the following varargs warning because the compiler sees possible heap pollution when the varargs parameter nums is assigned to the Object array obj:

```
warning: [varargs] Varargs method could cause heap
    pollution from non-reifiable varargs
parameter nums
                Object[] obj = nums;
                     ^

1 warning
```

You can suppress the unchecked and varargs warnings for a varargs method with a non-reifiable type parameter by using the @SuppressWarnings annotation as follows:

```
@SuppressWarnings({"unchecked", "varargs"})
public static void process(Wrapper<Long>...nums) {
    // Code goes here
}
```

Note that when you use the @SuppressWarnings annotation with a varargs method, it suppresses warnings only at the location of the method's declaration, not at the locations where the method is called.

Summary

Generics are the Java language features that allow you to declare types (classes and interfaces) that use type parameters. Type parameters are specified when the generic type is used. The type when used with the actual type parameter is known as a parameterized type. When a generic type is used without specifying its type parameters, it is called a raw type. For example, if Wrapper<T> is a generic class, Wrapper<String> is a parameterized type with String as the actual type parameter and Wrapper as the raw type. Type parameters can also be specified for constructors and methods. Generics allow you to write true polymorphic code in Java code using a type parameter that works for all types.

By default, a type parameter is unbounded, meaning that you can specify any type for the type parameter. For example, if a class is declared with a type parameter `<T>`, you can specify any type available in Java, such as `<String>`, `<Object>`, `<Person>`, `<Employee>`, `<Integer>`, etc., as the actual type for T. Type parameters in a type declaration can also be specified as having upper bounds or lower bounds. The declaration `Wrapper<U extends Person>` is an example of specifying an upper bound for the type parameter U that specifies that U can be of a type that is `Person` or a subtype of `Person`. The declaration `Wrapper<?super Person>` is an example of specifying a lower bound; it specifies that the type parameter is the type `Person` or a supertype of `Person`.

Java also lets you specify the wildcard, which is a question mark, as the actual type parameter. A wildcard as the actual parameter means the actual type parameter is unknown; for example, `Wrapper<?>` means that the type parameter T for the generic type `Wrapper<T>` is unknown.

The compiler attempts to infer the type of an expression using generics, depending on the context in which the expression is used. If the compiler cannot infer the type, it generates a compile-time error, and you will need to specify the type explicitly.

The supertype-subtype relationship does not exist with parameterized types. For example, `Wrapper<Long>` is not a subtype of `Wrapper<Number>`.

The generic type parameters are erased by the compiler using a process called *type erasure*. Therefore, the generic type parameters are not available at runtime. For example, the runtime type of `Wrapper<Long>` and `Wrapper<String>` are the same, which is `Wrapper`.

Exercises

Exercise 1

What are generics (or generic types), parameterized types, and raw types? Give an example of a generic type and its parameterized type.

Exercise 2

The `Number` class is the superclass of the `Long` class. The following snippet of code does not compile. Explain.

```
List<Number> list1= new ArrayList<>();
List<Long> list2= new ArrayList<>();
list1 = list2;  // A compile-time error
```

Exercise 3

Write the output when the following ClassNamePrinter class is run. Rewrite the code for the print() method of this class after the compiler erases the type parameter T during compilation:

```
// ClassNamePrinter.java
package com.jdojo.generics.exercises;
public class ClassNamePrinter {
    public static void main(String[] args) {
        ClassNamePrinter.print(10);
        ClassNamePrinter.print(10L);
        ClassNamePrinter.print(10.2);
    }
    public static <T extends Number> void
            print(T obj) {
        String className = obj.getClass().
            getSimpleName();
        System.out.println(className);
    }
}
```

Exercise 4

What are unbounded wildcards? Why does the following snippet of code not compile?

```
List<?> list = new ArrayList<>();
list.add("Hello"); // A compile-time error
```

Exercise 5

Consider the following incomplete declaration of the Util class:

```
// Util.java
package com.jdojo.generics.exercises;

import java.lang.reflect.Array;
import java.util.ArrayList;
import java.util.Arrays;
import java.util.List;
```

```
public class Util {
    public static void main(String[] args) {
        Integer[] n1 = {1, 2};
        Integer[] n2 = {3, 4};
        Integer[] m = merge(n1, n2);
        System.out.println(Arrays.toString(m));
        String[] s1 = {"one", "two"};
        String[] s2 = {"three", "four"};
        String[] t = merge(s1, s2);
        System.out.println(Arrays.toString(t));
        List<Number> list = new ArrayList<>();
        add(list, 10, 20, 30L, 40.5F, 50.9);
        System.out.println(list);
    }

    public static <T> T[] merge(T[] a, T[] b) {
    }
    public static /* Add type parameters here */ void
    add(List<T> list, U... elems) {
        /* Your code to add elems to list goes here */
    }
}
```

Complete the body of the merge() method, so it can concatenate the two arrays passed in as its parameters and return the concatenated array. Complete the add() method by specifying its type parameters and adding the code in its body. The first parameter to the method is a parameterized List<T>, and the second parameter is a varargs parameter of the type T or its descendant. That is, the second parameter type is any type whose objects can be added to the List<T>. Running the Util class should produce the following output:

```
[1, 2, 3, 4]
[one, two, three, four]
[10, 20, 30, 40.5, 50.9]
```

179

Exercise 6

Create a generic Stack<E> class. Its objects represent a stack that can store elements of its type parameter E. The following is a template for the class. You need to provide implementation for all its methods. Write test code to test all methods. Method names are standard method names for a stack. Any illegal access to the stack should throw a runtime exception.

```java
// Stack.java
package com.jdojo.generics.exercises;
import java.util.LinkedList;
import java.util.List;
public class Stack<E> {
    // Use LinkedList instead of ArrayList
    private final List<E> stack = new LinkedList<>();
    public void push(E e) {}
    public E pop() { }
    public E peek() { }
    public boolean isEmpty() { }
    public int size() { }
}
```

Exercise 7

What is heap pollution? What types of warnings does the compiler generate when it detects a possibility of heap pollution? How do you print such warnings during compilation? How do you suppress such warnings?

Exercise 8

Describe the reasons that the following declaration of the Test class does not compile:

```java
public class Test {
    public <T> void test(T t) {
        // More code goes here
    }
    public <U> void test(U u) {
        // More code goes here
    }
```

```
}public class Test {
    public <T> void test(T t) {
        // More code goes here
    }
    public <U> void test(U u) {
        // More code goes here
    }
}
```

CHAPTER 4

Lambda Expressions

In this chapter, you will learn:

- What lambda expressions are

- Why we need lambda expressions

- The syntax for defining lambda expressions

- Target typing for lambda expressions

- Commonly used built-in functional interfaces

- Method and constructor references

- Lexical scoping of lambda expressions

All example programs in this chapter are a member of a `jdojo.lambda` module, as declared in Listing 4-1.

Listing 4-1. The Declaration of a `jdojo.lambda` Module

```java
// module-info.java
module jdojo.lambda {
    exports com.jdojo.lambda;
}
```

What Is a Lambda Expression?

A lambda expression is an unnamed block of code (or an unnamed function) with a list of formal parameters and a body. Sometimes, a lambda expression is simply called a lambda. The body of a lambda expression can be a block statement or an expression.

© Kishori Sharan, Peter Späth 2021
K. Sharan and P. Späth, *More Java 17*, https://doi.org/10.1007/978-1-4842-7135-3_4

An arrow (->) is used to separate the list of parameters and the body. The term "lambda" has its origin in Lambda calculus that uses the Greek letter lambda (`lambda`) to denote a function abstraction. The following are some examples of lambda expressions in Java:

```
// Takes an int parameter and returns the parameter value
// incremented by 1
(int x) -> x + 1
// Takes two int parameters and returns their sum
(int x, int y) -> x + y
// Takes two int parameters and returns the maximum of
// the two
(int x, int y) -> { int max = x > y ? x : y;
                    return max;
                  }
// Takes no parameters and returns void
() -> { }
// Takes no parameters and returns a string "OK"
() -> "OK"
// Takes a String parameter and prints it on the standard
// output
(String msg) -> { System.out.println(msg); }
// Takes a parameter and prints it on the standard output
msg -> System.out.println(msg)
// Takes a String parameter and returns its length
(String str) -> str.length()
```

At this point, you will not be able to understand the syntax of lambda expressions completely. I cover the syntax in detail shortly. For now, just get the feel of it, keeping in mind that the syntax for lambda expressions is similar to the syntax for declaring methods.

Note   A lambda expression is not a method, although its declaration looks similar to a method. As the name suggests, a lambda expression is an expression that represents an instance of a functional interface.

Every expression in Java has a type, and so does a lambda expression. The type of a lambda expression is a functional interface type. When the abstract method of the functional interface is called, the body of the lambda expression is executed. Consider the lambda expression that takes a String parameter and returns its length:

```
(String str) -> str.length()
```

What is the type of this lambda expression? The answer is that we do not know. By looking at the lambda expression, all you can say is that it takes a String parameter and returns an int, which is the length of the String parameter. Its type can be any functional interface type with an abstract method that takes a String as a parameter and returns an int. The following is an example of such a functional interface:

```
@FunctionalInterface
interface StringToIntMapper {
    int map(String str);
}
```

The lambda expression represents an instance of the StringToIntMapper functional interface when it appears in the assignment statement, like so:

```
StringToIntMapper mapper =
    (String str) -> str.length();
```

In this statement, the compiler finds that the right side of the assignment operator is a lambda expression. To infer its type, it looks at the left side of the assignment operator that expects an instance of the StringToIntMapper interface; it verifies that the lambda expression conforms to the declaration of the map() method in the StringToIntMapper interface; finally, it infers that the type of the lambda expression is the StringToIntMapper interface type. When you call the map() method on the mapper variable passing a String, the body of the lambda expression is executed as shown in the following snippet of code:

```
StringToIntMapper mapper = (String str) -> str.length();
String name = "Kristy";
int mappedValue = mapper.map(name);
System.out.println("name=" + name +
    ", mapped value=" + mappedValue);

name=Kristy, mapped value=6
```

So far, you have not seen anything that you could not do in Java without using lambda expressions. The following snippet of code uses an anonymous class to achieve the same result as the lambda expression used in the previous example:

```
StringToIntMapper mapper = new StringToIntMapper() {
    @Override
    public int map(String str) {
        return str.length();
    }
};
String name = "Kristy";
int mappedValue = mapper.map(name);
System.out.println("name=" + name +
    ", mapped value=" + mappedValue);
```

```
name=Kristy, mapped value=6
```

At this point, a lambda expression may seem to be a concise way of writing an anonymous class, which is true as far as the syntax goes. There are some subtle differences in semantics between the two. I discuss those differences when I discuss more details later.

Note   Java is a strongly typed language, which means that the compiler must know the type of all expressions used in a Java program. A lambda expression by itself does not have a type, and, therefore, it cannot be used as a standalone expression. The type of a lambda expression is always inferred by the compiler by the context in which it is used.

Why Do We Need Lambda Expressions?

Java has supported object-oriented programming since the beginning. In object-oriented programming, the program logic is based on mutable objects. Methods of classes contain the logic. Methods are invoked on objects, which typically modify objects' states. In object-oriented programming, the order of method invocation matters as each method invocation may potentially modify the state of the object, thus producing side effects. Static analysis of the program logic is difficult as the program state depends on the order in which the code will be executed. Programming with mutating objects also poses a challenge in concurrent programming in which multiple parts of the program may attempt to modify the state of the same object concurrently.

As the processing power of computers has increased in recent years, so has the amount of data to be processed. Nowadays, it is common to process data as big as terabytes in size, requiring the need for parallel programming. Now it is common for computers to have a multicore processor that gives users the opportunity to run software programs faster; at the same time, this poses a challenge to programmers to write more parallel programs, taking advantage of all the available cores in the processor. Java has supported concurrent programming since the beginning. It added support for parallel programming in Java 7 through the fork/join framework, which was not easy to use.

Functional programming, which is based on Lambda calculus, existed long before object-oriented programming. It is based on the concept of functions, a block of code that accepts values, known as parameters, and the block of code is executed to compute a result. A function represents a functionality or operation. Functions do not modify data, including its input, thus producing no side effects; for this reason, the order of the execution of functions does not matter in functional programming. In functional programming, a higher-order function is an anonymous function that can be treated as a data object. That is, it can be stored in a variable and passed around from one context to another. It might be invoked in a context that did not necessarily define it. Note that a higher-order function is an anonymous function, so the invoking context does not have to know its name. A closure is a higher-order function packaged with its defining environment. A closure carries with it the variables in scope when it was defined, and it can access those variables even when it is invoked in a context other than the context in which those variables were defined.

In recent years, functional programming has become popular because of its suitability in concurrent, parallel, and event-driven programming. Modern programming languages such as C#, Groovy, Python, and Scala support functional programming. Java did not want to be left behind, and, hence, it introduced lambda expressions to support functional programming, which can be mixed with its already popular object-oriented features to develop robust, concurrent, parallel programs. Java adopted the syntax for lambda expressions that is very similar to the syntax used in other programming languages, such as C# and Scala.

In object-oriented programming, a function is called a method, and it is always part of a class. If you wanted to pass functionality around in Java, you needed to create a class, add a method to the class to represent the functionality, create an object of the class, and pass the object around. A lambda expression in Java is like a higher-order function in functional programming, which is an unnamed block of code representing a functionality that can be passed around like data. A lambda expression may capture the variables in its defining scope, and it may access those variables later in a context that did not define the captured variable. These features let you use lambda expressions to implement closures in Java.

So why and where do we need lambda expressions? Anonymous classes use a bulky syntax. Lambda expressions use a very concise syntax to achieve the same result. Lambda expressions are not a complete replacement for anonymous classes. You will still need to use anonymous classes in a few situations. Just to appreciate the conciseness of the lambda expressions, compare the following two statements from the previous section that create an instance of the StringToIntMapper interface; one uses an anonymous class, taking six lines of code, and another uses a lambda expression, taking just one line of code:

```
// Using an anonymous class
StringToIntMapper mapper = new StringToIntMapper() {
    @Override
    public int map(String str) {
        return str.length();
    }
};
// Using a lambda expression
StringToIntMapper mapper = (String str) -> str.length();
```

Syntax for Lambda Expressions

A lambda expression describes an anonymous function. The general syntax for using lambda expressions is very similar to declaring a method. The general syntax is

```
(<LambdaParametersList>) -> { <LambdaBody> }
```

A lambda expression consists of a list of parameters and a body separated by an arrow (->). The list of parameters is declared the same way as the list of parameters for methods. The list of parameters is enclosed in parentheses, as is done for methods. The body of a lambda expression is a block of code enclosed in braces. Like a method's body, the body of a lambda expression may declare local variables; use statements including break, continue, and return; throw exceptions; etc. Unlike a method, a lambda expression does not have the following four parts:

- A lambda expression does not have a name.

- A lambda expression does not have a return type. It is inferred by the compiler from the context of its use and from its body.

- A lambda expression does not have a throws clause. It is inferred from the context of its use and its body.

- A lambda expression cannot declare type parameters. That is, a lambda expression cannot be generic.

Table 4-1 contains some examples of lambda expressions and equivalent methods. I have given a suitable name to methods as you cannot have a method without a name in Java. The compiler infers the return type of lambda expressions.

Table 4-1. *Examples of Lambda Expressions and Equivalent Methods*

Lambda Expression	Equivalent Method
```(int x, int y) -> { return x + y; }```	```int sum(int x, int y) { return x + y; }```
```(Object x) -> { return x; }```	```Object identity(Object x) return x; }```

(*continued*)

Table 4-1. (*continued*)

Lambda Expression	Equivalent Method

`(int x, int y) -> {`
`  if (x > y)`
`    return x;`
`  } else {`
`    return y;`
`  }`
`}`
	`int getMax(int x, int y) {`
	`  if (x > y)`
	`    return x;`
	`  } else {`
	`    return y;`
	`  }`
	`}`

`(String msg) -> {`
`  System.out.println(msg);`
`}`
	`void print(String msg) {`
	`  System.out.println(msg);`
	`}`

`() -> {`
`  System.out.println(LocalDate.`
`now());`
`}`
	`void printCurrentDate() {`
	`  System.out.println(LocalDate.`
	`now());`
	`}`

`() -> {`
`  // No code goes here`
`}`
	`void doNothing() {`
	`  // No code goes here`
	`}`

One of the goals of lambda expressions is to keep its syntax concise and let the compiler infer the details. The following sections discuss the shorthand syntax for declaring lambda expressions.

Omitting Parameter Types

You can omit the declared type of the parameters. The compiler will infer the types of parameters from the context in which the lambda expression is used:

```
// Types of parameters are declared
(int x, int y) -> { return x + y; }
// Types of parameters are omitted
(x, y) -> { return x + y; }
```

If you omit the types of parameters, you must omit it for all parameters or for none. You cannot omit for some and not for others. The following lambda expression will not compile because it declares the type of one parameter and omits for the other:

```
// A compile-time error
(int x, y) -> { return x + y; }
```

Note   A lambda expression that does not declare the types of its parameters is known as an implicit lambda expression or an implicitly typed lambda expression. A lambda expression that declares the types of its parameters is known as an explicit lambda expression or an explicitly typed lambda expression.

Using Local Variable Syntax for Parameters

You can use the local variable syntax for the parameters in a lambda expression:

```
// A compile-time error
(var x, var y) -> { return x + y; }
```

The compiler will infer the types of parameters from the context in which the lambda expression is used, and it will remember each variable's type. The local variable syntax for lambda expression parameters was added to Java in JDK11.

Declaring a Single Parameter

Sometimes, a lambda expression takes only one parameter. You can omit the parameter type for a single parameter lambda expression as you can do for a lambda expression with multiple parameters. You can also omit the parentheses if you omit the parameter type in a single parameter lambda expression. The following are three ways to declare a lambda expression with a single parameter:

```
// Declares the parameter type
(String msg) -> { System.out.println(msg); }
// Omits the parameter type
(msg) -> { System.out.println(msg); }
// Omits the parameter type and parentheses
msg -> { System.out.println(msg); }
```

The parentheses can be omitted only if the single parameter also omits its type. The following lambda expression will not compile:

```
// Omits parentheses, but not the parameter type, which is not allowed.
String msg -> { System.out.println(msg); }
```

Declaring No Parameters

If a lambda expression does not take any parameters, you need to use empty parentheses:

```
// Takes no parameters
() -> { System.out.println("Hello"); }
```

It is not allowed to omit the parentheses when the lambda expression takes no parameter. The following declaration will not compile:

```
-> { System.out.println("Hello"); }
```

Parameters with Modifiers

You can use modifiers, such as `final`, in the parameter declaration for explicit lambda expressions. The following two lambda expressions are valid:

```
(final int x, final int y) -> { return x + y; }
(int x, final int y) -> { return x + y; }
```

The following lambda expression will not compile because it uses the final modifier in parameter declarations, but omits the parameter type:

```
(final x, final y) -> { return x + y; }
```

Declaring the Body of Lambda Expressions

The body of a lambda expression can be a block statement or a single expression. A block statement is enclosed in braces; a single expression is not enclosed in braces.

The body of a lambda expression is executed the same way as a method's body. A `return` statement or the end of the body returns the control to the caller of the lambda expression.

When an expression is used as the body, it is evaluated and returned to the caller. If the expression evaluates to void, nothing is returned to the caller. The following two lambda expressions are the same; one uses a block statement and the other an expression:

```
/ Uses a block statement. Takes two int parameters and
// returns their sum.
(int x, int y) -> { return x + y; }
// Uses an expression. Takes two int parameters and
// returns their sum.
(int x, int y) -> x + y
```

The following two lambda expressions are the same; one uses a block statement as the body and the other an expression that evaluates to void:

```
// Uses a block statement
(String msg) -> { System.out.println(msg); }
// Uses an expression
(String msg) -> System.out.println(msg)
```

Target Typing

Every lambda expression has a type, which is a functional interface type. In other words, a lambda expression represents an instance of a functional interface. Consider the following lambda expression:

```
(x, y) -> x + y
```

What is the type of this lambda expression? In other words, an instance of which functional interface does this lambda expression represent? We do not know the type of this lambda expression at this point. All we can say about this lambda expression with confidence is that it takes two parameters named x and y. We cannot tell its return type as the expression x + y, depending on the type of x and y, may evaluate to a number (int, long, float, or double) or a String. This is an implicit lambda expression, and, therefore, the compiler has to infer the types of two parameters using the context in which the expression is used. This lambda expression may be of different functional interface types depending on the context in which it is used.

193

There are two types of expressions in Java:

- Standalone expressions

- Poly expressions

A standalone expression is an expression whose type can be determined without knowing the context of its use. The following are examples of standalone expressions:

```
// The type of expression is String
new String("Hello")
// The type of expression is String (a String literal
// is also an expression)
"Hello"
// The type of expression is ArrayList<String>
new ArrayList<String>()
```

A poly expression is an expression that has different types in different contexts. The compiler determines the type. The contexts that allow the use of poly expressions are known as poly contexts. All lambda expressions in Java are poly expressions. You must use it in a context to know its type. For example, the expression new ArrayList<>() is a poly expression. You cannot tell its type unless you provide the context of its use. This expression is used in the following two contexts to represent two different types:

```
// The type of new ArrayList<>() is ArrayList<Long>
ArrayList<Long> idList = new ArrayList<>();
// The type of new ArrayList<>() is ArrayList<String>
ArrayList<String> nameList = new ArrayList<>();
```

The compiler infers the type of a lambda expression. The context in which a lambda expression is used expects a type, which is called the target type. The process of inferring the type of a lambda expression from the context is known as target typing. Consider the following pseudocode for an assignment statement, where a variable of type T is assigned a lambda expression:

```
T t = <LambdaExpression>;
```

The target type of the lambda expression in this context is T. The compiler uses the following rules to determine whether the <LambdaExpression> is assignment compatible with its target type T:

- T must be a functional interface type.

- The lambda expression has the same number and type of parameters as the abstract method of T. For an implicit lambda expression, the compiler will infer the types of parameters from the abstract method of T.

- The type of the returned value from the body of the lambda expression is assignment compatible to the return type of the abstract method of T.

- If the body of the lambda expression throws any checked exceptions, those exceptions must be compatible with the declared throws clause of the abstract method of T. It is a compile-time error to throw checked exceptions from the body of a lambda expression, if its target type's method does not contain a throws clause.

Let's look at a few examples of target typing. Consider two functional interfaces, Adder and Joiner, as shown in Listings 4-2 and 4-3, respectively.

Listing 4-2. A Functional Interface Named Adder

```
// Adder.java
package com.jdojo.lambda;
@FunctionalInterface
public interface Adder {
    double add(double n1, double n2);
}
```

Listing 4-3. A Functional Interface Named Joiner

```
// Joiner.java
package com.jdojo.lambda;
@FunctionalInterface
public interface Joiner {
    String join(String s1, String s2);
}
```

The add() method of the Adder interface adds two numbers. The join() method of the Joiner interface concatenates two strings. Both interfaces are used for trivial purposes; however, they will serve the purpose of demonstrating the target typing for lambda expressions very well. Consider the following assignment statement:

```
Adder adder = (x, y) -> x + y;
```

The type of the adder variable is Adder. The lambda expression is assigned to the variable adder, and, therefore, the target type of the lambda expression is Adder. The compiler verifies that Adder is a functional interface. The lambda expression is an implicit lambda expression. The compiler finds that the Adder interface contains a double add(double, double) abstract method. It infers the types for x and y parameters as double and double, respectively. At this point, the compiler treats this statement as shown:

```
Adder adder = (double x, double y) -> x + y;
```

If you write

```
Adder adder = (var x, var y) -> x + y;
```

the compiler will again know from the context that x and y are doubles. So we again have an implicit lambda expression. Compared to completely omitting the types the var name syntax a little better expresses that for the lambda expressions local variables get created, even though we are not interested in actually declaring the types.

The compiler now verifies the compatibility of the returned value from the lambda expression and the return type of the add() method. The return type of the add() method is double. The lambda expression returns x + y, which would be of a double as the compiler already knows that the types of x and y are double. The lambda expression does not throw any checked exceptions. Therefore, the compiler does not have to verify anything for that. At this point, the compiler infers that the type of the lambda expression is the type Adder.

Apply the rules of target typing for the following assignment statement:

```
Joiner joiner = (x, y) -> x + y;
```

This time, the compiler infers the type for the lambda expression as Joiner. Do you see an example of a poly expression where the same lambda expression (x, y) -> x + y is of the type Adder in one context and of the type Joiner in another?

Listing 4-4 shows how to use these lambda expressions in a program.

Listing 4-4. Examples of Using Lambda Expressions

```java
// TargetTypeTest.java
package com.jdojo.lambda;
public class TargetTypeTest {
    public static void main(String[] args)  {
        // Creates an Adder using a lambda expression
        Adder adder = (x, y) -> x + y;
        // Creates a Joiner using a lambda expression
        Joiner joiner = (x, y) -> x + y;
        // Adds two doubles
        double sum1 = adder.add(10.34, 89.11);
        // Adds two ints
        double sum2 = adder.add(10, 89);
        // Joins two strings
        String str = joiner.join("Hello", " lambda");
        System.out.println("sum1 = " + sum1);
        System.out.println("sum2 = " + sum2);
        System.out.println("str = " + str);
    }
}
```

```
sum1 = 99.45
sum2 = 99.0
str = Hello lambda
```

I now discuss the target typing in the context of method calls. You can pass lambda expressions as arguments to methods. Consider the code for the LambdaUtil class shown in Listing 4-5.

Listing 4-5. A LambdaUtil Class That Uses Functional Interfaces As an Argument in Methods

```java
// LambdaUtil.java
package com.jdojo.lambda;
```

```java
public class LambdaUtil {
    public void testAdder(Adder adder) {
        double x = 190.90;
        double y = 8.50;
        double sum = adder.add(x, y);
        System.out.print("Using an Adder:");
        System.out.println(x + " + " + y + " = " + sum);
    }
    public void testJoiner(Joiner joiner) {
        String s1 = "Hello";
        String s2 = "World";
        String s3 = joiner.join(s1,s2);
        System.out.print("Using a Joiner:");
        System.out.println("\"" + s1 + "\" + \"" + s2 +
            "\" = \"" + s3 + "\"");
    }
}
```

The LambdaUtil class contains two methods: testAdder() and testJoiner(). One method takes an Adder as an argument and another a Joiner as an argument. Both methods have simple implementations. Consider the following snippet of code:

```java
LambdaUtil util = new LambdaUtil();
util.testAdder((x, y) -> x + y);
```

The first statement creates an object of the LambdaUtil class. The second statement calls the testAdder() method on the object, passing a lambda expression of (x, y) -> x + y. The compiler must infer the type of the lambda expression. The target type of the lambda expression is the type Adder because the argument type of the testAdder(Adder adder) is Adder. The rest of the target typing process is the same as you saw in the assignment statement before. Finally, the compiler infers that the type of the lambda expression is Adder.

The program in Listing 4-6 creates an object of the LambdaUtil class and calls the testAdder() and testJoiner() methods.

Listing 4-6. Using Lambda Expressions As Method Arguments

```
// LambdaUtilTest.java
package com.jdojo.lambda;
public class LambdaUtilTest {
    public static void main(String[] args)  {
        LambdaUtil util = new LambdaUtil();
        // Call the testAdder() method
        util.testAdder((x, y) -> x + y);
        // Call the testJoiner() method
        util.testJoiner((x, y) -> x + y);
        // Call the testJoiner() method. The Joiner will
        // add a space between the two strings
        util.testJoiner((x, y) -> x + " " + y);
        // Call the testJoiner() method. The Joiner will
        // reverse the strings and join resulting
        // strings in reverse order adding a comma in
        //between
        util.testJoiner((x, y) -> {
            StringBuilder sbx = new StringBuilder(x);
            StringBuilder sby = new StringBuilder(y);
            sby.reverse().append(",").
                append(sbx.reverse());
            return sby.toString();
        });
    }
}
```

```
Using an Adder:190.9 + 8.5 = 199.4
Using a Joiner:"Hello" + "World" = "HelloWorld"
Using a Joiner:"Hello" + "World" = "Hello World"
Using a Joiner:"Hello" + "World" = "dlroW,olleH"
```

Notice the output of the `LambdaUtilTest` class. The `testJoiner()` method was called three times, and every time it printed a different result of joining the two strings "Hello" and "World". This is possible because different lambda expressions were passed to this method. At this point, you can say that you have parameterized the behavior of the testJoiner() method. That is, how the testJoiner() method behaves depends on its parameter. Changing the behavior of a method through its parameters is known as behavior parameterization. This is also known as passing code as data because you pass code (logic, functionality, or behavior) encapsulated in lambda expressions to methods as if it were data.

It is not always possible for the compiler to infer the type of a lambda expression. In some contexts, there is no way the compiler can infer the type of a lambda expression; those contexts do not allow the use of lambda expressions. Some contexts may allow using lambda expressions, but the use itself may be ambiguous to the compiler; one such case is passing lambda expressions to overloaded methods.

Consider the code for the LambdaUtil2 class shown in Listing 4-7. The code for this class is the same as for the LambdaUtil class in Listing 4-5, except that this class changed the names of the two methods to the same name, test(), making it an overloaded method.

Listing 4-7. A LambdaUtil2 Class That Uses Functional Interfaces As an Argument in Methods

```java
// LambdaUtil2.java
package com.jdojo.lambda;
public class LambdaUtil2 {
    public void test(Adder adder) {
        double x = 190.90;
        double y = 8.50;
        double sum = adder.add(x, y);
        System.out.print("Using an Adder:");
        System.out.println(x + " + " + y + " = " + sum);
    }
    public void test(Joiner joiner) {
        String s1 = "Hello";
        String s2 = "World";
        String s3 = joiner.join(s1,s2);
        System.out.print("Using a Joiner:");
        System.out.println("\"" + s1 + "\" + \"" + s2 +
            "\" = \"" + s3 + "\"");
    }
}
```

Consider the following snippet of code:

```
LambdaUtil2 util = new LambdaUtil2();
util.test((x, y) -> x + y); // A compile-time error
```

The second statement results in the following compile-time error:

```
Reference to test is ambiguous. Both method test(Adder) in
LambdaUtil2 and method test(Joiner) in LambdaUtil2 match.
```

The call to the test() method fails because the lambda expression is implicit, and it matches both versions of the test() method. The compiler does not know which method to use: test(Adder adder) or test(Joiner joiner). In such circumstances, you need to help the compiler by providing some more information. The following are some of the ways to help the compiler resolve the ambiguity:

- If the lambda expression is implicit, make it explicit by specifying the type of the parameters.

- Use a cast.

- Do not use the lambda expression directly as the method argument. First, assign it to a variable of the desired type, and then pass the variable to the method.

Let's discuss all three ways to resolve the compile-time error. The following snippet of code changes the lambda expression to an explicit lambda expression:

```
LambdaUtil2 util = new LambdaUtil2();
util.test((double x, double y) -> x + y);
// <- OK. Will call test(Adder adder)
```

Specifying the type of parameters in the lambda expression resolved the issue. The compiler has two candidate methods: test(Adder adder) and test(Joiner joiner). With the (double x, double y) parameter information, only the test(Adder adder) method matches.

The following snippet of code uses a cast to cast the lambda expression to the type Adder:

```
LambdaUtil2 util = new LambdaUtil2();
util.test((Adder)(x, y) -> x + y);
// <- OK. Will call test(Adder adder)
```

Using a cast tells the compiler that the type of the lambda expression is Adder and, therefore, helps it choose the test(Adder adder) method.

Consider the following snippet of code that breaks down the method call into two statements:

```
LambdaUtil2 util = new LambdaUtil2();
Adder adder = (x, y) -> x + y;
util.test(adder);
// <- OK. Will call test(Adder adder)
```

The lambda expression is assigned to a variable of type Adder, and the variable is passed to the test() method. Again, it helps the compiler choose the test(Adder adder) method based on the compile-time type of the adder variable.

The program in Listing 4-8 is similar to the one shown in Listing 4-6, except that it uses the LambdaUtil2 class. It uses explicit lambda expressions and a cast to resolve the ambiguous matches for lambda expressions.

Listing 4-8. Resolving Ambiguity During Target Typing

```
// LambdaUtil2Test.java
package com.jdojo.lambda;
public class LambdaUtil2Test {
    public static void main(String[] args) {
        LambdaUtil2 util = new LambdaUtil2();
        // Calls the testAdder() method
        util.test((double x, double y) -> x + y);
        // Calls the testJoiner() method
        util.test((String x, String y) -> x + y);
        // Calls the testJoiner() method. The Joiner will
        // add a space between the two strings
        util.test((Joiner) (x, y) -> x + " " + y);
        // Calls the testJoiner() method. The Joiner will
        // reverse the strings and join resulting strings
        // in reverse order adding a comma in between
        util.test((Joiner) (x, y) -> {
            StringBuilder sbx = new StringBuilder(x);
            StringBuilder sby = new StringBuilder(y);
```

```
        sby.reverse().append(",").
            append(sbx.reverse());
        return sby.toString();
    });
  }
}
```

```
Using an Adder:190.9 + 8.5 = 199.4
Using a Joiner:"Hello" + "World" = "HelloWorld"
Using a Joiner:"Hello" + "World" = "Hello World"
Using a Joiner:"Hello" + "World" = "dlroW,olleH"
```

Lambda expressions can be used only in the following contexts:

- Assignment context: A lambda expression may appear to the right side of the assignment operator in an assignment statement. For example:

  ```
  ReferenceType variable1 = LambdaExpression;
  ```

- Method invocation context: A lambda expression may appear as an argument to a method or constructor call. For example:

  ```
  util.testJoiner(LambdaExpression);
  ```

- Return context: A lambda expression may appear in a `return` statement inside a method, as its target type is the declared return type of the method. For example:

  ```
  return LambdaExpression;
  ```

- Cast context: A lambda expression may be used if it is preceded by a cast. The type specified in the cast is its target type. For example:

  ```
  (Joiner) LambdaExpression;
  ```

Functional Interfaces

A functional interface is simply an interface that has exactly one abstract method. The following types of methods in an interface do not count for defining a functional interface:

- Default methods

- static methods

- Public methods inherited from the Object class

Note that an interface may have more than one abstract method and can still be a functional interface if all but one of them is a redeclaration of the methods in the Object class. Consider the declaration of the Comparator class that is in the java.util package, as shown:

```
package java.util;
@FunctionalInterface
public interface Comparator<T> {
    // An abstract method declared in the interface
    int compare(T o1, T o2);
    // Re-declaration of the equals() method in the
    // Object class
    boolean equals(Object obj);
    // Many more static and default methods that are
    // not shown here.
}
```

The Comparator interface contains two abstract methods: compare() and equals(). The equals() method in the Comparator interface is a redeclaration of the equals() method of the Object class, and therefore it does not count against the one abstract method requirement for it to be a functional interface. The Comparator interface contains several default and static methods that are not shown here.

A lambda expression is used to represent an unnamed function as used in functional programming. A functional interface represents one type of functionality/operation in terms of its lone abstract method. This commonality is the reason why the target type of a lambda expression is always a functional interface.

Using the @FunctionalInterface Annotation

The declaration of a functional interface may optionally be annotated with the annotation @FunctionalInterface, which is in the java.lang package. So far, all functional interfaces declared in this chapter, such as Adder and Joiner, have been annotated with @FunctionalInterface. The presence of this annotation tells the compiler to make sure that the declared type is a functional interface. If the annotation @FunctionalInterface is used on a non-functional interface or other types such as classes, a compile-time error occurs. If you do not use the annotation @FunctionalInterface on an interface with one abstract method, the interface is still a functional interface, and it can be the target type for lambda expressions. Using this annotation gives you an additional assurance from the compiler. The presence of the annotation also protects you from inadvertently changing a functional interface into a non-functional interface, as the compiler will catch it.

The following declaration for an Operations interface will not compile, as the interface declaration uses the @FunctionalInterface annotation, and it is not a functional interface (defines two abstract methods):

```
@FunctionalInterface
public interface Operations {
    double add(double n1, double n2);
    double mult(double n1, double n2);
}
```

To compile the Operations interface, either remove one of the two abstract methods or remove the @FunctionalInterface annotation. The following declaration for a Test class will not compile, as @FunctionalInterface cannot be used on a type other than a functional interface:

```
@FunctionalInterface
public class Test {
    // Code goes here
}
```

Generic Functional Interface

A functional interface can have type parameters. That is, a functional interface can be generic. An example of a generic functional parameter is the Comparator interface with one type parameter T:

```
@FunctionalInterface
public interface Comparator<T> {
    int compare(T o1, T o2);
}
```

A functional interface may have a generic abstract method. That is, the abstract method may declare type parameters. The following is an example of a non-generic functional interface called Processor whose abstract method process() is generic:

```
@FunctionalInterface
public interface Processor {
    <T> void process(T[] list);
}
```

A lambda expression cannot declare type parameters, and, therefore, it cannot have a target type whose abstract method is generic. For example, you cannot represent the Processor interface using a lambda expression. In such cases, you need to use a method reference, which I discuss in the next section, or an anonymous class.

Let's look at a short example of a generic functional interface and instantiate it using lambda expressions. Listing 4-9 shows the code for a functional interface named Mapper.

Listing 4-9. A Mapper Functional Interface

```
// Mapper.java
package com.jdojo.lambda;
@FunctionalInterface
public interface Mapper<T> {
    // An abstract method
    int map(T source);
    // A generic static method
```

```
public static <U> int[] mapToInt(U[] list,
        Mapper<? super U> mapper) {
    int[] mappedValues = new int[list.length];
    for (int i = 0; i < list.length; i++) {
        // Map the object to an int
        mappedValues[i] = mapper.map(list[i]);
    }
    return mappedValues;
}
}
```

Mapper is a generic functional interface with a type parameter T. Its abstract method map() takes an object of type T as a parameter and returns an int. The mapToInt() method is a generic static method that accepts an array of type U and a Mapper of a type that is U itself or a supertype of U. The method returns an int array whose elements contain the mapped value for the corresponding elements passed as an array.

The program in Listing 4-10 shows how to use lambda expressions to instantiate the Mapper<T> interface. The program maps a String array and an Integer array to int arrays.

Listing 4-10. Using the Mapper Functional Interface

```
// MapperTest.java
package com.jdojo.lambda;
public class MapperTest {
    public static void main(String[] args) {
        // Map names using their length
        System.out.println(
            "Mapping names to their lengths:");
        String[] names = {"David", "Li", "Doug"};
        int[] lengthMapping = Mapper.mapToInt(names,
            (String name) -> name.length());
        printMapping(names, lengthMapping);
        System.out.println("\nMapping integers to " +
            "their squares:");
        Integer[] numbers = {7, 3, 67};
```

```
        int[] countMapping = Mapper.mapToInt(numbers,
            (Integer n) -> n * n);
        printMapping(numbers, countMapping);
    }
    public static void printMapping(Object[] from,
            int[] to) {
        for (int i = 0; i < from.length; i++) {
            System.out.println(from[i] + " mapped to " +
                to[i]);
        }
    }
}
```

```
Mapping names to their lengths:
David mapped to 5
Li mapped to 2
Doug mapped to 4
Mapping integers to their squares:
7 mapped to 49
3 mapped to 9
67 mapped to 4489
```

Intersection Type and Lambda Expressions

It is possible to declare an intersection type that is an intersection (or subtype) of multiple types (since Java 8). An intersection type may appear as the target type in a cast. An ampersand (&) is used between two types, such as (Type1 & Type2 & Type3), and it represents a new type that is an intersection of Type1, Type2, and Type3. Consider a marker interface called Sensitive, shown in Listing 4-11.

Listing 4-11. A Marker Interface Named Sensitive

```
// Sensitive.java
package com.jdojo.lambda;
public interface Sensitive {
    // It is a marker interface. So, no methods exist.
}
```

Suppose you have a lambda expression assigned to a variable of the Sensitive type:

```
Sensitive sen = (x, y) -> x + y;
// <- A compile-time error
```

This statement does not compile. The target type of a lambda expression must be a functional interface; Sensitive is not a functional interface. However, you should be able to make such an assignment, as a marker interface does not contain any methods. In such cases, you need to use a cast with an intersection type that creates a new synthetic type that is a subtype of all types. The following statement will compile:

```
Sensitive sen = (Sensitive & Adder) (x, y) -> x + y;
// <- OK
```

The intersection type Sensitive & Adder is still a functional interface, and, therefore, the target type of the lambda expression is a functional interface with one method from the Adder interface.

In Java, you can convert an object to a stream of bytes and restore the object back later. This is called serialization. A class must implement the java.io.Serializable marker interface for its objects to be serialized. If you want a lambda expression to be serialized, you will need to use a cast with an intersection type. The following statement assigns a lambda expression to a variable of the Serializable interface:

```
Serializable ser = (Serializable & Adder) (x, y) -> x + y;
```

Commonly Used Functional Interfaces

The java.util.function package contains many useful functional interfaces. They are listed in Table 4-2.

Table 4-2. *Functional Interfaces Declared in the java.util.function Package*

Interface Name	Method	Description
Function<T,R>	R apply(T t)	Represents a function that takes an argument of type T and returns a result of type R.
BiFunction<T,U,R>	R apply(T t, U u)	Represents a function that takes two arguments of types T and U and returns a result of type R.
Predicate<T>	boolean test(T t)	In mathematics, a predicate is a boolean-valued function that takes an argument and returns true or false. The function represents a condition that returns true or false for the specified argument.
BiPredicate<T,U>	boolean test(T t, U u)	Represents a predicate with two arguments.
Consumer<T>	void accept(T t)	Represents an operation that takes an argument, operates on it to produce some side effects, and returns no result.
BiConsumer<T,U>	void accept(T t, U u)	Represents an operation that takes two arguments, operates on them to produce some side effects, and returns no result.
Supplier<T>	T get()	Represents a supplier that returns a value.
UnaryOperator<T>	T apply(T t)	Inherits from Function<T,T>. Represents a function that takes an argument and returns a result of the same type.
BinaryOperator<T>	T apply(T t1, T t2)	Inherits from BiFunction<T,T,T>. Represents a function that takes two arguments of the same type and returns a result of the same.

The table shows only the generic versions of the functional interfaces. Several specialized versions of these interfaces exist. They have been specialized for frequently used primitive data types; for example, IntConsumer is a specialized version of

Consumer<T>. Some interfaces in the table contain convenience default and static methods. The table lists only the abstract method, not the default and static methods.

Using the **Function<T,R>** Interface

Six specializations of the Function<T,R> interface exist:

- IntFunction<R>

- LongFunction<R>

- DoubleFunction<R>

- ToIntFunction<T>

- ToLongFunction<T>

- ToDoubleFunction<T>

IntFunction<R>, LongFunction<R>, and DoubleFunction<R> take an int, a long, and a double as an argument, respectively, and return a value of type R. ToIntFunction<T>, ToLongFunction<T>, and ToDoubleFunction<T> take an argument of type T and return an int, a long, and a double, respectively. Similar specialized functions exist for other types of generic functions listed in the table.

Note   Your com.jdojo.lambda.Mapper<T> interface represents the same function type as ToIntFunction<T> in the java.util.function package. You created the Mapper<T> interface to learn how to create and use a generic functional interface. From now on, look at the built-in functional interfaces before creating your own; use them if they meet your needs.

The following snippet of code shows how to use the same lambda expression to represent a function that accepts an int and returns its square, using four variants of the Function<T, R> function type:

```
// Takes an int and returns its square
Function<Integer, Integer> square1 = x -> x * x;
IntFunction<Integer> square2 = x -> x * x;
ToIntFunction<Integer> square3 = x -> x * x;
UnaryOperator<Integer> square4 = x -> x * x;
```

```
System.out.println(square1.apply(5));
System.out.println(square2.apply(5));
System.out.println(square3.applyAsInt(5));
System.out.println(square4.apply(5));
```

25

25

25

25

The Function interface contains the following default and static methods:

- default <V> Function<T,V> andThen(Function<? super R,?
extends V> after)

- default <V> Function<V,R> compose(Function<? super V,?
extends T> before)

- static <T> Function<T,T> identity()

The andThen() method returns a composed Function that applies this function to the argument and then applies the specified after function to the result. The compose() function returns a composed function that applies the specified before function to the argument and then applies this function to the result. The identify() method returns a function that always returns its argument.

The following snippet of code demonstrates how to use default and static methods of the Function interface to compose new functions:

```
// Create two functions
Function<Long, Long> square = x -> x * x;
Function<Long, Long> addOne = x -> x + 1;
// Compose functions from the two functions
Function<Long, Long> squareAddOne = square.andThen(addOne);
Function<Long, Long> addOneSquare = square.compose(addOne);
// Get an identity function
Function<Long, Long> identity = Function.<Long>identity();
// Test the functions
long num = 5L;
```

```
System.out.println("Number: " + num);
System.out.println("Square and then add one: " +
    squareAddOne.apply(num));
System.out.println("Add one and then square: " +
    addOneSquare.apply(num));
System.out.println("Identity: " + identity.apply(num));

Number: 5
Square and then add one: 26
Add one and then square: 36
Identity: 5
```

You are not limited to composing a function that consists of two functions that are executed in a specific order. A function may be composed of as many functions as you want. You can chain lambda expressions to create a composed function in one expression. Note that when you chain lambda expressions, you may need to provide hints to the compiler to resolve the target type ambiguity that may arise. The following is an example of a composed function by chaining three functions. A cast is provided to help the compiler. Without the cast, the compiler will not be able to infer the target type:

```
// Square the input, add one to the result, and square
// the result
Function<Long, Long> chainedFunction =
    ((Function<Long, Long>)(x -> x * x))
                    .andThen(x -> x + 1)
                    .andThen(x -> x * x);
System.out.println(chainedFunction.apply(3L));

100
```

Using the Predicate<T> Interface

A predicate represents a condition that is either true or false for a given input. The Predicate interface contains the following default and static methods that let you compose a predicate based on other predicates using logical NOT, AND, and OR:

- default Predicate<T> negate()

- default Predicate<T> and(Predicate<? super T> other)

- default Predicate<T> or(Predicate<? super T> other)

- static <T> Predicate<T> isEqual(Object targetRef)

The negate() method returns a Predicate that is a logical negation of the original predicate. The and() method returns a short-circuiting logical AND predicate of this predicate and the specified predicate. The or() method returns a short-circuiting logical OR predicate of this predicate and the specified predicate. The isEqual() method returns a predicate that tests if the specified targetRef is equal to the specified argument for the predicate according to Objects.equals(Object o1, Object o2); if two inputs are null, this predicate evaluates to true. You can chain the calls to these methods to create complex predicates. The following snippet of code shows some examples of creating and using predicates:

```
// Create some predicates
Predicate<Integer> greaterThanTen = x -> x > 10;
Predicate<Integer> divisibleByThree = x -> x % 3 == 0;
Predicate<Integer> divisibleByFive = x -> x % 5 == 0;
Predicate<Integer> equalToTen = Predicate.isEqual(null);
// Create predicates using NOT, AND, and OR on other
// predicates
Predicate<Integer> lessThanOrEqualToTen =
    greaterThanTen.negate();
Predicate<Integer> divisibleByThreeAndFive =
    divisibleByThree.and(divisibleByFive);
Predicate<Integer> divisibleByThreeOrFive =
    divisibleByThree.or(divisibleByFive);
// Test the predicates
int num = 10;
System.out.println("Number: " + num);
System.out.println("greaterThanTen: " +
    greaterThanTen.test(num));
System.out.println("divisibleByThree: " +
    divisibleByThree.test(num));
System.out.println("divisibleByFive: " +
    divisibleByFive.test(num));
```

```
System.out.println("lessThanOrEqualToTen: " +
    lessThanOrEqualToTen.test(num));
System.out.println("divisibleByThreeAndFive: " +
    divisibleByThreeAndFive.test(num));
System.out.println("divisibleByThreeOrFive: " +
    divisibleByThreeOrFive.test(num));
System.out.println("equalsToTen: " +
    equalToTen.test(num));
```

```
Number: 10
greaterThanTen: false
divisibleByThree: false
divisibleByFive: true
lessThanOrEqualToTen: true
divisibleByThreeAndFive: false
divisibleByThreeOrFive: true
equalsToTen: false
```

Using Functional Interfaces

Functional interfaces are used in two contexts by two different types of users:

- By library designers for designing APIs

- By library users for using the APIs

Functional interfaces are used to design APIs by library designers. They are used to declare a parameter's type and return type in method declarations. They are used the same way non-functional interfaces are used (functional interfaces existed in Java since the beginning).

Library users use functional interfaces as target types for lambda expressions. That is, when a method in the API takes a functional interface as an argument, the user of the API should use a lambda expression to pass the argument. Using lambda expressions has the benefit of making the code concise and more readable.

In this section, I show you how to design APIs using functional interfaces and how to use lambda expressions to use the APIs. Functional interfaces have been used heavily in designing the Java library for the Collections and Streams APIs.

I use one enum and two classes in subsequent examples. The Gender enum, shown in Listing 4-12, contains two constants to represent the gender of a person. The Person class, shown in Listing 4-13, represents a person; it contains, apart from other methods, a getPersons() method that returns a list of persons.

Listing 4-12. A Gender enum

```java
// Gender.java
package com.jdojo.lambda;
public enum Gender {
    MALE, FEMALE
}
```

Listing 4-13. A Person Class

```java
// Person.java
package com.jdojo.lambda;
import java.time.LocalDate;
import java.util.ArrayList;
import java.util.List;
import static com.jdojo.lambda.Gender.MALE;
import static com.jdojo.lambda.Gender.FEMALE;

public class Person {
    private String firstName;
    private String lastName;
    private LocalDate dob;
    private Gender gender;
    public Person(String firstName, String lastName,
            LocalDate dob, Gender gender) {
        this.firstName = firstName;
        this.lastName = lastName;
        this.dob = dob;
        this.gender = gender;
    }
```

```java
public String getFirstName() {
    return firstName;
}
public void setFirstName(String firstName) {
    this.firstName = firstName;
}
public String getLastName() {
    return lastName;
}
public void setLastName(String lastName) {
    this.lastName = lastName;
}
public LocalDate getDob() {
    return dob;
}
public void setDob(LocalDate dob) {
    this.dob = dob;
}
public Gender getGender() {
    return gender;
}
public void setGender(Gender gender) {
    this.gender = gender;
}
@Override
public String toString() {
    return firstName + " " + lastName + ", " +
        gender + ", " + dob;
}
// A convenience method
public static List<Person> getPersons() {
    ArrayList<Person> list = new ArrayList<>();
    list.add(new Person("John", "Jacobs",
      LocalDate.of(1975, 1, 20), MALE));
```

```
        list.add(new Person("Wally", "Inman",
            LocalDate.of(1965, 9, 12), MALE));
        list.add(new Person("Donna", "Jacobs",
            LocalDate.of(1970, 9, 12), FEMALE));
        return list;
    }
}
```

The FunctionUtil class in Listing 4-14 is a utility class. Its methods apply a function on a List. List is an interface that is implemented by the ArrayList class. The forEach() method applies an action on each item in the list, typically producing side effects; the action is represented by a Consumer. The filter() method filters a list based on a specified Predicate. The map() method maps each item in the list to a value using a Function. As a library designer, you will design these methods using functional interfaces.

Listing 4-14. A FunctionUtil Class

```java
// FunctionUtil.java
package com.jdojo.lambda;
import java.util.ArrayList;
import java.util.List;
import java.util.function.Consumer;
import java.util.function.Function;
import java.util.function.Predicate;
public class FunctionUtil {
    // Applies an action on each item in a list
    public static <T> void forEach(List<T> list,
            Consumer<? super T> action) {
        for (T item : list) {
            action.accept(item);
        }
    }
    // Applies a filter to a list and returns the
    // filtered list items
```

```java
    public static <T> List<T> filter(List<T> list,
            Predicate<? super T> predicate) {
        List<T> filteredList = new ArrayList<>();
        for (T item : list) {
            if (predicate.test(item)) {
                filteredList.add(item);
            }
        }
        return filteredList;
    }
    // Maps each item in a list to a value
    public static <T, R> List<R> map(List<T> list,
            Function<? super T, R> mapper) {
        List<R> mappedList = new ArrayList<>();
        for (T item : list) {
            mappedList.add(mapper.apply(item));
        }
        return mappedList;
    }
}
```

You will now use the FunctionUtil class as a library user and use the functional interfaces as target types of lambda expressions. Listing 4-15 shows how to use the FunctionUtil class.

Listing 4-15. Using Functional Interfaces As Target Types of Lambda Expressions As Library Users

```java
// FunctionUtilTest.java
package com.jdojo.lambda;
import static com.jdojo.lambda.Gender.MALE;
import java.util.List;
public class FunctionUtilTest {
    public static void main(String[] args) {
        List<Person> list = Person.getPersons();
        // Use the forEach() method to print each person
        // in the list
```

```java
        System.out.println("Original list of persons:");
        FunctionUtil.forEach(list, p ->
            System.out.println(p));
        // Filter only males
        List<Person> maleList = FunctionUtil.filter(list,
            p -> p.getGender() == MALE);
        System.out.println("\nMales only:");
        FunctionUtil.forEach(maleList,
            p -> System.out.println(p));
        // Map each person to his/her year of birth
        List<Integer> dobYearList = FunctionUtil.map(list,
            p -> p.getDob().getYear());
        System.out.println("\nPersons mapped to year of " +
            "their birth:");
        FunctionUtil.forEach(dobYearList,
            year -> System.out.println(year));
        // Apply an action to each person in the list.
        // Add one year to each male's dob
        FunctionUtil.forEach(maleList,
            p -> p.setDob(p.getDob().plusYears(1)));
        System.out.println("\nMales only after adding " +
            "1 year to DOB:");
        FunctionUtil.forEach(maleList,
            p -> System.out.println(p));
    }
}

Original list of persons:
John Jacobs, MALE, 1975-01-20
Wally Inman, MALE, 1965-09-12
Donna Jacobs, FEMALE, 1970-09-12
Males only:
John Jacobs, MALE, 1975-01-20
Wally Inman, MALE, 1965-09-12
```

```
Persons mapped to year of their birth:
1975
1965
1970
Males only after adding 1 year to DOB:
John Jacobs, MALE, 1976-01-20
Wally Inman, MALE, 1966-09-12
```

The program gets a list of persons, applies a filter to the list to get a list of only males, maps persons to the year of their birth, and adds one year to each male's date of birth. It performs each of these actions using lambda expressions. Note the conciseness of the code; it uses only one line of code to perform each action. Most notable is the use of the forEach() method. This method takes a Consumer function. Then each item is passed to this function. The function can take any action on the item. You passed a Consumer that prints the item on the standard output as shown:

```
FunctionUtil.forEach(list,
    p -> System.out.println(p));
```

Typically, a Consumer applies an action on the item it receives to produce side effects. In this case, it simply prints the item, without producing any side effects.

Method References

A lambda expression represents an anonymous function that is treated as an instance of a functional interface. A method reference is a shorthand way to create a lambda expression using an existing method. Using method references makes your lambda expressions more readable and concise; it also lets you use the existing methods as lambda expressions. If a lambda expression contains a body that is an expression using a method call, you can use a method reference in place of that lambda expression.

Note   A method reference is not a new type in Java. It is not a function pointer as used in some other programming languages. It is simply shorthand for writing a lambda expression using an existing method. It can only be used where a lambda expression can be used.

Let's consider an example before I explain the syntax for method references. Consider the following snippet of code:

```java
import java.util.function.ToIntFunction;
...
ToIntFunction<String> lengthFunction = str ->
    str.length();
String name = "Ellen";
int len = lengthFunction.applyAsInt(name);
System.out.println("Name = " + name +
    ", length = " + len);
```

```
Name = Ellen, length = 5
```

The code uses a lambda expression to define an anonymous function that takes a String as an argument and returns its length. The body of the lambda expression consists of only one method call that is the length() method of the String class. You can rewrite the lambda expression using a method reference to the length() method of the String class, as shown:

```java
import java.util.function.ToIntFunction;
...
ToIntFunction<String> lengthFunction = String::length;
String name = "Ellen";
int len = lengthFunction.applyAsInt(name);
System.out.println("Name = " + name +
    ", length = " + len);
Name = Ellen, length = 5
```

The general syntax for a method reference is

```
<Qualifier>::<MethodName>
```

The <Qualifier> depends on the type of the method reference. Two consecutive colons act as a separator. The <MethodName> is the name of the method. For example, in the method reference String::length, String is the qualifier and length is the method name.

Note   A method reference does not call the method when it is declared. The method is called later when the method of its target type is called.

The syntax for method references allows specifying only the method name. You cannot specify the parameter types and return type of the method. Recall that a method reference is shorthand for a lambda expression. The target type, which is always a functional interface, determines the method's details. If the method is an overloaded method, the compiler will choose the most specific method based on the context. See Table 4-3.

Table 4-3.   *Types of Method References*

Syntax	Description
TypeName::staticMethod	A method reference to a static method of a class, an interface, or an enum.
objectRef::instanceMethod	A method reference to an instance method of the specified object.
ClassName::instanceMethod	A method reference to an instance method of an arbitrary object of the specified class.
TypeName. super::instanceMethod	A method reference to an instance method of the supertype of a particular object.
ClassName::new	A constructor reference to the constructor of the specified class.
ArrayTypeName::new	An array constructor reference to the constructor of the specified array type.

Using method references may be a little confusing in the beginning. The main point of confusion is the process of mapping the number and type of arguments in the actual method to the method reference. To help understand the syntax, I use a method reference and its equivalent lambda expression in all examples.

Static Method References

A static method reference uses a static method of a type as a lambda expression. The type could be a class, an interface, or an enum. Consider the following static method of the Integer class:

```
static String toBinaryString(int i)
```

The toBinaryString() method represents a function that takes an int as an argument and returns a String. You can use it in a lambda expression as shown:

```
// Using a lambda expression
Function<Integer,String> func1 =
    x -> Integer.toBinaryString(x);
System.out.println(func1.apply(17));
```

```
10001
```

The compiler infers the type of x as Integer and the return type of the lambda expression as String, by using the target type Function<Integer,String>.

You can rewrite this statement using a static method reference, as shown:

```
// Using a method reference
Function<Integer, String> func2 =
    Integer::toBinaryString;
System.out.println(func2.apply(17));
```

```
10001
```

The compiler finds a static method reference to the toBinaryString() method of the Integer class on the right side of the assignment operator. The toBinaryString() method takes an int as an argument and returns a String. The target type of the method reference is a function that takes an Integer as an argument and returns a String. The compiler verifies that after unboxing the Integer argument type of the target type to int, the method reference and target type are assignment compatible.

Consider another static method sum() in the Integer class:

```
static int sum(int a, int b)
```

The method reference would be Integer::sum. Let's use it in the same way you used the toBinaryString() method in the previous example:

```
Function<Integer,Integer> func2 = Integer::sum;
// <- A compile-time error

Error: incompatible types: invalid
        Function<Integer, Integer>
method sum in class Integer cannot
required: int,int
found: Integer
reason: actual and formal argument

method reference
func2 = Integer::sum;
be applied to given types

lists differ in length
```

The error message is stating that the method reference Integer::sum is not assignment compatible with the target type Function<Integer,Integer>. The sum(int, int) method takes two int arguments, whereas the target type takes only one Integer argument. The mismatch in the number of arguments caused the compile-time error.

To fix the error, the target type of the method reference Integer::sum should be a functional interface whose abstract method takes two int arguments and returns an int. Using a BiFunction<Integer,Integer, Integer> as the target type will work. The following snippet of code shows how to use a method reference Integer::sum as well as the equivalent lambda expression:

```
// Uses a lambda expression
BiFunction<Integer,Integer,Integer> func1 =
    (x, y) -> Integer.sum(x, y);
System.out.println(func1.apply(17, 15));
// Uses a method reference
BiFunction<Integer,Integer,Integer> func2 =
    Integer::sum;
System.out.println(func2.apply(17, 15));

32
32
```

Let's try using a method reference of the overloaded static method valueOf() of the Integer class. The method has three versions:

- static Integer valueOf(int i)

- static Integer valueOf(String s)

- static Integer valueOf(String s, int radix)

The following snippet of code shows how different target types will use the three different versions of the Integer.valueOf() static method. It is left as an exercise for readers to write the following snippet of code using lambda expressions:

```
// Uses Integer.valueOf(int)
Function<Integer,Integer> func1 = Integer::valueOf;

// Uses Integer.valueOf(String)
Function<String,Integer> func2 = Integer::valueOf;

// Uses Integer.valueOf(String, int)
BiFunction<String,Integer,Integer> func3 =
    Integer::valueOf;

System.out.println(func1.apply(17));
System.out.println(func2.apply("17"));
System.out.println(func3.apply("10001", 2));
```

```
17
17
17
```

The following is the last example in this category. The Person class, shown in Listing 4-13, contains a getPersons() static method that is declared as follows:

```
static List<Person> getPersons()
```

The method takes no argument and returns a List<Person>. A Supplier<T> represents a function that takes no arguments and returns a result of type T. The following snippet of code uses the method reference Person::getPersons as a Supplier<List<Person>>:

```
Supplier<List<Person>> supplier = Person::getPersons;
List<Person> personList = supplier.get();
FunctionUtil.forEach(personList,
    p -> System.out.println(p));
```

```
John Jacobs, MALE, 1975-01-20
Wally Inman, MALE, 1965-09-12
Donna Jacobs, FEMALE, 1970-09-12
```

Instance Method References

An instance method is invoked on an object's reference. The object reference on which an instance method is invoked is known as the *receiver* of the method invocation. The receiver of a method invocation can be an object reference or an expression that evaluates to an object's reference. The following snippet of code shows the receiver of the length() instance method of the String class:

```
String name = "Kannan";
// name is the receiver of the length() method
int len1 = name.length();
// "Hello" is the receiver of the length() method
int len2 = "Hello".length();
// (new String("Kannan")) is the receiver of the length()
// method
int len3 = (new String("Kannan")).length();
```

In a method reference of an instance method, you can specify the receiver of the method invocation explicitly, or you can provide it implicitly when the method is invoked. The former is called a *bound receiver*, and the latter is called an *unbound receiver*. The syntax for an instance method reference supports two variants:

- objectRef::instanceMethod

- ClassName::instanceMethod

For a bound receiver, use the `objectRef::instanceMethod` syntax. Consider the following snippet of code:

```
Supplier<Integer> supplier = () -> "Ellen".length();
System.out.println(supplier.get());
```

5

This statement uses a lambda expression that represents a function that takes no arguments and returns an `int`. The body of the expression uses a `String` object called "Ellen" to invoke the `length()` instance method of the `String` class. You can rewrite this statement using an instance method reference with the "Ellen" object as the bound receiver and using a `Supplier<Integer>` as the target type, as shown:

```
Supplier<Integer> supplier = "Ellen"::length;
System.out.println(supplier.get());
```

5

Consider the following snippet of code to represent a `Consumer<String>` that takes a `String` as an argument and returns void:

```
Consumer<String> consumer = str -> System.out.println(str);
consumer.accept("Hello");
```

Hello

This lambda expression invokes the `println()` method on the `System.out` object. This can be rewritten using a method reference with `System.out` as the bound receiver, as shown:

```
Consumer<String> consumer = System.out::println;
consumer.accept("Hello");
```

Hello

When the method reference `System.out::println` is used, the compiler looks at its target type, which is `Consumer<String>`. It represents a function type that takes a `String` as an argument and returns void. The compiler finds a `println(String)` method in the `PrintStream` class of the `System.out` object and uses that method for the method reference.

As the last example in this category, you will use the method reference `System.out::println` to print the list of persons, as shown:

```
List<Person> list = Person.getPersons();
FunctionUtil.forEach(list, System.out::println);
```

```
John Jacobs, MALE, 1975-01-20
Wally Inman, MALE, 1965-09-12
Donna Jacobs, FEMALE, 1970-09-12
```

For an unbound receiver, use the `ClassName::instanceMethod` syntax. Consider the following statement in which the lambda expression takes a `Person` as an argument and returns a `String`:

```
Function<Person,String> fNameFunc =
  (Person p) -> p.getFirstName();
```

This statement can be rewritten using the instance method reference, as shown:

```
Function<Person,String> fNameFunc = Person::getFirstName;
```

In the beginning, this is confusing for two reasons:

- The syntax is the same as the syntax for a method reference to a static method.

- It raises a question: Which object is the receiver of the instance method invocation?

The first confusion can be cleared up by looking at the method name and checking whether it is a static or an instance method. If the method is an instance method, the method reference represents an instance method reference.

The second confusion can be cleared up by keeping a rule in mind that the first argument to the function represented by the target type is the receiver of the method invocation. Consider an instance method reference called `String::length` that uses an unbound receiver. The receiver is supplied as the first argument to the `apply()` method, as shown:

```
Function<String,Integer> strLengthFunc = String::length;
String name = "Ellen";
// name is the receiver of String::length
```

```
int len = strLengthFunc.apply(name);
System.out.println("name = " + name +
    ", length = " + len);
name = Ellen, length = 5
```

The instance method `concat()` of the `String` class has the following declaration:

```
String concat(String str)
```

The method reference `String::concat` represents an instance method reference for a target type whose function takes two `String` arguments and returns a `String`. The first argument will be the receiver of the `concat()` method, and the second argument will be passed to the `concat()` method. The following snippet of code shows an example:

```
String greeting = "Hello";
String name = " Laynie";
// Uses a lambda expression
BiFunction<String,String,String> func1 =
    (s1, s2) -> s1.concat(s2);
System.out.println(func1.apply(greeting, name));
// Uses an instance method reference on an unbound
// receiver
BiFunction<String,String,String> func2 = String::concat;
System.out.println(func2.apply(greeting, name));

Hello Laynie
Hello Laynie
```

As the last example in this category, you will use the method reference `Person::getFirstName` that is an instance method reference on an unbound receiver, as shown:

```
List<Person> personList = Person.getPersons();
// Maps each Person object to its first name
List<String> firstNameList = FunctionUtil.map(personList,
    Person::getFirstName);
// Prints the first name list
FunctionUtil.forEach(firstNameList, System.out::println);
```

```
John
Wally
Donna
```

Supertype Instance Method References

The keyword super is used as a qualifier to invoke the overridden method in a class or an interface. The keyword is available only in an instance context. Use the following syntax to construct a method reference that refers to the instance method in the supertype and the method that's invoked on the current instance:

```
TypeName.super::instanceMethod
```

Consider the Priced interface and the Item class in Listings 4-16 and 4-17. The Priced interface contains a default method that returns 1.0. The Item class implements the Priced interface. It overrides the toString() method of the Object class and the getPrice() method of the Priced interface. I added three constructors to the Item class that display a message on the standard output. I use them in examples in the next section.

Listing 4-16. A Priced Interface with a Default Method of getPrice()

```java
// Priced.java
package com.jdojo.lambda;
public interface Priced {
    default double getPrice() {
        return 1.0;
    }
}
```

Listing 4-17. An Item Class That Implements the Priced Interface

```java
// Item.java
package com.jdojo.lambda;
import java.util.function.Supplier;
public class Item implements Priced {
    private String name = "Unknown";
    private double price = 0.0;
```

```java
    public Item() {
        System.out.println("Constructor Item() called.");
    }
    public Item(String name) {
        this.name = name;
        System.out.println("Constructor Item(String) " +
          "called.");
    }
    public Item(String name, double price) {
        this.name = name;
        this.price = price;
        System.out.println("Constructor " +
          "Item(String, double) called.");
    }
    public String getName() {
        return name;
    }
    public void setName(String name) {
        this.name = name;
    }
    public void setPrice(double price) {
        this.price = price;
    }
    @Override
    public double getPrice() {
        return price;
    }
    @Override
    public String toString() {
        return "name = " + getName() +
          ", price = " + getPrice();
    }
    public void test() {
        // Uses the Item.toString() method
        Supplier<String> s1 = this::toString;
```

```
    // Uses the Object.toString() method
    Supplier<String> s2 = Item.super::toString;
    // Uses the Item.getPrice() method
    Supplier<Double> s3 = this::getPrice;
    // Uses the Priced.getPrice() method
    Supplier<Double> s4 = Priced.super::getPrice;
    // Uses all method references and prints the
    // results
    System.out.println("this::toString: " + s1.get());
    System.out.println("Item.super::toString: " +
      s2.get());
    System.out.println("this::getPrice: " + s3.get());
    System.out.println("Priced.super::getPrice: " +
      s4.get());
  }
}
```

The test() method in the Item class uses four method references with a bound receiver. The receiver is the Item object on which the test() method is called.

- The method reference this::toString refers to the toString() method of the Item class.

- The method reference Item.super::toString refers to the toString() method of the Object class, which is the superclass of the Item class.

- The method reference this::getPrice refers to the getPrice() method of the Item class.

- The method reference Priced.super::getPrice refers to the getPrice() method of the Priced interface, which is the superinterface of the Item class.

The program in Listing 4-18 creates an object of the Item class and calls its test() method. The output shows the method being used by the four method references.

Listing 4-18. Testing the Item Class

```java
// ItemTest.java
package com.jdojo.lambda;
public class ItemTest {
    public static void main(String[] args) {
        Item apple = new Item("Apple", 0.75);
        apple.test();
    }
}
```

```
Constructor Item(String, double) called.
this::toString: name = Apple, price = 0.75
Item.super::toString: com.jdojo.lambda.Item@24d46ca6
this::getPrice: 0.75
Priced.super::getPrice: 1.0
```

Constructor References

Sometimes, the body of a lambda expression may be just an object creation expression. Consider the following two statements that use a `String` object creation expression as the body for lambda expressions:

```java
Supplier<String> func1 = () -> new String();
Function<String,String> func2 = str -> new String(str);
```

You can rewrite these statements by replacing the lambda expressions with constructor references as shown:

```java
Supplier<String> func1 = String::new;
Function<String,String> func2 = String::new;
```

The syntax for using a constructor is as follows:

- `ClassName::new`

- `ArrayTypeName::new`

234

The ClassName in ClassName::new is the name of the class that can be instantiated; it cannot be the name of an abstract class. The keyword new refers to the constructor of the class. A class may have multiple constructors. The syntax does not provide a way to refer to a specific constructor. The compiler selects a specific constructor based on the context. It looks at the target type and the number of arguments in the abstract method of the target type. The constructor whose number of arguments matches the number of arguments in the abstract method of the target type is chosen. Consider the following snippet of code that uses three constructors of the Item class, shown in Listing 4-17, in lambda expressions:

```
Supplier<Item> func1 = () -> new Item();
Function<String,Item> func2 = name -> new Item(name);
BiFunction<String,Double,Item> func3 =
    (name, price) -> new Item(name, price);
System.out.println(func1.get());
System.out.println(func2.apply("Apple"));
System.out.println(func3.apply("Apple", 0.75));

Constructor Item() called.
name = Unknown, price = 0.0
Constructor Item(String) called.
name = Apple, price = 0.0
Constructor Item(String, double) called.
name = Apple, price = 0.75
```

The following snippet of code replaces the lambda expressions with a constructor reference Item::new. The output shows the same constructors as before:

```
Supplier<Item> func1 = Item::new;
Function<String,Item> func2 = Item::new;
BiFunction<String,Double,Item> func3 = Item::new;
System.out.println(func1.get());
System.out.println(func2.apply("Apple"));
System.out.println(func3.apply("Apple", 0.75));
```

```
Constructor Item() called.
name = Unknown, price = 0.0
Constructor Item(String) called.
name = Apple, price = 0.0
Constructor Item(String, double) called.
name = Apple, price = 0.75
```

When the statement

```
Supplier<Item> func1 = Item::new;
```

is executed, the compiler finds that the target type `Supplier<Item>` does not accept an argument. Therefore, it uses the no-args constructor of the `Item` class. When the statement

```
Function<String,Item> func2 = Item::new;
```

is executed, the compiler finds that the target type `Function<String,Item>` takes a `String` argument. Therefore, it uses the constructor of the `Item` class that takes a `String` argument. When the statement

```
BiFunction<String,Double,Item> func3 = Item::new;
```

is executed, the compiler finds that the target type `BiFunction<String,Double,Item>` takes two arguments: a `String` and a `Double`. Therefore, it uses the constructor of the `Item` class that takes a `String` and a `double` argument.

The following statement generates a compile-time error, as the compiler does not find a constructor in the `Item` class that accepts a `Double` argument:

```
Function<Double,Item> func4 = Item::new;
// <- A compile-time error
```

Arrays in Java do not have constructors. There is a special syntax to use constructor references for arrays. Array constructors are treated to have one argument of int type that is the size of the array. The following snippet of code shows the lambda expression and its equivalent constructor reference for an `int` array:

```
// Uses a lambda expression
IntFunction<int[]> arrayCreator1 = size -> new int[size];
int[] empIds1 = arrayCreator1.apply(5);
```

```
// <- Creates an int array of five elements
// Uses an array constructor reference
IntFunction<int[]> arrayCreator2 = int[]::new;
int[] empIds2 = arrayCreator2.apply(5);
// <- Creates an int array of five elements
```

You can also use a Function<Integer,R> type to use an array constructor reference, where R is the array type:

```
// Uses an array constructor reference
Function<Integer,int[]> arrayCreator3 = int[]::new;
int[] empIds3 = arrayCreator3.apply(5);
// <- Creates an int array of five elements
```

The syntax for the constructor reference for arrays supports creating an array of multiple dimensions. However, you can specify the length for only the first dimension. The following statement creates a two-dimensional int array with the first dimension having the length of 5:

```
// Uses an array constructor reference
IntFunction<int[][]> TwoDimArrayCreator = int[][]::new;
int[][] matrix = TwoDimArrayCreator.apply(5);
// <- Creates an int[5][] array
```

You might be tempted to use a BiFunction<Integer,Integer,int[][]> to use a constructor reference for a two-dimensional array to supply the length for both dimensions. However, the syntax is not supported. Array constructors are supposed to accept only one parameter—the length of the first dimension. The following statement generates a compile-time error:

```
BiFunction<Integer,Integer,int[][]> arrayCreator =
    int[][]::new;
```

Generic Method References

Typically, the compiler figures out the actual type for generic type parameters when a method reference refers to a generic method. Consider the following generic method in the java.util.Arrays class:

```
static <T> List<T> asList(T... a)
```

The asList() method takes a varargs argument of type T and returns a List<T>. You can use Arrays::asList as a method reference. The syntax for the method reference allows you to specify the actual type parameter for the method just after the two consecutive colons. For example, if you are passing String objects to the asList() method, its method reference can be written as Arrays::<String>asList.

Note   The syntax for a method reference also supports specifying the actual type parameters for generic types. The actual type parameters are specified just before the two consecutive colons. For example, the constructor reference ArrayList<Long>::new specifies Long as the actual type parameter for the generic ArrayList<T> class.

The following snippet of code contains an example of specifying the actual type parameter for the generic method Arrays.asList(). In the code, Arrays::asList will work the same, as the compiler will infer String as the type parameter for the asList() method by examining the target type:

```
import java.util.Arrays;
import java.util.List;
import java.util.function.Function;
...
Function<String[],List<String>> asList =
    Arrays::<String>asList;
String[] namesArray = {"Jim", "Ken", "Li"};
List<String> namesList = asList.apply(namesArray);
for(String name : namesList) {
    System.out.println(name);
}

Jim
Ken
Li
```

Lexical Scoping

A scope is the part of a Java program within which a name can be used without a qualifier. Classes and methods define their own scope. Scopes may be nested. For example, a method scope does not exist independently, as a method is always part of another construct, for example, a class; an inner class appears inside the scope of another class; a local and an anonymous class appear inside the scope of a method.

Even though a lambda expression looks like a method declaration, it does not define a scope of its own. It exists in its enclosing scope. This is known as lexical scoping for lambda expressions. For example, when a lambda expression is used inside a method, the lambda expression exists in the scope of the method.

The meanings of the keywords this and super are the same inside the lambda expression and its enclosing method. Note that this is different from the meanings of these keywords inside a local and anonymous inner class in which the keyword this refers to the current instance of the local and anonymous inner class, not its enclosing class.

Listing 4-19 contains code for a functional interface named Printer that you will use to print messages in the examples in this section.

Listing 4-19. A Printer Functional Interface

```
// Printer.java
package com.jdojo.lambda;
@FunctionalInterface
public interface Printer {
    void print(String msg);
}
```

The program in Listing 4-20 creates two instances of the Printer interface: one using a lambda expression in the getLambdaPrinter() method and one using an anonymous inner class in the getAnonymousPrinter() method. Both instances use the keyword this inside the print() method. Both methods print the class name that the keyword this refers to. The output shows that the keyword this has the same meaning inside the getLambdaPrinter() method and the lambda expression. However, the keyword this has different meanings inside the getAnonymousPrinter() method and the anonymous class.

239

Listing 4-20. Testing Scope of a Lambda Expression and an Anonymous Class

```java
// ScopeTest.java
package com.jdojo.lambda;
public class ScopeTest {
    public static void main(String[] args) {
        ScopeTest test = new ScopeTest();
        Printer lambdaPrinter = test.getLambdaPrinter();
        lambdaPrinter.print("Lambda Expressions");
        Printer anonymousPrinter = test.
          getAnonymousPrinter();
        anonymousPrinter.print("Anonymous Class");
    }
    public Printer getLambdaPrinter() {
        System.out.println("getLambdaPrinter(): " +
          this.getClass());
        // Uses a lambda expression
        Printer printer = msg -> {
            // Here, this refers to the current object
            // of the ScopeTest class
            System.out.println(msg + ": " +
              this.getClass());
        };
        return printer;
    }
    public Printer getAnonymousPrinter() {
        System.out.println("getAnonymousPrinter(): " +
          this.getClass());
        // Uses an anonymous class
        Printer printer = new Printer() {
            @Override
            public void print(String msg) {
                // Here, this refers to the current
                // object of the anonymous class
```

```
                System.out.println(msg + ": " +
                    this.getClass());
            }
        };
        return printer;
    }
}
```

```
getLambdaPrinter(): class com.jdojo.lambda.ScopeTest
Lambda Expressions: class com.jdojo.lambda.ScopeTest
getAnonymousPrinter(): class com.jdojo.lambda.ScopeTest
Anonymous Class: class com.jdojo.lambda.ScopeTest\$1
```

Lexical scoping of a lambda expression means that variables declared in the lambda expression, including its parameters, exist in the enclosing scope. Simple names in a scope must be unique. It means that a lambda expression cannot redefine variables with the name that already exists in the enclosing scope.

The following code for a lambda expression inside the main() method generates a compile-time error, as its parameter name msg is already defined in the main() method's scope:

```
public class Test {
    public static void main(String[] args) {
        String msg = "Hello";
        // A compile-time error. The msg variable is
        // already defined and the lambda parameter is
        // attempting to redefine it.
        Printer printer = msg -> System.out.println(msg);
    }
}
```

The following code generates a compile-time error for the same reason that the local variable named msg is in scope inside the body of the lambda expression, and the lambda expression is attempting to declare a local variable with the same name msg:

```java
public class Test {
    public static void main(String[] args) {
        String msg = "Hello";
        Printer printer = msg1 -> {
            String msg = "Hi"; // A compile-time error
            System.out.println(msg1);
        };
    }
}
```

Variable Capture

Like a local and anonymous inner class, a lambda expression can access effectively final local variables. A local variable is effectively final in the following two cases:

- It is declared `final`.

- It is not declared `final`, but initialized only once.

In the following snippet of code, the `msg` variable is effectively final, as it has been declared `final`. The lambda expression accesses the variable inside its body:

```java
public Printer test() {
    final String msg = "Hello"; // msg is effectively final
    Printer printer = msg1 -> System.out.println(msg +
        " " + msg1);
    return printer;
}
```

In the following snippet of code, the `msg` variable is effectively final, as it is initialized once. The lambda expression accesses the variables inside its body:

```java
public Printer test() {
    String msg = "Hello"; // msg is effectively final
    Printer printer = msg1 ->
        System.out.println(msg + " " + msg1);
    return printer;
}
```

The following snippet of code is a slight variation of the previous example. The `msg` variable is effectively final, as it has been initialized only once:

```
public Printer test() {
    String msg;
    msg = "Hello"; // msg is effectively final
    Printer printer = msg1 ->
        System.out.println(msg + " " + msg1);
    return printer;
}
```

In the following snippet of code, the `msg` variable is not effectively final, as it is assigned a value twice. The lambda expression is accessing the `msg` variable that generates a compile-time error:

```
public Printer test() {
    // msg is not effectively final as it is changed later
    String msg = "Hello";
    // A compile-time error
    Printer printer = msg1 ->
        System.out.println(msg + " " + msg1);
    msg = "Hi";
    // <- msg is changed making it effectively non-final
    return printer;
}
```

The following snippet of code generates a compile-time error because the lambda expression accesses the `msg` variable that is declared lexically after its use. In Java, forward referencing of variable names in a method's scope is not allowed. Note that the `msg` variable is effectively final.

```
public Printer test() {
    // A compile-time error. The msg variable is not
    // declared yet.
    Printer printer = msg1 ->
        System.out.println(msg + " " + msg1);
    String msg = "Hello";  // msg is effectively final
    return printer;
}
```

Can you guess why the following snippet of code generates a compile-time error?

```
public Printer test() {
    String msg = "Hello";
    Printer printer = msg1 ->  {
        msg = "Hi " + msg1; // A compile-time error.
                            // Attempting to modify msg.
        System.out.println(msg);
    };
    return printer;
}
```

The lambda expression accesses the local variable msg. Any local variable accessed inside a lambda expression must be effectively final. The lambda expression attempts to modify the msg variable inside its body, and that causes the compile-time error.

Note   A lambda expression can access instance and class variables of a class whether they are effectively final or not. If instance and class variables are not final, they can be modified inside the body of the lambda expressions. A lambda expression keeps a copy of the local variables used in its body. If the local variables are reference variables, a copy of the references is kept, not a copy of the objects.

The program in Listing 4-21 demonstrates how to access the local and instance variables inside lambda expressions.

Listing 4-21. Accessing Local and Instance Variables Inside Lambda Expressions

```
// VariableCapture.java
package com.jdojo.lambda;
public class VariableCapture {
    private int counter = 0;
    public static void main(String[] args) {
        VariableCapture vc1 = new VariableCapture();
        VariableCapture vc2 = new VariableCapture();
        // Create lambdas
        Printer p1 = vc1.createLambda(1);
        Printer p2 = vc2.createLambda(100);
```

```
        // Execute the lambda bodies
        p1.print("Lambda #1");
        p2.print("Lambda #2");
        p1.print("Lambda #1");
        p2.print("Lambda #2");
        p1.print("Lambda #1");
        p2.print("Lambda #2");
    }
    public Printer createLambda(int incrementBy) {
        Printer printer = msg -> {
            // Accesses instance and local variables
            counter += incrementBy;
            System.out.println(msg + ": counter = " +
                counter);
        };
        return printer;
    }
}

Lambda #1: counter = 1
Lambda #2: counter = 100
Lambda #1: counter = 2
Lambda #2: counter = 200
Lambda #1: counter = 3
Lambda #2: counter = 300
```

The createLambda() method uses a lambda expression to create an instance of the Printer functional interface. The lambda expression uses the method's parameter incrementBy. Inside the body, it increments the instance variable counter and prints its value. The main() method creates two instances of the VariableCapture class and calls the createLambda() method on those instances by passing 1 and 100 as incrementBy values. The print() methods of the Printer objects are called three times for both instances. The output shows that the lambda expression captures the incrementBy value and increments the counter instance variable every time it is called.

Jumps and Exits

Statements such as break, continue, return, and throw are allowed inside the body of a lambda expression. These statements indicate jumps inside a method and exits from a method. Inside a lambda expression, they indicate jumps inside the body of the lambda expression and exits from the body of the lambda expressions. They indicate local jumps and exits in the lambda expressions. Non-local jumps and exits in lambda expressions are not allowed. The program in Listing 4-22 demonstrates the valid use of the break and continue statements inside the body of a lambda expression.

Listing 4-22. Using break and continue Statements Inside the Body of a Lambda Expression

```java
// LambdaJumps.java
package com.jdojo.lambda;
import java.util.function.Consumer;
public class LambdaJumps {
    public static void main(String[] args) {
        Consumer<int[]> printer = ids -> {
            int printedCount = 0;
            for (int id : ids) {
                if (id % 2 != 0) {
                    continue;
                }
                System.out.println(id);
                printedCount++;
                // Break out of the loop after printing 3
                // ids
                if (printedCount == 3) {
                    break;
                }
            }
        };
        // Print an array of 8 integers
        printer.accept(new int[]{1, 2, 3, 4, 5, 6, 7, 8});
    }
}
```

2

4

6

In the following snippet of code, the break statement is inside a for loop statement, and it is also inside the body of a lambda statement. If this break statement is allowed, it will jump out of the body of the lambda expression. This is the reason that the code generates a compile-time error:

```
public void test() {
    for(int i = 0; i < 5; i++) {
        Consumer<Integer> evenIdPrinter = id -> {
            if (id < 0) {
                // A compile-time error. Attempting to
                // break out of the lambda body
                break;
            }
        };
    }
}
```

Recursive Lambda Expressions

Sometimes, a function may invoke itself from its body. Such a function is called a recursive function. A lambda expression represents a function. However, a lambda expression does not support recursive invocations. If you need a recursive function, you need to use a method reference or an anonymous inner class.

The program in Listing 4-23 shows how to use a method reference when a recursive lambda expression is needed. It defines a recursive method called factorial() that computes the factorial of an integer. In the main() method, it uses the method reference RecursiveTest::factorial in place of a lambda expression.

Listing 4-23. Using a Method Reference When a Recursive Lambda Expression Is Needed

```java
// RecursiveTest.java
package com.jdojo.lambda;
import java.util.function.IntFunction;
public class RecursiveTest {
    public static void main(String[] args) {
        IntFunction<Long> factorialCalc =
          RecursiveTest::factorial;
        int n = 5;
        long fact = factorialCalc.apply(n);
        System.out.println("Factorial of " + n +
          " is " + fact);
    }
    public static long factorial(int n) {
        if (n < 0) {
            String msg = "Number must not be negative.";
            throw new IllegalArgumentException(msg);
        }
        if (n == 0) {
            return 1;
        } else {
            return n * factorial(n - 1);
        }
    }
}
```

```
factorial of 5 is 120
```

You can achieve the same results using an anonymous inner class as shown:

```java
IntFunction<Long> factorialCalc = new IntFunction<Long>() {
    @Override
    public Long apply(int n) {
        if (n < 0) {
            String msg = "Number must not be negative.";
```

```
            throw new IllegalArgumentException(msg);
        }
        if (n == 0) {
            return 1L;
        } else {
            return n * this.apply(n - 1);
        }
    }
};
```

Comparing Objects

The Comparator interface is a functional interface with the following declaration:

```
package java.util;
@FunctionalInterface
public interface Comparator<T> {
    int compare(T o1, T o2);
    /* Other methods are not shown. */
}
```

The Comparator<T> interface contains many default and static methods that can be used along with lambda expressions to create its instances. It is worth exploring the API documentation for the interface. In this section, I discuss the following two methods of the Comparator interface:

- static <T,U extends Comparable<? super U» Comparator<T>
  comparing(Function<? super T,? extends U> keyExtractor)

- default <U extends Comparable<? super U» Comparator<T>
  thenComparing(Function<? super T,? extends U> keyExtractor)

The comparing() method takes a Function and returns a Comparator. The Function should return a Comparable that is used to compare two objects. You can create a Comparator object to compare Person objects based on their first names, as shown:

```
Comparator<Person> firstNameComp =
    Comparator.comparing(Person::getFirstName);
```

The thenComparing() method is a default method. It is used to specify a secondary comparison if two objects are the same in sorting order based on the primary comparison. The following statement creates a Comparator<Person> that sorts Person objects based on their last names, first names, and DOBs:

```
Comparator<Person> lastFirstDobComp =
    Comparator.comparing(Person::getLastName)
            .thenComparing(Person::getFirstName)
            .thenComparing(Person::getDob);
```

The program in Listing 4-24 shows how to use the method references to create a Comparator object to sort Person objects. It uses the sort() default method of the List interface to sort the list of persons. The sort() method takes a Comparator as an argument. Thanks to lambda expressions and default methods in interfaces for making the sorting task so easy!

Listing 4-24. Sorting a List of Person Objects

```
/ ComparingObjects.java
package com.jdojo.lambda;
import java.util.Comparator;
import java.util.List;
public class ComparingObjects {
    public static void main(String[] args) {
        List<Person> persons = Person.getPersons();
        // Sort using the first name
        persons.sort(Comparator.comparing(
            Person::getFirstName));
        // Print the sorted list
        System.out.println("Sorted by the first name:");
        FunctionUtil.forEach(persons, System.out::println);
        // Sort using the last name, first name, and then
        // DOB
        persons.sort(Comparator.comparing(
            Person::getLastName)
                    .thenComparing(Person::getFirstName)
                    .thenComparing(Person::getDob));
```

```
    // Print the sorted list
    System.out.println("\nSorted by the last name, " +
        "first name, and dob:");
    FunctionUtil.forEach(persons, System.out::println);
  }
}
```

```
Sorted by the first name:
Donna Jacobs, FEMALE, 1970-09-12
John Jacobs, MALE, 1975-01-20
Wally Inman, MALE, 1965-09-12
Sorted by the last name, first name, and dob:
Wally Inman, MALE, 1965-09-12
Donna Jacobs, FEMALE, 1970-09-12
John Jacobs, MALE, 1975-01-20
```

Summary

A lambda expression is an unnamed block of code (or an unnamed function) with a list of formal parameters and a body. A lambda expression provides a concise way, as compared to anonymous inner classes, to create instances of functional interfaces. Lambda expressions and default methods in interfaces have given new life to the Java programming languages as far as expressiveness and fluency in Java programming go. The Java collection library has benefited the most from lambda expressions.

The syntax for defining lambda expressions is similar to declaring a method. A lambda expression may have a list of formal parameters and a body. A lambda expression is evaluated to an instance of a functional interface. The body of the lambda expression is not executed when the expression is evaluated. The body of the lambda expression is executed when the method of the functional interface is invoked.

One of the design goals of lambda expressions was to keep it concise and readable. The lambda expression syntax supports shorthand for common use cases. Method references are shorthand to specify lambda expressions that use existing methods.

A poly expression is an expression whose type depends on the context of its use. A lambda expression is always a poly expression. A lambda expression cannot be used by itself. Its type is inferred by the compiler from the context. A lambda expression can be used in assignments, method invocations, returns, and casts.

When a lambda expression occurs inside a method, it is lexically scoped. That is, a lambda expression does not define a scope of its own; rather, it occurs in the method's scope. A lambda expression may use the effectively final local variables of a method. A lambda expression may use the statements such as `break`, `continue`, `return`, and `throw`. The `break` and `continue` statements specify local jumps inside the body of the lambda expression. Attempting to jump outside the body of the lambda expression generates a compile-time error. The `return` and `throw` statements exit the body of the lambda expression.

Exercises

Exercise 1

What are lambda expressions and how are they related to functional interfaces?

Exercise 2

How does a lambda expression differ from an anonymous class? Can you always replace a lambda expression with an anonymous class and vice versa?

Exercise 3

Are the following two lambda expressions different?

```
a. (int x, int y) -> { return x + y; }
b. (int x, int y) -> x + y
```

Exercise 4

If someone shows you the following lambda expressions, explain the possible functions they may represent:

```
a. (int x, int y) -> x + y \\
b. (x, y) -> x + y \\
c. (String msg) -> { System.out.println(msg); }\\
d. () -> {}
```

Exercise 5

What kind of function the following lambda expression may represent?

```
x -> x;
```

Exercise 6

Will the following declaration of a MathUtil interface compile? Explain your answer.

```
@FunctionalInterface
public interface Operations {
    int factorial(int n);
    int abs(int n);
}
```

Exercise 7

Will the following statement compile? Explain your answer.

```
Object obj = x -> x + 1;
```

Exercise 8

Will the following statements compile? Explain your answer.

```
Function<Integer,Integer> f = x -> x + 1;
Object obj = f;
```

Exercise 9

What will be the output when you run the following Scope class?

```
// Scope.java
package com.jdojo.lambda.exercises;
import java.util.function.Function;
public class Scope {
    private static long n = 100;
    private static Function<Long,Long> f = n -> n + 1;
    public static void main(String[] args) {
        System.out.println(n);
        System.out.println(f.apply(n));
        System.out.println(n);
    }
}
```

Exercise 10

Why does the following method declaration not compile?

```
public static void test() {
    int n = 100;
    Function<Integer,Integer> f = n -> n + 1;
    System.out.println(f.apply(100));
}
```

Exercise 11

What will be the output when the following Capture class is run?

```
// Capture.java
package com.jdojo.lambda.exercises;
import java.util.function.Function;
public class Capture {
    public static void main(String[] args) {
        test();
        test();
    }
    public static void test() {
        int n = 100;
        Function<Integer,Integer> f = x -> n + 1;
        System.out.println(f.apply(100));
    }
}
```

Exercise 12

Assume that there is a Person class, which contains four constructors. One of the constructors is a no-args constructor. Given a constructor reference, Person::new, can you tell which constructor of the Person it refers to?

Exercise 13

Will the following declaration of the FeelingLucky interface compile? Notice that it has been annotated with @FunctionalInterface.

```
@FunctionalInterface
public interface FeelingLucky {
    void gamble();
```

```
    public static void hitJackpot() {
        System.out.println("You have won 80M dollars.");
    }
}
```

Exercise 14

Why does the following declaration of the Mystery interface not compile?

```
@FunctionalInterface
public interface Mystery {
    @Override
    String toString();
}
```

Exercise 15

What will be the output when the following PredicateTest class is run?

```
// PredicateTest.java
package com.jdojo.lambda.exercises;
import java.util.function.Predicate;
public class PredicateTest {
    public static void main(String[] args) {
        int[] nums = {1, 2, 3, 4, 5};
        filterThenPrint(nums, n -> n%2 == 0);
        filterThenPrint(nums, n -> n%2 == 1);
    }
    static void filterThenPrint(int[] nums,
            Predicate<Integer> p) {
        for(int x : nums) {
            if(p.test(x)) {
                System.out.println(x);
            }
        }
    }
}
```

Exercise 16

What will be the output when the following SupplierTest class is run? Explain your answer.

```java
/ SupplierTest.java
package com.jdojo.lambda.exercises;
import java.util.function.Supplier;
public class SupplierTest {
    public static void main(String[] args) {
        Supplier<Integer> supplier = () -> {
            int counter = 0;
            return ++counter;
        };
        System.out.println(supplier.get());
        System.out.println(supplier.get());
    }
}
```

Exercise 17

What will be the output when the following ConsumerTest class is run?

```java
// ConsumerTest.java
package com.jdojo.lambda.exercises;
import java.util.function.Consumer;
public class ConsumerTest {
    public static void main(String[] args) {
        Consumer<String> c1 = System.out::println;
        Consumer<String> c2 = s -> {};
        consume(c1, "Hello");
        consume(c2, "Hello");
    }
    static <T> void consume(Consumer<T> consumer,
            T item) {
        consumer.accept(item);
    }
}
```

CHAPTER 5

Threads

In this chapter, you will learn:

- What threads are

- How to create threads in Java

- How to execute your code in separate threads

- What the Java Memory Model is

- The lifecycle of threads

- How to use object monitors to synchronize access to a critical section by threads

- How to interrupt, stop, suspend, and resume threads

- Atomic variables, explicit locks, synchronizer, executor framework, fork/join framework, and thread-local variables

All example programs in this chapter are members of a `jdojo.threads` module, as declared in Listing 5-1.

Listing 5-1. The Declaration of a `jdojo.threads` Module

```
// module-info.java
module jdojo.threads {
    exports com.jdojo.threads;
}
```

What Is a Thread?

Threads are a vast topic. They deserve an entire book. This chapter does not discuss the concept of threads in detail. Rather, it discusses how to work with threads using Java

© Kishori Sharan, Peter Späth 2021
K. Sharan and P. Späth, *More Java 17*, https://doi.org/10.1007/978-1-4842-7135-3_5

constructs. Before I define the term thread, it is necessary to understand the meaning of some related terms, such as program, process, multitasking, sequential programming, concurrent programming, etc.

A program is an algorithm expressed in a programming language. A process is a running instance of a program with all system resources allocated by the operating system to that instance of the program. Typically, a process consists of a unique identifier, a program counter, executable code, an address space, open handles to system resources, a security context, and many other things. A program counter, also called an instruction pointer, is a value maintained in the CPU register that keeps track of the instruction being executed by the CPU. It is automatically incremented at the end of the execution of an instruction. You can also think of a process as a unit of activity (or a unit of work, or a unit of execution, or a path of execution) within an operating system. The concept of process allows one computer system to support multiple units of executions.

Multitasking is the ability of an operating system to execute multiple tasks (or processes) at once. On a single CPU machine, multitasking is not possible in a true sense because one CPU can execute instructions for only one process at a time. In such a case, the operating system achieves multitasking by dividing the single CPU's time among all running processes and switching between processes quickly enough to give an impression that all processes are running simultaneously. The switching of the CPU among processes is called a context switch. In a context switch, the running process is stopped, its state is saved, the state of the process that is going to get the CPU is restored, and the new process is run. It is necessary to save the state of the running process before the CPU is allocated to another process, so when this process gets the CPU again, it can start its execution from the same point where it left. Typically, the state of a process consists of a program counter, register values used by the process, and any other pieces of information that are necessary to restore the process later. An operating system stores a process state in a data structure, which is called a process control block or a switchframe. A context switch is rather an expensive task.

There are two types of multitasking: cooperative and preemptive. In cooperative multitasking, the running process decides when to release the CPU so that other processes can use the CPU. In preemptive multitasking, the operating system allocates a time slice to each process. Once a process has used up its time slice, it is preempted, and the operating system assigns the CPU to another process. In cooperative multitasking, a process may monopolize the CPU for a long time, and other processes may not get a chance to run. In preemptive multitasking, the operating system makes sure all processes get CPU time. UNIX, OS/2, and Windows (except Windows 3.x) use preemptive multitasking. Windows 3.x used cooperative multitasking.

Multiprocessing is the ability of a computer to use more than one processor simultaneously. Parallel processing is the ability of a system to simultaneously execute the same task on multiple processors. You may note that, for parallel processing, the task must be split up into subtasks, so that the subtasks can be executed on multiple processors simultaneously. Let's consider a program that consists of six instructions:

```
Instruction-1
Instruction-2
Instruction-3
Instruction-4
Instruction-5
Instruction-6
```

To execute this program completely, the CPU has to execute all six instructions. Suppose the first three instructions depend on each other. Assume that Instruction-2 uses the result of Instruction-1; Instruction-3 uses the result of Instruction-2. Assume that the last three instructions also depend on each other the same way the first three depend on each other. Suppose the first three and the last three instructions, as two groups, do not depend on each other. How would you like to execute these six instructions to get the best result? One of the ways to execute them is sequentially as they appear in the program. This gives you one sequence of execution in your program. Another way of executing them is to have two sequences of executions. One sequence of execution will execute Instruction-1, Instruction-2, and Instruction-3, and at the same time, another sequence of execution will execute Instruction-4, Instruction-5, and Instruction-6. The phrases "unit of execution" and "sequence of execution" mean the same; I use them interchangeably. These two scenarios are depicted in Figure 5-1.

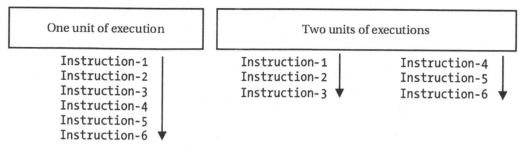

Figure 5-1. *Dividing a program into multiple units of execution*

Note that a process is also a unit of execution. Therefore, the two sets of instructions can be run as two processes to achieve concurrency in their execution. So far, we have assumed that the two sets of instructions are independent of each other. Suppose this assumption still holds true. What if the two sets of instructions access a shared memory; or, when both sets of instructions finish running, you need to combine the results from both to compute the final result? Processes are generally not allowed to access another process's address space. They must communicate using interprocess communication facilities such as sockets, pipes, etc. The very nature of a process—that it runs independent of other processes—may pose problems when multiple processes need to communicate or share resources. All modern operating systems let you solve this problem by allowing you to create multiple units of execution within a process, where all units of execution can share address space and resources allocated to the process. Each unit of execution within a process is called a thread.

Every process has at least one thread. A process can create multiple threads, if needed. The resources available to the operating system and its implementation determine the maximum number of threads a process can create. All threads within a process share all resources including the address space; they can also communicate with each other easily because they operate within the same process and they share the same memory. Each thread within a process operates independent of the other threads within the same process.

A thread maintains two things: a program counter and a stack. The program counter lets a thread keep track of the instruction that it is currently executing. It is necessary to maintain a separate program counter for each thread because each thread within a process may be executing different instructions at the same time. Each thread maintains its own stack to store the values of the local variables. A thread can also maintain its private memory, which cannot be shared with other threads, even if they are in the same process. The private memory maintained by a thread is called thread-local storage (TLS). Figure 5-2 depicts threads represented within a process.

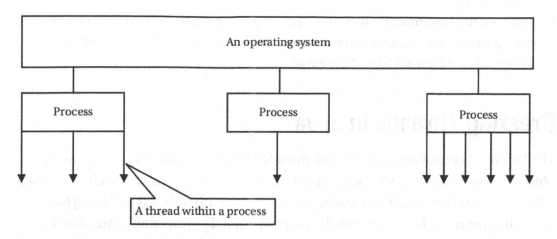

Figure 5-2. *Processes and threads*

In all modern operating systems, threads are scheduled on the CPU for execution, not the processes. Therefore, the CPU context switch occurs between the threads. The context switch between threads is less expensive compared to the context switch between processes. Because of the ease of communication, sharing resources among threads within a process, and a cheaper context switch, it is preferred to split a program into multiple threads, rather than multiple processes. Sometimes, a thread is also called a lightweight process. The program with six instructions as discussed previously can also be split into two threads within a process, as depicted in Figure 5-3. On a multiprocessor machine, multiple threads of a process may be scheduled on different processors, thus providing true concurrent executions of a program. A program that uses multiple threads is called a multi-threaded program.

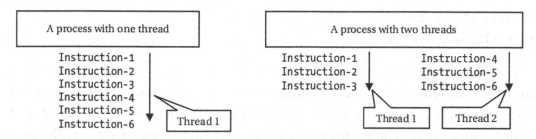

Figure 5-3. *Dividing the program logic to use two threads within a process*

You can think of the relationship between a process and threads as `Process = address space + resources + threads` where threads are units of execution within the process; they maintain their own unique program counter and stack; they share the process address space and resources; they are scheduled on a CPU independently and may execute on different CPUs, if available.

Creating Threads in Java

The Java API makes it easy to work with threads. It lets you represent a thread as an object. An object of the `java.lang.Thread` class represents a thread. Creating and using a thread in Java is as simple as creating an object of the `Thread` class and using that object in a program. Let's start with the simplest example of creating a thread in Java. There are at least two steps involved in working with a thread:

- Creating an object of the `Thread` class

- Invoking the `start()` method of the `Thread` class to start the thread

Creating an object of the `Thread` class is the same as creating an object of any other classes in Java. In its simplest form, you can use the no-args constructor of the `Thread` class to create a `Thread` object:

```
// Creates a thread object
Thread simplestThread = new Thread();
```

Creating an object of the `Thread` class allocates memory for that object on the heap. It does not start or run the thread. You must call the `start()` method of the `Thread` object to start the thread:

```
// Starts the thread
simplestThread.start();
```

The `start()` method returns after doing some housekeeping work. It puts the thread in the runnable state. In this state, the thread is ready to receive the CPU time. Note that invoking the `start()` method of a `Thread` object does not guarantee "when" this thread will start getting the CPU time. That is, it does not guarantee when the thread will start running. It just schedules the thread to receive the CPU time.

Let's write a simple Java program with these two statements, as shown in Listing 5-2. The program will not do anything useful. However, it will get you started using threads.

Listing 5-2. The Simplest Thread in Java

```
// SimplestThread.java
package com.jdojo.threads;
public class SimplestThread {
    public static void main(String[] args) {
        // Creates a thread object
        Thread simplestThread = new Thread();
        // Starts the thread
        simplestThread.start();
    }
}
```

When you run the SimplestThread class, you do not see any output. The program will start and finish silently. Even though you did not see any output, here are a few things the JVM did when the two statements in the main() method were executed:

- When the second statement, simplestThread.start(), is executed, the JVM scheduled this thread for execution.

- At some point in time, this thread got the CPU time and started executing. What code does a thread in Java start executing when it gets the CPU time?

- A thread in Java always starts its execution in a run() method. You can define the run() method to be executed by a thread when you create an object of the Thread class. In your case, you created an object of the Thread class using its no-args constructor. When you use the no-args constructor of the Thread class to create its object (as in new Thread()), the run() method of the Thread class is called when the thread starts its execution. The following sections in this chapter explain how to define your own run() method for a thread.

- The run() method of the Thread class checks how the object of the Thread class was created. If the thread object was created using the no-args constructor of the Thread class, it does not do anything and immediately returns. Therefore, in your program, when the thread got the CPU time, it called the run() method of the Thread class, which did not execute any meaningful code, and returned.

- When the CPU finishes executing the run() method, the thread is dead, which means the thread will not get the CPU time again.

Figure 5-4 depicts how the simplest thread example works.

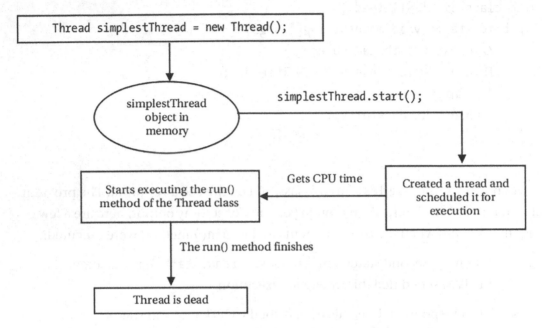

Figure 5-4. *The simplest thread execution*

There are two important points to add to the current discussion:

- When a thread is dead, it does not mean the thread object is garbage collected. Note that a thread is a unit of execution. "A thread is dead" means that the unit of execution that the thread represented has finished its work. However, the thread object representing the unit of execution still exists in memory. After the thread is dead, the object will be garbage collected based on the same garbage collection rules that are used for any other Java objects. Some restrictions exist that dictate the methods you can call on a dead thread. For example, you cannot call its start() method again. That is, a thread object can be started only once. However, you can still check if the thread is dead by calling the isAlive() method of the thread object.

- The thread does not get the CPU time in one go to execute the run() method. The operating system decides on the amount of time to allocate and when to allocate that time to the thread. This means that the multiple context switches may occur before the thread finishes executing the run() method.

Specifying Your Code for a Thread

There are three ways you can specify your code to be executed by a thread:

- By inheriting your class from the Thread class

- By implementing the Runnable interface in your class

- By using the method reference to a method that takes no parameters and returns void

---

Note   Inheriting your class from the Thread class may not be possible if your class already inherits from another class. In that case, you need to use the second method. You can use the third method from Java 8. Before Java 8, it was common to use an anonymous class to define a thread object where the anonymous class would either inherit from the Thread class or implement the Runnable interface.

Inheriting Your Class from the **Thread** Class

When you inherit your class from the Thread class, you should override the run() method and provide the code to be executed by the thread:

```
public class MyThreadClass extends Thread {
    @Override
    public void run() {
        System.out.println("Hello Java threads!");
    }
    // More code goes here
}
```

The steps to create a thread object and start the thread are the same:

```
MyThreadClass myThread = new MyThreadClass();
myThread.start();
```

The thread will execute the run() method of the MyThreadClass class.

Implementing the **Runnable** Interface

You can create a class that implements the java.lang.Runnable interface. Runnable is a functional interface, and it is declared in the java.lang package as follows:

```
@FunctionalInterface
public interface Runnable {
    void run();
}
```

A simple example implementation of Runnable would read

```
public class HelloRunnable implements Runnable {
    @Override
    public void run() {
        System.out.println("Hello Java threads!");
    }
}
```

```
// Creating an instance:
Runnable aRunnableObject = new HelloRunnable();
```

Instead, you can also use a lambda expression to create an instance of the Runnable interface:

```
Runnable aRunnableObject = () ->
    System.out.println("Hello Java threads!");
```

Create an object of the Thread class using the constructor that accepts a Runnable object:

```
Thread myThread = new Thread(aRunnableObject);
```

Start the thread by calling the start() method of the thread object:

```
myThread.start();
```

The thread will execute the code contained in the body of the lambda expression.

Using a Method Reference

To even further increase conciseness, you can use the method reference of a method (static or instance) that takes no parameters and returns void as the code to be executed by a thread. The following code declares a ThreadTest class that contains an execute() method. The method contains the code to be executed in a thread:

```
public class ThreadTest {
    public static void execute() {
        System.out.println("Hello Java threads!");
    }
}
```

The following snippet of code uses the method reference of the execute() method of the ThreadTest class to create a Runnable object:

```
Thread myThread = new Thread(ThreadTest::execute);
myThread.start();
```

The thread will execute the code contained in the execute() method of the ThreadTest class.

A Quick Example

Let's look at a simple example to print integers from 1 to 500 in a new thread. Listing 5-3 contains the code for the PrinterThread class that performs this task. When the class is run, it prints integers from 1 to 500 on the standard output.

Listing 5-3. Printing Integers from 1 to 500 in a New Thread

```
// PrinterThread.java
package com.jdojo.threads;
```

```
public class PrinterThread {
    public static void main(String[] args) {
        // Create a Thread object
        Thread t = new Thread(PrinterThread::print);
        // Start the thread
        t.start();
    }
    public static void print() {
        for (int i = 1; i <= 500; i++) {
            System.out.print(i + " ");
        }
    }
}
```

1 2 3 4 5 6 7 8 9 10 11 12 13 14 ... 497 498 499 500

I used a method reference to create the thread object in the example. You can use any of the other ways discussed earlier to create a thread object.

Using Multiple Threads in a Program

Using multiple threads in a Java program is as simple as creating multiple Thread objects and calling their start() method. Java does not have any upper limit on the number of threads that can be used in a program. It is limited by the operating system and the memory available to the program. Listing 5-4 uses two threads. Both threads print integers from 1 to 500. The code prints a new line after each integer. However, the output shows a space after each integer to keep the output short. Only partial output is shown.

Listing 5-4. Running Multiple Threads in a Program

```
// MultiPrinterThread.java
package com.jdojo.threads;
public class MultiPrinterThread {
    public static void main(String[] args) {
        // Create two Thread objects
        Thread t1 = new Thread(MultiPrinterThread::print);
        Thread t2 = new Thread(MultiPrinterThread::print);
```

```
    // Start both threads
    t1.start();
    t2.start();
  }
  public static void print() {
    for (int i = 1; i <= 500; i++) {
      System.out.println(i);
    }
  }
}
}
```

```
1   2   3   4   5   1   2   3   4   5   6   7   8   9   10   11   12   13
14   15   16   17   18   19   20   21   22   23   24   25   26   6   7
27   28   8   9   10   11   12   29   30   31   13   14   32   15   16
17   ...   496   497   498   499   500   424   425   ...   492   493
494   495   496   497   498   499   500
```

You will find some interesting things in the output. Every time you run this program, you may get different output. However, the nature of the output on your computer can be compared to the output shown here. On a very fast machine, the output may print 1 to 500 and 1 to 500. However, let's focus on the discussion assuming that your output is like the one shown.

The program created two threads. Each thread prints integers from 1 to 500. It starts the thread t1 first and the thread t2 second. You might expect that the thread t1 will start first to print integers from 1 to 500, and then the thread t2 will start to print integers from 1 to 500. However, it is obvious from the output that the program did not run the way you might have expected.

The start() method of the Thread class returns immediately. That is, when you call the start() method of a thread, the JVM takes note of your instruction to start the thread. However, it does not start the thread right away. It has to do some housekeeping before it can really start a thread. When a thread starts, it is up to the operating system to decide when and how much CPU time it will give to that thread. Therefore, as soon as the t1.start() and t2.start() methods return, your program enters the indeterminate realm. That is, both threads will start running; however, you do not know when they will start running and in what sequence they will run to execute their code. When you start multiple threads, you do not even know which thread will start running first. Looking at the output, you can observe that one of the threads started, and it got enough CPU time

269

to print integers from 1 to 5 before it was preempted. Another thread got CPU time to print from 1 to 26 before it was preempted. The second time, the first thread (the thread that started printing integers first) got the CPU time, and it printed only two integers, 6 and 7, and so on. You can see that both threads got CPU time. However, the amount of CPU time and the sequence in which they got the CPU time are unpredictable. Each time you run this program, you may get different output. The only guarantee that you get from this program is that all integers between 1 and 500 will be printed twice in some order.

Issues in Using Multiple Threads

Some issues are involved when you use multiple threads in a program. You need to consider these issues only if multiple threads have to coordinate based on some conditions or some shared resources.

In the previous sections, the examples involving threads were trivial. They simply printed some integers on the standard output. Let's look at a different kind of example that uses multiple threads, which access and modify the value of a variable. Listing 5-5 shows the code for the BalanceUpdate class.

Listing 5-5. Multiple Threads Modifying the Same Variable

```
// BalanceUpdate.java
package com.jdojo.threads;
public class BalanceUpdate {
    // Initialize balance to 100
    private static int balance = 100;
    public static void main(String[] args) {
        startBalanceUpdateThread();
        // <- Thread to update the balance value
        startBalanceMonitorThread();
        // <- Thread to monitor the balance value
    }
    public static void updateBalance() {
        // Add 10 to balance and subtract 10 from balance
        balance = balance + 10;
        balance = balance - 10;
    }
```

```java
    public static void monitorBalance() {
        int b = balance;
        if (b != 100) {
            System.out.println("Balance changed: " + b);
            System.exit(0); // Exit the program
        }
    }
    public static void startBalanceUpdateThread() {
        // Start a new thread that calls the
        // updateBalance() method in an infinite loop
        Thread t = new Thread(() -> {
            while (true) {
                updateBalance();
            }
        });
        t.start();
    }
    public static void startBalanceMonitorThread() {
        // Start a thread that monitors the balance value
        Thread t = new Thread(() -> {
            while (true) {
                monitorBalance();
            }
        });
        t.start();
    }
}
```

```
Balance changed: 110
```

A brief description of each component of this class follows:

- balance: It is a static variable of type int. It is initialized to 100.

- updateBalance(): It is a static method that adds 10 to the static variable balance and subtracts 10 from it. Upon completion of this method, the value of the static variable balance is expected to remain the same as 100.

- `startBalanceUpdateThread()`: It starts a new thread that keeps calling the `updateBalance()` method in an infinite loop. That is, once you call this method, a thread keeps adding 10 to the balance variable and subtracting 10 from it.

- `startBalanceMonitorThread()`: It starts a new thread that monitors the value of the `balance` static variable by repeatedly calling the `monitorBalance()` method. When the thread detects that the value of the `balance` variable is other than 100, it prints the current value and exits the program.

- `main()`: This method is used to run the program. It starts a thread that updates the `balance` class variable in a loop using the `updateBalance()` method. It also starts another thread that monitors the value of the `balance` class variable.

The program consists of two threads. One thread calls the `updateBalance()` method, which adds 10 to `balance` and subtracts 10 from it. That is, after this method finishes executing, the value of the `balance` variable is expected to remain unchanged. Another thread monitors the value of the `balance` variable. When it detects that the value of the `balance` variable is anything other than 100, it prints the new value and exits the program. Specifying zero in `System.exit(0)` method call indicates that you want to terminate the program normally.

Intuitively, the balance monitor thread should not print anything because the balance should always be 100, and the program should never end because both threads are using infinite loops. However, that is not the case. If you run this program, you will find, in a short time, the program prints the balance value other than 100 and exits.

Suppose on a particular machine the statement `balance = balance + 10;` is implemented as the following machine instructions assuming `register-1` as a CPU register:

```
register-1 = balance;
register-1 = register-1 + 10;
balance = register-1;
```

Similarly, assume that the statement `balance = balance - 10;` is implemented as the following machine instructions assuming `register-2` as another CPU register:

```
register-2 = balance;
register-2 = register-2 - 10;
balance = register-2;
```

When the `updateBalance()` method is invoked, the CPU has to execute six instructions to add 10 to and subtract 10 from the `balance` variable. When the balance update thread is in the middle of executing any of the first three instructions, the balance monitor thread will read the balance value as 100. When the balance update thread has finished executing the third instruction, the balance monitor thread will read its value as 110. The value 110 for the balance variable will be restored to 100 only when the balance update thread executes the sixth instruction. Note that if the balance monitor thread reads the value of the `balance` variable any time after the execution of the third instruction and before the execution of the sixth instruction by the balance update thread, it will read a value that is not the same as the value that existed at the start of the `updateBalance()` method execution. Table 5-1 shows how the value of the `balance` variable will be modified and read by the two threads.

In your program, the monitor thread was able to read the value of the `balance` variable as 110 because you allowed two threads to modify and read the value of the balance variable concurrently. If you allowed only one thread at a time to work with (modify or read) the `balance` variable, the balance monitor thread would never read the value of the balance variable other than 100.

Table 5-1. *Instruction Executions for Multiple Threads*

Statement (Suppose Balance Value Is 100 to Start With)	Instructions Being Executed by the Balance Update Thread	The Value of Balance Read by the Balance Monitor Thread
balance = balance + 10;	register-1 = balance;	100
	register-1 = register-1 + 10;	Before execution: 100
	balance = register-1;	After execution: 110
balance = balance - 10;	register-2 = balance;	110
	register-2 = register-2 - 10;	110
	balance = register-2;	Before execution: 110
		After execution: 100

The situation where multiple threads manipulate and access a shared data concurrently and the outcome depends on the order in which the execution of threads take place is known as a race condition. A race condition in a program may lead to unpredictable results. Listing 5-5 is an example of a race condition where the program output depends on the sequence of execution of the two threads.

To avoid a race condition in a program, you need to make sure that only one of the racing threads works with the shared data at a time. To solve this problem, you need to synchronize the access to the two methods updateBalance() and monitorBalance() of the BalanceUpdate class. That is, only one thread should access one of these two methods at a time. In other words, if one thread is executing the updateBalance() method, another thread that wants to execute the monitorBalance() method must wait until the thread executing the updateBalance() method is finished. Similarly, if one thread is executing the monitorBalance() method, another thread that wants to execute the updateBalance() method must wait until the thread executing the monitorBalance() method is finished. This will ensure that when a thread is in the process of updating the balance variable, no other threads will read the inconsistent value of the balance variable, and if a thread is reading the balance variable, no other threads will update the balance variable at the same time.

This kind of problem that needs synchronizing the access of multiple threads to a section of code in a Java program can be solved using the synchronized keyword. To understand the use of the synchronized keyword, I need to discuss the Java Memory Model in brief and the lock and wait sets of an object.

Java Memory Model

All program variables (instance fields, static fields, and array elements) in a program are allocated memory from the main memory of a computer. Each thread has a working memory (processor cache or registers). The Java Memory Model (JMM) describes how, when, and in what order program variables are stored to, and read from, the main memory. The JMM is described in the Java Language Specification in detail. You may visualize the JMM as depicted in Figure 5-5.

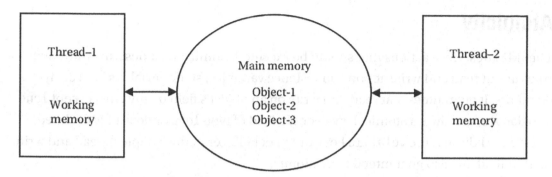

Figure 5-5. *The Java Memory Model*

Figure 5-5 shows two threads sharing the main memory. Let's assume that you have a Java program that is running two threads, thread-1 and thread-2, and each thread is running on different processors. Suppose thread-1 reads the value of an instance variable of object-1 in its working memory, updates the value, and does not write the updated value back to the main memory. Let's run through a few possible scenarios:

- What happens if thread-2 tries to read the value of the same instance variable of object-1 from the main memory? Would thread-2 read the old value from the main memory, or would it be able to read the updated value from the working memory of thread-1?

- Suppose thread-1 is in the middle of writing the updated value to the main memory, and at the same time, thread-2 is trying to read the same value from the main memory. Would thread-2 read the old value or some garbage value from the main memory because the value is not written back to the main memory completely?

The JMM answers all such questions. In essence, the JMM describes three important aspects of the execution of instructions in a Java program. They are as follows:

- Atomicity

- Visibility

- Ordering

Atomicity

The JMM describes actions that should be executed atomically. It describes atomicity rules about read and write actions on instance variables, static variables, and array elements. It guarantees that read and write on an object's field of any type, except long and double, are always atomic. However, if a field of type long or double is declared volatile (I discuss the volatile keyword in detail later in this chapter), read and write on that field are also guaranteed to be atomic.

Visibility

The JMM describes the conditions under which the effects produced by actions in one thread are visible to other threads. Mainly, it determines when a thread writes a value to a field, at what point the new value of that field can be visible to other threads. I discuss more about the visibility aspect of the JMM when I discuss locks, synchronization, and volatile variables later in this chapter. For completeness, the following are some of the visibility rules:

- When a thread reads the value of a field for the first time, it will read either the initial value of the field or some value that was written to that field by some other thread.

- A write to a volatile variable is always written to the main memory.

- A read on a volatile variable is always read from the main memory. That is, a volatile variable is never cached in the working memory of a thread. In effect, any write to a volatile variable is flushed to the main memory, immediately making the new value visible to other threads.

- When a thread terminates, the working memory of the thread is written to the main memory immediately. That is, after a thread terminates, all variables' values visible only to the terminated thread are made visible to all threads.

- When a thread enters a synchronized block, that thread reloads the values of all variables in its working memory. When a thread leaves a synchronized block, it writes all variables' values from its working memory to the main memory.

Ordering

The JMM describes in what order actions are performed within a thread and among threads. It guarantees that all actions performed within a thread are ordered. Actions in different threads are not guaranteed to be performed in any order. You may achieve some ordering while working with multiple threads by using the synchronization technique described later in this chapter.

Note   Each thread in a Java program uses two kinds of memory: working memory and main memory. A thread cannot access the working memory of another thread. Main memory is shared among the threads. Threads communicate with each other using the main memory. Every thread has its own stack, which is used to store local variables.

Object's Monitor and Thread Synchronization

In a multi-threaded program, a section of code that may have undesirable effects on the outcome of the program if executed by multiple threads concurrently is called a critical section. Often, the undesirable effects result from the concurrent use of a resource by multiple threads in the critical section. It is necessary to control the access to a critical section in a program so only one thread can execute the critical section at a time.

In a Java program, a critical section can be a block of statements or a method. Java has no built-in mechanism to identify a critical section in a program. However, Java has many built-in constructs that allow programmers to declare a critical section and to control and coordinate access to it. It is the programmer's responsibility to identify critical sections in a program and control the access to those critical sections by multiple threads. Controlling and coordinating the access to a critical section by multiple threads is known as thread synchronization. Thread synchronization is always a challenging task when writing a multi-threaded program. In Listing 5-5, the updateBalance() and monitorBalance() methods are critical sections, and you must synchronize the threads' access to these two methods to get a consistent output. Two kinds of thread synchronizations are built into the Java programming language:

- Mutual exclusion synchronization

- Conditional synchronization

In mutual exclusion synchronization, only one thread is allowed to have access to a section of code at a point in time. Listing 5-5 is an example of a program where mutual exclusion synchronization is needed so that only one thread can execute updateBalance() and monitorBalance() at a point in time. In this case, you can think of the mutual exclusion as an exclusive access to the balance variable by a thread.

The conditional synchronization allows multiple threads to work together to achieve a result. For example, consider a multi-threaded program to solve a producer/consumer problem. There are two threads in a program: one thread produces data (the producer thread), and another thread consumes the data (the consumer thread). The consumer thread must wait until the producer thread produces data and makes it available for consuming. The producer thread must notify the consumer thread when it produces data so the consumer thread can consume it. In other words, producer and consumer threads must coordinate/cooperate with each other to accomplish the task. During conditional synchronization, mutual exclusion synchronization may also be needed. Suppose the producer thread produces data one byte at a time and puts the data into a buffer whose capacity is also one byte. The consumer thread consumes data from the same buffer. In this case, only one of the threads should have access to the buffer at a time (a mutual exclusion). If the buffer is full, the producer thread must wait for the consumer thread to empty the buffer; if the buffer is empty, the consumer thread must wait for the producer thread to produce a byte of data and put it into the buffer (a conditional synchronization).

The mutual exclusion synchronization is achieved through a lock. A lock supports two operations: acquire and release. A thread that wants exclusive access to a resource must acquire the lock associated with that resource. As long as a thread possesses the lock to a resource, other threads cannot acquire the same lock. Once the thread that possesses the lock is finished with the resource, it releases the lock so another thread can acquire it.

The conditional synchronization is achieved through condition variables and three operations: wait, signal, and broadcast. Condition variables define the conditions on which threads are synchronized. The wait operation makes a thread wait on a condition to become true so it can proceed. The signal operation wakes up one of the threads that was waiting on the condition variables. The broadcast operation wakes up all threads that were waiting on the condition variables. Note that the difference between the signal operation and broadcast operation is that the former wakes up only one waiting thread, whereas the latter wakes up all waiting threads.

A monitor is a programming construct that has a lock, condition variables, and associated operations on them. Thread synchronization in a Java program is achieved using monitors. Every object in a Java program has an associated monitor.

A critical section in a Java program is defined with respect to an object's monitor. A thread must acquire the object's monitor before it can start executing the piece of code declared as a critical section. The synchronized keyword is used to declare a critical section. There are two ways to use the synchronized keyword:

- To declare a method as a critical section

- To declare a block of statements as a critical section

You can declare a method as a critical section by using the keyword synchronized before the method's return type, as shown:

```
public class CriticalSection {
    public synchronized void someMethod_1() {
        // Method code goes here
    }
    public static synchronized void someMethod_2() {
        // Method code goes here
    }
}
```

Note You can declare both an instance method and a static method as synchronized. A constructor cannot be declared as synchronized. A constructor is called only once by only one thread, which is creating the object. So it makes no sense to synchronize access to a constructor.

In the case of a synchronized instance method, the entire method is a critical section, and it is associated with the monitor of the object for which this method is executed. That is, a thread must acquire the object's monitor lock before executing the code inside a synchronized instance method of that object. For example:

```
// Create an object called cs1
CriticalSection cs1 = new CriticalSection();
// Execute the synchronized instance method. Before this
```

```
// method execution starts, the thread that is executing
// this statement must acquire the monitor lock of the cs1
// object
cs1.someMethod_1();
```

In the case of a synchronized static method, the entire method is a critical section, and it is associated with the class object that represents that class. That is, a thread must acquire the class object's monitor lock before executing the code inside a synchronized static method of that class. For example:

```
// Execute the synchronized static method. Before this
// method execution starts, the thread that is executing
// this statement must acquire the monitor lock of the
// CriticalSection.class object
CriticalSection.someMethod_2();
```

The syntax for declaring a block of code as a critical section is as follows:

```
synchronized(<objectReference>) {
    // one or more statements of the critical section
}
```

The <objectReference> is the reference of the object whose monitor lock will be used to synchronize the access to the critical section. This syntax is used to define part of a method body as a critical section. This way, a thread needs to acquire the object's monitor lock only, while executing a smaller part of the method's code, which is declared as a critical section.

Other threads can still execute other parts of the body of the method concurrently. Additionally, this method of declaring a critical section lets you declare a part or whole of a constructor as a critical section. Recall that you cannot use the keyword synchronized in the declaration part of a constructor. However, you can use it inside a constructor's body to declare a block of code as synchronized. The following snippet of code illustrates the use of the keyword synchronized:

```
public class CriticalSection2 {
    public synchronized void someMethod10() {
        // Method code goes here. Only one thread can
        // execute here at a time.
    }
```

```java
    public void someMethod11() {
        synchronized(this) {
            // Method code goes here. Only one thread
            // can execute here at a time.
        }
    }
    public void someMethod12() {
        // Some statements go here. Multiple threads can
        // execute here at a time.
        synchronized(this) {
            // Some statements go here. Only one thread
            // can execute here at a time.
        }
        // Some statements go here. Multiple threads can
        // execute here at a time.
    }
    public static synchronized void someMethod20() {
        // Method code goes here. Only one thread can
        // execute here at a time.
    }
    public static void someMethod21() {
        synchronized(CriticalSection2.class) {
            // Method code goes here. Only one thread can
            // execute here at a time.
        }
    }
    public static void someMethod_22() {
        // Some statements go here: section_1. Multiple
        // threads can execute here at a time.
        synchronized(CriticalSection2.class) {
            // Some statements go here: section_2. Only
            // one thread can execute here at a time.
        }
        // Some statements go here: section_3.  Multiple
        // threads can execute here at a time
    }
}
```

The `CriticalSection2` class has six methods: three instance methods and three class methods. The `someMethod10()` method is synchronized as the `synchronized` keyword is used in the method declaration. The `someMethod11()` method differs from the `someMethod10()` method only in the way it uses the `synchronized` keyword. It puts the entire method body inside the `synchronized` keyword as a block, which has practically the same effect as declaring the method `synchronized`. The method `someMethod12()` is different. It declares only part of the method's body as a `synchronized` block. There can be more than one thread that can execute `someMethod12()` concurrently. However, only one of them can be executing inside the `synchronized` block at one point in time. Other methods—`someMethod20()`, `someMethod21()`, and `someMethod22()`—are class methods, and they will behave the same way, except that the class's object monitor will be used to achieve the thread synchronization.

The process of acquiring and releasing an object's monitor lock is handled by the JVM. The only thing you need to do is declare a method (or a block) as `synchronized`. Before entering a `synchronized` method or block, the thread acquires the monitor lock of the object. On exiting the synchronized method or block, it releases the object's monitor lock. A thread that has acquired an object's monitor lock can acquire it again as many times as it wants. However, it must release the object's monitor lock as many times as it had acquired it in order for another thread to acquire the same object's monitor lock. Let's consider the following code for a `MultiLocks` class:

```
public class MultiLocks {
    public synchronized void method1() {
        // Some statements go here
        this.method2();
        // Some statements go here
    }
    public synchronized void method2() {
        // Some statements go here
    }
    public static synchronized void method3() {
        // Some statements go here
        MultiLocks.method4();
        // Some statements go here
    }
```

```
    public static synchronized void method4() {
        // Some statements go here
    }
}
```

The MultiLocks class has four methods, and all of them are synchronized. Two of them are instance methods, which are synchronized using the reference of the object on which the method call will be made. Two of them are class methods, which are synchronized using the reference of the class object of the MultiLocks class. If a thread wants to execute method1() or method2(), it must first acquire the monitor lock of the object on which the method is called. You are calling method2() from inside the method method1(). Since a thread that is executing method1() must already have acquired the object's monitor lock and a call to method2() requires the acquisition of the same lock, that thread will reacquire the same object's monitor lock automatically when it executes method2() from inside method1() without competing with other threads to acquire the object's monitor lock.

Therefore, when a thread executes method2() from inside method1(), it will have acquired the object's monitor lock twice. When it exits method2(), it will release the lock once; when it exits method1(), it will release the lock the second time; and then the object's monitor lock will be available for other threads for acquisition. The same argument applies to the call to method4() from inside method3() except that, in this case, the MultiLocks class object's monitor lock is involved in the synchronization. Consider calling method3() from method1(), like so:

```
public class MultiLocks {
    public synchronized void method1() {
        // Some statements go here
        this.method2();
        MultiLocks.method3();
        // Some statements go here
    }
    // Rest of the code remains the same as shown before
}
```

Suppose you call method1(), like so:

```
MultiLocks ml = new MultiLocks();
ml.method1();
```

When `ml.method1()` is executed, the executing thread must acquire the monitor lock of the object `ml`. However, the executing thread must acquire the monitor lock of the `MultiLocks.class` object to execute the `MultiLocks.method3()` method. Note that `ml` and `MultiLocks.class` are two different objects. The thread that wants to execute the `MultiLocks.method3()` method from the `method1()` method must possess both objects' monitor locks at the same time.

You can apply the same arguments to work with `synchronized` blocks. For example, you can have a snippet of code like this:

```
synchronized (objectReference) {
    // Trying to synchronize again on the same object is ok
    synchronized(objectReference) {
        // Some statements go here
    }
}
```

It is time to take a deeper look into the workings of thread synchronization using an object's monitor. Figure 5-6 depicts how multiple threads can use an object's monitor.

I use a doctor-patient analogy while discussing thread synchronization. Suppose a doctor has a clinic to treat patients. We know that it is very important to allow only one patient access to the doctor at a time. Otherwise, the doctor may mix up one patient's symptoms with another patient's symptoms; a patient with fever may get a prescription for a headache! Therefore, we will assume that only one patient can have access to the doctor at any point in time. It is the same assumption that only one thread (patient) can have access to an object's monitor (doctor) at a time.

Any patient who wants an access to the doctor must sign in and wait in the waiting room. Similarly, each object monitor has an entry set (waiting room for newcomers), and any thread that wants to acquire the object's monitor lock must enter the entry set first. If the patient signs in, they may get access to the doctor immediately, if the doctor is not treating a patient and there were no patients waiting for their turn in the waiting room. Similarly, if the entry set of an object's monitor is empty and there is no other thread that possesses the object's monitor lock, the thread entering the entry set acquires the object's monitor lock immediately. However, if there were patients waiting in the waiting room or one being treated by the doctor, the patient who signs in is blocked and must wait for the doctor to become available again. Similarly, if a thread enters the entry set, and other threads are already blocked in the entry set, or another thread already possesses the object's monitor lock, the thread that just signed in is said to be blocked and must wait in the entry set.

A thread entering the entry set is shown by the arrow labeled Enter. A thread itself is shown in Figure 5-6 using a circle. A circle with the text B shows a thread that is blocked in the entry set. A circle with the text R shows a thread that has acquired the object's monitor.

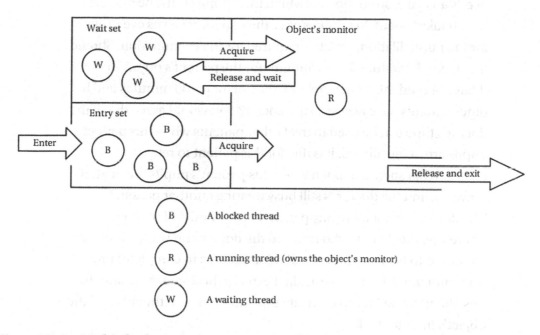

Figure 5-6. *Multiple threads using an object's monitor*

What happens to the threads that are blocked in the entry set? When do they get a chance to acquire the object's monitor? You can think about the patients blocked in the waiting room and getting their turn to be treated by the doctor. Many factors decide which patient will be treated next. First, the patient being treated must free the doctor before another patient can have access to the doctor. In Java, the thread that has the ownership of the object's monitor must release the object's monitor before any threads that are blocked in the entry set can have the ownership of the object's monitor. A patient may free the doctor for one of two reasons:

- The patient is done with their treatment and is ready to go home. This is a straightforward case of a patient freeing the doctor after their treatment is over.

- A patient is in the middle of their treatment. However, they must wait for some time in order for the doctor to resume their treatment. Let's assume that the clinic has a special waiting room (separate from the one where patients who just signed in wait) for those patients who are in the middle of their treatment. This case needs some explanation. Let's say that the doctor is an eye specialist and has some patients in their clinic. The patient who is being treated needs an eye examination for which their pupils must be dilated first. It takes about 30 minutes after the patient receives eye drops for full pupil dilation, which is required for the examination. Should the doctor be waiting for 30 minutes for the patient's pupils to dilate? Should this patient release the doctor for 30 minutes and let other patients have access to the doctor? You would agree that if the doctor's time can be used to treat other patients while this patient's pupils are being dilated, it is fine for this patient to release the doctor. What should happen when this patient's pupils are dilated, however, and the doctor is still busy treating another patient? The doctor cannot leave any patient in the middle of treatment. Therefore, the patient who released the doctor and waited for some condition to be true (here, the dilation process to complete) must wait until the doctor is free again. I explain this issue more later in this chapter, and I try to correlate this situation with threads and the object's monitor lock.

I must discuss another issue in the context of the doctor-patient example before I can compare this with the monitor-threads case. When the doctor is free and only one patient is waiting to get access to them, there is no problem. The sole patient waiting for the doctor will get access to them immediately. However, what happens when the doctor becomes available and there is more than one patient waiting to get access to them? Which one of the waiting patients should get access to the doctor first? Should it be the patient who came first (first in, first out or FIFO)? Should it be the patient who came in last (last in, first out or LIFO)? Should it be the patient who needs the least (or the most) amount of time for their treatment? Should it be the patient who is in the most serious condition? The answer depends on the policy followed by the clinic management.

Similar to a patient in the doctor-patient example, a thread can also release an object's monitor lock for two reasons:

- At this time, the thread has completed the work for which it had acquired the object's monitor lock. The arrow labeled "Release and Exit" in Figure 5-6 indicates this scenario in the diagram. When a thread simply exits a synchronized method/block, it releases the object's monitor lock it had acquired.

- The thread is in the middle of a task, and it needs to wait for some condition to be true to complete its remaining task. Let's consider the producer/consumer problem. Suppose the producer acquires the buffer object's monitor lock and wants to write some data into the buffer. However, it finds that the buffer is full and the consumer must consume the data and make the buffer empty before it can write to it. In this case, the producer must release the buffer object's monitor lock and wait until the consumer acquires the lock and empties the buffer. The same logic applies for the consumer when it acquires the buffer's monitor lock and finds that the buffer is empty. At that time, the consumer must release the lock and wait until the producer produces some data. This kind of temporarily releasing of the object's monitor lock and waiting for some condition to occur is shown in the diagram labeled as the "Release and Wait" arrow. An object can have multiple threads that can be in a "Release and Wait" state at the same time. All threads that have released the object's monitor lock and are waiting for some conditions to occur are put in a set called a wait set.

How is a thread placed in the wait set? Note that a thread can be placed in the wait set of an object monitor only if it once acquired the object's monitor lock. Once a thread has acquired the object's monitor lock, it must call the wait() method of the object in order to place itself into the wait set. This means a thread must always call the wait() method from inside a synchronized method or a block. The wait() method is defined in the java.lang.Object class, and it is declared final; that is, no other class in Java can override this method. You must consider the following two rules before you call the wait() method of an object.

Rule #1

The call to the wait() method must be placed inside a synchronized method (static or non-static) or a synchronized block.

Rule #2

The wait() method must be called on the object whose monitor the current thread has acquired. It throws a java.lang.InterruptedException. The code that calls this method must handle this exception. The wait() method throws an IllegalMonitorStateException when the current thread is not the owner of the object's monitor. The following snippet of code does not place the wait() method call inside a try-catch to keep the code simple and readable. For example, inside a synchronized non-static method, the call to the wait() method may look like the following:

```
public class WaitMethodCall {
    // Object that is used to synchronize a block
    private Object objectRef = new Object();
    public synchronized void someMethod_1() {
        // The thread running here has already acquired
        // the monitor lock on the object represented by
        // the reference this because it is a
        // synchronized non-static method

        // other statements go here
        while (some condition is true) {
            // It is ok to call the wait() method on this,
            // because the current thread possesses
            // monitor lock on this
            this.wait();
        }
        // other statements go here
    }
    public static synchronized void someMethod_2() {
        // The thread executing here has already acquired
        // the monitor lock on the class object represented
```

```
        // by the WaitMethodCall.class reference because it
        // is a synchronized static method

        while (some condition is true) {
            // It is ok to call the wait() method on
            // WaitMethodCall.class because the current
            // thread possesses monitor lock on
            // WaitMethodCall.class object
            WaitMethodCall.class.wait();
        }
        // other statements go here
    }
    public void someMethod_3() {
        // other statements go here
        synchronized(objectRef) {
            // Current thread possesses monitor lock of
            // objectRef
            while (some condition is true) {
                // It is ok to call the wait() method on
                // objectRef because the current thread
                // possesses monitor lock on objectRef
                objectRef.wait();
            }
        }
        // other statements go here
    }
}
```

Note that objectRef is an instance variable, and it is of the type java.lang.Object. Its only use is to synchronize threads' access to a block inside the someMethod_3() method. Since it is declared an instance variable, all threads calling someMethod_3() will use its monitor to execute the synchronized block. A common mistake made by beginners is to declare objectRef as a local variable inside a method and use it in a synchronized block. The following snippet of code shows such a mistake:

```
public void wrongSynchronizationMethod {
    // This objectRef is created every time a thread calls
    // this method
    Object objectRef = new Object();
    // It is a blunder to use objectRef for
    // synchronization below
    synchronized(objectRef) {
        // In fact, this block works as if there is no
        // synchronization, because every thread  creates a
        // new objectRef and acquires its monitor lock
        // immediately.
    }
}
```

With this snippet of code in mind, you must use an object reference that is common to all threads to synchronize access to a block.

Let's get back to the question of which patient will get access to the doctor when they become available again. Will it be a patient from the waiting room who is waiting after signing in or a patient from another waiting room who was waiting in the middle of their treatment? Before you answer this question, let's make it clear that there is a difference between the patients in the waiting room who are waiting after signing in and the patients waiting for some condition (e.g., dilation to complete) to occur in another waiting room. After signing in, patients wait on the availability of the doctor, whereas patients in the middle of their treatments wait on a particular condition to occur. For patients in the second category, a particular condition must hold before they can seek access to the doctor, whereas patients in the first category are ready to grab access to the doctor as soon as possible. Therefore, someone must notify a patient in the second category that a particular condition has occurred, and it is time for them to seek access to the doctor again to continue their treatment. Let's assume that this notification must come from a patient being currently treated by the doctor. That is, the patient who currently has access to the doctor notifies the patients waiting in the middle of their treatments to get ready to gain access to the doctor again. Note that it is just a notification that some condition has occurred, and it is delivered only to the patients waiting in the middle of their treatments. Whether the patient in the middle of their treatment will get access to the doctor right after the current patient is done with the doctor is not guaranteed. It only guarantees that the condition on which a patient was waiting holds at the time of notification, and the waiting patient may try to get access to the doctor to continue their treatment. Let's correlate this example to the monitor-threads example.

The threads in the entry set are blocked, and they are ready to grab access to the monitor as soon as possible. The threads in the wait set are waiting for some condition to occur. A thread that has ownership of the monitor must notify the threads waiting in the wait set about the fulfillment of the conditions on which they are waiting. In Java, the notification is made by calling the notify() and notifyAll() methods of the Object class. Like the wait() method, the notify() and notifyAll() methods are also declared final. Like the wait() method, these two methods must be called by a thread using an object whose monitor has already been acquired by the thread. If a thread calls these methods on an object before acquiring the object's monitor, an IllegalMonitorStateException is thrown. The call to the notify() method wakes up one thread from the wait set, whereas the call to the notifyAll() method wakes up all threads in the wait set. In the case of the notify() method call, the thread that is woken up is chosen arbitrarily. Note that when a thread calls the notify() or notifyAll() method, it still holds the lock on the object's monitor. Threads in the wait set are only woken up by the notify() or notifyAll() call. They do not acquire the object's monitor lock immediately. When the thread that called the notify() or notifyAll() method releases the object's monitor lock by "Release and Exit" or "Release and Wait," the woken up threads in the wait set compete with the threads in the entry set to acquire the object's monitor again. Therefore, a call to the notify() and notifyAll() serves only as a wake-up call for threads in the wait set, and it does not guarantee access to the object's monitor.

Note   There is no way to wake up a specific thread in the wait set. The call to notify() chooses a thread arbitrarily, whereas the call to notifyAll() wakes up all threads. Use notifyAll() when you are in doubt about which method to use.

The following snippet of code shows pseudocode for using the notifyAll() method along with the wait() method. You may observe that the call to the wait() and notify() methods is made on the same object, because if objectRef.wait() puts a thread in the wait set of the objectRef object, the objectRef.notify() or objectRef.notifyAll() method will wake that thread from the wait set of the objectRef object:

```java
public class WaitAndNotifyMethodCall {
    private Object objectRef = new Object();
    public synchronized void someMethod_1() {
        while (some condition is true) {
            this.wait();
        }
        if (some other condition is true) {
            // Notify all waiting threads
            this.notifyAll();
        }
    }
    public static synchronized void someMethod_2() {
        while (some condition is true) {
            WaitAndNotifyMethodCall.class.wait();
        }
        if (some other condition is true) {
            // Notify all waiting threads
            WaitAndNotifyMethodCall.class.notifyAll();
        }
    }

    public void someMethod_3() {
        synchronized(objectRef) {
            while (some condition is true) {
                objectRef.wait();
            }
            if (some other condition is true) {
                // Notify all waiting threads
                objectRef.notifyAll();
            }
        }
    }
}
```

Once a thread is woken up in the wait set, it has to compete with the threads in the entry set to acquire the monitor lock of the object. After a thread is woken up in the wait set and acquires the object's monitor lock, it has choices: to do some work and release the lock by invoking the wait() method (release and wait) again or to release the lock by exiting the synchronized section (release and exit). One important point to remember about the call to the wait() method is that, typically, a call to the wait() method is placed inside a loop. Here is the reason why it is necessary to do so. A thread looks for a condition to hold. It waits by calling the wait() method and placing itself in the wait set if that condition does not hold. The thread wakes up when it is notified by another thread, which calls the notify() or notifyAll() method. When the thread that woke up acquires the lock, the condition that held at the time of notification may not still hold. Therefore, it is necessary to check for the condition again, when the thread wakes up and acquires the lock, to make sure the condition it was looking for is true, and it can continue its work. For example, consider the producer/consumer problem. Suppose there is one producer and many consumers. Suppose a consumer calls the wait() method as follows:

```
if (buffer is empty) {
    buffer.wait();
}
buffer.consume();
```

Suppose the buffer is empty and all consumers are waiting in the wait set. The producer produces some data, and it calls the buffer.notifyAll() method to wake up all consumer threads in the wait set. All consumer threads wake up; however, only one will get a chance to acquire the monitor lock next. The first one acquires the lock and executes the buffer.consume() method to empty the buffer. When the next consumer acquires the monitor lock, it will also execute the buffer.consume() statement. However, the consumer that woke up and acquired the lock before this one had already emptied the buffer. The logical mistake in the previous snippet of code is that the call to the wait() method is placed inside an if statement instead of inside a loop. That is, after a thread wakes up, it is not checking if the buffer contains some data or not, before trying to consume the data. The corrected snippet of code is the following:

```
while (buffer is empty) {
    buffer.wait();
}
buffer.consume();
```

293

I answer one more question before you can see this big discussion about thread synchronization in action. The question is, "Which thread gets a chance to acquire the object's monitor lock when there are some blocked threads in the entry set and some woken up threads in the wait set?" Note that the threads that are in the wait set do not compete for the object's monitor until they are woken up by the notify() or notifyAll() call. The answer to this question is that it depends on the scheduler's algorithm of the operating system.

Listing 5-6 contains the code for the BalanceUpdateSynchronized class, which is a modified version of the BalanceUpdate class listed in Listing 5-5. The only difference between the two classes is the use of the synchronized keyword to declare the updateBalance() and monitorBalance() methods in the new class, so only one thread can enter one of the methods at a time. When you run the new class, you will not see any output because the monitorBalance() method will never see the value of the balance variable other than 100. You will need to terminate the program manually, for example, using Ctrl+C on Windows.

Listing 5-6. Synchronized Balance Update

```java
// BalanceUpdateSynchronized.java
package com.jdojo.threads;
public class BalanceUpdateSynchronized {
    // Initialize balance to 100
    private static int balance = 100;
    public static void main(String[] args) {
        startBalanceUpdateThread();
        // <- Thread to update the balance value
        startBalanceMonitorThread();
        // <- Thread to monitor the balance value
    }
    public static synchronized void updateBalance() {
        // Add 10 to balance and subtract 10 from balance
        balance = balance + 10;
        balance = balance - 10;
    }
```

```
    public static synchronized void monitorBalance() {
        int b = balance;
        if (b != 100) {
            System.out.println("Balance changed: " + b);
            System.exit(1); // Exit the program
        }
    }
    public static void startBalanceUpdateThread() {
        // Start a new thread that calls the
        // updateBalance() method in an infinite loop
        Thread t = new Thread(() -> {
            while (true) {
                updateBalance();
            }
        });
        t.start();
    }

    public static void startBalanceMonitorThread() {
        // Start a thread that monitors the balance value
        Thread t = new Thread(() -> {
            while (true) {
                monitorBalance();
            }
        });
        t.start();
    }
}
```

I show examples of using the wait() and notify() methods in the next section, which discusses the producer/consumer problem. The wait() method in the Object class is overloaded, and it has three versions:

- wait(): The thread waits in the object's wait set until another thread calls the notify() or notifyAll() method on the same object.

- `wait(long timeinMillis)`: The thread waits in the object's wait set until another thread calls the `notify()` or `notifyAll()` method on the same object or the specified amount of `timeinMillis` time has elapsed.

- `wait(long timeinMillis, long timeinNanos)`: This version lets you specify time in milliseconds and nanoseconds.

The Producer/Consumer Synchronization Problem

The producer/consumer is a typical thread synchronization problem that uses the `wait()` and `notify()` methods. I keep it simple.

The problem statement goes like this. There are four classes: `Buffer`, `Producer`, `Consumer`, and `ProducerConsumerTest`. An object of the `Buffer` class will have an integer data element that will be produced by the producer and consumed by the consumer. Therefore, in this example, a `Buffer` object can hold only one integer at a point in time. Your goal is to synchronize the access to the buffer, so the `Producer` produces a new data element only when the `Buffer` is empty, and the `Consumer` consumes the buffer's data only when it is available. The `ProducerConsumerTest` class is used to test the program.

Listings 5-7 to 5-10 contain the code for the four classes.

Listing 5-7. A Buffer Class for Producer/Consumer Synchronization

```
// Buffer.java
package com.jdojo.threads;
public class Buffer {
    private int data;
    private boolean empty;

    public Buffer() {
        this.empty = true;
    }
    public synchronized void produce(int newData) {
        // Wait until the buffer is empty
        while (!this.empty) {
            try {
                this.wait();
```

```java
            } catch (InterruptedException e) {
                e.printStackTrace();
            }
        }
        // Store the new data produced by the producer
        this.data = newData;
        // Set the empty flag to false, so the consumer
        // may consume the data
        this.empty = false;
        // Notify the waiting consumer in the wait set
        this.notify();
        System.out.println("Produced: " + newData);
    }
    public synchronized int consume() {
        // Wait until the buffer gets some data
        while (this.empty) {
            try {
                this.wait();
            } catch (InterruptedException e) {
                e.printStackTrace();
            }
        }
        // Set the empty flag to true, so that the
        // producer can store new data
        this.empty = true;
        // Notify the waiting producer in the wait set
        this.notify();
        System.out.println("Consumed: " + data);
        return data;
    }
}
```

Listing 5-8. A Producer Class for Producer/Consumer Synchronization

```java
// Producer.java
package com.jdojo.threads;
import java.util.Random;
public class Producer extends Thread {
    private final Buffer buffer;
    public Producer(Buffer buffer) {
        this.buffer = buffer;
    }
    @Override
    public void run() {
        Random rand = new Random();
        while (true) {
            // Generate a random integer and store it in
            // the buffer
            int n = rand.nextInt();
            buffer.produce(n);
        }
    }
}
```

Listing 5-9. A Consumer Class for Producer/Consumer Synchronization

```java
// Consumer.java
package com.jdojo.threads;
public class Consumer extends Thread {
    private final Buffer buffer;
    public Consumer(Buffer buffer) {
        this.buffer = buffer;
    }
    @Override
    public void run() {
        int data;
```

```
        while (true) {
            // Consume the data from the buffer. We are
            // not using the consumed data for any other
            // purpose here
            data = buffer.consume();
        }
    }
}
```

Listing 5-10. A ProducerConsumerTest Class to Test the Producer/Consumer Synchronization

```
// ProducerConsumerTest.java
package com.jdojo.threads;
public class ProducerConsumerTest {
    public static void main(String[] args) {
        // Create Buffer, Producer and Consumer objects
        Buffer buffer = new Buffer();
        Producer p = new Producer(buffer);
        Consumer c = new Consumer(buffer);
        // Start the producer and consumer threads
        p.start();
        c.start();
    }
}
Produced: 1872733184
Consumed: 1872733184
...
```

When you run the ProducerConsumerTest class, you may get different output. However, your output will look similar in the sense that two lines printed will be always of the following form, where XXX indicates an integer:

```
Produced: XXX
Consumed: XXX
```

In this example, the `Buffer` class needs some explanation. It has two instance variables:

- `private int data`

- `private boolean empty`

The producer uses the `data` instance variable to store the new data. The consumer reads it. The `empty` instance variable is used as an indicator whether the buffer is empty or not. In the constructor, it is initialized to `true`, indicating that the new buffer is empty.

It has two synchronized methods: `produce()` and `consume()`. Both methods are declared `synchronized` because the goal is to protect the `Buffer` object to be used by multiple threads concurrently. If the producer is producing new data by calling the `produce()` method, the consumer must wait to consume the data until the producer is done and vice versa. The producer thread calls the `produce()` method, passing the newly generated data to it. However, before the new data is stored in the `data` instance variable, the producer makes sure that the buffer is empty. If the buffer is not empty, it calls the `this.wait()` method to place itself in the wait set of the buffer object until the consumer notifies it using the `this.notify()` method inside the `consume()` method.

Once the producer thread detects that the buffer is empty, it stores the new data in the `data` instance variable, sets the `empty` flag to false, and calls `this.notify()` to wake up the consumer thread in the wait set to consume the data. At the end, it also prints a message on the console that data has been produced.

The `consume()` method of the `Buffer` class is similar to its counterpart, the `produce()` method. The only difference is that the consumer thread calls this method, and it performs logic that's opposite of the `produce()` method. For example, it checks if the buffer is not empty before consuming the data.

The `Producer` and `Consumer` classes inherit from the `Thread` class. They override the `run()` method of the `Thread` class. Both of them accept an object of the `Buffer` class in their constructor to use it in their `run()` method. The `Producer` class generates a random integer in its `run()` method inside an infinite loop and keeps writing it to the buffer. The `Consumer` class keeps consuming data from the buffer in an infinite loop.

The `ProducerConsumerTest` class creates all three objects (a buffer, a producer, and a consumer) and starts the producer and consumer threads. Since both classes (`Producer` and `Consumer`) use infinite loops inside the `run()` method, you have to terminate the program forcibly, such as by pressing `Ctrl+C`, if you are running this program from a Windows command prompt.

Which Thread Is Executing?

The Thread class has some useful static methods; one of them is the currentThread()
method. It returns the reference of the Thread object that calls this method. Consider the
following statement:

```
Thread t = Thread.currentThread();
```

The statement will assign the reference of the thread object that executes this statement
to the variable t. Note that a statement in Java can be executed by different threads at
different points in time during the execution of a program. Therefore, t may be assigned
the reference of a different Thread object when the statement is executed at different times
in the same program. Listing 5-11 demonstrates the use of the currentThread() method.
You may get the same text in the output, but in a different order.

Listing 5-11. Using the Thread.currentThread() Method

```java
// CurrentThread.java
package com.jdojo.threads;
public class CurrentThread extends Thread {
    public CurrentThread(String name) {
        super(name);
    }
    @Override
    public void run() {
        Thread t = Thread.currentThread();
        String threadName = t.getName();
        System.out.println("Inside run() method: " +
            threadName);
    }
    public static void main(String[] args) {
        CurrentThread ct1 = new CurrentThread(
            "Thread #1");
        CurrentThread ct2 = new CurrentThread(
            "Thread #2");
        ct1.start();
        ct2.start();
```

```
        // Let's see which thread is executing the
        // following statement
        Thread t = Thread.currentThread();
        String threadName = t.getName();
        System.out.println("Inside main() method: " +
            threadName);
    }
}
```

```
Inside main() method: main
Inside run() method: Thread #1
Inside run() method: Thread #2
```

Two different threads call the `Thread.currentThread()` method inside the `run()` method of the `CurrentThread` class. The method returns the reference of the thread executing the call. The program simply prints the name of the thread that is executing. It is interesting to note that when you called the `Thread.currentThread()` method inside the `main()` method, a thread named `main` executed the code. When you run a class, the JVM starts a thread named `main`, which is responsible for executing the `main()` method.

Letting a Thread Sleep

The `Thread` class contains a static `sleep()` method, which makes a thread sleep for a specified duration. It accepts a timeout as an argument. You can specify the timeout in milliseconds, or milliseconds and nanoseconds. The thread that executes this method sleeps for the specified amount of time. A sleeping thread is not scheduled by the operating system scheduler to receive the CPU time. If a thread has the ownership of an object's monitor lock before it goes to sleep, it continues to hold those monitor locks. The `sleep()` method may throw an `InterruptedException`, and your code should be ready to handle it. Listing 5-12 demonstrates the use of the `sleep()` method.

Listing 5-12. A Sleeping Thread

```java
// LetMeSleep.java
package com.jdojo.threads;
```

```java
public class LetMeSleep {
    public static void main(String[] args) {
        try {
            System.out.println(
                "I am going to sleep for 5 seconds.");
            Thread.sleep(5000);
            // <- The "main" thread will sleep
            System.out.println("I woke up.");
        } catch (InterruptedException e) {
            System.out.println(
                "Someone interrupted me in my sleep.");
        }
        System.out.println("I am done.");
    }
}
```

```
I am going to sleep for 5 seconds.
I woke up.
I am done.
```

Note   The TimeUnit enum in the java.util.concurrent package represents a measurement of time in various units such as milliseconds, seconds, minutes, hours, days, etc. It has some convenience methods. One of them is the sleep() method. The Thread.sleep() method accepts time in milliseconds. If you want a thread to sleep for five seconds, you need to call this method as Thread.sleep(5000) by converting the seconds into milliseconds. You can use the sleep() method of TimeUnit instead to avoid the time duration conversion, like so:

```
TimeUnit.SECONDS.sleep(5); // Same as Thread.sleep(5000)
```

I Will Join You in Heaven

I can rephrase this section heading as "I will wait until you die." That's right. A thread can wait for another thread to die (or terminate). Suppose there are two threads, t1 and t2. If the thread t1 executes t2.join(), thread t1 starts waiting until thread t2 is terminated. In other words, the call t2.join() blocks until t2 terminates. Using the join() method in a program is useful if one of the threads cannot proceed until another thread has finished executing.

Listing 5-13 has an example where you want to print a message on the standard output when the program has finished executing. The message to print is "We are done."

Listing 5-13. An Incorrect Way of Waiting for a Thread to Terminate

```java
// JoinWrong.java
package com.jdojo.threads;
public class JoinWrong {
    public static void main(String[] args) {
        Thread t1 = new Thread(JoinWrong::print);
        t1.start();
        System.out.println("We are done.");
    }
    public static void print() {
        for (int i = 1; i <= 5; i++) {
            try {
                System.out.println("Counter: " + i);
                Thread.sleep(1000);
            } catch (InterruptedException e) {
                e.printStackTrace();
            }
        }
    }
}
```

```
We are done.
Counter: 1
Counter: 2
Counter: 3
Counter: 4
Counter: 5
```

In the `main()` method, a thread is created and started. The thread prints integers from 1 to 5. It sleeps for one second after printing an integer. In the end, the `main()` method prints a message. It seems that this program should print the numbers from 1 to 5, followed by your last message. However, if you look at the output, it is in the reverse order. What is wrong with this program?

The JVM starts a new thread called `main` that is responsible for executing the `main()` method of the class that you run. In your case, the `main()` method of the `JoinWrong` class is executed by the `main` thread. This thread will execute the following statements:

```
Thread t1 =  new Thread(JoinWrong::print);
t1.start();
System.out.println("We are done.");
```

When the `t1.start()` method call returns, you have one more thread running in your program (thread `t1`) in addition to the main thread. The `t1` thread is responsible for printing the integers from 1 to 5, whereas the main thread is responsible for printing the message "We are done." Since there are two threads responsible for two different tasks, it is not guaranteed which task will finish first. What is the solution? You must make your main thread wait on the thread `t1` to terminate. This can be achieved by calling the `t1.join()` method inside the `main()` method.

Listing 5-14 contains the correct version of Listing 5-13 by using the `t1.join()` method call before printing the final message. When the main thread executes the `join()` method call, it waits until the `t1` thread is terminated. The `join()` method of the `Thread` class may throw an `InterruptedException`, and your code should be ready to handle it.

Listing 5-14. A Correct Way of Waiting for a Thread to Terminate

```java
// JoinRight.java
package com.jdojo.threads;
public class JoinRight {
    public static void main(String[] args) {
        Thread t1 = new Thread(JoinRight::print);
        t1.start();
        try {
            t1.join();
            // <- "main" thread waits until t1 is
            //    terminated
        } catch (InterruptedException e) {
            e.printStackTrace();
        }
        System.out.println("We are done.");
    }

    public static void print() {
        for (int i = 1; i <= 5; i++) {
            try {
                System.out.println("Counter: " + i);
                Thread.sleep(1000);
            } catch (InterruptedException e) {
                e.printStackTrace();
            }
        }
    }
}
```

```
Counter: 1
Counter: 2
Counter: 3
Counter: 4
Counter: 5
We are done.
```

The join() method of the Thread class is overloaded. Its other two versions accept a timeout argument. If you use the join() method with a timeout, the caller thread will wait until the thread on which it is called is terminated or the timeout has elapsed. If you replace the t1.join() statement in the JoinRight class with t1.join(1000), you will find that the output is not in the same order because the main thread will wait only for a second for the t1 thread to terminate before it prints the final message.

Can a thread join multiple threads? The answer is yes. A thread can join multiple threads like so:

```
t1.join(); // Join t1
t2.join(); // Join t2
t3.join(); // Join t3
```

You should call the join() method of a thread after it has been started. If you call the join() method on a thread that has not been started, it returns immediately. Similarly, if you invoke the join() method on a thread that is already terminated, it returns immediately.

Can a thread join itself? The answer is yes and no. Technically, it is allowed for a thread to join itself. However, a thread should not join itself in most circumstances. In such a case, a thread waits to terminate itself. In other words, the thread waits forever.

```
// "Bad" call (not if you know what you are doing) to
// join. It waits forever until another thread interrupts
// it.
Thread.currentThread().join();
```

If you write this statement, make sure that your program interrupts the waiting thread using some other threads. In such a case, the waiting thread will return from the join() method call by throwing an InterruptedException.

Be Considerate to Others and Yield

A thread may voluntarily give up the CPU by calling the static yield() method of the Thread class. The call to the yield() method is a hint to the scheduler that it may pause the running thread and give the CPU to other threads. A thread may want to call this method only if it executes in a long loop without waiting or blocking. If a thread frequently waits or blocks, the yield() method call is not very useful because this thread does not monopolize the CPU and other threads will get the CPU time when this thread is blocked or waiting. It is advisable not to depend on the yield() method because it is just a hint to the scheduler. It is not guaranteed to give a consistent result across different platforms. A thread that calls the yield() method continues to hold the monitor locks. Note that there is no guarantee as to when the thread that yields will get the CPU time again. You may use it like so:

```
// The run() method of a thread class
public void run() {
    while(true) {
        // do some processing here...
        Thread.yield(); // Let's yield to other threads
    }
}
```

Lifecycle of a Thread

A thread is always in one of the following six states:

- New
- Runnable
- Blocked
- Waiting
- Timed-waiting
- Terminated

All these states of a thread are JVM states. They do not represent the states assigned to a thread by an operating system.

When a thread is created and its start() method is not yet called, it is in the new state:

```
Thread t = new SomeThreadClass();
// <- t is in the new state
```

A thread that is ready to run or running is in the runnable state. In other words, a thread that is eligible for getting the CPU time is in a runnable state.

Note   The JVM combines two OS-level thread states: ready-to-run and running into a state called the runnable state. A thread in the ready-to-run OS state means it is waiting for its turn to get the CPU time. A thread in the running OS state means it is running on the CPU.

A thread is said to be in a blocked state if it was trying to enter (or reenter) a synchronized method or block, but the monitor is being used by another thread. A thread in the entry set that is waiting to acquire a monitor lock is in the blocked state. A thread in the wait set that is waiting to reacquire the monitor lock after it has been woken up is also in a blocked state.

A thread may place itself in a waiting state by calling one of the methods listed in Table 5-2. A thread may place itself in a timed-waiting state by calling one of the methods listed in Table 5-3. I discuss the parkNanos() and parkUntil() methods later in this chapter.

Table 5-2. *Methods That Place a Thread in Waiting State*

Method	Description
wait()	This is the wait() method of the Object class, which a thread may call if it wants to wait for a specific condition to hold. Recall that a thread must own the monitor's lock of an object to call the wait() method on that object. Another thread must call the notify() or notifyAll() method on the same object in order for the waiting thread to transition to the runnable state.
join()	This is the join() method of the Thread class. A thread that calls this method wants to wait until the thread on which this method is called terminates.
park()	This is the park() method of the LockSupport class, which is in the java.util.concurrent.locks package. A thread that calls this method may wait until a permit is available by calling the unpark() method on a thread. I cover the LockSupport class later in this chapter.

Table 5-3. *Methods That Place a Thread in a Timed-Waiting State*

Method	Description
sleep()	This method is in the Thread class.
wait (long millis) wait(long millis, int nanos)	These methods are in the Object class.
join(long millis) join(long millis, int nanos)	These methods are in the Thread class.
parkNanos (long nanos) parkNanos (Object blocker, long nanos)	These methods are in the LockSupport class, which is in the java.util.concurrent.locks package.
parkUntil (long deadline) parkUntil (Object blocker, long nanos)	These methods are in the LockSupport class, which is in the java.util.concurrent.locks package.

A thread that has completed its execution is said to be in the terminated state. A thread is terminated when it exits its run() method or its stop() method is called. A terminated thread cannot transition to any other state. You can use the isAlive() method of a thread after it has been started to know if it is alive or terminated.

You can use the getState() method of the Thread class to get the state of a thread at any time. This method returns one of the constants of the Thread.State enum type. Listings 5-15 and 5-16 demonstrate the transition of a thread from one state to another. The output of Listing 5-16 shows some of the states the thread transitions to during its lifecycle.

Listing 5-15. A ThreadState Class

```java
// ThreadState.java
package com.jdojo.threads;
public class ThreadState extends Thread {
    private boolean keepRunning = true;
    private boolean wait = false;
    private final Object syncObject;
    public ThreadState(Object syncObject) {
        this.syncObject = syncObject;
    }
```

```
    @Override
    public void run() {
        while (keepRunning) {
            synchronized (syncObject) {
                if (wait) {
                    try {
                        syncObject.wait();
                    } catch (InterruptedException e) {
                        e.printStackTrace();
                    }
                }
            }
        }
    }
    public void setKeepRunning(boolean keepRunning) {
        this.keepRunning = keepRunning;
    }
    public void setWait(boolean wait) {
        this.wait = wait;
    }
}
```

Listing 5-16. A ThreadStateTest Class to Demonstrate the States of a Thread

```
// ThreadStateTest.java
package com.jdojo.threads;
public class ThreadStateTest {
    public static void main(String[] args) {
        Object syncObject = new Object();
        ThreadState ts = new ThreadState(syncObject);
        System.out.println(
            "Before start()-ts.isAlive(): " +
            ts.isAlive());
        System.out.println("#1: " + ts.getState());
        // Start the thread
        ts.start();
```

```
        System.out.println(
            "After start()-ts.isAlive(): " +
            ts.isAlive());
        System.out.println("#2: " + ts.getState());
        ts.setWait(true);
        // Make the current thread sleep, so the thread
        // starts waiting
        sleepNow(100);
        synchronized (syncObject) {
            System.out.println("#3: " + ts.getState());
            ts.setWait(false);
            // Wake up the waiting thread
            syncObject.notifyAll();
        }
        // Make the current thread sleep, so ts thread
        // wakes up
        sleepNow(2000);
        System.out.println("#4: " + ts.getState());
        ts.setKeepRunning(false);
        // Make the current thread sleep, so the ts thread
        // will wake up
        sleepNow(2000);
        System.out.println("#5: " + ts.getState());
        System.out.println("At the end. ts.isAlive(): " +
            ts.isAlive());
    }
    public static void sleepNow(long millis) {
        try {
            Thread.currentThread().sleep(millis);
        } catch (InterruptedException e) {
        }
    }
}
```

```
Before start()-ts.isAlive(): false
#1: NEW
After start()-ts.isAlive(): true
#2: RUNNABLE
#3: WAITING
#4: RUNNABLE
#5: TERMINATED
At the end. ts.isAlive(): false
```

Priority of a Thread

A thread has a priority. The priority is indicated by an integer between 1 and 10. A thread with the priority of 1 is said to have the lowest priority. A thread with the priority of 10 is said to have the highest priority. There are three constants defined in the Thread class to represent three different thread priorities, as listed in Table 5-4.

Table 5-4. *Thread's Priority Constants Defined in the Thread Class*

Thread Priority Constant	Integer Value
MIN_PRIORITY	1
NORM_PRIORITY	5
MAX_PRIORITY	10

The priority of a thread is a hint to the scheduler that indicates the importance (or the urgency) with which it should schedule the thread. The higher priority of a thread indicates that the thread is of higher importance, and the scheduler should give priority in giving the CPU time to that thread. Note that the priority of a thread is just a hint to the scheduler; it is up to the scheduler to respect that hint. It is not recommended to depend on the thread priority for the correctness of a program. For example, if there are ten maximum priority threads and one minimum priority thread, that does not mean that the scheduler will schedule the minimum priority thread after all ten maximum priority threads have been scheduled and finished. This scheduling scheme will result in a thread starvation, where a lower priority thread will have to wait indefinitely or for a long time to get CPU time.

The setPriority() method of the Thread class sets a new priority for the thread. The getPriority() method returns the current priority for a thread. When a thread is created, its priority is set by default to the priority of the thread that creates the new thread.

Listing 5-17 demonstrates how to set and get the priority of a thread. It also demonstrates how a new thread gets the priority of the thread that creates it. In the example, threads t1 and t2 get the priority of the main thread at the time they are created.

Listing 5-17. Setting and Getting a Thread's Priority

```java
// ThreadPriority.java
package com.jdojo.threads;
public class ThreadPriority {
    public static void main(String[] args) {
        // Get the reference of the current thread
        Thread t = Thread.currentThread();
        System.out.println("main Thread Priority: " +
            t.getPriority());
        // Thread t1 gets the same priority as the main
        // thread at this point
        Thread t1 = new Thread();
        System.out.println("Thread(t1) Priority: " +
            t1.getPriority());
        t.setPriority(Thread.MAX_PRIORITY);
        System.out.println("main Thread Priority: " +
            t.getPriority());
        // Thread t2 gets the same priority as main
        // thread at this point, which is
        // Thread.MAX_PRIORITY (10)
        Thread t2 = new Thread();
        System.out.println("Thread(t2) Priority: " +
            t2.getPriority());
        // Change thread t2 priority to minimum
        t2.setPriority(Thread.MIN_PRIORITY);
```

```
        System.out.println("Thread(t2) Priority: " +
            t2.getPriority());
    }
}
```

```
main Thread Priority: 5
Thread(t1) Priority: 5
main Thread Priority: 10
Thread(t2) Priority: 10
Thread(t2) Priority: 1
```

Is It a Demon or a Daemon?

A thread can be a daemon thread or a user thread. The word "daemon" is pronounced the same as "demon." However, the word daemon in a thread's context has nothing to do with a demon!

A daemon thread is a kind of a service provider thread, whereas a user thread (or non-daemon thread) is a thread that uses the services of daemon threads. A service provider should not exist if there is no service consumer. The JVM applies this logic. When the JVM detects that all threads in an application are only daemon threads, it exits the application. Note that if there are only daemon threads in an application, the JVM does not wait for those daemon threads to finish before exiting the application.

You can make a thread a daemon thread by using the setDaemon() method by passing true as an argument. You must call the setDaemon() method of a thread before you start the thread. Otherwise, an IllegalThreadStateException is thrown. You can use the isDaemon() method to check if a thread is a daemon thread.

Note The JVM starts a garbage collector thread to collect all unused object's memory. The garbage collector thread is a daemon thread.

When a thread is created, its daemon property is the same as the thread that creates it. In other words, a new thread inherits the daemon property of its creator thread.

Listing 5-18 creates a thread and sets the thread as a daemon thread. The thread prints an integer and sleeps for some time in an infinite loop. At the end of the main() method, the program prints a message to the standard output stating that it is exiting the main() method. Since thread t is a daemon thread, the JVM will terminate the application when the main() method is finished executing. You can see this in the output. The application prints only one integer from the thread before it exits. You may get different output when you run this program.

Listing 5-18. A Daemon Thread Example

```java
// DaemonThread.java
package com.jdojo.threads;
public class DaemonThread {
    public static void main(String[] args) {
        Thread t = new Thread(DaemonThread::print);
        t.setDaemon(true);
        t.start();
        System.out.println("Exiting main method");
    }
    public static void print() {
        int counter = 1;
        while (true) {
            try {
                System.out.println("Counter: " +
                    counter++);
                Thread.sleep(2000); // sleep for 2 seconds
            } catch (InterruptedException e) {
                e.printStackTrace();
            }
        }
    }
}
```

```
Exiting main method
Counter: 1
```

Listing 5-19 is the same program as Listing 5-18, except that it sets the thread as a non-daemon thread. Since this program has a non-daemon (or a user) thread, the JVM will keep running the application, even after the main() method finishes. You have to stop this application manually because the thread runs in an infinite loop.

Listing 5-19. A Non-daemon Thread Example

```java
// NonDaemonThread.java
package com.jdojo.threads;
public class NonDaemonThread {
    public static void main(String[] args) {
        Thread t = new Thread(NonDaemonThread::print);
        // t is already a non-daemon thread because the
        // "main" thread that runs the main() method is a
        // non-daemon thread. You can verify it by using
        // t.isDaemon() method. It will return false.
        // Still we will use the following statement to
        // make it clear that we want t to be a non-daemon
        // thread.
        t.setDaemon(false);
        t.start();
        System.out.println("Exiting main method");
    }
    public static void print() {
        int counter = 1;
        while (true) {
            try {
                System.out.println("Counter: " +
                    counter++);
                Thread.sleep(2000); // sleep for 2 seconds
            } catch (InterruptedException e) {
                e.printStackTrace();
            }
        }
    }
}
```

```
Exiting main method
Counter: 1
Counter: 2
...
```

317

Am I Interrupted?

You can interrupt a thread that is alive by using the interrupt() method. This method invocation on a thread is just an indication to the thread that some other part of the program is trying to draw its attention. It is up to the thread how it responds to the interruption. Java implements the interruption mechanism using an interrupted status flag for every thread.

A thread could be in one of the two states when it is interrupted: running or blocked. If a thread is interrupted when it is running, its interrupted status is set by the JVM. The running thread can check its interrupted status by calling the Thread.interrupted() static method, which returns true if the current thread was interrupted. The call to the Thread.interrupted() method clears the interrupted status of a thread. That is, if you call this method again on the same thread and if the first call returned true, the subsequent calls will return false, unless the thread is interrupted after the first call but before the subsequent calls.

Listing 5-20 shows the code that interrupts the main thread and prints the interrupted status of the thread. Note that the second call to the Thread.interrupted() method returns false, as indicated in the output #3: false. This example also shows that a thread can interrupt itself. The main thread that is responsible for running the main() method is interrupting itself in this example.

Listing 5-20. A Simple Example of Interrupting a Thread

```java
// SimpleInterrupt.java
package com.jdojo.threads;
public class SimpleInterrupt {
    public static void main(String[] args) {
        System.out.println("#1: " + Thread.interrupted());
        // Now interrupt the main thread
        Thread.currentThread().interrupt();
        // Check if it has been interrupted
        System.out.println("#2: " + Thread.interrupted());
        // Check again if it has been interrupted
        System.out.println("#3: " + Thread.interrupted());
    }
}
```

```
#1: false
#2: true
#3: false
```

Let's look at another example of the same kind. This time, one thread will interrupt another thread. Listing 5-21 starts a thread that increments a counter until the thread is interrupted. At the end, the thread prints the value of the counter. The main() method starts the thread; it sleeps for one second to let the counter thread do some work; it interrupts the thread. Since the thread checks whether it has been interrupted or not before continuing in the while loop, it exits the loop once it is interrupted. You may get different output when you run this program.

Listing 5-21. A Thread Interrupting Another Thread

```java
// SimpleInterruptAnotherThread.java
package com.jdojo.threads;
public class SimpleInterruptAnotherThread {
    public static void main(String[] args) {
        Thread t = new Thread(
            SimpleInterruptAnotherThread::run);
        t.start();
        try {
            // Let the main thread sleep for 1 second
            Thread.currentThread().sleep(1000);
        } catch (InterruptedException e) {
            e.printStackTrace();
        }
        // Now interrupt the thread
        t.interrupt();
    }
    public static void run() {
        int counter = 0;
        while (!Thread.interrupted()) {
            counter++;
        }
```

```
        System.out.println("Counter: " + counter);
    }
}
```

Counter: 1313385352

The Thread class has a non-static isInterrupted() method that can be used to test if a thread has been interrupted. When you call this method, unlike the interrupted() method, the interrupted status of the thread is not cleared. Listing 5-22 demonstrates the difference between these methods.

Listing 5-22. Difference Between the interrupted() and isInterrupted() Methods

```java
// SimpleIsInterrupted.java
package com.jdojo.threads;
public class SimpleIsInterrupted {
    public static void main(String[] args) {
        // Check if the main thread is interrupted
        System.out.println("#1: " +
            Thread.interrupted());
        // Now interrupt the main thread
        Thread mainThread = Thread.currentThread();
        mainThread.interrupt();
        // Check if it has been interrupted
        System.out.println("#2: " +
            mainThread.isInterrupted());
        // Check if it has been interrupted
        System.out.println("#3: " +
            mainThread.isInterrupted());
        // Now check if it has been interrupted using the
        // static method which will clear the interrupted
        // status
        System.out.println("#4: " +
            Thread.interrupted());
```

```
        // Now, isInterrupted() should return false,
        // because previous statement Thread.interrupted()
        // has cleared the flag
        System.out.println("#5: " +
            mainThread.isInterrupted());
    }
}
```

```
#1: false
#2: true
#3: true
#4: true
#5: false
```

You may interrupt a blocked thread. Recall that a thread may block itself by executing one of the sleep(), wait(), and join() methods. If a thread blocked on these three methods is interrupted, an InterruptedException is thrown, and the interrupted status of the thread is cleared because the thread has already received an exception to signal the interruption.

Listing 5-23 starts a thread that sleeps for one second and prints a message until it is interrupted. The main thread sleeps for five seconds, so the sleeping thread gets a chance to sleep and print messages a few times. When the main thread wakes up, it interrupts the sleeping thread. You may get different output when you run the program.

Listing 5-23. Interrupting a Blocked Thread

```java
// BlockedInterrupted.java
package com.jdojo.threads;
public class BlockedInterrupted {
    public static void main(String[] args) {
        Thread t = new Thread(BlockedInterrupted::run);
        t.start();
        // main thread sleeps for 5 seconds
        try {
            Thread.sleep(5000);
```

```
        } catch (InterruptedException e) {
            e.printStackTrace();
        }
        // Interrupt the sleeping thread
        t.interrupt();
    }
    public static void run() {
        int counter = 1;
        while (true) {
            try {
                Thread.sleep(1000);
                System.out.println("Counter: " +
                    counter++);
            } catch (InterruptedException e) {
                System.out.println("I got interrupted!");
                // Terminate the thread by returning
                return;
            }
        }
    }
}

Counter: 1
Counter: 2
Counter: 3
Counter: 4
I got interrupted!
```

If a thread is blocked on an I/O, interrupting a thread does not really do anything if you are using the old I/O API. However, if you are using the new I/O API, your thread will receive a ClosedByInterruptException, which is declared in the java.nio.channels package.

Threads Work in a Group

A thread is always a member of a thread group. By default, the thread group of a thread is the group of its creator thread. The JVM creates a thread group called main and a thread in this group called main, which is responsible for running the main() method of the main class at startup. A thread group in a Java program is represented by an object of the ThreadGroup class. The getThreadGroup() method of the Thread class returns the reference to the ThreadGroup of a thread. Listing 5-24 demonstrates that, by default, a new thread is a member of the thread group of its creator thread.

Listing 5-24. Determining the Default Thread Group of a Thread

```java
// DefaultThreadGroup.java
package com.jdojo.threads;
public class DefaultThreadGroup {
    public static void main(String[] args) {
        // Get the current thread, which is called "main"
        Thread t1 = Thread.currentThread();
        // Get the thread group of the main thread
        ThreadGroup tg1 = t1.getThreadGroup();
        System.out.println(
            "Current thread's name: " +
            t1.getName());
        System.out.println(
            "Current thread's group name: " +
            tg1.getName());
        // Creates a new thread. Its thread group is the
        // same that of the main thread.
        Thread t2 = new Thread("my new thread");
        ThreadGroup tg2 = t2.getThreadGroup();
        System.out.println("New thread's name: " +
            t2.getName());
        System.out.println("New thread's group name: " +
            tg2.getName());
    }
}
```

```
Current thread's name: main
Current thread's group name: main
New thread's name: my new thread
New thread's group name: main
```

You can also create a thread group and place a new thread in that thread group. To place a new thread in your thread group, you must use one of the constructors of the Thread class that accepts a ThreadGroup object as an argument. The following snippet of code places a new thread in a particular thread group:

```
// Create a new ThreadGroup
ThreadGroup myGroup = new ThreadGroup("My Thread Group");
// Make the new thread a member of the myGroup thread group
Thread t = new Thread(myGroup, "myThreadName");
```

Thread groups are arranged in a tree-like structure. A thread group can contain another thread group. The getParent() method of the ThreadGroup class returns the parent thread group of a thread group. The parent of the top-level thread group is null.

The activeCount() method of the ThreadGroup class returns an estimate of the number of active threads in the group. The enumerate(Thread[] list) method of the ThreadGroup class can be used to get the threads in a thread group.

A thread group in a Java program can be used to implement a group-based policy that applies to all threads in a thread group. For example, by calling the interrupt() method of a thread group, you can interrupt all threads in the thread group and its subgroups.

Volatile Variables

I discussed the use of the synchronized keyword in previous sections. Two things happen when a thread executes a synchronized method/block:

- The thread must obtain the monitor lock of the object on which the method/block is synchronized.

- The thread's working copy of the shared variables is updated with the values of those variables in the main memory just after the thread gets the lock. The values of the shared variables in the main memory are updated with the thread's working copy value just before the thread releases the lock. That is, at the start and at the end of a synchronized method/block, the values of the shared variables in the thread's working memory and the main memory are synchronized.

What can you do to achieve only the second point without using a synchronized method/block? That is, how can you keep the values of variables in a thread's working memory in sync with their values in the main memory? The answer is the keyword `volatile`. You can declare a variable volatile like so:

```
volatile boolean flag = true;
```

For every read request for a volatile variable, a thread reads the value from the main memory. For every write request for a volatile variable, a thread writes the value to the main memory. In other words, a thread does not cache the value of a volatile variable in its working memory. Note that using a volatile variable is useful only in a multi-threaded environment for variables that are shared among threads. It is faster and cheaper than using a `synchronized` block.

You can declare only a class member variable (instance or static fields) as `volatile`. You cannot declare a local variable as `volatile` because a local variable is always private to the thread, which is never shared with other threads. You cannot declare a `volatile` variable `final` because the `volatile` keyword is used with a variable that changes.

You can use a `volatile` variable to stop a thread by using the variable's value as a flag. If the flag is set, the thread can keep running. If another thread clears the flag, the thread should stop. Since two threads share the flag, you need to declare it `volatile`, so that on every read the thread will get its updated value from the main memory.

Listing 5-25 demonstrates the use of a `volatile` variable. If the `keepRunning` variable is not declared `volatile`, the JVM is free to run the while loop in the `run()` method forever, as the initial value of `keepRunning` is set to `true` and a thread can cache this value in its working memory. Since the `keepRunning` variable is declared `volatile`, the JVM will read its value from the main memory every time it is used. When another thread updates the `keepRunning` variable's value to `false` using the `stopThread()` method, the next iteration of the while loop will read its updated value and stop the loop. Your program may work the same way as in Listing 5-25 even if you do not declare the `keepRunning` as `volatile`. However, according to the JVM specification, this behavior is not guaranteed. If the JVM specification is implemented correctly, using a `volatile` variable in this way ensures the correct behavior for your program.

Listing 5-25. Using a volatile Variable in a Multi-threaded Program

```java
// VolatileVariable.java
package com.jdojo.threads;
public class VolatileVariable extends Thread {
    private volatile boolean keepRunning = true;
    @Override
    public void run() {
        System.out.println("Thread started...");
        // keepRunning is volatile. So, for every read,
        // the thread reads its latest value from the main
        // memory
        while (keepRunning) {
            try {
                System.out.println("Going to sleep ...");
                Thread.sleep(1000);
            } catch (InterruptedException e) {
                e.printStackTrace();
            }
        }
        System.out.println("Thread stopped...");
    }
    public void stopThread() {
        this.keepRunning = false;
    }
    public static void main(String[] args) {
        // Create the thread
        VolatileVariable vv = new VolatileVariable();
        // Start the thread
        vv.start();
        // Let the main thread sleep for 3 seconds
        try {
            Thread.sleep(3000);
        } catch (InterruptedException e) {
            e.printStackTrace();
        }
```

```
    // Stop the thread
    System.out.println(
        "Going to set the stop flag to true...");
    vv.stopThread();
  }
}
```

```
Thread started...
Going to sleep ...
Going to sleep ...
Going to sleep ...
Going to set the stop flag to true...
Thread stopped...
```

Note   A `volatile` variable of long and double types is treated atomically for read and write purposes. Recall that a non-volatile variable of `long` and `double` types is treated non-atomically. That is, if two threads are writing two different values, say v1 and v2, to a non-volatile `long` or `double` variable, respectively, your program may see a value for that variable that is neither v1 nor v2. However, if that `long` or `double` variable is declared `volatile`, your program sees the value v1 or v2 at a given point in time. You cannot make array elements `volatile`.

Stopping, Suspending, and Resuming Threads

The stop(), suspend(), and resume() methods in the Thread class let you stop a thread, suspend a thread, and resume a suspended thread, respectively. These methods have been deprecated because their use is error-prone.

You can stop a thread by calling the stop() method. When the stop() method of a thread is called, the JVM throws a ThreadDeath error. Because of throwing this error, all monitors locked by the thread being stopped are unlocked. Monitor locks are used to protect some important shared resources (typically Java objects). If any of the shared resources protected by the monitors were in inconsistent states when the thread was stopped, other threads may see that inconsistent state of those resources. This will result in incorrect behavior of the program. This is the reason why the stop() method has been deprecated; you are advised not to use it in your program.

How can you stop a thread without using its stop() method? You can stop a thread by setting a flag that the running thread will check regularly. If the flag is set, the thread should stop executing. This way of stopping a thread was illustrated in Listing 5-25 in the previous section.

You can suspend a thread by calling its suspend() method. To resume a suspended thread, you need to call its resume() method. However, the suspend() method has been deprecated because it is error-prone, and it may cause a deadlock. Let's assume that the suspended thread holds the monitor lock of an object. The thread that will resume the suspended thread is trying to obtain the monitor lock of the same object. This will result in a deadlock. The suspended thread will remain suspended because there is no thread that will resume it, and the thread that will resume it will remain blocked because the monitor lock it is trying to obtain is held by the suspended thread. This is why the suspend() method has been deprecated. The resume() method is also deprecated because it is called in conjunction with the suspend() method. You can use a similar technique to simulate the suspend() and resume() methods of the Thread class in your program as you did to simulate the stop() method.

Listing 5-26 demonstrates how to simulate the stop(), suspend(), and resume() methods of the Thread class in your thread.

Listing 5-26. Stopping, Suspending, and Resuming a Thread

```
// StopSuspendResume.java
package com.jdojo.threads;
public class StopSuspendResume extends Thread {
    private volatile boolean keepRunning = true;
    private boolean suspended = false;
    public synchronized void stopThread() {
        this.keepRunning = false;
        // Notify the thread in case it is suspended when
        // this method is called, so  it will wake up and
        // stop.
        this.notify();
    }
```

```java
public synchronized void suspendThread() {
    this.suspended = true;
}
public synchronized void resumeThread() {
    this.suspended = false;
    this.notify();
}
@Override
public void run() {
    System.out.println("Thread started...");
    while (keepRunning) {
        try {
            System.out.println("Going to sleep...");
            Thread.sleep(1000);
            // Check for a suspended condition must be
            // made inside a synchronized block to call
            // the wait() method
            synchronized (this) {
                while (suspended) {
                    System.out.println("Suspended...");
                    this.wait();
                    System.out.println("Resumed...");
                }
            }
        } catch (InterruptedException e) {
            e.printStackTrace();
        }
    }
    System.out.println("Thread stopped...");
}
public static void main(String[] args) {
    StopSuspendResume t = new StopSuspendResume();
    // Start the thread
    t.start();
    // Sleep for 2 seconds
```

```
        try {
            Thread.sleep(2000);
        } catch (InterruptedException e) {
            e.printStackTrace();
        }
        // Suspend the thread
        t.suspendThread();
        // Sleep for 2 seconds
        try {
            Thread.sleep(2000);
        } catch (InterruptedException e) {
            e.printStackTrace();
        }
        // Resume the thread
        t.resumeThread();
        try {
            Thread.sleep(2000);
        } catch (InterruptedException e) {
            e.printStackTrace();
        }
        // Stop the thread
        t.stopThread();
    }
}

Thread started...
Going to sleep...
Going to sleep...
Going to sleep...
Suspended...
Resumed...
Going to sleep...
Going to sleep...
Going to sleep...
Thread stopped...
```

Note that you have two instance variables in the `StopSuspendResume` class. The suspended instance variable is not declared `volatile`. It is not necessary to declare it `volatile` because it is always accessed inside a `synchronized` method/block. The following code in the `run()` method is used to implement the suspend and resume features:

```
synchronized (this) {
    while (suspended) {
        System.out.println("Suspended...");
        this.wait();
        System.out.println("Resumed...");
    }
}
```

When the `suspended` instance variable is set to `true`, the thread calls the `wait()` method on itself to wait. Note the use of the `synchronized` block. It uses this as the object to synchronize. This is the reason that you can call `this.wait()` inside the `synchronized` block because you have obtained the lock on this object before entering the synchronized block. Once the `this.wait()` method is called, the thread releases the lock on this object and keeps waiting until another thread calls the `resumeThread()` method to notify it. I also use the `this.notify()` method call inside the `stopThread()` method because if the thread is suspended when the `stopThread()` method is called, the thread will not stop; rather, it will remain suspended.

The thread in this example sleeps for only one second in its `run()` method. Suppose your thread sleeps for an extended period. In such a case, calling the `stopThread()` method will not stop the thread immediately because the thread will stop only when it wakes up and checks its `keepRunning` instance variable value in its next loop iteration. In such cases, you can use the `interrupt()` method inside the `stopThread()` method to interrupt sleeping/waiting threads, and when an `InterruptedException` is thrown, you need to handle it appropriately.

If you use the technique used in Listing 5-26 to stop a thread, you may run into problems in some situations. The while loop inside the `run()` method depends on the `keepRunning` instance variable, which is set in the `stopThread()` method. The example in this listing is simple. It is just meant to demonstrate the concept of how to stop, suspend, and resume a thread. Suppose inside the run() method, your code waits for other resources like calling a method someBlockingMethodCall() as shown:

```
while (keepRunning) {
    try {
        someBlockingMethodCall();
    } catch (InterruptedException e) {
        e.printStackTrace();
    }
}
```

If you call the stopThread() method while this thread is blocked on the method call someBlockingMethodCall(), this thread will not stop until it returns from the blocked method call or it is interrupted. To overcome this problem, you need to change the strategy for how to stop a thread. It is a good idea to rely on the interruption technique of a thread to stop it prematurely. The stopThread() method can be changed as follows:

```
public void stopThread() {
    // interrupt this thread
    this.interrupt();
}
```

In addition, the while loop inside the run() method should be modified to check if the thread is interrupted. You need to modify the exception handling code to exit the loop if this thread is interrupted while it is blocked. The following snippet of code illustrates this logic:

```
public void run() {
    while (Thread.currentThread().isInterrupted())) {
        try {
            // Do the processing
        } catch (InterruptedException e) {
            // Stop the thread by exiting the loop
            break;
        }
    }
}
```

Spin-Wait Hints

Sometimes, one thread may have to wait for another thread to update a volatile variable. When the volatile variable is updated with a certain value, the first thread may proceed. If the wait could be longer, it is suggested that the first thread relinquish the CPU by sleeping or waiting and it be notified when it can resume work. However, making a thread sleep or wait has latency. For a short time wait and to reduce latency, it is common for a thread to wait in a loop by checking for a certain condition to be true. Consider the code in a class that uses a loop to wait for a volatile variable named dataReady to be true: volatile boolean dataReady;

```
...
@Override
public void run() {
    // Wait in a loop until data is ready
    while (!dataReady) {
        // No code
    }
    processData();
}
private void processData() {
    // Data processing logic goes here
}
```

The while loop in this code is called a spin-loop, busy-spin, busy-wait, or spin wait. The while loop keeps looping until the value of the dataReady variable becomes true.

While spin-wait is discouraged because of its unnecessary use of resources, it is commonly needed. In this example, the advantage is that the thread will start processing data as soon as the dataReady variable becomes true. However, you pay for performance and power consumption because the thread is actively looping.

Certain processors can be hinted that a thread is in a spin-wait and, if possible, can optimize the resource usage. For example, x86 processors support a PAUSE instruction to indicate a spin-wait. The instruction delays the execution of the next instruction for the thread for a finite small amount of time, thus improving resource usage.

The static onSpinWait() method of the Thread class can be used to give a hint to the processor that the caller thread is momentarily not able to proceed, so resource usage can be optimized. A possible implementation of this method may be no-op when the underlying platform does not support such hints.

Listing 5-27 contains sample code. Note that your program's semantics do not change by using a spin-wait hint. It may perform better if the underlying hardware supports the hint.

Listing 5-27. Sample Code for Using a Spin-Wait Hint to the Processor Using the static Thread.onSpinWait() Method

```java
// SpinWaitTest.java
package com.jdojo.misc;
public class SpinWaitTest implements Runnable {
    private volatile boolean dataReady = false;
    @Override
    public void run() {
        // Wait while data is ready
        while (!dataReady) {
            // use a spin-wait hint
            Thread.onSpinWait();
        }
        processData();
    }
    private void processData() {
        // Data processing logic goes here
    }
    public void setDataReady(boolean dataReady) {
        this.dataReady = dataReady;
    }
}
```

Handling an Uncaught Exception in a Thread

You can handle an uncaught exception thrown in your thread. It is handled using an object of a class that implements the nested Thread.UncaughtExceptionHandler interface. The interface contains one method: void uncaughtException(Thread t, Throwable e).

Here, t is the thread object reference that throws the exception, and e is the uncaught exception thrown. Listing 5-28 contains the code for a class whose object can be used as an uncaught exception handler for a thread.

Listing 5-28. An Uncaught Exception Handler for a Thread

```java
// CatchAllThreadExceptionHandler.java
package com.jdojo.threads;
public class CatchAllThreadExceptionHandler
        implements Thread.UncaughtExceptionHandler {
    @Override
    public void uncaughtException(Thread t,
            Throwable e) {
        System.out.println(
            "Caught Exception from Thread: " +
            t.getName());
    }
}
```

The class simply prints a message and the thread name stating that an uncaught exception from a thread has been handled. Typically, you may want to do some cleanup work or log the exception to a file or a database in the uncaughtException() method of the handler. The Thread class contains two methods to set an uncaught exception handler for a thread: one is a static setDefaultUncaughtExceptionHandler() method, and another is a non-static setUncaughtExceptionHandler() method. Use the static method to set a default handler for all threads in your application. Use the non-static method to set a handler for a particular thread. When a thread has an uncaught exception, the following steps are taken:

- If the thread sets an uncaught exception handler using the setUncaughtExceptionHandler() method, the uncaughtException() method of that handler is invoked.

335

- If a thread does not have an uncaught exception handler set, its thread group's uncaughtException() method is called. If the thread group has a parent thread group, it calls the uncaughtException() method of its parent. Otherwise, it checks if there is a default uncaught exception handler set. If it finds a default uncaught exception handler, it calls the uncaughtException() method on it. If it does not find a default uncaught exception handler, a message is printed on the standard error stream. It does not do anything if it does not find a default uncaught exception handler and a ThreadDeath exception is thrown.

Listing 5-29 demonstrates how to set a handler for uncaught exceptions in a thread. It creates an object of class CatchAllThreadExceptionHandler and sets it as a handler for the uncaught exceptions for the main thread. The main thread throws an unchecked exception in its last statement. The output shows that the handler handles the exception thrown in the main() method.

Listing 5-29. Setting an Uncaught Exception Handler for a Thread

```
// UncaughtExceptionInThread.java
package com.jdojo.threads;
public class UncaughtExceptionInThread {
    public static void main(String[] args) {
        CatchAllThreadExceptionHandler handler =
            new CatchAllThreadExceptionHandler();
        // Set an uncaught exception handler for the
        // main thread
        Thread.currentThread().
            setUncaughtExceptionHandler(handler);
        // Throw an exception
        throw new RuntimeException();
    }
}

Caught Exception from Thread: main
```

Thread Concurrency Packages

Although Java had support for multi-threading built into the language from the very beginning, it was not easy to develop a multi-threaded Java program that used an advanced level of concurrency constructs. For example, the synchronized keyword, used to lock an object's monitor, has existed since the beginning. However, a thread that tries to lock an object's monitor simply blocks if the lock is not available. In this case, developers had no choice but to back out. Wouldn't it be nice to have a construct that is based on a "try and lock" philosophy rather than a "lock or block" philosophy? In this strategy, if an object's monitor lock is not available, the call to lock the monitor returns immediately.

The java.util.concurrent package and its two subpackages, java.util. concurrent.atomic and java.util.concurrent.locks, include very useful concurrency constructs. You use them only when you are developing an advanced level multi-threaded program. I don't cover all concurrency constructs in this section because describing everything available in these packages could take more than a hundred pages. I briefly cover some of the most useful concurrency constructs available in these packages. You can broadly categorize these concurrency features into four categories:

- Atomic variables

- Locks

- Synchronizers

- Concurrent collections

Atomic Variables

Typically, when you need to share an updateable variable among threads, synchronization is used. Synchronization among multiple threads used to be achieved using the synchronized keyword, and it was based on an object's monitor. If a thread is not able to acquire an object's monitor, that thread is suspended and it has to be resumed later. This way of synchronization (suspending and resuming) uses a great deal of system resources. The problem is not in locking and unlocking the mechanism of the monitor lock; rather, it is in suspending and resuming threads. If there is no contention for acquiring a lock, using the synchronized keyword to synchronize threads does not hurt much.

An atomic variable uses a lock-free synchronization of a single variable. Note that if your program needs to synchronize on more than one shared variable, you still need to use the old synchronization methods. By lock-free synchronization, I mean that multiple threads can access a shared variable safely using no object monitor lock. JDK takes advantage of a hardware instruction called "compare and swap" (CAS) to implement the lock-free synchronization for one variable.

CAS

Compare And Swap is an internal instruction to maintain lock-free synchronization for single atomic variables.

CAS is based on three operands: a memory location M, an expected old value V, and a new value N. If the memory location M contains a value V, CAS updates it atomically to N; otherwise, it does not do anything. CAS always returns the current value at the location M that existed before the CAS operation started. The pseudocode for CAS is as follows:

```
CAS(M, V, N) {
    currentValueAtM = get the value at Location M;
    if (currentValueAtM == V) {
        set value at M to N;
    }
    return currentValueAtM;
}}
```

The CAS instruction is lock-free. It is directly supported in most modern computer hardware. However, CAS is not always guaranteed to succeed in a multi-threaded environment. CAS takes an optimistic approach by assuming that there are no other threads updating the value at location M; if location M contains value V, update it to N; if the value at location M is not V, do not do anything. Therefore, if multiple threads attempt to update the value at location M to different values simultaneously, only one thread will succeed, and the others will fail.

The synchronization using locks takes a pessimistic approach by assuming that other threads may be working with location M and acquires a lock before it starts working at location M, so that other threads will not access location M while one is working with it. In case CAS fails, the caller thread may try the action again or give up; the caller thread using CAS never blocks. However, in the case of synchronization using a lock, the caller thread may have to be suspended and resumed if it could not acquire the lock. Using synchronization, you also run the risk of a deadlock, a livelock, and other synchronization-related failures.

Atomic variable classes are named like `AtomicXxx` and can be used to execute multiple instructions on a single variable atomically without using any lock. Here, `Xxx` is replaced with different words to indicate different classes that are used for different purposes; for example, the `AtomicInteger` class is used to represent an `int` variable, which is supposed to be manipulated atomically. Twelve classes in the Java class library support read-modify-write operations on a single variable atomically. They are in the `java.util.concurrent.atomic` package. They can be categorized in four categories, which are discussed in the following sections.

Scalar Atomic Variable Classes

The `AtomicInteger`, `AtomicLong`, and `AtomicBoolean` classes support operations on primitive data types `int`, `long`, and `boolean`, respectively.

If you need to work with other primitive data types, use the `AtomicInteger` class. You can use it directly to work with the `byte` and `short` data types. Use it to work with the `float` data type by using the `Float.floatToIntBits()` method to convert a `float` value to the `int` data type and the `AtomicInteger.floatValue()` method to convert an `int` value to the `float` data type.

You can use the `AtomicLong` class to work with the `double` data type by using the `Double.doubleToLongBits()` method to convert a `double` value to the `long` data type and the `AtomicLong.doubleValue()` method to convert the `long` value to the `double` data type.

The `AtomicReference<V>` class is used to work with a reference data type when a reference variable needs to be updated atomically.

Atomic Array Classes

There are three classes—called `AtomicIntegerArray`, `AtomicLongArray`, and `AtomicReferenceArray <E>`—that represent an array of `int`, `long`, and reference types whose elements can be updated atomically.

Atomic Field Updater Classes

There are three classes—called AtomicLongFieldUpdater, AtomicIntegerFieldUpdater, and AtomicReferenceFieldUpdater<T,V>—that can be used to update a volatile field of a class atomically using reflection. These classes have no constructors. To get a reference to an object of these classes, you need to use their factory method called newUpdater().

Atomic Compound Variable Classes

CAS works by asking "Is the value at location M still V?" If the answer is yes, it updates the value at location M from V to N. In a typical scenario, one thread may read the value from location M as V. By the time this thread tries to update the value from V to N, another thread has changed the value at location M from V to P, and back from P to V. Therefore, the call CAS(M, V, N) will succeed because the value at location M is still V, even though it was changed (v to P and back to V) twice after the thread read the value V last time. In some cases, it is fine. The thread that wants to update the value at location M does not care if the old value V that it read last time was updated before its own update as long as the value at location M is V at the time it is updating the value to N. However, in some cases, it is not acceptable. If a thread reads the value V from a location M, this thread wants to make sure that after it read the value, no other thread has updated the value. In such cases, CAS needs to ask "Has the value at location M changed since I last read it as V?" To achieve this functionality, you need to store a pair of values: the value you want to work with and its version number. Each update will also update the version number. The AtomicMarkableReference and AtomicStampedReference classes fall into this category of atomic compound variable class.

Let's look at a simple example that uses an atomic class. If you want to write a class to generate a counter using built-in Java synchronization, it will resemble the code shown in Listing 5-30.

Listing 5-30. A Counter Class That Uses Synchronization

```
// SynchronizedCounter.java
package com.jdojo.threads;
public class SynchronizedCounter {
    private long value;
```

```
    public synchronized long next() {
        return ++value;
    }
}
```

You would rewrite the SynchronizedCounter class using the AtomicLong class, as shown in Listing 5-31.

Listing 5-31. A Counter Class Using an Atomic Variable

```
// AtomicCounter.java
package com.jdojo.threads;
import java.util.concurrent.atomic.AtomicLong;
public class AtomicCounter {
    private final AtomicLong value = new AtomicLong(0L);
    public long next() {
        return value.incrementAndGet();
    }
}
```

Note that the AtomicCounter class does not use any explicit synchronization. It takes advantage of CAS hardware instruction. The call to the incrementAndGet() method inside the next() method of the AtomicCounter class is performed atomically for you.

You can also use an object of the AtomicLong class as a thread-safe counter object like so:

```
AtomicLong aCounter = new AtomicLong(0L);
```

Then you can use the aCounter.incrementAndGet() method to generate a new counter. The incrementAndGet() method of the AtomicLong class increments its current value and returns the new value. You also have its counterpart method called getAndIncrement(), which increments its value and returns its previous value.

The AtomicXxx variable classes have a compareAndSet() method. It is a variant of compare and swap (CAS). The only difference is that the compareAndSet() method returns a boolean. It returns true if it succeeds; otherwise, it returns false. The following is the pseudocode representation of the compareAndSet() method:

```
compareAndSet(M, V, N) {
    // Call CAS (see CAS pseudocode) if CAS succeeded,
    // return true; otherwise, return false.
    return (CAS(M, V, N) == V)
}
```

Explicit Locks

The explicit locking mechanism can be used to coordinate access to shared resources in a multi-threaded environment without using the synchronized keyword. The Lock interface, which is declared in the java.util.concurrent.locks package, defines the explicit locking operations. The ReentrantLock class, in the same package, is the concrete implementation of the Lock interface. The Lock interface contains the following methods:

- void lock();

- Condition newCondition();

- void lockInterruptibly() throws InterruptedException;

- boolean tryLock();

- boolean tryLock(long time, TimeUnit unit) throws InterruptedException;

- void unlock();

The use of the lock() method to acquire a lock behaves the same as the use of the synchronized keyword. The use of the synchronized keyword requires that a thread should acquire and release an object's monitor lock in the same block of code. When you use the synchronized keyword to acquire an object's monitor lock, the lock is released by the JVM when the program leaves the block in which the lock was acquired. This feature makes working with intrinsic locks very simple and less error-prone. However, in the case of the Lock interface, the restriction of acquiring and releasing the lock in the same block of code does not apply. This makes it a little flexible to use; however, it is more error-prone because the responsibility of acquiring as well as releasing the lock is on the developer. It is not difficult to acquire the lock and forget to release it, resulting in hard-to-find bugs. You must make sure that you release the lock by calling the unlock() method of the Lock interface after you are done with the lock. You can use the lock() and unlock() methods in their simplest form, shown in Listing 5-32.

Listing 5-32. Using an Explicit Lock in Its Simplest Form

```java
// SimpleExplicitLock.java
package com.jdojo.threads;
import java.util.concurrent.locks.Lock;
import java.util.concurrent.locks.ReentrantLock;
public class SimpleExplicitLock {
    // Instantiate the lock object
    private final Lock myLock = new ReentrantLock();
    public void updateResource() {
        // Acquire the lock
        myLock.lock();
        try {
            // Logic for updating/reading the shared
            // resource goes here
        } finally {
            // Release the lock
            myLock.unlock();
        }
    }
}
```

Note the use of a try-finally block to release the lock in the updateResource() method. The use of a try-finally block is necessary in this case because no matter how you finish returning from this method after you call myLock.lock(), you would like to release the lock. This can be assured only if you place the call to the unlock() method inside the finally block.

You may wonder why you would use the code structure listed in Listing 5-32 when you could have used the synchronized keyword to achieve the same effect, like so:

```
public void updateResource() {
    // Acquire the lock and the lock will be released
    // automatically by the JVM when your code exits the
    // block
    synchronized (this) {
        // Logic for updating/reading the shared
        // resource goes here
    }
}
```

You are correct in thinking that using the synchronized keyword would have been better in this case. It is much simpler and less error-prone to use the synchronized keyword in such situations. The power of using the new Lock interface becomes evident when you come across situations where using the synchronized keyword is not possible or very cumbersome. For example, if you want to acquire the lock in the updateResource() method and release it in some other methods, you cannot use the synchronized keyword. If you need to acquire two locks to work with a shared resource and if only one lock is available, you want to do something else rather than waiting for the other lock to become available. If you use the synchronized keyword or the lock() method of the Lock interface to acquire a lock, the call blocks if the lock is not available immediately, which gives you no option to back off once you asked for the lock. Such blocked threads cannot be interrupted either. The two methods of the Lock interface, tryLock() and lockInterruptibly(), give you the ability to try to acquire a lock (rather than acquire a lock or block). The thread that has acquired the lock can be interrupted if it is blocked. The syntax to acquire and release a lock using the Lock interface should use a try-finally or a try-catch-finally block structure, to avoid unintended bugs, by placing the unlock() call in a finally block.

You will solve a classic synchronization problem known as the dining philosophers problem using the explicit lock constructs. The problem goes like this: five philosophers spend all of their time either thinking or eating. They sit around a circular table with five chairs and five forks, as shown in Figure 5-7. There are only five forks, and all five philosophers need to pick the two nearest (one from their left and one from their right) forks to eat.

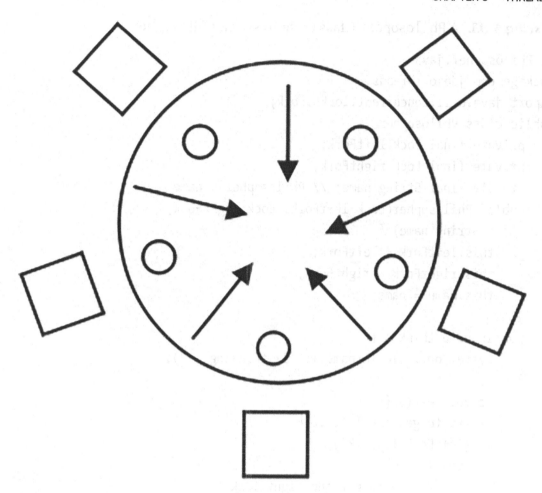

Figure 5-7. *Five philosophers at a dining table*

Once a philosopher finishes eating, he puts down both forks and starts thinking. A philosopher cannot pick up a fork if his neighbor is using it. What happens if each of the five philosophers picks up one fork from his right and waits for his left fork to be released by his neighbor? This would be a deadlock situation, and no philosopher would be able to eat. This deadlock condition can be avoided easily by using the tryLock() method of the Lock interface. This method returns immediately, and it never blocks. If the lock is available, it gets the lock and returns true. If the lock is not available, it returns false. The class in Listing 5-33 can be used to model the philosophers assuming that an object of the ReentrantLock class represents a fork.

Listing 5-33. A Philosopher Class to Represent a Philosopher

```java
// Philosopher.java
package com.jdojo.threads;
import java.util.concurrent.locks.Lock;
public class Philosopher {
    private final Lock leftFork;
    private final Lock rightFork;
    private final String name; // Philosopher's name
    public Philosopher(Lock leftFork, Lock rightFork,
            String name) {
        this.leftFork = leftFork;
        this.rightFork = rightFork;
        this.name = name;
    }
    public void think() {
        System.out.println(name + " is thinking...");
    }
    public void eat() {
        // Try to get the left fork
        if (leftFork.tryLock()) {
            try {
                // try to get the right fork
                if (rightFork.tryLock()) {
                    try {
                        // Got both forks. Eat now
                        System.out.println(name +
                            " is eating...");
                    } finally {
                        // release the right fork
                        rightFork.unlock();
                    }
                }
```

```
        } finally {
            // release the left fork
            leftFork.unlock();
        }
    }
}
```

To create philosophers, you would use code like:

```
Lock fork1 = new ReentrantLock();
Lock fork2 = new ReentrantLock();
...
Lock fork5 = new ReentrantLock();
Philosopher p1 = new Philosopher(fork1, fork2, "John");
Philosopher p2 = new Philosopher(fork2, fork3, "Wallace");
...
Philosopher p5 = new Philosopher(fork5, fork1, "Charles");
```

It is left for the reader as an exercise to complete the code and run all five philosophers in five different threads to simulate the dining philosophers problem. You can also think about how to use the synchronized keyword to solve the same problem. Read the code in the eat() method carefully. It tries to get the left and right forks one at a time. If you can get only one fork and not the other, you put down the one you got so others can have it. The code in the eat() method has only the logic to get the forks. In a real program, if you cannot get both forks, you would like to wait for some time and try again to pick up the forks. You will have to write that logic.

You can specify the fairness of a lock when you instantiate the ReentrantLock class. The fairness indicates the way of allocating the lock to a thread when multiple threads are waiting to get the lock. In a fair lock, threads acquire the lock in the order they request it. In a non-fair lock, jumping ahead by a thread is allowed. For example, in a non-fair lock, if some threads are waiting for a lock and another thread, which requests the same lock later, gets the lock before the waiting threads, if the lock becomes available at the time the second thread requested it. This may sound a little strange because it is not fair to the waiting threads to leave them waiting and granting the lock to the thread that requested it later. However, it has a performance gain. The overhead of suspending and resuming a thread is reduced using non-fair locking. The tryLock() method of the ReentrantLock class always uses a non-fair lock. You can create fair and non-fair locks as follows:

```
Lock nonFairLock1 = new ReentrantLock();
    // <- A non-fair lock (Default is non-fair)
Lock nonFairLock2 = new ReentrantLock(false);
    // <- A non-fair lock
Lock fairLock2 = new ReentrantLock(true);
    // <- A fair lock
```

A ReentrantLock provides a mutually exclusive locking mechanism. That is, only one thread can own the ReentrantLock at a time. If you have a data structure guarded by a ReentrantLock, a writer thread as well as a reader thread must acquire the lock one at a time to modify or to read the data. This restriction of ReentrantLock, to be owned by only one thread at a time, may downgrade the performance if your data structure is read frequently and modified infrequently. In such situations, you may want multiple reader threads to have concurrent access to the data structure. However, if the data structure is being modified, only one writer thread should have the access to the data structure. The read-write lock allows you to implement this kind of locking mechanism using an instance of the ReadWriteLock interface. It has two methods: one to get the reader lock and another to get the writer lock, as shown:

```
public interface ReadWriteLock {
    Lock readLock();
    Lock writeLock();
}
```

A ReentrantReadWriteLock class is an implementation of the ReadWriteLock interface. Only one thread can hold the write lock of ReentrantReadWriteLock, whereas multiple threads can hold its read lock. Listing 5-34 demonstrates the usage of ReentrantReadWriteLock. Note that in the getValue() method, you use read lock so multiple threads can read the data concurrently. The setValue() method uses a write lock so only one thread can modify the data at a given time.

Note   The ReadWriteLock allows you to have a read and a write version of the same lock. Multiple threads can own a read lock as long as another thread does not own the write lock. However, only one thread can own the write lock at a time.

Listing 5-34. Using a ReentrantReadWriteLock to Guard a Read-Mostly Data Structure

```java
// ReadMostlyData.java
package com.jdojo.threads;
import java.util.concurrent.locks.Lock;
import java.util.concurrent.locks.ReentrantReadWriteLock;
public class ReadMostlyData {
    private int value;
    private final ReentrantReadWriteLock rwLock =
        new ReentrantReadWriteLock();
    private final Lock rLock = rwLock.readLock();
    private final Lock wLock = rwLock.writeLock();
    public ReadMostlyData(int value) {
        this.value = value;
    }
    public int getValue() {
        // Use the read lock, so multiple threads may
        // read concurrently
        rLock.lock();
        try {
            return this.value;
        } finally {
            rLock.unlock();
        }
    }
    public void setValue(int value) {
        // Use the write lock, so only one thread can
        // write at a time
        wLock.lock();
```

```
    try {
        this.value = value;
    } finally {
        wLock.unlock();
    }
  }
}
```

Synchronizers

I discussed how to coordinate access to a critical section by multiple threads using a mutually exclusive mechanism of intrinsic locks and explicit locks. Some classes known as synchronizers are used to coordinate the control flow of a set of threads in a situation that needs other than mutually exclusive access to a critical section. A synchronizer object is used with a set of threads. It maintains a state, and depending on its state, it lets a thread pass through or forces it to wait. This section discusses the following types of synchronizers:

- Semaphores

- Barriers

- Phasers

- Latches

- Exchangers

Other classes can also act as synchronizers, such as a blocking queue.

Semaphores

A semaphore is used to control the number of threads that can access a resource. A synchronized block also controls the access to a resource that is the critical section. So, how is a semaphore different from a synchronized block? A synchronized block allows only one thread to access a resource (a critical section), whereas a semaphore allows N threads (N can be any positive number) to access a resource.

If N is set to one, a semaphore can act as a synchronized block to allow a thread to have mutually exclusive access to a resource. A semaphore maintains a number of virtual permits. To access a resource, a thread acquires a permit, and it releases the permit when it is done with the resource. If a permit is not available, the requesting thread is blocked until a permit becomes available. You can think of a semaphore's permit as a token.

Let's discuss a daily life example of using a semaphore. Suppose there is a restaurant with three dining tables. Only three people can eat in that restaurant at a time. When a person arrives at the restaurant, they must take a token for a table. When they are done eating, they will return the token. Each token represents a dining table. If a person arrives at the restaurant when all three tables are in use, they must wait until a table becomes available. If a table is not available immediately, you have a choice to wait until one becomes available or to go to another restaurant. Let's simulate this example using a semaphore. You will have a semaphore with three permits. Each permit will represent a dining table. The Semaphore class in the java.util.concurrent package represents the semaphore synchronizer. You create a semaphore using one of its constructors:

```
final int MAX_PERMITS = 3;
Semaphore s = new Semaphores(MAX_PERMITS);
```

Another constructor for the Semaphore class takes fairness as the second argument:

```
final int MAX_PERMITS = 3;
Semaphore s = new Semaphores(MAX_PERMITS, true);
   // <- A fair semaphore
```

The fairness of a semaphore has the same meaning as that for locks. If you create a fair semaphore, in the situation of multiple threads asking for permits, the semaphore will guarantee first in, first out (FIFO). That is, the thread that asked for the permit first will get the permit first.

To acquire a permit, use the acquire() method. It returns immediately if a permit is available. It blocks if a permit is not available. The thread can be interrupted while it is waiting for the permit to become available. Other methods of the Semaphore class let you acquire one or multiple permits in one go.

To release a permit, use the release() method.

Listing 5-35 contains the code for a Restaurant class. It takes the number of tables available in a restaurant as an argument in its constructor and creates a semaphore, which has the number of permits that is equal to the number of tables. A customer uses its getTable() and returnTable() methods to get and return a table, respectively. Inside the getTable() method, you acquire a permit. If a customer calls the getTable() method and no table is available, they must wait until one becomes available. This class depends on a RestaurantCustomer class that is declared in Listing 5-36.

Listing 5-35. A Restaurant Class, Which Uses a Semaphore to Control Access to Tables

```java
// Restaurant.java
package com.jdojo.threads;
import java.util.concurrent.Semaphore;
public class Restaurant {
    private final Semaphore tables;
    public Restaurant(int tablesCount) {
        // Create a semaphore using number of tables we
        // have
        this.tables = new Semaphore(tablesCount);
    }
    public void getTable(int customerID) {
        try {
            System.out.println("Customer #" + customerID
                + " is trying to get a table.");
            // Acquire a permit for a table
            tables.acquire();
            System.out.println("Customer #" + customerID
                + " got a table.");
        } catch (InterruptedException e) {
            e.printStackTrace();
        }
    }
    public void returnTable(int customerID) {
        System.out.println("Customer #" + customerID +
            " returned a table.");
        tables.release();
    }
}
```

```
    public static void main(String[] args) {
        // Create a restaurant with two dining tables
        Restaurant restaurant = new Restaurant(2);
        // Create five customers
        for (int i = 1; i <= 5; i++) {
            RestaurantCustomer c = new RestaurantCustomer(
                restaurant, i);
            c.start();
        }
    }
}
```

```
Customer #4 is trying to get a table.
Customer #5 is trying to get a table.
Customer #1 is trying to get a table.
Customer #3 is trying to get a table.
```

Listing 5-36 contains the code for a RestaurantCustomer class whose object represents a customer in a restaurant. The run() method of the customer thread gets a table from the restaurant, eats for a random amount of time, and returns the table to the restaurant. When you run the Restaurant class, you may get similar but not the same output. You may observe that you have created a restaurant with only two tables, and five customers are trying to eat. At any given time, only two customers are eating, as shown by the output.

Listing 5-36. A RestaurantCustomer Class to Represent a Customer in a Restaurant

```
// RestaurantCustomer.java
package com.jdojo.threads;
import java.util.Random;
class RestaurantCustomer extends Thread {
    private final Restaurant r;
    private final int customerID;
    private static final Random random = new Random();
```

```java
    public RestaurantCustomer(Restaurant r,
            int customerID) {
        this.r = r;
        this.customerID = customerID;
    }
    @Override
    public void run() {
        r.getTable(this.customerID); // Get a table
        try {
            // Eat for some time. Use number between 1
            // and 30 seconds
            int eatingTime = random.nextInt(30) + 1;
            System.out.println("Customer #"
                    + this.customerID
                    + " will eat for "
                    + eatingTime + " seconds.");
            Thread.sleep(eatingTime * 1000);
            System.out.println("Customer #"
                    + this.customerID
                    + " is done eating.");
        } catch (InterruptedException e) {
            e.printStackTrace();
        } finally {
            r.returnTable(this.customerID);
        }
    }
}
```

A semaphore is not limited to the number of permits it was created with. Each release() method adds one permit to it. Therefore, if you call the release() method more than the times you call its acquire() method, you end up having more permits than the one you started with. A permit is not acquired on a per-thread basis. One thread can acquire a permit from a semaphore, and another can return it. This leaves the burden of the correct usage of acquiring and releasing a permit on the developers. A semaphore has other methods to acquire a permit, which will let you back off instead of forcing you to wait if a permit is not immediately available, such as the tryAcquire() and acquireUninterruptibly() methods.

Barriers

A barrier is used to make a group of threads meet at a barrier point. A thread from a group arriving at the barrier waits until all threads in that group arrive. Once the last thread from the group arrives at the barrier, all threads in the group are released. You can use a barrier when you have a task that can be divided into subtasks; each subtask can be performed in a separate thread, and each thread must meet at a common point to combine their results. Figures 5-8 through 5-11 depict how a barrier synchronizer lets a group of three threads meet at the barrier point and lets them proceed.

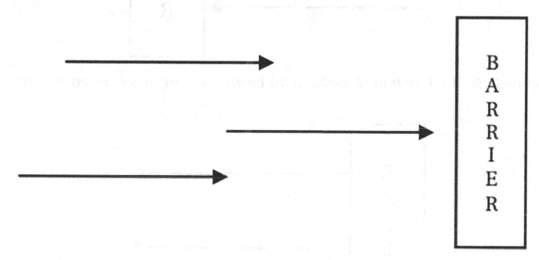

Figure 5-8. *Three threads arriving at a barrier*

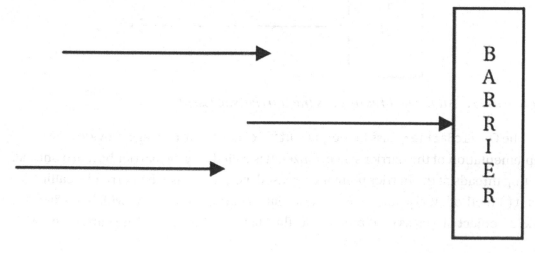

Figure 5-9. *One thread waits for the two other threads to arrive at the barrier*

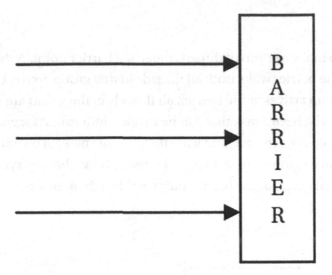

Figure 5-10. *All three threads arrive at the barrier and are then released at once*

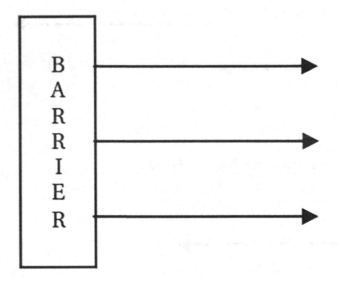

Figure 5-11. *All three threads pass the barrier successfully*

The CyclicBarrier class in the java.util.concurrent package provides the implementation of the barrier synchronizer. It is called a cyclic barrier because once all waiting threads at the barrier point are released, you can reuse the barrier by calling its reset() method. It also allows you to associate a barrier action to it, which is a Runnable task (an object of a class that implements the Runnable interface). The barrier action is executed just before all threads are released. You can think of the barrier action as a "party time" when all threads meet at the barrier, but before they are released. Here are the steps you need to perform to use a barrier in a program:

1. Create an object of the `CyclicBarrier` class with the number of threads in the group:

    ```
    CyclicBarrier barrier = new CyclicBarrier(5);
    // <- 5 threads
    ```

    If you want to execute a barrier action when all threads meet at the barrier, you can use another constructor of the `CyclicBarrier` class:

    ```
    // Assuming a BarrierAction class implements the
    // Runnable interface
    Runnable barrierAction = new BarrierAction();
    CyclicBarrier barrier = new CyclicBarrier(
        5, barrierAction);
    ```

2. When a thread is ready to wait at the barrier, the thread executes the `await()` method of the `CyclicBarrier` class. The `await()` method comes in two flavors. One lets you wait for all other threads unconditionally, and the other lets you specify a timeout.

The program in Listing 5-37 demonstrates how to use a cyclic barrier. You may get different output. However, the sequence of events will be the same: all three threads will work for some time, wait at the barrier for others to arrive, have a party time, and pass the barrier.

Listing 5-37. A Class That Demonstrates How to Use a `CyclicBarrier` in a Program

```
// MeetAtBarrier.java
package com.jdojo.threads;
import java.util.Random;
import java.util.concurrent.CyclicBarrier;
import java.util.concurrent.BrokenBarrierException;
```

```java
public class MeetAtBarrier extends Thread {
    private final CyclicBarrier barrier;
    private final int ID;
    private static final Random random = new Random();
    public MeetAtBarrier(int ID, CyclicBarrier barrier) {
        this.ID = ID;
        this.barrier = barrier;
    }
    @Override
    public void run() {
        try {
            // Generate a random number between 1 and 30
            // to wait
            int workTime = random.nextInt(30) + 1;
            System.out.println("Thread #" + ID
                    + " is going to work for "
                    + workTime + " seconds");
            // Yes. Sleeping is working for this thread!!!
            Thread.sleep(workTime * 1000);
            System.out.println("Thread #" + ID
                    + " is waiting at the barrier...");
            // Wait at barrier for other threads in group
            // to arrive
            this.barrier.await();
            System.out.println("Thread #" + ID
                    + " passed the barrier...");
        } catch (InterruptedException e) {
            e.printStackTrace();
        } catch (BrokenBarrierException e) {
            System.out.println("Barrier is broken...");
        }
    }
```

```
public static void main(String[] args) {
    // Create a barrier for a group of three threads
    // with a barrier action
    String msg =
        "We are all together. It's party time...";
    Runnable barrierAction = () ->
        System.out.println(msg);
    CyclicBarrier barrier =
        new CyclicBarrier(3, barrierAction);
    for (int i = 1; i <= 3; i++) {
        MeetAtBarrier t =
            new MeetAtBarrier(i, barrier);
        t.start();
    }
}
}
```

```
Thread #2 is going to work for 15 seconds
Thread #3 is going to work for 2 seconds
Thread #1 is going to work for 30 seconds
Thread #3 is waiting at the barrier...
Thread #2 is waiting at the barrier...
Thread #1 is waiting at the barrier...
We are all together. It's party time...
Thread #3 passed the barrier...
Thread #2 passed the barrier...
Thread #1 passed the barrier...
```

You might have noticed that inside the run() method of the MeetAtBarrier class, you are catching BrokenBarrierException. If a thread times out or it is interrupted while waiting at the barrier point, the barrier is considered broken. The thread that times out is released with a TimeoutException, whereas all waiting threads at the barrier are released with a BrokenBarrierException.

Note   The await( ) method of the CyclicBarrier class returns the arrival index of the thread calling it. The last thread to arrive at the barrier has an index of zero, and the first has an index of the number of threads in the group minus one. You can use this index to do any special processing in your program. For example, the last thread to arrive at the barrier may log the time when a particular round of computation is finished by all participating threads.

Phasers

The Phaser class in the java.util.concurrent package provides an implementation for another synchronization barrier called phaser. A Phaser provides functionality similar to the CyclicBarrier and CountDownLatch synchronizers. I cover the CountDownLatch synchronizer in the next section. However, it is more powerful and flexible. It provides the following features:

- Like a CyclicBarrier, a Phaser is also reusable.

- Unlike a CyclicBarrier, the number of parties to synchronize on a Phaser can change dynamically. In a CyclicBarrier, the number of parties is fixed at the time the barrier is created. However, in a Phaser, you can add or remove parties at any time.

- A Phaser has an associated phase number, which starts at zero. When all registered parties arrive at a Phaser, the Phaser advances to the next phase, and the phase number is incremented by one. The maximum value of the phase number is Integer.MAX_VALUE. After its maximum value, the phase number restarts at zero.

- A Phaser has a termination state. All synchronization methods called on a Phaser in a termination state return immediately without waiting for an advance. The Phaser class provides different ways to terminate a phaser.

- A Phaser has three types of parties count: a registered parties count, an arrived parties count, and an unarrived parties count. The registered parties count is the number of parties that are registered for synchronization. The arrived parties count is the number of parties that have arrived at the current phase of the phaser. The unarrived parties count is the number of parties that have not yet arrived at the current phase of the phaser. When the last party arrives, the phaser advances to the next phase. Note that all three types of party counts are dynamic.

- Optionally, a Phaser lets you execute a phaser action when all registered parties arrive at the phaser. Recall that a CyclicBarrier lets you execute a barrier action, which is a Runnable task. Unlike a CyclicBarrier, you specify a phaser action by writing code in the onAdvance() method of your Phaser class. It means you need to use your own phaser class by inheriting it from the Phaser class and override the onAdvance() method to provide a Phaser action. I discuss an example of this kind shortly.

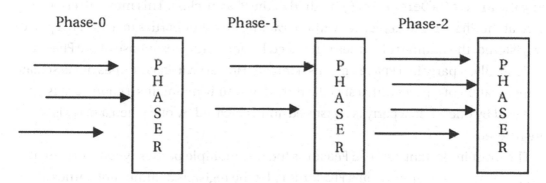

Figure 5-12. *A Phaser with three phases with a different number of parties in each phase*

Figure 5-12 shows a phaser with three phases. It synchronizes on a different number of parties in each phase. An arrow in the figure represents a party.

There are several steps to work with a Phaser. You can create a Phaser with no initially registered party using its default constructor:

```
// A phaser with no registered parties
Phaser phaser = new Phaser();
```

Another constructor lets you register parties when the Phaser is created:

```
// A phaser with 5 registered parties
Phaser phaser = new Phaser(5);
```

A Phaser may be arranged in a tree-like structure. Other constructors let you create a Phaser by specifying the parent of the newly created Phaser. Once you have created a Phaser, the next step is to register parties that are interested in synchronizing on the phaser. You can register a party in the following ways:

- By specifying the number of parties to register in the constructor of the Phaser class when you create a Phaser object

- By using the register() method of the Phaser class to register one party at a time

- By using the bulkRegister(int parties) method of the Phaser class to register the specified number of parties in bulk

The registered parties of a Phaser may change at any time by registering new parties or deregistering the already registered parties. You can deregister a registered party using the arriveAndDeregister() method of the Phaser class. This method lets a party arrive at the Phaser and deregister without waiting for other parties to arrive. If a party is deregistered, the number of parties is reduced by one in the next phase of the Phaser.

Typically, a party in a Phaser means a thread. However, a Phaser does not associate the registration of a party with a specific thread. It simply maintains a count that is increased by one when a party is registered and decreased by one when a party is deregistered.

The most important part of a Phaser is the way multiple parties synchronize on it. A typical way to synchronize on a Phaser is to let the registered number of parties arrive and wait at the Phaser for other registered parties to arrive. Once the last registered party arrives at the Phaser, all parties advance to the next phase of the Phaser.

The arriveAndAwaitAdvance() method of the Phaser class lets a party arrive at the Phaser and waits for other parties to arrive before it can proceed.

The arriveAndDeregister() method of the Phaser class lets a party arrive at the Phaser and deregister without waiting for other parties to arrive. Upon deregistration, the number of parties required to advance to the future phase reduces by one. Typically, the arriveAndDeregister() method is used by a controller party whose job is to control the advance of other parties without participating in the advance itself. Typically, the controller party registers itself with the Phaser and waits for some conditions to occur; when the required condition occurs, it arrives and deregisters itself from the Phaser so parties can synchronize on the Phaser and advance.

Let's walk through an example of using a Phaser to synchronize a group of tasks so they can all start at the same time. An instance of the StartTogetherTask class, shown in Listing 5-38, represents a task in this example.

Listing 5-38. A StartTogetherTask Class to Represent Tasks That Start Together by Synchronizing on a Phaser

```java
// StartTogetherTask.java
package com.jdojo.threads;
import java.util.Random;
import java.util.concurrent.Phaser;
public class StartTogetherTask extends Thread {
    private final Phaser phaser;
    private final String taskName;
    private static Random rand = new Random();
    public StartTogetherTask(String taskName,
            Phaser phaser) {
        this.taskName = taskName;
        this.phaser = phaser;
    }
    @Override
    public void run() {
        System.out.println(taskName + ":Initializing...");
        // Sleep for some time between 1 and 5 seconds
        int sleepTime = rand.nextInt(5) + 1;
        try {
            Thread.sleep(sleepTime * 1000);
        } catch (InterruptedException e) {
            e.printStackTrace();
        }
        System.out.println(taskName + ":Initialized...");
        // Wait for all parties to arrive to start the task
```

```
        phaser.arriveAndAwaitAdvance();
        System.out.println(taskName + ":Started...");
    }
}
```

The StartTogetherTask class inherits from the Thread class. Its constructor accepts a task name and a Phaser instance. In its run() method, it prints a message that it is initializing. It fakes its initialization by sleeping for a random period of 1 to 5 seconds. After that, it prints a message that it is initialized. At this stage, it waits on a Phaser advance by calling the arriveAndAwaitAdvance() method of the Phaser. This method will block until all registered parties arrive at the Phaser. When this method returns, it prints a message that the task has started. Listing 5-39 contains the code to test three tasks of StartTogetherTask type.

Listing 5-39. Testing Some Objects of the StartTogetherTask Class with a Phaser

```
// StartTogetherTaskTest.java
package com.jdojo.threads;
import java.util.concurrent.Phaser;
public class StartTogetherTaskTest {
    public static void main(String[] args) {
        // Start with 1 registered party
        Phaser phaser = new Phaser(1);
        // Let's start three tasks
        final int TASK_COUNT = 3;
        for (int i = 1; i <= TASK_COUNT; i++) {
            // Register a new party with the phaser for
            // each task
            phaser.register();
            // Now create the task and start it
            String taskName = "Task #" + i;
            StartTogetherTask task =
                new StartTogetherTask(taskName, phaser);
            task.start();
        }
```

```
        // Now, deregister the self, so all tasks can
        // advance
        phaser.arriveAndDeregister();
    }
}
```

```
Task #3:Initializing...
Task #2:Initializing...
Task #1:Initializing...
Task #3:Initialized...
Task #1:Initialized...
Task #2:Initialized...
Task #2:Started...
Task #1:Started...
Task #3:Started...
```

First, the program creates a Phaser object by specifying 1 as the initially registered party:

```
// Start with 1 registered party
Phaser phaser = new Phaser(1);
```

You register a task with the Phaser one at a time. If a task (or a party) is registered and started before other tasks are registered, the first task will advance the phaser because there will be one registered party and it will arrive at the phaser by itself. Therefore, you need to start with one registered party in the beginning. It acts like the controller party for other tasks.

You create three tasks in a loop. Inside the loop, you register a party (that represents a task) with the Phaser, create a task, and start it. Once you are done setting up the tasks, you call the arriveAndDeregister() method of the Phaser. This takes care of one extra party that you had registered when you created the Phaser. This method makes a party arrive at the Phaser and deregister without waiting for other registered parties to arrive. After this method call is over, it is up to the three tasks to arrive at the Phaser and advance. Once all three tasks arrive at the Phaser, they will all advance at the same time, thus making them start at the same time. You may get different output. However, the last three messages in the output will always be about starting the three tasks.

If you do not want to use an additional party to act as a controller, you need to register all tasks in advance to make this program work correctly. You can rewrite the code in the main() method of the StartTogetherTaskTest class as follows:

```
public static void main(String[] args) {
    // Start with 0 registered party
    Phaser phaser = new Phaser();
    // Let's start three tasks
    final int TASK_COUNT = 3;
    // Initialize all tasks in one go
    phaser.bulkRegister(TASK_COUNT);
    for(int i = 1; i <= TASK_COUNT; i++) {
        // Now create the task and start it
        String taskName = "Task #" + i;
        StartTogetherTask task =
            new StartTogetherTask(taskName, phaser);
        task.start();
    }
}
```

This time, you create a Phaser with no registered party. You register all the parties using the bulkRegister() method in one go. Note that you do not register a party inside the loop anymore. The new code has the same effect as the old one. It is just a different way to write the same logic.

Like a CyclicBarrier, a Phaser lets you execute an action upon a phase advance using its onAdvance() method. You will need to create your own phaser class by inheriting it from the Phaser class and override the onAdvance() method to write your custom Phaser action. On each phase advance, the onAdvance() method of the phaser is invoked. The onAdvance() method in the Phaser class is declared as follows. The first argument is the phase number, and the second is the number of registered parties:

```
protected boolean onAdvance(int phase, int registeredParties)
```

Besides defining a phase advance action, the onAdvance() method of the Phaser class also controls the termination state of a Phaser. A Phaser is terminated if its onAdvance() method returns true. You can use the isTerminated() method of the Phaser class to check if a phaser is terminated or not. You can also terminate a phaser using its forceTermination() method.

Listing 5-40 demonstrates how to add a Phaser action. This is a trivial example. However, it demonstrates the concept of adding and executing a Phaser action. It uses an anonymous class to create a custom Phaser class. The anonymous class overrides the onAdvance() method to define a Phaser action. It simply prints a message in the onAdvance() method as the Phaser action. It returns false, which means the phaser will not be terminated from the onAdvance() method. Later, it registers itself as a party and triggers a phase advance using the arriveAndDeregister() method. On every phase advance, the Phaser action that is defined by the onAdvance() method is executed.

Listing 5-40. Adding a Phaser Action to a Phaser

```
// PhaserActionTest.java
package com.jdojo.threads;
import java.util.concurrent.Phaser;
public class PhaserActionTest {
    public static void main(String[] args) {
        // Create a Phaser object using an anonymous class
        // and override its onAdvance() method to define a
        // phaser action
        Phaser phaser = new Phaser() {
            @Override
            protected boolean onAdvance(int phase,
                  int parties) {
                System.out.println(
                    "Inside onAdvance(): phase = "
                    + phase + ", Registered Parties = "
                    + parties);
                // Do not terminate the phaser by returning
                // false
                return false;
            }
        };
        // Register the self (the "main" thread) as a party
        phaser.register();
        // Phaser is not terminated here
```

```
        System.out.println("#1: isTerminated(): " +
            phaser.isTerminated());
        // Since we have only one party registered, this
        // arrival will advance the phaser and registered
        // parties reduces to zero
        phaser.arriveAndDeregister();
        // Trigger another phase advance
        phaser.register();
        phaser.arriveAndDeregister();
        // Phaser is still not terminated
        System.out.println("#2: isTerminated(): " +
            phaser.isTerminated());
        // Terminate the phaser
        phaser.forceTermination();
        // Phaser is terminated
        System.out.println("#3: isTerminated(): " +
            phaser.isTerminated());
    }
}
```

```
#1: isTerminated(): false
Inside onAdvance(): phase = 0, Registered Parties = 0
Inside onAdvance(): phase = 1, Registered Parties = 0
#2: isTerminated(): false
#3: isTerminated(): true
```

Let's consider using a Phaser to solve a complex task. This time, the Phaser works in multiple phases by synchronizing multiple parties in each phase. Multiple tasks generate random integers in each phase and add them to a List. After the Phaser is terminated, you compute the sum of all the randomly generated integers.

Listing 5-41 contains the code for a task. Let's call this task AdderTask. In its run() method, it creates a random integer between 1 and 10, adds the integer to a List, and waits for a Phaser to advance. It keeps adding an integer to the list in each phase of the Phaser until the Phaser is terminated.

Listing 5-41. An AdderTask Class Whose Instances Can Be Used with a Phaser to Generate Some Integers

```java
// AdderTask.java
package com.jdojo.threads;
import java.util.List;
import java.util.Random;
import java.util.concurrent.Phaser;
public class AdderTask extends Thread {
    private final Phaser phaser;
    private final String taskName;
    private final List<Integer> list;
    private static Random rand = new Random();
    public AdderTask(String taskName, Phaser phaser,
            List<Integer> list) {
        this.taskName = taskName;
        this.phaser = phaser;
        this.list = list;
    }
    @Override
    public void run() {
        do {
            // Generate a random integer between 1 and 10
            int num = rand.nextInt(10) + 1;
            System.out.println(taskName + " added " +
                num);
            // Add the integer to the list
            list.add(num);
            // Wait for all parties to arrive at the phaser
            phaser.arriveAndAwaitAdvance();
        } while (!phaser.isTerminated());
    }
}
```

Listing 5-42 creates a `Phaser` by inheriting an anonymous class from the `Phaser` class. In its `onAdvance()` method, it terminates the phaser after the second advance, which is controlled by the `PHASE_COUNT` constant, or if the registered parties reduce to zero. You use a synchronized `List` to gather the random integers generated by the adder tasks. You plan to use three adder tasks, so you register four parties (one more than the number of tasks) with the phaser. The additional party will be used to synchronize each phase. It waits for each phase advance until the `Phaser` is terminated. At the end, the sum of the random integers generated by all adder tasks is computed and displayed on the standard output. You may get different output.

Listing 5-42. A Program to Use Multiple `AdderTask` Tasks with a `Phaser`

```
// AdderTaskTest.java
package com.jdojo.threads;

import java.util.List;
import java.util.ArrayList;
import java.util.Collections;
import java.util.concurrent.Phaser;

public class AdderTaskTest {
    public static void main(String[] args) {
        final int PHASE_COUNT = 2;
        Phaser phaser = new Phaser() {
            @Override
            public boolean onAdvance(int phase,
                    int parties) {
                // Print the phaser details
                System.out.println("Phase:" + phase
                        + ", Parties:"
                        + parties
                        + ", Arrived:"
                        + this.getArrivedParties());
                boolean terminatePhaser = false;
                // Terminate the phaser when we reach the
                // PHASE_COUNT or there is no registered
                // party
```

```
        if (phase >= PHASE_COUNT - 1 ||
                parties == 0) {
            terminatePhaser = true;
        }
        return terminatePhaser;
    }
};
// Use a synchronized List
List<Integer> list = Collections.synchronizedList(
    new ArrayList<>());
// Let's start three tasks
final int ADDER_COUNT = 3;
// Register parties one more than the number of
// adder tasks. The extra party will synchronize to
// compute the result of all generated integers by
// all adder tasks
phaser.bulkRegister(ADDER_COUNT + 1);
for (int i = 1; i <= ADDER_COUNT; i++) {
    // Create the task and start it
    String taskName = "Task #" + i;
    AdderTask task = new AdderTask(taskName,
        phaser, list);
    task.start();
}
// Wait for the phaser to terminate, so we can
// compute the sum of all generated integers by the
// adder tasks
while (!phaser.isTerminated()) {
    phaser.arriveAndAwaitAdvance();
}
// Phaser is terminated now. Compute the sum
int sum = 0;
for (Integer num : list) {
    sum = sum + num;
}
```

```
        System.out.println("Sum = " + sum);
    }
}
```

```
Task #2 added 2
Task #1 added 2
Task #3 added 5
Phase:0, Parties:4, Arrived:4
Task #3 added 5
Task #1 added 1
Task #2 added 7
Phase:1, Parties:4, Arrived:4
Sum = 22
```

Latches

A latch works similar to a barrier in the sense that it also makes a group of threads wait until it reaches its terminal state. Once a latch reaches its terminal state, it lets all threads pass through. Unlike a barrier, it is a one-time object. Once it has reached its terminal state, it cannot be reset and reused. A latch can be used in situations where a number of activities cannot proceed until a certain number of one-time activities have completed. For example, a service should not start until all services that it depends on have started.

The CountDownLatch class in the java.util.concurrent package provides the implementation of a latch. It is initialized to a count using its constructor. All threads that call the await() method of the latch object are blocked until the latch's countDown() method is called as many times as its count is set. When the number of calls to the countDown() method is the same as its count, it reaches its terminal state, and all blocked threads are released. Once a latch reaches its terminal state, its await() method returns immediately. You can think of the count that is set for the latch as the same as the number of events that a group of thread will wait to occur. Each occurrence of an event will call its countDown() method.

Listings 5-43 and 5-44 contain classes that represent a helper service and a main service, respectively. The main service depends on helper services to start. After all helper services have started, only then can the main service start.

Listing 5-43. A Class to Represent a Helper Service

```java
// LatchHelperService.java
package com.jdojo.threads;
import java.util.concurrent.CountDownLatch;
import java.util.Random;
public class LatchHelperService extends Thread {
    private final int ID;
    private final CountDownLatch latch;
    private final Random random = new Random();
    public LatchHelperService(int ID,
            CountDownLatch latch) {
        this.ID = ID;
        this.latch = latch;
    }
    @Override
    public void run() {
        try {
            int startupTime = random.nextInt(30) + 1;
            System.out.println("Service #" + ID
                    + " starting in "
                    + startupTime + " seconds...");
            Thread.sleep(startupTime * 1000);
            System.out.println("Service #" + ID
                    + " has started...");
        } catch (InterruptedException e) {
            e.printStackTrace();
        } finally {
            // Count down on the latch to indicate that
            // it has started
            this.latch.countDown();
        }
    }
}
```

Listing 5-44. A Class to Represent the Main Service That Depends on Helper Services to Start

```
// LatchMainService.java
package com.jdojo.threads;
import java.util.concurrent.CountDownLatch;
public class LatchMainService extends Thread {
    private final CountDownLatch latch;
    public LatchMainService(CountDownLatch latch) {
        this.latch = latch;
    }
    @Override
    public void run() {
        try {
            System.out.println(
                "Main service is waiting for helper " +
                "services to start...");
            latch.await();
            System.out.println(
                "Main service has started...");
        } catch (InterruptedException e) {
            e.printStackTrace();
        }
    }
}
```

Listing 5-45 lists a program to test the concept of helper and main services with a latch. You create a latch that is initialized to two. The main service thread is started first, and it calls the latch's await() method to wait for the helper service to start. Once both helper threads call the countDown() method of the latch, the main service starts. The output explains the sequence of events clearly.

Listing 5-45. A Class to Test the Concept of a Latch with Helper and Main Services

```java
// LatchTest.java
package com.jdojo.threads;
import java.util.concurrent.CountDownLatch;
public class LatchTest {
    public static void main(String[] args) {
        // Create a countdown latch with 2 as its counter
        CountDownLatch latch = new CountDownLatch(2);
        // Create and start the main service
        LatchMainService ms = new LatchMainService(latch);
        ms.start();
        // Create and start two helper services
        for (int i = 1; i <= 2; i++) {
            LatchHelperService lhs =
                new LatchHelperService(i, latch);
            lhs.start();
        }
    }
}
```

```
Main service is waiting for helper services to start...
Service #1 starting in 12 seconds...
Service #2 starting in 2 seconds...
Service #2 has started...
Service #1 has started...
Main service has started...
```

Exchangers

An exchanger is another form of a barrier. Like a barrier, an exchanger lets two threads wait for each other at a synchronization point. When both threads arrive, they exchange an object and continue their activities. This is useful in building a system where two independent parties need to exchange information from time to time. Figures 5-13 through 5-15 depict how an exchanger works with two threads and lets them exchange an object.

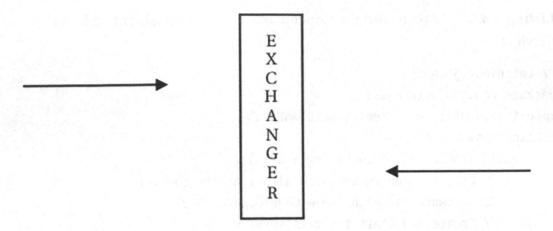

Figure 5-13. *Two threads perform their work independently*

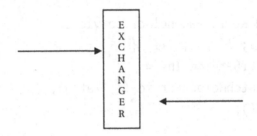

Figure 5-14. *One thread arrives at the exchange point and waits for another thread to arrive*

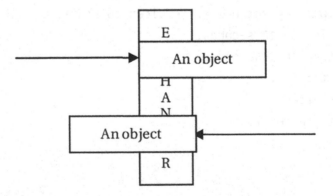

Figure 5-15. *Two threads meet at the exchange point and exchange objects*

The Exchanger<V> class provides an implementation for an exchanger synchronizer. It has one constructor, which takes no arguments. The type parameter V is the type of Java object that will be exchanged between two parties. You can create an exchanger that will let two threads exchange a Long as follows:

```
Exchanger<Long> exchanger = new Exchanger<>();
```

The Exchanger class has only one method, exchange(). When a thread is ready to exchange an object with another thread, it calls the exchange() method of the exchanger and waits for another thread to exchange the object. A thread that is waiting to exchange an object may be interrupted.

Another overloaded version of the exchange() method accepts a timeout period. If the timeout period is specified, the thread calling this method will wait for another thread to exchange an object until the timeout period is elapsed. The exchange() method takes the object to pass on to another thread as an argument, and it returns the object passed by another thread. You call the exchange() method like so:

```
objectReceived = exchanger.exchange(objectedPassed);
```

Listings 5-46 to 5-48 demonstrate the use of an exchanger in building a producer/consumer system that exchanges a buffer, which is an ArrayList of Integer objects. To declare an array list of integer objects, you have to declare it as follows:

```
ArrayList<Integer> buffer = new ArrayList<Integer>();
```

In Listing 5-48, you have created an exchanger as

```
Exchanger<ArrayList<Integer>> exchanger =
        new Exchanger<ArrayList<Integer>>();
```

The type declaration Exchanger<ArrayList<Integer» indicates that the exchanger will let two threads exchange objects of type ArrayList<Integer>. You can also note that the type declarations in the ExchangerProducer and ExchangerConsumer classes match the previous declaration. The producer fills up the data and waits for some time to give the users the impression that it is really filling up data. It waits for the consumer to exchange the filled buffer with an empty buffer from the consumer. The consumer does the opposite. It waits for the producer to exchange the buffer. When it gets a full buffer from the producer, it empties the buffer and again waits for the producer to exchange its empty buffer for a full one. Since the producer and consumer run in infinite loops, the program will not end. You will have to end the program manually. You will get a similar output to that shown in Listing 5-48.

Listing 5-46. A Producer Thread That Will Use an Exchanger to Exchange Data with a Consumer

```java
// ExchangerProducer.java
package com.jdojo.threads;
import java.util.concurrent.Exchanger;
import java.util.ArrayList;
import java.util.Random;
public class ExchangerProducer extends Thread {
    private final Exchanger<ArrayList<Integer>> exchanger;
    private ArrayList<Integer> buffer = new ArrayList<>();
    private final int bufferLimit;
    private final Random random = new Random();
    private int currentValue = 0; // to produce values
    public ExchangerProducer(
            Exchanger<ArrayList<Integer>> exchanger,
            int bufferLimit) {
        this.exchanger = exchanger;
        this.bufferLimit = bufferLimit;
    }
    @Override
    public void run() {
        // keep producing integers
        while (true) {
            try {
                System.out.println(
                    "Producer is filling the buffer" +
                    " with data...");
                // Wait for some time by sleeping
                int sleepTime = random.nextInt(20) + 1;
                Thread.sleep(sleepTime * 1000);
```

```
                // Fill the buffer
                this.fillBuffer();
                System.out.println(
                    "Producer has produced:" + buffer);
                // Let's wait for the consumer to
                // exchange data
                System.out.println(
                    "Producer is waiting to exchange" +
                    " the data...");
                buffer = exchanger.exchange(buffer);
            } catch (InterruptedException e) {
                e.printStackTrace();
            }
        }
    }
    public void fillBuffer() {
        for (int i = 1; i <= bufferLimit; i++) {
            buffer.add(++currentValue);
        }
    }
}
```

Listing 5-47. A Consumer Thread That Will Use an Exchanger to Exchange Data with a Producer

```
// ExchangerConsumer.java
package com.jdojo.threads;
import java.util.concurrent.Exchanger;
import java.util.ArrayList;
import java.util.Random;
public class ExchangerConsumer extends Thread {
    private final Exchanger<ArrayList<Integer>> exchanger;
    private ArrayList<Integer> buffer = new ArrayList<>();
    private final Random random = new Random();
```

```java
    public ExchangerConsumer(
        Exchanger<ArrayList<Integer>> exchanger) {
      this.exchanger = exchanger;
    }
    @Override
    public void run() {
      // keep consuming the integers
      while (true) {
        try {
          // Let's wait for the consumer to exchange
          // data
          System.out.println(
              "Consumer is waiting to exchange" +
              " the data...");
          buffer = exchanger.exchange(buffer);
          System.out.println(
              "Consumer has received:" + buffer);
          System.out.println(
              "Consumer is emptying data from" +
              " the buffer...");
          // Wait for some time by sleeping
          int sleepTime = random.nextInt(20) + 1;
          // Sleep for some time
          Thread.sleep(sleepTime * 1000);
          // Empty the buffer
          this.emptyBuffer();
        } catch (InterruptedException e) {
          e.printStackTrace();
        }
      }
    }
    public void emptyBuffer() {
      buffer.clear();
    }
}
```

Listing 5-48. A Class to Test a Producer/Consumer System with an Exchanger

```java
// ExchangerProducerConsumerTest.java
package com.jdojo.threads;
import java.util.concurrent.Exchanger;
import java.util.ArrayList;
public class ExchangerProducerConsumerTest {
    public static void main(String[] args) {
        Exchanger<ArrayList<Integer>> exchanger =
            new Exchanger<>();
        // The producer will produce 5 integers at a time
        ExchangerProducer producer =
            new ExchangerProducer(exchanger, 5);
        ExchangerConsumer consumer =
            new ExchangerConsumer(exchanger);
        producer.start();
        consumer.start();
    }
}
```

```
Producer is filling the buffer with data...
Consumer is waiting to exchange the data...
Producer has produced:[1, 2, 3, 4, 5]
Producer is waiting to exchange the data...
Producer is filling the buffer with data...
Consumer has received:[1, 2, 3, 4, 5]
Consumer is emptying data from the buffer...
...
```

The Executor Framework

A task is a logical unit of work, and typically a thread is used to represent and execute a task. Many aspects of task execution should be considered before modeling it in a program. A few aspects of a task are as follows:

- How it is created.

- How it is submitted for execution.

- How it is executed. Is it executed synchronously or asynchronously?

- The time at which it is executed. Is it executed immediately upon submission or queued?

- Which thread executes it? Is it executed in the thread that submits it or in another thread?

- How do we get the result of a task when it is finished executing?

- How do we know the error that occurs during its execution?

- Does it depend on other tasks to finish its execution?

A task may be represented as a Runnable. If you want to manage tasks using threads, follow the steps described next. You can create a class to represent a task:

```
public class MyTask implements Runnable {
    public void run() {
        // Task processing logic goes here
    }
}
```

You create tasks as follows:

```
MyTask task1 = new MyTask();
MyTask task2 = new MyTask();
MyTask task3 = new MyTask();
```

To execute the tasks, you use threads as follows:

```
Thread t1 = new Thread(task1);
Thread t2 = new Thread(task2);
Thread t3 = new Thread(task3);
t1.start();
t2.start();
t3.start();
```

If you want to get the result of a task execution, you have to write additional code. You may notice that managing tasks like this is difficult, if not impossible. There is another aspect of task execution that is very important: how many threads should be created to execute a group of tasks? One approach would be to create a thread per task. Creating a thread per task has the following disadvantages:

- Creating and destroying threads requires overhead and takes time, which in turn delays the start of the execution of the tasks.

- Each thread consumes resources. If the number of threads is more than the available CPUs, other threads will be sitting idle and will consume resources.

- Each platform has a limit on how many maximum threads it can support. If an application exceeds that limit, it may even crash! Another approach is to create one thread and let it handle the execution of all tasks. This is another extreme case, which has the following disadvantages:

- Having one thread executing all tasks makes it a sequential executor.

- This policy is deadlock-prone if one task submits another task and it depends on the result of the task it has submitted.

- If you have long-running tasks, other tasks waiting for their execution seem to be unresponsive because of the long time it will take to start the pending tasks.

The executor framework attempts to solve all of these problems of task execution. The framework provides a way to separate task submission from task execution. You create a task and submit it to an executor. The executor takes care of the execution details of the task. It provides configurable policies to control many aspects of the task execution.

The Executor interface in the java.util.concurrent package is the foundation for the executor framework. The interface contains only one method, as shown:

```
public interface Executor {
    void execute (Runnable command);
}
```

You can use the executor framework to execute the previously mentioned three tasks as follows:

```
// Get an executor instance.
Executor executor = Executors.newCachedThreadPool();
// Submit three tasks to the executor
executor.execute(task1);
executor.execute(task2);
executor.execute(task3);
```

Note that when you used an executor, you did not create three threads to execute the three tasks. The executor will decide that for you. You just called the execute() method of the executor to submit a task. The executor will manage the threads that will execute the tasks and other details about the task execution.

The executor framework provides a class library to select the policies on the thread usage to execute the tasks. You can choose to run all tasks in one thread, in a fixed number of threads, or in a variable number of threads. In fact, you can choose a thread pool to execute your tasks, and the thread pool is configurable as to how many threads will be in the pool and how those threads will be maintained. In any case, all threads in the pool are reused as they become available. Using a thread pool to execute the submitted tasks has two important advantages:

- The overhead of creating new threads and destroying them when you are done with them is reduced. The executor reuses the threads from the thread pool.

- If a thread is available in the thread pool at the time of a task submission, the task may start immediately. This eliminates the time delay between the thread creation and the task execution.

It is important to mention another interface called ExecutorService at this point. It provides some advanced features of an executor, which include managing the shutdown of the executor and checking the status of the submitted tasks. It inherits from the Executor interface. Some of the important methods of this interface are shutdown(), shutdownNow(), submit(), and awaitTermination(). I discuss them shortly.

It is important that you shut down the executor when it is no longer needed. The executor framework creates non-daemon threads to execute the tasks. Generally, when a thread is done executing a task, it is not destroyed. Rather, it is kept in the thread pool for reuse in the future—whether a thread is destroyed or kept depends on the thread pool configuration. A Java application will not exit if some non-daemon threads are still alive. Therefore, if you forget to shut down the executor, your application may never exit.

How does an executor handle a task execution? To avoid a detailed and lengthy discussion, here is a simple explanation. You specify the type of thread pool that the executor should use to manage the tasks at the time you create the executor. All tasks that you submit to an executor are queued in a queue known as the work queue. As a thread becomes available, it removes a task from the work queue and executes it. When a thread is done executing a task, depending on your thread pool type, your executor either destroys the thread or puts it back into the pool so it can be reused to execute another task. You have a number of options to decide on what kind of thread pool to use for an executor:

- You can use one of the factory methods of the Executors class to get an executor, which has a preconfigured thread pool and lets you reconfigure it, if you desire so. You will use this approach to get an executor in your examples. You can also use this class to get a preconfigured executor that cannot be reconfigured. The comm only used methods of the Executors class to get an executor service are as follows:

  - newCachedThreadPool(): It returns an ExecutorService object. The thread pool reuses the previously created threads if they are available. Otherwise, it creates a new thread to execute a task. It destroys and removes idle threads from the pool. The thread pool has characteristics of expanding and shrinking depending on the workload.

  - newFixedThreadPool(int nThreads): It returns an ExecutorService object. The thread pool maintains a fixed number of threads. At any time, the thread pool will have the maximum nThread number of threads. If a task arrives in the work queue and all threads are busy executing other tasks, the task has to wait for its execution until a thread becomes available. If a thread is terminated because of an unexpected failure during a task execution, it is replaced with a new thread.

- newSingleThreadExecutor(): It returns an ExecutorService object. The thread pool maintains only one thread to execute all tasks. It guarantees that only one task will be executed at a time. If the lone thread dies unexpectedly, it is replaced with a new one.

- You can instantiate the ThreadPoolExecutor class and configure the thread pool.

- You can create your own executor from scratch.

Listing 5-49 contains the complete code for a RunnableTask class.

Listing 5-49. A Runnable Task

```java
// RunnableTask.java
package com.jdojo.threads;
import java.util.Random;
public class RunnableTask implements Runnable {
    private final int taskId;
    private final int loopCounter;
    private final Random random = new Random();
    public RunnableTask(int taskId, int loopCounter) {
        this.taskId = taskId;
        this.loopCounter = loopCounter;
    }
    @Override
    public void run() {
        for (int i = 1; i <= loopCounter; i++) {
            try {
                int sleepTime = random.nextInt(10) + 1;
                System.out.println("Task #" + this.taskId
                        + " - Iteration #" + i
                        + " is going to sleep for "
                        + sleepTime + " seconds.");
                Thread.sleep(sleepTime * 1000);
```

```
        } catch (InterruptedException e) {
            System.out.println("Task #" + this.taskId
                    + " has been interrupted.");
            break;
        }
    }
  }
}
```

An object of the RunnableTask class represents a task in your program. You will have a task that will sleep for some time and print a message on the standard output. The time to sleep will be determined randomly between 1 and 10 seconds. Every task will be assigned a task ID and a loop counter. The task ID is used to identify the task. The loop counter is used to control the loop inside the run() method. Listing 5-50 contains the complete code to test the Runnable task class.

Listing 5-50. A Class to Test an Executor to Run Some Runnable Tasks

```
// RunnableTaskTest.java
package com.jdojo.threads;
import java.util.concurrent.Executors;
import java.util.concurrent.ExecutorService;
public class RunnableTaskTest {
    public static void main(String[] args) {
        final int THREAD_COUNT = 3;
        final int LOOP_COUNT = 3;
        final int TASK_COUNT = 5;
        // Get an executor with three threads in its
        // thread pool
        ExecutorService exec =
            Executors.newFixedThreadPool(THREAD_COUNT);
        // Create five tasks and submit them to the
        // executor
```

```
        for (int i = 1; i <= TASK_COUNT; i++) {
            RunnableTask task =
                new RunnableTask(i, LOOP_COUNT);
            exec.submit(task);
        }
        // Let's shutdown the executor
        exec.shutdown();
    }
}
```

```
Task #1 - Iteration #1 is going to sleep for 9 seconds.
Task #2 - Iteration #1 is going to sleep for 2 seconds.
Task #3 - Iteration #1 is going to sleep for 7 seconds.
Task #2 - Iteration #2 is going to sleep for 5 seconds.
Task #2 - Iteration #3 is going to sleep for 7 seconds.
Task #3 - Iteration #2 is going to sleep for 2 seconds.
...
```

The RunnableTaskTest class creates an Executor with three threads. It creates five instances of the RunnableTask class—each task making three iterations in its run() method. All five tasks are submitted to the Executor. You have used an executor with its thread pool with a fixed number of threads. Your executor will have only three threads in its thread pool to execute only three tasks at a time. When the executor is done with one of the first three tasks, it starts the fourth one. Note the exec.shutdown() method call to shut down the executor after submitting all tasks. The shutdownNow() method call of the executor attempts to stop the executing tasks by interrupting it and discards the pending tasks. It returns the list of all pending tasks that were discarded. If you replace the exec. shutdown() to exec.shutdownNow() in the main() method, you may get an output similar to the one shown:

```
Task #1 - Iteration #1 is going to sleep for 7 seconds.
Task #2 - Iteration #1 is going to sleep for 10 seconds.
Task #3 - Iteration #1 is going to sleep for 9 seconds.
Task #2 has been interrupted.
Task #3 has been interrupted.
Task #1 has been interrupted.
```

Result-Bearing Tasks

How do you get the result of a task when it is complete? The task that can return a result upon its execution has to be represented as an instance of the `Callable<V>` interface:

```
public interface Callable<V> {
    V call() throws Exception;
}
```

The type parameter V is the type of the result of the task. Note that the `run()` method of the Runnable interface cannot return a value, and it cannot throw any checked exception. The `call()` method of the Callable interface can return a value of any type. It also allows you to throw an exception.

Let's redo your `RunnableTask` class from Listing 5-49 as `CallableTask`, which is shown in Listing 5-51.

Listing 5-51. A Callable Task

```
// CallableTask.java
package com.jdojo.threads;
import java.util.Random;
import java.util.concurrent.Callable;
public class CallableTask implements Callable<Integer> {
    private final int taskId;
    private final int loopCounter;
    private final Random random = new Random();
    public CallableTask(int taskId, int loopCounter) {
        this.taskId = taskId;
        this.loopCounter = loopCounter;
    }
    @Override
    public Integer call() throws InterruptedException {
        int totalSleepTime = 0;
        for (int i = 1; i <= loopCounter; i++) {
            try {
                int sleepTime = random.nextInt(10) + 1;
```

```
                System.out.println("Task #" + this.taskId
                        + " - Iteration #" + i
                        + " is going to sleep for "
                        + sleepTime + " seconds.");
                Thread.sleep(sleepTime * 1000);
                totalSleepTime = totalSleepTime +
                    sleepTime;
            } catch (InterruptedException e) {
                System.out.println("Task #" + this.taskId
                        + " has been interrupted.");
                throw e;
            }
        }
        return totalSleepTime;
    }
}
```

The call() method of the task returns the sum of all its sleeping periods. Listing 5-52 illustrates the use of the Callable task. You may get different output every time you run the program.

Listing 5-52. A Class to Demonstrate How to Use a Callable Task with an Executor

```
// CallableTaskTest.java
package com.jdojo.threads;

import java.util.concurrent.Executors;
import java.util.concurrent.ExecutorService;
import java.util.concurrent.Future;
import java.util.concurrent.ExecutionException;

public class CallableTaskTest {
    public static void main(String[] args) {
        // Get an executor with three threads in its
        // thread pool
        ExecutorService exec =
            Executors.newFixedThreadPool(3);
```

```
        // Create the callable task with loop counter as 3
        CallableTask task = new CallableTask(1, 3);
        // Submit the callable task to executor
        Future<Integer> submittedTask = exec.submit(task);
        try {
            Integer result = submittedTask.get();
            System.out.println(
                "Task's total sleep time: " + result +
                " seconds");
        } catch (ExecutionException e) {
            System.out.println(
                "Error in executing the task.");
        } catch (InterruptedException e) {
            System.out.println(
                "Task execution has been interrupted.");
        }
        // Let's shutdown the executor
        exec.shutdown();
    }
}
```

```
Task #1 - Iteration #1 is going to sleep for 6 seconds.
Task #1 - Iteration #2 is going to sleep for 5 seconds.
Task #1 - Iteration #3 is going to sleep for 4 seconds.
Task's total sleep time: 15 seconds
```

I explain the logic in the two listings step by step.

The CallableTask class defines the call() method, which contains the logic for task processing. It sums up all the sleep times for the task and returns it.

The CallableTaskTest class uses an executor with three threads in its thread pool.

The ExecutorService.submit() method returns a Future<V> object. Future is an interface that lets you track the progress of the task that you submit. It contains the following methods:

- boolean cancel(boolean mayInterruptIfRunning)

- V get() throws InterruptedException, ExecutionException

- V get(long timeout, TimeUnit unit) throws
  InterruptedException, ExecutionException, TimeoutException

- boolean isCancelled()

- boolean isDone()

The get() method returns the result of the task execution, which is the same as the returned value from the call() method of a Callable object. If the task has not yet finished executing, the get() method blocks. You can use another version of the get() method to specify a timeout period for waiting for the result of a task execution.

The cancel() method cancels a submitted task. Its call has no effect on a completed task. It accepts a boolean argument to indicate if the executor should interrupt the task if the task is still running. If you use cancel(true) to cancel a task, make sure the task responds to the interruption properly.

The isDone() method tells you if the task has finished executing. It returns true if the task is finished executing normally, it has been cancelled, or it had an exception during its execution.

In the CallableTaskTest class, you keep the returned Future object in the submittedTask variable. The Future<Integer> declaration indicates that your task returns an Integer object as its result:

```
Future<Integer> submittedTask = exec.submit(task);
```

Another important method call is the get() method on submittedTask:

```
Integer result = submittedTask.get();
```

I placed the call to the get() method in a try-catch block because it may throw an exception. If the task has not finished executing, the get() method will block. The program prints the result of the task execution, which is the total time that the task spent sleeping during its execution.

Finally, you shut down the executor using its shutdown() method.

Scheduling a Task

The executor framework lets you schedule a task that will run in the future. You can run a task to execute after a given delay or periodically. Scheduling a task is done using an instance of the ScheduledExecutorService interface, which you can get using one of the static factory methods of the Executors class. You can also use the concrete implementation of this interface, which is the ScheduledThreadPoolExecutor class. To get an instance of the ScheduledExecutorService interface, use the following snippet of code:

```
// Get scheduled executor service with 3 threads
ScheduledExecutorService sexec =
    Executors.newScheduledThreadPool(3);
```

To schedule a task (say task1) after a certain delay (say 10 seconds), use

```
sexec.schedule(task1, 10, TimeUnit.SECONDS);
```

To schedule a task (say task2) after a certain delay (say 10 seconds), and repeat after a certain period (say 25 seconds), use

```
sexec.scheduleAtFixedRate(task2, 10, 25,
    TimeUnit.SECONDS);
```

After a 10-second delay, task2 will execute for the first time. Subsequently, it will keep executing after 10 + 25 seconds, 10 + 2 * 25 seconds, 10 + 3 * 25 seconds, and so on.

You can also schedule a task with a set delay period between the end of an execution and the start of the next execution. To schedule task3 for the first time after 40 seconds, and every 60 seconds after every execution finishes, use

```
sexec.scheduleWithFixedDelay(task3, 40, 60,
    TimeUnit.SECONDS);
```

The ScheduledExecutorService interface does not provide a method to schedule a task using an absolute time. However, you can schedule a task to execute at an absolute time using the following technique. Suppose scheduledDateTime is the date and time at which you want to execute the task:

```
import java.time.LocalDateTime;
import static java.time.temporal.ChronoUnit.SECONDS;
import java.util.concurrent.TimeUnit;
...
LocalDateTime scheduledDateTime =
    get the scheduled date and time for the task...
```

```
// Compute the delay from the time you schedule the task
long delay = SECONDS.between(LocalDateTime.now(),
    scheduledDateTime);
// Schedule the task
sexec.schedule(task, delay, TimeUnit.MILLISECONDS);
```

Note   The submit() method of ExecutorService submits the task for immediate execution. You can submit a task for immediate execution using the ScheduledExecutorService.schedule() method by specifying an initial delay of zero. A negative initial delay schedules a task for immediate execution.

Listing 5-53 contains the code for a Runnable task. It simply prints the date and time when it is run.

Listing 5-53. A Scheduled Task

```
// ScheduledTask.java
package com.jdojo.threads;
import java.time.LocalDateTime;
public class ScheduledTask implements Runnable {
    private final int taskId;
    public ScheduledTask(int taskId) {
        this.taskId = taskId;
    }
    @Override
    public void run() {
        LocalDateTime now = LocalDateTime.now();
        System.out.println("Task #" + this.taskId +
            " ran at " + now);
    }
}
```

Listing 5-54 demonstrates how to schedule a task. The second task has been scheduled to run repeatedly. To let it run a few times, make the main thread sleep for 60 seconds before you shut down the executor. Shutting down an executor discards any pending tasks. A good way to stop a scheduled task that repeats is to cancel it after a certain delay using another scheduled task. You may get different output when you run the ScheduledTaskTest class.

Listing 5-54. A Class to Test Scheduled Task Executions Using the Executor Framework

```java
// ScheduledTaskTest.java
package com.jdojo.threads;
import java.util.concurrent.Executors;
import java.util.concurrent.ScheduledExecutorService;
import java.util.concurrent.TimeUnit;
public class ScheduledTaskTest {
    public static void main(String[] args) {
        // Get an executor with 3 threads
        ScheduledExecutorService sexec =
            Executors.newScheduledThreadPool(3);
        // Task #1 and Task #2
        ScheduledTask task1 = new ScheduledTask(1);
        ScheduledTask task2 = new ScheduledTask(2);
        // Task #1 will run after 2 seconds
        sexec.schedule(task1, 2, TimeUnit.SECONDS);
        // Task #2 runs after 5 seconds delay and keep
        // running every 10 seconds
        sexec.scheduleAtFixedRate(task2, 5, 10,
            TimeUnit.SECONDS);
        // Let the current thread sleep for 60 seconds
        // and shut down the executor that will cancel
        // the task #2 because it is scheduled
        // to run after every 10 seconds
        try {
            TimeUnit.SECONDS.sleep(60);
        } catch (InterruptedException e) {
            e.printStackTrace();
        }
```

```
        // Shut down the executor
        sexec.shutdown();
    }
}
```

```
Task #1 ran at 2020-10-07T10:47:48.800387200
Task #2 ran at 2020-10-07T10:47:51.753682400
Task #2 ran at 2020-10-07T10:48:01.754210400
Task #2 ran at 2020-10-07T10:48:11.754739100
Task #2 ran at 2020-10-07T10:48:21.755259400
Task #2 ran at 2020-10-07T10:48:31.755795600
Task #2 ran at 2020-10-07T10:48:41.756322800
```

Handling Uncaught Exceptions in a Task Execution

What happens when an uncaught exception occurs during a task execution? The
executor framework handles occurrences of such uncaught exception nicely for you. If
you execute a Runnable task using the execute() method of an Executor, any uncaught
runtime exceptions will halt the task execution, and the exception stack trace will be
printed on the console, as shown in the output of Listing 5-55.

Listing 5-55. Printing the Runtime Stack Trace from the execute() Method of
the Executor

```java
// BadRunnableTask.java
package com.jdojo.threads;
import java.util.concurrent.ExecutorService;
import java.util.concurrent.Executors;
public class BadRunnableTask {
    public static void main(String[] args) {
        Runnable badTask = () -> {
            throw new RuntimeException(
                "The task threw an exception...");
        };
        ExecutorService exec = Executors.
            newSingleThreadExecutor();
```

```
        exec.execute(badTask);
        exec.shutdown();
    }
}
Exception in thread "pool-1-thread-1" java.lang.
    RuntimeException: The task threw an exception...
        at jdojo.threads/com.jdojo.threads.
            BadRunnableTask.
            lambda$main$0(BadRunnableTask.java:10)
        at java.base/java.util.concurrent.
            ThreadPoolExecutor.runWorker(
            ThreadPoolExecutor.java:1167)
        at java.base/java.util.concurrent.
            ThreadPoolExecutor\$Worker.
            run(ThreadPoolExecutor.java:641)
        at java.base/java.lang.Thread.run(
            Thread.java:844)
```

If you are submitting a task using the submit() method of the ExecutorService, the executor framework handles the exception and indicates that to you when you use the get() method to get the result of the task execution. The get() method of the Future instance throws an ExecutionException, wrapping the actual exception as its cause. Listing 5-56 illustrates this kind of example. You can use the get() method of the Future instance even if you submit a Runnable task. On successful execution of the task, the get() method will return null. If an uncaught exception is thrown during the task execution, it throws an ExecutionException.

Listing 5-56. Future's get() Method Throws ExecutionException, Wrapping the Actual Exception Thrown in Task Execution As Its Cause

```
// BadCallableTask.java
package com.jdojo.threads;

import java.util.concurrent.ExecutorService;
import java.util.concurrent.Executors;
import java.util.concurrent.Callable;
import java.util.concurrent.Future;
import java.util.concurrent.ExecutionException;
```

```java
public class BadCallableTask {
    public static void main(String[] args) {
        Callable<Object> badTask = () -> {
            throw new RuntimeException(
                "The task threw an exception...");
        };
        // Create an executor service
        ExecutorService exec = Executors.
            newSingleThreadExecutor();
        // Submit a task
        Future submittedTask = exec.submit(badTask);
        try {
            // The get method should throw
            // ExecutionException
            Object result = submittedTask.get();
        } catch (ExecutionException e) {
            System.out.println(
                "Execution exception has occurred: "
                + e.getMessage());
            System.out.println(
                "Execution exception cause is: "
                + e.getCause().getMessage());
        } catch (InterruptedException e) {
            e.printStackTrace();
        }
        exec.shutdown();
    }
}
```

```
Execution exception has occurred:
    java.lang.RuntimeException:
    The task threw an exception...
Execution exception cause is:
    The task threw an exception...
```

Executor's Completion Service

In the previous sections, I explained how to fetch the result of a task execution using a Future object. To fetch the result of a submitted task, you must keep the reference of the Future object returned from the executor, as demonstrated in Listing 5-52. However, if you have a number of tasks that you have submitted to an executor and you want to know their results as they become available, you need to use the completion service of the executor. It is represented by an instance of the CompletionService<V> interface. It combines an executor and a blocking queue to hold the completed task references. The ExecutorCompletionService<V> class is a concrete implementation of the CompletionService<V> interface. Here are the steps to use it:

1. Create an executor object:

    ```
    ExecutorService exec = Executors.
        newScheduledThreadPool(3);
    ```

2. Create an object of the ExecutorCompletionService class, passing the executor created in the previous step to its constructor:

    ```
    ExecutorCompletionService CompletionService =
        new ExecutorCompletionService(exec);
    ```

    The executor completion service uses a blocking queue internally to hold the completed task. You can also use your own blocking queue to hold the completed tasks.

3. The take() method of the completion service returns the reference of a completed task. It blocks if no completed task is present. If you do not want to wait, in case there is no completed task, you can use the poll() method, which returns null if there is no completed task in the queue. Both methods remove the completed task from the queue if they find one.

Listings 5-57 to 5-59 illustrate the use of the completion service. An instance of the TaskResult class represents the result of a task. It was necessary to have a custom object like a TaskResult to represent the result of a task because the completion service just tells you that a task is completed and you get its result. It does not tell you which task is completed. To identify the task that was completed, you need to identify the task in the result of the task. Your SleepingTask returns a TaskResult from its call() method by embedding the task ID and the total sleeping time for the task.

Listing 5-57. A Class to Represent the Result of a Task

```java
// TaskResult.java
package com.jdojo.threads;
public class TaskResult {
    private final int taskId;
    private final int result;
    public TaskResult(int taskId, int result) {
        this.taskId = taskId;
        this.result = result;
    }
    public int getTaskId() {
        return taskId;
    }
    public int getResult() {
        return result;
    }
    @Override
    public String toString() {
        return "Task Name: Task #" + taskId +
            ", Task Result:" + result + " seconds";
    }
}
```

Listing 5-58. A Class Whose Object Represents a Callable Task and Produces a TaskResult As Its Result

```java
// SleepingTask.java
package com.jdojo.threads;
import java.util.Random;
import java.util.concurrent.Callable;
```

```java
public class SleepingTask implements Callable<TaskResult> {
    private int taskId;
    private int loopCounter;
    private Random random = new Random();
    public SleepingTask(int taskId, int loopCounter) {
        this.taskId = taskId;
        this.loopCounter = loopCounter;
    }
    @Override
    public TaskResult call() throws InterruptedException {
        int totalSleepTime = 0;
        for (int i = 1; i <= loopCounter; i++) {
            try {
                int sleepTime = random.nextInt(10) + 1;
                System.out.println("Task #" + this.taskId
                    + " - Iteration #" + i
                    + " is going to sleep for "
                    + sleepTime + " seconds.");
                Thread.sleep(sleepTime * 1000);
                totalSleepTime = totalSleepTime +
                    sleepTime;
            } catch (InterruptedException e) {
                System.out.println("Task #" + this.taskId
                        + " has been interrupted.");
                throw e;
            }
        }
        return new TaskResult(taskId, totalSleepTime);
    }
}
```

Listing 5-59. A Class to Test the Completion Service

```java
// CompletionServiceTest.java
package com.jdojo.threads;

import java.util.concurrent.Future;
import java.util.concurrent.Executors;
import java.util.concurrent.ExecutorService;
import java.util.concurrent.ExecutionException;
import java.util.concurrent.ExecutorCompletionService;

public class CompletionServiceTest {
    public static void main(String[] args) {
        // Get an executor with three threads in its thread
        // pool
        ExecutorService exec = Executors.
            newFixedThreadPool(3);

        // Completed task returns an object of the
        // TaskResult class
        ExecutorCompletionService<TaskResult>
        completionService
            = new ExecutorCompletionService<>(exec);
        // Submit five tasks and each task will sleep three
        // times for a random period between 1 and 10
        // seconds
        for (int i = 1; i <= 5; i++) {
            SleepingTask task = new SleepingTask(i, 3);
            completionService.submit(task);
        }
        // Print the result of each task as they are
        // completed
        for (int i = 1; i <= 5; i++) {
            try {
                Future<TaskResult> completedTask =
                    completionService.take();
                TaskResult result = completedTask.get();
```

```
            System.out.println("Completed a task - " +
                result);
        } catch (ExecutionException ex) {
            System.out.println(
                "Error in executing the task.");
        } catch (InterruptedException ex) {
            System.out.println("Task execution" +
                " has been interrupted.");
        }
    }
    // Let's shut down the executor
    exec.shutdown();
    }
}

Task #3 - Iteration #1 is going to sleep for 3 seconds.
...
Task #4 - Iteration #1 is going to sleep for 5 seconds.
Completed a task - Task Name: Task #2, Task Result:15
    seconds
...
Completed a task - Task Name: Task #4, Task Result:15
    seconds
Completed a task - Task Name: Task #5, Task Result:18
    seconds
```

The Fork/Join Framework

The fork/join framework is an implementation of the executor service whose focus is to solve those problems efficiently, which may use the divide-and-conquer algorithm by taking advantage of the multiple processors or multiple cores on a machine. The framework helps solve the problems that involve parallelism. Typically, the fork/join framework is suitable in a situation where

- A task can be divided in multiple subtasks that can be executed in parallel.

- When subtasks are finished, the partial results can be combined to get the final result.

The fork/join framework creates a pool of threads to execute the subtasks. When a thread is waiting on a subtask to finish, the framework uses that thread to execute other pending subtasks of other threads. The technique of an idle thread executing other threads' task is called work-stealing. The framework uses the work-stealing algorithm to enhance the performance. The following four classes in the `java.util.concurrent` package are central to learning the fork/join framework:

- `ForkJoinPool`

- `ForkJoinTask<V>`

- `RecursiveAction`

- `RecursiveTask<V>`

An instance of the `ForkJoinPool` class represents a thread pool. An instance of the `ForkJoinTask` class represents a task. The `ForkJoinTask` class is an abstract class. It has two concrete subclasses: `RecursiveAction` and `RecursiveTask`. Java 8 added an abstract subclass of the `ForkJoinTask` class that is called `CountedCompleter<T>`. The framework supports two types of tasks:

- A task that does not yield a result and a task that yields a result. An instance of the `RecursiveAction` class represents a task that does not yield a result.

- An instance of the `RecursiveTask` class represents a task that yields a result.

A `CountedCompleter` task may or may not yield a result. Both classes, `RecursiveAction` and `RecursiveTask`, provide an abstract `compute()` method. Your class whose object represents a fork/join task should inherit from one of these classes and provide an implementation for the `compute()` method. Typically, the logic inside the `compute()` method is written similar to the following:

```
if (Task is small) {
    Solve the task directly.
} else {
    Divide the task into subtasks.
    Launch the subtasks asynchronously (the fork stage).
```

```
    Wait for the subtasks to finish (the join stage).
    Combine the results of all subtasks.
}
```

The following two methods of the ForkJoinTask class provide two important features during a task execution:

- The fork() method launches a new subtask from a task for an asynchronous execution.

- The join() method lets a task wait for another task to complete.

Steps in Using the Fork/Join Framework

Using the fork/join framework involves the following five steps.

Step 1: Declaring a Class to Represent a Task

Create a class inheriting from the RecursiveAction or RecursiveTask class. An instance of this class represents a task that you want to execute. If the task yields a result, you need to inherit it from the RecursiveTask class. Otherwise, you will inherit it from the RecursiveAction class. The RecursiveTask is a generic class. It takes a type parameter, which is the type of the result of your task. A MyTask class that returns a Long result may be declared as follows:

```
public class MyTask extends RecursiveTask<Long> {
    // Code for your task goes here
}
```

Step 2: Implementing the compute() Method

The logic to execute your task goes inside the compute() method of your class. The return type of the compute() method is the same as the type of the result that your task returns. The declaration for the compute() method of the MyTask class looks like the following:

```
public class MyTask extends RecursiveTask<Long> {
    public Long compute() {
        // Logic for the task goes here
    }
}
```

Step 3: Creating a Fork/Join Thread Pool

You can create a pool of worker threads to execute your task using the `ForkJoinPool` class. The default constructor of this class creates a pool of threads, which has the same parallelism as the number of processors available on the machine:

```
ForkJoinPool pool = new ForkJoinPool();
```

Other constructors let you specify the parallelism and other properties of the pool.

Step 4: Creating the Fork/Join Task

You need to create an instance of your task:

```
MyTask task = MyTask();
```

Step 5: Submitting the Task to the Fork/Join Pool for Execution

You need to call the `invoke()` method of the `ForkJoinPool` class, passing your task as an argument. The `invoke()` method will return the result of the task if your task returns a result. The following statement will execute your task:

```
long result = pool.invoke(task);
```

A Fork/Join Example

Let's consider a simple example of using the fork/join framework. Your task will generate a few random integers and compute their sum. Listing 5-60 shows the complete code for your task.

Listing 5-60. A ForkJoinTask Class to Compute the Sum of a Few Random Integers

```
// RandomIntSum.java
package com.jdojo.threads;

import java.util.ArrayList;
import java.util.List;
import java.util.Random;
import java.util.concurrent.RecursiveTask;
```

```java
public class RandomIntSum extends RecursiveTask<Long> {
    private static final Random randGenerator =
        new Random();
    private final int count;
    public RandomIntSum(int count) {
        this.count = count;
    }
    @Override
    protected Long compute() {
        long result = 0;
        if (this.count <= 0) {
            return 0L; // We do not have anything to do
        }
        if (this.count == 1) {
            // Compute the number directly and return the
            // result
            return (long) this.getRandomInteger();
        }
        // Multiple numbers. Divide them into many single
        // tasks. Keep the references of all tasks to call
        // their join() method later
        List<RecursiveTask<Long>> forks =
            new ArrayList<>();
        for (int i = 0; i < this.count; i++) {
            RandomIntSum subTask = new RandomIntSum(1);
            subTask.fork(); // Launch the subtask
            // Keep the subTask references to combine the
            // results later
            forks.add(subTask);
        }
        // Now wait for all subtasks to finish and combine
        // the results
        for (RecursiveTask<Long> subTask : forks) {
            result = result + subTask.join();
        }
```

```
        return result;
    }
    public int getRandomInteger() {
        // Generate the next random integer between
        // 1 and 100
        int n = randGenerator.nextInt(100) + 1;
        System.out.println("Generated a random integer: " +
            n);
        return n;
    }
}
```

The RandomIntSum class inherits from the RecursiveTask<Long> class because it yields a result of the type Long. The result is the sum of all random integers. It declares a randGenerator instance variable that is used to generate random numbers. The count instance variable stores the number of random numbers that you want to use. The value for the count instance variable is set in the constructor.

The getRandomInteger() method generates a random integer between 1 and 100, prints the integer value on the standard output, and returns the random integer.

The compute() method contains the main logic to perform the task. If the number of random numbers to use is one, it computes the result and returns it to the caller. If the number of random numbers is more than one, it launches as many subtasks as the number of random numbers. Note that if you use ten random numbers, it will launch ten subtasks because each random number can be computed independently. Finally, you need to combine the results from all subtasks. Therefore, you need to keep the references of the subtask for later use. You used a List to store the references of all subtasks. Note the use of the fork() method to launch a subtask. The following snippet of code performs this logic:

```
List<RecursiveTask<Long>> forks = new ArrayList<>();
for(int i = 0; i < this.count; i++) {
    RandomIntSum subTask = new RandomIntSum(1);
    subTask.fork(); // Launch the subtask
    // Keep the subTask references to combine the
    // results at the end
    forks.add(subTask);
}
```

Once all subtasks are launched, you need to wait for all subtasks to finish and combine all random integers to get the sum. The following snippet of code performs this logic. Note the use of the join() method, which will make the current task wait for the subtask to finish:

```
for(RecursiveTask<Long> subTask : forks) {
    result = result + subTask.join();
}
```

Finally, the compute() method returns the result, which is the sum of all the random integers. Listing 5-61 has the code to execute a task, which is an instance of the RandomIntSum class. You may get different output.

Listing 5-61. Using a Fork/Join Pool to Execute a Fork/Join Task

```
// ForkJoinTest.java
package com.jdojo.threads;
import java.util.concurrent.ForkJoinPool;
public class ForkJoinTest {
    public static void main(String[] args) {
        // Create a ForkJoinPool to run the task
        ForkJoinPool pool = new ForkJoinPool();
        // Create an instance of the task
        RandomIntSum task = new RandomIntSum(3);
        // Run the task
        long sum = pool.invoke(task);
        System.out.println("Sum is " + sum);
    }
}
```

```
Generated a random integer: 26
Generated a random integer: 5
Generated a random integer: 68
Sum is 99
```

This is a very simple example of using the fork/join framework. You are advised to explore the fork/join framework classes to know more about the framework. Inside the compute() method of your task, you can have complex logic to divide tasks into subtasks. Unlike in this example, you may not know in advance how many subtasks you need to launch. You may launch a subtask that may launch another subtask and so on.

Thread-Local Variables

A thread-local variable provides a way to maintain a separate value for a variable for each thread. The ThreadLocal<T> class in the java.lang package provides the implementation of a thread-local variable. It has five methods:

- T get()

- protected T initialValue()

- void remove()

- void set(T value)

- static <S> ThreadLocal<S> withInitial(Supplier<? extends S> supplier)

The get() and set() methods are used to get and set the value for a thread-local variable, respectively. The initialValue() method is used to set the initial value of the variable, and it has a protected access. To use it, you need to subclass the ThreadLocal class and override this method. You can remove the value by using the remove() method. The withInitial() method lets you create a ThreadLocal with an initial value.

Let's create a CallTracker class, shown in Listing 5-62, to keep track of the number of times a thread calls its call() method.

Listing 5-62. A Class That Uses a ThreadLocal Object to Track Calls to Its Method

```java
// CallTracker.java
package com.jdojo.threads;
public class CallTracker {
    // threadLocal variable is used to store counters for
    // all threads
    private static final ThreadLocal<Integer>
        threadLocal = new ThreadLocal<Integer>();
```

```
public static void call() {
    Integer counterObject = threadLocal.get();
    // Initialize counter to 1
    int counter = 1;
    if (counterObject != null) {
        counter = counterObject + 1;
    }
    // Set the new counter
    threadLocal.set(counter);
    // Print how many times this thread has called
    // this method
    String threadName = Thread.currentThread().
        getName();
    System.out.println("Call counter for " +
        threadName + " = " + counter);
    }
}
```

The get() method of the ThreadLocal class works on a thread basis. It returns the value set by the set() method by the same thread, which is executing the get() method. If a thread calls the get() method the very first time, it returns null. The program sets the call counter for the caller thread to 1 if it is its first call. Otherwise, it increments the call counter by 1. It sets the new counter back in the threadLocal object. In the end, the call() method prints a message about how many times the current thread has called this method.

Listing 5-63 uses the CallTracker class in three threads. Each thread calls this method a random number of times between 1 and 5. You can observe in the output that the counter is maintained for each thread's call separately. You may get different output.

Listing 5-63. A Test Class for the CallTracker Class

```
// CallTrackerTest.java
package com.jdojo.threads;
import java.util.Random;
public class CallTrackerTest {
    public static void main(String[] args) {
        // Let's start three threads to the
        // CallTracker.call() method
```

```
        new Thread(CallTrackerTest::run).start();
        new Thread(CallTrackerTest::run).start();
        new Thread(CallTrackerTest::run).start();
    }
    public static void run() {
        Random random = new Random();
        // Generate a random value between 1 and 5
        int counter = random.nextInt(5) + 1;
        // Print the thread name and the generated random
        // number by the thread
        System.out.println(Thread.currentThread().getName()
                + " generated counter: " + counter);
        for (int i = 0; i < counter; i++) {
            CallTracker.call();
        }
    }
}
```

```
Thread-0 generated counter: 4
Thread-1 generated counter: 2
Thread-2 generated counter: 3
Call counter for Thread-0 = 1
Call counter for Thread-2 = 1
Call counter for Thread-1 = 1
Call counter for Thread-2 = 2
Call counter for Thread-0 = 2
Call counter for Thread-2 = 3
Call counter for Thread-1 = 2
Call counter for Thread-0 = 3
Call counter for Thread-0 = 4
```

The initialValue() method sets the initial value of the thread-local variable for each thread. If you have set the initial value, the call to the get() method, before you call the set() method, will return that initial value. It is a protected method. You must override it in a subclass. You can set the initial value for the call counter to 1000 by using an anonymous class as shown:

```
// Create an anonymous subclass ThreadLocal class and
// override its initialValue()
// method to return 1000 as the initial value
private static ThreadLocal<Integer> threadLocal =
    new ThreadLocal<Integer>() {
        @Override
        public Integer initialValue() {
            return 1000;
        }
    };
```

Subclassing the ThreadLocal class just to have an instance of ThreadLocal with an initial value was overkill. Finally, the class designers realized it (in Java 8) and provided a factory method called withInitial() in the ThreadLocal class that can specify an initial value. The method is declared as follows:

```
public static <S> ThreadLocal<S> withInitial(Supplier<? extends S> supplier)
```

The specified supplier provides the initial value for the ThreadLocal. The get() method of the supplier is used to get the initial value. You can rewrite this logic and replace the anonymous class with a lambda expression as follows:

```
// Create a ThreadLocal with an initial value of 1000
ThreadLocal<Integer> threadLocal = T
    hreadLocal.withInitial(() -> 1000);
```

Having a Supplier as the supplier for the initial value, you can generate the initial value lazily and based on some logic. The following statement creates a ThreadLocal with the initial value as the second part of the current time when the initial value is retrieved:

```
// Return the second part of the current time as the
// initial value
ThreadLocal<Integer> threadLocal =
    ThreadLocal.withInitial(() ->
        LocalTime.now().getSecond()
    );
```

You can use the `remove()` method to reset the value of the thread-local variable for a thread. After the call to the `remove()` method, the first call to the `get()` method works as if it were called the first time by returning the initial value.

The typical use of a thread-local variable is to store user ID, transaction ID, or transaction context for a thread. The thread sets those values in the beginning, and any code during the execution of that thread can use those values. Sometimes, a thread may start child threads that may need to use the value set for a thread-local variable in the parent thread. You can achieve this by using an object of the `InheritableThreadLocal<T>` class, which is inherited from the `ThreadLocal` class. The child thread inherits its initial value from the parent thread. However, the child thread can set its own value using the `set()` method.

Setting Stack Size of a Thread

Each thread in a JVM is allocated its own stack. A thread uses its stack to store all local variables during its execution. Local variables are used in constructors, methods, or blocks (static or non-static). The stack size of each thread will limit the number of threads that you can have in a program. Local variables are allocated memory on stack during their scope. Once they are out of scope, the memory used by them is reclaimed. It is essential to optimize the stack size of a thread in your program if it uses too many threads. If the stack size is too big, you can have a fewer number of threads in your program. The number of threads will be limited by the available memory to the JVM. If the stack size is too small to store all local variables used at a time, you may encounter a `StackOverflowError`. To set the stack size for each thread, you can use a non-standard JVM option called `-Xss<size>`, where `<size>` is the size of the thread stack. To set the stack size to `512` KB, you can use a command, like so:

```
java -Xss512k <other-arguments>
```

Summary

A thread is a unit of execution in a program. An instance of the `Thread` class represents a thread in a Java program. The thread starts its execution in the `run()` method of the `Thread` class or its subclass. To execute your code in a thread, you need to subclass the `Thread` class and override its `run()` method; you can also use an instance of the

Runnable interface as the target for a thread. Beginning with Java 8, you can use a method reference of any method that takes no parameters and returns void as the target for a thread. A thread is scheduled by using the start() method of the Thread class.

There are two types of threads: daemon and non-daemon. A non-daemon thread is also known as a user thread. The JVM exits when only threads running in the JVM are all daemon threads.

Each thread in Java has a priority that is an integer between 1 and 10, 1 being the lowest priority and 10 being the highest priority. The priority of a thread is a hint, which can be ignored, to the operating system about its importance for getting the CPU time.

In a multi-threaded program, a section of code that may have undesirable effects on the outcome of the program if executed by multiple threads concurrently is called a critical section. You can mark a critical section in a Java program using the synchronized keyword. Methods can also be declared as synchronized. Only one synchronized instance method of an object can be executed at a time by any threads. Only one synchronized class method of a class can be executed at a time by any threads.

A thread in a Java program goes through a set of states that determines its lifecycle. A thread can be in any one of these states: new, runnable, blocked, waiting, timed-waiting, or terminated. States are represented by constants of the Thread.State enum. Use the getState() method of the Thread class to get the current state of the thread.

A thread can be interrupted, stopped, suspended, and resumed. A stopped thread or a thread that has finished executing cannot be restarted.

Atomic variables, explicit locks, the synchronizer, the executor framework, and the fork/join framework are provided as class libraries to the Java developers to assist in developing concurrent applications. Atomic variables are variables that can be atomically updated without using explicit synchronization. Explicit locks have features that let you acquire locks and back off if the locks are not available. The executor framework helps schedule tasks. The fork/join framework is written on top of the executor framework to assist in working with tasks that can be divided in subtasks, and finally their results can be combined.

Thread-local variables are implemented through the ThreadLocal<T> class. They store values based on threads. They are suitable for values that are local to threads and that cannot be seen by other threads.

Exercises

Exercise 1

What is a thread? Can threads share memory? What is thread-local storage?

Exercise 2

What is a multi-threaded program?

Exercise 3

What is the name of the class whose objects represent threads in Java programs?

Exercise 4

Suppose you create an object of the `Thread` class:

```
Thread t = new Thread();
```

What do you need to do next so that this `Thread` object will get CPU time?

Exercise 5

What is a race condition when using multiple threads? How do you avoid a race condition in your program?

Exercise 6

What is a critical section in a program?

Exercise 7

What is the effect of using the `synchronized` keyword in a method's declaration?

Exercise 8

What is thread synchronization? How is thread synchronization achieved in a Java program?

Exercise 9

What are an entry set and a wait set of an object?

Exercise 10

Describe the user of the `wait()`, `notify()`, and `notifyAll()` methods in thread synchronization.

Exercise 11

What method of the `Thread` class do you use to check if a thread is terminated or alive?

Exercise 12

Describe the following six states of a thread: new, runnable, blocked, waiting, timed-waiting, and terminated. What method in the `Thread` class returns the state of a thread?

Exercise 13

Can you restart a thread by calling its `start()` method after the thread is terminated?

Exercise 14

What is thread starvation?

Exercise 15

What is a daemon thread? What happens when the JVM detects that there are only daemon threads running in the application? Are the main thread and garbage collector thread daemon threads?

Exercise 16

How do you interrupt a thread? What is the difference in calling the instance `isInterrupted()` method and `static interrupted()` method of the `Thread` class? What happens when a blocked thread is interrupted?

Exercise 17

What is a thread group? What is the default thread group of a thread? How do you get an estimate of active threads in a thread group?

Exercise 18

Describe the use of volatile variables in Java programs.

Exercise 19

What is the difference between using an `AtomicLong` variable and a `long` variable with a `synchronized` getter and setter?

Exercise 20

What are semaphores, barriers, phasers, latches, and exchangers? Name the classes in Java that represent instances of these synchronizers.

Exercise 21

What is the executor framework? What is the difference between an instance of the `Executor` interface and an instance of the `ExecutorService` interface? What class do you use to get a preconfigured `Executor` instance?

Exercise 22

If you want to submit a result-bearing task to an `Executor`, the task needs to be an instance of which interface: `Runnable` or `Callable<T>`?

Exercise 23

What does an instance of the `Future<T>` interface represent?

Exercise 24

What is the difference in using the `shutdown()` and `shutdownNow()` methods to shut down an executor?

Exercise 25

What is the fork/join framework?

Exercise 26

Describe the use of the `ThreadLocal<T>` class.

Exercise 27

What JVM option do you use to set the Java thread's stack size?

Exercise 28

Create a class inheriting it from the `Thread` class. When an instance of the class is run as a thread, it should print text like 1<name> 2<name> ...N<name> where <name> is the name of the thread you specify and N is the upper limit on the number of integers starting from 1 to be printed. For example, if you create an instance of your class with 100 and "A," it should print 1A 2A 3A ...100A. Create three threads of your class and run them simultaneously.

Exercise 29

Create a class named `BankAccount`. An instance of this class represents a bank account. It should contain three methods: `deposit()`, `withdraw()`, and `balance()`. They deposit, withdraw, and return the balance in the account. Its `balance` instance variable should store the balance in the account, and it is initialized to 100. The balance in the account must not go below 100. Do not use any thread synchronization constructs or keywords in this class. Create an instance of the `BankAccount` class. Pass this instance to four threads—two threads should deposit money, and two should withdraw money. The deposit and withdrawal amount should be selected randomly between 1 and 10. Start another thread, a monitor thread, that keeps calling the `balance()` method to check if the balance goes below 100. When the balance goes below 100, it should print a message and exit the application.

Exercise 30

Create another copy of the `BankAccount` class and name it `Account`. Use thread synchronization to guard the access to the `balance` instance variable in the `Account` class, so its value never goes below 100. Run the same number of threads as in the previous exercise for five minutes. This time, the monitor thread should not print any message. After five minutes, all your threads should be interrupted, and your threads should respond to the interruption by finishing its task. This way, your application should exit normally after five minutes.

CHAPTER 6

Streams

In this chapter, you will learn:

- What streams are

- Differences between collections and streams

- How to create streams from different types of data sources

- How to represent an optional value using the `Optional` class

- Applying different types of operations on streams

- Collecting data from streams using collectors

- Grouping and partitioning a stream's data

- Finding and matching data in streams

- How to work with parallel streams

All example programs in this chapter are members of a `jdojo.streams` module, as declared in Listing 6-1.

Listing 6-1. The Declaration of a `jdojo.streams` Module

```java
// module-info.java
module jdojo.streams {
    exports com.jdojo.streams;
}
```

© Kishori Sharan, Peter Späth 2021

K. Sharan and P. Späth, *More Java 17*, https://doi.org/10.1007/978-1-4842-7135-3_6

What Are Streams?

An aggregate operation computes a single value from a collection of values. The result of an aggregate operation may be simply a primitive value, an object, or a void. Note that an object may represent a single entity such as a person or a collection of values such as a list, a set, a map, etc.

A stream is a sequence of data elements supporting sequential and parallel aggregate operations. Computing the sum of all elements in a stream of integers, mapping all names in a list to their lengths, etc. are examples of aggregate operations on streams.

Looking at the definition of streams, it seems that they are like collections. So, how do streams differ from collections? Both are abstractions for a collection of data elements. Collections focus on storage of data elements for efficient access, whereas streams focus on aggregate computations on data elements from a data source that is typically, but not necessarily, collections.

In this section, I discuss the following features of streams, comparing them with collections when necessary:

- Streams have no storage.

- Streams can represent a sequence of infinite elements.

- The design of streams is based on internal iteration.

- Streams are designed to be processed in parallel with no additional work from the developers.

- Streams are designed to support functional programming.

- Streams support lazy operations.

- Streams can be ordered or unordered.

- Streams cannot be reused.

The following sections present brief snippets of code using streams. The code is meant to give you a feel for the Streams API and to compare the Streams API with the Collections API. You do not need to understand the code fully at this point. I explain it later in detail.

Streams Have No Storage

A collection is an in-memory data structure that stores all its elements. All elements must exist in memory before they are added to the collection. A stream has no storage; it does not store elements. A stream pulls elements from a data source on demand and passes them to a pipeline of operations for processing.

Infinite Streams

A collection cannot represent a group of infinite elements, whereas a stream can. A collection stores all its elements in memory, and therefore it is not possible to have an infinite number of elements in a collection. Having a collection of an infinite number of elements will require an infinite amount of memory, and the storage process will continue forever. A stream pulls its elements from a data source that can be a collection, a function that generates data, an I/O channel, etc. Because a function can generate an infinite number of elements and a stream can pull data from it on demand, it is possible to have a stream representing a sequence of infinite data elements.

Internal Iteration vs. External Iteration

Collections are based on external iteration. You obtain an iterator for a collection and process elements of the collections in serial using the iterator. Suppose you have a list of integers from 1 to 5. You would compute the sum of the squares of all odd integers in the list as follows:

```
List<Integer> numbers = List.of(1, 2, 3, 4, 5);
int sum = 0;
for (int n : numbers) {
    if (n % 2 == 1) {
        int square = n * n;
        sum = sum + square;
    }
}
```

This example uses a for-each loop that performs an external iteration on the list of integers. Simply put, the client code (the for loop in this case) pulls the elements out of the collection and applies the logic to get the result. Consider the following snippet of code that uses a stream to compute the sum of the squares of all odd integers in the same list:

```
int sum = numbers.stream()
                 .filter(n -> n % 2 == 1)
                 .map(n -> n * n)
                 .reduce(0, Integer::sum);
```

Did you notice the power and the simplicity of streams? You replaced five statements with just one statement. However, the code brevity is not the point that I want to make. The point is that you did not iterate over the elements in the list when you used the stream. The stream did that for you internally. This is what I meant by internal iteration supported by streams. You specify to a stream what you want by passing an algorithm using lambda expressions to the stream, and the stream applies your algorithm to its data element by iterating over its elements internally and gives you the result.

Using external iteration, typically, produces sequential code; that is, the code can be executed only by one thread. For example, when you wrote the logic to compute the sum using a for-each loop, the loop must be executed only by one thread. All modern computers come with a multicore processor. Wouldn't it be nice to take advantage of the multicore processor to execute the logic in parallel? The Java library provides a fork/join framework to divide a task into subtasks recursively and execute the subtasks in parallel, taking advantage of a multicore processor. However, the fork/join framework is not so simple to use, especially for beginners.

Streams come to your rescue! They are designed to process their elements in parallel without you even noticing it! This does not mean that streams automatically decide for you when to process their elements in serial or parallel. You just need to tell a stream that you want to use parallel processing, and the stream will take care of the rest. Streams take care of the details of using the fork/join framework internally. You can compute the sum of squares of odd integers in the list in parallel, like so:

```
int sum = numbers.parallelStream()
                 .filter(n -> n % 2 == 1)
                 .map(n -> n * n)
                 .reduce(0, Integer::sum);
```

All you had to do was replace the method called `stream()` with `parallelStream()`. The Streams API uses multiple threads to filter the odd integers, compute their squares, and add them to compute partial sums. Finally, it joins the partial sums to give you the result. In this example, you have only five elements in the list, and using multiple threads to process them is overkill. You will not use parallel processing for such a trivial computation. I have presented this example to drive home the point that parallelizing your computation using streams is free; you get it by just using a different method name! The second point is that parallelizing the computation was made possible because of the internal iteration provided by the stream.

Streams are designed to use internal iteration. They provide an `iterator()` method that returns an Iterator to be used for external iteration of its elements. You will "never" need to iterate elements of a stream yourself using its iterator. If you ever need it, here is how to use it:

```
// Get a list of integers from 1 to 5
List<Integer> numbers = List.of(1, 2, 3, 4, 5);
...
// Get an iterator from the stream
Iterator<Integer> iterator = numbers.stream().iterator();

// That's not normally the way you'd use streams!
while(iterator.hasNext()) {
    int n = iterator.next();
    ...
}
```

Imperative vs. Functional

Collections support imperative programming, whereas streams support declarative programming. This is an offshoot of collections supporting external iteration, whereas streams support internal iteration. When you use collections, you need to know "what" you want and "how" to get it; this is the feature of imperative programming. When you use streams, you specify only "what" you want in terms of stream operations; the "how" part is taken care of by the Streams API. The Streams API supports functional programming. Operations on a stream produce a result without modifying the data source. Like in functional programming, when you use streams, you specify "what" operations you want to perform on its elements using the built-in methods provided by the Streams API, typically by passing a lambda expression to those methods, customizing the behavior of those operations.

Stream Operations

A stream supports two types of operations:

- Intermediate operations

- Terminal operations

Intermediate operations are also known as lazy operations. Terminal operations are also known as eager operations. Operations are known as lazy and eager based on the way they pull the data elements from the data source. A lazy operation on a stream does not process the elements of the stream until another eager operation is called on the stream.

Streams connect through a chain of operations forming a stream pipeline. A stream is inherently lazy until you call a terminal operation on it. An intermediate operation on a stream produces another stream. When you call a terminal operation on a stream, the elements are pulled from the data source and pass through the stream pipeline. Each intermediate operation takes elements from an input stream and transforms the elements to produce an output stream. The terminal operation takes inputs from a stream and produces the result. Figure 6-1 shows a stream pipeline with a data source, three streams, and three operations. The filter and map operations are intermediate operations, and the reduce operation is a terminal operation.

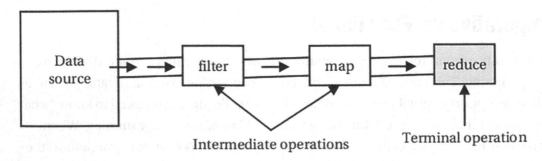

Figure 6-1. *A stream pipeline*

In the figure, the first stream (on the left) pulls data from the data source and becomes the input source for the filter operation. The filter operation produces another stream containing data for which the filter condition is true. The stream produced by the filter operation becomes the input for the map operation. The map operation produces another stream that contains the mapped data. The stream produced by the map operation becomes the input for the reduce operation. The reduce operation is a terminal operation. It computes and returns the result, and then the stream processing is over.

Note   I use the phrase "a stream pulls/consumes elements from its data source" in the preceding discussion. This does not mean that the stream removes the elements from the data source; it only reads them. Streams are designed to support functional programming in which data elements are read and operations on the read data elements produce new data elements. However, the data elements are not modified (or at least should not be modified).

Stream processing does not start until a terminal operation is called. If you just call intermediate operations on a stream, nothing exciting happens, except that they create another stream of objects in memory, without reading data from the data source. This implies that you must use a terminal operation on a stream for it to process the data to produce a result. This is also the reason that the terminal operation is called a result-bearing operation, and intermediate operations are also called nonresult-bearing operations.

You saw the following code that uses a pipeline of stream operations to compute the sum of the squares of odd integers from 1 to 5:

```
List<Integer> numbers = List.of(1, 2, 3, 4, 5);
int sum = numbers.stream()
                 .filter(n -> n % 2 == 1)
                 .map(n -> n * n)
                 .reduce(0, Integer::sum);
```

Figures 6-2 through 6-5 show the states of the stream pipeline as operations are added. Notice that no data flows through the stream until the reduce operation is called. The last figure shows the integers in the input stream for an operation and the mapped (or transformed) integers produced by the operation. The reduce terminal operation produces the result 35.

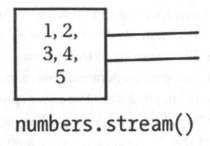

Figure 6-2. *The stream pipeline after the stream object is created*

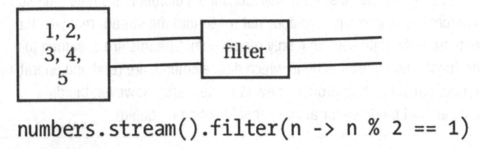

Figure 6-3. *The stream pipeline after the filter operation is called*

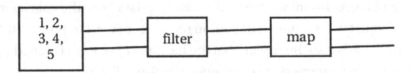

Figure 6-4. *The stream pipeline after the map operation is called*

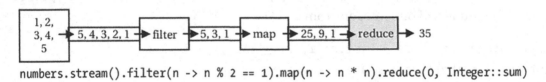

Figure 6-5. *The stream pipeline after the reduce operation is called*

Ordered Streams

A stream can be ordered or unordered. An ordered stream preserves the order of its elements. The Streams API lets you convert an ordered stream into an unordered stream. A stream can be ordered because it represents an ordered data source such as a list or a sorted set. You can also convert an unordered stream into an ordered stream by applying an intermediate operation such as sorting.

A data source is said to have an encounter order if the order in which the elements are traversed by an iterator is predictable and meaningful. For example, arrays and lists always have an encounter order that is from the element at index 0 to the element at the last index. All ordered data sources have an encounter order for their elements. Streams based on data sources having an encounter order also have an encounter order for their elements. Sometimes, a stream operation may impose an encounter order on an otherwise unordered stream. For example, a HashSet does not have an encounter order for its elements. However, applying a sort operation on a stream based on a HashSet imposes an encounter order so that elements are yielded in sorted order.

Streams Are Not Reusable

Unlike collections, streams are not reusable. They are one-shot objects. A stream cannot be reused after calling a terminal operation on it. If you need to perform a computation on the same elements from the same data source again, you must recreate the stream pipeline. A stream implementation may throw an IllegalStateException if it detects that the stream is being reused.

Architecture of the Streams API

Figure 6-6 shows a class diagram for the stream-related interfaces. Stream-related interfaces and classes are in the java.util.stream package.

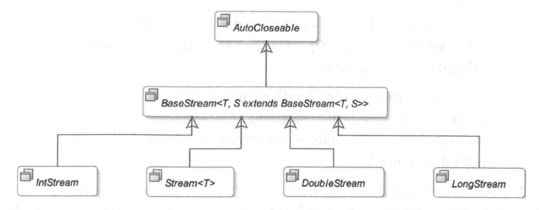

Figure 6-6. *A class diagram for stream-related interfaces in the Streams API*

All stream interfaces inherit from the BaseStream interface, which inherits from the AutoCloseable interface from the java.lang package. In practice, most streams use collections as their data source, and collections do not need to be closed. When a stream is based on a closeable data source such as a file I/O channel, you may create the instance of the stream using a try-with-resources statement to get it closed automatically. Methods common to all types of streams are declared in the BaseStream interface as follows:

- Iterator<T> iterator(): It returns an iterator for the stream. You will almost never need to use this method in your code. This is a terminal operation. After calling this method, you cannot call any other methods on the stream.

- S sequential(): It returns a sequential stream. If the stream is already sequential, it returns itself. Use this method to convert a parallel stream into a sequential stream. This is an intermediate operation.

- S parallel(): It returns a parallel stream. If the stream is already parallel, it returns itself. Use this method to convert a parallel stream into a sequential stream. This is an intermediate operation.

- boolean isParallel(): It returns true if the stream is parallel, false otherwise. The result is unpredictable when this method is called after invoking a terminal stream operation method.

- S unordered(): It returns an unordered version of the stream. If the stream is already unordered, it returns itself. This is an intermediate operation.

- void close(): It closes the stream. You do not need to close collection-based streams. Operating on a closed stream throws an IllegalState-Exception.

- S onClose(Runnable closeHandler): It returns an equivalent stream with an additional close handler. Close handlers are run when the close() method is called on the stream and are executed in the order they were added.

The Stream<T> interface represents a stream of the element type T; for example, a Stream<Person> represents a stream of Person objects. The interface contains methods representing intermediate and terminal operations such as `filter()`, `map()`, `reduce()`, `collect()`, `max()`, `min()`, etc. When you work with streams, you will use these methods most of the time. I discuss each method in detail shortly.

Note that the `Stream<T>` interface takes a type parameter T, which means that you can use it only to work with the elements of the reference type. If you have to work with a stream of primitive type such as `int`, `long`, etc., using `Stream<T>` will involve an additional cost of boxing and unboxing the elements when primitive values are needed. For example, adding all elements of a `Stream<Integer>` will require unboxing all `Integer` elements to int. The designers of the Streams API realized this, and they provided three specialized stream interfaces called `IntStream`, `LongStream`, and `DoubleStream` to work with primitives; these interfaces contain methods to deal with primitive values. Note that you do not have stream interfaces representing other primitive types such as `float`, `short`, etc. because the three stream types can be used to work with other primitive type values.

A Quick Example

Let's look at a quick example of using streams. The code reads a list of integers and computes the sum of the squares of all odd integers in the list.

The `stream()` method in the `Collection` interface returns a sequential stream where the `Collection` acts as the data source. The following snippet of code creates a `List<Integer>` and obtains a `Stream<Integer>` from the list:

```
// Get a list of integers from 1 to 5
List<Integer> numbersList = List.of(1, 2, 3, 4, 5);
// Get a stream from the list
Stream<Integer> numbersStream = numbersList.stream();
```

The `filter()` method of the `Stream<T>` interface takes a `Predicate<? super T>` as an argument and returns a `Stream<T>` with elements of the original stream for which the specified `Predicate` returns `true`. The following statement obtains a stream of only odd integers:

```
// Get a stream of odd integers
Stream<Integer> oddNumbersStream =
    numbersStream.filter(n -> n % 2 == 1);
```

Notice the use of the lambda expression as the argument for the `filter()` method. The lambda expression returns `true` if the element in the stream is not divisible by 2.

The `map()` method of the `Stream<T>` interface takes `Function<? super T,? extends R>` as an argument. Each element in the stream is passed to this `Function`, and a new stream is generated containing the returned values from the `Function`. The following statement takes all odd integers and maps them to their squares:

```
// Get a stream of the squares of odd integers
Stream<Integer> squaredNumbersStream =
    oddNumbersStream.map(n -> n * n);
```

Finally, you need to add the squares of all odd integers to get the result. The `reduce(T identity, BinaryOperator<T> accumulator)` method of the `Stream<T>` interface performs a reduction operation on the stream to reduce the stream to a single value. It takes an initial value and an accumulator that is a `BinaryOperator<T>` as arguments. The first time, the accumulator receives the initial value and the first element of the stream as arguments and returns a value. The second time, the accumulator receives the value returned from its previous call and the second element from the stream. This process continues until all elements of the stream have been passed to the accumulator. The returned value from the last call of the accumulator is returned from the `reduce()` method. The following snippet of code performs the sum of all integers in the stream:

```
// Sum all integers in the stream
int sum = squaredNumbersStream.
    reduce(0, (n1, n2) -> n1 + n2);
```

The `Integer` class contains a static `sum()` method to perform the sum of two integers. You can rewrite the previous statement using a method reference, like so:

```
// Sum all integers in the stream
int sum = squaredNumbersStream.
    reduce(0, Integer::sum);
```

In this example, I break down each operation on the stream into a single statement. You cannot use the returned streams from intermediate operations, except to apply other operations on them. Typically, you care about the result of the terminal operation, not the intermediate streams. Streams are designed to support method chaining to avoid temporary variables, which you used in this example. You can combine these statements into one statement as follows:

```java
// Sum the squares of all odd integers in the numbers list
int sum = numbersList.stream()
                .filter(n -> n % 2 == 1)
                .map(n -> n * n)
                .reduce(0, Integer::sum);
```

I chain all method calls on streams to form only one statement in subsequent examples. Listing 6-2 contains the complete program for this example. Note that you are working with only integers in this example. For better performance, you could have used an IntStream in this example. I show you how to use an IntStream later.

Listing 6-2. Computing the Sum of the Squares of All Odd Integers from 1 to 5

```java
// SquaredIntsSum.java
package com.jdojo.streams;
import java.util.List;
public class SquaredIntsSum {
    public static void main(String[] args) {
        // Get a list of integers from 1 to 5
        List<Integer> numbers = List.of(1, 2, 3, 4, 5);
        // Compute the sum of the squares of all odd
        // integers in the list
        int sum = numbers.stream()
                        .filter(n -> n % 2 == 1)
                        .map(n -> n * n)
                        .reduce(0, Integer::sum);
        System.out.println("Sum = " + sum);
    }
}

Sum = 35
```

I show many examples of performing aggregate operations on different types of streams. Most of the time, it is easier to explain the stream operations using streams of numbers and strings. I show some real-world examples of using streams by using a stream of Person objects. Listing 6-3 contains the declaration for the Person class.

Listing 6-3. A Person Class

```java
// Person.java
package com.jdojo.streams;
import java.time.LocalDate;
import java.time.Month;
import java.util.List;
public class Person {
    // An enum to represent the gender of a person
    public static enum Gender {
        MALE, FEMALE
    }
    private long id;
    private String name;
    private Gender gender;
    private LocalDate dob;
    private double income;

    public Person(long id, String name, Gender gender,
            LocalDate dob, double income) {
        this.id = id;
        this.name = name;
        this.gender = gender;
        this.dob = dob;
        this.income = income;
    }
    public long getId() {
        return id;
    }
    public void setId(long id) {
        this.id = id;
    }
```

```java
public String getName() {
    return name;
}
public void setName(String name) {
    this.name = name;
}
public Gender getGender() {
    return gender;
}
public boolean isMale() {
    return this.gender == Gender.MALE;
}

public boolean isFemale() {
    return this.gender == Gender.FEMALE;
}
public void setGender(Gender gender) {
    this.gender = gender;
}
public LocalDate getDob() {
    return dob;
}
public void setDob(LocalDate dob) {
    this.dob = dob;
}
public double getIncome() {
    return income;
}
public void setIncome(double income) {
    this.income = income;
}
public static List<Person> persons() {
    Person ken = new Person(1, "Ken",
            Gender.MALE,
            LocalDate.of(
               1970, Month.MAY, 4), 6000.0);
```

```java
        Person jeff = new Person(2, "Jeff",
                Gender.MALE,
                LocalDate.of(
                  1970, Month.JULY, 15), 7100.0);
        Person donna = new Person(3, "Donna",
                Gender.FEMALE,
                LocalDate.of(
                  1962, Month.JULY, 29), 8700.0);
        Person chris = new Person(4, "Chris",
                Gender.MALE,
                LocalDate.of(
                  1993, Month.DECEMBER, 16), 1800.0);
        Person laynie = new Person(5, "Laynie",
                Gender.FEMALE,
                LocalDate.of(
                  2012, Month.DECEMBER, 13), 0.0);
        Person lee = new Person(6, "Li",
                Gender.MALE,
                LocalDate.of(
                  2001, Month.MAY, 9), 2400.0);
        // Create a list of persons
        List<Person> persons = List.of(
            ken, jeff, donna, chris, laynie, lee);
        return persons;
    }
    @Override
    public String toString() {
        String str = String.format(
                "(%s, %s, %s, %s, %.2f)",
                id, name, gender, dob, income);
        return str;
    }
}
```

The `Person` class contains a static `Gender` enum to represent the gender of a person. The class declares five instance variables (`id`, `name`, `gender`, `dob`, and `income`), getters, and setters. The `isMale()` and `isFemale()` methods have been declared to be used as method references in lambda expressions. You will use a list of people frequently, and, for that purpose, the class contains a static method called `persons()` to get a list of people.

Creating Streams

There are many ways to create streams. Many existing classes in the Java libraries have received new methods that return a stream. Based on the data source, stream creation can be categorized as follows:

- Streams from values

- Empty streams

- Streams from function

- Streams from arrays

- Streams from collection

- Streams from files

- Streams from other sources

Streams from Values

The Stream interface contains the following three static methods to create a sequential Stream from a single value and multiple values:

- `<T> Stream<T> of(T t)`

- `<T> Stream<T> of(T...values)`

- `<T> Stream<T> ofNullable(T t)`

The following snippet of code creates two streams:

```
// Creates a stream with one string element
Stream<String> stream = Stream.of("Hello");
// Creates a stream with four string elements
Stream<String> stream = Stream.of(
    "Ken", "Jeff", "Chris", "Ellen");
```

The ofNullable() method returns a stream with a single value if the specified value is non-null. Otherwise, it returns an empty stream:

```
String str = "Hello";
// Stream s1 will have one element "Hello"
Stream<String> s1 = Stream.ofNullable(str);
str = null;
// Stream s2 is an empty stream because str is null
Stream<String> s2 = Stream.ofNullable(str);
```

You created a List<Integer> and called its stream() method to get a stream object in Listing 6-2. You can rewrite that example using the Stream.of() method as follows:

```
import java.util.stream.Stream;
...
// Compute the sum of the squares of all odd integers in
// the list
int sum = Stream.of(1, 2, 3, 4, 5)
                .filter(n -> n % 2 == 1)
                .map(n -> n * n)
                .reduce(0, Integer::sum);
System.out.println("Sum = " + sum);

Sum = 35
```

Note that the second version of the of() method takes a varargs argument, and you can use it to create a stream from an array of objects as well. The following snippet of code creates a stream from a String array:

```
String[] names  = {"Ken", "Jeff", "Chris", "Ellen"};
// Creates a stream of four strings in the names array
Stream<String> stream = Stream.of(names);
```

Note   The Stream.of() method creates a stream whose elements are of reference type. If you want to create a stream of primitive values from an array of primitive types, you need to use the Arrays.stream() method, which I explain shortly.

The following snippet of code creates a stream of strings from a String array returned from the split() method of the String class:

```
String str  = "Ken,Jeff,Chris,Ellen";
// The stream will contain 4 elements:
// "Ken", "Jeff", "Chris", and "Ellen"
Stream<String> stream = Stream.of(str.split(","));
```

The Stream interface also supports creating a stream using the builder pattern using the Stream.Builder<T> interface whose instance represents a stream builder. The builder() static method of the Stream interface returns a stream builder:

```
// Gets a stream builder
Stream.Builder<String> builder = Stream.builder();
```

The Stream.Builder<T> interface contains the following methods:

- void accept(T t)

- Stream.Builder<T> add(T t)

- Stream<T> build()

The accept() and add() methods add elements to the stream being built. You might wonder about the existence of two methods in the builder to add elements. The Stream. Builder<T> interface inherits from the Consumer<T> interface, and therefore it inherits the accept() method from the Consumer<T> interface. You can pass a builder's instance to a method that accepts a consumer, and the method can add elements to the builder using the accept() method.

The add() method returns the reference to the builder that makes it suitable for adding multiple elements using method chaining. Once you are done adding elements, call the build() method to create the stream. You cannot add elements to the stream after you call the build() method; doing so results in an IllegalStateException runtime exception. The following snippet of code uses the builder pattern to create a stream of four strings:

```
Stream<String> stream = Stream.<String>builder()
    .add("Ken")
    .add("Jeff")
    .add("Chris")
    .add("Ellen")
.build();
```

Note that the code specifies the type parameter as String when it obtains the builder Stream.<String>builder(). The compiler fails to infer the type parameter if you do not specify it. If you obtain the builder separately, the compiler will infer the type as String, as shown:

```
// Obtain a builder
Stream.Builder<String> builder = Stream.builder();
// Add elements and build the stream
Stream<String> stream = builder.add("Ken")
    .add("Jeff")
    .add("Chris")
    .add("Ellen")
.build();
```

The IntStream interfaces contain four static methods that let you create IntStream from values:

- IntStream of(int value)

- IntStream of(int... values)

- IntStream range(int start, int end)

- IntStream rangeClosed(int start, int end)

The of() methods let you create an IntStream by specifying individual values. The range() and rangeClosed() methods produce an IntStream that contains ordered integers between the specified start and end. The specified end is exclusive in the range() method, whereas it is inclusive in the rangeClosed() method. The following snippet of code uses both methods to create an IntStream having integers 1, 2, 3, 4, and 5 as their elements:

```
// Create an IntStream containing 1, 2, 3, 4, and 5
IntStream oneToFive = IntStream.range(1, 6);
// Create an IntStream containing 1, 2, 3, 4, and 5
IntStream oneToFive = IntStream.rangeClosed(1, 5);
```

The LongStream interface also contains range() and rangeClosed() methods, which take arguments of type long and return a LongStream. The LongStream and DoubleStream interfaces also contain of() methods, which work with the long and double values and return a LongStream and a DoubleStream, respectively.

Empty Streams

An empty stream is a stream with no elements. The Stream interface contains an empty() static method to create an empty sequential stream:

```
// Creates an empty stream of strings
Stream<String> stream = Stream.empty();
```

The IntStream, LongStream, and DoubleStream interfaces also contain an empty() static method to create an empty stream of primitive types. Here is one example:

```
// Creates an empty stream of integers
IntStream numbers = IntStream.empty();
```

Streams from Functions

An infinite stream is a stream with a data source capable of generating an infinite number of elements. Note that I am saying that the data source should be "capable of generating" an infinite number of elements, not that the data source should have or contain an infinite number of elements. It is impossible to store an infinite number of elements of any kind because of memory and time constraints. However, it is possible to have a function that can generate an infinite number of values on demand. The Stream interface contains the following two static methods to generate an infinite stream:

- `<T> Stream<T> iterate(T seed, Predicate<? super T> hasNext, Unary-Operator<T> next)`

- `<T> Stream<T> iterate(T seed, UnaryOperator<T> f)`

- `<T> Stream<T> generate(Supplier<? extends T> s)`

The `iterate()` method creates a sequential ordered stream, whereas the `generate()` method creates a sequential unordered stream. The following sections show you how to use these methods.

The stream interfaces for primitive values `IntStream`, `LongStream`, and `DoubleStream` also contain `iterate()` and `generate()` static methods that take parameters specific to their primitive types. For example, these methods are defined as follows in the `IntStream` interface:

- `static IntStream iterate(int seed, IntPredicate hasNext, IntUnaryOperator next)`

- `IntStream iterate(int seed, IntUnaryOperator f)`

- `IntStream generate(IntSupplier s)`

The first version of the `iterate()` method is declared as follows:

```
static <T> Stream<T> iterate(
    T seed,
    Predicate<? super T> hasNext,
    UnaryOperator<T> next)
```

The method takes three arguments: a seed, a predicate, and a function. It produces elements by iteratively applying the `next` function as long as the `hasNext` predicate is true. The `seed` argument is the initial element. Calling this method is similar to using a for loop as follows:

```
for (int index = seed;
     hasNext.test(index);
     index = next.applyAsInt(index)) {
  // index is the next element in the stream
}
```

The following snippet of code produces a stream of integers from 1 to 10:

```
Stream<Integer> nums =
    Stream.iterate(1, n -> n <= 10, n -> n + 1);
```

The second version of the iterate() method is declared as follows:

```
static <T> Stream<T> iterate(T seed, UnaryOperator<T> f)
```

The method takes two arguments: a seed and a function. The first argument is a seed that is the first element of the stream. The second element is generated by applying the function to the first element. The third element is generated by applying the function on the second element and so on. Its elements are seed, f(seed), f(f(seed)), f(f(f(seed))), and so on. The following statement creates an infinite stream of natural numbers and an infinite stream of all odd natural numbers:

```
// Creates a stream of natural numbers
Stream<Long> naturalNumbers =
    Stream.iterate(1L, n -> n + 1);
// Creates a stream of odd natural numbers
Stream<Long> oddNaturalNumbers =
    Stream.iterate(1L, n -> n + 2);
```

What do you do with an infinite stream? You understand that it is not possible to consume all elements of an infinite stream. This is simply because the stream processing will take forever to complete. Typically, you convert the infinite stream into a fixed-size stream by applying a limit operation that truncates the input stream to be no longer than a specified size. The limit operation is an intermediate operation that produces another stream. You apply the limit operation using the limit(long maxSize) method of the Stream interface. The following snippet of code creates a stream of the first 10 natural numbers:

```
// Creates a stream of the first 10 natural numbers
Stream<Long> tenNaturalNumbers =
    Stream.iterate(1L, n -> n + 1).
    limit(10);
```

You can apply a forEach operation on a stream using the forEach(Consumer<? super T> action) method of the Stream interface. The method returns void.

It is a terminal operation. The following snippet of code prints the first five odd natural numbers on the standard output:

```
Stream.iterate(1L, n -> n + 2)
    .limit(5)
    .forEach(System.out::println);
```

1
3
5
7
9

Let's look at a realistic example of creating an infinite stream of prime numbers. Listing 6-4 contains a utility class called PrimeUtil. The class contains two utility methods. The next() instance method returns the next prime number after the last found prime number. The next(long after) static method returns the prime number after the specified number. The isPrime() static method checks if a number is a prime number.

Listing 6-4. A Utility Class to Work with Prime Numbers

```
// PrimeUtil.java
package com.jdojo.streams;
public class PrimeUtil {
    // Used for a stateful PrimeUtil
    private long lastPrime = 0L;
    // Computes the prime number after the last generated
    // prime
    public long next() {
        lastPrime = next(lastPrime);
        return lastPrime;
    }
    // Computes the prime number after the specified
    // number
    public static long next(long after) {
        long counter = after;
        // Keep looping until you find the next prime
```

```
            // number
            while (!isPrime(++counter));
            return counter;
        }
        // Checks if the specified number is a prime number
        public static boolean isPrime(long number) {
            // <= 1 is not a prime number
            if (number <= 1) {
                return false;
            }
            // 2 is a prime number
            if (number == 2) {
                return true;
            }
            // Even numbers > 2 are not prime numbers
            if (number % 2 == 0) {
                return false;
            }

            long maxDivisor = (long) Math.sqrt(number);
            for (int counter = 3;
                    counter <= maxDivisor;
                    counter += 2) {
                if (number % counter == 0) {
                    return false;
                }
            }
            return true;
        }
    }
}
```

The following snippet of code creates an infinite stream of prime numbers and prints the first five prime numbers on the standard output:

```
Stream.iterate(2L, PrimeUtil::next)
        .limit(5)
        .forEach(System.out::println);
```

```
2
3
5
7
11
```

There is another way to get the first five prime numbers. You can generate an infinite stream of natural numbers, apply a filter operation to pick only the prime numbers, and limit the filtered stream to five. The following snippet of code shows this logic using the isPrime() method of the PrimeUtil class:

```
// Print the first 5 prime numbers
Stream.iterate(2L, n -> n + 1)
      .filter(PrimeUtil::isPrime)
      .limit(5)
      .forEach(System.out::println);
```

```
2
3
5
7
11
```

Sometimes, you may want to discard some elements of a stream. This is accomplished using the skip operation. The skip(long n) method of the Stream interface discards (or skips) the first n elements of the stream. This is an intermediate operation. The following snippet of code uses this operation to print five prime numbers, skipping the first 100 prime numbers:

```
Stream.iterate(2L, PrimeUtil::next)
      .skip(100)
      .limit(5)
      .forEach(System.out::println);
```

```
547
557
563
569
571
```

Using everything you have learned about streams, can you write a stream pipeline to print five prime numbers that are greater than 3000? This is left as an exercise for the readers.

The generate(Supplier<? extends T> s) method uses the specified Supplier to generate an infinite sequential unordered stream. The following snippet of code prints five random numbers greater than or equal to 0.0 and less than 1.0 using the random() static method of the Math class. You may get different output:

```
Stream.generate(Math::random)
      .limit(5)
      .forEach(System.out::println);
```

```
0.05958352209327644
0.8122226657626394
0.5073323815997652
0.9327951597282766
0.4314430923877808
```

If you want to use the generate() method to generate an infinite stream in which the next element is generated based on the value of the previous element, you need to use a Supplier that stores the last generated element. Note that a PrimeUtil object can act as a Supplier whose next() instance method remembers the last generated prime number. The following snippet of code prints five prime numbers after skipping the first 100:

```
Stream.generate(new PrimeUtil()::next)
      .skip(100)
      .limit(5)
      .forEach(System.out::println);
```

```
547
557
563
569
571
```

The Random class in the java.util package contains specially tailored methods to work with streams. So we have methods like ints(), longs(), and doubles() that return infinite IntStream, LongStream, and DoubleStream, respectively, which contain random numbers of the int, long, and double types. The following snippet of code prints five random int values from an IntStream returned from the ints() method of the Random class:

```
// Print five random integers
new Random().ints()
           .limit(5)
           .forEach(System.out::println);
```

```
-1147567659
285663603
-412283607
412487893
-22795557
```

You may get different output every time you run the code. You can use the nextInt() method of the Random class as the Supplier in the generate() method to achieve the same result:

```
// Print five random integers
Stream.generate(new Random()::nextInt)
      .limit(5)
      .forEach(System.out::println);
```

If you want to work with only primitive values, you can use the generate() method of the primitive type stream interfaces. For example, the following snippet of code prints five random integers using the generate() static method of the IntStream interface:

```
IntStream.generate(new Random()::nextInt)
        .limit(5)
        .forEach(System.out::println);
```

How would you generate an infinite stream of repeating values? For example, how would you generate an infinite stream of zeroes? The following snippet of code shows you how to do this:

```
IntStream zeroes = IntStream.generate(() -> 0);
```

Streams from Arrays

The Arrays class in the java.util package contains an overloaded stream() static method to create sequential streams from arrays. You can use it to create an IntStream from an int array, a LongStream from a long array, a DoubleStream from a double array, and a Stream<T> from an array of the reference type T. The following snippet of code creates an IntStream and a Stream<String> from an int array and a String array:

```
// Creates a stream from an int array with elements
// 1, 2, and 3
IntStream numbers = Arrays.stream(new int[]{1, 2, 3});
// Creates a stream from a String array with elements
// "Ken", and "Jeff"
Stream<String> names = Arrays.stream(
    new String[] {"Ken", "Jeff"});
```

Note   You can create a stream from a reference type array using two methods: Arrays.stream(T[] t) and Stream.of(T...t). Providing two methods in the library to accomplish the same thing is intentional.

Streams from Collections

The Collection interface contains the stream() and parallelStream() methods that create sequential and parallel streams from a Collection, respectively. The following snippet of code creates streams from a set of strings:

```
import java.util.HashSet;
import java.util.Set;
import java.util.stream.Stream;
...
// Create and populate a set of strings
Set<String> names = Set.of("Ken", "jeff");
// Create a sequential stream from the set
Stream<String> sequentialStream = names.stream();
// Create a parallel stream from the set
Stream<String> parallelStream = names.parallelStream();
```

Streams from Files

There are many methods in the classes of the `java.io` and `java.nio.file` packages to support I/O operations using streams. For example:

- You can read text from a file as a stream of strings in which each element represents one line of text from the file.

- You can obtain a stream of `JarEntry` from a `JarFile`.

- You can obtain the list of entries in a directory as a stream of `Path`.

- You can obtain a stream of `Path` that is a result of a file search in a specified directory.

- You can obtain a stream of `Path` that contains the file tree of a specified directory.

I show some examples of using streams with file I/O in this section. Refer to the API documentation for the `java.nio.file.Files`, `java.io.BufferedReader`, and `java.util.jar.JarFile` classes for more details on the stream-related methods.

The `BufferedReader` and `Files` classes contain a `lines()` method that reads a file lazily and returns the contents as a stream of strings. Each element in the stream represents one line of text from the file. The file needs to be closed when you are done with the stream. Calling the `close()` method on the stream will close the underlying file. Alternatively, you can create the stream in a try-with-resources statement so the underlying file is closed automatically.

The program in Listing 6-5 shows how to read contents of a file using a stream. It also walks the entire file tree for the current working directory and prints the entries in the directory. The program assumes that you have the `luci1.txt` file, which is supplied with the source code, in the current working directory. If the file does not exist, an error message with the absolute path of the expected file is printed. You may get different output when you run the program.

Listing 6-5. Performing File I/O Using Streams

```
// IOStream.java
package com.jdojo.streams;
```

```java
import java.io.IOException;
import java.nio.file.Files;
import java.nio.file.Path;
import java.nio.file.Paths;
import java.util.stream.Stream;

public class IOStream {
    public static void main(String[] args) {
        // Read the contents of the file luci1.txt
        readFileContents("luci1.txt");
        // Print the file tree for the current working
        // directory
        listFileTree();
    }
    public static void readFileContents(String filePath) {
        Path path = Paths.gct(filcPath);
        if (!Files.exists(path)) {
            System.out.println("The file "
                    + path.toAbsolutePath()
                    + " does not exist.");
            return;
        }
        try (Stream<String> lines = Files.lines(path)) {
            // Read and print all lines
            lines.forEach(System.out::println);
        } catch (IOException e) {
            e.printStackTrace();
        }
    }
    public static void listFileTree() {
        Path dir = Paths.get("");
        System.out.printf("%nThe file tree for %s%n",
            dir.toAbsolutePath());
        try (Stream<Path> fileTree = Files.walk(dir)) {
            fileTree.forEach(System.out::println);
        } catch (IOException e) {
```

```
        e.printStackTrace();
    }
  }
}
```

STRANGE fits of passion have I known:
And I will dare to tell,
But in the lover's ear alone,
What once to me befell.

The file tree for C:\Java9LanguageFeatures
build
build\modules
build\modules\com
build\modules\com\jdojo
...

Streams from Other Sources

Many classes that hold some kind of contents provide methods that return the data they represent in a stream. Two such methods that you may use frequently are explained next:

- The chars() method in the CharSequence interface returns an IntStream whose elements are int values representing the characters of the CharSequence. You can use the chars() method on a String, a StringBuilder, and a StringBuffer to obtain a stream of characters of their contents as these classes implement the CharSequence interface.

- The splitAsStream(CharSequence input) method of the java.util.regex. Pattern class returns a stream of String whose elements match the pattern.

Let's look at an example in both categories. The following snippet of code creates a stream of characters from a string, filters out all digits and whitespace, and prints the remaining characters:

```
String str = "5 apples and 25 oranges";
str.chars()
    .filter(n -> !Character.isDigit((char)n)
                && !Character.isWhitespace((char)n))
    .forEach(n -> System.out.print((char)n));
```

applesandoranges

The following snippet of code obtains a stream of strings by splitting a string using a regular expression (","). The matched strings are printed on the standard output:

```
String str = "Ken,Jeff,Lee";
Pattern.compile(",")
       .splitAsStream(str)
       .forEach(System.out::println);
```

Ken

Jeff

Lee

Representing an Optional Value

In Java, null is used to represent "nothing" or an "empty" result. Most often, a method returns null if it does not have a result to return. This has been a source of frequent NullPointerException in Java programs. Consider printing a person's year of birth, like so:

```
Person ken = new Person(1, "Ken", Person.Gender.MALE,
    null, 6000.0);
int year = ken.getDob().getYear();
// <- Throws a NullPointerException
System.out.println("Ken was born in the year " + year);
```

The code throws a NullPointerException at runtime. The problem is in the return value of the ken.getDob() method that returns null. Calling the getYear() method on a null reference results in the NullPointerException. So, what is the solution? In fact, unless you want to replace Java by a new language, there is no real solution to this on a language level. But Java provides a library construct which helps to avoid

NullPointerExceptions. There exists an Optional<T> class in the java.util package to deal with NullPointerExceptions gracefully. Methods that may return nothing should return an Optional instead of null.

An Optional is a container object that may or may not contain a non-null value. Its isPresent() method returns true if it contains a non-null value, and false otherwise. Its get() method returns the non-null value if it contains a non-null value, and throws a NoSuchElementException otherwise. This implies that when a method returns an Optional, you must, as a practice, check if it contains a non-null value before asking it for the value. If you use the get() method before making sure it contains a non-null value, you may get a NoSuchElementException instead of getting a NullPointerException. This is why I said in the previous paragraph that there is no real solution to the NullPointerException. However, returning an Optional is certainly a better way to deal with null, as developers will get used to using the Optional objects in the way they are designed to be used.

How do you create an Optional<T> object? The Optional<T> class provides the following static factory methods to create its objects:

- <T> Optional<T> empty(): Returns an empty Optional. That is, the Optional returned from this method does not contain a non-null value.

- <T> Optional<T> of(T value): Returns an Optional containing the specified value as the non-null value. If the specified value is null, it throws a NullPointerException.

- <T> Optional<T> ofNullable(T value): Returns an Optional containing the specified value if the value is non-null. If the specified value is null, it returns an empty Optional.

The following snippet of code shows how to create Optional objects:

```
// Create an empty Optional
Optional<String> empty = Optional.empty();
// Create an Optional for the string "Hello"
Optional<String> str = Optional.of("Hello");
// Create an Optional with a String that may be null
String nullableString = "";
// <- get a string that may be null...
Optional<String> str2 = Optional.of(nullableString);
```

The following snippet of code prints the value in an `Optional` if it contains a non-null value:

```
// Create an Optional for the string "Hello"
Optional<String> str = Optional.of("Hello");
// Print the value in Optional
if (str.isPresent()) {
    String value = str.get();
    System.out.println("Optional contains " + value);
} else {
    System.out.println("Optional is empty.");
}

Optional contains Hello
```

You can use the `ifPresent(Consumer<? super T> action)` method of the `Optional` class to take an action on the value contained in the `Optional`. If the `Optional` is empty, this method does not do anything. You can rewrite the previous code to print the value in an `Optional` as follows. Note that if the `Optional` were empty, the code would not print anything:

```
// Create an Optional for the string "Hello"
Optional<String> str = Optional.of("Hello");
// Print the value in the Optional, if present
str.ifPresent(value ->
    System.out.println("Optional contains " + value));

Optional contains Hello
```

The following are four methods to get the value of an `Optional`:

- `T get()`: Returns the value contained in the `Optional`. If the `Optional` is empty, it throws a `NoSuchElementException`.

- `T orElse(T defaultValue)`: Returns the value contained in the `Optional`. If the `Optional` is empty, it returns the specified `defaultValue`.

- T orElseGet(Supplier<? extends T> defaultSupplier): Returns the value contained in the Optional. If the Optional is empty, it returns the value returned from the specified defaultSupplier.

- <X extends Throwable> T orElseThrow(Supplier<? extends X> exceptionSupplier) throws X extends Throwable: Returns the value contained in the Optional. If the Optional is empty, it throws the exception returned from the specified exceptionSupplier.

The Optional<T> class describes a non-null reference type value or its absence. The java.util package contains three more classes named OptionalInt, OptionalLong, and OptionalDouble to deal with optional primitive values. They contain similarly named methods that apply to primitive data types, except for getting their values. They do not contain a get() method. To return their values, the OptionalInt class contains a getAsInt(), the OptionalLong class contains a getAsLong(), and the OptionalDouble class contains a getAsDouble() method. Like the get() method of the Optional class, the getters for primitive optional classes also throw a NoSuchElementException when they are empty. Unlike the Optional class, they do not contain an ofNullable() factory method because primitive values cannot be null. The following snippet of code shows how to use the OptionalInt class:

```
// Create an empty OptionalInt
OptionalInt empty = OptionalInt.empty();
// Use an OptionalInt to store 287
OptionalInt number = OptionalInt.of(287);
if (number.isPresent()){
    int value = number.getAsInt();
    System.out.println("Number is " + value);
} else {
    System.out.println("Number is absent.");
}

Number is 287
```

Several methods in the Streams API return an instance of the Optional, OptionalInt, OptionalLong, and OptionalDouble when they do not have anything to return. For example, all types of streams let you compute the maximum element in the stream. If the stream is empty, there is no maximum element. Note that in a stream pipeline, you may start with a non-empty stream and end up with an empty stream because of filtering or other operations such as limit, skip, etc. For this reason, the max() method in all stream classes returns an optional object. The program in Listing 6-6 shows how to get the maximum integer from IntStream.

Listing 6-6. Working with Optional Values

```java
// OptionalTest.java
package com.jdojo.streams;

import java.util.Comparator;
import java.util.Optional;
import java.util.OptionalInt;
import java.util.stream.IntStream;
import java.util.stream.Stream;

public class OptionalTest {
    public static void main(String[] args) {
        // Get the maximum of odd integers from the stream
        OptionalInt maxOdd = IntStream.of(10, 20, 30)
                                .filter(n -> n % 2 == 1)
                                .max();
        if (maxOdd.isPresent()) {
            int value = maxOdd.getAsInt();
            System.out.println("Maximum odd integer is " +
                value);
        } else {
            System.out.println("Stream is empty.");
        }

        // Get the maximum of odd integers from the stream
        OptionalInt numbers = IntStream.of(
                1, 10, 37, 20, 31)
            .filter(n -> n % 2 == 1)
            .max();
```

```
        if (numbers.isPresent()) {
            int value = numbers.getAsInt();
            System.out.println("Maximum odd integer is " +
                value);
        } else {
            System.out.println("Stream is empty.");
        }
        // Get the longest name
        Optional<String> name =
            Stream.of("Ken", "Ellen", "Li")
            .max(Comparator.comparingInt(String::length));
        if (name.isPresent()) {
            String longestName = name.get();
            System.out.println("Longest name is " +
                longestName);
        } else {
            System.out.println("Stream is empty.");
        }
    }
}
Stream is empty.
Maximum odd integer is 37
Longest name is Ellen
```

In addition, the Optional<T> class contains the following methods:

- void ifPresentOrElse(Consumer<? super T> action, Runnable empty-Action)

- Optional<T> or(Supplier<? extends Optional<? extends T» supplier)

- Stream<T> stream()

Before I describe these methods and present a complete program showing their use, consider the following list of an Optional<Integer>:

```
List<Optional<Integer>> optionalList = List.of(
    Optional.of(1),
    Optional.empty(),
    Optional.of(2),
    Optional.empty(),
    Optional.of(3));
```

The list contains five Optional elements, two of which are empty and three contain values as 1, 2, and 3. I refer to this list in the subsequent discussion.

The ifPresentOrElse() method lets you provide two alternate courses of actions. If a value is present, it performs the specified action with the value.

Otherwise, it performs the specified emptyAction. The following snippet of code iterates over all the elements in the list using a stream to print the value if Optional contains a value and an "Empty" string if Optional is empty:

```
optionalList.stream()
        .forEach(p -> p.ifPresentOrElse(
                System.out::println,
                () -> System.out.println("Empty")));
```

```
1
Empty
2
Empty
3
```

The or() method returns the Optional itself if the Optional contains a non-null value. Otherwise, it returns the Optional returned by the specified supplier. The following snippet of code creates a stream from a list of Optional and uses the or() method to map all empty Optionals to an Optional with a value of zero:

```
optionalList.stream()
            .map(p -> p.or(() -> Optional.of(0)))
            .forEach(System.out::println);
```

```
Optional[1]
Optional[0]
Optional[2]
Optional[0]
Optional[3]
```

The stream() method returns a sequential stream of elements containing the value present in the Optional. If the Optional is empty, it returns an empty stream. Suppose you have a list of Optional and you want to collect all present values in another list. You can achieve this as follows:

```
// Print the values in all non-empty Optionals
optionalList.stream()
            .filter(Optional::isPresent)
            .map(Optional::get)
            .forEach(System.out::println);
```

```
1
2
3
```

You had to use a filter to filter out all empty Optionals and map the remaining Optionals to their values. With the new stream() method, you can combine the filter() and map() operations into one flatMap() operation as shown. I discuss flattening streams in detail in the "Flattening Streams" section later in this chapter.

```
// Print the values in all non-empty Optionals
optionalList.stream()
            .flatMap(Optional::stream)
            .forEach(System.out::println);
```

```
1
2
3
```

Applying Operations to Streams

Table 6-1 lists some of the commonly used stream operations, their types, and descriptions. The Stream interface contains a method with the same name as the name of the operation in the table. You have seen some of these operations in previous sections. Subsequent sections cover them in detail.

Table 6-1. *List of Commonly Used Stream Operations Supported by the Streams API*

Operation	Type	Description
Distinct	Intermediate	Returns a stream consisting of the distinct elements of this stream. Elements e1 and e2 are considered equal if e1.equals(e2) returns true.
Filter	Intermediate	Returns a stream consisting of the elements of this stream that match the specified predicate.
flatMap	Intermediate	Returns a stream consisting of the results of applying the specified function to the elements in this stream. The function produces a stream for each input element, and the output streams are flattened. Performs one-to-many mapping.
Limit	Intermediate	Returns a stream consisting of the elements in this stream, truncated to be no longer than the specified size.
Map	Intermediate	Returns a stream consisting of the results of applying the specified function to the elements in this stream. Performs one-to-one mapping.
peek	Intermediate	Returns a stream whose elements consist of this stream. It applies the specified action as it consumes elements of this stream. It is mainly used for debugging purposes.
Skip	Intermediate	Discards the first N elements in the stream and returns the remaining stream. If this stream contains fewer than N elements, an empty stream is returned.
dropWhile	Intermediate	Returns the elements of the stream, discarding the elements from the beginning for which a predicate is true. This operation was added to the Streams API in Java 9.

(continued)

Table 6-1. (*continued*)

Operation	Type	Description
takeWhile	Intermediate	Returns elements from the beginning of the stream, which match a predicate, discarding the rest of the elements. This operation was added to the Streams API in Java 9.
sorted	Intermediate	Returns a stream consisting of the elements in this stream, sorted according to natural order or the specified Comparator. For an ordered stream, the sort is stable.
allMatch	Terminal	Returns true if all elements in the stream match the specified predicate, false otherwise. Returns true if the stream is empty.
anyMatch	Terminal	Returns true if any element in the stream matches the specified predicate, false otherwise. Returns false if the stream is empty.
findAny	Terminal	Returns any element from the stream. An empty Optional is returned for an empty stream.
findFirst	Terminal	Returns the first element of the stream. For an ordered stream, it returns the first element in the encounter order; for an unordered stream, it returns any element.
noneMatch	Terminal	Returns true if no elements in the stream match the specified predicate, false otherwise. Returns true if the stream is empty.
forEach	Terminal	Applies an action for each element in the stream.
Reduce	Terminal	Applies a reduction operation to compute a single value from the stream.

Debugging a Stream Pipeline

You apply a sequence of operations on a stream. Each operation transforms the elements of the input stream, either producing another stream or a result. Sometimes, you may need to look at the elements of the streams as they pass through the pipeline. You can do so by using the peek(Consumer<? super T> action) method of the Stream<T> interface that is meant only for debugging purposes. It produces a stream after applying an action on each input element. The `IntStream`, `LongStream`, and `DoubleStream` methods also contain a `peek()` method that takes an `IntConsumer`, a `LongConsumer`, and a `DoubleConsumer` as an argument. Typically, you use a lambda expression with the `peek()` method to log messages describing elements being processed. The following snippet of code uses the `peek()` method at three places to print the elements passing through the stream pipeline:

```
int sum = Stream.of(1, 2, 3, 4, 5)
    .peek(e -> System.out.println("Taking integer: "
        + e))
    .filter(n -> n % 2 == 1)
    .peek(e -> System.out.println("Filtered integer: "
        + e))
    .map(n -> n * n)
    .peek(e -> System.out.println("Mapped integer: "
        + e))
    .reduce(0, Integer::sum);
System.out.println("Sum = " + sum);

Taking integer: 1
Filtered integer: 1
Mapped integer: 1
Taking integer: 2
Taking integer: 3
Filtered integer: 3
Mapped integer: 9
Taking integer: 4
Taking integer: 5
Filtered integer: 5
Mapped integer: 25
Sum = 35
```

Notice that the output shows the even numbers being taken from the data source, but not passing the filter operation.

Applying the ForEach Operation

The forEach operation takes an action for each element of the stream. The action may simply print each element of the stream to the standard output or increase the income of every person in a stream by 10%. The Stream<T> interface contains two methods to perform the forEach operation:

- void forEach(Consumer<? super T> action)

- void forEachOrdered(Consumer<? super T> action)

IntStream, LongStream, and DoubleStream also contain the same methods, except that their parameter type is the specialized consumer types for primitives; for example, the parameter type for the forEach() method in the IntStream is IntConsumer.

Why do you have two methods to perform the forEach operation? Sometimes, the order in which the action is applied for the elements in a stream is important, and sometimes it is not. The forEach() method does not guarantee the order in which the action for each element in the stream is applied. The forEachOrdered() method performs the action in the encounter order of elements defined by the stream. Use the forEachOrdered() method for a parallel stream only when necessary because it may slow down processing. The following snippet of code prints the details of females in the person list:

```
Person.persons()
      .stream()
      .filter(Person::isFemale)
      .forEach(System.out::println);
```

```
(3, Donna, FEMALE, 1962-07-29, 8700.00)
(5, Laynie, FEMALE, 2012-12-13, 0.00)
```

The program in Listing 6-7 shows how to use the forEach() method to increase the income of all females by 10%. The output shows that only Donna got an increase because another female named Laynie had 0.0 income before.

Listing 6-7. Applying the ForEach Operation on a List of Persons

```
// ForEachTest.java
package com.jdojo.streams;
import java.util.List;
```

```java
public class ForEachTest {
    public static void main(String[] args) {
        // Get the list of persons
        List<Person> persons = Person.persons();
        // Print the list
        System.out.println(
            "Before increasing the income: " + persons);
        // Increase the income of females by 10%
        persons.stream()
            .filter(Person::isFemale)
            .forEach( ->
                p.setIncome(p.getIncome() * 1.10));
        // Print the list again
        System.out.println(
            "After increasing the income: " + persons);
    }
}
```

```
Before increasing the income:
    [(1, Ken, MALE, 1970-05-04, 6000.00),
     (2, Jeff, MALE, 197007-15, 7100.00),
     (3, Donna, FEMALE, 1962-07-29, 8700.00),
     (4, Chris, MALE, 1993-12-16,1800.00),
     (5, Laynie, FEMALE, 2012-12-13, 0.00),
     (6, Li, MALE, 2001-05-09, 2400.00)]
After increasing the income:
    [(1, Ken, MALE, 1970-05-04, 6000.00),
     (2, Jeff, MALE, 197007-15, 7100.00),
     (3, Donna, FEMALE, 1962-07-29, 9570.00),
     (4, Chris, MALE, 1993-12-16,1800.00),
     (5, Laynie, FEMALE, 2012-12-13, 0.00),
     (6, Li, MALE, 2001-05-09, 2400.00)]
```

Applying the Map Operation

A map operation (also known as mapping) applies a function to each element of the input stream to produce another stream (also called an output stream or a mapped stream). The number of elements in the input and output streams is the same. The operation does not modify the elements of the input stream—at least it is not supposed to.

Figure 6-7 depicts the application of the map operation on a stream. It shows element e1 from the input stream being mapped to element et1 in the mapped stream, element e2 mapped to et2, etc.

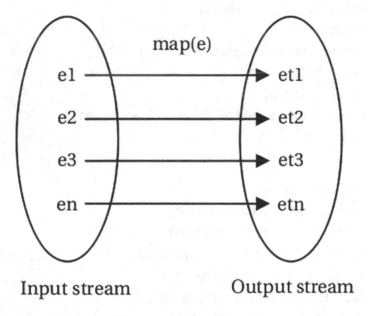

Figure 6-7. *A pictorial view of the map operation*

Mapping a stream to another stream is not limited to any specific type of elements. You can map a stream of T to a stream of type S, where T and S may be the same or different types. For example, you can map a stream of Person to a stream of int where each Person element in the input stream maps to the Person's ID in the mapped stream. You can apply the map operation on a stream using one of the following methods of the Stream<T> interface:

- `<R> Stream<R> map(Function<? super T,? extends R> mapper)`

- `DoubleStream mapToDouble(ToDoubleFunction<? super T> mapper)`

- IntStream mapToInt(ToIntFunction<? super T> mapper)

- LongStream mapToLong(ToLongFunction<? super T> mapper)

The map operation takes a function as an argument. Each element from the input stream is passed to the function. The returned value from the function is the mapped element in the mapped stream. Use the map() method to perform the mapping to reference type elements. If the mapped stream is of a primitive type, use other methods; for example, use the mapToInt() method to map a stream of a reference type to a stream of int. The IntStream, LongStream, and DoubleStream interfaces contain similar methods to facilitate mapping of one type of stream to another. The methods supporting the map operation on an IntStream are as follows:

- IntStream map(IntUnaryOperator mapper)

- DoubleStream mapToDouble(IntToDoubleFunction mapper)

- LongStream mapToLong(IntToLongFunction mapper)

- <U> Stream<U> mapToObj(IntFunction<? extends U> mapper)

The following snippet of code creates an IntStream whose elements are integers from 1 to 5, maps the elements of the stream to their squares, and prints the mapped stream on the standard output. Note that the map() method used in the code is the map() method of the IntStream interface:

```
IntStream.rangeClosed(1, 5)
        .map(n -> n * n)
        .forEach(System.out::println);

1
4
9
16
25
```

The following snippet of code maps the elements of a stream of people to their names and prints the mapped stream. Note that the map() method used in the code is the map() method of the Stream interface:

```
Person.persons()
      .stream()
      .map(Person::getName)
      .forEach(System.out::println);
```

```
Ken
Jeff
Donna
Chris
Laynie
Li
```

Flattening Streams

In the previous section, you saw the map operation that facilitates a one-to-one mapping. Each element of the input stream is mapped to an element in the output stream. The Streams API also supports one-to-many mapping through the `flatMap` operation. It works as follows:

1. It takes an input stream and produces an output stream using a mapping function.

2. The mapping function takes an element from the input stream and maps the element to a stream. The type of input element and the elements in the mapped stream may be different. This step produces a stream of streams. Suppose the input stream is a `Stream<T>` and the mapped stream is `Stream<Stream<R>>` where T and R may be the same or different.

3. Finally, it flattens the output stream (i.e., a stream of streams) to produce a stream. That is, the `Stream<Stream<R>>` is flattened to `Stream<R>`.

It takes some time to understand the flat map operation. Suppose that you have a stream of three numbers: 1, 2, and 3. You want to produce a stream that contains the numbers and the squares of the numbers. You want the output stream to contain 1, 1, 2, 4, 3, and 9. The following is the first, incorrect attempt to achieve this:

```
Stream.of(1, 2, 3)
      .map(n -> Stream.of(n, n * n))
      .forEach(System.out::println);
```

```
java.util.stream.ReferencePipeline$Head@372f7a8d
java.util.stream.ReferencePipeline$Head@2f92e0f4
java.util.stream.ReferencePipeline\$Head@28a418fc
```

Are you surprised by the output? You do not see numbers in the output. The input stream to the map() method contains three integers: 1, 2, and 3. The map() method produces one element for each element in the input stream. In this case, the map() method produces a Stream<Integer> for each integer in the input stream. It produces three Stream<Integer>s. The first stream contains 1 and 1; the second one contains 2 and 4; the third one contains 3 and 9. The forEach() method receives the Stream<Integer> object as its argument and prints the string returned from the toString() method of each Stream<Integer>. You can call the forEach() on a stream, so let's nest its call to print the elements of the stream of streams, like so:

```
Stream.of(1, 2, 3)
      .map(n -> Stream.of(n, n * n))
      .forEach(e -> e.forEach(System.out::println));
```

```
1
1
2
4
3
9
```

You were able to print the numbers and their squares. But you have not achieved the goal of getting those numbers in a Stream<Integer>. They are still in the Stream<Stream<Integer». The solution is to use the flatMap() method instead of the map() method. The following snippet of code does this:

```
Stream.of(1, 2, 3)
      .flatMap(n -> Stream.of(n, n * n))
      .forEach(System.out::println);
```

1

1

2

4

3

9

Figure 6-8 shows the pictorial view of how the `flatMap()` method works in this example. If you still have doubts about the workings of the `flatMap` operation, you can think of its name in the reverse order. Read it as mapFlat, which means "map the elements of the input stream to streams, and then flatten the mapped streams."

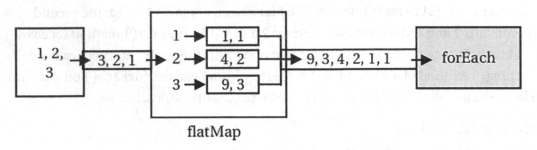

Figure 6-8. *Flattening a stream using the flatMap method*

Let's take another example of the flat map operation. Suppose you have a stream of strings. How will you count the number of the Es in the strings? The following snippet of code shows you how to do it:

```
long count = Stream.of("Ken", "Jeff", "Ellen")
          .map(name -> name.chars())
          .flatMap(intStream -> intStream.
              mapToObj(n -> (char)n))
          .filter(ch -> ch == 'e' || ch == 'E')
          .count();
System.out.println("Es count: " + count);

Es count: 4
```

The code maps the strings to IntStream. Note that the chars() method of the String class returns an IntStream, not a Stream<Character>. The output of the map() method is Stream<IntStream>. The flatMap() method maps the Stream<IntStream> to Stream<Stream<Character» and, finally, flattens it to produce a Stream<Character>. So, the output of the flatMap() method is Stream<Character>. The filter() method filters out any characters that are not an E or e. Finally, the count() method returns the number of elements in the stream. The main logic is to convert the Stream<String> to a Stream<Character>. You can achieve the same using the following code as well:

```
long count = Stream.of("Ken", "Jeff", "Ellen")
        .flatMap(name ->
            IntStream.range(0, name.length())
            .mapToObj(name::charAt))
        .filter(ch -> ch == 'e' || ch == 'E')
        .count();
```

The IntStream.range() method creates an IntStream that contains the indexes of all characters in the input string. The mapToObj() method converts the IntStream into a Stream<Character> whose elements are the characters in the input string.

Applying the Filter Operation

The filter operation is applied on an input stream to produce another stream, which is known as the filtered stream. The filtered stream contains all elements of the input stream for which a predicate evaluates to true. A predicate is a function that accepts an element of the stream and returns a boolean value. Unlike a mapped stream, the filtered stream is of the same type as the input stream.

The filter operation produces a subset of the input stream. If the predicate evaluates to false for all elements of the input stream, the filtered stream is an empty stream. Figure 6-9 shows a pictorial view of applying a filter operation to a stream. The figure shows that two elements (e1 and en) from the input stream made it to the filtered stream, and the other two elements (e2 and e3) were filtered out.

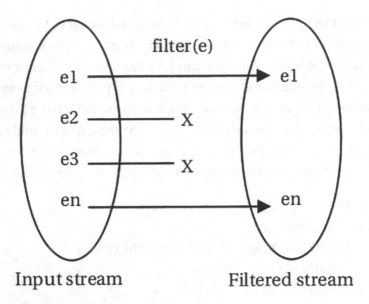

Figure 6-9. *A pictorial view of the filter operation*

You can apply a filter operation to a stream using the `filter()` method of the `Stream`, `IntStream`, `LongStream`, and `DoubleStream` interfaces. The method accepts a `Predicate`. The Streams API offers different flavors of the filter operations, which I discuss after a few examples of using the `filter()` method.

Note   In a map operation, the new stream contains the same number of elements with different values from the input stream. In a filter operation, the new stream contains a different number of elements with the same values from the input stream.

The following snippet of code uses a stream of people and filters in only females. It maps the females to their names and prints them to the standard output:

```
Person.persons()
    .stream()
    .filter(Person::isFemale)
    .map(Person::getName)
    .forEach(System.out::println);
Donna
Laynie
```

The following snippet of code applies two filter operations to print the names of all males having income more than 5000.0:

```
Person.persons()
    .stream()
    .filter(Person::isMale)
    .filter(p -> p.getIncome() > 5000.0)
    .map(Person::getName)
    .forEach(System.out::println);
```

Ken
Jeff

You could have accomplished the same using the following statement that uses only one filter operation that includes both predicates for filtering into one predicate:

```
Person.persons()
    .stream()
    .filter(p -> p.isMale() && p.getIncome() > 5000.0)
    .map(Person::getName)
    .forEach(System.out::println);
```

Ken
Jeff

The following methods can be used to apply filter operations to streams:

- `Stream<T> skip(long count)`
- `Stream<T> limit(long maxCount)`
- `default Stream<T> dropWhile(Predicate<? super T> predicate)`
- `default Stream<T> takeWhile(Predicate<? super T> predicate)`

The skip() method returns the elements of the stream after skipping the specified count elements from the beginning. The limit() method returns elements from the beginning of the stream that are equal to or less than the specified maxCount. One of these methods drops elements from the beginning, and another takes elements from the beginning dropping the remaining. Both work based on the number of elements. The dropWhile() and takeWhile() are like skip() and limit() methods, respectively; however, they work on a Predicate rather than on the number of elements.

You can think of the dropWhile() and takeWhile() methods similar to the filter() method with an exception. The filter() method evaluates the predicate on all elements, whereas the dropWhile() and takeWhile() methods evaluate the predicate on elements from the beginning on the stream until the predicate evaluates to false.

For an ordered stream, the dropWhile() method returns the elements of the stream discarding the elements from the beginning for which the specified predicate is true. Consider the following ordered stream of integers:

```
1, 2, 3, 4, 5, 6, 7
```

If you use a predicate in the dropWhile() method that returns true for an integer less than 5, the method will drop the first four elements and return the rest:

```
Stream.of(1, 2, 3, 4, 5, 6, 7)
        .dropWhile(e -> e < 5)
        .forEach(System.out::println);
```

```
5
6
7
```

For an unordered stream, the behavior of the dropWhile() method is non-deterministic. It may choose to drop any subset of elements matching the predicate. The current implementation drops the matching elements from the beginning until it finds a non-matching element. The following snippet of code uses the dropWhile() method on an unordered stream, and only one of the elements matching the predicate is dropped:

```
Stream.of(1, 5, 6, 2, 3, 4, 7)
      .dropWhile(e -> e < 5)
      .forEach(System.out::println);
```

```
5
6
2
3
4
7
```

There are two extreme cases for the dropWhile() method. If the first element does not match the predicate, the method returns the original stream. If all elements match the predicate, the method returns an empty stream.

The takeWhile() method works the same way as the dropWhile() method, except that it returns the matching elements from the beginning of the stream and discards the rest.

Caution   Use the dropWhile() and takeWhile() methods with ordered, parallel streams with great care because you may see a performance hit. In an ordered, parallel stream, elements must be ordered and returned from all threads before these methods can return. These methods perform best with sequential streams.

Applying the Reduce Operation

The reduce operation combines all elements of a stream to produce a single value by applying a combining function repeatedly. It is also called a reduction operation or a fold. Computing the sum, maximum, average, count, etc. of elements of a stream of integers are examples of reduce operations. Collecting elements of a stream in a List, Set, or Map is also an example of the reduce operation.

The reduce operation takes two parameters called a seed (also called an initial value) and an accumulator. The accumulator is a function. If the stream is empty, the seed is the result. Otherwise, the seed represents a partial result. The partial result and an element are passed to the accumulator, which returns another partial result. This repeats until all elements are passed to the accumulator. The last value returned from the accumulator is the result of the reduce operation. Figure 6-10 shows a pictorial view of the reduce operation.

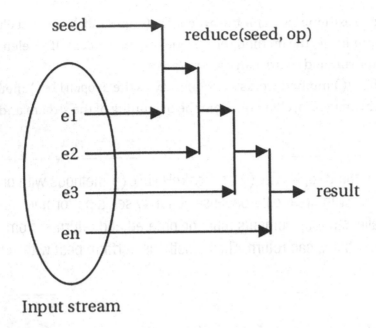

Input stream

Figure 6-10. A pictorial view of applying the reduce operation

The stream-related interfaces contain two methods called reduce() and collect() to perform generic reduce operations. Methods such as sum(), max(), min(), count(), etc. are also available to perform specialized reduce operations. Note that the specialized methods are not available for all types of streams. For example, having a sum() method in the Stream<T> interface does not make sense because adding reference type elements, such as adding two people, is meaningless. So, you will find methods like sum() only in IntStream, LongStream, and DoubleStream interfaces. Counting the number of elements in a stream makes sense for all types of streams. So, the count() method is available for all types of streams. I discuss the reduce() method in this section. I discuss the collect() method in several subsequent sections.

Let's consider the following snippet of code, which performs the reduce operation in the imperative programming style. The code computes the sum of all integers in a list:

```
// Create the list of integers
List<Integer> numbers = List.of(1, 2, 3, 4, 5);
// Declare an accumulator called sum and initialize
// (or seed) it to zero
int sum = 0;
```

```
for(int num : numbers) {
    // Accumulate the partial result in sum
    sum = sum + num;
}
// Print the result
System.out.println(sum);
```

```
15
```

The code declares a variable named sum and initializes the variable to 0. If there is no element in the list, the initial value of sum becomes the result. The for-each loop traverses the list and keeps storing the partial results in the sum variable, using it as an accumulator. When the for-each loop finishes, the sum variable contains the result. As pointed out at the beginning of this chapter, such a for loop has no room for parallelization; the entire logic must be executed in a single thread.

Consider another example that computes the sum of incomes of persons in a list:

```
// Declare an accumulator called sum and initialize
// it to zero
double sum = 0.0;
for(Person person : Person.persons()) {
    // Map the Person to his income double
    double income = person.getIncome();
    // Accumulate the partial result in sum
    sum = sum + income;
}
System.out.println(sum);
```

This time, you had to perform an additional step to map the Person to their income before you could accumulate the partial results in the sum variable.

The Stream<T> interface contains a reduce() method to perform the reduce operation. The method has three overloaded versions:

- T reduce(T identity, BinaryOperator<T> accumulator)

- <U> U reduce(U identity, BiFunction<U,? super T,U> accumulator, BinaryOperator<U> combiner)

- Optional<T> reduce(BinaryOperator<T> accumulator)

The first version of the reduce() method takes an identity and an accumulator as arguments and reduces the stream to a single value of the same type. You can rewrite the example of computing the sum of integers in a list as follows:

```
List<Integer> numbers = List.of(1, 2, 3, 4, 5);
int sum = numbers.stream()
                .reduce(0, Integer::sum);
System.out.println(sum);
```

15

Let's attempt to do the same with the second example, which computes the sum of the incomes. The following code generates a compile-time error. Only the relevant part of the error message is shown:

```
double sum = Person.persons()
                .stream()
                .reduce(0.0, Double::sum);

error: no suitable method found for
    reduce(double,Double::sum)
    .reduce(0.0, Double::sum);
    ^
    method Stream.reduce(Person,BinaryOperator
    <Person>) is not applicable
      (argument mismatch;
    double cannot be converted to Person) ...
```

The stream() method in Person.persons().stream() returns a Stream<Person>, and, therefore, the reduce() method is supposed to perform a reduction on the Person objects. However, the first argument to the method is 0.0, which implies that the method is attempting to operate on the Double type, not the Person type. This mismatch in the expected argument type Person and the actual argument type Double resulted in the error.

You wanted to compute the sum of the incomes of all people. You need to map the stream of people to a stream of their incomes using the map operation as follows:

```
double sum = Person.persons()
                    .stream()
                    .map(Person::getIncome)
                    .reduce(0.0, Double::sum);
System.out.println(sum);
```

26000.0

Performing a map-reduce operation is typical in functional programming. The second version of the reduce method, shown again for easy reference, lets you perform a map operation, followed by a reduce operation.

```
<U> U reduce(U identity,
    BiFunction<U,? super T,U> accumulator,
    BinaryOperator<U> combiner)
```

Note that the second argument, which is the accumulator, takes an argument whose type may be different from the type of the stream. This is used for the map operation as well as for accumulating the partial results. The third argument is used for combining the partial results when the reduce operation is performed in parallel, which I elaborate on shortly. The following snippet of code prints the sum of the incomes of all people:

```
double sum = Person.persons()
    .stream()
    .reduce(0.0, (partialSum, person) ->
        partialSum + person.getIncome(), Double::sum);
System.out.println(sum);
```

26000.0

If you examine the code, the second argument to the reduce() method is sufficient to produce the desired result in this case. So, what is the purpose of the third argument, Double::sum, which is the combiner? In fact, the combiner was not used in the reduce() operation at all, even if you specified it. You can verify that the combiner was not used using the following code, which prints a message from the combiner:

```
double sum = Person.persons()
    .stream()
    .reduce(0.0, (partialSum, person) ->
        partialSum + person.getIncome(),
        (a, b) -> {
            System.out.println(
                "Combiner called: a = " + a + "b = " + b );
            return a + b;
        });
System.out.println(sum);
```

26000.0

The output proves that the combiner was not called. Why do you need to provide the combiner when it is not used? It is used when the reduce operation is performed in parallel. In that case, each thread will accumulate the partial results using the accumulator. At the end, the combiner is used to combine the partial results from all threads to get the result. The following snippet of code shows how the sequential reduce operation works. The code prints a message at several steps along with the current thread name that is performing the operation:

```
double sum = Person.persons()
    .stream()
    .reduce(0.0,
        (Double partialSum, Person p) -> {
            double accumulated = partialSum + p.getIncome();
            System.out.println(
                Thread.currentThread().getName() +
                " - Accumulator: partialSum = " +
                partialSum + ", person = " + p +
                ", accumulated = " + accumulated);
            return accumulated;
        },
        (a, b) -> {
            double combined = a + b;
```

```
            System.out.println(
              Thread.currentThread().getName() +
              " - Combiner: a = " + a + ", b = " + b +
              ", combined = " + combined);
          return combined;
        });
System.out.println(sum);

main - Accumulator: partialSum = 0.0,
  person = (1, Ken, MALE, 1970-05-04, 6000.00),
  accumulated = 6000.0
main - Accumulator: partialSum = 6000.0,
  person = (2, Jeff, MALE, 1970-07-15, 7100.00),
  accumulated = 13100.0
main - Accumulator: partialSum = 13100.0,
  person = (3, Donna, FEMALE, 1962-07-29, 8700.00),
  accumulated = 21800.0
main - Accumulator: partialSum = 21800.0,
  person = (4, Chris, MALE, 1993-12-16, 1800.00),
  accumulated = 23600.0
main - Accumulator: partialSum = 23600.0,
  person = (5, Laynie, FEMALE, 2012-12-13, 0.00),
  accumulated = 23600.0
main - Accumulator: partialSum = 23600.0,
  person = (6, Li, MALE, 2001-05-09, 2400.00),
  accumulated = 26000.0
26000.0
```

The output shows that the accumulator was sufficient to produce the result, and the combiner was never called. Notice that there was only one thread named main that processed all people in the stream.

Let's turn the stream into a parallel stream, keeping all the debugging messages. The following code uses a parallel stream to get the sum of the incomes of all people. You may get different output containing a different message, but the sum value would be the same as 26000.0.

```
double sum = Person.persons()
    .parallelStream()
    .reduce(0.0,
        (Double partialSum, Person p) -> {
            double accumulated = partialSum + p.getIncome();
            System.out.println(
                Thread.currentThread().getName() +
                " - Accumulator: partialSum = " +

                partialSum + ", person = " + p +
                ", accumulated = " + accumulated);
          return accumulated;
        },
        (a, b) -> {
            double combined = a + b;
            System.out.println(
              Thread.currentThread().getName() +
              " - Combiner: a = " + a + ", b = " + b +
              ", combined = " + combined);
          return combined;
        });
System.out.println(sum);

ForkJoinPool.commonPool-worker-4 -
  Accumulator: partialSum = 0.0,
  person = (5, Laynie, FEMALE, 2012-12-13, 0.00),
  accumulated = 0.0
ForkJoinPool.commonPool-worker-2 -
  Accumulator: partialSum = 0.0,
  person = (6, Li, MALE, 2001-05-09, 2400.00),
  accumulated = 2400.0
ForkJoinPool.commonPool-worker-1 -
  Accumulator: partialSum = 0.0,
  person = (2, Jeff, MALE, 1970-07-15, 7100.00),
  accumulated = 7100.0
ForkJoinPool.commonPool-worker-2 -
  Combiner: a = 0.0, b = 2400.0, combined = 2400.0
```

```
ForkJoinPool.commonPool-worker-5 -
  Accumulator: partialSum = 0.0,
  person = (3, Donna, FEMALE, 1962-07-29, 8700.00),
  accumulated = 8700.0
main - Accumulator: partialSum = 0.0,
  person = (4, Chris, MALE, 1993-12-16, 1800.00),
  accumulated = 1800.0
ForkJoinPool.commonPool-worker-3 -
  Accumulator: partialSum = 0.0,
  person = (1, Ken, MALE, 1970-05-04, 6000.00),
  accumulated = 6000.0
main - Combiner: a = 1800.0, b = 2400.0,
  combined = 4200.0
ForkJoinPool.commonPool-worker-5 -
  Combiner: a = 7100.0, b = 8700.0, combined = 15800.0
ForkJoinPool.commonPool-worker-5 -
  Combiner: a = 6000.0, b = 15800.0, combined = 21800.0
ForkJoinPool.commonPool-worker-5 -
  Combiner: a = 21800.0, b = 4200.0, combined = 26000.0
26000.0
```

The output shows that six threads (five fork/join worker threads and one main thread) performed the parallel reduce operation. They all performed partial reduction using the accumulator to obtain partial results. Finally, the partial results were combined using the combiner to get the result.

Sometimes, you cannot specify a default value for a reduce operation. Suppose you want to get a maximum integer value from a stream of integers. If the stream is empty, you cannot default the maximum value to 0. In such a case, the result is not defined. The third version of the reduce(BinaryOperator<T> accumulator) method is used to perform such a reduction operation. The method returns an Optional<T> that wraps the result or the absence of a result. If the stream contains only one element, that element is the result. If the stream contains more than one element, the first two elements are passed to the accumulator, and subsequently the partial result and the remaining elements are passed to the accumulator. The following snippet of code computes the maximum of integers in a stream:

```java
Optional<Integer> max = Stream.of(1, 2, 3, 4, 5)
                              .reduce(Integer::max);
if (max.isPresent()) {
    System.out.println("max = " + max.get());
} else {
    System.out.println("max is not defined.");
}
```

```
max = 5
```

The following snippet of code tries to get the maximum of integers in an empty stream:

```java
Optional<Integer> max = Stream.<Integer>empty()
                              .reduce(Integer::max);
if (max.isPresent()) {
    System.out.println("max = " + max.get());
} else {
    System.out.println("max is not defined.");
}
```

```
max is not defined.
```

The following snippet of code prints the details of the highest earner in the person's list:

```java
Optional<Person> person = Person.persons()
    .stream()
    .reduce((p1, p2) ->
        p1.getIncome() > p2.getIncome() ? p1 : p2);
if (person.isPresent()) {
    System.out.println(
        "Highest earner: " + person.get());
} else {
    System.out.println(
        "Could not get the highest earner.");
}
```

```
Highest earner: (3, Donna, FEMALE, 1962-07-29, 8700.00)
```

To compute the sum, max, min, average, etc. of a numeric stream, you do not need to use the reduce() method. You can map the non-numeric stream into one of the three numeric stream types (IntStream, LongStream, or DoubleStream) and use the specialized methods for these purposes. The following snippet of code prints the sum of the incomes of all people. Note the use of the mapToDouble() method that converts a Stream<Person> to a DoubleStream. The sum() method is called on the DoubleStream.

```
double totalIncome = Person.persons()
    .stream()
    .mapToDouble(Person::getIncome)
    .sum();
System.out.println("Total Income: " + totalIncome);

Total Income : 26000.0
```

To get the minimum and maximum values of a stream, use the min() and max() methods of the specific stream. These methods in the Stream<T> interface take a Comparator as an argument and return an Optional<T>. They do not take any arguments in the IntStream, LongStream, and DoubleStream interfaces and return OptionalInt, OptionalLong, and OptionalDouble, respectively. The following snippet of code prints the details of the highest earner in a list of people:

```
Optional<Person> person = Person.persons()
    .stream()
    .max(Comparator.comparingDouble(Person::getIncome));
if (person.isPresent()) {
    System.out.println(
        "Highest earner: " + person.get());
} else {
    System.out.println(
        "Could not get the highest earner.");
}

Highest earner: (3, Donna, FEMALE, 1962-07-29, 8700.00)
```

The following snippet of code prints the highest income in the person list using the `max()` method of the `DoubleStream`:

```
OptionalDouble income = Person.persons()
    .stream()
    .mapToDouble(Person::getIncome)
    .max();
if (income.isPresent()) {
    System.out.println(
        "Highest income: " + income.getAsDouble());
} else {
    System.out.println(
        "Could not get the highest income.");
}
```

```
Highest income: 8700.0
```

How will you get the highest earner among males and the highest among females in one stream pipeline? So far, you have learned how to compute a single value using the reduce operation. In this case, you need to group the people into two groups, males and females, and then compute the person with the highest income in each group. I show you how to perform grouping and collect multiple values when I discuss the `collect()` method in the next section.

Streams support a count operation through the `count()` method, which simply returns the number of elements in the stream as a `long`. The following snippet of code prints the number of elements in the stream of people:

```
long personCount = Person.persons()
    .stream()
    .count();
System.out.println("Person count: " + personCount);
```

```
Person count: 6
```

The count operation is a specialized reduce operation. Were you thinking of using the `map()` and `reduce()` methods to count the number of elements in a stream? The easier way is to map each element in the stream to 1 and compute the sum. This approach does not use the `reduce()` method. Here is how you do this:

```
long personCount = Person.persons()
    .stream()
    .mapToLong(p -> 1L)
    .sum();
```

The following snippet of code uses the map() and reduce() methods to implement
the count operation:

```
long personCount = Person.persons()
    .stream()
    .map(p -> 1L)
    .reduce(0L, Long::sum);
```

The following snippet of code uses only the reduce() method to implement the
count operation:

```
long personCount = Person.persons()
    .stream()
    .reduce(0L, (partialCount, person) ->
        partialCount + 1L,
        Long::sum);
```

Note   This section showed you many ways to perform the same reduction
operation on a stream. Some ways may perform better than others depending on
the stream type and the parallelization used. Use primitive type streams whenever
possible to avoid the overhead of unboxing; use parallel streams whenever
possible to take advantage of the multicores available on the machine.

Collecting Data Using Collectors

So far, you have been applying reduction on a stream to produce a single value (a
primitive value or a reference value) or void. For example, you used the reduce()
method of the Stream<Integer> interface to compute a long value that is the sum of its
elements. There are several cases in which you want to collect the results of executing a
stream pipeline into a collection such as a List, a Set, a Map, etc. Sometimes, you may

want to apply complex logic to summarize the stream's data. For example, you may want to group people by their gender and compute the highest earner in every gender group. This is possible using the collect() method of the Stream<T> interface. The collect() method is overloaded with two versions:

- <R> R collect(Supplier<R> supplier, BiConsumer<R,? super T> accumulator, BiConsumer<R,R> combiner)

- <R,A> R collect(Collector<? super T,A,R> collector): The method uses a mutable reduction operation. It uses a mutable container such as a mutable Collection to compute the results from the input stream. The first version of the collect() method takes three arguments:

    – A supplier that supplies a mutable container to store (or collect) the results

    – An accumulator that accumulates the results into the mutable container

    – A combiner that combines the partial results when the reduction operation takes place in parallel

---

Note   The container to collect the data using the collect() method need not be a Collection. It can be any mutable object that can accumulate results, such as a StringBuilder.

Suppose you have a stream of people and you want to collect the names of all of the people in an ArrayList<String>. Here are the steps to accomplish this.

First, you need to have a supplier that will return an ArrayList<String> to store the names. You can use either of the following statements to create the supplier:

```
// Using a lambda expression
Supplier<ArrayList<String>> supplier =
    () -> new ArrayList<>();
// Using a constructor reference
Supplier<ArrayList<String>> supplier =
    ArrayList::new;
```

Second, you need to create an accumulator that receives two arguments. The first argument is the container returned from the supplier, which is the `ArrayList<String>` in this case. The second argument is the element of the stream. Your accumulator should simply add the names to the list. You can use either of the following statements to create an accumulator:

```
// Using a lambda expression
BiConsumer<ArrayList<String>, String> accumulator =
    (list, name) -> list.add(name);
// Using a method reference
BiConsumer<ArrayList<String>, String> accumulator =
    ArrayList::add;
```

Finally, you need a combiner that will combine the results of two `ArrayList<String>`s into one `ArrayList<String>`. Note that the combiner is used only when you collect the results using a parallel stream. In a sequential stream, the accumulator is sufficient to collect all results. Your combiner will be simple; it will add all the elements of the second list to the first list using the `addAll()` method. You can use either of the following statements to create a combiner:

```
// Using a lambda expression
BiConsumer<ArrayList<String>,
        ArrayList<String>> combiner =
    (list1, list2) -> list1.addAll(list2);
// Using a method reference
BiConsumer<ArrayList<String>,
        ArrayList<String>> combiner =
    ArrayList::addAll;
```

Now you are ready to use the `collect()` method to collect the names of all people in a list using the following snippet of code:

```
List<String> names = Person.persons()
    .stream()
    .map(Person::getName)
    .collect(ArrayList::new,
            ArrayList::add,
            ArrayList::addAll);
System.out.println(names);
```

```
[Ken, Jeff, Donna, Chris, Laynie, Li]
```

You can use a similar approach to collect data in a Set and a Map. It seems to be a lot of plumbing just to collect data in a simple collection like a list. Another version of the `collect()` method provides a simpler solution. It takes an instance of the Collector interface as an argument and collects the data for you. The Collector interface is in the `java.util.stream` package, and it is declared as follows. Only abstract methods are shown:

```
public interface Collector<T,A,R> {
    Supplier<A> supplier();
    BiConsumer<A,T> accumulator();
    BinaryOperator<A> combiner();
    Function<A,R> finisher();
    Set<Collector.Characteristics> characteristics();
}
```

The Collector interface takes three type parameters called T, A, and R, where T is the type of input elements, A is the type of the accumulator, and R is the type of the result. The first three methods look familiar; you just used them in the previous example. The `finisher` is used to transform the intermediate type A to result type R. The characteristics of a Collector describe the properties that are represented by the constants of the `Collector.Characteristics` enum.

The designers of the Streams API realized that rolling out your own collector is too much work. They provided a utility class called Collectors that provides out-of-the-box implementations for commonly used collectors. Three of the most commonly used methods of the Collectors class are `toList()`, `toSet()`, and `toCollection()`.

The toList() method returns a Collector that collects the data in a List; the toSet() method returns a Collector that collects data in a Set; the toCollection() takes a Supplier that returns a Collection to be used to collect data. The following snippet of code collects all names of people in a List<String>:

```
List<String> names = Person.persons()
    .stream()
    .map(Person::getName)
    .collect(Collectors.toList());
System.out.println(names);
```

[Ken, Jeff, Donna, Chris, Laynie, Li]

Notice that this time you achieved the same result in a much cleaner way.

The following snippet of code collects all names in a Set<String>. Note that a Set keeps only unique elements.

```
Set<String> uniqueNames = Person.persons()
    .stream()
    .map(Person::getName)
    .collect(Collectors.toSet());
System.out.println(uniqueNames);
```

[Donna, Ken, Chris, Jeff, Laynie, Li]

The output is not in a particular order because a Set does not impose any ordering on its elements. You can collect names in a sorted set using the toCollection() method as follows:

```
SortedSet<String> uniqueSortedNames= Person.persons()
    .stream()
    .map(Person::getName)
    .collect(Collectors.toCollection(TreeSet::new));
System.out.println(uniqueSortedNames);
```

[Chris, Donna, Jeff, Ken, Laynie, Li]

Recall that the toCollection() method takes a Supplier as an argument that is used to collect the data. In this case, you have used the constructor reference TreeSet::new as the Supplier. This has an effect of using a TreeSet, which is a sorted set, to collect the data.

You can also sort the list of names using the sorted operation. The sorted() method of the Stream interface produces another stream containing the same elements in a sorted order. The following snippet of code shows how to collect sorted names in a list:

```
List<String> sortedName = Person.persons()
    .stream()
    .map(Person::getName)
    .sorted()
    .collect(Collectors.toList());
System.out.println(sortedName);
```

```
[Chris, Donna, Jeff, Ken, Laynie, Li]
```

Note that the code applies the sorting before it collects the names. The collector notices that it is collecting an ordered stream (sorted names) and preserves the ordering during the collection process.

You will find many static methods in the Collectors class that return a Collector meant to be used as a nested collector. One of these methods is the counting() method that returns the number of input elements. Here is an example of counting the number of people in the streams:

```
long count = Person.persons()
    .stream()
    .collect(Collectors.counting());
System.out.println("Person count: " + count);
```

```
Person count: 6
```

You may argue that you could have achieved the same result using the count() method of the Stream interface as follows:

```
long count = Person.persons()
    .stream()
    .count();
System.out.println("Persons count: " + count);
```

```
Persons count: 6
```

When do you use the `Collectors.counting()` method instead of the `Stream.count()` method to count the number of elements in a stream? As mentioned before, collectors can be nested. You will see examples of nested collectors shortly. These methods in the `Collectors` class are meant to be used as nested collectors, not in this case just to count the number of elements in the stream. Another difference between the two is their type: the `Stream.count()` method represents an operation on a stream, whereas the `Collectors. counting()` method returns a `Collector`. Listing 6-8 shows the complete program to collect sorted names in a list.

Listing 6-8. Collecting Results into a Collection

```
// CollectTest.java
package com.jdojo.streams;
import java.util.List;
import java.util.stream.Collectors;
public class CollectTest {
    public static void main(String[] args) {
        List<String> sortedNames = Person.persons()
            .stream()
            .map(Person::getName)
            .sorted()
            .collect(Collectors.toList());
        System.out.println(sortedNames);
    }
}

[Chris, Donna, Jeff, Ken, Laynie, Li]
```

Collecting Summary Statistics

In a data-centric application, you need to compute the summary statistics on a group of numeric data. For example, you may want to know the maximum, minimum, sum, average, and count of the incomes of all people. The `java.util` package contains three classes to collect statistics:

- `DoubleSummaryStatistics`

- LongSummaryStatistics

- IntSummaryStatistics

These classes do not necessarily need to be used with streams. You can use them to compute the summary statistics on any group of numeric data. Using these classes is simple: create an object of the class, keep adding numeric data using the accept() method, and, finally, call the getter methods such as getCount(), getSum(), getMin(), getAverage(), and getMax() to get the statistics for the group of data. Listing 6-9 shows how to compute the statistics on a number of double values.

Listing 6-9. Computing Summary Statistics on a Group of Numeric Data

```
// SummaryStats.java
package com.jdojo.streams;
import java.util.DoubleSummaryStatistics;
public class SummaryStats {
    public static void main(String[] args) {
        DoubleSummaryStatistics stats =
            new DoubleSummaryStatistics();
        stats.accept(100.0);
        stats.accept(500.0);
        stats.accept(400.0);
        // Get stats
        long count = stats.getCount();
        double sum = stats.getSum();
        double min = stats.getMin();
        double avg = stats.getAverage();
        double max = stats.getMax();
        System.out.printf("count=%d, sum=%.2f, " +
                "min=%.2f, max=%.2f, average=%.2f%n",
                count, sum, min, max, avg);
    }
}
```

```
count=3, sum=1000.00, min=100.00, max=500.00,
average=333.33
```

The summary statistics classes were designed to be used with streams. They contain a `combine()` method that combines two summary statistics. Can you guess its use? Recall that you need to specify a combiner when you collect data from a stream, and this method can act as a combiner for two summary statistics. The following snippet of code computes the summary statistics for incomes of all people:

```
DoubleSummaryStatistics incomeStats =
    Person.persons()
        .stream()
        .map(Person::getIncome)
        .collect(DoubleSummaryStatistics::new,
                DoubleSummaryStatistics::accept,
                DoubleSummaryStatistics::combine);
System.out.println(incomeStats);
```

```
DoubleSummaryStatistics{count=6, sum=26000.000000,
min=0.000000, average=4333.333333,
max=8700.000000}
```

The `Collectors` class contains methods to obtain a collector to compute the summary statistics of the specific type of numeric data. The methods are named `summarizingDouble()`, `summarizingLong()`, and `summarizingInt()`. They take a function to be applied on the elements of the stream and return a `DoubleSummaryStatistics`, a `LongSummaryStatistics`, and an `IntSummaryStatistics`, respectively. You can rewrite the code for the previous example as follows:

```
DoubleSummaryStatistics incomeStats =
    Person.persons()
        .stream()
        .collect(Collectors.summarizingDouble(Person::getIncome));
System.out.println(incomeStats);
```

```
DoubleSummaryStatistics{count=6, sum=26000.000000, min=0.000000,
average=4333.333333,
max=8700.000000}
```

The `Collectors` class contains methods such as `counting()`, `summingXxx()`, `averagingXxx()`, `minBy()`, and `maxBy()` that return a collector to perform a specific type of summary computation on a group of numeric data that you get in one shot using the `summarizingXxx()` method. Here, Xxx can be `Double`, `Long`, and `Int`.

Collecting Data in Maps

You can collect data from a stream into a `Map`. The `toMap()` method of the `Collectors` class returns a collector to collect data in a `Map`. The method is overloaded and it has three versions:

- `toMap(Function<? super T,? extends K> keyMapper, Function<? super T,? extends U> valueMapper)`

- `toMap(Function<? super T,? extends K> keyMapper, Function<? super T,? extends U> valueMapper, BinaryOperator<U> mergeFunction)`

- `toMap(Function<? super T,? extends K> keyMapper, Function<? super T,? extends U> valueMapper, BinaryOperator<U> mergeFunction, Supplier<M> mapSupplier)`

The first version takes two arguments. Both arguments are `Functions`. The first argument maps the stream elements to keys in the map. The second argument maps stream elements to values in the map. If duplicate keys are found, an `IllegalStateException` is thrown. The following snippet of code collects a person's data in a `Map<long,String>` whose keys are the person's IDs and values are the person's names:

```
Map<Long,String> idToNameMap = Person.persons()
    .stream()
    .collect(Collectors.toMap(Person::getId,
Person::getName));
System.out.println(idToNameMap);
```

```
{1=Ken, 2=Jeff, 3=Donna, 4=Chris, 5=Laynie, 6=Li}
```

Suppose you want to collect a person's name based on gender. The following is the first, incorrect attempt, which throws an `IllegalStateException`. Only partial output is shown.

```
Map<Person.Gender,String> genderToNamesMap =
    Person.persons()
    .stream()
    .collect(Collectors.toMap(Person::getGender,
                              Person::getName));
```

```
Exception in thread "main"
java.lang.IllegalStateException: Duplicate key Ken ...
```

The runtime is complaining about the duplicate keys because `Person::getGender` will return the gender of the person as the key, and you have multiple males and females in the stream.

The solution is to use the second version of the `toMap()` method to obtain the collection. It lets you specify a merge function as a third argument. The merge function is passed the old and new values for the duplicate key. The function is supposed to merge the two values and return a new value that will be used for the key. In your case, you can concatenate the names of all males and females. The following snippet of code accomplishes this:

```
Map<Person.Gender,String> genderToNamesMap =
    Person.persons()
    .stream()
    .collect(Collectors.toMap(
            Person::getGender,
            Person::getName,
            (oldValue, newValue) ->
                String.join(", ", oldValue, newValue)));
System.out.println(genderToNamesMap);
```

```
{FEMALE=Donna, Laynie, MALE=Ken, Jeff, Chris, Li}
```

The first two versions of the `toMap()` method create the Map for you. The third version lets you pass a `Supplier` to provide a Map yourself. I do not cover an example of using this version of the `toMap()` method.

Armed with two examples of collecting the data in maps, can you think of the logic for collecting data in a map that summarizes the number of people by gender? Here is how you accomplish this:

```
Map<Person.Gender, Long> countByGender = Person.persons()
    .stream()
    .collect(Collectors.toMap(
            Person::getGender,
            p -> 1L,
            (oldCount, newCount) -> oldCount + 1));
System.out.println(countByGender);
```

```
{MALE=4, FEMALE=2}
```

The key mapper function remains the same. The value mapper function is p -> 1L, which means when a person belonging to a gender is encountered the first time, its value is set to 1. In case of a duplicate key, the merge function is called that simply increments the old value by 1.

The last example in this category that collects the highest earner by gender in a Map is shown in Listing 6-10.

Listing 6-10. Collecting the Highest Earner by Gender in a Map

```
// CollectIntoMapTest.java
package com.jdojo.streams;
import java.util.Map;
import java.util.function.Function;
import java.util.stream.Collectors;
public class CollectIntoMapTest {
    public static void main(String[] args) {
        Map<Person.Gender, Person> highestEarnerByGender =
            Person.persons()
              .stream()
              .collect(Collectors.toMap(
                    Person::getGender,
                    Function.identity(),
```

```
                (oldPerson, newPerson) ->
                    newPerson.getIncome() >
                    oldPerson.getIncome() ?
                    newPerson:oldPerson));
          System.out.println(highestEarnerByGender);
    }
}

{ FEMALE=(3, Donna, FEMALE, 1962-07-29, 8700.00),
  MALE=(2, Jeff, MALE, 1970-07-15, 7100.00)
}
```

The program stores the Person object as the value in the map. Note the use of Function.identity() as the function to map values. This method returns an identity function that simply returns the value that was passed to it. You could have used a lambda expression of person -> person in its place. The merge function compares the income of the person already stored as the value for a key. If the new person has more income than the existing one, it returns the new person.

Collecting data into a map is a very powerful way of summarizing data. You will see maps again when I discuss grouping and partitioning of data shortly.

Note   The toMap() method returns a non-concurrent map that has performance overhead when streams are processed in parallel. It has a companion method called toConcurrentMap() that returns a concurrent collector that should be used when streams are processed in parallel.

Joining Strings Using Collectors

The joining() method of the Collectors class returns a collector that concatenates the elements of a stream of CharSequence and returns the result as a String. The concatenation occurs in the encounter order. The joining() method is overloaded, and it has three versions:

- joining()

- joining(CharSequence delimiter)

- joining(CharSequence delimiter, CharSequence prefix, CharSequence suffix)

The version with no arguments simply concatenates all elements. The second version uses a delimiter between two elements. The third version uses a delimiter, a prefix, and a suffix. The prefix is added to the beginning of the result, and the suffix is added to the end of the result. Listing 6-11 shows how to use the joining() method.

Listing 6-11. Joining a Stream of CharSequence Using a Collector

```java
// CollectJoiningTest.java
package com.jdojo.streams;
import java.util.List;
import java.util.stream.Collectors;
public class CollectJoiningTest {
    public static void main(String[] args) {
        List<Person> persons = Person.persons();
        String names = persons.stream()
            .map(Person::getName)
            .collect(Collectors.joining());
        String delimitedNames = persons.stream()
            .map(Person::getName)
            .collect(Collectors.joining(", "));
        String prefixedNames = persons.stream()
            .map(Person::getName)
            .collect(Collectors.joining(
                ", ", "Hello ", ". Goodbye."));
        System.out.println("Joined names: " + names);
        System.out.println("Joined, delimited names: " +
            delimitedNames);
        System.out.println(prefixedNames);
    }
}
```

```
Joined names: KenJeffDonnaChrisLaynieLi
Joined, delimited names:
    Ken, Jeff, Donna, Chris, Laynie, Li
Hello Ken, Jeff, Donna, Chris, Laynie, Li. Goodbye.
```

Grouping Data

Grouping data for reporting purposes is common. For example, you may want to know the average income by gender, the youngest person by gender, etc. In previous sections, you used the toMap() method of the Collectors class to get collectors that can be used to group data in maps. The groupingBy() method of the Collectors class returns a collector that groups the data before collecting them in a Map. If you have worked with SQL statements, it is similar to using a "group by" clause. The groupingBy() method is overloaded, and it has three versions:

- groupingBy(Function<? super T,? extends K> classifier)

- groupingBy(Function<? super T,? extends K> classifier,
  super T,A,D> downstream)

- groupingBy(Function<? super T,? extends K> classifier,
  Supplier<M> mapFactory, Collector<? super T,A,D>
  downstream)

I discuss the first and second versions. The third version is the same as the second one, except that it lets you specify a Supplier that is used as the factory to get the Map. In the first two versions, the collector takes care of creating the Map for you.

Note   The groupingBy() method returns a non-concurrent map that has performance overhead when the stream is processed in parallel. It has a companion method called groupingByConcurrent() that returns a concurrent collector that should be used in parallel stream processing for better performance.

In the most generic version, the groupingBy() method takes two parameters:

- A classifier that is a function to generate the keys in the map

- A collector that performs a reduction operation on the values associated with each key

The first version of the groupingBy() method returns a collector that collects data into a Map<K, List<T», where K is the return type of the classifier function and T is the

type of elements in the input stream. Note that the value of a grouped key in the map is a list of elements from the stream. The following snippet of code collects the list of people by gender:

```
Map<Person.Gender, List<Person>> personsByGender =
    Person.persons()
        .stream()
        .collect(Collectors.groupingBy(
                Person::getGender));
System.out.println(personsByGender);
```

```
{FEMALE=[(3, Donna, FEMALE, 1962-07-29, 8700.00),
  (5, Laynie, FEMALE, 2012-12-13, 0.00)],
MALE=[(1, Ken, MALE, 1970-05-04, 6000.00),
  (2, Jeff, MALE, 1970-07-15, 7100.00),
  (4, Chris, MALE, 1993-12-16, 1800.00),
  (6, Li, MALE, 2001-05-09, 2400.00)]}
```

Suppose you want to get a list of names grouped by gender. You need to use the second version of the groupingBy() method that lets you perform a reduction operation on the values of each key. Notice that the type of the second argument is Collector. The Collectors class contains many methods that return a Collector that you will be using as the second argument.

Let's try a simple case where you want to group people by gender and count the number of people in each group. The counting() method of the Collectors class returns a Collector to count the number of elements in a stream. The following snippet of code accomplishes this:

```
Map<Person.Gender, Long> countByGender =
    Person.persons()
        .stream()
        .collect(Collectors.groupingBy(
            Person::getGender,
            Collectors.counting()));
System.out.println(countByGender);
```

```
{MALE=4, FEMALE=2}
```

Let's get back to the example of listing a person's name by gender. You need to use the `mapping()` method of the `Collectors` class to get a collector that will map the list of people in the value of a key to their names and join them. The signature of the `mapping()` method is as follows:

```
mapping(Function<? super T,? extends U> mapper,
        Collector<? super U,A,R> downstream)
```

Notice the type of the second argument of the `mapping()` method. It is another `Collector`. This is where dealing with grouping data gets complex. You need to nest collectors inside collectors. To simplify the grouping process, you break down the things you want to perform on the data. You have already grouped people by their gender. The value of each key in the map was a `List<Person>`. Now you want to reduce the `List<Person>` to a `String` that contains a comma-separated list of the names of all the people. You need to think about this operation separately to avoid confusion. You can accomplish this reduction as follows:

1. Use a function to map each person to their name. This function could be as simple as a method reference like `Person::getName`. Think of the output of this step as a stream of person names in a group.

2. What do you want to do with the stream of names generated in the first step? You may want to collect them in a `String`, a `List`, a `Set`, or some other data structure. In this case, you want to join the names of people, so you use the collector returned from the `joining()` method of the `Collectors` class.

The following snippet of code shows how to group the names of people by gender:

```
Map<Person.Gender, String> namesByGender =
    Person.persons()
          .stream()
          .collect(Collectors.groupingBy(Person::getGender,
              Collectors.mapping(
                  Person::getName,
                  Collectors.joining(", "))));
System.out.println(namesByGender);

{MALE=Ken, Jeff, Chris, Li, FEMALE=Donna, Laynie}
```

501

The code collects the names for a group in a comma-separated `String`. Can you think of a way to collect the names in a `List`? It is easy to accomplish this. Use the collector returned by the `toList()` method of the `Collectors` class, like so:

```
Map<Person.Gender, List<String>> namesByGender =
    Person.persons()
        .stream()
        .collect(Collectors.groupingBy(Person::getGender,
            Collectors.mapping(
                Person::getName,
                Collectors.toList())));
System.out.println(namesByGender);
```

```
{FEMALE=[Donna, Laynie], MALE=[Ken, Jeff, Chris, Li]}
```

Groups can be nested. Let's create a report that groups people by gender. Within each gender group, it creates another group based on the month of their births and lists the names of the people born in this group. This is a very simple computation to perform. You already know how to group people by gender.

All you need to do is perform another grouping on the values of the keys, which is simply another collector obtained using the `groupingBy()` method again. In this case, the value for a key in the map representing the top-level grouping (by gender) is a `Map`. Listing 6-12 contains the complete code to accomplish this.

Notice the use of the static imports to import the static methods from the `Collectors` class for better code readability. The program assumes that every person has a date of birth.

Listing 6-12. Using Nested Groupings

```
// NestedGroupings.java
package com.jdojo.streams;

import java.time.Month;
import java.util.Map;
import static java.util.stream.Collectors.groupingBy;
import static java.util.stream.Collectors.mapping;
import static java.util.stream.Collectors.joining;
```

```java
public class NestedGroupings {
    public static void main(String[] args) {
        Map<Person.Gender, Map<Month, String>>
        personsByGenderAndDobMonth
            = Person.persons()
                .stream()
                .collect(groupingBy(Person::getGender,
                    groupingBy(p ->
                        p.getDob().getMonth(),
                    mapping(Person::getName,
                        joining(", ")))));
        System.out.println(personsByGenderAndDobMonth);
    }
}
```

```
{FEMALE={DECEMBER=Laynie, JULY=Donna},
MALE={DECEMBER=Chris, JULY=Jeff, MAY=Ken, Li}}
```

Notice that the output has two top-level groups based on gender: Male and Female. With each gender group, there are nested groups based on the month of the person's birth. For each month group, you have a list of those born in that month. For example, Ken and Li were born in the month of May and they are males, so they are listed in the output together.

As the final example in this section, let's summarize the income of people grouped by gender. The program in Listing 6-13 computes the summary statistics of income by gender. I used static imports to use the method names from the `Collectors` class to keep the code a bit cleaner. Looking at the output, you can tell the average income of females is 25 dollars more than that of males. You can keep nesting groups inside another group. There is no limit on levels of nesting for groups.

Listing 6-13. Summary Statistics of Income Grouped by Gender

```java
// IncomeStatsByGender.java
package com.jdojo.streams;

import java.util.DoubleSummaryStatistics;
import java.util.Map;
```

```
import static
    java.util.stream.Collectors.groupingBy;
import static
    java.util.stream.Collectors.summarizingDouble;

public class IncomeStatsByGender {
    public static void main(String[] args) {
        Map<Person.Gender, DoubleSummaryStatistics>
        incomeStatsByGender =
            Person.persons()
              .stream()
              .collect(
                    groupingBy(Person::getGender,
                    summarizingDouble(Person::getIncome)));
        System.out.println(incomeStatsByGender);
    }
}

{MALE=DoubleSummaryStatistics{count=4, sum=17300.000000,
min=1800.000000,average=4325.000000, max=7100.000000},
FEMALE=DoubleSummaryStatistics{count=2, sum=8700.000000,
min=0.000000, average=4350.000000, max=8700.000000}}
```

Partitioning Data

Partitioning data is a special case of grouping data. Grouping data is based on the keys returned from a function. There are as many groups as the number of distinct keys returned from the function. Partitioning collects data into two groups: for one group, a condition is true; for the other, the same condition is false. The partitioning condition is specified using a Predicate. By now, you might have guessed the name of the method in the Collectors class that returns a collector to perform the partitioning. The method is partitioningBy(). It is overloaded and it has two versions:

- partitioningBy(Predicate<? super T> predicate)

- partitioningBy(Predicate<? super T> predicate, Collector<?
  super T,A,D> downstream)

Like the `groupingBy()` method, the `partitioningBy()` method also collects data in a `Map` whose keys are always of the type `Boolean`. Note that the `Map` returned from the collector always contains two entries: one with the key value as true and another with the key value as false.

The first version of the `partitioningBy()` method returns a collector that performs the partitioning based on the specified predicate. The values for a key are stored in a `List`. If the predicate evaluates to `true` for an element, the element is added to the list for the key with a `true` value; otherwise, the value is added to the list of values for the key with a `false` value. The following snippet of code partitions people based on whether the person is a male:

```
Map<Boolean, List<Person>> partitionedByMaleGender =
    Person.persons()
          .stream()
          .collect(Collectors.partitioningBy(
              Person::isMale));
System.out.println(partionedByMaleGender);

{false=[(3, Donna, FEMALE, 1962-07-29, 8700.00),
  (5, Laynie, FEMALE, 2012-12-13, 0.00)],
true=[(1, Ken, MALE, 1970-05-04, 6000.00),
  (2, Jeff, MALE, 1970-07-15, 7100.00),
  (4, Chris, MALE, 1993-12-16, 1800.00),
  (6, Li, MALE, 2001-05-09, 2400.00)]}
```

The second version of the method lets you specify another collector that can perform a reduction operation on the values for each key. You have seen several examples of this kind in the previous section when you grouped data using the `groupingBy()` method. The following snippet of code partitions people into male and non-male and collects their names in a comma-separated string:

```
Map<Boolean,String> partionedByMaleGender =
    Person.persons()
          .stream()
```

```
        .collect(Collectors.partitioningBy(
            Person::isMale,
            Collectors.mapping(Person::getName,
                Collectors.joining(", ")))));
System.out.println(partionedByMaleGender);
```

```
{false=Donna, Laynie, true=Ken, Jeff, Chris, Li}
```

Adapting the Collector Results

So far, you have seen collectors doing great work on their own: you specify what you
want, and the collector does all the work for you. There is one more type of collector that
collects the data and lets you modify the result before and after collecting the data. You
can adapt the result of the collector to a different type; you can filter the elements after
they are grouped but before they are collected; you map elements as they are grouped,
but before they are collected. The following static methods in the Collectors class
return such collectors:

- `<T,A,R,RR> Collector<T,A,RR> collectingAndThen(Collector
  <T,A,R> downstream, Function<R,RR> finisher)`

- `<T,A,R> Collector<T,?,R> filtering(Predicate<? super T>
  predicate, Collector<? super T,A,R> downstream)`

- `<T,U,A,R> Collector<T,?,R> flatMapping(Function<? super
  T,? extends Stream<? extends U» mapper, Collector<? super
  U,A,R> downstream)`

The filtering() and flatMapping() methods were added to the Collectors class
in Java 9.

The collectingAndThen() method lets you modify the results of a collector after
the collector has collected all elements. Its first argument is a collector that collects
the data. The second argument is a finisher that is a function. The finisher is passed a
result, and it is free to modify the result, including its type. The return type of such a
collector is the return type of the finisher. One of the common uses for the finisher is to
return an unmodifiable view of the collected data. Here is an example that returns an
unmodifiable list of person names:

```
List<String> names = Person.persons()
    .stream()
    .map(Person::getName)
    .collect(Collectors.collectingAndThen(
        Collectors.toList(),
        result ->
            Collections.unmodifiableList(result)));
System.out.println(names);
```

```
[Ken, Jeff, Donna, Chris, Laynie, Li]
```

The collector collects the names in a mutable list, and the finisher wraps the mutable list in an unmodifiable list. Let's take another example of using the finisher. Suppose you want to print a calendar that contains the names of people by the month of their dates of birth. You have already collected the list of names grouped by months of their birth. You may have a month that doesn't contain any birthdays. However, you want to print the month's name anyway and just add "None." Here is the first attempt:

```
Map<Month,String> dobCalendar = Person.persons()
    .stream()
    .collect(groupingBy(p -> p.getDob().getMonth(),
            mapping(Person::getName, joining(", "))));
dobCalendar.entrySet().forEach(System.out::println);
```

```
MAY=Ken, Li
DECEMBER=Chris, Laynie
JULY=Jeff, Donna
```

This calendar has three issues:

- It is not sorted by month.

- It does not include all months.

- It is modifiable. The returned Map from the collect() method is modifiable.

You can fix all three issues by using the collector returned from the collectingAndThen() method and specifying a finisher. The finisher will add the missing months in the map, convert the map to a sorted map, and, finally, wrap the map in an unmodifiable map. The collect() method returns the map returned from the finisher. Listing 6-14 contains the complete code.

Listing 6-14. Adapting the Collector Result

```java
// DobCalendar.java
package com.jdojo.streams;

import java.time.Month;
import java.util.Collections;
import java.util.Map;
import java.util.TreeMap;
import static
  java.util.stream.Collectors.collectingAndThen;
import static
  java.util.stream.Collectors.groupingBy;
import static
  java.util.stream.Collectors.joining;
import static
  java.util.stream.Collectors.mapping;

public class DobCalendar {
    public static void main(String[] args) {
        Map<Month, String> dobCalendar = Person.persons()
            .stream().collect(collectingAndThen(
                groupingBy(p -> p.getDob().getMonth(),
                mapping(Person::getName, joining(", "))),
                result -> {
                    // Add missing months
                    for (Month m : Month.values()) {
                        result.putIfAbsent(m, "None");
                    }
                    // Return a sorted, unmodifiable map
                    return Collections.unmodifiableMap(
                        new TreeMap<>(result));
                }));
```

```
        dobCalendar.entrySet().
            forEach(System.out::println);
    }
}
```

```
JANUARY=None
FEBRUARY=None
MARCH=None
APRIL=None
MAY=Ken, Li
JUNE=None
JULY=Jeff, Donna
AUGUST=None
SEPTEMBER=None
OCTOBER=None
NOVEMBER=None
DECEMBER=Chris, Laynie
```

The filtering() method lets you group the elements, apply a filter in each group, and collect the filtered elements. The following snippet of code shows you how to group people by gender and collect only those people who make more than 8000.00:

```
Map<Person.Gender, List<Person>> makingOver8000 =
    Person.persons()
    .stream()
    .collect(groupingBy(
        Person::getGender,
        filtering(p ->
            p.getIncome() > 8000.00, toList())));
System.out.println(makingOver8000);
```

```
{MALE=[], FEMALE=[(3, Donna, FEMALE, 1962-07-29, 8700.00)]}
```

Notice an empty list in the male group. In the collector, two groups were collected: male and female. The filtering( ) method filtered out all elements in the male group, so you got an empty list. If you had used the filter() method on the original stream to filter out people making 8000.00 or less, you would not have seen the male group in the output because the collector would have not seen the male group at all.

You have already seen the use of the collector returned by the `mapping()` function of the `Collectors` class in the "Grouping Data" section, which lets you apply a function to each element before accumulating the elements in a collector. The `flatMapping()` method lets you apply a flat mapping function on each element. Consider the list of people in Table 6-2. Suppose you want to summarize the table's data by grouping people by their gender and the list of unique languages spoken by people of each gender type.

Table 6-2. *A List of People, Their Genders, and the List of Languages They Speak*

Name	Gender	Language
Ken	Male	English, French
Jeff	Male	Spanish, Wu
Donna	Female	English, French
Chris	Male	Wu, Lao
Laynie	Female	English, German
Li	Male	English

For this example, I use a `Map.Entry<String,Set<String>>` instance to represent a row in this table. I use only gender and spoken languages in each row of the table, ignoring the person's name. Listing 6-15 contains the complete code.

Listing 6-15. Applying a Flat Mapping Operation After Grouping

```java
// FlatMappingTest.java
package com.jdojo.streams;

import java.util.List;
import java.util.Map;
import java.util.Map.Entry;
import static java.util.Map.entry;
import java.util.Set;
import static java.util.stream.Collectors.flatMapping;
import static java.util.stream.Collectors.groupingBy;
import static java.util.stream.Collectors.toSet;
```

```java
public class FlatMappingTest {
    public static void main(String[] args) {
        // Represent the gender and the list of spoken
        // languages
        List<Entry<String, Set<String>>> list = List.of(
            entry("Male", Set.of("English", "French")),
            entry("Male", Set.of("Spanish", "Wu")),
            entry("Female", Set.of("English", "French")),
            entry("Male", Set.of("Wu", "Lao")),
            entry("Female", Set.of("English", "German")),
            entry("Male", Set.of("English")));
        Map<String, Set<String>> langByGender =
            list.stream()
            .collect(groupingBy(Entry::getKey,
                flatMapping(e ->
                    e.getValue().stream(), toSet())));
        System.out.println(langByGender);
    }
}
```

```
{Female=[English, French, German],
Male=[English, French, Spanish, Lao, Wu]}
```

The Entry::getKey method reference is used to group the elements of the list by gender. The first argument maps each entry in the list to a Stream<String>, which contains the languages spoken for that element. The flatMapping() method flattens the stream produced and collects the results, which are the names of the spoken languages in a Set<String>, giving you a unique list of spoken languages by gender.

Finding and Matching in Streams

The Streams API supports different types of find and match operations on stream elements. For example, you can check if any elements in the stream match a predicate, if all elements match a predicate, etc. The following methods in the Stream interface are used to perform find and match operations:

- boolean allMatch(Predicate<? super T> predicate)

- `boolean anyMatch(Predicate<? super T> predicate)`

- `boolean noneMatch(Predicate<? super T> predicate)`

- `Optional<T> findAny()`

- `Optional<T> findFirst()`

The primitive type streams such as `IntStream`, `LongStream`, and `DoubleStream` also contain the same methods that work with a predicate and an optional one for primitive types. For example, the `allMatch()` method in the `IntStream` takes an `IntPredicate` as an argument, and the `findAny()` method returns an `OptionalInt`.

All find and match operations are terminal operations. They are also short-circuiting operations. A short-circuiting operation may not have to process the entire stream to return the result. For example, the `allMatch()` method checks if the specified predicate is `true` for all elements in the stream. It is sufficient for this method to return `false` if the predicate evaluates to `false` for one element. Once the predicate evaluates to false for one element, it stops further processing (short-circuits) of elements and returns the result as `false`. The same argument goes for all other methods. Note that the return type of the `findAny()` and `findFirst()` methods is `Optional<T>` because these methods may not have a result if the stream is empty.

The program in Listing 6-16 shows how to perform find and match operations on streams. The program uses sequential stream because the stream size is very small. Consider using a parallel stream if the match has to be performed on large streams. In that case, any thread can find a match or not find a match to end the matching operations.

Listing 6-16. Performing Find and Match Operations on Streams

```java
// FindAndMatch.java
package com.jdojo.streams;
import java.util.List;
import java.util.Optional;
public class FindAndMatch {
public static void main(String[] args) {
        // Get the list of persons
        List<Person> persons = Person.persons();
        // Check if all persons are males
```

```java
        boolean allMales = persons.stream()
            .allMatch(Person::isMale);
        System.out.println("All males: " + allMales);
        // Check if any person was born in 1970
        boolean anyoneBornIn1970 = persons.stream()
            .anyMatch(p -> p.getDob().getYear() == 1970);
        System.out.println("Anyone born in 1970: " +
            anyoneBornIn1970);
        // Check if any person was born in 1955
        boolean anyoneBornIn1955 = persons.stream()
            .anyMatch(p -> p.getDob().getYear() == 1955);
        System.out.println("Anyone born in 1955: " +
            anyoneBornIn1955);
        // Find any male
        Optional<Person> anyMale = persons.stream()
            .filter(Person::isMale)
            .findAny();
        if (anyMale.isPresent()) {
            System.out.println("Any male: " +
                anyMale.get());
        } else {
            System.out.println("No male found.");
        }
        // Find the first male
        Optional<Person> firstMale = persons.stream()
            .filter(Person::isMale)
            .findFirst();
        if (firstMale.isPresent()) {
            System.out.println("First male: " +
                anyMale.get());
        } else {
            System.out.println("No male found.");
        }
    }
}
```

```
All males: false
Anyone born in 1970: true
Anyone born in 1955: false
Any male: (1, Ken, MALE, 1970-05-04, 6000.00)
First male: (1, Ken, MALE, 1970-05-04, 6000.00)
```

Parallel Streams

Streams can be sequential or parallel. Operations on a sequential stream are processed in serial using one thread. Operations on a parallel stream are processed in parallel using multiple threads. You do not need to take additional steps to process streams because they are sequential or parallel. All you need to do is call the appropriate method that produces a sequential or parallel stream. Everything else is taken care of by the Streams API. This is why I stated in the beginning of this chapter that you get parallelism in stream processing "almost" for free.

Most of the methods in the Streams API produce sequential streams by default. To produce a parallel stream from a collection, such as a List or a Set, you need to call the parallelStream() method of the Collection interface. Use the parallel() method on a stream to convert a sequential stream into a parallel stream. Conversely, use the sequential() method on a stream to convert a parallel stream into a sequential stream. The following snippet of code shows serial processing of the stream pipeline because the stream is sequential:

```
String names = Person
    .persons()                 // The data source
    .stream()                  // Produces a sequential stream
    .filter(Person::isMale)    // Processed in serial
    .map(Person::getName)      // Processed in serial
    .collect(Collectors.
        joining(", "));        // Processed in serial
```

The following snippet of code shows parallel processing of the stream pipeline because the stream is parallel:

```
String names = Person
    .persons()               // The data source
    .parallelStream()        // Produces a parallel stream
    .filter(Person::isMale)  // Processed in parallel
    .map(Person::getName)    // Processed in parallel
    .collect(Collectors.
        joining(", "));      // Processed in parallel
```

The following snippet of code shows processing of the stream pipeline in mixed mode because the operations in the pipeline produce serial and parallel streams:

```
String names = Person
    .persons()               // The data source
    .stream()                // Produces a sequential stream
    .filter(Person::isMale)  // Processed in serial
    .parallel()              // Produces a parallel stream
    .map(Person::getName)    // Processed in parallel
    .collect(Collectors.
        joining(", "));      // Processed in parallel
```

The operations following a serial stream are performed serially, and the operations following a parallel stream are performed in parallel. You get parallelism when processing streams for free. So when do you use parallelism in stream processing? Do you get the benefits of parallelism whenever you use it? The answer is no. There are some conditions that must be met before you should use parallel streams. Sometimes, using parallel streams may result in worse performance.

The Streams API uses the fork/join framework to process parallel streams. The fork/join framework uses multiple threads. It divides the stream elements into chunks; each thread processes a chunk of elements to produce a partial result, and the partial results are combined to give you the result. Starting up multiple threads, dividing the data into chunks, and combining partial results take up CPU time. This overhead is justified by the overall time to finish the task. For example, a stream of six people is going to take longer to process in parallel than in serial. The overhead of setting up the threads and coordinating them for such a small amount of work is not worth it.

You have seen the use of an Iterator for traversing elements of collections. The Streams API uses a Spliterator (a splittable iterator) to traverse elements of streams. Spliterator is a generalization of Iterator. An iterator provides sequential access to data elements. A Spliterator provides sequential access and decomposition of data elements. When you create a Spliterator, it knows the chunk of data it will process. You can split a Spliterator into two: each will get its own chunk of data to process. The Spliterator is an interface in the java.util package. It is used heavily for splitting stream elements into chunks to be processed by multiple threads. As the user of the Streams API, you will never have to work directly with a Spliterator. The data source of the streams provides a Spliterator. Parallel processing of a stream is faster if the Spliterator can know the size of the streams. Streams can be based on a data source that may have a fixed size or an unknown size. Splitting the stream elements into chunks is not possible if the size of the stream cannot be determined. In such cases, even though you can use a parallel stream, you may not get the benefits of parallelism.

Another consideration in parallel processing is the ordering of elements. If elements are ordered, threads need to keep the ordering at the end of the processing. If ordering is not important for you, you can convert an ordered stream into an unordered stream using the unordered() method.

Spliterators divide the data elements into chunks. It is important that the data source for the stream does not change during stream processing; otherwise, the result is not defined. For example, if your stream uses a list/set as the data source, do not add or remove elements from the list/set when the stream is being processed.

Stream processing is based on functional programming that does not modify data elements during processing. It creates new data elements rather than modifying them. The same rule holds for stream processing, particularly when it is processed in parallel. The operations in a stream pipeline are specified as lambda expressions that should not modify the mutable states of the elements being processed.

Let's take an example of counting the prime numbers in a big range of natural numbers, say from 2 to 214748364. The number 214748364 is one tenth of Integer.MAX_ VALUE. The following snippet of code performs the counting in serial:

```
// Process the stream in serial
long count = IntStream.rangeClosed(2, Integer.MAX_VALUE/10)
                    .filter(PrimeUtil::isPrime)
                    .count();
```

The code took 758 seconds to finish. Let's try converting the stream to a parallel stream as follows:

```
// Process the stream in parallel
long count = IntStream.rangeClosed(2, Integer.MAX_VALUE/10)
                      .parallel()
                      .filter(PrimeUtil::isPrime)
                      .count();
```

This time, the code took only 181 seconds, which is roughly 24% of the time it took when it was processed in serial. This is a significant gain. Both pieces of code were run on a machine with a processor that had eight cores. The code may take a different amount of time to complete on your machine.

Summary

A stream is a sequence of data elements supporting sequential and parallel aggregate operations. Collections in Java focus on data storage and access to the data, whereas streams focus on computations on data. Streams do not have storage. They get the data from a data source, which is most often a collection. However, a stream can get its data from other sources, such as file I/O channel, a function, etc. A stream can also be based on a data source that is capable of generating infinite data elements.

Streams are connected through operations forming a pipeline. Streams support two types of operations: intermediate and terminal operations. An intermediate operation on a stream produces another stream that can serve as an input stream for another intermediate operation. A terminal operation produces a result in the form of a single value. A stream cannot be reused after a terminal operation is invoked on it.

Some operations on streams are called short-circuiting operations. A short-circuiting operation does not necessarily have to process all data in the stream. For example, findAny is a short-circuiting operation that finds any element in the stream for which the specified predicate is true. Once an element is found, the operation discards the remaining elements in the stream.

Streams are inherently lazy. They process data on demand. Data is not processed when intermediate operations are invoked on a stream. Invocation of a terminal operation processes the stream data.

A stream pipeline can be executed in serial or in parallel. By default, streams are serial. You can convert a serial stream into a parallel stream by calling the stream's parallel() method. You can convert a parallel stream into a serial stream by calling the stream's sequential() method.

The Streams API supports most of the operations supported in the functional programming such as `filter`, `map`, `forEach`, `reduce`, `allMatch`, `anyMatch`, `findAny`, `findFirst`, etc. Streams contain a `peek()` method for debugging purposes that lets you take an action on every element passing through the stream. The Streams API provides collectors that are used to collect data in collections, such as a `map`, a `list`, a `set`, etc. The `Collectors` class is a utility class that provides several implementations of collectors. Mapping, grouping, and partitioning of a stream's data can be easily performed using the `collect()` method of streams and using the collector provided.

Parallel streams take advantage of multicore processors. They use the fork/join framework to process the stream's element in parallel.

Exercises

Exercise 1

What are streams and aggregate operations on streams?

Exercise 2

How do streams differ from collections?

Exercise 3

Fill in the blanks:

a. Collections have storage, whereas streams have _____ storage.

b. Collections support external iteration, whereas streams support _____ iteration.

c. Collections support imperative programming, whereas streams support _____ programming.

d. Collections support a finite number of elements, whereas streams support _____ number of elements.

e. Streams support sequential and _____ processing of its elements.

f. A stream does not start pulling elements from its data source until a _____ operation is called on the stream.

g. Once a terminal operation is called on a stream, the stream _____ be reused.

Exercise 4

Describe the difference between intermediate and terminal operations on streams.

Exercise 5

Create a `Stream<Integer>` of all integers from 10 to 30 and compute the sum of all integers in the list.

Exercise 6

Complete the following snippet of code, which computes the sum of characters in a list of names using a stream:

```
List<String> names = List.of(
    "Mo", "Jeff", "Li", "Dola");
int sum = names.stream()
    ./* your code goes here */;
System.out.println("Total characters: " + sum);
```

The expected output is as follows:

```
Total characters: 12
```

Exercise 7

Complete the following snippet of code, which creates two empty `Stream<String>`s.

You are supposed to use different methods of the `Stream` interface to complete the code:

```
Stream<String> noNames1 = Stream.
    /* Your code goes here */;
Stream<String> noNames2 = Stream.
    /* Your code goes here */;
```

Exercise 8

What method of the `Stream` interface is used to limit the number of elements in a stream to a specified size?

Exercise 9

What method of the `Stream` interface is used to skip a specified number of elements in a stream?

Exercise 10

Describe the characteristics of the stream produced by the following snippet of code:

```
Stream<Integer> stream = Stream.
    generate(() -> 1969);
```

Exercise 11

What is the use of the instances of the Optional<T> class?

Exercise 12

Complete the following snippet of code, which is supposed to print the names of people along with the number of characters in the names in the non-empty Optionals in the list:

```
List<Optional<String>> names = List.of(
    Optional.of("Ken"),
    Optional.empty(),
    Optional.of("Li"),
    Optional.empty(),
    Optional.of("Toto"));
names.stream()
    .flatMap(/* Your code goes here */)
    .forEach(/* Your code goes here */);
```

The expected output is as follows:

```
Ken: 3
Li: 2
Toto: 4
```

Exercise 13

What is the use of the peek() method in the Stream interface?

Exercise 14

What is the use of the map() and flatMap() methods in the Stream interface?

Exercise 15

Compare the filter and map operations on a stream with respect to the type of elements and number of elements in the input and output streams of these operations.

Exercise 16

What is a reduction operation on a stream? Name three commonly used reduction operations on streams.

Exercise 17

Write the logic to compute the sum of all integers in the following array using a parallel stream and the reduce() method of the Stream interface:

```
int[] nums = {1, 2, 3, 4, 5, 6, 7, 8, 9, 10};
```

Exercise 18

Complete the following snippet of code to print the unique non-null values in a map:

```
Map<Integer, String> map = new HashMap<>();
map.put(1, "One");
map.put(2, "One");
map.put(3, null);
map.put(4, "Two");
map.entrySet()
    .stream()
    .flatMap(/* Your code goes here */)
    ./* Your code goes here */
    .forEach(System.out::println);
```

The expected output is as follows:

```
One
Two
```

Exercise 19

Complete the missing piece of code in the following snippet of code, which is supposed to count the number of even and odd integers in a list of integers:

```
List<Integer> list = List.of(
    10, 19, 20, 40, 45, 50);
Map<String,Long> oddEvenCounts = list.stream()
        .map(/* Your code goes here */)
        .collect(/* Your code goes here */);
System.out.println(oddEvenCounts);
```

The expected output is as follows:

```
{Even=4, Odd=2}
```

Exercise 20

The following snippet of code is supposed to print a sorted list of odd integers in the list, which are separated by colons. Complete the missing pieces of the code:

```
List<Integer> list = List.of(5, 1, 2, 7, 3, 4, 8);
String str = list.stream()
            ./* Multiple method calls go here */;
System.out.println(str);
```

The expected output is as follows:

```
1:3:5:7
```

CHAPTER 7

Implementing Services

In this chapter, you will learn:

- What services, service interfaces, and service providers are

- How to implement a service in Java

- How to use a Java interface as a service implementation

- How to load service providers using the `ServiceLoader` class

- How to use the `uses` statement in a module declaration to specify the service interface that the current module discovers and loads using the `ServiceLoader` class

- How to use the `provides` statement to specify a service provider provided by the current module

- How to discover, filter, and select service providers based on their type without instantiating them

What Is a Service?

A specific functionality provided by an application (or a library) is known as a *service*. For example, you can have different libraries providing a *prime number service*, which can check if a number is a prime and generate the next prime after a given number. Applications and libraries providing implementations for a service are known as *service providers*. Applications using the service are called *service consumers* or *clients*. How does a client use the service? Does a client know all service providers? Does a client get a service without knowing any service providers? I answer these questions in this chapter.

Earlier versions of Java (SE 6 onward) already provided a mechanism to allow for loose coupling between service providers and service consumers. That is, a service

© Kishori Sharan, Peter Späth 2021
K. Sharan and P. Späth, *More Java 17*, https://doi.org/10.1007/978-1-4842-7135-3_7

consumer can use a service provided by a service provider without knowing the service provider. With the module system, this architectural pattern became more standardized and more straightforwardly to apply to Java projects.

In Java, a *service* is defined by a set of interfaces and classes. The service contains an interface or an abstract class that defines the functionality provided by the service, and it is known as the *service provider interface* or simply *service interface*. Note that the term "interface" in "service provider interface" and "service interface" does not refer to an interface construct in Java. A service interface can be a Java interface or an abstract class. It is possible, but not recommended, to use a concrete class as a service interface. Sometimes, a service interface is also called a *service type*—the type that is used to identify the service.

A specific implementation of a *service* is known as a *service provider*. There can be multiple service providers for a service interface. Typically, a service provider consists of several interfaces and classes to provide an implementation for the service interface.

The JDK contains a `java.util.ServiceLoader<S>` class whose sole purpose is to discover and load service providers at runtime for a service interface of type S. The `ServiceLoader` class allows decoupling of service providers from service consumers. A service consumer knows only the service interface; the `ServiceLoader` class makes the instances of the service providers that are implementing the service interface available to consumers. Figure 7-1 shows a pictorial view of the arrangement of a service, service providers, and a service consumer.

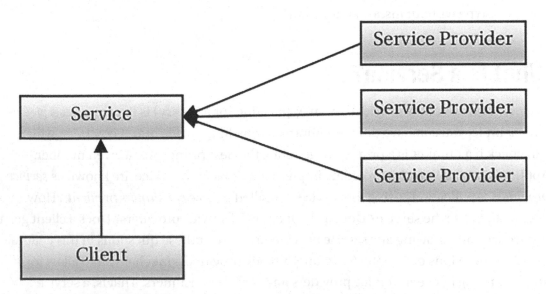

Figure 7-1. *The arrangement of a service, service providers, and a service consumer*

Typically, the service will use the ServiceLoader class to load all service providers and make them available to service consumers (or clients). This architecture allows for a plugin mechanism in which a service provider can be added or removed without affecting the service and service consumers. Service consumers know only about the service interface. They do not know about any specific implementations (service providers) of the service interface.

Note I suggest reading the documentation for the java.util.ServiceLoader class for a complete understanding of the service-loading facility.

In this chapter, I use a service and three service providers. Their modules, class/interface names, and brief descriptions are listed in Table 7-1.

Table 7-1. *Modules, Classes, and Interfaces Used in the Chapter Examples*

Module	Classes/Interfaces	Description
jdojo.prime	PrimeChecker	It acts as a service, a service interface, and a service provider. It provides a default implementation for the service interface.
jdojo.prime.faster	FasterPrimeChecker	A service provider.
jdojo.prime.probable	ProbablePrimeChecker	A service provider.
jdojo.prime.client	Main	A service consumer.

Figure 7-2 shows the classes/interfaces arranged as services, service providers, and service consumers, which can be compared with Figure 7-1.

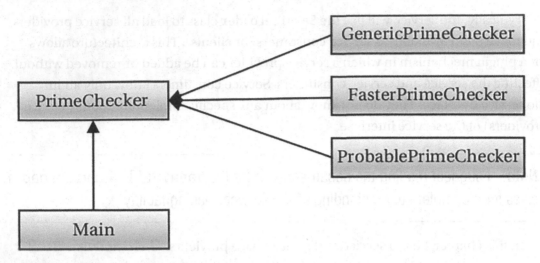

Figure 7-2. *The arrangement of a service, three service providers, and a service consumer*

Discovering Services

In order for a service to be used, its providers need to be discovered and loaded. The ServiceLoader class does the work of discovering and loading the service providers. The module that discovers and loads service providers must contain a uses statement in its declaration, which has the following syntax:

uses <service-interface>;

Here, <service-interface> is the name of the service interface, which is a Java interface name, a class name, or an annotation type name. If a module uses the ServiceLoader<S> class to load the instances of service providers for a service interface named S, the module declaration must contain the following statement:

uses S;

In my opinion, the statement name, uses, seems to be a misnomer. At first glance, it seems that the current module will use the specified service. However, that is not the case. A service is used by the clients, not by the module defining the service. A more intuitive statement name would have been discovers or loads. You can understand its meaning correctly if you read its definition as: the module having the uses statement *uses* the ServiceLoader class to load the service providers for this service interface.

You do not need to use the uses statement in client modules unless your client modules load the service providers for services. It is unusual for client modules to load services.

A module may discover and load more than one service. The following module declaration uses two uses statements indicating that it will discover and load services identified by the com.jdojo.PrimeChecker and com.jdojo.CsvParser interfaces:

```
module jdojo.loader {
    uses com.jdojo.PrimeChecker;
    uses com.jdojo.CsvParser:
    // Other module statements go here
}
```

A module declaration allows import statements. For better readability, you can rewrite this module declaration as follows:

```
// Import types from other packages
import com.jdojo.PrimeChecker;
import com.jdojo.CsvParser:
module jdojo.loader {
    uses PrimeChecker;
    uses CsvParser:
    // Other module statements go here
}
```

The service interface specified in a uses statement may be declared in the current module or in another module. If it is declared in another module, the service interface must be accessible to the code in the current module; otherwise, a compile-time error occurs. For example, the com.jdojo.CsvParser service interface used in the uses statement in the previous declaration may be declared in the jdojo.loader module or another module, say jdojo.csvUtil. In the latter case, the com.jdojo.CsvParser interface must be accessible to the jdojo.loader module.

Service provider discovery occurs at runtime. Modules that discover service providers typically do not (and need not) declare compile-time dependency on the service provider modules because it is not possible to know all provider modules in advance. Another reason for service discoverer modules not declaring dependency on service provider modules is to keep the service provider and service consumer decoupled.

Providing Service Implementations

A module that provides implementations for a service interface must contain a provides statement. If a module contains a service provider, but does not contain a provides statement in its declaration, this service provider will not be loaded through the ServiceLoader class. That is, a provides statement in a module declaration is a way to tell the ServiceLoader class, "Hey! I provide an implementation for a service. You can use me as a service provider whenever you need that service." The syntax for a provides statement is as follows:

```
provides <service-interface> with
    <service-implementation-name>;
```

(You can of course write this in a single line.)

Here, the provides clause specifies the name of the service interface, and the with clause specifies the name of the class that implements the service provider interface. A service provider may specify an interface as an implementation for a service interface. This may sound incorrect, but it is true. I provide an example in this chapter where an interface serves as a service provider implementation type. The following module declaration contains two provides statements:

```
module com.jdojo.provider {
    provides com.jdojo.PrimeChecker with
        com.jdojo.impl.PrimeCheckerFactory;
    provides com.jdojo.CsvParser with
        com.jdojo.impl.CsvFastParser;
    // Other module statements go here
}
```

The first provides statement declares that com.jdojo.impl.PrimeCheckerFactory is one possible implementation for the service interface named com.jdojo.PrimeChecker. The second provides statement declares that com.jdojo.impl.CsvFastParser is one possible implementation for the service interface named com.jdojo.CsvParser. The implementations PrimeCheckerFactory and CsvParser usually are classes, but it is also possible to use interfaces.

A module can contain any combination of uses and provides statements—the same module can provide implementation for a service and discover the same service; it can only provide implementation for one or more services, or it can provide implementation for one service and discover another type of service. The following module declaration discovers and provides the implementation for the same service:

```
module com.jdojo.parser {
    uses com.jdojo.XmlParser;
    provides com.jdojo.XmlParser with
        com.jdojo.xml.impl.XmlParserFactory;
    // Other module statements go here
}
```

Note   The service implementation class/interface specified in the with clause of the provides statement must be declared in the current module. Otherwise, a compile-time error occurs.

The `ServiceLoader` class creates instances of the service implementation. When the service implementation is an interface, it calls the interface's `provider()` static method to get an instance of the provider. The service implementation (a class or an interface) must follow these rules:

- If the service implementation implicitly or explicitly declares a public constructor with no formal parameters, that constructor is called the *provider constructor.*

- If the service implementation contains a public static method named `provider` with no formal parameters, this method is called the *provider method.*

- The return type of the provider method must be the service interface type or its subtype.

- If the service implementation does not contain the provider method, the type of the service implementation must be a class with a provider constructor, and the class must be of the service interface type or its subtype.

When the `ServiceLoader` class is requested to discover and load a service provider, it checks whether the service implementation contains the provider method. If the provider method is found, the returned value of the method is the service returned by the `ServiceLoader` class. If the provider method is not found, it instantiates the service implementation using the provider constructor. If the service implementation contains neither the provider method nor the provider constructor, a compile-time error occurs.

With these rules, it is possible to use a Java interface as a service implementation. The interface should have a public static method named `provider` that returns an instance of the service interface type.

The following sections walk you through the steps to implement a service using modules. The last section explains how to make the same service work in a non-modular environment.

Defining the Service Interface

In this section, you develop a service called *prime checker*. I keep the service simple, so you can focus on working with the service provider mechanism in Java, rather than writing complex code to implement the service functionality. Requirements for this service are as follows:

- The service should provide an API to check if a number is a prime.

- Clients should be able to know the names of the available service providers. The name of a service provider will be the fully qualified name of the service provider class or interface.

- The service should provide a default implementation of the service interface.

- Clients should be able to retrieve a service instance without specifying the name of the service provider. In this case, the default service provider is returned.

- Clients should be able to retrieve a service instance by specifying a service provider fully qualified name. If a service provider with the specified name does not exist, `null` is returned.

Let's design the service. The functionality provided by the service will be represented by an interface named `PrimeChecker`. It contains one method:

```
public interface PrimeChecker {
    boolean isPrime(long n);
}
```

The isPrime() method returns true if the specified argument is a prime, and it returns false otherwise. All service providers will implement the PrimeChecker interface. The PrimeChecker interface is our service interface (or service type).

Obtaining Service Provider Instances

The service needs to provide APIs to the clients to retrieve instances of the service providers. The service needs to discover and load all service providers before it can give them to clients. Service providers are loaded using the ServiceLoader class. The class has no public constructor. You can use one of its load() methods to get its instances. You need to specify the class reference of the service interface to the load() method. The ServiceLoader class contains an iterator() method that returns an Iterator for all service providers of a specific service interface loaded by this ServiceLoader. The ServiceLoader class also implements the Iterable interface, so you can also iterate over all the service providers using a for-each statement. The following snippet of code shows you how to load and iterate through all service provider instances for PrimeChecker:

```
// Load the service providers for PrimeChecker
ServiceLoader<PrimeChecker> loader =
    ServiceLoader.load(PrimeChecker.class);
// Iterate through all service provider instances
Iterator<PrimeChecker> iterator = loader.iterator();
if (iterator.hasNext()) {
    PrimeChecker checker = iterator.next();
    // Use the prime checker here...
}
```

The following snippet of code shows you how to use a ServiceLoader instance in a for-each statement to iterate over all service provider instances:

```
ServiceLoader<PrimeChecker> loader =
    ServiceLoader.load(PrimeChecker.class);
for (PrimeChecker checker : loader) {
    // checker is your service provider instance
}
```

At times, you'll want to select providers based on their class names. For example, you may want to select only those prime service providers whose fully qualified class name starts with com.jdojo. Typical logic to achieve this would be to use the iterator returned by the iterator() method of the ServiceLoader class. However, this is costly. The iterator instantiates a provider before returning. JDK9 added a new stream() method to the ServiceLoader class:

```
public Stream<ServiceLoader.Provider<S>> stream()
```

The method returns a stream of instances of the ServiceProvider.Provider<S> interface, which is declared as a nested interface in the ServiceLoader class as follows:

```
public static interface Provider<S> extends Supplier<S> {
    // Returns a Class reference of the class of the
    // service provider
    Class<? extends S> type();
    @Override
    S get();
}
```

An instance of the ServiceLoader.Provider interface represents a service provider. Its type() method returns the Class object of the service implementation. The get() method returns an instance of the service provider.

How does the ServiceLoader.Provider interface help? When you use the stream() method, each element in the stream is of the ServiceLoader.Provider type. You can filter the stream based on the class name or type of the provider, which will not instantiate the provider. You can use the type() method in your filters. When you find the desired provider, call the get() method to instantiate the provider. This way, you instantiate a provider when you know you need it, not when you are iterating through all providers. The following is an example of using the stream() method of the ServiceLoader class. It gives you a list of all prime service providers whose class name starts with com.jdojo:

```
static List<PrimeChecker> startsWith(String prefix) {
    return ServiceLoader.load(PrimeChecker.class)
            .stream()
            .filter((Provider p) ->
                p.type().getName().startsWith(prefix))
```

```
        .map(Provider::get)
        .collect(Collectors.toList());
}
```

Your prime checker service is supposed to let clients find a service provider using the service provider class or interface name. You can provide a newInstance(String providerName) method using the stream() method of the ServiceLoader class as follows:

```
static PrimeChecker newInstance(String providerName) {
    // Try to find the first service provider with the
    // specified providerName
    Optional<Provider<PrimeChecker>> optional =
        ServiceLoader.load(PrimeChecker.class)
            .stream()
            .filter((Provider p) ->
                p.type().getName().equals(providerName))
            .findFirst();
    PrimeChecker checker = null;
    // Instantiate the provider if we found one
    if (optional.isPresent()) {
        Provider<PrimeChecker> provider = optional.get();
        checker = provider.get();
    }
    return checker;
}
```

There is a big difference between using the Iterator and the stream() method of the ServiceLoader class to find a service provider. The Iterator supplies you with the instance of the service provider, which you can use to determine the details of the actual service provider implementation class. A service provider may use the provider constructor or the provider method to supply its instances. The stream() method does not create service provider instances. Rather, it looks at the provider constructors and provider methods to give you the type of the service provider implementation. If you use the provider constructor, the stream() method knows the actual class name of the service implementation. If you use the provider method, the stream() method does not (and cannot) peek inside the provider method to see the actual implementation class type. In this case, it simply looks at the return type of the provider method, and its `type()` method returns the `Class` reference of that return type. Consider the following provider method implementation of the `PrimeChecker` service type:

```
// FasterPrimeChecker.java
package com.jdojo.prime.faster;
import com.jdojo.prime.PrimeChecker;
public class FasterPrimeChecker implements PrimeChecker {
    // No provider constructor
    private FasterPrimeChecker() {
        // No code
    }
    // Define a provider method
    public static PrimeChecker provider() {
        return new FasterPrimeChecker();
    }
    @Override
    public boolean isPrime(long n) {
        // More code goes here
    }
}
```

Suppose the `FasterPrimeChecker` class is available as a service provider. When you use the `stream()` method of the `ServiceLoader` class, you will get a `ServiceLoader.Provider` element for this service provider whose `type()` method will return the `Class` reference of the `com.jdojo.prime.PrimeChecker` interface, which is the return type of the `provider()` method. When you call the `get()` method of the `ServiceLoader.Provider` instance, it will call the `provider()` method and return the reference of an object of the `FasterPrimeChecker` class as it is returned from the `provider()` method. If you try to write the following code to find the `FasterPrimeChecker` provider, it will fail:

```
String providerName =
    "com.jdojo.prime.faster.FasterPrimeChecker";
Optional<Provider<PrimeChecker>> optional =
    ServiceLoader.load(PrimeChecker.class)
        .stream()
```

```
        .filter((Provider p) ->
            p.type().getName().equals(providerName))
        .findFirst();
```

If you want to find this service provider by its class name using the stream() method of the ServiceLoader class, you can change the return type of the provider() method as shown:

```java
// FasterPrimeChecker.java
package com.jdojo.prime.faster;
import com.jdojo.prime.PrimeChecker;
public class FasterPrimeChecker implements PrimeChecker {
    // No provider constructor
    private FasterPrimeChecker() {
        // No code
    }
    // Define a provider method
    public static FasterPrimeChecker provider() {
        return new FasterPrimeChecker();
    }
    @Override
    public boolean isPrime(long n) {
        // More code goes here
    }
}
```

Defining the Service

You can create a class to provide the discovering, loading, and retrieving features for your service. But since it is possible to add static methods to interfaces, you can also use interfaces for the same purpose. Let's add two static methods to the service interface:

```java
public interface PrimeChecker {
    // Part of the service interface
    boolean isPrime(long n);
    // Part of the service
    static PrimeChecker newInstance() { /*...*/ };
```

```
static PrimeChecker newInstance(String providerName) {
    /*...*/ };
static List<PrimeChecker> providers() { /*...*/ };
static List<String> providerNames(/*...*/);
}
```

The newInstance() method will return an instance of the PrimeChecker that is the default service provider. The newInstance(String providerName) method will return the instance of a service provider with the specified provider name. The providers() method will return all provider instances, whereas the providerNames() method will return a list of all provider names.

Notice that your PrimeChecker interface is going to serve two purposes:

- It serves as a service interface with the isPrime() method as the only method in that service interface. Clients will use the PrimeChecker interface as the service type.

- It serves as a service with the two versions of the newInstance() method, the providers() method, and the providerNames() method.

At this point, you had a choice to have a separate service class, say a PrimeService class, with newInstance(), providers(), and providerNames() methods in it—leaving only the isPrime() method in the PrimeChecker interface. If you decided to do so, clients would have used the PrimeService class to obtain a service provider.

Note   Adding methods to interfaces somewhat thwarts the original notion of an interface. Strictly spoken, there should be a clear distinction between interfaces describing methods and classes which implement such methods and contain actually executable code. It is up to you if you want to use such interface methods with code given inside the interface declaration itself, or if you want to provide special infrastructure classes that allow for instantiating services.

Listing 7-1 contains the complete code for the PrimeChecker interface.

Listing 7-1. A Service Provider Interface Named PrimeChecker

```java
// PrimeChecker.java
package com.jdojo.prime;
import java.util.ArrayList;
import java.util.List;
import java.util.Optional;
import java.util.ServiceLoader;
import java.util.ServiceLoader.Provider;
import java.util.stream.Collectors;
public interface PrimeChecker {
    boolean isPrime(long n);
    static PrimeChecker newInstance() {
        // Return the default service provider
        String defaultSP =
            "com.jdojo.prime.impl.GenericPrimeChecker";
        return newInstance(defaultSP);
    }
    static PrimeChecker newInstance(String providerName) {
        Optional<Provider<PrimeChecker>> optional =
            ServiceLoader.load(PrimeChecker.class)
                .stream()
                .filter((Provider p) ->
                    p.type().getName().
                        equals(providerName))
                .findFirst();
        PrimeChecker checker = null;
        if (optional.isPresent()) {
            Provider<PrimeChecker> provider =
                optional.get();
            checker = provider.get();
        }
        return checker;
    }
```

```
    static List<PrimeChecker> providers() {
        List<PrimeChecker> providers = new ArrayList<>();
        ServiceLoader<PrimeChecker> loader =
            ServiceLoader.load(PrimeChecker.class);
        for (PrimeChecker checker : loader) {
            providers.add(checker);
        }
        return providers;
    }
    static List<String> providerNames() {
        List<String> providers =
            ServiceLoader.load(PrimeChecker.class)
                .stream()
                .map((Provider p) -> p.type().getName())
                .collect(Collectors.toList());
        return providers;
    }
}
```

The declaration of the `jdojo.prime` module is shown in Listing 7-2. It exports the `com.jdojo.prime` package because other service provider modules need to use the PrimeChecker interface.

Listing 7-2. The Declaration of the jdojo.prime Module

```
// module-info.java
module jdojo.prime {
    exports com.jdojo.prime;
    uses com.jdojo.prime.PrimeChecker;
}
```

You need to use a `uses` statement with the fully qualified name of the PrimeChecker interface because the code in this module will use the ServiceLoader class to load the service providers for this interface. You are not done with the declaration of the `jdojo.prime` module yet. You will add a default service provider to this module in the next section.

Defining Service Providers

In the next sections, you will create three service providers for the PrimeChecker service interface. The first service provider will be your default prime checker service provider. You will package it with the jdojo.prime module. You will call the second service provider as a *faster prime checker provider*. You will call the third service provider as the *probable prime checker provider*. Later, you will create a client to test the service. You will have a choice to use one of these service providers or all of them.

These service providers will implement algorithms to check whether a given number is a prime. It will be helpful for you to understand the definition of a prime number. A positive integer that is not divisible without a remainder unless you divide it by 1 or itself, is called a prime. 1 is not a prime. A few examples of primes are 2, 3, 5, 7, and 11.

Defining a Default Prime Service Provider

In this section, you will define a default service provider for the PrimeChecker service. Defining a service provider for a service is achieved simply by creating a class that implements the service interface. For our example, you will be creating a class named GenericPrimeChecker that implements the PrimeChecker interface and will contain a provider constructor.

This service provider will be defined in the same module, jdojo.prime, which also contains your service interface. Listing 7-3 contains the complete code for a class named GenericPrimeChecker. It implements the PrimeChecker interface, and hence its instances can be used as a service provider. Notice that I have placed this class in the com.jdojo.prime.impl package, just to keep the public interface and private implementation separate. The isPrime() method of the class checks whether the specified parameter is a prime. The implementation of this method is not optimal. The next service provides a better implementation.

Listing 7-3. A Service Implementation Class for the PrimeChecker Service Interface

```
// GenericPrimeChecker.java
package com.jdojo.prime.impl;
import com.jdojo.prime.PrimeChecker;
```

```java
public class GenericPrimeChecker implements PrimeChecker {
    @Override
    public boolean isPrime(long n) {
        if (n <= 1) {
            return false;
        }
        if (n == 2) {
            return true;
        }
        if (n % 2 == 0) {
            return false;
        }
        for (long i = 3; i < n; i += 2) {
            if (n % i == 0) {
                return false;
            }
        }
        return true;
    }
}
```

To make the GenericPrimeChecker class available to the ServiceLoader class as a
service provider for the PrimeChecker service interface, you need to include a provides
statement in the jdojo.prime module's declaration. Listing 7-4 contains the modified
version of the jdojo.prime module's declaration.

Listing 7-4. The Modified Declaration of the jdojo.prime Module

```java
// module-info.java
module jdojo.prime {
    exports com.jdojo.prime;
    uses com.jdojo.prime.PrimeChecker;
    provides com.jdojo.prime.PrimeChecker
        with com.jdojo.prime.impl.GenericPrimeChecker;
}
```

The `provides` statement specifies that this module provides an implementation for the `PrimeChecker` interface, and its `with` clause specifies the name of the implementation class. The implementation class must fulfill the following conditions:

- It must be a public concrete class or a public interface. It can be a top-level or nested static class. It cannot be an inner class or an `abstract` class.

- It must provide either the provider constructor or the provider method. You have a pubic no-args constructor, which serves as the provider constructor. This constructor is used by the `ServiceLoader` class to instantiate the service provider using reflection.

- An instance of the implementation class must be assignment compatible with the service provider interface.

If any of these conditions are not met, a compile-time error occurs. Note that you do not need to export the `com.jdojo.prime.impl` package that contains the service implementation class because no client is supposed to directly depend on a service implementation. Clients need to reference only the service interface, not any specific service implementation classes. The `ServiceLoader` class can access and instantiate the implementation class without the package containing the service implementation being exported by the module.

Note   If a module uses a `provides` statement, the specified service Interface may be in the current module or another accessible module. The service implementation class/interface specified in the `with` clause must be defined in the current module.

That's all you have for this module. Compile and package this module as a modular JAR. At this point, there is nothing to test.

Defining a Faster Prime Service Provider

In this section, you will define another service provider for the PrimeChecker service interface. Let's call this a *faster* service provider because you will implement a faster algorithm to check for a prime. This service provider will be defined in a separate module named jdojo.prime.faster, and the service implementation class is called FasterPrimeChecker.

Listing 7-5 contains the module declaration, which is similar to the one we had for the jdojo.prime module. This time, only the class name in the with clause has changed.

Listing 7-5. The Module Declaration for the com.jdojo.prime.faster Module

```
// module-info.java
module jdojo.prime {
    exports com.jdojo.prime;
    uses com.jdojo.prime.PrimeChecker;
    provides com.jdojo.prime.PrimeChecker
        with com.jdojo.prime.impl.GenericPrimeChecker;
}
```

The FasterPrimeChecker class will need to implement the PrimeChecker interface, which is in the jdojo.prime module. The requires statement is needed to read the jdojo.prime module.

Listing 7-6 contains the code for the FasterPrimeChecker class whose isPrime() method executes faster than the isPrime() method of the GenericPrimeChecker class. This time, the method loops through all the odd numbers starting at 3 and ending at the square root of the number being tested for a prime.

Listing 7-6. An Implementation for the PrimeChecker Service Interface

```
// FasterPrimeChecker.java
package com.jdojo.prime.faster;
import com.jdojo.prime.PrimeChecker;
public class FasterPrimeChecker implements PrimeChecker {
    // No provider constructor
    private FasterPrimeChecker() {
        // No code
    }
    // Define a provider method
    public static FasterPrimeChecker provider() {
        return new FasterPrimeChecker();
    }
```

```
@Override
public boolean isPrime(long n) {
    if (n <= 1) {
        return false;
    }
    if (n == 2) {
        return true;
    }
    if (n % 2 == 0) {
        return false;
    }
    long limit = (long) Math.sqrt(n);
    for (long i = 3; i <= limit; i += 2) {
        if (n % i == 0) {
            return false;
        }
    }
    return true;
}
}
```

Note the difference between the GenericPrimeChecker and FasterPrimeChecker classes, as shown in Listings 7-3 and 7-6. The GenericPrimeChecker class contains a default constructor that serves as the provider constructor. It does not contain the provider method. The FasterPrimeChecker class makes the no-args constructor private, which does not qualify the constructor to be the provider constructor. The FasterPrimeChecker class provides the provider method instead, which is declared as follows:

```
public static FasterPrimeChecker provider() { /*...*/ }
```

When the ServiceLoader class needs to instantiate the faster prime service, it will call this method. The method is very simple—it creates and returns an object of the FasterPrimeChecker class.

That's all you need for this module at this time. To compile this module, the jdojo. prime module needs to be in the module path. Compile and package this module as a modular JAR. At this point, there is nothing to test.

Defining a Probable Prime Service Provider

In this section, I show you how to use a Java interface as a service implementation. You will define another service provider for the PrimeChecker service interface. Let's call this a *probable* prime service provider because it tells you that a number is probably a prime. This service provider will be defined in a separate module named jdojo.prime. probable, and the service implementation interface is called ProbablePrimeChecker.

The service is about checking for a prime number. The java.math.BigInteger class contains a method named isProbablePrime(int certainty). If the method returns true, the number may be a prime. If the method returns false, the number is certainly not a prime. The certainty parameter determines the degree to which the method makes sure the number is prime before returning true. The higher the value of the certainty parameter, the higher the cost this method incurs and the higher the probability that the number is a prime when the method returns true.

Listing 7-7 contains the module declaration, which is similar to the ones we had before for the jdojo.prime.faster module. This time, only the class/ interface name in the with clause has changed. Listing 7-8 contains the code for the ProbablePrimeChecker class.

Listing 7-7. The Module Declaration for the com.jdojo.prime.probable Module

```
// module-info.java
module jdojo.prime.probable {
    requires jdojo.prime;
    provides com.jdojo.prime.PrimeChecker
        with com.jdojo.prime.probable.ProbablePrimeChecker;
}
```

Listing 7-8. An Implementation Interface for the PrimeChecker Service Interface

```
// ProbablePrimeChecker.java
package com.jdojo.prime.probable;
import com.jdojo.prime.PrimeChecker;
import java.math.BigInteger;
public interface ProbablePrimeChecker
        extends PrimeChecker {
    // A provider method
```

```
public static ProbablePrimeChecker provider() {
    int certainty = 1000;
    ProbablePrimeChecker checker = n ->
        BigInteger.valueOf(n).
        isProbablePrime(certainty);
    return checker;
    }
}
```

The ProbablePrimeChecker interface extends the PrimeChecker interface and consists of only one method, which is the provider method:

```
public static ProbablePrimeChecker provider() {/*...*/}
```

When the ServiceLoader class needs to instantiate the probable prime service, it will call this method. The method is very simple—it creates and returns an instance of the ProbablePrimeChecker interface. It uses a lambda expression to create the provider. The isPrime() method uses the BigInteger class to check whether the number is a probable prime.

Listing 7-9 contains an alternative declaration of the ProbablePrimeChecker interface as a service provider.

Listing 7-9. An Alternative Declaration of the ProbablePrimeChecker Interface

```
// ProbablePrimeChecker.java
package com.jdojo.prime.probable;
import com.jdojo.prime.PrimeChecker;
import java.math.BigInteger;
public interface ProbablePrimeChecker {
    // A provider method
    public static PrimeChecker provider() {
        int certainty = 1000;
        PrimeChecker checker = n ->
            BigInteger.valueOf(n).
            isProbablePrime(certainty);
        return checker;
    }
}
```

This time, the interface does not extend the PrimeChecker interface. To be a service implementation, its provider method must return an instance of the service interface (the PrimeChecker interface) or its subtype. By declaring the return type of the provider method as PrimeChecker, you have fulfilled this requirement. Declaring the ProbablePrimeChecker interface, as shown in Listing 7-9, has one drawback that you cannot find this service provider by its class name, com.jdojo.probable. ProbablePrimeChecker, using the stream() method of the ServiceLoader class without instantiating the service provider. The type() method of ServiceLoader.Provider will return the Class reference of the com.jdojo.prime.PrimeChecker interface, which is the return type of the provider() method. I use the declaration of this interface as shown in Listing 7-8.

That's all you have for this module. To compile this module, you need to add the jdojo.prime module to the module path. Compile and package this module as a modular JAR. At this point, there is nothing to test.

Testing the Prime Service

In this section, you test the service by creating a client application, which will be defined in a separate module named jdojo.prime.client. Listing 7-10 contains the module declaration.

Listing 7-10. The Declaration of the jdojo.prime.client Module

```
// module-info.java
module jdojo.prime.client {
    requires jdojo.prime;
}
```

The client module needs to know only about the service interface. In this case, the jdojo.prime module defines the service interface. Therefore, the client module reads the service interface module and nothing else. In the real world, the client module will be much more complex than this, and it may read other modules as well. Figure 7-3 shows the module graph for the jdojo.prime.client module.

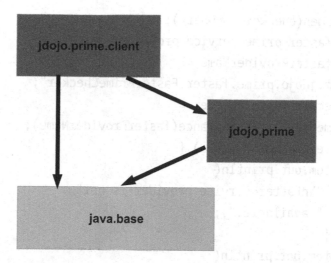

Figure 7-3. *The module graph for the com.jdojo.prime.client module*

Listing 7-11 contains the code for the client that uses the PrimeChecker service.

Listing 7-11. A Main Class to Test the PrimeChecker Service

```java
// Main.java
package com.jdojo.prime.client;
import com.jdojo.prime.PrimeChecker;
public class Main {
    public static void main(String[] args) {
        // Numbers to be checked for prime
        long[] numbers = {3, 4, 121, 977};
        // Use the default service provider
        PrimeChecker checker = PrimeChecker.newInstance();
        System.out.println(
            "Using default service provider:");
```

```
        checkPrimes(checker, numbers);
        // Try faster prime service provider
        String fasterProviderName =
            "com.jdojo.prime.faster.FasterPrimeChecker";
        PrimeChecker fasterChecker =
            PrimeChecker.newInstance(fasterProviderName);
        if (fasterChecker == null) {
            System.out.println(
                "\nFaster service provider is not" +
                " available.");
        } else {
            System.out.println(
                "\h nUsing faster service provider:");
            checkPrimes(fasterChecker, numbers);
        }
        // Try probable prime service provider
        String probableProviderName =
            "com.jdojo.prime.probable.ProbablePrimeChecker";
        PrimeChecker probableChecker =
            PrimeChecker.newInstance(probableProviderName);
        if (probableChecker == null) {
            System.out.println(
                "\nProbable service provider is not" +
                " available.");
        } else {
            System.out.println(
                "\nUsing probable service provider:");
            checkPrimes(probableChecker, numbers);
        }
    }
    public static void checkPrimes(PrimeChecker checker,
            long... numbers) {
        for (long n : numbers) {
            if (checker.isPrime(n)) {
                System.out.printf(
                    "%d is a prime.%n", n);
```

```
        } else {
            System.out.printf(
                "%d is not a prime.%n", n);
        }
    }
  }
}
```

The checkPrimes() method takes a PrimeChecker instance and varargs long numbers. It uses the PrimeChecker to check whether numbers are prime and prints corresponding messages. The main() method retrieves the default PrimeChecker service provider instance and the instances of the faster and probable service providers. It uses all three service providers' instances to check the same set of numbers to be prime. Compile and package the module's code. Run the Main class with only two modules, jdojo.prime and jdojo.prime.client, in the module path, as follows (remove line break and spaces after ";"):

```
C:\Java9LanguageFeatures>java ^
--module-path dist\jdojo.prime.jar;
            dist\jdojo.prime.client.jar ^
--module jdojo.prime.client/com.jdojo.prime.client.Main

Using default service provider:
3 is a prime.
4 is not a prime.
121 is not a prime.
977 is a prime.
Faster service provider is not available.
Probable service provider is not available.
```

There was only one service provider in the module path, which was the default service provider packaged with the jdojo.prime module. Therefore, attempts to retrieve the faster and probable service providers failed. This is evident from the output.

Note   When the module system encounters a `uses` statement in a module declaration in a resolved module, it scans the module path to find all modules that contain `provides` statements specifying implementations for the service interface specified in the `uses` statement. In this sense, a `uses` statement in a module indicates an indirect optional dependency on other modules, which is resolved automatically for you. Therefore, to use a service provider, just drop the service provider module on the module path; it will be discovered and loaded by the `ServiceLoader` class.

Let's run the same command by also including the `jdojo.prime.faster` module to the module path as follows (remove line break and spaces after ";"):

```
C:\Java9LanguageFeatures>java ^
--module-path dist\jdojo.prime.jar;
    dist\jdojo.prime.client.jar;
    dist\jdojo.prime.faster.jar ^
--module jdojo.prime.client/com.jdojo.prime.client.Main

Using default service provider:
3 is a prime.
4 is not a prime.
121 is not a prime.
977 is a prime.
Using faster service provider:
3 is a prime.
4 is not a prime.
121 is not a prime.
977 is a prime.
Probable service provider is not available.
```

This time, you had two service providers on the module path, and both were found by the runtime, which is evident from the output.

The following command includes the `jdojo.prime`, `jdojo.prime.faster`, and `jdojo.prime.probable` modules on the module path. All three service providers will be found, which is evident from the output (remove line break and spaces after ";"):

```
C:\Java9LanguageFeatures>java ^
--module-path dist\jdojo.prime.jar;
    dist\jdojo.prime.client.jar;
    dist\jdojo.prime.faster.jar;
    dist\jdojo.prime.probable.jar ^
--module jdojo.prime.client/com.jdojo.prime.client.Main

Using default service provider:
3 is a prime.
4 is not a prime.
121 is not a prime.
977 is a prime.
Using faster service provider:
3 is a prime.
4 is not a prime.
121 is not a prime.
977 is a prime.
Using probable service provider:
3 is a prime.
4 is not a prime.
121 is not a prime.
977 is a prime.
```

This is how modules are resolved in this case:

- The main class is in the jdojo.prime.client module, so this module is the root module, and it is resolved first.

- The jdojo.prime.client module reads the jdojo.prime module, so the jdojo.prime module is resolved.

- The jdojo.prime module contains a uses statement that specifies com.jdojo.prime.PrimeChecker as the service interface type. The runtime scans all modules in the module path to check if any of them contains a provides statement specifying the same service interface. It finds the jdojo.prime, jdojo.prime.faster, and jdojo.prime. probable modules containing such provides statements. The jdojo. prime module was already resolved in the previous step. The jdojo. prime.faster and jdojo.probable modules are resolved at this time.

551

You can see the module resolution process using the -show-module-resolution command-line option as follows. A partial output is shown (remove line break and spaces after ";"):

```
C:\Java9LanguageFeatures>java ^
--module-path dist\jdojo.prime.jar;
    dist\jdojo.prime.client.jar;
    dist\jdojo.prime.faster.jar;
    dist\jdojo.prime.probable.jar ^
--show-module-resolution ^
--module jdojo.prime.client/com.jdojo.prime.client.Main

root jdojo.prime.client ...
jdojo.prime.client requires jdojo.prime ...
jdojo.prime binds jdojo.prime.probable ...
jdojo.prime binds jdojo.prime.faster...
...
```

Testing Prime Service in Legacy Mode

Not all applications will be migrated to use modules. Your modular JARs for the prime service may be used along with other JARs on the class path. Suppose you placed all modular JARs for the prime service in the C:\Java9LanguageFeatures\lib directory. Run the com.jdojo.prime.client.Main class by placing the four modular JARs on the class path using the following command (remove line break and spaces after ";"):

```
C:\Java9Revealed>java ^
--class-path lib\com.jdojo.prime.jar;
    lib\com.jdojo.prime.client.jar;
    lib\com.jdojo.prime.faster.jar;
    lib\com.jdojo.prime.generic.jar;
    lib\com.jdojo.prime.probable.jar ^
com.jdojo.prime.client.Main
```

```
Using default service provider:
Exception in thread "main" java.lang.NullPointerException
        at com.jdojo.prime.client.Main.checkPrimes
            (Main.java:39)
        at com.jdojo.prime.client.Main.main
            (Main.java:14)
```

The output indicates that using the legacy mode—the pre-JDK9 mode by placing all modular JARs on the class path—did not find any of the service providers. In legacy mode, the service provider discovery mechanism is different. The ServiceLoader class scans all JARs on the class path looking for files in the META-INF/services directory. The file name is the fully qualified service interface name. The file path looks like this:

```
META-INF/services/<service-interface>
```

The content of this file is the list of the fully qualified names of the service provider implementation classes/interfaces. Each class name needs to be on a separate line. You can use a single-line comment in the file. Text on a line starting from a # character is considered a comment.

The service interface name is com.jdojo.prime.PrimeChecker, so the modular JARs for the three service providers will have a file named com.jdojo.prime.PrimeChecker with the following path:

```
META-INF/services/com.jdojo.prime.PrimeChecker
```

You need to add the META-INF/services directory to the root of the source code directory. If you are using an IDE such as NetBeans, the IDE will take care of packaging the file for you. Listings 7-12 to 7-14 contain the contents of this file for the modular JARs for the three prime service provider modules.

Listing 7-12. Contents of the META-INF/services/com.jdojo.prime.
PrimeChecker File in the Modular JAR for the com.jdojo.prime Module

```
# The generic service provider implementation class name
com.jdojo.prime.impl.GenericPrimeChecker
```

Listing 7-13. Contents of the META-INF/services/com.jdojo.prime.
PrimeChecker File in the Modular JAR for the com.jdojo.prime.faster Module

```
# The faster service provider implementation class name
com.jdojo.prime.faster.FasterPrimeChecker
```

Listing 7-14. Contents of the META-INF/services/com.jdojo.prime.
PrimeChecker File in the Modular JAR for the com.jdojo.prime.probable Module

```
# The probable service provider implementation interface
# name
com.jdojo.prime.probable.ProbablePrimeChecker
```

Recompile and repackage the modular JARs for the generic and faster prime checker
service providers. Run the following command (remove line break and spaces after ";"):

```
C:\Java9LanguageFeatures>java ^
--class-path lib\jdojo.prime.jar;
    lib\jdojo.prime.client.jar;
    lib\jdojo.prime.faster.jar;
    lib\jdojo.prime.probable.jar ^
com.jdojo.prime.client.Main

Using default service provider:
3 is a prime.
4 is not a prime.
121 is not a prime.
977 is a prime.
Exception in thread "main"
    java.util.ServiceConfigurationError:
    com.jdojo.prime.
PrimeChecker:
com.jdojo.prime.faster.FasterPrimeChecker
Unable to get public no-arg  constructor
...
```

```
Caused by: java.lang.NoSuchMethodException:
  com.jdojo.prime.faster.
FasterPrimeChecker.<init>()
...
```

A partial output is shown. The output indicates a runtime exception when the ServiceLoader class tries to instantiate the faster prime service provider. You will get the same error when an attempt is made to instantiate the probable prime service provider. Adding information about a service in the META-INF/services directory is the legacy way of implementing services. For backward compatibility, the service implementation must be a class with a public no-args constructor. Recall that you provided a provider constructor only for the GenericPrimeChecker class. Therefore, the default prime checker service provider works and the other two do not work in legacy mode. You can add a provider constructor to the FasterPrimeChecker class to make it work. However, it is not possible to add a provider constructor to an interface, and the ProbablePrimeChecker will not work in the class path mode. You must load it from an explicit module to make it work.

Summary

A specific functionality provided by an application (or a library) is known as a *service*. Applications and libraries providing implementations of a service are known as service providers. Applications using the service provided by those service providers are called *service consumers* or *clients*.

In Java, a *service* is defined by a set of interfaces and classes. The service contains an interface or an abstract class that defines the functionality provided by the service, and it is known as the *service provider interface, service interface,* or *service type*. A specific implementation of a service interface is known as a *service provider*. There can be multiple service providers for a single service interface. A service provider may be a class or an interface.

The JDK contains a java.util.ServiceLoader<S> class whose sole purpose is to discover and load service providers of type S at runtime for a specified service interface. If a JAR (modular or non-modular) containing a service provider is placed on the class path, the ServiceLoader class uses the META-INF/services directory to find the service providers. The name of the file in this directory should be the same as the fully qualified name of the service interface. The file contains the fully qualified name of the service provider implementation classes—one class name per line. The file can use a # character as the start of single-line comments. The ServiceLoader class scans all META-INF/ services directories on the class path to discover service providers.

In a modularized environment, the META-INF/services directory is not needed. A module that uses the ServiceLoader class to discover and load the service providers needs to specify the service interface using a uses statement. The service interface specified in a uses statement may be declared in the current module or any module accessible to the current module. You can use the iterator() method of the ServiceLoader class to iterate over all service providers. The stream() method provides a stream of elements that are instances of the ServiceLoader.Provider interface. You can use the stream to filter and select a specific type of providers based on the provider's class names without having to instantiate all providers.

A module that contains a service provider needs to specify the service interface and its implementation class using a provides statement. The implementation class must be declared in the current module.

Exercises

Exercise 1

What are services, service interfaces, and service providers in Java?

Exercise 2

Write the declaration for a module named M, which loads service providers of a service interface whose fully qualified name is p.S.

Exercise 3

Write the declaration for a module named N, which provides the implementation of a service interface p.S. The fully qualified name of the service implementation class is q.C.

Exercise 4

How many types of services can a module load using the ServiceLoader class?

Exercise 5

How many service implementations of a service type can a module provide?

Exercise 6

When do you use the java.util.ServiceLoader<S> class?

Exercise 7

When do you use the nested java.util.ServiceLoader.Provider<S> interface?

Exercise 8

You can discover and load service providers of a specific type using the `iterator()` method or the `stream()` method of the `ServiceLoader` class. Which method has better performance when you have to select a service provider based on the name of the service provider implementation class or interface?

Exercise 9

What are the provider constructor and provider method? If both are available, which one is used when services are loaded from modular JARs?

Exercise 10

What steps would you take while defining a service packaged in a modular JAR that should also work when placed in the class path?

CHAPTER 8

Network Programming

In this chapter, you will learn:

- What network programming is
- What the network protocol suite is
- What an IP address is and what the different IP addressing schemes are
- Special IP addresses and their uses
- What port numbers are and how they are used
- Using TCP and UDP client and server sockets for communication between remote computers
- The definitions of URI, URL, and URN and how to represent them in Java programs
- How to use non-blocking sockets
- How to use asynchronous socket channels
- Datagram-oriented socket channels and multicast datagram channels

All example programs in this chapter are members of a `jdojo.net` module, as declared in Listing 8-1.

Listing 8-1. The Declaration of a jdojo.net Module

```
// module-info.java
module jdojo.net {
    exports com.jdojo.net;
}
```

© Kishori Sharan, Peter Späth 2021
K. Sharan and P. Späth, *More Java 17*, https://doi.org/10.1007/978-1-4842-7135-3_8

The first few sections in this chapter are intended to give a quick overview of basics related to network technologies for those readers who do not have a computer science background. If you understand terms like IP address, port number, and network protocol suites, you may skip these sections and start reading from the "Socket API and Client-Server Paradigm" section.

What Is Network Programming?

A network is a group of two or more computers or other types of electronic devices such as printers that are linked together with a goal to share information. Each device linked to a network is called a *node*. A computer that is linked to a network is called a *host*. Network programming in Java involves writing Java programs that facilitate the exchange of information between processes running on different computers on the network.

Java makes it easy to write network programs. Sending a message to a process running on another computer is as simple as writing data to a local file system. Similarly, receiving a message that was sent from a process running in another computer is as simple as reading data from a local file system. Most of the programs in this chapter involve reading and writing data over the network, and they are similar to file I/O. You learn about a few new classes in this chapter that facilitate the communication between two computers on a network.

You do not need to have advanced level knowledge of networking technologies to understand or write Java programs in this chapter. This chapter covers high-level details of a few things that are involved in network communication.

A network can be categorized based on different criteria. Based on the geographical area that a network is spread over, it is categorized as follows:

- Local Area Network (LAN): It covers a small area such as a building or a block of buildings.

- Campus Area Network (CAN): It covers a campus such as a university campus, interconnecting multiple LANs within that campus.

- Metropolitan Area Network (MAN): It covers more geographical area than a LAN. Usually, it covers a city.

- Wide Area Network (WAN): It covers a larger geographical area such as a region of a country or multiple regions in different countries in the world.

When two or more networks are connected using routers (also known as gateways), it is called *internetworking*, and the resulting combined network is called an *internetwork*, in short, *internet* (note the lowercase i in *internet*). The global internetwork, which encompasses all networks in the world connected together, is referred to as the *Internet* (note the uppercase I in Internet).

Based on the topology (the arrangement of nodes in a network), a network may be categorized as *star, tree, ring, bus, hybrid,* etc.

Based on the technology a network uses to transmit the data, it can be categorized as *Ethernet, LocalTalk, Fiber Distributed Data Interface (FDDI), Token Ring, Asynchronous Transfer Mode (ATM),* etc.

I do not cover any details about the different kinds of networks. Refer to any standard textbook on networks to learn more about networks and network technologies in detail.

Communication between two processes on a computer is simple, and it is achieved using interprocess communication as defined by the operating system. It is a very tedious task when two processes running on two different computers on an internet need to communicate. You need to consider many aspects of the communication before such two processes may start communicating. Some of the points that you need to consider are as follows:

- The two computers may be using different technologies such as different operating systems, different hardware, etc.

- They may be on two different networks that use different network technologies.

- They may be separated by many other networks, which may be using different technologies. That is, two computers are not on two networks that are interconnected directly. You need to consider not just two networks, but all networks that the data from one computer must pass to reach another computer.

- They may be a few miles apart or on other sides of the globe. How do you transmit the information efficiently without worrying about the distance between the two computers?

- One computer may not understand the information sent by the other computer.

- The information sent over a network may be duplicated, delayed, or lost. How should the receiver and the sender handle these abnormal situations?

Simply put, two computers on a network communicate using messages (sequences of 0s and 1s).

There must be well-defined rules to handle the previously mentioned issues (and many more). The set of rules to handle a specific task is known as a *protocol*. Many types of tasks are involved in handling network communication. There is a protocol defined to handle each specific task. There is a stack of protocols (also called *protocol suite*) that are used together to handle a network communication.

Network Protocol Suite

Modern networks are called *packet switching networks* because they transmit data in chunks called *packets*. Each packet is transmitted independent of other packets. This makes it easy to transmit the packets from the same computer to the same destination using different routes. However, it may become a problem if a computer sends two packets to a remote computer and the second packet arrives before the first one. For this reason, each packet also has a packet number along with its destination address. There are rules to rearrange the out-of-order arrival of the packets at the destination computer. The following discussion attempts to explain some of the mechanisms that are used to handle packets in a network communication.

Figure 8-1 shows a layered protocol suite called the *Internet Reference Model* or *TCP/IP Layering Model*. This is the most widely used protocol suite. Each layer in the model performs a well-defined task. The main advantage of having a layered protocol model is that any layer can be changed without affecting others. A new protocol can be added to any layer without changing other layers.

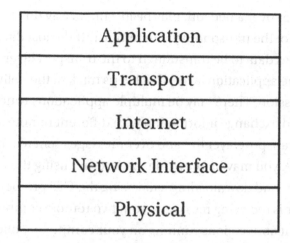

Figure 8-1. *The Internet protocol suite showing its five protocol layers*

Each layer knows about only the layer immediately above and below it. Each layer has two interfaces—one for the layer above it and one for the layer below it. For example, the transport layer has interfaces to the application layer and internet layer. That is, the transport layer knows how to communicate only with the application layer and the internet layer. It knows nothing about the network interface layer or the physical layer.

A user application such as a Java program uses the application layer to communicate to a remote application. The user application has to specify the protocol that it wants to use to communicate with the remote application. A protocol in an application layer defines the rules for formatting messages and associating the meaning to the information contained in the messages such as the message type, describing whether it is a request or a response, etc. After the application layer formats the message, it hands over the message to the transport layer. The examples of protocols in an application layer are the Hypertext Transfer Protocol (HTTP), File Transfer Protocol (FTP), Gopher, Telecommunication Network (Telnet), Simple Mail Transfer Protocol (SMTP), and Network News Transfer Protocol (NNTP).

The transport layer protocol handles the ways messages are transported from one application on one computer to another application on the remote computer. It controls the data flow, error handling during data transmission, and connections between two applications. For example, a user application may hand over a very large chunk of data to the transport layer to transmit to a remote application. The remote computer may not be able to handle that large amount of data at once. It is the responsibility of the transport layer to pass a suitable amount of data at a time to the remote computer, so the remote application can handle the data according to its capacity. The data passed to the remote computer over a network may be lost on its way due to various reasons. It is the responsibility of the transport layer to retransmit the lost data. Note that the application layer passes data to be transmitted to the transport layer only once. It is the transport layer (not the application layer) that keeps track of the delivered and the lost data during a transmission. There may be multiple applications running, all of which use different protocols and exchange information with different remote applications. It is the responsibility of the transport layer to hand over messages sent to a remote application correctly. For example, you may be browsing the Internet using the HTTP protocol from one remote web server and downloading a file using the FTP protocol from another FTP server. Your computer is receiving messages from two remote computers, and they are meant for two different applications running on your computer—one web browser to receive HTTP data and one FTP application to receive FTP data. It is the responsibility of the transport layer to pass the incoming data to the appropriate application. You can see how different layers of the protocol suite play different roles in data transmission over the network. Depending on the transport layer protocol being used, the transport layer adds relevant information to the message and passes it to the next layer, which is the internet layer. The examples of protocols used in the transport layer are the Transmission Control Protocol (TCP), User Datagram Protocol (UDP), and Stream Control Transmission Protocol (SCTP).

The internet layer accepts the messages from the transport layer and prepares a packet suitable for sending over the internet. It includes the Internet Protocol (IP). The packet prepared by the IP is also known as an IP datagram. It consists of a header and a data area, apart from other pieces of information. The header contains the sender's IP address, destination IP address, time to live (TTL, which is an integer), a header checksum, and many other pieces of information specified in the protocol. The IP prepares the message into datagrams, which are ready to be transmitted over the internet. The TTL in the IP datagram header specifies how long, in terms of the number of routers, an IP datagram can keep traveling before it needs to be discarded. Its size is one byte and its value could be between 1 and 255. When an IP datagram reaches a router in its route to the destination, the router decrements the TTL value by one. If the decremented value is zero, the router discards the datagram and sends an error message back to the sender using the Internet Control Message Protocol (ICMP). If the TTL value is still a positive number, the router forwards the datagram to the next router. The IP uses an address scheme, which assigns a unique address to each computer. The address is called an IP address. I discuss the IP addressing scheme in detail in the next section.

The internet layer hands over the IP datagram to the next layer, which is the network interface layer. The examples of protocols in an internet layer are the Internet Protocol (IP), Internet Control Message Protocol (ICMP), Internet Group Management Protocol (IGMP), and Internet Protocol Security (IPsec).

The network interface layer prepares a packet to be transmitted on the network. The packet is called a *frame*. The network interface layer sits just on top of the physical layer, which involves the hardware. Note that the IP layer uses the IP address to identify the destination on a network. An IP address is a virtual address, which is completely maintained in software. The hardware is unaware of the IP address, and it does not know how to transmit a frame using an IP address. The hardware must be given the hardware address, also called the *Media Access Control* (MAC) address, of the destination that it needs to transmit the frame to. This layer resolves the destination hardware address from the IP address and places it in the frame header. It hands over the frame to the physical layer. The examples of protocols in a network interface layer are the Open Shortest Path First (OSPF), Point-to-Point Protocol (PPP), Point-to-Point Tunneling Protocol (PPTP), and Layer 2 Tunneling Protocol (L2TP).

The physical layer consists of the hardware. It is responsible for converting the bits of information into signals and transmitting the signal over the wire.

Note   Packet is a generic term that is used to mean an independent chunk of data in network programming. Each layer of the protocol also uses a specific term to mean the packet it deals with. For example, a packet is called a segment in the TCP layer; it is called a datagram in the IP layer; it is called a frame in the network interface and physical layers. Each layer adds a header (sometimes also a trailer) to the packet it receives from the layer before it while preparing the packet to be transmitted over the network. Each layer performs the reverse action when it receives a packet from the layer below it. It removes the header from the packet; performs some actions, if needed; and hands over the packet to the layer above it.

When a packet sent by an application reaches the remote computer, it has to pass through the same layer of protocols in the reverse order. Each layer will remove its header, perform some actions, and pass the packet to the layer immediately above it. Finally, the packet reaches the remote application in the same format it started from the application on the sender's computer. Figure 8-2 shows the transmission of packets from the sender and the receiver computer. P1, P2, P3, and P4 are the packets in different formats of the same data. A protocol layer at a destination receives the same packet from the layer immediately below it, which the same protocol layer had passed to the layer immediately below it on the sender's computer.

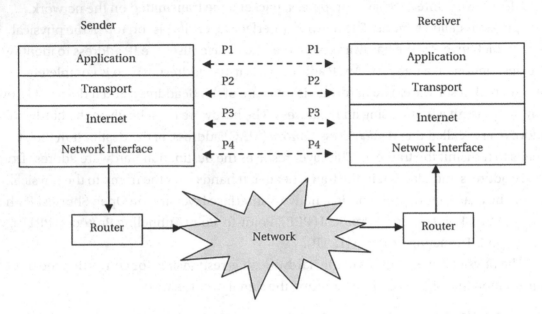

Figure 8-2. *Transmission of packets through the protocol layers on the sender and receiver computers*

IP Addressing Scheme

IP uses a unique address, called an IP address, to route an IP datagram to the destination. An IP address uniquely identifies a connection between a computer and a router. Normally, it is understood that an IP address identifies a computer. However, it should be emphasized that it identifies a connection between a computer and a router, not just a computer. A router is also assigned an IP address. A computer can be connected to multiple networks using multiple routers, and each connection between the computer and the router will have a unique IP address. In such cases, the computer will be assigned multiple IP addresses, and the computer is known as *multihomed*. Multihoming increases the availability of the network connection to a computer. If one network connection fails, the computer can use other available network connections.

An IP address contains two parts—a network identifier (I call it a prefix) and a host identifier (I call it a suffix). The prefix identifies a network on the Internet uniquely; the suffix identifies a host uniquely within that network. It is possible for two hosts to have IP addresses with the same suffix as long as they have a different prefix.

There are two versions of an Internet Protocol—IPv4 (or simply IP) and IPv6, where v4 and v6 stand for version 4 and version 6. IPv6 is also known as the Internet Protocol next generation (IPng). Note that there is no IPv5. When IP was in its full swing of popularity, it was at version 4. Before IPng was assigned a version number 6, version 5 was already assigned to another protocol called the Internet Stream Protocol (ST).

Both IPv4 and IPv6 use an IP address to identify a host on a network. However, the addressing schemes in the two versions differ significantly. The next two sections explain the addressing schemes used by IPv4 and IPv6.

Since an IP address must be unique, its assignment is controlled by an organization called the *Internet Assigned Numbers Authority* (IANA). IANA assigns a unique address to each network that belongs to an organization. The organization uses the network address and a unique number to form a unique IP address for each host on the network. IANA divides the IP address allocations to five Regional Internet Registry (RIR) organizations, which allocate IP addresses in specific regions as listed in Table 8-1. You can find more information on how to get a network address in your area from IANA at www.iana.com.

Table 8-1. *Regional Internet Registries for Allocating Network IP Addresses*

Regional Internet Registry Organization Name	Regions Covered
African Network Information Centre (AfriNIC)	Africa Region
Asia/Pacific Network Information Centre (APNIC)	Asia-Pacific Region
American Registry for Internet Numbers (ARIN)	North America Region
Latin American and Caribbean Internet Address Registry (LACNIC)	Latin America and some Caribbean Islands
Réseaux IP Européens Network Coordination Centre (RIPE NCC)	Europe, the Middle East, and Central Asia

IPv4 Addressing Scheme

IPv4 (or simply IP) uses a 32-bit number to represent an IP address. An IP address contains two parts—a prefix and a suffix. The prefix identifies a network, and the suffix identifies a host on the network, as shown in Figure 8-3.

```
0 1 2 3 4 5 6 7 8 9 10 ... 21 22 23 24 25 26 27 28 29 30 31
              Prefix            |         Suffix
|                               |                           |
```

Figure 8-3. *IPv4 addressing scheme*

It is not easy for humans to remember a 32-bit number in binary format. IPv4 allows you to work with an alternate form using four decimal numbers. Each decimal number is in the range from 0 to 255. Programs take care of converting decimal numbers into a 32-bit binary number that will be used by the computer. The decimal number format of IPv4 is called a dotted decimal format because a dot is used to separate two decimal numbers. Each decimal number represents the value contained in 8 bits of the 32-bit number. For example, an IPv4 address of 1100 0000 1010 1000 0000 0001 1110 0111 in the binary format can be represented as 192.168.1.231 in the dotted decimal format. The process of converting binary IPv4 to its decimal equivalent is shown in Figure 8-4. In 192.168.1.231, the part 192.168.1 identifies the network address (the prefix), and the part 231 (the suffix) identifies the host on that network.

32-bit Binary Representation	11000000	10101000	00000001	11100111
Decimal Value of Each Octet	192	168	1	231
Parts of IPv4 Address	Prefix			Suffix
Alternate Representation of IPv4	192.168.1.231			

Figure 8-4. *Parts of an IPv4 address in binary and decimal formats*

How do you know that 192.168.1 represents a prefix in an IPv4 address 192.168.1.231? A rule governs the value of a prefix and a suffix in an IPv4.

More precisely, the IPv4 address space is divided in five categories called network classes, named A, B, C, D, and E. A class type defines how many bits of the 32 bits will be used to represent the network address part of an IP address. The leading bit (or bits) in the prefix defines the class of the IP address. This is also known as a *self-identifying* or *classful* IP address because you can tell which class it belongs to by looking at the IP address.

Table 8-2 lists the five network classes and their characteristics in IPv4. The leading bits in an IP address identify the class of the network. For example, if an IP address looks like 0XXX, where XXX is the last 31 bits of the 32 bits, it belongs to the class A network; if an IP address looks like 110XXX, where XXX is the last 29 bits of 32 bits, it belongs to the class C network. There can be only 128 networks of class A type, and each network can have 16777214 hosts. The number of hosts that a class A network can have is very big, and it is very unlikely that a network will have that many hosts. In a class C type of network, the maximum number of hosts that a network can have is limited to 254.

Table 8-2. *Five Classes of IPv4 in the Classful Addressing Scheme*

Network Class	Prefix	Suffix	Leading Bits in Prefix	Number of Networks	Number of Hosts per Network
A	8 bits	24 bits	0	128	16777214
B	16 bits	16 bits	10	16384	65534
C	24 bits	8 bits	110	2097152	254
D	Not defined	Not defined	1110	Not defined	Not defined
E	Not defined	Not defined	1111	Not defined	Not defined

What happens if an organization is assigned a network address from class C and it has only ten hosts to attach to the network? The remaining slots in the IP addresses in that network remain unused. Recall that the host (or suffix) part in an IP address must be unique within the network (the prefix part). On the other hand, if an organization needs to connect 300 computers to a network, it needs to get two class C network addresses because getting a class B network address, which can accommodate 65534 hosts, will again waste a great many IP addresses.

Note that if the number of bits allocated for a suffix is N, the number of hosts that can be used is 2N - 2. Two bit patterns—all 0s and all 1s—cannot be used for a host address. They are used for special purposes. This is the reason a class C network can have a maximum of 254 hosts and not 256. Class D addresses are used as multicast addresses. Class E addresses are reserved.

The fast growth of the Internet and the large number of IP addresses not being used prompted for a new addressing scheme. This scheme is simply based on one criterion—one should be able to use an arbitrary boundary between the prefix and suffix parts of an IP address, instead of predefined boundaries at 8, 16, and 24 bits. This will keep the unused addresses at a minimum. For example, if an organization needs a network number for a network with only 20 hosts, that organization can use only a 27-bit prefix and a 5-bit suffix.

Two terminologies called *subnetting* and *supernetting* are used to describe the situations when some bits from the suffix are used for the prefix and some bits from the prefix are used as the suffix. When bits from the suffix are used as the prefix, essentially, it creates more network addresses at the cost of host addresses. The extra network addresses are called *subnets*. Subnetting is achieved by using a number called a *subnet mask* or an *address mask*. A subnet mask is a 32-bit number that is used to compute the network address from an IP address. Using a subnet mask eliminates the restriction that the class of a network must predefine the network number part of the IP address. A logical AND is performed on the IP address and the subnet mask to compute the network number. In this scheme of addressing, an IP address is always specified with its subnet mask. A forward slash and subnet mask follows an IP address. For example, 140.10.11.9/255.255.0.0 denotes an IP address of 140.10.11.9 with a subnet mask 255.255.0.0. It is possible to use any subnet mask whose four decimal parts range from 0 to 255. In this example, 140.10.11.9 is a class B address. A class B address uses 16 bits for the prefix and 16 bits for the suffix. Let's take 6 bits off the suffix and add it to the prefix. Now, the prefix is 22 bits, and the suffix is only 10 bits. By doing this, you have created additional network numbers at the cost of host numbers. To describe an IP address in this scheme of subnetting, you need to use a subnet mask of 255.255.252.0. If you write an IP address using this subnet mask as 140.10.11.9/255.255.252.0, the network address is computed as 140.10.8.0, like so:

```
IP Address: 10001100 00001010 00001011 00001001
Subnet Mask: 11111111 11111111 11111100 00000000
-------------------------------------------------
Logical AND: 10001100 00001010 00001000 00000000
              (140)     (10)      (8)      (0)
```

Classless Inter-Domain Routing (CIDR) is another IPv4 addressing scheme in which an IPv4 address is specified as four dotted decimal numbers along with another decimal number separated by a forward slash such as 192.168.1.231/24, where the last number

24 denotes the prefix length (or number of bits used for a network number) in the 32-bit IPv4 address. Note that the CIDR addressing scheme lets you define the prefix/suffix boundary at any bits in 32-bit IPv4. By moving the bits from the prefix to the suffix, you can combine multiple networks and increase the number of hosts per network. This is called *supernetting*. You can create supernets as well as subnets using CIDR notation.

Some IP addresses in an IPv4 addressing scheme are reserved for broadcast and multicast IP addresses. I discuss broadcasting and multicasting later in this chapter.

IPv6 Addressing Scheme

IPv6 is a new version of IP, and it is the successor for IPv4. The address space in IPv4 was running out of addresses in the fast-growing Internet world. IPv6 is aimed at providing enough address space, so that every computer in the world may get a unique IP address in the decades to come. Here are some of the main features of IPv6:

- IPv6 uses a 128-bit number for an IP address instead of a 32-bit number used in IPv4.

- It has different header formats for IP packets than IPv4. IPv4 has only one header per datagram, whereas IPv6 has one base header followed by multiple variable-length extension headers per datagram.

- IPv6 supports datagrams of a bigger size than IPv4.

- In IPv4, the routers performed an IP packet fragmentation. In IPv6, the sender host is supposed to perform a packet fragmentation rather than the routers. This means that the host that uses IPv6 must know in advance the path of the maximum transmission unit (MTU) that is the minimum of the maximum packet size allowed by all networks to the destination host. The IP datagram's fragmentation occurs when it has to enter a network that has a lower size transmission capacity than the network the datagram is leaving. In IPv4, the fragmentation is performed by the router, which detects a lower transmission capacity network in the route. Since IPv6 allows only the host to perform the fragmentation, the host must discover the minimum size datagram that can be routed through all possible routes from the source to the destination host.

- IPv6 supports specifying routing information for the datagrams in the headers so that routers can use it to route the datagrams through a specific route. This feature is helpful in delivering time-critical information.

- IPv6 is extensible. Any number of extension headers can be added to an IPv6 datagram, which can be interpreted in a new way.

IPv6 uses a 128-bit IP address. It uses an easy-to-understand notation to represent an IP address in a textual form. The 128 bits are divided into 8 fields of 16 bits each. Each field is written in hexadecimal form and separated by a colon. The following are some examples of IPv6 addresses:

- `F6DC:0:0:4015:0:BA98:C0A8:1E7`

- `F6DC:0:0:7678:0:0:0:A21D`

- `F6DC:0:0:0:0:0:0:A21D`

- `0:0:0:0:0:0:0:1`

It is common to have many fields in an IPv6 address with zero values, especially for all IPv4 addresses. The IPv6 address notation lets you compress contiguous fields of zero values by using two consecutive colons. You can use two colons to suppress contiguous zero value fields only once in an address. The previous IPv6 address may be rewritten using the zero compression technique:

- `F6DC::4015:0:BA98:C0A8:1E7`

- `F6DC:0:0:7678::A21D`

- `F6DC::A21D`

- `::1`

Note that we could suppress only one of the two sets of contiguous zero fields in the second address, `F6DC:0:0:7678::A21D`. Rewriting it as `F6DC::7678::A21D` would be invalid because it uses two colons more than once. You can use two colons to suppress contiguous zero fields, which may occur in the beginning, middle, or end of the address string. If an address contains all zeroes in it, you can represent it simply as `::`.

You can also mix hexadecimal and decimal formats in an IPv6 address. The notation is useful when you have an IPv4 address and want to write it in IPv6 format. You can write the first six 16-bit fields using a hexadecimal notation as described previously and use dotted decimal notation for IPv4 for the last two 16-bit fields. The mixed notation takes the form X:X:X:X:X:X:D.D.D.D, where an X is a hexadecimal number and a D is a decimal number. You can rewrite the previous IPv6 addresses using this notation as follows:

- F6DC::4015:0:BA98:192.168.1.231

- F6DC:0:0:7678::0.0.162.29

- F6DC::0.0.162.29

- ::0.0.0.1

Unlike IPv4, IPv6 does not assign IP addresses based on network classes. Like IPv4, it uses CIDR addresses, so that the boundary between the prefix and suffix in an IP address can be specified at any arbitrary bit. For example, ::1 can be represented in CIDR notation as ::1/128, where 128 is the prefix length.

Note   An IPv6 address should be enclosed in brackets ([ ]) when it is used inside a literal string as part of a URL. This rule does not apply to IPv4. For example, If you are accessing a web server on a loopback address using an IPv4 address, you can use a URL like http://127.0.0.1/index.html. In an IPv6 address notation, you need to use a URL like http://[::1]/index.html. Make sure your browser supports IPv6 address notation in its URLs before using it.

Special IP Addresses

Some IP addresses are used for special purposes. Some of such IP addresses are as follows:

- Loopback IP address

- Unicast IP address

- Multicast IP address

- Anycast IP address

- Broadcast IP address

- Unspecified IP address

The following sections describe the use of these special IP addresses in detail.

Loopback IP Address

You need at least two computers connected via a network to test or run a network program. Sometimes, it may not be feasible or desirable to set up a network when you want to test your network program during the development phase of your project. The designers of IP realized this need.

There is a provision in the IP addressing scheme to treat an IP address as a loopback address to facilitate testing of network programs using only one computer. When the Internet layer in the protocol suite detects a loopback IP address as the destination for an IP datagram, it does not pass over the packet to the protocol layer below it (i.e., network interface layer). Rather, it turns around (or loops back, hence the name *loopback address*) and routes the packet back to the transport layer on the same computer. The transport layer will deliver the packet to the destination process on the same host as it would have done had the packet come from a remote host. A loopback IP address makes testing of a network program using one computer possible. Figure 8-5 depicts the way an Internet packet, which is addressed to a loopback IP address, is processed by the IP. The packet never leaves the source computer. It is intercepted by the internet layer and routed back to the same computer it started from.

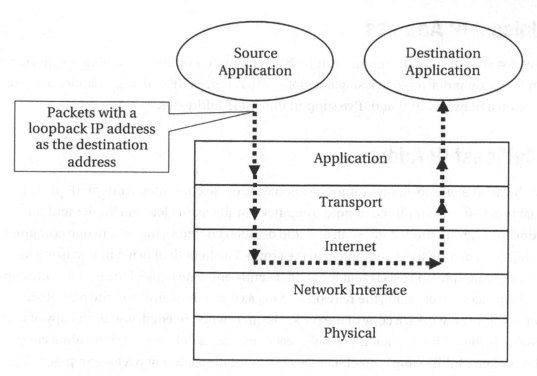

Figure 8-5. *An Internet packet that has a loopback IP address as its destination is routed back to the same*

Loopback IP addresses are reserved addresses, and the IP is required not to forward a packet with a loopback IP address as its destination address to the network interface layer.

In an IPv4 addressing scheme, 127.X.X.X block is reserved for loopback addresses, where X is a decimal number between 0 and 255. Typically, 127.0.0.1 is used as a loopback address in IPv4. However, you are not limited to using only 127.0.0.1 as the only loopback address. If you wish, you can also use 127.0.0.2 or 127.3.5.11 as a valid loopback address. Typically, the name localhost is mapped to a loopback address of 127.0.0.1 on a computer.

In an IPv6 addressing scheme, there is only one loopback address, which is sufficient to perform any local testing for a network program. It is 0:0:0:0:0:0:0:1 or simply ::1.

Unicast IP Address

Unicast is a one-to-one communication between two computers on a network in which an IP packet is delivered to a single remote host. A unicast IP address identifies a unique host on a network. IPv4 and IPv6 support unicast IP addresses.

Multicast IP Address

Multicast is a one-to-many communication where one computer sends an IP packet that is delivered to multiple remote computers. Multicasting lets you implement the concept of group interaction such as audio or video conferencing, where one computer sends information to all computers in the group. The benefit of using multicasting in place of multiple unicasts is that the sender sends only one copy of the packet. One copy of the packet travels along the network as long as it can. If receivers of the packet are on multiple networks, a copy of the packet is made when needed, and each copy of the packet is routed independently. Finally, each receiver is delivered an individual copy of the packet. Multicasting is an efficient way of communication between group members as it reduces network traffic.

An IP packet has only one destination IP address. How is an IP packet delivered to multiple hosts using multicasting? IP contains some addresses in its address space as multicast addresses. If a packet is addressed to a multicast address, the packet will be delivered to multiple hosts. The concept of multicast packet delivery is the same as a group membership for an activity. When a group is formed, the group is given a group ID. Any information addressed to that group ID is delivered to all group members. In a multicast communication, a multicast IP address (similar to a group ID) is used. Multicast packets are addressed to that multicast address. Each interested host registers its IP address with the local router that it is interested in communication made on that multicast address. The registration process between a host and the local router is accomplished using an Internet Group Management Protocol (IGMP). When the router receives a packet with a multicast address, it delivers a copy of the packet to each host registered with it for that multicast address. A receiver may choose to leave the multicast group any time by informing the router.

A multicast packet may travel through many routers before it finds its way to the receiver hosts. All receivers of a multicast packet may not be on the same network. There are many protocols, such as the Distance Vector Multicast Routing Protocol (DVMRP), that deal with routing of multicast packets.

Both IPv4 and IPv6 support multicast addressing. In IPv4, class D network addresses are used for multicasting. That is, the four highest order bits are 1110 in a multicast address in IPv4. In IPv6, a multicast address has the first 8 bits set to 1. That is, a multicast address in IPv6 always starts with FF. For example, FF0X:0:0:0:0:0:2:0000 is a multicast address in IPv6.

Anycast IP Address

Anycast is a one-to-one-from-a-group communication where one computer sends a packet to a group of computers, but the packet is delivered to exactly one computer in the group. IPv4 does not support anycasting. IPv6 supports anycasting. In anycasting, the same address is assigned to multiple computers. When a router receives a packet, which is addressed to an anycast address, it delivers the packet to the nearest computer. Anycasting is useful when a service has been replicated at many hosts, and you want to provide the service at the nearest host to the client. Sometimes, anycast addressing is also called *cluster addressing*. An anycast address is used from the unicast address space. You cannot distinguish a unicast address from an anycast address by looking at their bit arrangements. When the same unicast address is assigned to multiple hosts, it is treated as an anycast address. Note that the router must know about the hosts that are assigned an anycast address, so that it can deliver the packets addressed to that anycast address to one of the nearest hosts.

Broadcast IP Address

Broadcast is a one-to-all communication where one computer sends a packet and that packet is delivered to all computers on the network. IPv4 assigns some addresses as broadcast addresses. When all 32 bits are set to 1, it forms a broadcast address, and the packet is delivered to all hosts on the local subnet. When all bits in the host address are set to 1 and a network address is specified, it forms a broadcast address for the specified network number. For example, 255.255.255.255 is a broadcast address for a local subnet, and 192.168.1.255 is a broadcast address for a network 192.168.1.0. IPv6 does not have a broadcast address. You need to use a multicast address as the broadcast address in IPv6.

Unspecified IP Address

0.0.0.0 in IPv4 and :: in IPv6 (note that :: denotes a 128-bit IPv6 address with all bits set to zero) are known as unspecified addresses. A host uses this address as a source address to indicate that it does not have an IP address yet, such as during the boot up process when it is not assigned an IP address yet.

Port Numbers

A port number is a 16-bit unsigned integer ranging from 0 to 65535. Sometimes, a port number is also referred to simply as a *port*. A computer runs many processes, which communicate with other processes running on remote computers. When the transport layer receives an incoming packet from the Internet layer, it needs to know which process (running in the application layer) on that computer should this packet be delivered to. A port number is a logical number that is used by the transport layer to recognize a destination process for a packet on a computer.

Each incoming packet to the transport layer has a protocol; for example, the TCP protocol handler in the transport layer handles a TCP packet, and the UDP protocol handler in the transport layer handles a UDP packet.

In the application layer, a process uses a separate protocol of each communication channel it wants to communicate on with a remote process. A process uses a unique port number for each communication channel it opens for a specific protocol and registers that port number with the specific protocol module in the transport layer. Therefore, a port number must be unique for a specific protocol. For example, process P1 can use a port number 1988 for a TCP protocol, and another called process P2 can use the same port number 1988 on the same computer for a UDP protocol. A process on a host uses the protocol and the port number of the remote process to send data to the remote process.

How does a process on a computer start communicating with a remote process? For example, when you visit Yahoo's website, you simply enter http://www.yahoo.com as the web page address. In this web page address, http indicates the application layer protocol, which uses TCP as a transport layer protocol, and www.yahoo.com is the machine name, which is resolved to an IP address using a Domain Name System (DNS). The machine identified by www.yahoo.com may be running many processes, which may use the http protocol. Which process on www.yahoo.com does your web browser connect to? Since many people use Yahoo's website, it needs to run its http service at a well-known port, so that everyone can use that port to connect to it. Typically, the http web server runs at port 80. You can use http://www.yahoo.com:80, which is the same as using http://www.yahoo.com. It is not always necessary to run the http web server at port 80. If you do not run your http web server at port 80, people who want to use your http service must know the port you are using. IANA is responsible for recommending which port numbers to use for well-known services. IANA divides the port numbers into three ranges:

- Well-known ports: 0–1023

- Registered ports: 1024–49151

- Dynamic and/or private ports: 49152–65535

Well-known port numbers are used by most commonly used services provided globally such as HTTP, FTP, etc. Table 8-3 lists some of the well-known ports that are used for well-known application layer protocols. Generally, you need administrative privileges to use a well-known port on a computer.

Table 8-3. *Partial List of Well-Known Ports Used for Some Application Layer Protocols*

Application Layer Protocol	Port Number
echo	7
FTP	21
Telnet	23
SMTP	25
HTTP	80
HTTPS	443
POP3	110
NNTP	119

An organization (or a user) can register a port number with IANA in the registered port range to be used by an application. For example, the 1099 (TCP/UDP) port has been registered for the RMI Registry (RMI stands for Remote Method Invocation).

Any application can use a port number from a dynamic/private port number range.

Socket API and Client-Server Paradigm

I have not yet started discussing Java classes that make network communication possible in a Java program. In this section, I cover sockets and the client-server paradigm that is used in a network communication between two remote hosts.

I covered briefly the different lower layers of protocols and their responsibilities in the previous sections. It is time to move up in the protocol stack and discuss the interaction between the application layer and the transport layer. How does an application use these protocols to communicate with a remote application? Operating systems provide an application program interface (API) called a *socket*, which lets two remote applications communicate, taking advantage of lower-level protocols in the protocol stack. A socket is not another layer of protocol. It is an interface between the transport layer and the application layer. It provides a standard way of communication between the two layers, which in turn provides a standard way of communication between two remote applications. There are two kinds of sockets:

- A connection-oriented socket

- A connectionless socket

A connection-oriented socket is also called a *stream socket*. A connectionless socket is also called a *datagram socket*. Note that the data is always sent one datagram at a time from one host to another on the Internet using IP datagrams.

The Transmission Control Protocol (TCP), which is used in a transport layer, is one of the most widely used protocols to provide connection-oriented sockets. The application hands over data to a TCP socket, and the TCP takes care of streaming the data to the destination host. The TCP takes care of all issues like ordering, fragmentation, assembly, lost data detection, duplicate data transmission, etc., on both sides of the communication, which gives the impression to the applications that data is flowing like a continuous stream of bytes from the source application to the destination application. No physical connection at the hardware level exists between two hosts that use TCP sockets. It is all implemented in software. Sometimes, it is also called a *virtual connection*. The combination of two sockets uniquely defines a connection.

In a connection-oriented socket communication, the client and the server create a socket at their ends, establish a connection, and exchange information. TCP takes care of the errors that may occur during data transmission. TCP is also known as a reliable transport level protocol because it guarantees the delivery of the data. If it could not deliver the data for some reasons, it will inform the sender application about the error conditions. After it sends the data, it waits for an acknowledgment from the receiver to make sure that the data reached the destination. However, the reliability that TCP offers comes at a price. The overhead as compared to a connectionless protocol is much more significant, and it is slower. TCP makes sure that a sender sends the amount of data to the receiver, which can be handled by the receiver's buffer size. It also handles traffic congestion over the network. It slows down the data transmission when it detects traffic congestion. Java supports TCP sockets.

The User Datagram Protocol (UDP), which is used in a transport layer, is the most widely used protocol that provides a connectionless socket. It is unreliable, but much faster. It lets you send limited sized data—one packet at a time—which is different from TCP, which lets you send data as a stream of any size, handling the details of segmenting them in appropriate size of packets. Data delivery is not guaranteed when you send data using UDP. However, it is still used in many applications, and it works very well. The sender sends a UDP packet to a destination and forgets about it. If the receiver gets it, it gets it. Otherwise, there is no way to know—for the receiver—that there was a UDP packet sent to it. You can compare the communication used in TCP and UDP to the communication used in a telephone and mailing a letter. A telephone conversation is reliable, and it offers acknowledgment between two parties that are communicating. When you mail a letter, you do not know when the addressee receives it, or if they received it at all. There is another important difference between UDP and TCP. UDP does not guarantee the ordering of data. That is, if you send five packets to a destination using UDP, those five packets may arrive in any order. However, TCP guarantees that packets will be delivered in the order they were sent. Java supports UDP sockets.

Which protocol should you use: TCP or UDP? It depends on how the application will be used. If data integrity is of utmost significance, you should use TCP. If speed is prioritized over lower data integrity, you should use UDP. For example, a file transfer application should use TCP, whereas a video conferencing application should use UDP. If you lose video data of a few pixels, it does not matter much to the video conference. It can continue. However, if you lose a few bytes of data when a file is being transferred, that file may not be usable at all.

How do two remote applications start communicating? Which application initiates the communication? How does an application know that a remote application is interested in communicating with it? Have you ever dialed a customer service number of a company to talk to a customer service representative? If you have talked to a company's customer service representative, you already have experienced two remote applications communicate. I refer to the mechanism of using a company's customer service to explain remote communication in this section. You and a company's representative are at two remote locations. You need a service and the company provides that service. In other words, you are the client, and the company is a service provider (or a server). You do not know when you will need a service from the company. The company provides a customer service phone number, so you can contact the company. There is one more thing the company does. What is it that the company must do to provide you a service? Can you guess? It waits for your calls at the phone number that it gave you. The communication has to happen between you and the company, and the company has already taken one step forward in that communication by *passively* waiting for your call. As soon as you dial the company's number, a connection is established, and you exchange information with the company's representative. Both of you hang up, at the end, to discontinue the communication. The network communication using sockets is similar to the communication that happens between you and the company's representative. If you understand this example of communication, understanding sockets is easy.

Two remote applications use a pair of sockets to communicate. You need two endpoints for any communication to occur. A socket is a communication endpoint on each side of the communication channel. Communication over a pair of sockets follows a typical client-server communication paradigm. One application creates a socket and passively waits to be contacted by another remote application. The application that waits for a remote application to contact it is called a *server application* or simply a *server*. Another application creates a socket and initiates the communication with the waiting server application. This is called a *client application* or simply a *client*. Many other steps must be performed before a client and a server can exchange information. For example, a server must advertise the location and other details about itself so a client may contact it.

A socket passes through different states. Each state marks an event. It is the state of the socket that tells you what a socket can do and what it cannot do. Generally, a socket's lifecycle is described by eight primitives listed in Table 8-4.

Table 8-4. *Typical Socket Primitives and Their Descriptions*

Primitives	Description
Socket	Creates a socket, which is used by an application to serve as a communication endpoint.
Bind	Associates a local address to the socket. The local address includes an IP address and a port number. The port number must be a number between 0 and 65535. It should be unique for the protocol being used for the socket on the computer. For example, if a TCP socket uses port 12456, a UDP socket can also use the same port number 12456.
Listen	Defines the size of its wait queue for a client request. It is performed only by a connection-oriented server socket.
Accept	Waits for a client request to arrive. It is performed only by a connection-oriented server socket.
Connect	Attempts to establish a connection to a server socket, which is waiting on an accept primitive. It is performed by a connection-oriented client socket.
Send/Sendto	Sends data. Usually, send indicates a send operation on a connection-oriented socket, and Sendto indicates a send operation on a connectionless socket.
Receive/ReceiveFrom	Receives data. They are counterparts of Send and Sendto.
Close	Closes a connection.

The following sections elaborate each socket primitive.

The Socket Primitive

A server creates a socket by specifying what kind of socket it is: a stream socket or a datagram socket.

The Bind Primitive

The bind primitive associates the socket to a local IP address and a port number. Note that a host can have multiple IP addresses. A socket can be bound to one of the IP addresses of the host or all of them. Binding a socket to all available IP addresses for the host is also known as binding to a wildcard address. Binding reserves the port number for this socket. No other socket can use that port number for communication. The bound port will be used by the transport protocol (TCP as well as UDP) to route the data intended for this socket. I explain more about transferring data between the transport layer and a socket a little later in this section. For now, it is sufficient to understand that, in binding, the socket tells the transport layer that here is my IP address and port number, and if you get any data addressed to this address, please pass that data to me. The IP address and the port number to which a socket is bound are called the *local address* and the *local port* for the socket, respectively.

The Listen Primitive

A server informs the operating system to place the socket in a passive mode so it waits for the incoming client requests. At this point, the server is not yet ready to accept any client request. A server also specifies a wait queue size for the socket. When a client contacts the server at this socket, the client request is placed in that queue. Initially, the queue is empty. If a client contacts the server at this socket and the wait queue is full, the client's request is rejected.

The Accept Primitive

A server informs the operating system that this socket is ready to accept client requests. This step is not performed if the server is using a socket using a connectionless transport protocol such as UDP. This step is performed for TCP server sockets. When a socket sends an accept message to the operating system, it blocks until it receives a client request for a new connection.

The Connect Primitive

Only a connection-oriented client socket performs this step. This is the most important phase in a socket communication. The client socket sends a request to the server socket to establish a connection. The server socket has issued `accept` and has been waiting for a client request to arrive. The client socket sends the IP address and the port number of the server socket. Recall that a server socket binds an IP address and a port number before it starts listening and accepting connections from outside. Along with its request, a client socket also sends its own IP address and the port number to which it is already bound.

An important question arises at this point. How does the transport layer such as TCP know that the packet (in the form of a request for a connection) that came from a client has to be handed over to the server socket? During the binding phase, a socket specifies its local IP address and a local port number as well as a remote IP address and a remote port number. If the server socket wants to accept a connection only from a specific remote host IP address and port number, it can do so. Usually, the server socket will accept a connection from any client, and it will specify an unspecified IP address and a zero port number as its remote address. A server socket passes five pieces of information—a local IP address, a local port number, a remote IP address, a remote port number, and a buffer—to the transport layer. The transport layer stores them for future use in a special structure called a *Transmission Control Block* (TCB). When a packet from outside arrives at the transport layer, it looks up its TCB based on the four pieces of information contained in the incoming packet, <source IP address, source port number, destination IP address, destination port number>. Recall that the client sends the source and destination addresses in each TCP packet to the server. The transport layer attempts to find a buffer that is associated with the source and destination addresses. If it finds a buffer, it transfers the incoming data to the buffer and notifies the socket that there is some information for it in the buffer. If the server socket is accepting requests from any client (all zeroes in the remote address), the data from any client will be routed to its buffer.

Once a server socket detects a request from a client, it creates a new socket with the remote client's address information. The new socket is bound using a <local IP address, local port number (the same as the server socket's port number), remote IP address, and remote port number>, and a new buffer is created and bound to this combined addresses. In fact, two buffers are created for a socket: one for the incoming data and one for the outgoing data. At this point, a server socket lets the new socket communicate with the client socket that requested a connection. The server socket itself can close itself (accepting no more client requests for a connection), or it can start waiting again to accept another client request for a connection.

After a connection is established between two sockets (a client and a server), they can exchange information. A TCP connection supports a full duplex connection. That is, data can be sent or received in both directions simultaneously.

A client socket knows its local IP address, local port number, remote IP address, and remote port number before it attempts to connect to a server. At the client end, the creation of a TCB follows similar rules.

Once the client and server sockets are in place, two sockets (the client socket and the server socket dedicated to the client) define a connection.

A server socket acts like a receptionist sitting at the front desk in an office (server). A client comes in and talks to the receptionist first. A connection request comes from a client to the server and contacts the server socket first. The receptionist hands over the client to another staff. At this point, the job of the receptionist is over with that client. They continue their work of waiting to welcome another client coming to the office. Meanwhile, the first client can continue talking to another staff as long as they need. Similarly, the server socket creates a new socket and assigns that new socket to the client for further communication. As soon as the server socket assigns a new socket to the client, its job is over with that client. It will wait for another incoming request for connection from another client. Note that apart from many other details, a socket has five important pieces of information associated with it: a protocol, a local IP address, a local port number, a remote IP address, and a remote port number.

The Send/Sendto Primitive

It is the stage when a socket sends data.

The Receive/ReceiveFrom Primitive

It is the stage when a socket receives data.

The Close Primitive

It is time to say goodbye. Finally, the server and client sockets close the connection.

Subsequent sections discuss Java classes that support different kinds of sockets to facilitate network programming. Java classes that are related to network programming are in the `java.net`, `javax.net`, and `javax.net.ssl` packages.

Representing a Machine Address

An Internet Protocol uses the IP addresses of machines to deliver packets. Using IP addresses in a program is not always easy because of its numeric format. You may be able to memorize and use IPv4 addresses because they are only four decimal numbers in length. Memorizing and using IPv6 addresses is a little more difficult because they are eight numbers in a hexadecimal format. Every computer also has a name such as www. yahoo.com. Using a computer name in your program makes your life much easier. Java provides classes that let you use a computer name or an IP address in a Java program. If you use a computer name, Java takes care of resolving the computer name to its IP address using a Domain Name System (DNS).

An object of the InetAddress class represents an IP address. It has two subclasses, Inet4Address and Inet6Address, which represent IPv4 and IPv6 addresses, respectively. The InetAddress class does not have a public constructor. It provides the following factory methods to create its object. They are as follows—all of them throw a checked UnknownHostException:

- `static InetAddress[] getAllByName(String host)`

- `static InetAddress getByAddress(byte[] addr)`

- `static InetAddress getByAddress(String host, byte[] addr)`

- `static InetAddress getByName(String host)`

- `static InetAddress getLocalHost()`

- `static InetAddress getLoopbackAddress()`

The host argument refers to a computer name or an IP address in the standard format. The addr argument refers to the parts of an IP address as a byte array. If you specify an IPv4 address, addr must be a 4-element byte array. For IPv6 addresses, it should be a 16-element byte array. The InetAddress class takes care of resolving the host name to an IP address using DNS.

Sometimes, a host may have multiple IP addresses. The getAllByName() method returns all addresses as an array of InetAddress objects.

Typically, you create an object of the InetAddress class using one of these factory methods and pass that object to other methods during a socket creation and connection. The following snippet of code demonstrates some of its uses. You will need to handle exceptions when you use the InetAddress class or its subclasses.

```
// Get the IP address of the yahoo web server
InetAddress yahooAddress = InetAddress.
    getByName("www.yahoo.com");
// Get the loopback IP address
InetAddress loopbackAddress = InetAddress.
    getByName(null);
/* Get the address of the local host. Typically, a name
   "localhost" is mapped to a loopback address. Here, we
   are trying to get the IP address of the local computer
   where this code executes and not the loopback address.
*/
InetAddress myComputerIPAddress =
    InetAddress.getLocalHost();
```

The following snippet of code shows how to print the computer name and IP address of the computer on which the code is executed:

```
try {
    InetAddress addr = InetAddress.getLocalHost();
    System.out.println("My computer name: " +
        addr.getHostName());
    System.out.println("My computer IP address: " +
        addr.getHostAddress());
} catch (UnknownHostException e) {
    e.printStackTrace();
}
```

Listing 8-2 demonstrates the use of the InetAddress class and some of its methods. You may get a different output when you run the program.

Listing 8-2. Demonstrating the Use of the InetAddress Class

```
// InetAddressTest.java
package com.jdojo.net;
import java.io.IOException;
import java.net.InetAddress;
```

```java
public class InetAddressTest {
    public static void main(String[] args) {
        // Print www.yahoo.com address details
        printAddressDetails("www.yahoo.com");
        // Print the loopback address details
        printAddressDetails(null);
        // Print the loopback address details using IPv6
        // format
        printAddressDetails("::1");
    }
    public static void printAddressDetails(String host) {
        System.out.println("Host name: " + host);
        try {
            InetAddress addr = InetAddress.getByName(host);
            System.out.println("Host IP Address: " +
                addr.getHostAddress());
            System.out.println("Canonical Host Name: " +
                addr.getCanonicalHostName());
            int timeOutinMillis = 10000;
            System.out.println("isReachable(): " +
                addr.isReachable(timeOutinMillis));
            System.out.println("isLoopbackAddress(): " +
                addr.isLoopbackAddress());
        } catch (IOException e) {
            e.printStackTrace();
        } finally {
            System.out.println(
                "-------------------------------\n");
        }
    }
}
```

```
Host name: www.yahoo.com
Host IP Address: 98.138.252.39
Canonical Host Name:
    media-router-fp2.prod.media.vip.ne1.yahoo.com
```

```
isReachable(): true
isLoopbackAddress(): false
--------------------------------
Host name: null
Host IP Address: 127.0.0.1
Canonical Host Name: 127.0.0.1
isReachable(): true
isLoopbackAddress(): true
--------------------------------
Host name: ::1
Host IP Address: 0:0:0:0:0:0:0:1
Canonical Host Name: 0:0:0:0:0:0:0:1
isReachable(): true
isLoopbackAddress(): true
--------------------------------
```

Representing a Socket Address

A socket address contains two parts, an IP address and a port number. An object of the InetSocketAddress class represents a socket address. You can use the following constructors to create an object of the InetSocketAddress class:

- InetSocketAddress(InetAddress addr, int port)

- InetSocketAddress(int port)

- InetSocketAddress(String hostname, int port)

All constructors will attempt to resolve a host name to an IP address. If a host name could not be resolved, the socket address will be flagged as unresolved, which you can test using the isUnresolved() method. If you do not want this class to resolve the address when creating its object, you can use the following factory method to create the socket address:

```
static InetSocketAddress createUnresolved(
    String host, int port)
```

The getAddress() method of the InetSocketAddress class returns an InetAddress. If a host name is not resolved, the getAddress() method returns null. If you use an unresolved InetSocketAddress object with a socket, an attempt is made to resolve the host name during the bind process.

Listing 8-3 shows how to create resolved and unresolved InetSocketAddress objects. You may get a different output when you run the program.

Listing 8-3. Creating an InetSocketAddress Object

```java
// InetSocketAddressTest.java
package com.jdojo.net;
import java.net.InetSocketAddress;
public class InetSocketAddressTest {
    public static void main(String[] args) {
        InetSocketAddress addr1 = new InetSocketAddress(
            "::1", 12889);
        printSocketAddress(addr1);
        InetSocketAddress addr2 = InetSocketAddress.
            createUnresolved("::1", 12881);
        printSocketAddress(addr2);
    }
    public static void
    printSocketAddress(InetSocketAddress sAddr) {
        System.out.println("Socket Address: " +
            sAddr.getAddress());
        System.out.println("Socket Host Name: " +
            sAddr.getHostName());
        System.out.println("Socket Port: " +
            sAddr.getPort());
        System.out.println("isUnresolved(): " +
            sAddr.isUnresolved());
        System.out.println();
    }
}
```

```
Socket Address: /0:0:0:0:0:0:0:1
Socket Host Name: 0:0:0:0:0:0:0:1
Socket Port: 12889
isUnresolved(): false
Socket Address: null
Socket Host Name: ::1
Socket Port: 12881
isUnresolved(): true
```

Creating a TCP Server Socket

An object of the ServerSocket class represents a TCP server socket. A ServerSocket object is used to accept a connection request from a remote client. The ServerSocket class provides many constructors. You can use the no-args constructor to create an unbound server socket and use its bind() method to bind it to a local port and a local IP address. The following snippet of code shows you how to create a server socket:

```
// Create an unbound server socket
ServerSocket serverSocket = new ServerSocket();
// Create a socket address object
InetSocketAddress endPoint = new InetSocketAddress(
    "localhost", 12900);
// Set the wait queue size to 100
int waitQueueSize = 100;
// Bind the server socket to localhost at port 12900
// with a wait queue size of 100
serverSocket.bind(endPoint, waitQueueSize);
```

There is no separate listen() method in the ServerSocket class that corresponds to the listen socket primitive. Its bind() method takes care of specifying the waiting queue size for the socket.

You can combine the create, bind, and listen operations in one step by using any of the following constructors of the ServerSocket class. The default value for the wait queue size is 50. The default value for a local IP address is the wildcard address, which means all IP addresses of the server machine.

- ServerSocket(int port)

- ServerSocket(int port, int waitQueueSize)

- ServerSocket(int port, int waitQueueSize, InetAddress
  bindAddr)

You can combine the socket creation and bind steps into one statement as shown:

```
// Create a server socket at port 12900, with 100 as the
// wait queue size at the localhost loopback address
ServerSocket serverSocket =
    new ServerSocket(12900, 100, InetAddress.
getByName("localhost"));
```

Once a server socket is created and bound, it is ready to accept incoming connection requests from remote clients. To accept a remote connection request, you need to call the accept() method on the server socket. The accept() method call blocks until a request from a remote client arrives in its wait queue. When the server socket receives a request for a connection, it reads the remote IP address and the remote port number from the request and creates a new *active* socket. The reference of the newly created active socket is returned from the accept() method. An object of the Socket class represents the new active socket. The accept() method returns a new *active* socket because it is not a *passive* socket like a server socket, which waits for a remote request. It is an active socket because it is created for an active communication with the remote client. Sometimes, this active socket is also called a *connection socket* because it handles the data transmission on a connection:

```
// Wait for a new remote connection request
Socket activeSocket = serverSocket.accept();
```

Once the server socket returns from the accept() method call, the number of sockets in the server application increases by one. You have one passive server socket and one more active socket. The new active socket is the endpoint at the server for the new client connection. At this point, you need to handle the communication with the client using the new active socket.

Now you are ready to read and write data on the connection represented by the new socket. A Java TCP socket provides a full duplex connection. It lets you read data from the connection as well as write data to the connection. The Socket class contains two methods called getInputStream() and getOutputStream() for this purpose. The getInputStream() method returns an InputStream object that you can use to read data from the connection. The getOutputStream() method returns an OutputStream object that you can use to write data to the connection. You use InputStream and OutputStream objects as if you are reading from and writing to a file on a local file system. I assume that you are familiar with Java I/O. When you are done with reading/writing data on the connection, you close the InputStream/OutputStream, and finally close the socket. The following snippet of code reads a message from a client and echoes the message to the client. Note that the server and the client must agree on the format of the message before they start communicating. The following snippet of code assumes that the client sends one line of text at a time:

```
// Create a buffered reader and a buffered writer from
// the socket's input and output streams, so that we can
// read/write one line at a time
BufferedReader br = new BufferedReader(
    new InputStreamReader(activeSocket.
        getInputStream()));
BufferedWriter bw = new BufferedWriter(
    new OutputStreamWriter(activeSocket.
        getOutputStream()));
```

You can use br and bw the same way you will use them to read from a file or write to a file. An attempt to read from an input stream blocks until data becomes available on the connection.

```
// Read one line of text from the connection
String inMsg = br.readLine();
// Write some text to the output buffer
bw.write("Hello from server");
bw.flush();
```

At the end, close the connection using the socket's close() method. Closing the socket also closes its input and output streams. In fact, you can close one of the three (the input stream, the output stream, or the socket), and the other two will be closed automatically. An attempt to read/write on a closed socket throws a java.net. SocketException. You can check if a socket is closed by using its isClosed() method, which returns true if the socket is closed.

```
// Close the socket
activeSocket.close();
```

Note   Once you close a socket, you cannot reuse it. You must create a new socket and bind it before using the new socket.

A server handles two kinds of work: accepting new connection requests and responding to already connected clients. If responding to a client takes a very small amount of time, you can use the strategy as shown:

```
ServerSocket serverSocket = ...;
// <- create a server socket here;
while(true) {
    Socket activeSocket = serverSocket.accept();
    // Handle the client request on activeSocket here
}
```

This strategy handles one client at a time. It is suitable only if the number of concurrent incoming connections is very low and a client's request takes a very small amount of time to respond. If a client request takes a significant amount of time to respond, all other clients will have to wait before they can be served.

Another strategy to work with multiple client requests is to handle each client's request in a separate thread so the server can serve multiple clients at the same time. The following pseudocode outlines this strategy:

```
ServerSocket serverSocket = ...;
// <- create a server socket here;
while(true) {
    Socket activeSocket = serverSocket.accept();
    Runnable runnable = () -> {
        // Handle the client request on the activeSocket
        // here
    };
    new Thread(runnable).start(); // start a new thread
}
```

This strategy seems to work fine until you have too many threads that are created for concurrent client connections. Another strategy that works well in most of the situations is to have a thread pool to serve all client connections. If all threads in the pool are busy serving clients, the request should wait until a thread becomes free to serve it.

Listing 8-4 contains the complete code for an echo server. It creates a new thread to handle each client request. You can run the echo server program now. However, it is not going to do much as you do not have a client program to connect to it. You will see it in action after you learn how to create the TCP client socket in the next section.

Listing 8-4. An Echo Server Based on TCP Sockets

```java
// TCPEchoServer.java
package com.jdojo.net;
import java.io.BufferedReader;
import java.io.BufferedWriter;
import java.io.IOException;
import java.io.InputStreamReader;
import java.io.OutputStreamWriter;
import java.net.InetAddress;
import java.net.ServerSocket;
import java.net.Socket;
public class TCPEchoServer {
    public static void main(String[] args) {
        try {
            // Create a Server socket
            ServerSocket serverSocket =
                new ServerSocket(12900, 100,
                    InetAddress.getByName("localhost"));
            System.out.println("Server started at: " +
                serverSocket);
            // Keep accepting client connections in an
            // infinite loop
            while (true) {
                System.out.println(
                    "Waiting for a connection...");
                // Accept a connection
                final Socket activeSocket =
                    serverSocket.accept();
                System.out.println(
                    "Received a connection from " +
                    activeSocket);
```

```java
                // Create a new thread to handle the new
                // connection
                Runnable runnable = () ->
                    handleClientRequest(activeSocket);
                new Thread(runnable).start();
                // <- start a new thread
            }
        } catch (IOException e) {
            e.printStackTrace();
        }
    }
    public static void handleClientRequest(Socket socket) {
        BufferedReader socketReader = null;
        BufferedWriter socketWriter = null;
        try {
            // Create a buffered reader and writer for
            // the socket
            socketReader = new BufferedReader(
                new InputStreamReader(
                    socket.getInputStream()));
            socketWriter = new BufferedWriter(
                new OutputStreamWriter(
                    socket.getOutputStream()));
            String inMsg = null;
            while ((inMsg = socketReader.readLine())
                    != null) {
                System.out.println(
                    "Received from client: " + inMsg);
                // Echo the received message to the client
                String outMsg = inMsg;
                socketWriter.write(outMsg);
                socketWriter.write("\n");
                socketWriter.flush();
            }
```

```
        } catch (IOException e) {
            e.printStackTrace();
        } finally {
            try {
                socket.close();
            } catch (IOException e) {
                e.printStackTrace();
            }
        }
    }
}
```

Creating a TCP Client Socket

An object of the Socket class represents a TCP client socket. You have already seen how an object of the Socket class works with a TCP server socket. For a server socket, you got an object of the Socket class as the return value from the server socket's accept() method. For a client socket, you will have to perform three steps: create, bind, and connect. The Socket class provides many constructors that let you specify the remote IP address and port number. These constructors bind the socket to a local host and an available port number. The following snippet of code shows how to create a TCP client socket:

```
// Create a client socket, which is bound to the
// localhost at any available port
// connected to remote IP 192.168.1.2 at port 3456
Socket socket = new Socket("192.168.1.2", 3456);

// Create an unbound client socket. bind it, and
// connect it.
Socket socket = new Socket();

socket.bind(new InetSocketAddress("localhost", 14101));
socket.connect(new InetSocketAddress("localhost", 12900));
```

Once you get a connected `Socket`, you can use its input and output streams using the `getInputStream()` and `getOutputStream()` methods, respectively. You can read/write on the connection the same way you would read/write from/to a file using the input and output streams.

Listing 8-5 contains the complete code for an echo client application. It receives input from the user, sends the input to the echo server as listed in Listing 8-4, and prints the server's response on the standard output. Both applications, the echo server and the echo client, must agree on the format of the messages that they will be exchanging. They exchange one line of text at a time. It is important to note that you must append a new line with every message that is sent across the connection because you are using the `readLine()` method of the `BufferedReader` class, which returns only when it encounters a new line. The client application must use the same IP address and port number where the server socket is accepting the connection.

Listing 8-5. An Echo Client Based on TCP Sockets

```
// TCPEchoClient.java
package com.jdojo.net;
import java.io.BufferedReader;
import java.io.BufferedWriter;
import java.io.IOException;
import java.io.InputStreamReader;
import java.io.OutputStreamWriter;
import java.net.Socket;
public class TCPEchoClient {
    public static void main(String[] args) {
        Socket socket = null;
        BufferedReader socketReader = null;
        BufferedWriter socketWriter = null;
        try {
            // Create a socket that will connect to
            // localhost at port 12900.
            // Note that the server must also be running
            // at localhost and 12900.
            socket = new Socket("localhost", 12900);
```

```java
System.out.println("Started client socket at "
        + socket.getLocalSocketAddress());
// Create a buffered reader and writer using
// the socket's input and output streams
socketReader = new BufferedReader(
    new InputStreamReader(
        socket.getInputStream()));
socketWriter = new BufferedWriter(
    new OutputStreamWriter(
        socket.getOutputStream()));
// Create a buffered reader for user's input
BufferedReader consoleReader =
    new BufferedReader(
        new InputStreamReader(System.in));
String promptMsg =
    "Please enter a message (Bye to quit):";
String outMsg = null;
System.out.print(promptMsg);
while ((outMsg = consoleReader.readLine())
        != null) {
    if (outMsg.equalsIgnoreCase("bye")) {
        break;
    }
    // Add a new line to the message to the
    // server, because the server reads one
    // line at a time.
    socketWriter.write(outMsg);
    socketWriter.write("\n");
    socketWriter.flush();
    // Read and display the message from the
    // server
    String inMsg = socketReader.readLine();
    System.out.println("Server: " + inMsg);
    System.out.println(); // Print a blank line
    System.out.print(promptMsg);
}
```

```
        } catch (IOException e) {
            e.printStackTrace();
        } finally {
            // Finally close the socket
            if (socket != null) {
                try {
                    socket.close();
                } catch (IOException e) {
                    e.printStackTrace();
                }
            }
        }
    }
}
```

Putting a TCP Server and Clients Together

Figure 8-6 shows the setup in which three clients are connected to a server. Two Socket objects, one at each end, represent a connection. The ServerSocket object in the server keeps waiting for incoming connection requests from a client.

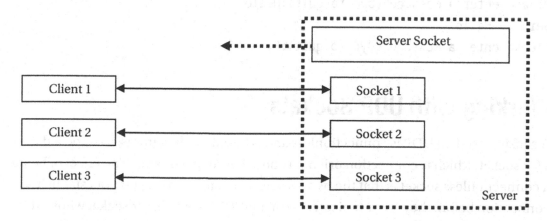

Figure 8-6. *A client-server setup using ServerSocket and socket objects*

Listings 8-4 and 8-5 list the complete program for a TCP echo server and client application. You need to run the TCPEchoServer class first and then the TCPEchoClient class. The server application waits for the client application to connect. The client application prompts the user to enter a text message on the console. Once the user enters a text message and presses the Enter key, the client application sends that text to the server. The server responds back with the same message. Both applications print the details about the conversation to the standard output. The following are the outputs for an echo server and an echo client. You can run multiple instances of the TCPEchoClient application. The server application handles each client connection in a separate thread.

The following is a sample output for the server application:

```
Server started at: ServerSocket[addr=localhost/
    127.0.0.1,port=0,localport=12900]
Waiting for a connection ...
Received a connection from Socket[addr=/127.0.0.1,
    port=1698,localport=12900]
Waiting for a connection ...
Received from client: Hello
```

The following is a sample output for the client application:

```
Started client socket at /127.0.0.1:53498
Please enter a message (Bye to quit):Hello
Server: Hello
Please enter a message (Bye to quit):Bye
```

Working with UDP Sockets

A socket based on UDP is connectionless and is based on datagrams, as opposed to a TCP socket, which is connection oriented and is based on streams. The effect of being a connectionless socket is that the two sockets (client and server) do not establish a connection before they communicate. Recall that TCP has a server socket whose sole function was to listen for a connection request from remote clients. Because UDP is a connectionless protocol, there will not be a server socket when you work with UDP. In TCP sockets, the impression of having a stream-oriented data transmission between the client and server was produced by TCP in the transport layer because of its connection-oriented features. TCP maintained the state of the data being transmitted on each side of the connection. The implication of UDP being a connectionless protocol is that each side (client and server) sends or receives a chunk of data without any prior knowledge of communication between them. In a communication using UDP, each chunk of data that is sent to the same destination is independent of the previously sent data. The chunk of data that is sent using UDP is called a datagram or a UDP packet. Each UDP packet contains data, destination IP address, and destination port number. UDP is an unreliable protocol because it does not guarantee the delivery and the order of delivery of packets to the intended recipient.

Note   Although UDP is a connectionless protocol, you can build a connection-oriented communication using UDP in your application. You will need to write the logic that will handle the lost packets, out-of-order packet delivery, and many more things. TCP provides all these features at the transport layer, and your application does not have to worry about them.

Writing an application using UDP sockets is easier than writing an application using TCP sockets. You have to deal with only two classes:

- DatagramPacket

- DatagramSocket

An object of the DatagramPacket class represents a UDP datagram that is the unit of data transmission over a UDP socket. An object of the DatagramSocket class represents a UDP socket that is used to send or receive a datagram packet. Here are the steps you need to perform to work with UDP sockets:

- Create an object of the DatagramSocket class and bind it to a local IP address and a local port number.

- Create an object of the DatagramPacket class to hold the destination address and the data to be transmitted.

- Use the send(DatagramPacket packet) method of the DatagramSocket class to send the datagram packet to its destination. On the receiving end, use the receive(DatagramPacket packet) method to read the datagram packet.

You can use one of the constructors to create an object of the DatagramSocket class. All of them will create the socket and bind it to a local IP address and a local port number. Note that a UDP socket does not have a remote IP address and a remote port number because it is never connected to a remote socket. It can receive/send a datagram packet from/to any UDP socket.

```
// Create a UDP Socket bound to a port number 15900
// at localhost
DatagramSocket udpSocket =
    new DatagramSocket(15900, "localhost");
```

The DatagramSocket class provides a bind() method, which lets you bind the socket to a local IP address and a local port number. Typically, you do not need to use this method because you specify the socket address to which it needs to be bound in its constructor, as you just did.

A DatagramPacket contains three things: a destination IP address, a destination port number, and the data. The constructors for the DatagramPacket class fall into two categories. Constructors in one of the categories let you create a DatagramPacket object to receive a packet. They require only the buffer size, offset, and length of data in that buffer. Constructors in the other category let you create a DatagramPacket object to send a packet. They require you to specify the destination address along with the data. If you have created a DatagramPacket without specifying the destination address, you can set the destination address afterward using the setAddress() and setPort() methods.

Constructors of the DatagramPacket class to create a packet to receive data are as follows:

- DatagramPacket(byte[] buffer, int length)

- DatagramPacket(byte[] buffer, int offset, int length)

Constructors of the DatagramPacket class to create a packet to send data are as follows:

- DatagramPacket(byte[] buffer, int length, InetAddress address, int port)

- DatagramPacket(byte[] buffer, int offset, int length, InetAddress address, int port)

- DatagramPacket(byte[] buffer, int length, SocketAddress address)

- DatagramPacket(byte[] buffer, int offset, int length, SocketAddress address)

The following snippet of code demonstrates some of the ways to create a datagram packet:

```
// Create a packet to receive 1024 bytes of data
byte[] data = new byte[1024];
DatagramPacket packet =
    new DatagramPacket(data, data.length);
// Create a packet that a has buffer size of 1024, but it
// will receive data starting at offset 8 (offset zero
// means the first element in the array) and it will
// receive only 32 bytes of data.
byte[] data2 = new byte[1024];
DatagramPacket packet2 = new DatagramPacket(data2, 8, 32);
// Create a packet to send 1024 bytes of data that has a
// destination address of "localhost" and port 15900.
// Will need to populate data3 array before sending the
// packet.
byte[] data3 = new byte[1024];
DatagramPacket packet3 = new DatagramPacket(data3, 1024,
    InetAddress.getByName("localhost"), 15900);
// Create a packet to send 1024 bytes of data that has a
// destination address of "localhost" and port 15900.
// Will need to populate data4 array before sending the
// packet. The code sets the destination address by
// calling methods on the packet instead of specifying
// it in its constructor.
byte[] data4 = new byte[1024];
DatagramPacket packet4 = new DatagramPacket(data4, 1024);
packet4.setAddress(InetAddress.getByName("localhost"));
packet4.setPort(15900);
```

It is very important to understand that data in the packet always has offset and length specified. You need to use those two pieces of information while reading the data from a packet. Suppose that a receivedPacket object reference represents a DatagramPacket that you have received from a remote UDP socket. The getData() method of the DatagramPacket class returns the buffer (a byte array) of the packet. A packet can have a bigger buffer than the size of the received data from a remote client. In such cases, you must use the offset and the length to read the data from the buffer that was received without touching the garbage data in the buffer. If a packet's buffer size is smaller than the size of the data received, the extra bytes are silently ignored. You should use the code similar to the following to read data that a socket receives. The point is that you should use data in the receiving buffer starting from its specified offset and as many bytes as indicated by its length property:

```
// Get the packet's buffer, offset, and length
byte[] dataBuffer = receivedPacket.getData();
int offset = receivedPacket.getOffset();
int length = receivedPacket.getLength();
// Copy the received data using offset and length to
// receivedData array, which will hold all good data
byte[] receivedData = new byte[length];
System.arraycopy(dataBuffer, offset,
    receivedData, 0,
    length);
```

Creating a UDP socket (client as well as server) is as simple as creating an object of the DatagramSocket class. You can use its send() method to send a packet. You can use the receive() method to receive a packet from a remote socket. The receive() method blocks until a packet arrives. You supply an empty datagram packet to the receive() method. The socket populates it with information that it receives from the remote socket. If the supplied datagram packet has a smaller data buffer size than that of the received datagram packet, the received data is truncated silently to fit into the supplied datagram packet. If the supplied datagram packet has a bigger data buffer size than that of the received one, the socket will copy the received data to the supplied data buffer in its segment indicated by its offset and length properties without touching the other parts of the buffer. Note that the available data buffer size is not the size of the byte array. Rather, it is defined by the length property. For example, suppose you have a datagram packet with a byte array of 32 elements with an offset of 2 and a data buffer length of 8. If you pass this datagram packet to the receive() method, the maximum of 8 bytes of received data will be copied. The data will be copied from the third element in the buffer to the eleventh element as indicated by the offset 2 and the length 8, respectively.

```
// Create a UDP socket bound to a port number 15900 at
// localhost
DatagramSocket socket =
    new DatagramSocket(15900,
        InetAddress.getByName("localhost"));
// Send a packet assuming that you have a datagram packet
// in p
socket.send(p);
// Receive a packet
DatagramPacket p2 =
    new DatagramPacket(new byte[1024], 1024);
socket.receive(p2);
```

Creating a UDP Echo Server

Creating an echo server using UDP is very easy. It takes only four lines of real code. Use the following steps to create a UDP echo server:

- Create a DatagramSocket object to represent a UDP socket.

- Create a DatagramPacket object to receive the packet from a remote client.

- Call the receive() method of the socket to wait for a packet to arrive.

- Call the send() method of the socket passing the same packet that you received.

When a UDP packet is received by a server, it contains the sender's address. You do not need to change anything in the packet to echo back the same message to the sender of the packet. When you prepare a datagram packet for sending, you need to set a destination address. When the packet arrives at its destination, it contains its sender's address. This is useful in case the receiver wants to respond to the sender of the datagram packet.

The following snippet of code shows you how to write a UDP echo server:

```
DatagramSocket socket =
    new DatagramSocket(15900);
DatagramPacket packet =
    new DatagramPacket(new byte[1024], 1024);
while(true) {
    // Receive the packet
    socket.receive(packet);
    // Send back the same packet to the sender
    socket.send(packet);
}
```

Listing 8-6 contains the expanded version of the same code for a UDP echo server. It contains the same basic logic as shown previously. Additionally, it contains the code to handle errors and print the packet's details on the standard output.

Listing 8-6. An Echo Server Based on UDP Sockets

```
// UDPEchoServer.java
package com.jdojo.net;
import java.io.IOException;
import java.net.DatagramPacket;
import java.net.DatagramSocket;
import java.net.InetAddress;
public class UDPEchoServer {
    public static void main(String[] args) {
        final int LOCAL_PORT = 15900;
        final String SERVER_NAME = "localhost";
        try {
            DatagramSocket udpSocket = new DatagramSocket(
                LOCAL_PORT,
                InetAddress.getByName(SERVER_NAME));
            System.out.println(
                "Created UDP server socket at " +
                udpSocket.getLocalSocketAddress() +
                "...");
```

```java
            // Wait for a message in a loop and echo the
            // same message to the sender
            while (true) {
                System.out.println(
                    "Waiting for a UDP packet" +
                    " to arrive...");
                // Prepare a packet to hold the received
                // data
                DatagramPacket packet =
                    new DatagramPacket(
                        new byte[1024], 1024);
                // Receive a packet
                udpSocket.receive(packet);
                // Print the packet details
                displayPacketDetails(packet);
                // Echo the same packet to the sender
                udpSocket.send(packet);
            }
        } catch (IOException e) {
            e.printStackTrace();
        }
    }
    public static void
    displayPacketDetails(DatagramPacket packet) {
        // Get the message
        byte[] msgBuffer = packet.getData();
        int length = packet.getLength();
        int offset = packet.getOffset();
        int remotePort = packet.getPort();
        InetAddress remoteAddr = packet.getAddress();
        String msg = new String(
            msgBuffer, offset, length);
```

```
        System.out.println(
            "Received a packet:[IP Address="
            + remoteAddr + ", port=" + remotePort
            + ", message=" + msg + "]");
    }
}
```

Listing 8-7 contains the program for the client application that uses a UDP socket to send/receive messages to/from the UDP echo server. Note that the client and server exchange one line of text at a time.

Listing 8-7. An Echo Client Based on UDP Sockets

```java
// UDPEchoClient.java
package com.jdojo.net;
import java.io.BufferedReader;
import java.io.InputStreamReader;
import java.net.DatagramPacket;
import java.net.DatagramSocket;
import java.net.InetAddress;
import java.net.UnknownHostException;
public class UDPEchoClient {
    public static void main(String[] args) {
        DatagramSocket udpSocket = null;
        BufferedReader br = null;
        try {
            // Create a UDP socket at localhost using an
            // available port
            udpSocket = new DatagramSocket();
            String msg = null;
            // Create a buffered reader to get an input
            // from a user
            br = new BufferedReader(
                new InputStreamReader(System.in));
            String promptMsg =
                "Please enter a message (Bye to quit):";
            System.out.print(promptMsg);
```

```java
        while ((msg = br.readLine()) != null) {
            if (msg.equalsIgnoreCase("bye")) {
                break;
            }
            // Prepare a packet to send to the server
            DatagramPacket packet =
                UDPEchoClient.getPacket(msg);
            // Send the packet to the server
            udpSocket.send(packet);
            // Wait for a packet from the server
            udpSocket.receive(packet);
            // Display the packet details received
            // from the server
            displayPacketDetails(packet);
            System.out.print(promptMsg);
        }
    } catch (Exception e) {
        e.printStackTrace();
    } finally {
        // Close the socket
        if (udpSocket != null) {
            udpSocket.close();
        }
    }
}
public static void
displayPacketDetails(DatagramPacket packet) {
    byte[] msgBuffer = packet.getData();
    int length = packet.getLength();
    int offset = packet.getOffset();
    int remotePort = packet.getPort();
    InetAddress remoteAddr = packet.getAddress();
    String msg = new String(msgBuffer, offset, length);
    System.out.println(
        "[Server at IP Address=" + remoteAddr
        + ", port=" + remotePort + "]: " + msg);
```

```
        // Add a line break
        System.out.println();
    }
    public static DatagramPacket
    getPacket(String msg) throws UnknownHostException {
        // We will send and accept a message of 1024
        // bytes in length.
        // Longer messages will be truncated
        final int PACKET_MAX_LENGTH = 1024;
        byte[] msgBuffer = msg.getBytes();
        int length = msgBuffer.length;
        if (length > PACKET_MAX_LENGTH) {
            length = PACKET_MAX_LENGTH;
        }
        DatagramPacket packet =
            new DatagramPacket(msgBuffer, length);
        // Set the destination address and the port number
        int serverPort = 15900;
        final String SERVER_NAME = "localhost";
        InetAddress serverIPAddress =
            InetAddress.getByName(SERVER_NAME);
        packet.setAddress(serverIPAddress);
        packet.setPort(serverPort);
        return packet;
    }
}
```

To test the UDP echo application, you need to run the UDPEchoServer and UDPEchoClient classes. You need to run the server first. The client application will prompt you to enter a message. Enter a text message and press the Enter key to send that message to the server. The server will echo the same message. Both applications display the messages being exchanged on the standard output. They also display the packet details, such as the sender's IP address and port number. The server application uses port number 15900, and the client application uses any available UDP port on the computer. If you get an error, it means that port number 15900 is in use, so you need to change the port number in the server program and use the new port number in the client program to address the packet. The server is designed to handle multiple clients at a time. You can run multiple instances of the UDPEchoClient class. Note that the server runs in an infinite loop, and you must stop the server application manually.

The following is a sample log on the server console:

```
Created UDP server socket at /127.0.0.1:15900...
Waiting for a UDP packet to arrive...
Received a packet:[IP Address=/127.0.0.1,
    port=61119, message=Hello]
Waiting for a UDP packet to arrive...
Received a packet:[IP Address=/127.0.0.1,
    port=61119, message=Nice talking to you]
Waiting for a UDP packet to arrive...
```

The following is a sample log on the client console:

```
Please enter a message (Bye to quit):
    Hello
[Server at IP Address=localhost/127.0.0.1,
    port=15900]: Hello
Please enter a message (Bye to quit):
    Nice talking to you
[Server at IP Address=localhost/127.0.0.1, port=15900]:
    Nice talking to you
Please enter a message (Bye to quit):
    Bye
```

A Connected UDP Socket

UDP sockets do not support an end-to-end connection like the TCP sockets. The DatagramSocket class contains a connect() method. This method allows an application to restrict sending and receiving of UDP packets to a specific IP address at a specific port number. Consider the following snippet of code:

```
InetAddress localIPAddress =
    InetAddress.getByName("192.168.11.101");
int localPort = 15900;
```

```
DatagramSocket socket =
    new DatagramSocket(localPort, localIPAddress);
// Connect the socket to a remote address
InetAddress remoteIPAddress =
    InetAddress.getByName("192.168.12.115");
int remotePort = 17901;
socket.connect(remoteIPAddress, remotePort);
```

The socket is bound to the local IP address 192.168.11.101 and local UDP port number 15900. It is connected to a remote IP address of 192.188.12.15 and a remote UDP port number 17901. It means that the socket object can be used to send/receive a datagram packet only to/from another UDP socket running at an IP address of 192.168.12.115 at the port number 17901. After you have called the connect() method on a UDP socket, you do not need to set the destination IP address and the port number for the outgoing datagram packets. The socket will add the destination IP address and port number that were used in the connect() method's call to all outgoing packets. If you do supply a destination address with a packet before you send it, the socket will make sure the destination address supplied in the packet is the same as the remote address used in the connect() method call. Otherwise, the send() method will throw an IllegalArgumentException.

Using the connect() method of a UDP socket has two advantages:

- It sets the destination address for the outgoing packets every time you send a packet.

- It restricts the socket to communicate only to the remote host whose IP address was used in the connect() method's call.

Now you understand that UDP sockets are connectionless, and you do not have a real connection using a UDP socket. The connect() method in the DatagramSocket class does not provide any kind of connection for UDP sockets. Rather, it is useful for restricting the communication to a specific remote UDP socket.

UDP Multicast Sockets

Java supports UDP multicast sockets that can receive datagram packets sent to a multicast IP address. An object of the MulticastSocket class represents a multicast socket. Working with a MulticastSocket socket is similar to working with a `DatagramSocket` with one difference—a multicast socket is based on a group membership. After you have created and bound a multicast socket, you need to call its `joinGroup(InetAddress multiCastIPAddress)` method to make this socket a member of the multicast group defined by the specified multicast IP address, `multiCastIpAddress`. Once it becomes a member of a multicast group, any datagram packet sent to that group will be delivered to this socket. There can be multiple members in a multicast group. A multicast socket can be a member of multiple multicast groups. If a member decides not to receive a multicast packet from a group, it can leave the group by calling the `leaveGroup(InetAddress multiCastIPAddress)` method.

In IPv4, any IP address in the range `224.0.0.0` to `239.255.255.255` can be used as a multicast address to send a datagram packet. The IP address `224.0.0.0` is reserved, and you should not use it in your application. A multicast IP address cannot be used as a source address for a datagram packet, which implies that you cannot bind a socket to a multicast address.

A socket itself does not have to be a member of a multicast group to send a datagram packet to a multicast address.

In Java, the IP multicast capability is part of the `DatagramChannel` class. Refer to the "Multicasting Using Datagram Channels" section later in this chapter on how to use a datagram channel for IP multicasting.

Listing 8-8 contains a program that creates a multicast socket that receives datagram packets addressed to the `230.1.1.1` multicast IP address.

Listing 8-8. A UDP Multicast Socket That Receives UDP Multicast Messages

```
// UDPMultiCastReceiver.java
package com.jdojo.net;
import java.io.IOException;
import java.net.DatagramPacket;
import java.net.InetAddress;
import java.net.MulticastSocket;
public class UDPMultiCastReceiver {
    public static void main(String[] args) {
        int mcPort = 18777;
        String mcIPStr = "230.1.1.1";
        MulticastSocket mcSocket = null;
        InetAddress mcIPAddress = null;
```

```
        try {
            mcIPAddress = InetAddress.getByName(mcIPStr);
            mcSocket = new MulticastSocket(mcPort);
            System.out.println(
                "Multicast Receiver running at:"
                + mcSocket.getLocalSocketAddress());
            // Join the group
            mcSocket.joinGroup(mcIPAddress);
            DatagramPacket packet =
                new DatagramPacket(new byte[1024], 1024);
            while (true) {
                System.out.println(
                    "Waiting for a multicast message...");
                mcSocket.receive(packet);
                String msg = new String(
                    packet.getData(),
                    packet.getOffset(),
                    packet.getLength());
                System.out.println(
                    "[Multicast Receiver] Received:" +
                    msg);
            }
        } catch (Exception e) {
            e.printStackTrace();
        } finally {
            if (mcSocket != null) {
                try {
                    mcSocket.leaveGroup(mcIPAddress);
                    mcSocket.close();
                } catch (IOException e) {
                    e.printStackTrace();
                }
            }
        }
    }
}
```

Listing 8-9 contains a program that sends a message to the same multicast address. Note that you can run multiple instances of the UDPMulticastReceiver class, and all of them will become a member of the same multicast group. When you run the UDPMulticastSender class, it will send a message to the group, and all members in the group will receive a copy of the same message. The UDPMulticastSender class uses a DatagramSocket, not a MulticastSocket, to send a multicast message.

Listing 8-9. A UDP Datagram Socket, a Multicast Sender Application

```java
// UDPMultiCastSender.java
package com.jdojo.net;
import java.net.DatagramPacket;
import java.net.DatagramSocket;
import java.net.InetAddress;
public class UDPMultiCastSender {
    public static void main(String[] args) {
        int mcPort = 18777;
        String mcIPStr = "230.1.1.1";
        DatagramSocket udpSocket = null;
        try {
            // Create a datagram socket
            udpSocket = new DatagramSocket();
            // Prepare a message
            InetAddress mcIPAddress =
                InetAddress.getByName(mcIPStr);
            byte[] msg = "Hello multicast socket".
                getBytes();
            DatagramPacket packet =
                new DatagramPacket(msg, msg.length);
            packet.setAddress(mcIPAddress);
            packet.setPort(mcPort);
            udpSocket.send(packet);
            System.out.println(
                "Sent a multicast message.");
            System.out.println(
                "Exiting application");
```

```
        } catch (Exception e) {
            e.printStackTrace();
        } finally {
            if (udpSocket != null) {
                try {
                    udpSocket.close();
                } catch (Exception e) {
                    e.printStackTrace();
                }
            }
        }
    }
}
```

To see multicast in action, run one or more instances of the UDPMulticastReceiver class followed by one instance of the UDPMulticastSender class. The following is a sample output when the UDPMulticastReceiver class is run. Note that the program receives a multicast message when the UDPMulticastSender is run:

```
Multicast Receiver running at:
    0.0.0.0/0.0.0.0:18777
Waiting for a multicast message...
[Multicast Receiver] Received:
    Hello multicast socket
Waiting for a multicast message...
```

The following is a sample output when the UDPMulticastSender class is run:

```
Sent a multicast message.
Exiting application
```

URI, URL, and URN

A Uniform Resource Identifier (URI) is a sequence of characters that identifies a resource. The Request for Comments (RFC) 3986 defines the generic syntax for a URI. The full text of this RFC is available at www.ietf.org/rfc/rfc3986.txt. A resource identifier can identify a resource by a location, a name, or both. This section gives an overview of the URI. If you are interested in details about the URI, you are advised to read RFC3986.

A URI that uses a location to identify a resource is called a Uniform Resource Locator (URL). For example, `http://www.yahoo.com/index.html` represents a URL that identifies a document named `index.html` at the host `www.yahoo.com`. Another example of a URL is `mailto:ksharan@jdojo.com` in which the `mailto` protocol instructs the application that interprets it to open up an email application to send an email to the email address specified in the URL. In this case, the URL is not locating any resources. Rather, it is identifying the details of an email. You can also set the subject and the body parts of an email using the `mailto` protocol. Therefore, a URL does not always imply a location of a resource. Sometimes, the resource may be abstract, as in the case of the `mailto` protocol. Once you locate a resource using a URL, you can perform some operations, such as retrieve, update, or delete, on the resource. The details of how the operations are performed depend on the scheme being used in the URL. A URL just identifies the parts of a resource location and scheme to locate it, not the details of any operations that can be performed on the resource.

A URI that uses a name to identify a resource is called a Uniform Resource Name (URN). For example, `URN:ISBN:978-1-4302-6661-7` represents a URN, which identifies a book using an International Standard Book Number (ISBN) namespace.

A URL and a URN are subsets of a URI. Therefore, the discussion about a URI applies to both the URL and the URN. The detailed syntax of a URI depends on the scheme it uses. In this section, I cover a generic syntax of the URI, which is typically a URL. The next section explores the Java classes that are used to represent URIs and URLs in Java programs.

A URI can be absolute or relative. A relative URI is always interpreted in the context of another absolute URI, which is called the base URI. In other words, you must have an absolute URI to make a relative URI meaningful. An absolute URI has the following generic format:

```
<scheme>:<scheme-specific-part>
```

The `<scheme-specific-part>` depends on the `<scheme>`. For example, an `http` scheme uses one format, and a `mailto` scheme uses another format. Another generic form of a URI is as follows. Typically, but not necessarily, it represents a URL:

```
<scheme>://<authority><path>?<query>#<fragment>
```

Here, `<scheme>` indicates a method to access a resource. It is the protocol name such as `http`, `ftp`, etc. We all use the term "protocol" for what is termed a "scheme" in the URI specification. If the term "scheme" throws you off, you can read it as "protocol" whenever it appears in this section. The `<scheme>` and `<path>` parts are required in a URI. All other parts are optional. The `<path>` part may be an empty string.

The `<authority>` part indicates the server name (or IP address) or a scheme-specific registry. If the `<authority>` part represents a server name, it may be written in the form of `<userinfo>@host:port`. If an `<authority>` is present in a URI, it begins with two forward slashes; it is an optional part. For example, a URL that identifies a file in a local file system on a machine uses the `file` scheme as `file:///c:/documents/welcome.doc`.

The URI syntax uses a hierarchical syntax in its `<path>` part, which locates the resource on the server. Multiple parts of the `<path>` are separated by a forward slash (`/`).

The `<query>` part indicates that the resource is obtained by executing the specified query. It consists of name-value pairs separated by an ampersand (`&`). The name and value are separated by an equals sign (`=`). For example, `id=123&rate=5.5` is a query, which has two parts, `id` and `rate`.

The value for `id` is `123` and the value for `rate` is `5.5`.

The `<fragment>` part identifies a secondary resource, typically a subset of the primary resource identified by another part of the URI.

The following is an example of a URI, which is also broken into parts:

```
URI:        http://www.jdojo.com/java/intro.html?
            id=123#conclusion
Scheme:     http
Authority:  www.jdojo.com
Path:       /java/intro.html
Query:      id=123
Fragment:   conclusion
```

The URI represents a URL that refers to a document named `intro.html` on the `www.jdojo.com` server. The scheme `http` indicates that the document can be retrieved using the `http` protocol. The query `id=123` indicates that the document is obtained by executing this query. The fragment part `conclusion` can be interpreted differently by different applications that use the document. In the case of an HTML document, the fragment part is interpreted by the web browser as the part of the main document.

Not all parts of a URI are mandatory. Which parts are mandatory and which parts are optional depend on the scheme that is used. One of the goals of using a URI to identify a resource was to make it universally readable. For this reason, there is a well-defined set of characters that can be used to represent a URI. The URI syntax uses some reserved characters that have special meaning, and they can only be used in specific parts of a URI. In other parts, the reserved characters need to be escaped. A character is escaped by using a percent character followed by its ASCII value in a hexadecimal format. For example, the ASCII value of space is 32 in decimal format, and it is 20 in hexadecimal format. If you want to use a space character in a URI, you must use %20, which is the escaped form for a space. Since the percent sign is used as part of an escape character, you must use %25 to represent a % character in a URI (25 is the hexadecimal value for number 37 in decimal. The ASCII value for % is 37 in decimal). For example, if you want to use a value of 5.2% in a query, the following is an invalid URI:

```
http://www.jdojo.com/details?rate=5.2%
```

To make it a valid URI, you need to escape the percent sign character as %25 as shown:

```
http://www.jdojo.com/details?rate=5.2%25
```

It is important to understand the usage of a relative URI. A relative URI is always interpreted in the context of an absolute URI, which is called the base URI. An absolute URI starts with a scheme. A relative URI inherits some parts of its base URI. Let's consider a URI that refers to an HTML document as shown:

```
http://www.jdojo.com/java/intro.html
```

The document referred to in the URI is intro.html. Its path is /java/intro.html. Suppose two documents named brief_intro.html and detailed_intro.html reside (physically or logically) in the same path hierarchy as intro.html. The following are the absolute URIs for all three documents:

- http://www.jdojo.com/java/intro.html
- http://www.jdojo.com/java/brief_intro.html
- http://www.jdojo.com/java/detailed_intro.html

If you are already in the `intro.html` context, it will be easier to refer to the other two documents using their names instead of their absolute URI. What does it mean by being in the `intro.html` context? When you use the `http://www.jdojo.com/java/intro.html` URI to identify a resource, it has three parts: a scheme (`http`), a server name (`www.jdojo.com`), and a document path (`/java/intro.html`). The path indicates that the document is under the `java` path hierarchy, which in turn is at the root of the path hierarchy. All details—scheme, server name, path details, excluding the document name itself (`intro.html`)—make up the context for the `intro.html` document. If you look at the URI for the other two documents listed previously, you will notice that all details about them are the same as for `intro.html`. In other words, you can state that the context for the other two documents is the same as for `intro.html`. In this case, with an absolute URI of the `intro.html` document as the base URI, the relative URIs for the other two documents are their names: `brief_intro.html` and `detailed_intro.html`. It can be listed as follows:

- Base URI: `http://www.jdojo.com/java/intro.html`

- Relative URI: `brief_intro.html`

- Relative URI: `detailed_intro.html`

In the list, the two relative URIs inherit the scheme, server name, and path hierarchy from the base URI. It is to be emphasized that a relative URI never makes sense without specifying its base URI.

When a relative URI has to be used, it must be resolved to its equivalent absolute URI. The URI specification lays down rules to resolve a relative URI. I discuss some of the most commonly used forms of relative URIs and their resolutions. There are two special characters used to define the `<path>` part of a URI. They are a dot and two dots. A dot means the current path hierarchy. Two dots mean one up in the path hierarchy. You must have seen these two sets of characters being used in a file system to mean the current directory and parent directory. You can think of their meanings in a URI the same way, but a URI does not assume any directory hierarchy. In a URI, a path is considered as hierarchical, and it is not tied to a file system hierarchical structure at all. However, in practice, when you work with web-based applications, URLs are usually mapped to a file system hierarchical structure. In the normalized form of a URI, dots are replaced appropriately. For example, `s://sn/a/./b` is normalized to `s://sn/a/b`, and `s://sn/a/../b` is normalized to `s://sn/b`. The non-normalized and normalized forms refer to the same URL. The normalized form has extra characters removed. By just looking at the two URIs, you cannot say that they are referring to the same resource or not. You must normalize them before you compare them for equality. During the comparison process, the scheme, server name, and hexadecimal digits are considered case-insensitive. Here are some rules to resolve a relative URI:

- If a URI starts with a scheme, it is considered an absolute URI.

- If a relative URI starts with an authority, it inherits a scheme from its base URI.

- If a relative URI is an empty string, it is the same as the base URI.

- If a relative URI has a fragment part only, the resolved URI uses the new fragment. If a base URI had a fragment, it is replaced with the fragment of the relative URI. Otherwise, the fragment of the relative URI is added to the base URI.

- A relative URI's path does not start with a forward slash (/). If the base URI has a path, remove the last component of the path in the base URI and append the relative URI. Note that the last component of the path may be an empty string, as in http://www.abc.com/.

- If a relative URL starts with a path, which in turn starts with a forward slash (/), the base URI's path is replaced with the relative URI's path.

Table 8-5 contains examples of using these rules. The examples in the table conform to the rules followed in Java URI and URL classes. Java rules deviate slightly in a few cases from the rules set in the URI specification.

Table 8-5. *Examples of How a Relative URI Is Resolved to an Absolute URI Using a Base URI*

Base URI	Relative URI	Resolved URI Relative	Description of the Relative URI
h://sn/a/b/c	http://sn2/ fooh://sn2/foo	It is an absolute URI.	
h://sn/a/b/c	//sn2/h/k h://sn2/h/k	It starts with an authority.	
h://sn/a/b/c		h://sn/a/b/c	It is an empty string.
h://sn/a/b/c	#k	h://sn/a/b/c#k	It contains a fragment only.
h://sn/a/b/c#a	#k	h://sn/a/b/c#k	It contains a fragment only.
h://sn/a/b/	Foo	h://sn/a/b/foo	The path does not start with a /.
h://sn/a/b/c	Foo	h://sn/a/b/foo	The path does not start with a /.
h://sn/a/b/c?d=3	Foo	h://sn/a/b/foo	The path does not start with a /.
h://sn/	Foo	h://sn/foo	The path does not start with a /.
h://sn	Foo	h://sn/foo	The path does not start with a /.
h://sn/a/b/	/foo	h://sn/foo	The path starts with a /.
h://sn/a/b/c	/foo	h://sn/foo	The path starts with a /.
h://sn/a/b/c?d=3	/foo	h://sn/foo	The path starts with a /.
h://sn/	/foo	h://sn/foo	The path starts with a /.
h://sn/	/foo	h://sn/foo	The path starts with a /.

Note   You can also use a host name or an IP address as an authority in a URI. IPv4 can be used in its dotted decimal format such as http://192.168.10.178/ docs/toc.html. IPv6 must be enclosed in brackets such as http:// [1283::8:800:200C:A43A]/docs/toc.html.

URI and URL As Java Objects

Java represents URIs and URLs as objects. It provides the following four classes that you can use to work with URIs and URLs as objects in a Java program:

- `java.net.URI`

- `java.net.URL`

- `java.net.URLEncoder`

- `java.net.URLDecoder`

An object of the URI class represents a URI. An object of the URL class represents a URL. URLEncoder and URLDecoder are utility classes that help encode and decode URI strings. I cover other Java classes in the next sections that are used to retrieve the resource identified by a URL.

The URI class has many constructors, which let you create a URI object from combinations of parts (scheme, authority, path, query, and fragment) of a URI. All constructors throw a checked exception, URISyntaxException, if strings, which you use to construct a URI object, may not be in conformity with the URI specification.

```
// Create a URI object
URI baseURI = new URI("http://www.yahoo.com");
// Create a URI with relative URI string and resolve it
// using baseURI
URI relativeURI = new URI("welcome.html");
URI resolvedRelativeURI = baseURI.resolve(relativeURI);
```

Listing 8-10 demonstrates how to use the URI class in a Java program.

Listing 8-10. A Sample Class That Demonstrates the Use of the java.net.URI Class

```
// URITest.java
package com.jdojo.net;
import java.net.URI;
import java.net.URISyntaxException;
```

```java
public class URITest {
    public static void main(String[] args) {
        String baseURIStr =
            "http://www.jdojo.com/javaintro.html?"
            + "id=25&rate=5.5%25#foo";
        String relativeURIStr = "../sports/welcome.html";
        try {
            URI baseURI = new URI(baseURIStr);
            URI relativeURI = new URI(relativeURIStr);
            // Resolve the relative URI with respect to
            // the base URI
            URI resolvedURI = baseURI.resolve(relativeURI);
            printURIDetails(baseURI);
            printURIDetails(relativeURI);
            printURIDetails(resolvedURI);
        } catch (URISyntaxException e) {
            e.printStackTrace();
        }
    }
    public static void printURIDetails(URI uri) {
        System.out.println("URI:" + uri);
        System.out.println("Normalized:"
                + uri.normalize());
        String parts = "[Scheme=" + uri.getScheme()
                + ", Authority=" + uri.getAuthority()
                + ", Path=" + uri.getPath()
                + ", Query:" + uri.getQuery()
                + ", Fragment:" + uri.getFragment()
                + "]";
        System.out.println(parts);
        System.out.println();
    }
}
```

```
URI:http://www.jdojo.com/javaintro.html?
    id=25&rate=5.5%25#foo
Normalized:http://www.jdojo.com/javaintro.html?
    id=25&rate=5.5%25#foo
[Scheme=http,
  Authority=www.jdojo.com,
  Path=/javaintro.html,
  Query:id=25&rate=5.5%,
Fragment:foo]
URI:../sports/welcome.html
Normalized:../sports/welcome.html
[
  Scheme=null,
  Authority=null,
  Path=../sports/welcome.html,
  Query:null,
  Fragment:null
]
URI:http://www.jdojo.com/../sports/welcome.html
Normalized:http://www.jdojo.com/../sports/welcome.html
[
  Scheme=http,
  Authority=www.jdojo.com,
  Path=/../sports/welcome.html,
  Query:null,
  Fragment:null
]
```

You can also get a URL object from a URI object using its toURL() method as shown:

```
URL baseURL = baseURI.toURL();
```

You can also create a URI object using the create(String str) static method of the URI class. The create() method does not throw a checked exception. It throws a runtime exception. Therefore, its use will not force you to handle the exception. You should use this method only when you know that a URI string is well formed:

```
URI uri2 = URI.create("http://www.yahoo.com");
```

An instance of the `java.net.URL` class represents a URL in a Java program. Although every URL is also a URI, Java does not inherit the URL class from the URI class. Java uses the term protocol to refer to the scheme part in the URI specification. You can create a URL object by providing a string that has all URL's parts concatenated or by providing the parts separately. If strings that you supply to create a URL object are not valid, the constructors of the URL class will throw a `MalformedURLException` checked exception.

Listing 8-11 demonstrates how to create a URL object. The URL class lets you create an absolute URL from a relative URL and a base URL using one of its constructors.

Listing 8-11. A Sample Class That Demonstrates the Use of the java.net.URL Class

```
// URLTest.java
package com.jdojo.net;
import java.net.URL;
public class URLTest {
    public static void main(String[] args) {
        String baseURLStr =
            "http://www.ietf.org/rfc/rfc3986.txt";
        String relativeURLStr = "rfc2732.txt";
        try {
            URL baseURL = new URL(baseURLStr);
            URL resolvedRelativeURL =
                new URL(baseURL, relativeURLStr);
            System.out.println(
                "Base URL:" + baseURL);
            System.out.println(
                "Relative URL String:" +
                relativeURLStr);
            System.out.println(
                "Resolved Relative URL:" +
                resolvedRelativeURL);
        } catch (Exception e) {
            e.printStackTrace();
        }
    }
}
```

```
Base URL:http://www.ietf.org/rfc/rfc3986.txt
Relative URL String:rfc2732.txt
Resolved Relative URL:http://www.ietf.org/rfc/rfc2732.txt
```

Typically, you create a URL object to retrieve the resource identified by the URL. Note that you can create an object of the URL class as long as the URL is well formed textually, and the protocol to handle the URL is available. The successful creation of a URL object in a Java program does not guarantee the existence of the resource at the server specified in the URL. The URL class provides methods that you can use in conjunction with other classes to retrieve the resource identified by the URL.

The URL class makes sure that it can handle the protocol specified in the URL string. For example, it will not let you create a URL object with a string as ppp://www.sss.com/ unless you develop and supply it a protocol handler for a protocol named ppp. I cover how to retrieve the resource identified by a URL in the next section.

Sometimes, you do not know the parts of the URL string in advance. You get the parts of the URL at runtime as input from other parts of the program or from the user. In such cases, you will need to encode the parts of the URL before you can use them to create a URL object. Sometimes, you get a string in encoded form, and you want it to be decoded. An encoded string will have all the restricted characters properly escaped.

The URLEncoder and URLDecoder classes are used to encode and decode strings, respectively. The URLEncoder.encode(String source, String encoding) static method is used to encode a source string using the specified encoding. The URLDecoder.decode(String source, String encoding) static method is used to decode a source string using a specified encoding. The following snippet of code shows how to encode/decode strings. Typically, you encode/decode the value part of name-value pairs in the query part of a URL. Note that you should never attempt to encode the entire URL string. Otherwise, it will encode some of the reserved characters such as a forward slash, and the resulting URL string will be invalid.

```
String source = "this is a test for 2.5% and &" ;
String encoded = URLEncoder.encode(source, "utf-8");
String decoded = URLDecoder.decode(encoded, "utf-8");
System.out.println("Source: " + source);
System.out.println("Encoded: " + encoded);
System.out.println("Decoded: " + decoded);
```

```
Source: this is a test for 2.5% and &
Encoded: this+is+a+test+for+2.5%25+and+%26
Decoded: this is a test for 2.5% and &
```

Accessing the Contents of a URL

A URL has a protocol that is used to communicate with the remote application that hosts the URL's contents. For example, the URL http://www.yahoo.com/index.html uses the http protocol. In a URL, you specify a protocol that is used by the application layer in the protocol suite. When you need to access the URL's contents, the computer will use some kind of protocols from lower layers in the protocol suite (transport, Internet layers, etc.) to communicate with the remote host. The http application layer protocol uses TCP/IP protocols in lower layers. In a distributed application, it is very frequent that you need to retrieve (or read) the resource (could be text, html content, image files, audio/video files, or any other kind of information) identified by a URL. Although it is possible to open a socket every time you need to read the contents of a URL, it is time consuming and cumbersome for programmers. After all, programmers need some way to be more productive than writing repetitive code for what seems to be a routine job. Java designers realized this need, and they have provided a very easy (yes, it is very easy) way to read/write data from/to a URL. This section explores some of the ways, from very simple to quite complex, to read/write data from/to a URL.

As the data passes from one layer to another in the protocol suite, each layer adds a header to the data. Since a URL uses a protocol in the application layer, it also contains its own header. The format of the header depends on the protocol being used. When the http request is sent to a remote host, the application layer in the source host adds the http header to the data. The remote host has an application layer that handles the http protocol, and it uses the header information to interpret the contents. In summary, a URL data will have two parts: a header part and a content part. The URL class along with some other classes lets you read/write both header and content parts of a URL. I start with the simplest case of reading the contents of a URL.

Before you read/write from/to a URL, you need to have a working URL that you can access. You can read content of any URL that is publicly available on the Internet. For this discussion, I use a website at www.httpbin.org/ that provides several URLs for testing purposes. This website provides several endpoints for testing purposes. Visit this website for the complete list of endpoints. Table 8-6 contains two of such endpoints that you will use in the examples in this section.

Table 8-6. *Useful Endpoints at* `www.httpbin.org` *Used in the Examples*

URL	Description
`http://www.httpbin.org/get`	Accepts an HTTP GET request and returns the parameters passed to this URL in JSON format. If you pass a year parameter with a value of 1969 to this endpoint, your URL would look as follows: `http://www.httpbin.org/get?year=1069`
`http://www.httpbin.org/post`	Accepts an HTTP POST request and returns the same POST data passed to this URL in JSON format.

The URL class lets you read the contents (not header) of a URL by just writing two lines of code as shown:

```
URL url = new URL("your URL string goes here");
InputStream ins = url.openStream();
```

Listing 8-12 contains the complete program that reads the contents of the URL `http://httpbin.org/get?year=1969`. The output shows that the server returned the passed GET parameter (year=1969) in the args object. If you want to use the POST method to send a request to a URL, you will need to use the URLConnection class, which I explain next. I have formatted the output for better readability.

Listing 8-12. A Simple URL Content Reader Program

```java
// SimpleURLContentReader.java
package com.jdojo.net;
import java.io.BufferedReader;
import java.io.IOException;
import java.io.InputStreamReader;
import java.net.URL;
```

```java
public class SimpleURLContentReader {
    public static void main(String[] args) {
        String urlStr = "http://httpbin.org/get?year=1969";
        String content = getURLContent(urlStr);
        System.out.println(content);
    }
    public static String getURLContent(String urlStr) {
        BufferedReader br = null;
        try {
            URL url = new URL(urlStr);
            // Get the input stream wrapped into a
            // BufferedReader
            br = new BufferedReader(
                new InputStreamReader(
                    url.openStream()));
            StringBuilder sb = new StringBuilder();
            String msg = null;
            while ((msg = br.readLine()) != null) {
                sb.append(msg);
                sb.append("\n");
                // <- Append a new line
            }
            return sb.toString();
        } catch (IOException e) {
            e.printStackTrace();
        } finally {
            if (br != null) {
                try {
                    br.close();
                } catch (IOException e) {
                    e.printStackTrace();
                }
            }
        }
```

```
            // If we get here it means there was an error
            return null;
        }
    }
```

```
{
  "args": {
    "year": "1969"
  },
  "headers": {
    "Accept": "text/html, image/gif,
        image/jpeg, *; q=.2, */*; q=.2",
    "Connection": "close",
    "Host": "httpbin.org",
    "User-Agent": "Java/9"
  },
  "origin": "50.58.251.82",
  "url": "http://httpbin.org/get?year=1969"
}
```

Once you get the input stream, you can use it for reading the content of the URL. Another way of reading the content of a URL is by using the getContent() method of the URL class. Since getContent() can return any kind of content, its return type is the Object type. You will need to check what kind of object it returns before you use the contents of the object. For example, it may return an InputStream object, and in that case, you will need to read data from the input stream. The following are the two versions of the getContent() method:

- final Object getContent() throws IOException

- final Object getContent(Class[] classes) throws IOException

The second version of the method lets you pass an array of class type. It will attempt to convert the content object to one of the classes you pass to it in the specified order. If the content object does not match any of the types, it will return null. You will still need to write if statements to know what type of object was returned from the getContent() method, as shown:

```
URL baseURL = new URL ("your url string goes here");
Class[] c = new Class[] {
    String.class,
    BufferedReader.class,
    InputStream.class
};
Object content = baseURL.getContent(c);
if (content == null) {
    // Contents are not of any of the three kinds
} else if (content instanceof String) {
    // You got a string
} else if (content instanceof BufferedReader) {
    // You got a reader
} else if (content instanceof InputStream) {
    // You got an input stream
}
```

If you read the contents of a URL using the openStream() or getContent() method, the URL class handles many of the complexities of using sockets internally. The downside of this approach is that you do not have any control over the connection settings. You cannot write data to the URL using this approach. Also, you do not have access to the header information for the protocol used in a URL. Don't despair; Java provides another class named URLConnection that lets you do these in a simple and concise manner.

URLConnection is an abstract class, and you cannot create its object directly. You need to use the openConnection() method of the URL object to get a URLConnection object. The URL class will handle the creation of a URLConnection object, which will be appropriate to handle the data for the protocol used in the URL. The following snippet of code shows how to use a URLConnection object to read and write data to a URL:

```
URL url = new URL("your URL string goes here");
// Get a connection object
URLConnection connection = url.openConnection();
// Indicate that you will be writing to the connection
connection.setDoOutput(true);
```

```
// Get output/input streams to write/read data
OutputStream ous = connection.getOutputStream();
InputStream ins = connection.getInputStream();
// <- Caution. Read below
```

The openConnection() method of the URL class returns a URLConnection object, which is not connected to the URL source yet. You must set all connection-related parameters to this object before it is connected. For example, if you want to write data to the URL, you must call the setDoOutput(true) method on the connection object before it is connected. A URLConnection object gets connected when you call its connect() method. However, it is connected implicitly when you call its methods that require a connection. For example, writing data to a URL and reading the URL's data or header fields will connect the URLConnection object automatically, if it is not already connected.

Here are a few things you must follow if you want to avoid problems when you work with a URLConnection to read and write data to a URL:

- When you are only reading data from a URL, you can get the input stream using its getInputStream() method. Use the input stream to read data. It will use a GET method for the request to the remote host. That is, if you are passing some parameters to the URL, you must do so by adding the query part to the URL.

- If you are writing as well as reading data from a URL, you must call the setDoOutput(true) before you connect. You must finish writing the data to the URL before you start reading the data. Writing data to a URL will change the request method to POST. You cannot even get the input stream before you finish writing data to the URL. In fact, the getInputStream() method sends a request to the remote host. Your intention is to send the data to the remote host and read the response from the remote host. This one gets as tricky as it can. Here is a little more explanation, using a snippet of code, assuming that connection is a URLConnection object:

```
// Incorrect - 1. Get input and output streams
// you must get the output stream first
InputStream ins = connection.getInputStream();
OutputStream ous = connection.getOutputStream();
// Incorrect - 2. Get output and input streams
```

```
// you must get the output stream and finish writing
// before you should get the input stream
OutputStream ous = connection.getOutputStream();
InputStream ins = connection.getInputStream();
// Correct. Get output stream and get done with it.
// And, then get the input stream and read data.
OutputStream ous = connection.getOutputStream();
// Write logic to write data using ous object here.
// Make sure you are done writing data before you
// call the getInputStream() method as shown below
InputStream ins = connection.getInputStream();
// Write logic to read data
```

- Using the getInputStream() method and reading header fields, using any method such as getHeaderField(String headerName), have the same effect. The URL's server supplies both header and content. A URLConnection must send the request to get them.

Listing 8-13 contains the complete code that writes/reads data to/from the http://www.httpbin/post URL.

Listing 8-13. A URL Reader/Writer Class That Writes/Reads Data to/from a URL

```
// URLConnectionReaderWriter.java
package com.jdojo.net;
import java.io.BufferedReader;
import java.io.BufferedWriter;
import java.io.IOException;
import java.io.InputStream;
import java.io.InputStreamReader;
import java.io.OutputStream;
import java.io.OutputStreamWriter;
import java.io.UnsupportedEncodingException;
import java.net.URL;
import java.net.URLConnection;
import java.net.URLEncoder;
import java.util.Map;
```

```java
public class URLConnectionReaderWriter {
    public static String
    getURLContent(String urlStr, String input) {
        BufferedReader br = null;
        BufferedWriter bw = null;
        try {
            URL url = new URL(urlStr);
            URLConnection connection =
                url.openConnection();
            // Must call setDoOutput(true) to indicate
            // that you will write to the connection. By
            // default, it is false.
            // By default, setDoInput() is set to true.
            connection.setDoOutput(true);
            // Now, connect to the remote object
            connection.connect();
            // Write data to the URL first before reading
            // the response
            OutputStream ous = connection.getOutputStream();
            bw = new BufferedWriter(
                new OutputStreamWriter(ous));
            bw.write(input);
            bw.flush();
            bw.close();
            // Must be placed after writing the data.
            // Otherwise, it will result in error, because
            // if write is performed, read must be performed
            // after the write.
            printRequestHeaders(connection);
            InputStream ins = connection.getInputStream();
            // Wrap the input stream into a reader
            br = new BufferedReader(
                new InputStreamReader(ins));
            StringBuilder sb = new StringBuilder();
            String msg = null;
```

```java
        while ((msg = br.readLine()) != null) {
            sb.append(msg);
            sb.append("\n");
            // <- Append a new line
        }
        return sb.toString();
    } catch (IOException e) {
        e.printStackTrace();
    } finally {
        if (br != null) {
            try {
                br.close();
            } catch (IOException e) {
                e.printStackTrace();
            }
        }
    }
    // If we arrive here it means there was an error
    return null;
}
public static void
printRequestHeaders(URLConnection connection) {
    Map headers = connection.getHeaderFields();
    System.out.println("Request Headers are:");
    System.out.println(headers);
    System.out.println();
}
public static void main(String[] args) {
    // Change the URL to point to the echo_params.jsp
    // page on your web server
    String urlStr = "http://www.httpbin.org/post";
    String query = null;
    try {
        // Encode the query. We need to encode only
        // the value of the name parameter. Other
        // names and values are fine
```

```
            query = "id=789&name=" +
                URLEncoder.encode("John & Co.", "utf-8");
            // Get the content and display it on the console
            String content = getURLContent(urlStr, query);
            System.out.println(
                "Returned data from the server is:");
            System.out.println(content);
        } catch (UnsupportedEncodingException e) {
            e.printStackTrace();
        }
    }
}
```

Request Headers are:
```
{
  null=[HTTP/1.1 200 OK],
  X-Processed-Time=[0.000935077667236],
  Server=[meinheld/0.6.1],
  Access-Control-Allow-Origin=[*],
  Access-Control-Allow-Credentials=[true],
  Connection=[keep-alive],
  Content-Length=[462],
  Date=[Wed, 03 Jan 2018 19:37:10 GMT],
  Via=[1.1 vegur],
  X-Powered-By=[Flask],
  Content-Type=[application/json]
}
```
Returned data from the server is:
```
{
  "args": {},
  "data": "",
  "files": {},
  "form": {
    "id": "789",
    "name": "John & Co."
  },
```

```
"headers": {
  "Accept": "text/html, image/gif, image/jpeg, *;
            q=.2, */*; q=.2",
  "Connection": "close",
  "Content-Length": "24",
  "Content-Type": "application/x-www-form-urlencoded",
  "Host": "www.httpbin.org",
  "User-Agent": "Java/9"
},
"json": null,
"origin": "50.58.251.82",
"url": "http://www.httpbin.org/post"
}
```

This time, you are using the POST method to send data to the URL. Note that the data that you send has been encoded using the URLEncoder class. You needed to encode only the value of the name field, which is "John & Co." because the ampersand in the value will conflict with the name-value pair separator in the query string. The program has plenty of comments to warn you of any dangers if you change the sequence of any statements.

The program prints information about all headers that are returned in a java.util. Map object. The URLConnection class provides several ways to get the header field's values. For commonly used headers, it provides a direct method. For example, the methods called getContentLength(), getContentType(), and getContentEncoding() return the value of the header fields that indicate length, type, and encoding of the URL's contents, respectively. If you know the header field name or its index, you can use the getHeaderField(String headerName) or getHeaderField(int headerIndex) method to get its value. The getHeaderFields() method returns a Map object whose keys represent the header field names, and the values represent the header field values. Use caution when reading a header field because it has the same effect on the URLConnection object as reading the contents. If you wish to write data to a URL, you must first write the data before you can read the header fields.

Java lets you read the contents of a JAR file using the jar protocol. Suppose you have a JAR file called myclasses.jar, which has a class file whose path is myfolder/Abc. class. You can get a JarURLConnection from a URL and use its methods to access the JAR file data. Note that you can only read JAR file contents from a URL. You cannot write to a JAR file URL. The following snippet of code shows how to get a `JarURLConnection` object. You will need to use its methods to get the JAR-specific data:

```
String str =
    "jar:http://www.abc.com/myclasses.jar!/myfolder/" +
    "Abc.class";
URL url = new URL(str);
JarURLConnection connection = (JarURLConnection)
    url.openConnection();
// Use the connection object to access any jar related
// data.
```

Note You have read many words of caution in this section about using a URLConnection object. Here is one more: a URLConnection object must be used for only one request. It works on the concept of obtain-use-and-throw. If you wish to write or read data from a URL multiple times, you must call the URL's openConnection() each time separately.

Non-blocking Socket Programming

In previous sections, I explained TCP and UDP sockets. The `connect()`, `accept()`, `read()`, and `write()` methods of the `Socket` and `ServerSocket` classes block until the operation is complete. For example, a client socket's thread is blocked if it calls the `read()` method to read data from a server until the data is available. Would it not be nice if you could call the `read()` method on a client socket and start doing something else until the data from the server arrives? When data is available from the server, the client socket will be notified, which will read the data at an appropriate time. Another big issue that you face with socket programming is the scalability of a server application. In previous sections, I suggested that you would need to create a new thread to handle each client connection, or you would have a pool of threads to handle all client connections. Both ways, you will be creating and maintaining a bunch of threads in your program. Wouldn't it be nice if you didn't have to deal with threads in a server program to handle multiple clients? Non-blocking socket channels offer all of these nice features. As always, a good feature has a price tag associated with it; so too with the non-blocking socket channel. It has a bit of a learning curve. You are used to programming where things happen sequentially. With non-blocking socket channels, you will need to change your mindset about the way you think about performing things in a program. Changing your mindset takes time. Your program will be performing multiple things that will not be performed sequentially. If you are learning Java for the first time, you can skip this section and revisit it later when you gain some more experience in writing complex Java programs.

It is assumed that you have a good understanding of socket programming using ServerSocket and Socket classes. It is further assumed that you have a basic understanding of *New Input/Output* in Java using buffers and channels. This section uses some classes that are contained in java.nio, java.nio.channels, and java.nio. charset packages.

Let's start by comparing classes that are involved in blocking and non-blocking socket communications. Table 8-7 lists the main classes that are used in blocking and non-blocking socket applications.

Table 8-7. *Comparison of Classes Involved in Blocking and Non-blocking Socket Programming*

Classes Used in Blocking Socket-Based Communication	Classes Used in Non-blocking Socket-Based Communications
ServerSocket	ServerSocketChannel The ServerSocket class still exists behind the scenes.
Socket	SocketChannel The Socket class still exists behind the scenes.
InputStream OutputStream	No corresponding classes exist. A SocketChannel is used to read/write data.
No corresponding classes exist.	Selector
No corresponding class exists.	SelectionKey

You will work with a ServerSocketChannel object primarily to accept a new connection request in a server instead of using a ServerSocket. The ServerSocket has not disappeared. It is still at play behind the scenes. If you need the reference of the

ServerSocket object being used internally, you can get it by using the socket() method of the ServerSocketChannel object. You can think of a ServerSocketChannel object as a wrapper for a ServerSocket object.

You will work with a SocketChannel to communicate between a client and a server instead of a Socket. A Socket object is still at play behind the scenes. You can get the reference of the Socket object using the socket() method of the SocketChannel class. You can think of a SocketChannel object as a wrapper for a Socket object.

Before I start discussing the mechanism that is used by the non-blocking sockets to give you a more efficient and scalable application interface, it would be helpful to look at a real-world example. Let's discuss the way orders are placed and served in a fast food restaurant. Suppose the restaurant expects a maximum of ten customers and a minimum of zero customers at any time. A customer comes to the restaurant, places their order, and is served the food. How many servers should that restaurant employ? In the best case, it may employ only one server that can handle receiving orders from all customers and serving their food. In the worst case, it can have ten servers—one server reserved for one customer. In the latter case, if there are only three customers in the restaurant, seven servers will be idle.

Let's take the middle path in the restaurant management. Let's have a few servers in the kitchen to cook and one server at the counter to receive orders. A customer comes and places an order with the server at the counter, the customer gets an order ID, the customer leaves the counter, the server at the counter passes on the order to one of the servers in the kitchen, and the server starts taking an order from the next customer. At this point, the customer is free to do something else while their order is being prepared. The server at the counter is dealing with other customers. Servers in the kitchen are busy preparing the food according to the orders placed. No one is waiting for anyone. As soon as the food item in an order is ready, the server at the counter receives it from the server in the kitchen and calls the order number so the customer who placed that order will pick up their food. A customer may get their food in multiple installments. They can eat the food that they have been served while the remaining items in their order are being prepared in the kitchen. This architecture is the most efficient architecture you can have in a restaurant. It keeps everyone busy most of the time and makes efficient use of the resources. This is the approach that non-blocking socket channels follow.

Another approach would be that the customer comes in, places their order, and waits until their order is complete and is served, and then the next customer places their order, and so on. This is the approach that blocking sockets follow. If you understand the approach taken by the fast food restaurant for the efficient use of resources, you can understand the non-blocking socket channels easily. I compare the people used in the restaurant example with objects used in non-blocking sockets in the following discussion.

Let's first discuss the situation on the server side. The server side is your restaurant. The person at the counter, who interfaces with all customers, is called a *selector*. A selector is an object of the Selector class. Its sole job is to interact with the outside world. It sits between remote clients interacting with the server and the things inside the server. A remote client never interacts with objects working inside the server, as a customer in the restaurant never interacts directly with servers in the kitchen. Figure 8-7 shows the architecture of non-blocking socket channel communication. It shows where the selector fits into the architecture.

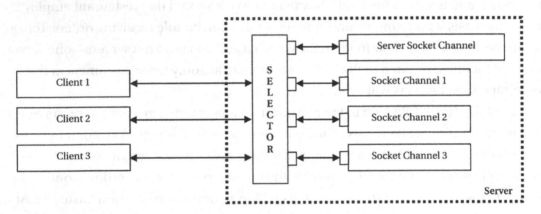

Figure 8-7. *Architecture of non-blocking client-server sockets*

You cannot create a selector object directly using its constructor. You need to call its open() static method to get a selector object as shown:

```
// Get a selector object
Selector selector = Selector.open();
```

A ServerSocketChannel is used to listen for a new connection request from clients. Again, you cannot create a new ServerSocketChannel object using its constructor. You need to call its open() static method as shown:

```
// Get a server socket channel
ServerSocketChannel ssChannel = ServerSocketChannel.open();
```

By default, a server socket channel or a socket channel is a blocking channel. You need to configure it to make it a non-blocking channel as shown:

```
// Configure the server socket channel to be non-blocking
ssChannel.configureBlocking(false);
```

Your server socket channel needs to be bound to a local IP address and a local port number, so a remote client may contact it for new connections. You bind a server socket channel using its bind() method, which is part of the ServerSocketChannel and the SocketChannel classes:

```
InetAddress hostIPAddress =
    InetAddress.getByName("localhost");
int port = 19000;
ssChannel.bind(new InetSocketAddress(hostIPAddress, port));
```

The most important step is taken now. The server socket has to register itself with the selector showing interest in some kind of operation. It is like a pizza maker in a restaurant letting the server at the counter know that they are ready to make pizza for customers, and they need to be notified when an order for pizza is placed. There are four kinds of operations for which you can register a channel with the selector. They are defined as integer constants in the SelectionKey class listed in Table 8-8.

Table 8-8. *Operations Recognized by the Selector*

Operation Type	Value (Constants in SelectionKey Class)	Who Can Register for This Operation	Description
Connect	OP_CONNECT	SocketChannel at client	Selector will notify about the connect operation progress.
Accept	OP_ACCEPT	ServerSocketChannel at server	Selector will notify when a client request for a new connection arrives.
Read	OP_READ	SocketChannel at client and server	Selector will notify when the channel is ready to read some data.
Write	OP_WRITE	SocketChannel at client and server	Selector will notify when the channel is ready to write some data.

A ServerSocketChannel only listens for accepting a new client connection request, and therefore it can register for only one operation as shown:

```
// Register the server socket channel with the selector
// for accept operation
ssChannel.register(selector, SelectionKey.OP_ACCEPT);
```

The register() method of ServerSocketChannel returns an object of type SelectionKey. You can think of this object as a registration certificate with the selector. You can store this key object in a variable if you need to use it later. The example ignores it. The selector has a copy of your key (registration details) and will use it in the future to notify you of any operation for which your channel is ready.

At this point, your selector is ready to intercept an incoming request for a client connection and pass it on to the server socket channel. Suppose a client attempts to connect to the server socket channel at this time. How does interaction between the selector and the server socket channel take place? When the selector detects that there is a registered key with it, which is ready for an operation, it places that key (an object of the SelectionKey class) in a separate group called the *ready set*. A java.util.Set object represents a ready set. You can determine the number of keys in a ready state by calling the select() method of a Selector object:

```
// Get the key count in the ready set
int readyCount = selector.select();
```

Once you get at least one ready key in the ready set, you need to get the key and look at the details. You can get all ready keys from the ready set as shown:

```
// Get the set of ready keys
Set readySet = selector.selectedKeys();
```

Note that you register a key for one or more operations. You need to look at the key details for its readiness for a particular operation. If a key is ready for accepting a new connection request, its isAcceptable() method will return true. If a key is ready for a connection operation, its isConnectable() method will return true. If a key is ready for read and write operations, its isReadable() and isWritable() methods will return true. You may observe that there is a method to check for the readiness for each operation type. When you are processing a ready set, you will also need to remove the key from the ready set. Here is some typical code that processes the ready set in a server application. An infinite loop is typical on a server application because you need to keep looking for the next ready set once you are done with the current ready set:

```
while(true) {
    // Get the count of keys in the ready set. If ready
    // key count is greater than zero, process each key
    // in the ready set.
}
```

The following snippet of code shows the typical logic that you can use to process all keys in a ready set:

```
SelectionKey key = null;
Iterator iterator = readySet.iterator();
while (iterator.hasNext()) {
    // Get the next ready selection key object
    key = (SelectionKey)iterator.next();
    // Remove the key from ready set
    iterator.remove();
    // Process the key according to the operation
    if (key.isAcceptable()) {
        // Process new connection
    }
    if (key.isReadable()) {
        // Read from the channel
    }
    if (key.isWritable()) {
        // Write to the channel
    }
}
```

How do you accept a connection request from a remote client on a server socket channel? The logic is similar to accepting a remote connection request using a ServerSocket object. A SelectionKey object has a reference to the ServerSocketChannel that registered it. You can get to the ServerSocketChannel object of a SelectionKey object using its channel() method. You need to call the accept()

method on the ServerSocketChannel object to accept a new connection request. The accept() method returns an object of the SocketChannel class that is used to communicate (read and write) with a remote client. You need to configure the new SocketChannel object to be a non-blocking socket channel. The most important point that you need to understand is that the new SocketChannel object must register itself for read, write, or both operations with the selector to start reading/writing data on the connection channel. The following snippet of code shows the logic to accept a remote connection request:

```
ServerSocketChannel ssChannel =
    (ServerSocketChannel)key.channel();
SocketChannel sChannel = (SocketChannel)ssChannel.accept();
sChannel.configureBlocking(false);
// Register only for read. Your message is small and you
// write it back to the client as soon as you read it.
sChannel.register(key.selector(), SelectionKey.OP_READ);
```

If you wish to register the socket channel with a selector for a read and a write, you can do so as shown:

```
// Register for read and write
sChannel.register(key.selector(),
    SelectionKey.OP_READ | SelectionKey.OP_WRITE);
```

Once your socket channel is registered with the selector, it will be notified through the selector's ready set when it receives any data from the remote client or when you can write data to the remote client on its channel.

If data becomes available on a socket channel, the key.isReadable() will return true for this socket channel. A typical read operation looks as follows. You must have a basic understanding of Java NIO (New Input/Output) to read data using channels and buffers.

```
SocketChannel sChannel = (SocketChannel) key.channel();
ByteBuffer buffer = ByteBuffer.allocate(1024);
int bytesCount = sChannel.read(buffer);
String msg = "";
```

```
if (bytesCount > 0) {
    buffer.flip();
    Charset charset = Charset.forName("UTF-8");
    CharsetDecoder decoder = charset.newDecoder();
    CharBuffer charBuffer = decoder.decode(buffer);
    msg = charBuffer.toString();
    System.out.println("Received Message: " + msg);
}
```

If you can write to a channel, the selector will place the associated key in its ready set whose isWritable() method will return true. Again, you need to understand Java NIO to use the ByteBuffer object to write data on a channel.

```
SocketChannel sChannel = (SocketChannel)key.channel();
String msg =
    "message to be sent to remote client goes here";
ByteBuffer buffer = ByteBuffer.wrap(msg.getBytes());
sChannel.write(buffer);
```

What happens on a client side is easy to understand. You start with getting a selector object, and you get a SocketChannel object by calling the SocketChannel.open() method. At this point, you need to configure the socket channel to be non-blocking before you connect to the server. Now you are ready to register your socket channel with the selector. Typically, you register with the selector for connect, read, and write operations. Processing the ready set of the selector is done the same way you processed the ready set of the selector in the server application. The code for reading and writing to the channel is similar to the server-side code. The following snippet of code shows the typical logic used in a client application:

```
InetAddress serverIPAddress =
    InetAddress.getByName("localhost");
int port = 19000;
InetSocketAddress serverAddress =
    new InetSocketAddress(serverIPAddress, port);
// Get a selector
Selector selector = Selector.open();
```

```
// Create and configure a client socket channel
SocketChannel channel = SocketChannel.open();
channel.configureBlocking(false);
// Connect to the server
channel.connect(serverAddress);
// Register the channel for connect, read and write
// operations
int operations = SelectionKey.OP_CONNECT |
    SelectionKey.OP_READ |
    SelectionKey.OP_WRITE;
channel.register(selector, operations);
// Process the ready set of the selector here
```

When you get a connect operation on a client-side SocketChannel, it may mean either a successful or failed connection. You can call the finishConnect() method on the SocketChannel object to finish the connection process. If the connection has failed, the finishConnect() call will throw an IOException. Typically, you handle a connect operation as follows:

```
if (key.isConnectable()) {
    try {
        // Call to finishConnect() is in a loop as it is
        // non-blocking for your channel
        while(channel.isConnectionPending()) {
            channel.finishConnect();
        }
    } catch (IOException e) {
        // Cancel the channel's registration with the
        // selector
        key.cancel();
        e.printStackTrace();
    }
}
```

It is time to build an echo client application and an echo server application using these channels. Listings 8-14 and 8-15 contain the complete code for a non-blocking socket channel for an echo server and an echo client, respectively.

You need to run the NonBlockingEchoServer class first and then one or more instances of the NonBlockingEchoClient class. They work similar to your other two echo client-server programs. Note that, this time, you may not see the messages from the server just after you enter a message in the client application. The client application sends a message to the server, and it does not wait for the message to be echoed back. Rather, it processes the server message when the socket channel receives the notification from the selector. Therefore, it is possible to get the two messages echoed back from the server at one time. Exception handling has been left out in these examples to keep the code simple and readable.

Listing 8-14. A Non-blocking Socket Channel Echo Server Program

```java
// NonBlockingEchoServer.java
package com.jdojo.net;
import java.io.IOException;
import java.net.InetAddress;
import java.net.InetSocketAddress;
import java.nio.ByteBuffer;
import java.nio.CharBuffer;
import java.nio.channels.SelectionKey;
import java.nio.channels.Selector;
import java.nio.channels.ServerSocketChannel;
import java.nio.channels.SocketChannel;
import java.nio.charset.Charset;
import java.nio.charset.CharsetDecoder;
import java.util.Iterator;
import java.util.Set;
public class NonBlockingEchoServer {
    public static void main(String[] args)
            throws Exception {
        InetAddress hostIPAddress =
            InetAddress.getByName("localhost");
        int port = 19000;
        // Get a selector
        Selector selector = Selector.open();
```

```
        // Get a server socket channel
        ServerSocketChannel ssChannel =
            ServerSocketChannel.open();
        // Make the server socket channel non-blocking
        // and bind it to an address
        ssChannel.configureBlocking(false);
        ssChannel.socket().bind(
            new InetSocketAddress(hostIPAddress, port));
        // Register a socket server channel with the
        // selector for accept operation, so that it can
        // be notified when a new connection request
        // arrives
        ssChannel.register(selector,
            SelectionKey.OP_ACCEPT);
        // Now we will keep waiting in a loop for any kind
        // of request that arrives to the server -
        // connection, read, or write request. If a
        // connection request comes in, we will accept the
        // request and register a new socket channel with
        // the selector for read and write operations. If
        // read or write requests come in, we will forward
        // that request to the registered channel.
        while (true) {
            if (selector.select() <= 0) {
                continue;
            }
            processReadySet(selector.selectedKeys());
        }
    }
    public static void
    processReadySet(Set readySet) throws Exception {
        SelectionKey key = null;
        Iterator iterator = null;
        iterator = readySet.iterator();
```

```
    while (iterator.hasNext()) {
        // Get the next ready selection key object
        key = (SelectionKey) iterator.next();
        // Remove the key from the ready key set
        iterator.remove();
        // Process the key according to the operation
        // it is ready for
        if (key.isAcceptable()) {
            processAccept(key);
        }
        if (key.isReadable()) {
            String msg = processRead(key);
            if (msg.length() > 0) {
                echoMsg(key, msg);
            }
        }
    }
}
public static void
processAccept(SelectionKey key) throws IOException {
    // This method call indicates that we got a new
    // connection request. Accept the connection
    // request and register the new socket channel
    // with the selector, so that client can
    // communicate on a new channel
    ServerSocketChannel ssChannel =
        (ServerSocketChannel)key.channel();
    SocketChannel sChannel =
        (SocketChannel) ssChannel.accept();
    sChannel.configureBlocking(false);
    // Register only for read. Our message is small
    // and we write it back to the client as soon
    // as we read it
    sChannel.register(key.selector(),
        SelectionKey.OP_READ);
}
```

```java
    public static String
    processRead(SelectionKey key) throws Exception {
        SocketChannel sChannel =
            (SocketChannel) key.channel();
        ByteBuffer buffer = ByteBuffer.allocate(1024);
        int bytesCount = sChannel.read(buffer);
        String msg = "";
        if (bytesCount > 0) {
            buffer.flip();
            Charset charset = Charset.forName("UTF-8");
            CharsetDecoder decoder = charset.newDecoder();
            CharBuffer charBuffer = decoder.decode(buffer);
            msg = charBuffer.toString();
            System.out.println("Received Message: " + msg);
        }
        return msg;
    }
    public static void
    echoMsg(SelectionKey key, String msg)
    throws IOException {
        SocketChannel sChannel =
            (SocketChannel) key.channel();
        ByteBuffer buffer =
            ByteBuffer.wrap(msg.getBytes());
        sChannel.write(buffer);
    }
}
```

Listing 8-15. A Non-blocking Socket Channel Echo Client Program

```java
// NonBlockingEchoClient.java
package com.jdojo.net;
import java.io.BufferedReader;
import java.io.IOException;
import java.io.InputStreamReader;
import java.net.InetAddress;
```

```java
import java.net.InetSocketAddress;
import java.nio.ByteBuffer;
import java.nio.CharBuffer;
import java.nio.channels.SelectionKey;
import java.nio.channels.Selector;
import java.nio.channels.SocketChannel;
import java.nio.charset.Charset;
import java.nio.charset.CharsetDecoder;
import java.util.Iterator;
import java.util.Set;
public class NonBlockingEchoClient {
    private static BufferedReader userInputReader = null;
    public static void main(String[] args)
            throws Exception {
        InetAddress serverIPAddress =
            InetAddress.getByName("localhost");
        int port = 19000;
        InetSocketAddress serverAddress =
            new InetSocketAddress(serverIPAddress, port);
        // Get a selector
        Selector selector = Selector.open();
        // Create and configure a client socket
        // channelHello
        try (SocketChannel channel =
                SocketChannel.open()) {
            channel.configureBlocking(false);
            channel.connect(serverAddress);
            // Register the channel for connect, read and
            // write operations
            int operations =
                SelectionKey.OP_CONNECT |
                SelectionKey.OP_READ |
                SelectionKey.OP_WRITE;
            channel.register(selector, operations);
```

```
            userInputReader =
                new BufferedReader(
                    new InputStreamReader(System.in));
            while (true) {
                if (selector.select() > 0) {
                    boolean doneStatus =
                        processReadySet(
                            selector.selectedKeys());
                    if (doneStatus) {
                        break;
                    }
                }
            }
        }
    }
    public static boolean
    processReadySet(Set readySet) throws Exception {
        SelectionKey key = null;
        Iterator iterator = null;
        iterator = readySet.iterator();
        while (iterator.hasNext()) {
            // Get the next ready selection key object
            key = (SelectionKey) iterator.next();
            // Remove the key from the ready key set
            iterator.remove();
            if (key.isConnectable()) {
                boolean connected = processConnect(key);
                if (!connected) {
                    return true; // Exit
                }
            }
            if (key.isReadable()) {
                String msg = processRead(key);
                System.out.println("[Server]: " + msg);
            }
```

```java
        if (key.isWritable()) {
            String msg = getUserInput();
            if (msg.equalsIgnoreCase("bye")) {
                return true; // Exit
            }
            processWrite(key, msg);
        }
    }
    return false; // Not done yet
}
public static boolean
processConnect(SelectionKey key) {
    SocketChannel channel =
        (SocketChannel) key.channel();
    try {
        // Call the finishConnect() in a loop as it is
        // non-blocking for your channel
        while (channel.isConnectionPending()) {
            channel.finishConnect();
        }
    } catch (IOException e) {
        // Cancel the channel's registration with the
        // selector
        key.cancel();
        e.printStackTrace();
        return false;
    }
    return true;
}
public static String
processRead(SelectionKey key) throws Exception {
    SocketChannel sChannel =
        (SocketChannel) key.channel();
    ByteBuffer buffer = ByteBuffer.allocate(1024);
    sChannel.read(buffer);
    buffer.flip();
```

```
        Charset charset = Charset.forName("UTF-8");
        CharsetDecoder decoder = charset.newDecoder();
        CharBuffer charBuffer = decoder.decode(buffer);
        String msg = charBuffer.toString();
        return msg;
    }
    public static void
    processWrite(SelectionKey key, String msg)
    throws IOException {
        SocketChannel sChannel =
            (SocketChannel) key.channel();
        ByteBuffer buffer =
            ByteBuffer.wrap(msg.getBytes());
        sChannel.write(buffer);
    }
    public static String
    getUserInput() throws IOException {
        String promptMsg =
            "Please enter a message(Bye to quit): ";
        System.out.print(promptMsg);
        String userMsg = userInputReader.readLine();
        return userMsg;
    }
}
```

Socket Security Permissions

You can control the access for a Java program to use sockets using an instance of
the java.net.SocketPermission class. The generic format used to grant a socket
permission in a Java policy file is as follows:

```
grant {
    permission java.net.SocketPermission
        "target", "actions";
};
```

The target is of the form `<host name>:<port range>`. The possible values of actions are `accept`, `connect`, `listen`, and `resolve`.

The `listen` action is meaningful only when "localhost" is used as the host name. The `resolve` action refers to a DNS lookup, and it is implied if any of the other three actions is present.

A host name could be either a DNS name or an IP address. You can use an asterisk (*) as a wildcard character in the DNS host name. If an asterisk is used, it must be used as the leftmost character in the DNS name. If the host name consists only of an asterisk, it refers to any host. The "localhost" for the host name refers to the local machine. You can indicate the port range for the host name in different formats, as described in Table 8-9. Here, N1 and N2 indicate port numbers (0 to 65535), and it is assumed that N1 is less than N2. Table 8-9 lists the format used for indicating the port range.

Table 8-9. *The <port range> Format for java.net.*
SocketPermission Security Settings

Port Range Value	Description
N1	Only one port number—N1
N1-N2	Port numbers from N1 to N2
N1-	Port numbers from N1 and greater
-N1	Port numbers from N1 and less

The following are examples of using a `java.net.SocketPermission` in a Java policy file:

```
// Grant to all codebase
grant {
    // Permission to connect with 192.168.10.123
    // at port 5000
    permission java.net.SocketPermission
        "192.168.10.123:5000", "connect";
    // Connect permission to any host at port 80
    permission java.net.SocketPermission
        "*:80", "connect";
```

```
// All socket permissions to on port >= 1024
// on the localhost
permission java.net.SocketPermission
    "localhost:1024-", "listen, accept, connect";
};
```

Asynchronous Socket Channels

Java has support for asynchronous socket operations such as connect, read, and write. The asynchronous socket operations are performed using the following two socket channel classes:

- `java.nio.channels.AsynchronousServerSocketChannel`

- `java.nio.channels.AsynchronousSocketChannel`

An AsynchronousServerSocketChannel serves as a server socket that listens for new incoming client connections. Once it accepts a new client connection, the interaction between the client and the server is handled by an AsynchronousSocketChannel at both ends. Asynchronous socket channels are set up very similar to the synchronous sockets. The main difference between the two setups is that the request for an asynchronous socket operation returns immediately and the requestor is notified when the operation is completed, whereas in a synchronous socket operation the request for a socket operation blocks until it is complete. Because of the asynchronous nature of the operations with the asynchronous socket channels, the code to handle the completion or failure of a socket operation is a bit complex.

In an asynchronous socket channel, you request an operation using one of the methods of the asynchronous socket channel classes. The method returns immediately. You receive a notification about the completion or failure of the operation later. The methods that allow you to request asynchronous operations are overloaded. One version returns a Future object that lets you check the status of the requested operation. Another version of those methods lets you pass a CompletionHandler. When the requested operation completes successfully, the completed() method of the CompletionHandler is called. When the requested operation fails, the failed() method of the CompletionHandler is called. The following snippet of code demonstrates both approaches of handling the completion/failure of a requested asynchronous socket operation. It shows how a server socket channel accepts a client connection asynchronously:

```
/* Using a Future Object */
// Get a server socket channel instance
AsynchronousServerSocketChannel server =
    ... /* get a server instance */;
// Bind the socket to a host and a port
server.bind(your_host, your_port);
// Start accepting a new client connection. Note that the
// accept() method returns immediately by returning a
// Future object
Future<AsynchronousSocketChannel> result = server.accept();
// Wait for the new client connection by calling the get()
// method of the Future object. Alternatively, you can poll
// the Future object periodically using its isDone() method
AsynchronousSocketChannel newClient = result.get();
// Handle the newClient here and call the server.accept()
// again to accept another client connection

/* Using a CompletionHandler Object */
// Get a server socket channel instance
AsynchronousServerSocketChannel server =
    ... /* get a server instance */;
// Bind the socket to a host and a port
server.bind(your_host, your_port);
// Start accepting a new client connection. The accept()
// method returns immediately. The completed() or failed()
// method of the ConnectionHandler will be called upon
// completion or failure of the requested operation
YourAnyClass attach = ...; // Get an attachment
server.accept(attach, new ConnectionHandler());
```

This version of the accept() method accepts an object of any class as an attachment. It could be a null reference. The attachment is passed to the completed() and failed() methods of the completion handler, which is an object of ConnectionHandler in this case. The ConnectionHandler class may look as follows:

```
private static class ConnectionHandler
    implements CompletionHandler
              <AsynchronousSocketChannel, YourAnyClass> {
    @Override
    public void
    completed(AsynchronousSocketChannel client,
            YourAnyClass attach) {
        // Handle the new client connection here and again
        // start accepting a new client connection
    }
    @Override
    public void
    failed(Throwable e, YourAnyClass attach) {
        // Handle the failure here
    }
}
```

In this section, I cover the following three steps in detail. During the discussion, I build an application that consists of an echo server and a client. Clients will send messages to the server asynchronously, and the server will echo back the message to the client asynchronously. It is assumed that you are familiar working with buffers and channels.

- Setting up an asynchronous server socket channel

- Setting up an asynchronous client socket channel

- Putting the asynchronous server and client socket channels in action

Setting Up an Asynchronous Server Socket Channel

An instance of the AsynchronousServerSocketChannel class is used as an asynchronous server socket channel to listen to the new incoming client connections. Once a connection to a client is established, an instance of the AsynchronousSocketChannel class is used to communicate with the client. The static open() method of the AsynchronousServerSocketChannel class returns an object of the AsynchronousServerSocketChannel class, which is not yet bound:

```
// Create an asynchronous server socket channel object
AsynchronousServerSocketChannel server =
    AsynchronousServerSocketChannel.open();
// Bind the server to the localhost and the port 8989
String host = "localhost";
int port = 8989;
InetSocketAddress sAddr =
    new InetSocketAddress(host, port);
server.bind(sAddr);
```

At this point, your server socket channel can be used to accept a new client connection by calling its accept() method as follows. The code uses two classes, Attachment and ConnectionHandler, which are described later.

```
// Prepare the attachment
Attachment attach = new Attachment();
attach.server = server;
// Accept new connections
server.accept(attach, new ConnectionHandler());
```

Typically, a server application runs indefinitely. You can make the server application run forever by waiting on the main thread in the main() method as follows:

```
try {
    // Wait indefinitely until someone interrupts the
    // main thread
    Thread.currentThread().join();
} catch (InterruptedException e) {
    e.printStackTrace();
}
```

You will use the completion handler mechanism to handle the completion/failure notification for the server socket channel. An object of the following Attachment class will be used to serve as an attachment to the completion handler. An attachment object is used to pass the context for the server socket that may be used inside the completed() and failed() methods of the completion handler:

```
class Attachment {
    AsynchronousServerSocketChannel server;
    AsynchronousSocketChannel client;
    ByteBuffer buffer;
    SocketAddress clientAddr;
    boolean isRead;
}
```

You need a CompletionHandler implementation to handle the completion of an accept() call. Let's call your class as ConnectionHandler as shown:

```
private static class ConnectionHandler
    implements CompletionHandler
            <AsynchronousSocketChannel, Attachment> {
    @Override
    public void
    completed(AsynchronousSocketChannel client,
            Attachment attach) {
        try {
            // Get the client address
            SocketAddress clientAddr =
                client.getRemoteAddress();
            System.out.format(
                "Accepted a connection from %s%n",
                clientAddr);
            // Accept another connection
            attach.server.accept(attach, this);
            // Handle the client connection by invoking an
            // asyn read
            Attachment newAttach = new Attachment();
            newAttach.server = attach.server;
            newAttach.client = client;
            newAttach.buffer = ByteBuffer.allocate(2048);
            newAttach.isRead = true;
            newAttach.clientAddr = clientAddr;
            // Create a new completion handler for reading
            // to and writing from the new client
```

```
            ReadWriteHandler readWriteHandler =
                new ReadWriteHandler();
            // Read from the client
            client.read(newAttach.buffer, newAttach,
                readWriteHandler);
        } catch (IOException e) {
            e.printStackTrace();
        }
    }
}
@Override
public void failed(Throwable e, Attachment attach) {
    System.out.println(
        "Failed to accept a connection.");
    e.printStackTrace();
}
}
```

The ConnectionHandler class is simple. In its failed() method, it prints the exception stack trace. In its completed() method, it prints a message that a new client connection has been established and starts listening for another new client connection by calling the accept() method on the server socket again. Note the reuse of the attachment in another accept() method call inside the completed() method. It uses the same CompletionHandler object again. Note that the attach.server.accept(attach, this) method call uses the keyword this to refer to the same instance of the completion handler. At the end, it prepares a new instance of the Attachment class, which wraps the details of handling (reading and writing) the new client connection, and calls the read() method on the client socket to read from the client. Note that the read() method uses another completion handler, which is an instance of the ReadWriteHandler class. The code for the ReadWriteHandler is as follows:

```
private static class ReadWriteHandler
        implements CompletionHandler<Integer, Attachment> {
    @Override
    public void
```

```
completed(Integer result, Attachment attach) {
    if (result == -1) {
        try {
            attach.client.close();
            System.out.format(
                "Stopped listening to the client %s%n",
                attach.clientAddr);
        } catch (IOException ex) {
            ex.printStackTrace();
        }
        return;
    }
    if (attach.isRead) {
        // A read to the client was completed
        // Get the buffer ready to read from it
        attach.buffer.flip();
        int limits = attach.buffer.limit();
        byte bytes[] = new byte[limits];
        attach.buffer.get(bytes, 0, limits);
        Charset cs = Charset.forName("UTF-8");
        String msg = new String(bytes, cs);
        // Print the message from the client
        System.out.format(
            "Client at %s says: %s%n",
            attach.clientAddr, msg);
        // Let us echo back the same message to the
        // client
        attach.isRead = false; // It is a write
        // Prepare the buffer to be read again
        attach.buffer.rewind();
        // Write to the client again
        attach.client.write(attach.buffer,
            attach, this);
    } else {
```

```
            // A write to the client was completed.
            // Perform another read from the client.
            attach.isRead = true;
            // Prepare the buffer to be filled in
            attach.buffer.clear();
            // Perform a read from the client
            attach.client.read(attach.buffer, attach,
                this);
        }
    }
    @Override
    public void
    failed(Throwable e, Attachment attach) {
        e.printStackTrace();
    }
}
```

The first argument called `result` of the `completed()` method is the number of bytes that is read from or written to the client. Its value of –1 indicates the end of stream, and in that case, the client socket is closed. If a read operation was completed, it displays the read text on the standard output and writes back the same text to the client. If a write operation to a client was completed, it performs a read on the same client.

Listing 8-16 contains the complete code for your asynchronous server socket channel. It uses three inner classes: one for the attachment, one for the connection completion handler, and one for the read/write completion handler. The `AsyncEchoServerSocket` class can be run now. However, it will not do any work as it needs a client to connect to it to echo back messages that are sent from the client. You will develop your asynchronous client socket channel in the next section, and then, in the subsequent section, you will test both server and client socket channels together.

Listing 8-16. A Server Application That Uses an Asynchronous Server Socket Channel

```
// AsyncEchoServerSocket.java
package com.jdojo.net;
import java.io.IOException;
import java.net.SocketAddress;
```

```java
import java.nio.ByteBuffer;
import java.nio.charset.Charset;
import java.net.InetSocketAddress;
import java.nio.channels.CompletionHandler;
import java.nio.channels.AsynchronousSocketChannel;
import java.nio.channels.AsynchronousServerSocketChannel;
public class AsyncEchoServerSocket {
    private static class Attachment {
        AsynchronousServerSocketChannel server;
        AsynchronousSocketChannel client;
        ByteBuffer buffer;
        SocketAddress clientAddr;
        boolean isRead;
    }
    private static class ConnectionHandler implements
            CompletionHandler
            <AsynchronousSocketChannel, Attachment> {
        @Override
        public void
        completed(AsynchronousSocketChannel client,
                Attachment attach) {
            try {
                // Get the client address
                SocketAddress clientAddr = client.
                    getRemoteAddress();
                System.out.format(
                    "Accepted a connection from %s%n",
                    clientAddr);
                // Accept another connection
                attach.server.accept(attach, this);
                // Handle the client connection by using
                // an asyn read
                ReadWriteHandler rwHandler =
                    new ReadWriteHandler();
```

```java
            Attachment newAttach = new Attachment();
            newAttach.server = attach.server;
            newAttach.client = client;
            newAttach.buffer = ByteBuffer.
                allocate(2048);
            newAttach.isRead = true;
            newAttach.clientAddr = clientAddr;
            client.read(newAttach.buffer, newAttach,
                rwHandler);
        } catch (IOException e) {
            e.printStackTrace();
        }
    }
    @Override
    public void
    failed(Throwable e, Attachment attach) {
        System.out.println(
            "Failed to accept a connection.");
        e.printStackTrace();
    }
}
private static class ReadWriteHandler
        implements CompletionHandler
        <Integer, Attachment> {
    @Override
    public void
    completed(Integer result, Attachment attach) {
        if (result == -1) {
            try {
                attach.client.close();
                System.out.format(
                    "Stopped listening to the" +
                    " client %s%n",
                    attach.clientAddr);
```

```
        } catch (IOException ex) {
            ex.printStackTrace();
        }
        return;
    }
    if (attach.isRead) {
        // A read to the client was completed.
        // Get the buffer ready to read from it
        attach.buffer.flip();
        int limits = attach.buffer.limit();
        byte bytes[] = new byte[limits];
        attach.buffer.get(bytes, 0, limits);
        Charset cs = Charset.forName("UTF-8");
        String msg = new String(bytes, cs);
        // Print the message from the client
        System.out.format(
            "Client at %s says: %s%n",
            attach.clientAddr, msg);
        // Let us echo back the same message to
        // the client
        attach.isRead = false; // It is a write
        // Prepare the buffer to be read again
        attach.buffer.rewind();
        // Write to the client
        attach.client.write(attach.buffer,
            attach, this);
    } else {
        // A write to the client was completed.
        // Perform another read.
        attach.isRead = true;
        // Prepare the buffer to be filled in
        attach.buffer.clear();
```

```java
                // Perform a read from the client
                attach.client.read(attach.buffer,
                    attach, this);
            }
        }
        @Override
        public void
        failed(Throwable e, Attachment attach) {
            e.printStackTrace();
        }
    }
    public static void main(String[] args) {
        try (AsynchronousServerSocketChannel server
                = AsynchronousServerSocketChannel.open()) {
            // Bind the server to the localhost and the
            // port 8989
            String host = "localhost";
            int port = 8989;
            InetSocketAddress sAddr
                    = new InetSocketAddress(host, port);
            server.bind(sAddr);
            // Display a message that server is ready
            System.out.format(
                "Server is listening at %s%n", sAddr);
            // Prepare the attachment
            Attachment attach = new Attachment();
            attach.server = server;
            // Accept new connections
            server.accept(attach,
                new ConnectionHandler());
            try {
                // Wait until the main thread is
                // interrupted
                Thread.currentThread().join();
```

```
        } catch (InterruptedException e) {
            e.printStackTrace();
        }
    } catch (IOException e) {
        e.printStackTrace();
    }
  }
}
```

Setting Up an Asynchronous Client Socket Channel

An instance of the AsynchronousSocketChannel class is used as an asynchronous client socket channel in a client application. The static open() method of the AsynchronousSocketChannel class returns an open channel of the AsynchronousSocketChannel type that is not yet connected to a server socket channel. The channel's connect() method is used to connect to a server socket channel. The following snippet of code shows how to create an asynchronous client socket channel and connect it to a server socket channel. It uses a Future object to handle the completion of the connection to the server:

```
// Create an asynchronous socket channel
AsynchronousSocketChannel channel =
    AsynchronousSocketChannel.open();
// Connect the channel to the server
String serverName = "localhost";
int serverPort = 8989;
SocketAddress serverAddr =
    new InetSocketAddress(serverName, serverPort);
Future<Void> result = channel.connect(serverAddr);
System.out.println("Connecting to the server...");
// Wait for the connection to complete
result.get();
// Connection to the server is complete now
System.out.println("Connected to the server...");
```

Once the client socket channel is connected to a server, you can start reading from the server and writing to the server using the channel's `read()` and `write()` methods asynchronously. Both methods let you handle the completion of the operation using a `Future` object or a `CompletionHandler` object. You will use an `Attachment` class as shown to pass the context to the completion handler:

```
class Attachment {
    AsynchronousSocketChannel channel;
    ByteBuffer buffer;
    Thread mainThread;
    boolean isRead;
}
```

In the `Attachment` class, the `channel` instance variable holds the reference to the client channel. The `buffer` instance variable holds the reference to the data buffer. You will use the same data buffer for reading and writing. The `mainThread` instance variable holds the reference to the main thread of the application. When the client channel is done, you can interrupt the waiting main thread, so the client application terminates. The `isRead` instance variable indicates if the operation is a read or a write. If it is `true`, it means it is a read operation. Otherwise, it is a write operation.

Listing 8-17 contains the complete code for an asynchronous client socket channel. It uses two inner classes called `Attachment` and `ReadWriteHandler`. An instance of the `Attachment` class is used as an attachment to the `read()` and `write()` asynchronous operations. An instance of the `ReadWriteHandler` class is used as a completion handler for the `read()` and `write()` operations. Its `getTextFromUser()` method prompts the user to enter a message on the standard input and returns the user-entered message. The `completed()` method of the completion handler checks if it is a read or a write operation. If it is a read operation, it prints the text that was read from the server on the standard output. It prompts the user for another message. If the user enters Bye, it terminates the application by interrupting the waiting main thread. Note that the channel is closed automatically when the program exits the `try` block because it is opened inside a `try-with-resources` block in the `main()` method.

Listing 8-17. An Asynchronous Client Socket Channel

```java
// AsyncEchoClientSocket.java
package com.jdojo.net;
import java.io.BufferedReader;
import java.io.IOException;
import java.io.InputStreamReader;
import java.net.InetSocketAddress;
import java.net.SocketAddress;
import java.nio.ByteBuffer;
import java.nio.charset.Charset;
import java.util.concurrent.Future;
import java.nio.channels.CompletionHandler;
import java.util.concurrent.ExecutionException;
import java.nio.channels.AsynchronousSocketChannel;
public class AsyncEchoClientSocket {
    private static class Attachment {
        AsynchronousSocketChannel channel;
        ByteBuffer buffer;
        Thread mainThread;
        boolean isRead;
    }
    private static class ReadWriteHandler
        implements CompletionHandler<Integer, Attachment>
    {
        @Override
        public void
        completed(Integer result, Attachment attach) {
            if (attach.isRead) {
                attach.buffer.flip();
                // Get the text read from the server
                Charset cs = Charset.forName("UTF-8");
                int limits = attach.buffer.limit();
                byte bytes[] = new byte[limits];
                attach.buffer.get(bytes, 0, limits);
                String msg = new String(bytes, cs);
```

```java
        // A read from the server was completed
        System.out.format(
            "Server Responded: %s%n", msg);
        // Prompt the user for another message
        msg = this.getTextFromUser();
        if (msg.equalsIgnoreCase("bye")) {
            // Interrupt the main thread, so the
            // program terminates
            attach.mainThread.interrupt();
            return;
        }
        // Prepare buffer to be filled in again
        attach.buffer.clear();
        byte[] data = msg.getBytes(cs);
        attach.buffer.put(data);
        // Prepared buffer to be read
        attach.buffer.flip();
        attach.isRead = false; // It is a write
        // Write to the server
        attach.channel.write(
            attach.buffer, attach, this);
    } else {
        // A write to the server was completed.
        // Perform another read from the server
        attach.isRead = true;
        // Prepare the buffer to be filled in
        attach.buffer.clear();
        // Read from the server
        attach.channel.read(attach.buffer,
            attach, this);
    }
}
```

```java
        @Override
        public void
        failed(Throwable e, Attachment attach) {
            e.printStackTrace();
        }
        private String getTextFromUser() {
            System.out.print(
                "Please enter a message (Bye to quit):");
            String msg = null;
            BufferedReader consoleReader =
                new BufferedReader(
                    new InputStreamReader(System.in));
            try {
                msg = consoleReader.readLine();
            } catch (IOException e) {
                e.printStackTrace();
            }
            return msg;
        }
    }
    public static void main(String[] args) {
        // Use a try-with-resources to open a channel
        try (AsynchronousSocketChannel channel =
                AsynchronousSocketChannel.open()) {
            // Connect the client to the server
            String serverName = "localhost";
            int serverPort = 8989;
            SocketAddress serverAddr =
                new InetSocketAddress(serverName,
                    serverPort);
            Future<Void> result = channel.
                connect(serverAddr);
            System.out.println(
                "Connecting to the server...");
            // Wait for the connection to complete
            result.get();
```

```
        // Connection to the server is complete now
        System.out.println(
            "Connected to the server...");
        // Start reading from and writing to the server
        Attachment attach = new Attachment();
        attach.channel = channel;
        attach.buffer = ByteBuffer.allocate(2048);
        attach.isRead = false;
        attach.mainThread = Thread.currentThread();
        // Place the "Hello" message in the buffer
        Charset cs = Charset.forName("UTF-8");
        String msg = "Hello";
        byte[] data = msg.getBytes(cs);
        attach.buffer.put(data);
        attach.buffer.flip();
        // Write to the server
        ReadWriteHandler readWriteHandler =
            new ReadWriteHandler();
        channel.write(attach.buffer, attach,
            readWriteHandler);
        // Let this thread wait for ever on its own
        // death until interrupted
        attach.mainThread.join();
    } catch (ExecutionException | IOException e) {
        e.printStackTrace();
    } catch (InterruptedException e) {
        System.out.println(
            "Disconnected from the server.");
    }
  }
}
```

Putting the Server and the Client Together

At this point, your asynchronous server and client programs are ready. You need to use the following steps to run the server and the client.

Run the `AsyncEchoServerSocket` class as listed in Listing 8-16. You should get a message on the standard output as follows:

```
Server is listening at localhost/127.0.0.1:8989
```

If you get this message, you need to proceed to the next step. If you do not get this message, it is most likely that the port 8989 is being used by another process. In such a case, you should get the following error message:

```
java.net.BindException: Address already in use: bind
```

If you get the "`Address already in use`" error message, you need to change the port value in the `AsyncEchoServerSocket` class from 8989 to some other value and retry running the `AsyncEchoServerSocket` class. If you change the port number in the server program, you must also change the port number in the client program to match the server port number. The server socket channel listens at a port, and the client must connect to the same port on which the server is listening.

Before proceeding with this step, make sure that you were able to perform the previous step successfully. Run one or more instances of the `AsyncEchoClientSocket` class that is listed in Listing 8-17. You should get the following message on the standard output if the client application was able to connect to the server successfully:

```
Connecting to the server...
Connected to the server...
Server Responded: Hello
Please enter a message (Bye to quit):
```

You might receive the following error message when you attempt to run the `AsyncEchoClientSocket` class:

```
Connecting to the server...
java.util.concurrent.ExecutionException:
    java.io.IOException: The remote system refused
the network connection.
```

Typically, this error message indicates one of the following problems:

- The server is not running. If this is the case, make sure that the server is running.

- The client is attempting to connect to the server on a different host and port than the host and the port on which the server is listening. If this is the case, make sure that the server and the client are using the same host names (or IP addresses) and the port numbers.

You need to stop the server program manually such as by pressing Ctrl+C keys on the command prompt on Windows.

Datagram-Oriented Socket Channels

An instance of the java.nio.channels.DatagramChannel class represents a datagram channel. By default, it is blocking. You can configure it to be non-blocking by using the configureBlocking(false) method.

To create a DatagramChannel, you need to invoke one of its open() static methods. If you want to use it for IP multicasting, you need to specify the address type (or protocol family) of the multicast group as an argument to its open() method. The open() method creates a DatagramChannel, which is not connected. If you want your datagram channel to send and receive datagrams only to a specific remote host, you need to use its connect() method to connect the channel to that specific host. A datagram channel that is not connected may send datagrams to and receive datagrams from any remote host. The following sections outline the steps that are typically needed to send/receive datagrams using a datagram channel.

Creating the Datagram Channel

You can create a datagram channel using the open() method of the DatagramChannel class. The following snippet of code shows three different ways to create a datagram channel:

```
// Create a new datagram channel to send/receive datagram
DatagramChannel channel = DatagramChannel.open();
// Create a datagram channel to receive datagrams from a
// multicast group
// that uses IPv4 address type
DatagramChannel ipv4MulticastChannel =
    DatagramChannel.open(StandardProtocolFamily.INET);
// Create a datagram channel to receive datagrams from a
// multicast group that uses IPv6 address type
DatagramChannel iPv6MulticastChannel =
    DatagramChannel.open(StandardProtocolFamily.INET6);
```

Setting the Channel Options

You can set the channel options using the setOption() method of the DatagramChannel class. Some options must be set before binding the channel to a specific address, whereas some can be set after the binding. The following snippet of code shows how to set the channel options. The socket options are defined as constants in the StandardSocketOptions class. Refer to the Javadoc for the StandardSocketOptions class for the complete list of socket options, which are supported by all types of sockets. Table 8-10 contains the list of socket options with their descriptions supported by a DatagramChannel.

Table 8-10. *Standard Socket Options*

Socket Option Name	Description
SO_SNDBUF	The size of the socket send buffer in bytes. Its value is of Integer type.
SO_RCVBUF	The size of the socket receive buffer in bytes. Its value is of Integer type.
SO_REUSEADDR	For datagram sockets, it allows multiple programs to bind to the same address. Its value is of Boolean type. This option should be enabled for IP multicasting using the datagram channels.
SO_BROADCAST	Allows transmission of broadcast datagrams. Its value is of type Boolean.

(*continued*)

Table 8-10. (*continued*)

Socket Option Name	Description
IP_TOS	The Type of Service (ToS) octet in the Internet Protocol (IP) header. Its value is of the Integer type.
IP_MULTICAST_IF	The network interface for Internet Protocol (IP) multicast datagrams. Its value is a reference of the NetworkInterface type.
IP_MULTICAST_TTL	The time to live for Internet Protocol (IP) multicast datagrams. Its value is of type Integer in the range of 0 to 255.
IP_MULTICAST_LOOP	Loopback for Internet Protocol (IP) multicast datagrams. Its value is of type Boolean.

There exist three methods, setOption(), getOption(), and supportedOptions(), inside the Socket, ServerSocket, and DatagramSocket classes. These methods let you set the socket option, query the value of a socket option, and get a set of supported socket options by a socket. Refer to the Javadoc for these classes for more details on how to use these methods.

To bind multiple sockets to the same socket address, you need to set the SO_REUSEADDR option for the socket as follows:

```
channel.setOption(StandardSocketOptions.SO_REUSEADDR, true)
```

Bind the datagram channel to a specific local address and port using the bind() method of the DatagramChannel class. If you use null as the bind address, this method will bind the socket to an available address automatically. The following snippet of code shows how to bind a datagram channel:

```
// Bind the channel to any available address automatically
channel.bind(null);
// Bind the channel to "localhost" and port 8989
InetSocketAddress sAddr =
    new InetSocketAddress("localhost", 8989);
channel.bind(sAddr);
```

Sending Datagrams

To send a datagram to a remote host, use the send() method of the DatagramChannel class. The method accepts a ByteBuffer and a remote SocketAddress. If you call the send() method on an unbound datagram channel, the send() method binds the channel automatically to an available address:

```
// Prepare a message to send
String msg = "Hello";
ByteBuffer buffer = ByteBuffer.wrap(msg.getBytes());
// Pack the remote address and port into an object
InetSocketAddress serverAddress =
    new InetSocketAddress("localhost", 8989);
// Send the message to the remote host
channel.send(buffer, serverAddress);
```

The receive() method of the DatagramChannel class lets a datagram channel receive a datagram from a remote host. This method requires you to provide a ByteBuffer to receive the data. The received data is copied to the specified ByteBuffer at its current position. If the ByteBuffer has less space available than the received data, the extra data is discarded silently. The receive() method returns the address of the remote host. If the datagram channel is in a non-blocking mode, the receive() method returns immediately by returning null. Otherwise, it waits until it receives a datagram.

```
// Prepare a ByteBufer to receive data
ByteBuffer buffer = ByteBuffer.allocate(1024);
// Wait to receive data from a remote host
SocketAddress remoteAddress = channel.receive(buffer);
```

Finally, close the datagram channel using its close() method:

```
// Close the channel
channel.close();
```

Listing 8-18 contains a program that acts as an echo server. Listing 8-19 has a program that acts as a client. The echo server waits for a message from a remote client. It echoes the message that it receives from the remote client. You need to start the echo server program before starting the client program. You can run multiple client programs simultaneously. A sample output is shown for both client and server programs.

Listing 8-18. An Echo Server Based on the Datagram Channel

```java
// DGCEchoServer.java
package com.jdojo.net;
import java.io.IOException;
import java.net.InetSocketAddress;
import java.net.SocketAddress;
import java.nio.ByteBuffer;
import java.nio.channels.DatagramChannel;
public class DGCEchoServer {
    public static void main(String[] args) {
        // Create a datagram channel and bind it to
        // localhost at port 8989
        try (DatagramChannel server =
                DatagramChannel.open()) {
            InetSocketAddress sAddr =
                new InetSocketAddress("localhost", 8989);
            server.bind(sAddr);
            ByteBuffer buffer = ByteBuffer.allocate(1024);
            // Wait in an infinite loop for a client to
            // send data
            while (true) {
                System.out.println(
                    "Waiting for a message from"
                    + " a remote host at " + sAddr);
                // Wait for a client to send a message
                SocketAddress remoteAddr =
                    server.receive(buffer);
                // Prepare the buffer to read the message
                buffer.flip();
                // Convert the buffer data into a String
                int limits = buffer.limit();
                byte bytes[] = new byte[limits];
                buffer.get(bytes, 0, limits);
                String msg = new String(bytes);
```

```
                System.out.println(
                    "Client at " + remoteAddr +
                    " says: " + msg);
                // Reuse the buffer to echo the message to
                // the client
                buffer.rewind();
                // Send the message back to the client
                server.send(buffer, remoteAddr);
                // Prepare the buffer to receive the next
                // message
                buffer.clear();
            }
        } catch (IOException e) {
            e.printStackTrace();
        }
    }
}
```

```
Waiting for a message from a remote host
    at localhost/127.0.0.1:8989
Client at /127.0.0.1:62644 says: Hello
Waiting for a message from a remote host
    at localhost/127.0.0.1:8989
```

Listing 8-19. A Client Program Based on the Datagram Channel

```java
// DGCEchoClient.java
package com.jdojo.net;
import java.io.IOException;
import java.net.InetSocketAddress;
import java.nio.ByteBuffer;
import java.nio.channels.DatagramChannel;
public class DGCEchoClient {
    public static void main(String[] args) {
        // Create a new datagram channel
```

```
        try (DatagramChannel client =
                DatagramChannel.open()) {
            // Bind the client to any available local
            // address and port
            client.bind(null);
            // Prepare a message for the server
            String msg = "Hello";
            ByteBuffer buffer =
                ByteBuffer.wrap(msg.getBytes());
            InetSocketAddress serverAddress =
                new InetSocketAddress("localhost", 8989);
            // Send the message to the server
            client.send(buffer, serverAddress);
            // Reuse the buffer to receive a response from
            // the server
            buffer.clear();
            // Wait for the server to respond
            client.receive(buffer);
            // Prepare the buffer to read the message
            buffer.flip();
            // Convert the buffer into a string
            int limits = buffer.limit();
            byte bytes[] = new byte[limits];
            buffer.get(bytes, 0, limits);
            String response = new String(bytes);
            // Print the server message on the standard
            // output
            System.out.println("Server responded: " +
                response);
        } catch (IOException e) {
            e.printStackTrace();
        }
    }
}

Server responded: Hello
```

Multicasting Using Datagram Channels

Java provides support for IP multicasting using a datagram channel. A datagram channel that is interested in receiving multicast datagrams joins a multicast group. The datagrams that are sent to a multicast group are delivered to all its members. The following sections outline the steps that are typically needed to set up a client application that is interested in receiving a multicast datagram.

Creating the Datagram Channel

Create a datagram channel to use a specific multicast address type as follows. In your application, you will be using IPv4 or IPv6, not both.

```
// Need to use INET protocol family for an IPv4 addressing
// scheme
DatagramChannel client =
    DatagramChannel.open(StandardProtocolFamily.INET);

// Need to use INET6 protocol family for an IPv6
// addressing scheme
DatagramChannel client =
    DatagramChannel.open(StandardProtocolFamily.INET6);
```

Setting the Channel Options

Set the options for the client channel using the setOption() method as shown:

```
// Let other sockets reuse the same address
client.setOption(StandardSocketOptions.SO_REUSEADDR, true);
```

Binding the Channel

Bind the client channel to a local address and a port as shown:

```
int MULTICAST_PORT = 8989;
client.bind(new InetSocketAddress(MULTICAST_PORT));
```

Setting the Multicast Network Interface

Set the socket option IP_MULTICAST_IF that specifies the network interface on which the client channel will join the multicast group:

```
// Get the reference of a network interface named "eth1"
NetworkInterface interf =
    NetworkInterface.getByName("eth1");
// Set the IP_MULTICAST_IF option
client.setOption(StandardSocketOptions.IP_MULTICAST_IF,
    interf);
```

Listing 8-20 contains the complete program that prints the names of all network interfaces available on your machine. It also prints whether a network interface supports multicast and whether it is up. You may get a different output when you run the code on your machine. You will need to use the name of one of the available network interfaces that supports multicast, and that network interface should be up. For example, as shown in the output, the network interface named eth2 is up and supports multicast on my machine, so I used eth2 as the network interface for working with multicast messages.

Listing 8-20. Listing the Available Network Interface on a Machine

```
// ListNetworkInterfaces.java
package com.jdojo.net;
import java.net.NetworkInterface;
import java.net.SocketException;
import java.util.Enumeration;
public class ListNetworkInterfaces {
    public static void main(String[] args) {
        try {
            Enumeration<NetworkInterface> e =
                NetworkInterface.getNetworkInterfaces();
            while (e.hasMoreElements()) {
                NetworkInterface nif = e.nextElement();
```

```
                System.out.println("Name: "
                    + nif.getName()
                    + ", Supports Multicast: "
                    + nif.supportsMulticast()
                    + ", isUp(): " + nif.isUp());
            }
        } catch (SocketException ex) {
            ex.printStackTrace();
        }
    }
}
```

```
Name: lo, Supports Multicast: true, isUp(): true
Name: eth0, Supports Multicast: true, isUp(): false
Name: net0, Supports Multicast: true, isUp(): false
Name: wlan0, Supports Multicast: true, isUp(): false
Name: net1, Supports Multicast: true, isUp(): false
Name: wlan1, Supports Multicast: true, isUp(): false
Name: wlan2, Supports Multicast: true, isUp(): false
Name: eth1, Supports Multicast: true, isUp(): false
Name: wlan3, Supports Multicast: true, isUp(): false
Name: wlan4, Supports Multicast: true, isUp(): false
Name: eth2, Supports Multicast: true, isUp(): true
Name: eth3, Supports Multicast: true, isUp(): false
Name: eth4, Supports Multicast: true, isUp(): false
Name: eth5, Supports Multicast: true, isUp(): false
Name: eth6, Supports Multicast: true, isUp(): false
Name: wlan5, Supports Multicast: true, isUp(): false
Name: wlan6, Supports Multicast: true, isUp(): false
Name: wlan7, Supports Multicast: true, isUp(): false
Name: wlan8, Supports Multicast: true, isUp(): false
Name: wlan9, Supports Multicast: true, isUp(): false
Name: wlan10, Supports Multicast: true, isUp(): false
Name: wlan11, Supports Multicast: true, isUp(): false
Name: wlan12, Supports Multicast: true, isUp(): false
Name: wlan13, Supports Multicast: true, isUp(): false
```

```
Name: wlan14, Supports Multicast: true, isUp(): false
Name: wlan15, Supports Multicast: true, isUp(): false
Name: wlan16, Supports Multicast: true, isUp(): false
Name: wlan17, Supports Multicast: true, isUp(): false
```

Joining the Multicast Group

Now it is time to join the multicast group using the join() method as follows. Note that you must use a multicast IP address for the group:

```
String MULTICAST_IP = "239.1.1.1";
// Join the multicast group on interf interface
InetAddress group = InetAddress.getByName(MULTICAST_IP);
MembershipKey key = client.join(group, interf);
```

The join() method returns an object of the MembershipKey class that represents the membership of the datagram channel with the multicast group. If a datagram channel is not interested in receiving multicast datagrams anymore, it can use the drop() method of the key to drop its membership from the multicast group.

Note   A datagram channel may decide to receive multicast datagrams only from selective sources. You can use the block(InetAddress source) method of the MembershipKey class to block a multicast datagram from the specified source address. Its unblock(InetAddress source) lets you unblock a previously blocked source address.

Receiving a Message

At this point, receiving datagrams that are addressed to the multicast group is just a matter of calling the receive() method on the channel as shown:

```
// Prepare a buffer to receive the message from the
// multicast group
ByteBuffer buffer = ByteBuffer.allocate(1048);
// Wait to receive a message from the multicast group
client.receive(buffer);
```

After you are done with the channel, you can drop its membership from the group as shown:

```
// We are no longer interested in receiving multicast
// message from the group. So, we need to drop the
// channel's membership from the group
key.drop();
```

Closing the Channel

Finally, you need to close the channel using its close() method as shown:

```
// Close the channel
client.close();
```

To send a message to a multicast group, you do not need to be a member of that multicast group. You can send a datagram to a multicast group using the send() method of the DatagramChannel class.

Listing 8-21 contains a class with three constants that are used in the subsequent two classes to build the multicast application. The constants contain the multicast IP address, multicast port number, and multicast network interface name that will be used in the subsequent example. Make sure that the value eth1 for the MULTICAST_INTERFACE_ NAME constant is the network interface name on your machine that supports multicast and it is up. You can get the list of all network interfaces on your machine by running the program in Listing 8-20.

Listing 8-21. A DatagramChannel-Based Multicast Client Program

```
// DGCMulticastUtil.java
package com.jdojo.net;
public class DGCMulticastUtil {
    public static final String MULTICAST_IP = "239.1.1.1";
    public static final int MULTICAST_PORT = 8989;
    /* You need to change the following network interface
       name "eth2" to the network interface name that
       supports multicast and is up on your machine.
```

```
    Please run the ListNetworkInterfaces class to
    get the list of all available network interface on
    your machine.
  */
  public static final String MULTICAST_INTERFACE_NAME =
      "eth2";
}
```

Listing 8-22 contains a program that joins a multicast group as a member. It waits for a message from a multicast group to arrive, prints the message, and quits. Listing 8-23 contains a program that sends a message to the multicast group. You can run multiple instances of the DGCMulticastClient class and then run the DGCMulticastServer class. All client instances should receive and print the same message on the standard output.

Listing 8-22. A DatagramChannel-Based Multicast Client Program

```java
// DGCMulticastClient.java
package com.jdojo.net;
import java.io.IOException;
import java.net.InetAddress;
import java.net.InetSocketAddress;
import java.net.NetworkInterface;
import java.net.StandardProtocolFamily;
import java.net.StandardSocketOptions;
import java.nio.ByteBuffer;
import java.nio.channels.DatagramChannel;
import java.nio.channels.MembershipKey;
public class DGCMulticastClient {
    public static void main(String[] args) {
        MembershipKey key = null;
        // Create, configure and bind the client datagram
        // channel
        try (DatagramChannel client =
                DatagramChannel.open(
                    StandardProtocolFamily.INET)) {
```

```
            // Get the reference of a network interface
            NetworkInterface interf =
                NetworkInterface.getByName(
                    DGCMulticastUtil.
                    MULTICAST_INTERFACE_NAME);
        client.setOption(
            StandardSocketOptions.SO_REUSEADDR,
            true);
        client.bind(
            new InetSocketAddress(
                DGCMulticastUtil.MULTICAST_PORT));
        client.setOption(
            StandardSocketOptions.IP_MULTICAST_IF,
            interf);
        // Join the multicast group on the interf
        // interface
        InetAddress group =
            InetAddress.getByName(
                DGCMulticastUtil.MULTICAST_IP);
        key = client.join(group, interf);
        // Print some useful messages for the user
        System.out.println(
            "Joined the multicast group:" + key);
        System.out.println(
            "Waiting for a message from the"
            + " multicast group....");
        // Prepare a data buffer to receive a message
        // from the multicast group
        ByteBuffer buffer = ByteBuffer.allocate(1048);
        // Wait to receive a message from the
        // multicast group
        client.receive(buffer);
        // Convert the message in the ByteBuffer
        // into a string
```

```
                buffer.flip();
                int limits = buffer.limit();
                byte bytes[] = new byte[limits];
                buffer.get(bytes, 0, limits);
                String msg = new String(bytes);
                System.out.format(
                    "Multicast Message:%s%n", msg);
            } catch (IOException e) {
                e.printStackTrace();
            } finally {
                // Drop the membership from the multicast
                // group
                if (key != null) {
                    key.drop();
                }
            }
        }
    }
}
```

```
Joined the multicast group:<239.1.1.1,eth3>
Waiting for a message from the multicast group....
Multicast Message:Hello from multicast!
```

Listing 8-23. A DatagramChannel-Based Multicast Program That Sends a
Message to a Multicast Group

```java
// DGCMulticastServer.java
package com.jdojo.net;
import java.io.IOException;
import java.net.InetSocketAddress;
import java.net.NetworkInterface;
import java.net.StandardSocketOptions;
import java.nio.ByteBuffer;
import java.nio.channels.DatagramChannel;
```

```java
public class DGCMulticastServer {
    public static void main(String[] args) {
        // Get a datagram channel object to act as a server
        try (DatagramChannel server =
                DatagramChannel.open()) {
            // Bind the server to any available local
            // address
            server.bind(null);
            // Set the network interface for outgoing
            // multicast data
            NetworkInterface interf =
                NetworkInterface.getByName(
                    DGCMulticastUtil.
                    MULTICAST_INTERFACE_NAME);
            server.setOption(
                StandardSocketOptions.IP_MULTICAST_IF,
                interf);
            // Prepare a message to send to the multicast
            // group
            String msg = "Hello from multicast!";
            ByteBuffer buffer =
                ByteBuffer.wrap(msg.getBytes());
            // Get the multicast group reference to send
            // data to
            InetSocketAddress group =
                new InetSocketAddress(
                    DGCMulticastUtil.MULTICAST_IP,
                    DGCMulticastUtil.MULTICAST_PORT);
            // Send the message to the multicast group
            server.send(buffer, group);
            System.out.println(
                "Sent the multicast message: " + msg);
```

```
        } catch (IOException e) {
            e.printStackTrace();
        }
    }
}
```

Sent the multicast message: Hello from multicast!

Further Reading

Network programming in Java is a vast topic. There are a few books written especially on this topic. This chapter covers only the basics of the network programming support that is available in Java. Java also supports secured socket communications using a Secured Socket Layer (SSL) protocol. The classes for secured socket communication programming are in the `javax.net.ssl` package. This chapter does not cover SSL sockets. I have not covered many of the options for sockets that you can use in your Java programs. If you want to do advanced level network programming in Java, it is recommended that you read a book that devotes itself solely to network programming in Java after you finish this chapter.

Summary

A network is a group of two or more computers or other types of electronic devices such as printers, linked together with a goal to share information. Each device linked to a network is called a node. A computer that is linked to a network is called a host. Network programming in Java involves writing Java programs that facilitate exchange of information between processes running on different computers on the network.

The communication between two remote hosts is performed by a layered protocol suite called the Internet Reference Model or TCP/IP Layering Model. The protocol suite consists of five layers named application, transport, internet, network interface, and physical. A user application such as a Java program uses the application layer to communicate to a remote application. The transport layer protocol handles the ways messages are transported from one application on one computer to another application on a remote computer. The internet layer accepts the messages from the transport layer and prepares a packet suitable for sending over the internet. It includes the Internet Protocol (IP). The packet prepared by IP is also known as an IP datagram, and it consists of a header and a data area, apart from other pieces of information. The network interface layer prepares a packet to be transmitted on the network. The packet is called a frame. The network interface layer sits on top of the physical layer, which involves the hardware. The physical layer consists of the hardware. It is responsible for converting the bits of information into signals and transmitting the signal over the wire.

An IP address uniquely identifies a connection between a computer and a router. There are two versions of an Internet Protocol—IPv4 (or simply IP) and IPv6, where v4 and v6 stand for version 4 and version 6. IPv6 is also known as the Internet Protocol next generation (IPng). An object of the InetAddress class represents an IP address in Java programs. The InetAddress class has two subclasses, Inet4Address and Inet6Address, which represent IPv4 and IPv6 addresses, respectively.

A port number is a 16-bit unsigned integer ranging from 0 to 65535 that is used to uniquely identify a process for a specific protocol.

An object of the InetSocketAddress class represents a socket address that combines an IP address and a port number.

An object of the ServerSocket class represents a TCP server socket for accepting connections from remote hosts. An object of the Socket class represents a server/client socket. The client and server applications exchange information using objects of the Socket class. The Socket class provides the getInputStream() and getOutputStream() methods to obtain the input and output streams of the socket, respectively. The input stream of the socket is used to read the data from the socket, and the output stream of the socket is used to write data to the socket.

An object of the DatagramPacket class represents a UDP datagram that is the unit of data transmission over a UDP socket. An object of the DatagramSocket class represents a UDP server/client socket.

A Uniform Resource Identifier (URI) is a sequence of characters that identifies a resource. A URI that uses a location to identify a resource is called a Uniform Resource Locator (URL). A URI that uses a name to identify a resource is called a Uniform Resource Name (URN). A URL and a URN are subsets of a URI. An object of the java.net.URI class represents a URI in Java. An object of the java.net.URL class represents a URL in Java. Java provides classes to access the contents identified by a URL.

Java supports non-blocking socket channels using the ServerSocketChannel, SocketChannel, Selector, and SelectionKey classes in the java.nio.channels package.

Java also supports asynchronous socket channels through the
AsynchronousServerSocketChannel and AsynchronousSocketChannel classes in the
java.nio.channels package.

Java supports datagram-oriented socket channel through the DatagramChannel class.
IP multicasting is also supported on datagram channels.

Exercises

Exercise 1

What is network programming in Java?

Exercise 2

What are the network types: LAN, CAN, MAN, and WAN?

Exercise 3

What is a network protocol?

Exercise 4

What is an IP address? Can a computer have more than one IP address?

Exercise 5

How many bytes are used to represent an IP address in IPv4 and IPv6? Describe the
textual format of representing IP addresses in IPv4 and IPv6 formats.

Exercise 6

You have an IP address of 0.0.0.0, which is in IPv4 format. How will you rewrite this
IP address in IPv6 format?

Exercise 7

Describe the use of the following address types: loopback IP address, unicast IP
address, multicast IP address, anycast IP address, broadcast IP address, and unspecified
IP address.

Exercise 8

What is a port number and why is it used?

Exercise 9

What is a socket? What is the difference between a connection-oriented socket and
a connectionless socket? Give an example of a protocol that supports these types of
sockets.

Exercise 10

What does an instance of the InetAddress class represent? Write a program that prints the computer name and the IP address of the computer on which the program is executed.

Exercise 11

What does an instance of the InetSocketAddress class represent?

Exercise 12

What do the instances of the ServerSocket and Socket classes represent?

Exercise 13

What do the instances of the DatagramSocket and DatagramPacket classes represent?

Exercise 14

UDP sockets do not support an end-to-end connection like the TCP sockets. The DatagramSocket class, which represents UDP sockets, contains a connect() method. What is the purpose of this connect() method?

Exercise 15

What do the instances of the MulticastSocket class represent? Does a socket have to be a member of a multicast group to send a datagram packet to a multicast address?

Exercise 16

What are URI, URL, and URN? How do you represent them in a Java program?

CHAPTER 9

Java Remote Method Invocation

In this chapter, you will learn:

- What Java Remote Method Invocation (RMI) is and the RMI architecture

- How to develop and package RMI server and client applications

- How to start the `rmiregistry`, RMI server, and client applications

- How to troubleshoot and debug RMI applications

- Dynamic class downloading in an RMI application

- Garbage collections of remote objects in RMI applications

An RMI application contains classes and interfaces that fall into three parts:

- Server part

- Client part

- Common part, which is present in both the client and server

You will package three parts of the example application in this chapter into three modules named `jdojo.rmi.common`, `jdojo.rmi.server`, and `jdojo.rmi.client`. The declarations for these modules are shown in Listings 9-1 to 9-3.

Listing 9-1. The Declaration of a jdojo.rmi.common Module

```
// module-info.java
module jdojo.rmi.common {
    requires java.rmi;
    exports com.jdojo.rmi.common;
}
```

© Kishori Sharan, Peter Späth 2021
K. Sharan and P. Späth, *More Java 17*, https://doi.org/10.1007/978-1-4842-7135-3_9

Listing 9-2. The Declaration of a jdojo.rmi.server Module

```
// module-info.java
module jdojo.rmi.server {
    requires java.rmi;
    requires jdojo.rmi.common;
    exports com.jdojo.rmi.server;
}
```

Listing 9-3. The Declaration of a jdojo.rmi.client Module

```
// module-info.java
module jdojo.rmi.client {
    requires java.rmi;
    requires jdojo.rmi.common;
    exports com.jdojo.rmi.client;
}
```

The RMI-related classes and interfaces are in the `java.rmi` module. Your module that contains RMI programs needs to read the `java.rmi` module. The `jdojo.rmi.common` module contains types that will be used by the server and client applications, and this is the reason that the `jdojo.rmi.server` and `jdojo.rmi.client` modules read the `jdojo.rmi.common` module.

What Is Java Remote Method Invocation?

Java supports a variety of application architectures that determine how and where the application code is deployed and executed. In the simplest application architecture, all Java code resides on a single machine, and one JVM manages all Java objects and the interaction among them. This is an example of a standalone application, where all that is needed is a machine that can launch a JVM. Java also supports a distributed application architecture in which the application's code and execution can be distributed among multiple machines.

In Chapter 8, you learned network programming in Java that involves at least two JVMs running on different machines that execute the Java code for the client and server sockets. Typically, sockets are used to transfer data between two applications. In socket programming, it is possible for the client program to send a message to the server program. The server program creates a Java object, invokes a method on that object, and returns the result of the method invocation to the client program. Finally, the client program reads the result using sockets. In such cases, the client is able to invoke a method on a Java object that resides in a different JVM. This possibility opens up doors for new application architectures, called *distributed programming*, in which an application may utilize multiple machines, running multiple JVMs to process the business logic. Although it is possible to invoke a method on an object that resides in a different JVM (possibly on a different machine too) using socket programming, it is not easy to code. To achieve this, Java provides a separate mechanism called Java Remote Method Invocation (Java RMI).

Java RMI enables a Java application to invoke a method on a Java object in a remote JVM. I use the term "remote object" to refer to a Java object that is created and managed by a JVM, other than the JVM that manages the Java code that calls methods on that "remote object." Typically, a remote object also implies that it is managed by a JVM that runs on a machine other than the machine from which it is accessed. However, it is not a requirement for a Java object to be a remote object that it should exist in a JVM on a different machine. For learning purposes, you will use one machine to deploy the remote object in one JVM and launch another application in a different JVM to access the remote object. RMI lets you treat the remote object as if it is a local object. Internally, it uses sockets to handle access to the remote object and to invoke its methods.

An RMI application consists of two programs, a client and a server, that run in two different JVMs. The server program creates Java objects and makes them accessible to the remote client programs to invoke methods on those objects. The client program needs to know the location of the remote objects on the server, so it can invoke methods on them. The server program creates a remote object and registers (or binds) its reference to an RMI registry. An RMI registry is a name service that is used to bind a remote object reference to a name, so a client can get the reference of the remote object using a name-based lookup in the registry. An RMI registry runs in a separate process from the server program. It is supplied as a tool called `rmiregistry`. When you install a JDK/JRE on your machine, it is copied in the `bin` sub-directory under the JDK/JRE installation directory.

After the client program gets the remote reference of a remote object, it invokes methods using that reference as if it were a reference to a local object. RMI technology takes care of the details of invoking the methods on the remote reference in the server program running on a different JVM on a different machine. In an RMI application, Java code is written in terms of interfaces. The server program contains implementations for the interfaces. The client program uses interfaces along with the remote object references to invoke methods on the remote object that exists in the server's JVM. All Java library classes supporting Java RMI are in the `java.rmi` package and its subpackages.

The RMI Architecture

Figure 9-1 shows the RMI architecture in a simplified form. A rectangular box in the figure represents a component in an RMI application. An arrow line shows a message sent from one component to another in the direction of the arrow. The ovals showing numbers from 1 to 11 represent the sequence of steps that take place in a typical RMI application. I explain these steps in detail in this section.

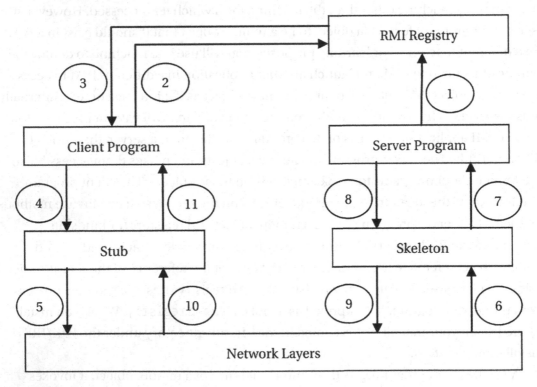

Figure 9-1. *The RMI architecture*

Let's assume that you have developed all Java classes and interfaces that are needed for an RMI application. In this section, I walk you through all the steps that are involved when you run an RMI application. You will develop the Java code that is needed for each step in the next few sections.

The first step involved in an RMI application is to create a Java object in the server. The object will be used as the remote object. There is an additional step that needs to be performed to make an ordinary Java object a remote object. The step is known as *exporting* the remote object. When an ordinary Java object is exported as a remote object, it becomes ready to receive/handle calls from remote clients. The export process produces a remote object reference (also called a stub). The remote reference knows the details about the exported object such as its location and methods that can be called remotely. This step is not labeled in the figure. It happens inside the server program. When this step finishes, the remote object has been created in the server and is ready to receive a remote method invocation.

The next step is performed by the server to register (or bind) the remote reference with an RMI registry. The server chooses a unique name for each remote reference it registers with an RMI registry. A remote client will need to use the same name to look up the remote reference in the RMI registry. This is labeled as #1 in the figure. When this step finishes, the RMI registry has registered the remote object reference, and a client interested in invoking a method on the remote object may ask for its reference from the RMI registry.

Note   For security reasons, an RMI registry and the server must run on the same machine so that a server can register the remote references with the RMI registry. If this restriction is not imposed, a hacker may register their own harmful Java objects to your RMI registry from their machine.

This step involves the interaction between a client and an RMI registry. Typically, a client and an RMI registry run on two different machines. The client sends a lookup request to the RMI registry for a remote reference. The client uses a name to look up the remote reference in the RMI registry. The name is the same as the name used by the server to bind the remote reference in the RMI registry in step #1. The lookup step is labeled as #2 in the figure. The RMI registry returns the remote reference (or stub) to the client labeled as step #3 in the figure. If a remote reference is not bound in the RMI registry with the name used by the client in the lookup request, the RMI registry throws a

NotBoundException. If this step finishes successfully, the client has received the remote reference (or stub) of the remote object.

In this step, the client invokes a method on the stub. It is shown as step #4 in the figure. At this point, the stub connects to the server and transmits the information required to invoke the method on the remote object, such as the name of the method, the method's arguments, etc. The stub knows about the server location and the details about how to contact the remote object on the server. This step is labeled as step #5 in the figure. Many different layers at the network level are involved in transmitting information emanating from the stub to the server.

A skeleton is the server-side counterpart of a stub on the client side. Its job is to receive the data sent by the stub. This is shown as step #6 in the figure. After a skeleton receives the data, it reassembles the data into a more meaningful format and invokes the method on the remote object, which is shown as step #7 in the figure. Once the remote method call is over on the server, the skeleton receives the result of the method call (step #8) and transmits the information back to the stub (step #9) through the network layers. The stub receives the result of the remote method invocation (step #10), reassembles the result, and passes the result to the client program (step #11).

Steps #4 through #11 may be repeated to call the same or different methods on the same remote object. If a client wants to call a method on a different remote object, it will have to first perform steps #2 and #3 before initiating a remote method call.

It is typical in an RMI application that a client contacts an RMI registry to get the stub of a remote object in the beginning. If the client needs the stub of another remote object running in the server, it may get it by calling a method on the stub that it already has. Note that a remote object's method can also return a stub to a remote client. This way, a remote client may perform a lookup in the RMI registry only once at startup. The Java code that you write for an RMI application is no different from that of a non-RMI application, except for looking up for a remote object reference in the RMI registry.

Developing an RMI Application

This section walks you through the steps to write the Java code to develop an RMI application. You will develop a remote utility RMI application that will let you perform three things: echo a message from the server, get the current date and time from the server, and add two integers. The following steps are involved in writing an RMI application:

- Writing a remote interface.

- Implementing the remote interface in a class. An object of this class serves as the remote object.

- Writing a server program. It creates an object of the class that implements the remote interface and registers it with the RMI registry.

- Writing a client program that accesses the remote object on the server.

Writing the Remote Interface

A remote interface is like any other Java interface whose methods are meant to be called from a remote client running in a different JVM. It has four special requirements:

- It must extend the marker Remote interface.

- All methods in a remote interface must throw a RemoteException or an exception, which is its superclass such as IOException or Exception. The RemoteException is a checked exception. A remote method can also throw any number of other application-specific exceptions.

- A remote method may accept the reference of a remote object as a parameter. It may also return the reference of a remote object as its return value. If a method in a remote interface accepts or returns a remote object reference, the parameter or return type must be declared of the type Remote rather than of the type of the class that implements the Remote interface.

- A remote interface may only use three data types in its method's parameters or return value. It could be a primitive type, a remote object, or a serializable non-remote object. A remote object is passed by reference, whereas a non-remote serializable object is passed by copy. An object is serializable if its class implements the java.io.Serializable interface.

You will name your remote interface RemoteUtility. Listing 9-4 contains the code for the RemoteUtility remote interface, which is a member of the jdojo.rmi.common module. It contains three methods called echo(), getServerTime(), and add(), which provide your three intended functionalities.

Listing 9-4. A RemoteUtility Interface

```
// RemoteUtility.java
package com.jdojo.rmi.common;
import java.rmi.Remote;
import java.rmi.RemoteException;
import java.time.ZonedDateTime;
public interface RemoteUtility extends Remote {
    // Echoes a string message back to the client
    String echo(String msg) throws RemoteException;
    // Returns the current date and time to the client
    ZonedDateTime getServerTime() throws RemoteException;
    // Adds two integers and returns the result to the
    // client
    int add(int n1, int n2) throws RemoteException;
}
```

Implementing the Remote Interface

This step involves creating a class that implements the remote interface. You will name the class RemoteUtilityImpl. It will implement the RemoteUtility remote interface and will provide implementations for three methods: echo(), getServerTime(), and add(). You can have any number of other methods in this class. The only thing you must do is provide implementations for all methods defined in the RemoteUtility remote interface. The remote client will be able to call only remote methods of this class. If you define methods in this class other than those defined in the remote interface, those methods are not available for remote method invocations. However, you can use the additional methods to implement the remote methods. Listing 9-5 contains the code for the RemoteUtilityImpl class, which is a member of the jdojo.rmi.server module.

Listing 9-5. An Implementation Class for the RemoteUtility Remote Interface

```java
// RemoteUtilityImpl.java
package com.jdojo.rmi.server;
import com.jdojo.rmi.common.RemoteUtility;
import java.time.ZonedDateTime;
public class RemoteUtilityImpl implements RemoteUtility {
    public RemoteUtilityImpl() {
    }
    @Override
    public String echo(String msg) {
        return msg;
    }
    @Override
    public ZonedDateTime getServerTime() {
        return ZonedDateTime.now();
    }
    @Override
    public int add(int n1, int n2) {
        return n1 + n2;
    }
}
```

The remote object implementation class is very simple. It implements the RemoteUtility interface and provides implementations for three methods of the interface. Note that these methods in the RemoteUtilityImpl class do not declare that they throw a RemoteException. The requirement to declare that all remote methods throw a RemoteException is for the remote interface, not the class implementing the remote interface.

There are two ways to write your implementation class for a remote interface. One way is to inherit it from the java.rmi.server.UnicastRemoteObject class. Another way is to inherit it from no class or any class other than the UnicastRemoteObject class. Listing 9-5 took the latter approach. It did not inherit the RemoteUtilityImpl class from any class.

What difference does it make if the implementation class for a remote interface inherits from the UnicastRemoteObject class or some other class? The implementation class of a remote interface is used to create remote objects whose methods are invoked remotely. The object of this class must go through an export process, which makes it suitable for a remote method invocation. The constructors for the UnicastRemoteObject class export the object automatically for you. So, if your implementation class inherits from the UnicastRemoteObject class, it will save you one step in the entire process later. Sometimes, your implementation class must inherit from another class, and that will force you not to inherit it from the UnicastRemoteObject class. One thing you need to note is that the constructors for the UnicastRemoteObject class throw a RemoteException. If you inherit the remote object implementation class from the UnicastRemoteObject class, the implementation class's constructor must throw a RemoteException in its declaration.

Listing 9-6 rewrites the RemoteUtilityImpl class by inheriting it from the UnicastRemoteObject class. There are two new things in this implementation—it uses the extends clause in the class declaration, and it uses a throws clause in the constructor declaration. Everything else remains the same. I discuss the difference in using the implementation of the RemoteUtilityImpl class shown in Listings 9-5 and 9-6 when you write the server program later in this chapter.

Listing 9-6. Rewriting the RemoteUtilityImpl Class by Inheriting It from the UnicastRemoteObject Class

```
// RemoteUtilityImpl.java
package com.jdojo.rmi.server;
import com.jdojo.rmi.common.RemoteUtility;
import java.rmi.RemoteException;
import java.rmi.server.UnicastRemoteObject;
import java.time.ZonedDateTime;
public class RemoteUtilityImpl
        extends UnicastRemoteObject
        implements RemoteUtility {
    // Must throw the RemoteException
    public RemoteUtilityImpl() throws RemoteException {
    }
```

```
    @Override
    public String echo(String msg) {
        return msg;
    }
    @Override
    public ZonedDateTime getServerTime() {
        return ZonedDateTime.now();
    }
    @Override
    public int add(int n1, int n2) {
        return n1 + n2;
    }
}
```

Writing the RMI Server Program

The responsibility of a server program is to create the remote object and make it accessible to remote clients. A server program performs the following things:

- Installs the security manager

- Creates and exports the remote object

- Registers the remote object with the RMI registry application

The subsequent sections discuss these steps in detail.

You need to make sure that the server code is running under a security manager. An RMI program cannot download Java classes from remote locations if it is not running with a security manager. Without a security manager, it can only use local Java classes. In both RMI servers and RMI clients, programs may need to download class files from remote locations. You will look at examples of downloading Java classes from remote locations shortly. When you run a Java program under a security manager, you must also control access to the privileged resources through a Java policy file. The following snippet of code shows how to install a security manager if it is not already installed. You can use an object of the `java.lang.SecurityManager` class or `java.rmi.RMISecurityManager` class to install a security manager.

```
SecurityManager secManager = System.getSecurityManager();
if (secManager == null) {
    System.setSecurityManager(new SecurityManager());
}
```

A security manager controls the access to privileged resources through a policy file. You will need to set appropriate permissions to access the resources used in a Java RMI application. For this example, you will give all permissions to all code. However, you should use a properly controlled policy file in a production environment. The entry that you need to make in the policy file to grant all permissions is as follows:

```
grant {
    permission java.security.AllPermission;
};
```

Typically, a Java policy file resides in the user's home directory on a computer, and it is named .java.policy. Note that the file name starts with a dot.

The next step the RMI server program performs is to create an object of the class that implements the remote interface, which will serve as a remote object. In your case, you will create an object of the RemoteUtilityImpl class:

```
RemoteUtilityImpl remoteUtility = new RemoteUtilityImpl();
```

You need to export the remote object, so remote clients can invoke its remote methods. If your remote object class (RemoteUtility class in this case) inherits from the UnicastRemoteObject class, you do not need to export it. It is exported automatically when you create it. If your remote object's class does not inherit from the UnicastRemoteObject class, you need to export it explicitly using one of the exportObject() static methods of the UnicastRemoteObject class. When you export a remote object, you can specify a port number where it can listen for a remote method invocation. By default, it listens at port 0, which is an anonymous port. The following statement exports a remote object:

```
int port = 0;
RemoteUtility remoteUtilityStub = (RemoteUtility)
    UnicastRemoteObject.exportObject(remoteUtility, port);
```

The exportObject() method returns the reference of the exported remote object, which is also called a stub or a remote reference. You need to keep the reference of the stub, so you can register it with an RMI registry.

The final step that the server program performs is to register (or bind) the remote object reference with an RMI registry using a name. An RMI registry is a separate application that provides a name service. To register a remote reference with an RMI registry, you must first locate it. An RMI registry runs on a machine at a specific port. By default, it runs on port 1099. Once you locate the registry, you need to call its bind() method to bind the remote reference. You can also use its rebind() method, which will replace an old binding if it already exists for the specified name. The name used is a String. You will use the name MyRemoteUtility as the name for your remote reference. It is better to follow a naming convention for binding a reference object in the RMI registry to avoid name collisions.

```
Registry registry =
    LocateRegistry.getRegistry("localhost", 1099);
String name = "MyRemoteUtility";
registry.rebind(name, remoteUtilityStub);
```

That is all needed to write a server program. Listing 9-7 contains the complete code for the RMI server, which is a member of the jdojo.rmi.server module. It assumes that the RemoteUtilityImpl class does not inherit from the UnicastRemoteObject class, as listed in Listing 9-5.

Listing 9-7. An RMI Remote Server Program

```
// RemoteServer.java
package com.jdojo.rmi.server;
import com.jdojo.rmi.common.RemoteUtility;
import java.rmi.RemoteException;
import java.rmi.registry.LocateRegistry;
import java.rmi.registry.Registry;
import java.rmi.server.UnicastRemoteObject;
public class RemoteServer {
    public static void main(String[] args) {
        SecurityManager secManager =
            System.getSecurityManager();
```

```
        if (secManager == null) {
            System.setSecurityManager(
                new SecurityManager());
        }
        try {
            RemoteUtilityImpl remoteUtility =
                new RemoteUtilityImpl();
            // Export the object as a remote object
            int port = 0; // An anonymous port
            RemoteUtility remoteUtilityStub =
                (RemoteUtility) UnicastRemoteObject.
                exportObject(remoteUtility, port);
            // Locate the registry
            Registry registry =
                LocateRegistry.
                getRegistry("localhost", 1099);
            // Bind the exported remote reference in the
            // registry
            String name = "MyRemoteUtility";
            registry.rebind(name, remoteUtilityStub);
            System.out.println(
                "Remote server is ready...");
        } catch (RemoteException e) {
            e.printStackTrace();
        }
    }
}
```

If you use the implementation of the RemoteUtilityImpl class listed in Listing 9-6, you will need to modify the code in Listing 9-7. The code in the try-catch block will change to the code as follows. All other code will remain the same:

```
RemoteUtilityImpl remoteUtility = new RemoteUtilityImpl();
// No need to export the object
// Locate the registry
Registry registry = LocateRegistry.
```

```
        getRegistry("localhost", 1099);
// Bind the exported remote reference in the registry
String name = "MyRemoteUtility";
registry.rebind(name, remoteUtility);
System.out.println("Remote server is ready...");
```

You are not ready to start your server program yet. I discuss how to start an RMI application in the sections that follow.

For security reasons, you can bind a remote reference to an RMI registry only from the RMI server program that is running on the same machine as the RMI registry. Otherwise, a hacker may be able to bind any arbitrary and potentially harmful remote references to your RMI registry. By default, the getRegistry() static method of the LocateRegistry class returns a stub for a registry that runs on the same machine at port 1099. You may just use the following code to locate a registry in the server program:

```
// Get a registry stub for a local machine at port 1099
Registry registry = LocateRegistry.getRegistry();
```

Note that the call to the LocateRegistry.getRegistry() method does not try to connect to a registry application. It just returns a stub for the registry. It is the subsequent call on this stub, bind(), rebind(), or any other method call that attempts to connect to the registry application.

Writing the RMI Client Program

The RMI client program calls the methods on remote objects, which exist on the remote server. The first thing that a client program must do is to know the location of the remote object. It is the RMI server program that creates and knows the location of the remote object. It is the responsibility of the server program to publish the location details of the remote object so a client can locate it and use it. The server program publishes the remote object's location details by binding it with an RMI registry and gives it a name, which is MyRemoteUtility in your case. The client program contacts the RMI registry and performs a name-based lookup to get the remote reference. After getting the remote reference, the client program calls methods on the remote reference, which are executed in the server. Typically, the RMI client program performs the following:

- It makes sure that it is running under a security manager:

```
SecurityManager secManager =
    System.getSecurityManager();
if (secManager == null) {
    System.setSecurityManager(
    new SecurityManager());
```

- It locates the registry where the remote reference has been bound by the server. You must know the machine name or IP address, and the port number at which the RMI registry is running. In a real-world RMI program, you would not be using localhost in the client program to locate the registry. Rather, an RMI registry will be running on a separate machine. For this example, you will run all three programs—RMI registry, server, and client—on the same machine:

```
// Locate the registry
Registry registry =
    LocateRegistry.getRegistry(
        "localhost", 1099);
```

- It performs the lookup in the registry using the lookup() method of the Registry interface. It passes the name of the bound remote reference to the lookup() method and gets back the remote reference (or stub). Note that the lookup() method must use the same name that was used to bind/rebind a remote reference by the server. The lookup() method returns a Remote object. You must cast it to the type of your remote interface. The following snippet of code casts the returned remote reference from the lookup() method to the RemoteUtility interface type:

```
String name = "MyRemoteUtility";
RemoteUtility remoteUtilStub =
    (RemoteUtility) registry.
    lookup(name);
```

- It calls methods on the remote reference (or stub). The client program treats the `remoteUtilStub` reference as if it is a reference to a local object. Any method call made on it is sent to the server for execution. All remote methods throw a `RemoteException`. You must handle the `RemoteException` when you call any remote method.

```
// Call the echo() method
String reply = remoteUtilStub.echo(
    "Hello from the RMI client.");
...
```

Listing 9-8 contains the complete code for your client program, which is a member of the `jdojo.rmi.client` module. Do not run this program yet. You will go through the step-by-step process in the next few sections to run your RMI application. You may notice that writing RMI code is not complex. It is the plumbing of different components in RMI that is complex.

Listing 9-8. An RMI Remote Client Program

```java
// RemoteClient.java
package com.jdojo.rmi;

import com.jdojo.rmi.common.RemoteUtilily;
import java.rmi.RemoteException;
import java.rmi.registry.LocateRegistry;
import java.rmi.registry.Registry;
import java.rmi.server.UnicastRemoteObject;
public class RemoteClient {
    public static void main(String[] args) {
        SecurityManager secManager =
            System.getSecurityManager();
        if (secManager == null) {
            System.setSecurityManager(
                new SecurityManager());
        }
```

```java
    try {
        // Locate the registry
        Registry registry =
            LocateRegistry.getRegistry(
                "localhost", 1099);
        String name = "MyRemoteUtility";
        RemoteUtility remoteUtilStub =
            (RemoteUtility) registry.
            lookup(name);
        // Call the echo() method
        String reply = remoteUtilStub.echo(
            "Hello from the RMI client.");
        System.out.println("Reply: " +
            reply);
    } catch (RemoteException e) {
        e.printStackTrace();
    } catch (NotBoundException e) {
        e.printStackTrace();
    }
  }
}
```

Separating the Server and Client Code

It is important that you separate the code for the server and client programs in an RMI application. The server program needs to have the following three components:

- The remote interface

- The implementation class for the remote interface

- The server program

The client program needs to have the following two components:

- The remote interface

- The client program

You were prepared for this client-server code separation from the very beginning of this chapter. To achieve this, you will deploy the `jdojo.rmi.server` and `jdojo.rmi.common` modules to the server machine, and you will deploy `jdojo.rmi.client` and `jdojo.rmi.common` modules to the client machine. I refer to these modular JARs as `jdojo.rmi.server.jar`, `jdojo.rmi.client.jar`, and `jdojo.rmi.common.jar` in subsequent sections when you run the RMI application.

Running the RMI Application

You need to start all programs involved in an RMI application in the following specific sequence:

- Run the RMI registry.

- Run the RMI server program.

- Run the RMI client program.

Refer to the "Troubleshooting an RMI Application" section later in this chapter if you have any problem in running any of the programs.

Your server and client programs use security managers. You must have your Java policy file properly configured before you can run the RMI application successfully. You can grant all security permissions to an RMI application for learning purposes. You can do so by creating a text file named `rmi.policy` (you can use any other file name you want) and entering the following content, which grants all permissions to all code:

```
grant {
    permission java.security.AllPermission;
};
```

When you run the RMI client or server program, you need to set the `rmi.policy` file as your Java security policy file using the `java.security.policy` JVM option. It is assumed that you have saved the `rmi.policy` file in the `C:\mypolicy` folder on Windows:

```
java - Djava.security.policy=^
file:///C:/mypolicy/rmi.policy <other-options>
```

This approach of setting a Java policy file has a temporary effect. It should be used only for learning purposes. You will need to set a fine-grained security in a production environment.

Running the RMI Registry

The RMI registry application is supplied with the JDK/JRE installation. It is copied in the bin subfolder of the respective installation main folder. On the Windows platform, it is the rmiregistry.exe executable file. You can run the RMI registry by starting the rmiregistry application using a command prompt. It accepts a port number on which it will run. By default, it runs on port 1099. The following command starts it at port 1099 using a command prompt on Windows:

```
C:\java9\bin> rmiregistry
```

The following command starts the RMI registry at port 8967:

```
C:\java9\bin> rmiregistry 8967
```

The rmiregistry application does not print any startup message on the prompt. Usually, it is started as a background process.

Most likely, the command is not going to work on your machine. Using this command, you will be able to start the rmiregistry successfully. However, you will get ClassNotFoundException when you run the RMI server application in the next section. The rmiregistry application needs access to some of the classes (the registered ones) used in the RMI server application. There are three ways to make the classes available to rmiregistry:

- Set the CLASSPATH appropriately.

- Set the java.rmi.server.codebase JVM property to the URL that contains the classes needed by the rmiregistry.

- Set the JVM property named java.rmi.server.useCodebaseOnly to false. This property is set to true by default. If this property is set to false, the rmiregistry can download the needed class files from the server.

The following command adds the JARs containing the server classes and common interfaces to the CLASSPATH, before starting the rmiregistry:

```
C:\java9\bin> SET CLASSPATH=^
C:\Java9APIsAndModules\dist\jdojo.rmi.common.jar;^
C:\Java9APIsAndModules\dist\jdojo.rmi.server.jar
C:\java9\bin> rmiregistry
```

Instead of setting the CLASSPATH to make classes available to the rmiregistry, you can also set the java.rmi.server.codebase JVM property that is a space-separated list of URLs, as shown:

```
C:\java9\bin> rmiregistry ^
-J-Djava.rmi.server.codebase=^
file:///C:/Java9APIsAndModules/dist/jdojo.rmi.common.jar ^
file:///C:/Java9APIsAndModules/dist/jdojo.rmi.server.jar
```

The following command resets the CLASSPATH and sets the java.rmi.server. useCodebaseOnly property for the JVM to false so the rmiregistry will download any class files needed from the RMI server. Your example will work using this command:

```
C:\java9\bin> SET CLASSPATH=
C:\java9\bin> rmiregistry ^
-J-Djava.rmi.server.useCodebaseOnly=false
```

Running the RMI Server

The RMI registry must be running before you can run the RMI server. Recall that the server runs under a security manager that requires you to grant permissions to perform certain actions in a Java policy file. Make sure that you have entered the required grants in a policy file. You can use the following command to run the server program. The command text is entered in one line; it has been shown in multiple lines for clarity. Each part in the command text should be separated by a space, not a new line. In the command, you will need to change the path to the JAR and policy files that will reflect their paths on your machine:

```
C:\Java9APIsAndModules>java --module-path ^
dist\jdojo.rmi.common.jar;dist\jdojo.rmi.server.jar ^
```

```
-Djava.security.policy=file:///C:/mypolicy/rmi.policy ^
-Djava.rmi.server.codebase=^
file:///C:/Java9APIsAndModules/dist/jdojo.rmi.common.jar ^
--module ^
jdojo.rmi.server/com.jdojo.rmi.server.RemoteServer

Remote server is ready...
```

You need to set a `java.rmi.server.codebase` property. This is used by an RMI registry and a client program if they need to download class files that they do not have. The value of this property is a URL, which can point to a local file system, a web server, an FTP server, or any other resource. The URL may point to a JAR file, as it does in this case, or it can point to a directory. If it points to a directory, the URL must end with a forward slash. The following command uses a folder as its codebase. If an RMI registry and a client need any class files, they will attempt to download the class files from the URL `file:///C:/myrmi/classes/`.

```
java -Djava.rmi.server.codebase=^
file:///C:/myrmi/classes/ <other-options>
```

You can also set a `java.rmi.server.codebase` property to point to a web server, where you can store your necessary class files as shown:

```
java -Djava.rmi.server.codebase=^
http://www.jdojo.com/rmi/classes/ <other-options>
```

If you store class files at multiple locations, you can specify all locations separated by a space as follows:

```
java -Djava.rmi.server.codebase=^
  "http://www.jdojo.com/rmi/classes/
   ftp://www.jdojo.com/rmi/some/classes/c.jar" ^
<other-options>
```

It specifies one location as a directory and another as a JAR file. One uses the `http` protocol and another `ftp`. The two values are separated by a space, and they are on one line, not on two lines as shown. A `ClassNotFoundException` may occur when you run the server or client program, which is most likely caused by an incorrect setting for the `java.rmi.server.codebase` property or by not setting this property at all.

Running an RMI Client Program

After the RMI registry and server applications are started successfully, it is time to start the RMI client application. You can use the following command to run the client program:

```
C:\Java9APIsAndModules>java ^
--module-path ^
dist\jdojo.rmi.common.jar;dist\jdojo.rmi.client.jar ^
-Djava.rmi.server.codebase=^
file:///C:/Java9APIsAndModules/dist/jdojo.rmi.common.jar ^
-Djava.security.policy=file:///C:/mypolicy/rmi.policy ^
--module ^
jdojo.rmi.client/com.jdojo.rmi.client.RemoteClient

Reply: Hello from the RMI client.
```

For this example, you do not have to include a `java.rmi.server.codebase` option when you run the previous command. However, you will need to include this option if your client program uses parameters in remote methods, and the class files for those parameter types are not available on the server. In that case, the server will download those class files from the specified `java.rmi.server.codebase` option.

You should be able to see an output on the console when the client program runs successfully. You may get a different output when you run the program because it prints the current date and time with the zone information for the server machine running the server application.

Troubleshooting an RMI Application

It is very likely that you will get many errors before you will be able to run the RMI application the first time. This section lists a few errors that you may receive. It will also list some possible causes for those errors and some possible solutions. It is not possible to list all possible errors that you might get when you attempt to run an RMI application. You should be able to figure out most of the errors by looking at the stack prints of the errors.

java.rmi.server.ExportException

You get an ExportException when you try to run the rmiregistry application or the server application. The exception stack trace will be similar to the one shown if you get this exception when you attempt to run the rmiregistry application:

```
java.rmi.server.ExportException:
    Port already in use: 1099; nested exception is:
    java.net.BindException: Address already in use:
    JVM_Bind...
```

It states that the port number 1099 (may be a different number in your case) is already in use. Maybe you have already started the rmiregistry application at port 1099 (which is the default port number for an rmiregistry application), or some other application is using the port 1099. You can do one of the following two things to fix this problem:

- You can stop the application that is using the port 1099.

- You can start the rmiregistry application at a port other than 1099.

If you get an ExportException when you run the server program, it is caused by the failure of the export process of the remote object. There are many reasons for the export process to fail. The following exception stack trace (partial trace is shown) is caused by exporting the same remote object twice:

```
java.rmi.server.ExportException:
    object already exported
  at sun.rmi.transport.ObjectTable.putTarget(
    ObjectTable.java:189)
  at sun.rmi.transport.Transport.exportObject(
    Transport.java:92)...
```

Check your server program and make sure that you are exporting your remote object only once. It is a common mistake to inherit the remote object implementation class from the UnicastRemoteObject class and use the exportObject() method of the UnicastRemoteObject class to export the remote object. When you inherit the remote object's implementation class from the UnicastRemoteObject class, the remote object, which you create, is exported automatically. If you try to export it again using the exportObject() method, you will get this exception. I have stressed this point a few times when discussing the remote interface implementation class. When you are developing an RMI application, remember the saying, "To err is programmer, to punish, Java." Even a little mistake in the setup of an RMI program may take hours to detect and fix.

java.security.AccessControlException

You get this exception when your Java policy file does not have grant entries that are necessary to run the RMI application. The following is the partial stack trace of an exception, which is caused when you attempt to run the server program, and it attempts to bind a remote object to the RMI registry:

```
java.security.AccessControlException:
    access denied (java.net.SocketPermission
127.0.0.1:1099 connect,resolve)...
```

Communications among registry, server, and client are performed using sockets. You must grant appropriate socket permission in the Java policy file for security, so that the three components of your RMI application may be able to communicate. Most of the security-related exceptions can be fixed by granting appropriate permissions in the Java policy file.

java.lang.ClassNotFoundException

You get a ClassNotFoundException exception when a class file that is needed by Java runtime is not found. You must have received this exception many times by now. Most of the time, you receive this exception when the CLASSPATH is not appropriately set. In an RMI application, this exception may be the cause for another exception. The following stack trace shows that the java.rmi.ServerException exception was thrown, which has its cause in a ClassNotFoundException exception:

```
java.rmi.ServerException:
    RemoteException occurred in server thread;
    nested exception is:
        java.rmi.UnmarshalException:
        error unmarshalling arguments;
```

```
        nested exception is:
            java.lang.ClassNotFoundException:
            com.jdojo.rmi.RemoteUtility
...
Caused by: java.lang.ClassNotFoundException:
    com.jdojo.rmi.RemoteUtility
  at java.net.URLClassLoader$1.run(
    URLClassLoader.java:220)
  at java.net.URLClassLoader$1.run(
    URLClassLoader.java:209)
```

This type of exception is thrown when the `java.rmi.server.codebase` option is not set properly or not set at all when you run the server or the client application.

This exception was thrown when the server program was started without using the `java.rmi.server.codebase` option and the `rmiregistry` application was run without setting the CLASSPATH. When you try to bind/rebind a remote reference with an `rmiregistry` application, the server application sends the remote reference to the `rmiregistry` application. The `rmiregistry` application must load the class before it can represent the remote reference as a Java object in its JVM. At this time, the `rmiregistry` will try to download the required class files from the location that was specified at the server startup using the `java.rmi.server.codebase` property.

If you get this exception when you run the client program, make sure you have set the `java.rmi.server.codebase` property when you run the client program.

Please check the CLASSPATH and `java.rmi.server.codebase` property when you run the server and the client program to avoid this exception.

You get a `ClassNotFoundException` when you run the client program because the server was not able to find some class definitions that were required in unmarshalling the client call on the server side. The sample partial stack trace of the exception is shown:

```
java.rmi.ServerException:
    RemoteException occurred in server thread;
    nested exception is:
        java.rmi.UnmarshalException:
        error unmarshalling arguments;
        nested exception is: java.lang.
            ClassNotFoundException:
```

```
            com.jdojo.rmi.client.Square
    at sun.rmi.server.UnicastServerRef.dispatch(
        UnicastServerRef.java:336)
    at sun.rmi.transport.Transport$1.run(
        Transport.java:159)...
```

A remote method defined in a remote interface may accept a parameter, which may be of an interface or a class type. The client may pass an object of a class that implements the interface or an object of a subclass of type defined in the remote interface's method signature. If the class definition does not exist on the server, the server will attempt to download the class using the `java.rmi.server.codebase` property that was set in the client application. You need to make sure the class for which you are getting this error (the exception stack trace shows `com.jdojo.rmi.client.Square` as the class name) is in the `CLASSPATH` of the server JVM or set the `java.rmi.server.codebase` property when you run the remote client, so that this class can be downloaded by the sever.

Debugging an RMI Application

You can turn on RMI logging for an RMI server application by setting the JVM property named `java.rmi.server.logCalls` to `true`. By default, it is set to `false`. The following command launches your `RemoteServer` application setting the `java.rmi.server.logCalls` property to `true`:

```
C:\Java9APIsAndModules>java ^
--module-path ^
dist\jdojo.rmi.common.jar;dist\jdojo.rmi.server.jar ^
-Djava.rmi.server.logCalls=true ^
-Djava.security.policy=file:///C:/mypolicy/rmi.policy ^
-Djava.rmi.server.codebase=^
file:///C:/Java9APIsAndModules/dist/jdojo.rmi.common.jar ^
--module ^
jdojo.rmi.server/com.jdojo.rmi.server.RemoteServer
```

When the `java.rmi.server.logCalls` property for the server JVM is set to `true`, all incoming calls to the server and stack trace of any exceptions that are thrown during execution of an incoming call are logged to the standard error.

The RMI runtime also lets you log the incoming calls in a server application to a file, irrespective of the value set for the java.rmi.server.logCalls property for the server JVM. You can log all incoming call details to a file using the setLog(OutputStream out) static method of the java.rmi.server.RemoteServer class. Typically, you set the file output stream for logging in the beginning of the server program code such as the very first statement in the main() method of your com.jdojo.rmi.server.RemoteServer class. The following snippet of code enables call logging in a remote server application to a C:\rmilogs\rmi.log file. You can disable call logging by using null as the OutputStream in the setLog() method:

```
try {
    java.io.OutputStream os =
        new java.io.FileOutputStream(
            "C:\\rmilogs\\rmi.log");
    java.rmi.server.RemoteServer.setLog(os);
} catch (FileNotFoundException e) {
    System.err.println(
        "Could not enable incoming calls logging.");
    e.printStackTrace();
}
```

When a security manager is installed on the server, the running code, which enables logging to a file, must have a java.util.logging.LoggingPermission with permission target as "control". The following grant entry in the Java policy file will grant this permission. You will also have to grant the "write" permission to the log file (C:\rmilogs\rmi.log in this example) in the Java policy file:

```
grant {
    permission java.io.FilePermission
        "c:\\rmilogs\\rmi.log", "write";
    permission java.util.logging.LoggingPermission
        "control";
};
```

If you want to get debugging information about an RMI client application, set a non-standard sun.rmi.client.logCalls property to true when you launch the RMI client application. It will display the debugging information on the standard error.

Since this property is not part of a public specification, it may be removed in future releases. You need to refer to the RMI specification for more details on debugging options. You can find the RMI specification at `https://docs.oracle.com/javase/8/docs/technotes/guides/rmi/faq.html`.

If you still have problems compiling and running your RMI application, you can refer to the web page at `https://docs.oracle.com/javase/8/docs/technotes/guides/rmi/faq.html`. This web page provides answers to several frequently asked questions while working with RMI applications.

Dynamic Class Downloading

The JVM loads the class definition before it can create an object of a class. It uses a class loader to load a class at runtime. A class loader is an instance of the `java.lang.ClassLoader` class. A class loader must locate the bytecodes for a class before it can load its definition into the JVM. A Java class loader is capable of loading the bytecodes of a class from any location such as a local file system and a network. There could be multiple class loaders in one JVM, and they could be system or custom defined.

The JVM creates a class loader at startup, which is called a *bootstrap* class loader. The bootstrap class loader is responsible for loading initial classes required for basic JVM functions. Class loaders are organized in a tree-like structure based on a parent-child relationship. The bootstrap class loader has no parent. All other class loaders have the bootstrap class loader as their direct or indirect parent. In a typical class loading process, when a class loader is asked to load the bytecode for a class, it asks its parent to load the class, which in turn asks its parent and so on, until the bootstrap class loader gets the request to load the class. If none of the parent class loaders is able to load the class, the class loader that received the initial request to load the class will attempt to load the class.

The RMI runtime uses a special RMI class loader that is responsible for loading the classes in an RMI application. When an object is being passed around in an RMI application from one JVM to another, the sending JVM has to serialize and marshal the object, and the receiving JVM has to deserialize and unmarshal it. The sending JVM adds the value of the property `java.rmi.server.codebase` to the object's serialized stream. When the object stream is received at the other end, the receiving JVM must load the class definition of the object using a class loader before it can convert the object stream into a Java object. The JVM instructs the RMI class loader to load the class definition of the object, which it has received in a stream form. The class loader attempts to load the class definition from its JVM CLASSPATH. If the class definition is not found using the CLASSPATH, the class loader uses the value of the java.rmi.server.codebase property from the object's stream to load the class definition.

Note that the java.rmi.server.codebase property is set in one JVM, and it is used to download the class definition in another JVM. This property can be set when you run the RMI server or client program. When one side (server or client) transmits an object to another side, which does not have the bytecode to represent the class definition for the object being received, the sending side must have set the java.rmi.server.codebase property at the time of sending the object, so that the receiving end can download the class bytecode using this property. The value for the java.rmi.server.codebase property is a space-separated list of URLs.

Downloading code from an RMI server to the client may be fine from a security point of view. Sometimes, it may not be considered safe to download code from a client to the server. By default, downloading the classes from remote JVMs is disabled. RMI lets you enable/disable this feature by using a java.rmi.server.useCodebaseOnly property. By default, it is set to true. If it is set to true, the JVM's class loader will load classes only from local CLASSPATH or locally set java.rmi.server.codebase property. That is, if it is set to true, the class loader will not read the value of java.rmi.server.codebase from the received object's stream to download the class definition. Rather, it will look for the class definition in its JVM CLASSPATH and use URLs that are set as the value of the java.rmi.server.codebase property for its own JVM. That is, when the java.rmi.server.useCodebaseOnly property is set to true, the RMI class loader ignores the value for the codebase that is sent from the sending JVM in an object's stream. The property name useCodebaseOnly seems to be a misnomer. It could have conveyed its meaning better had it been named useLocallySetCodebaseOnly. Here is how you can set this property when you run the RMI server:

```
java -Djava.rmi.server.codebase=^
"http://www.myurl.com/rmiclasses" ^
    -Djava.rmi.server.useCodebaseOnly=true ^
    <other-options> ^
    com.jdojo.rmi.RemoteServer
```

Note   The default value for the `java.rmi.server.codebase` property is set to true. It means, by default, the application is not allowed to download classes from other JVMs.

There are two implications of setting the `java.rmi.server.useCodebaseOnly` property to `true`:

- If the server needs a class as part of a remote call from a client, it will always look in its CLASSPATH, or it will use the value of `java.rmi.server.codebase` that you set for the server program. In the previous example, all classes in the server must be found in its CLASSPATH or at the URL `http://www.myurl.com/rmiclasses`.

- If a client needs to use a new class type in a remote method call, the new class type must be known to the server in advance because the server will never use the client's instruction (set by using the `java.rmi.server.codebase` property at the client side) about the location from where to download the required new classes. This means that you must make the new classes that will be used by a remote client available in the server's CLASSPATH or at the URLs specified as the `java.rmi.server.codebase` property for the server. This situation may arise when a remote method accepts an interface type and the client sends an object of a class that implements that interface. In this case, the server may not have the same definition of the new implementation of the interface as the client.

The previous argument applies to running an RMI client application as well if you set the `java.rmi.server.useCodebaseOnly` property to `true` for the JVM running the RMI client application. If this property is set to `true` for the client application, you must make all required classes available to the client either by placing them in its CLASSPATH or placing them at URLs and setting the URLs as the value for the `java.rmi.server.codebase` property at the client side.

Garbage Collection of Remote Objects

In an RMI application, remote objects are created in the JVM on the server. The RMI registry and remote clients keep references of the remote objects. Does a remote object ever get garbage collected? And, if it does get garbage collected, when does it happen and how does it happen? Garbage collection of a local object is easy. A local object is created and referenced in the same JVM. It is an easy task for a garbage collector to determine that a local object is no longer referenced in the JVM.

In an RMI application, you need a garbage collector that can keep track of the references of a remote object in remote JVMs. Suppose an RMI server creates a remote object of the RemoteUtilityImpl class, and five clients get its remote reference. An RMI registry is also a client that gets the remote reference as part of the bind/rebind process. When and how does the server garbage collect the lone object of the RemoteUtilityImpl class, which is being referenced by five clients?

The JVM on the server, which has the remote object, and the five JVMs at five different clients must interact, so the remote object in the server's JVM can be garbage collected when it is no longer used by any remote clients. Let's ignore the local references of the remote object in the server JVM for this discussion. The interaction between a remote client and an RMI server depends on many unreliable factors. For example, the network may go down, and a remote client may not be able to communicate with the server. The second consideration is who initiates the interaction between the remote client and the server? Is it the server that keeps asking a remote client if it has a live remote reference? Is it the remote client who keeps telling the server that it still has a live remote reference? The responsibility of the interaction between the client and the server is shared by both. The remote client needs to update the server about the aliveness of its remote references. If the server does not hear from any clients for a specific period of time, it takes a unilateral decision to make the remote object a candidate for a future garbage collection.

The RMI garbage collector is based on reference count. A reference count has an associated lease. A lease has a time period for which it is valid. When a remote client (including an RMI registry) gets a reference to a remote object, it sends a message to the RMI runtime on the server requesting a lease for that remote object reference. The server grants a lease for a specified time period to that client. The server increments the reference count for that remote object by one and sends back the lease to the client.

By default, an RMI server grants a lease for ten minutes for a remote object. Now, the following are some possibilities:

- The client may be done with the remote object reference within the time period for which it had acquired the lease from the server.

- The client may want to renew the lease for another extended time period.

- The client crashes. The server does not receive any message from the client, and the lease period for a remote reference that was acquired by the client expires.

Let's look at each possibility. A client sends messages to the server on three different occasions. It sends a message the very first time it receives a remote reference. It tells the server that it has a reference of the remote object. The second time, it sends a message to the server when it wants to renew the lease for a remote reference. The third time, it sends a message to the server when it is done with the remote reference. In fact, when a remote reference is garbage collected in a client application, it sends a message to the server that it is done with the remote object. Internally, there are only two types of messages that a remote client sends to a server: dirty and clean. The *dirty* message is sent to get a lease, and the *clean* message is sent to remove/cancel the lease. These two messages are sent from a remote client to a server using the `dirty()` and `clean()` methods of the `java.rmi.dgc.DGC` interface. As a developer, you do not have any control over these messages (sending or receiving) except that you can customize the lease time period. The lease time period controls the frequency of these messages sent to the server.

When a client is done with a remote object reference, it sends a message to the server that it is done with it. The message is sent when the remote reference in the client's JVM is garbage collected. Therefore, it is important that you set the remote reference in the client program code to `null` as soon as you are done with it. Otherwise, the server will keep holding on to the remote object, even if it is no longer used by the remote client. You do not have any control on the timing of this message, which is sent from the remote client to the server. All you can do to expedite this message sending is to set the remote object reference in the client code to `null`, so the garbage collector will attempt to garbage collect it and send a clean message to the server.

The RMI runtime keeps track of the leases for remote references in a remote client JVM. When a lease is halfway through its expiration period, the remote client sends a lease renewal request to the server and gets the lease renewed. When a lease for a remote client is renewed for a remote reference, the server keeps track of the lease expiration time, and it will not garbage collect the remote object. It is important that you understand the importance of setting the lease period for a remote reference. If it is too small, a significant amount of network bandwidth will be used for renewing the lease frequently. If it is too large, the server will keep the remote object alive for a longer time in case a client is done with its remote reference, and it does not inform the server to cancel the lease. I discuss shortly how to set a lease period value in an RMI application.

If the server does not hear anything from a remote client about the lease of a remote reference that the client had acquired, after the expiration of the lease period, it simply cancels the lease and decrements the reference count for that remote object by one. This unilateral decision that is made by the server is important to handle the cases of ill-behaved remote clients (not telling the server that it is done with a remote reference) or any network/system hiccups that may prevent the remote client from communicating with the server.

When all clients are done with a remote reference of a remote object, its reference count in the server will go down to zero. A remote client is considered done with a remote reference when either its lease is expired or it has sent a clean message to the server. In this case, the RMI runtime will reference the remote object using a *weak reference*, so if there is no local reference to the remote object, it may be garbage collected.

By default, the lease period is set for ten minutes. You can set the lease period using the java.rmi.dgc.leaseValue property when you start the RMI server. The value for the lease period is specified in milliseconds. The following command starts the server program with a lease period set to 5 minutes (300000 milliseconds):

```
C:\Java9APIsAndModules>java --module-path ^
dist\jdojo.rmi.common.jar;dist\jdojo.rmi.server.jar ^
-Djava.security.policy=file:///C:/mypolicy/rmi.policy ^
-Djava.rmi.dgc.leaseValue=300000 ^
-Djava.rmi.server.codebase=^
file:///C:/Java9APIsAndModules/dist/jdojo.rmi.common.jar ^
--module ^
jdojo.rmi.server/com.jdojo.rmi.server.RemoteServer

Remote server is ready...
```

Except for setting the lease time period, everything is handled by the RMI runtime. The RMI runtime gives you one more piece of information about the garbage collection of a remote object. It can tell you when the reference count of the remote object has gone down to zero. It is important to get this notification if a remote object holds some resources that you would like to free when no remote client is referencing it. To get this notification, you need to implement the `java.rmi.server.Unreferenced` interface in your remote object implementation class. Its declaration is as follows:

```
public interface Unreferenced {
    void unreferenced()
}
```

The `unreferenced()` method is called when the remote reference count for a remote object becomes zero. If you want to get a notification in your example for the `RemoteUtility` remote object, you need to modify the declaration of the `RemoteUtilityImpl` class, as shown in Listing 9-9.

Listing 9-9. A Modified Version of the RemoteUtilityImpl Class That Implements the Unreferenced Interface

```
// RemoteUtilityImpl.java
package com.jdojo.rmi.server;
import com.jdojo.rmi.common.RemoteUtility;
import java.rmi.server.Unreferenced;
import java.time.ZonedDateTime;
public class RemoteUtilityImpl implements
        RemoteUtility, Unreferenced {
    public RemoteUtilityImpl() {
    }
    @Override
    public String echo(String msg) {
        return msg;
    }
    @Override
    public ZonedDateTime getServerTime() {
        return ZonedDateTime.now();
    }
```

```
    @Override
    public int add(int n1, int n2) {
        return n1 + n2;
    }
    @Override
    public void unreferenced() {
        System.out.println(
            "RemoteUtility unreferenced at: " +
            ZonedDateTime.now());
    }
}
```

You may notice that, this time, the RemoteUtilityImpl class implements the Unreferenced interface and provides implementation for the unreferenced() method, which prints a message to the standard output with the time when its reference count becomes zero. The unreferenced() method will be called by the RMI runtime. To test that the unreferenced() method is called, you can start the RMI registry application and then start the RMI server application. The RMI registry will keep renewing the lease for the remote object. As long as an RMI registry is running, you will never see the unreferenced() method being called. You need to shut down the RMI registry application and wait for the remote object reference's lease to expire or to be cancelled by the RMI registry when you shut it down. After the RMI registry is shut down, you will see the message on the standard output for the server program that will be printed by the unreferenced() method.

An RMI registry should be used just as a bootstrap means to start the remote client. Later on, the remote client can receive a remote object's reference as a method call to another remote object. If a remote client receives a remote object reference by a remote method call on a remote object, that remote object's reference need not be registered with the RMI registry. In this case, after the last remote client is finished with the remote reference, the server will garbage collect the remote object instead of keeping it in memory when it is bound to an RMI registry.

Summary

Java Remote Method Invocation (RMI) allows a program running in one JVM to invoke methods on Java objects running in another JVM. RMI provides an API to develop distributed applications using the Java programming language.

An RMI application involves three applications running in three JVMs: the `rmiregistry` application, a server application, and a client application. The `rmiregistry` application is shipped with the JDK. You are responsible for developing the server and client applications. The server application creates Java objects called remote objects and registers them with the `rmiregistry` for later name lookup by clients. The client application looks up the remote object in the `rmiregistry` using a logical name and gets back a reference of the remote object. The client application invokes methods on the remote object reference that is sent to the server application for execution of the method on the remote object. The result of the method invocation is sent back from the server application to the client application.

An RMI application must follow a few rules to develop the classes and interfaces involved in the remote communication. You need to create an interface (called remote interface) that must inherit from the `Remote` interface. All methods in the interface must include a `throws` clause that throws at least the `RemoteException`. The class for the remote object must implement the remote interface. The server application creates an object of the class implementing the remote interface, exports the object to give a status of a real remote object, and registers it with the `rmiregistry`. The client application needs only the remote interface.

If any of the three applications needs classes that are not locally available, they can download them dynamically at runtime. For a JVM to download classes dynamically, the `java.rmi.server.useCodebaseOnly` property must be set to `false`. By default, it is set to `true`, which disables dynamic downloading of the classes in a JVM. Along with a remote object reference, the JVM also receives the value of a property named `java.rmi.server.codebase`, which is the URL from where the JVM may download (if permitted by its own `java.rmi.server.useCodebaseOnly` property setting) the classes needed to work with the remote object reference.

There are several components working together in an RMI application that make it hard to debug. You can log all calls to the RMI server by running it with the JVM property `java.rmi.server.logCalls` set to `true`. All calls to the server will be logged to a standard error. You can also log RMI server calls to a file.

RMI provides automatic garbage collection for remote objects running in the RMI server. The garbage collection of remote objects is based on reference counts and leases. When the client application gets the reference of the remote object, it also obtains a lease for the remote object from the server application. The lease is valid for a period. The client application keeps renewing the lease periodically as long as it keeps the remote object reference. The server application keeps track of the reference count and the leases for the remote objects. When the client application is done with the remote reference, it sends a message to the server application, and the server application reduces the reference count for the remote object by one. When the reference count of the remote object reduces to zero in the server application, the remote object is garbage collected.

Exercises

Exercise 1

What is Java Remote Method Invocation?

Exercise 2

What is the fully qualified name of the interface that every remote interface must extend?

Exercise 3

What steps do you need to perform in your RMI server program after you create a remote object, so the remote object is available for a client to use?

Exercise 4

What is RMI registry and where is it located?

Exercise 5

In an RMI application, can an RMI registry and RMI server be deployed to two different machines? If your answer is no, explain why.

Exercise 6

Describe the typical sequence of steps an RMI client program needs to perform to call a method on a remote object.

Exercise 7

An RMI application involves three layers of applications: client, RMI registry, and server. In what order must these applications be run?

Exercise 8

Describe the use of the `java.rmi.server.codebase` command-line option while running an RMI client and server application.

Exercise 9

What is the effect of using the `java.rmi.server.logCalls=true` command-line option while running an RMI server program?

Exercise 10

How do you log remote calls in an RMI server application to a file?

Exercise 11

What is the effect of using the `java.rmi.server.useCodebaseOnly=true` command-line option while running an RMI application?

Exercise 12

Briefly explain how remote objects are garbage collected.

Exercise 13

Describe the steps to get notified when a remote object is no longer being referenced.

CHAPTER 10

Scripting in Java

In this chapter, you will learn:

- What scripting in Java is
- How to execute scripts from Java and how to pass parameters to scripts
- How the ScriptContext is used in executing scripts
- How to use the Java programming language in scripts
- How to implement a script engine

All example programs in this chapter are members of a jdojo.script module, as declared in Listing 10-1, unless specified otherwise.

Listing 10-1. The Declaration of a jdojo.script Module

```
// module-info.java
module jdojo.script {
    requires java.scripting;
    requires jdk.unsupported;
    // <- needed for GraalVM JavaScript
    exports com.jdojo.script;
}
```

The scripting support in JDK is in the java.scripting module. Your module using the Java Scripting API needs to read the java.scripting module as the jdojo.script module does.

© Kishori Sharan, Peter Späth 2021
K. Sharan and P. Späth, *More Java 17*, https://doi.org/10.1007/978-1-4842-7135-3_10

What Is Scripting in Java?

Some believe that the Java Virtual Machine (JVM) can execute programs written only in the Java programming language, which is not true. The JVM executes language-neutral bytecode. It can execute programs written in any programming language, if the program can be compiled into Java bytecode.

A *scripting language* is a programming language that provides the ability to write *scripts* that are evaluated (or interpreted) by a runtime environment called a *script engine* (or an interpreter). A script is a sequence of characters that is written using the syntax of a scripting language and used as the source for a program executed by an interpreter. The interpreter parses the scripts; produces intermediate code, which is an internal representation of the program; and executes the intermediate code. The interpreter stores the variables used in a script in data structures called *symbol tables*.

Typically, unlike in a compiled programming language, the source code (called a script) in a scripting language is not compiled, but is interpreted at runtime. However, scripts written in some scripting languages may be compiled into Java bytecode that can be run by the JVM.

Java has included scripting support to the Java platform that lets a Java application execute scripts written in scripting languages such as JavaScript, Groovy, Jython, JRuby, etc. Two-way communication is supported. It also lets scripts access Java objects created by the host application. The Java runtime and a scripting language runtime can communicate and use each other's features.

Support for scripting languages in Java comes through the Java Scripting API. All classes and interfaces in the Java Scripting API are in the `javax.script` package, which is in the `java.scripting` module.

Using a scripting language in a Java application provides several advantages:

- Most scripting languages are dynamically typed, which makes it simpler to write programs.

- They provide a quicker way to develop and test small applications.

- Customization by end users is possible.

- A scripting language may provide domain-specific features that are not available in Java.

Scripting languages have some disadvantages as well. For example, dynamic typing is good to write simpler code; however, it turns into a disadvantage when a type is interpreted incorrectly, and you have to spend a lot of time debugging it.

Scripting support in Java lets you take advantage of both worlds: it allows you to use the Java programming language for developing statically typed, scalable, and high-performance parts of the application and use a scripting language that fits the domain-specific needs for other parts.

I use the term *script engine* frequently in this chapter. A *script engine* is a software component that executes programs written in a scripting language. Typically, but not necessarily, a script engine is an implementation of an interpreter for a scripting language. Interpreters for several scripting languages have been implemented in Java. They expose programming interfaces so a Java program may interact with them.

JDK used to be co-bundled with a script engine called Nashorn JavaScript. However, Nashorn was removed in Oracle's JDK15, although you can still find it in OpenJDK 16. We don't talk about Nashorn in this chapter.

Java can execute scripts in any scripting language that provides an implementation for a script engine. For example, Java can execute scripts written in GraalVM JavaScript, Groovy, Jython, JRuby, etc. Examples in this chapter use the Groovy language.

Note   As a substitute for the Nashorn JavaScript engine, you might consider using the JavaScript script engine provided with GraalVM. Unfortunately, this one doesn't work well with OpenJDK 17.

Installing Script Engines in Maven

In case you are using Maven as a build tool, installing scripting engines is easy. All you need to do is to add a non-standard repository and certain dependencies in your pom.xml:

```
<project xmlns="http://maven.apache.org/POM/4.0.0"
  xmlns:xsi="http://www.w3.org/2001/XMLSchema-instance"
  xsi:schemaLocation=
      "http://maven.apache.org/POM/4.0.0
       https://maven.apache.org/xsd/maven-4.0.0.xsd">
  <modelVersion>4.0.0</modelVersion>
```

```xml
  <groupId>your.project.group.id</groupId>
  <artifactId>your.project.artifact.id</artifactId>
  <version>your.project.version</version>

<dependencies>
  <dependency>
    <groupId>org.codehaus.groovy</groupId>
    <artifactId>groovy-jsr223</artifactId>
    <version>3.0.8</version>
  </dependency>

  <!-- Other script engines:-->
  <dependency>
    <groupId>org.scijava</groupId>
    <artifactId>scripting-jython</artifactId>
    <version>1.0.0</version>
  </dependency>
  <dependency>
    <groupId>org.scijava</groupId>
    <artifactId>scripting-jruby</artifactId>
    <version>0.3.1</version>
  </dependency>
  <dependency>
    <groupId>org.graalvm.js</groupId>
    <artifactId>js-scriptengine</artifactId>
    <version>21.1.0</version>
  </dependency>
  <dependency>
    <!-- needed for GraalVM.js -->
    <groupId>org.graalvm.truffle</groupId>
    <artifactId>truffle-api</artifactId>
    <version>21.1.0</version>
  </dependency>
  ...
</dependencies>
```

```
<repositories>
  <repository>
    <id>Maven Repo</id>
    <url>
https://repo1.maven.org/maven2/
    </url>
  </repository>
  <repository>
    <id>Maven Repo 2</id>
    <url>
http://maven.imagej.net/content/repositories/releases/
    </url>
  </repository>
</repositories>

...
</project>
```

Of course, you can comment out or remove scripting engines you don't need.

Executing Your First Script

In this section, you will use Groovy to print a message on the standard output. The same steps can be used to print a message using any other scripting languages, with one difference: you will need to use the scripting language–specific code to print the message. You need to perform the following three steps to run a script in Java:

- Create a script engine manager.

- Get an instance of a script engine from the script engine manager.

- Call the eval() method of the script engine to execute a script.

A script engine manager is an instance of the **ScriptEngineManager** class:

```
// Create an script engine manager
ScriptEngineManager manager = new ScriptEngineManager();
```

An instance of the ScriptEngine interface represents a script engine in a Java program. The getEngineByName(String engineShortName) method of the ScriptEngineManager returns an instance of a script engine. To get an instance of the Groovy engine, use Groovy as the short name of the engine as shown:

```
// Get the reference of the Groovy engine
ScriptEngine engine =
    manager.getEngineByName("Groovy");
```

Note   The short name of a script engine is case-sensitive. Sometimes, a script engine has multiple short names. Groovy engine has the following short names: groovy, Groovy. You can use any of these short names of an engine to get its instance using the getEngineByName() method of the ScriptEngineManager class. Just watch out for possible name clashes with other scripting engines.

In Groovy, the println() function prints a message on the standard output. A string literal in Groovy is a sequence of characters enclosed in single or double quotes. The following snippet of code stores a Groovy script in a Java String object that prints Hello Scripting! to the standard output:

```
// Store a Groovy script in a String
String script = "println('Hello Scripting!')";
```

If you want to use double quotes to enclose the string literal in Groovy, the statement will look as shown:

```
// Store a Groovy script in a String
String script = "println(\"Hello Scripting!\")";
```

or

```
// Store a Groovy script in a String
String script = """println("Hello Scripting!")""";
```

To execute the script, you need to pass the script to the eval() method of the script engine. A script engine may throw a ScriptException when it runs a script. For this reason, you need to handle this exception when you call the eval() method of the ScriptEngine. The following snippet of code executes the script stored in the script variable:

```
try {
    engine.eval(script);
} catch (ScriptException e) {
    e.printStackTrace();
}
```

Listing 10-2 contains the complete code for the program to print a message on the standard output.

Listing 10-2. Printing a Message on the Standard Output Using Groovy

```
// HelloScripting.java
package com.jdojo.script;
import javax.script.ScriptEngine;
import javax.script.ScriptEngineManager;
import javax.script.ScriptException;
public class HelloScripting {
    public static void main(String[] args) {
        // Create a script engine manager
        ScriptEngineManager manager =
            new ScriptEngineManager();
        // Obtain a Groovy script engine from the manager
        ScriptEngine engine =
            manager.getEngineByName("Groovy");
        // Store the Groovy script in a String
        String script = """
            println('Hello Scripting!')
        """;
        try {
            // Execute the script
            engine.eval(script);
```

```
        } catch (ScriptException e) {
            e.printStackTrace();
        }
    }
}
```

```
Hello Scripting!
```

Using Other Scripting Languages

It is very simple to use a scripting language, other than Groovy, in a Java program. You need to perform only one task before you can use a script engine: include the JAR files for a particular script engine in your application module path. Implementors of the script engines provide those JAR files.

Java's service provider mechanism will list all script engines whose modular JAR or JAR files have been included in the application's module path. An instance of the ScriptEngineFactory interface is used to create and describe a script engine. The provider of a script engine provides an implementation for the ScriptEngineFactory interface. The getEngineFactories() method of the ScriptEngineManager returns a List<ScriptEngineFactory> of all available script engine factories. The getScriptEngine() method of the ScriptEngineFactory returns an instance of the ScriptEngine. Several other methods of the factory return metadata about the engine.

Listing 10-3 shows how to print details of all available script engines. The output shows that the script engine for Groovy is available. It is available because I have added the org.codehaus.groovy:groovy-jsr223:3.0.8 artifact to the Maven project, which leads to including all the JARs necessary to the module path on my machine. This program is helpful when you have included a script engine in the module path, and you want to know the short name of the script engine. You may get a different output when you run the program.

Listing 10-3. Listing All Available Script Engines

```java
// ListingAllEngines.java
package com.jdojo.script;
import java.util.List;
import javax.script.ScriptEngineFactory;
import javax.script.ScriptEngineManager;
```

```java
public class ListingAllEngines {
    public static void main(String[] args) {
        ScriptEngineManager manager =
            new ScriptEngineManager();
        // Get the list of all available engines
        List<ScriptEngineFactory> list =
            manager.getEngineFactories();
        // Print the details of each engine
        for (ScriptEngineFactory f : list) {
            System.out.println("Engine Name:" +
                f.getEngineName());
            System.out.println("Engine Version:" +
                f.getEngineVersion());
            System.out.println("Language Name:" +
                f.getLanguageName());
            System.out.println("Language Version:" +
                f.getLanguageVersion());
            System.out.println("Engine Short Names:" +
                f.getNames());
            System.out.println("Mime Types:" +
                f.getMimeTypes());
            System.out.println(
                "---------------------------");
        }
    }
}
```

```
ScriptEngineFactory Info
Script Engine: Groovy Scripting Engine (2.0)
Engine Alias: groovy
Engine Alias: Groovy
Language: Groovy (3.0.8)
```

Listing 10-4 shows how to print a message on the standard output using JavaScript, Groovy, Jython, and JRuby. If a script engine is not available, the program prints a message to that effect. You may get a different output.

Listing 10-4. Printing a Message on the Standard Output Using Different
Scripting Languages

```java
// HelloEngines.java
package com.jdojo.script;
import javax.script.ScriptEngine;
import javax.script.ScriptEngineManager;
import javax.script.ScriptException;
public class HelloEngines {
    public static void main(String[] args) {
        // Get the script engine manager
        ScriptEngineManager manager =
            new ScriptEngineManager();
        // Try executing scripts in JavaScript, Groovy,
        // Jython, and JRuby
        execute(manager, "JavaScript",
            "print('Hello JavaScript')");
        execute(manager, "Groovy",
            "println('Hello Groovy')");
        execute(manager, "jython",
            "print 'Hello Jython'");
        execute(manager, "jruby",
            "puts('Hello JRuby')");
    }
    public static void
    execute(ScriptEngineManager manager, String engineName,
            String script) {
        // Try getting the engine
        ScriptEngine engine =
            manager.getEngineByName(engineName);
        if (engine == null) {
            System.out.println(engineName +
                " is not available.");
            return;
        }
```

```
        // If we get here, it means we have the engine
        // installed. So, run the script
        try {
            engine.eval(script);
        } catch (ScriptException e) {
            e.printStackTrace();
        }
    }
}
```

```
JavaScript is not available.
Hello Groovy
jython is not available.
jruby is not available.
```

Exploring the javax.script Package

The Java Scripting API in Java consists of a small number of classes and interfaces. They are in the `javax.script` package in the `java.scripting` module. This section contains a brief description of classes and interfaces in this package. I discuss their usage in subsequent sections.

The ScriptEngine and ScriptEngineFactory Interfaces

The `ScriptEngine` interface is the main interface in the Java Scripting API whose instances facilitate the execution of scripts written in a particular scripting language.

The implementer of the `ScriptEngine` interface also provides an implementation of the `ScriptEngineFactory` interface. A `ScriptEngineFactory` performs two tasks:

- It creates instances of the script engine.

- It provides information about the script engine such as engine name, version, language, etc.

The AbstractScriptEngine Class

AbstractScriptEngine is an abstract class. It provides a partial implementation for the ScriptEngine interface. You will not use this class directly unless you are implementing a script engine.

The ScriptEngineManager Class

The ScriptEngineManager class provides a discovery and instantiation mechanism for script engines. It also maintains a mapping of key-value pairs as an instance of the Bindings interface storing state that is shared by all script engines that it creates.

The Compilable Interface and the CompiledScript Class

The Compilable interface may optionally be implemented by a script engine that allows compiling scripts for their repeated execution without recompilation.

The CompiledScript class is declared abstract. It is extended by the providers of a script engine. It stores a script in a compiled form, which may be executed repeatedly without recompilation. Note that using a ScriptEngine to execute a script repeatedly causes the script to recompile every time, thus slowing down the performance. A script engine is not required to support script compilation. It must implement the Compilable interface if it supports script compilation.

The Invocable Interface

The Invocable interface may optionally be implemented by a script engine that may allow invoking procedures, functions, and methods in scripts that have been compiled previously.

The Bindings Interface and the SimpleBindings Class

An instance of a class that implements the Bindings interface is a mapping of key-value pairs with a restriction that a key must be a non-null, non-empty String. It extends the java.util.Map interface. The SimpleBindings class is an implementation of the Bindings interface.

The ScriptContext Interface and the SimpleScriptContext Class

An instance of the ScriptContext interface acts as a bridge between the Java host application and the script engine. It is used to pass the execution context of the Java host application to the script engine. The script engine may use the context information while executing a script. A script engine may store its state in an instance of a class that implements the ScriptContext interface, which may be accessible to the Java host application.

The SimpleScriptContext class is an implementation of the ScriptContext interface.

The ScriptException Class

The ScriptException class is an exception class. A script engine throws a ScriptException if an error occurs during the execution, compilation, or invocation of a script. The class contains three useful methods called getLineNumber(), getColumnNumber(), and getFileName(). These methods report the line number, the column number, and the file name of the script in which the error occurs. The ScriptException class overrides the getMessage() method of the Throwable class and includes the line number, column number, and the file name in the message that it returns.

Discovering and Instantiating Script Engines

You can create a script engine using a ScriptEngineFactory or ScriptEngineManager. Who is actually responsible for creating a script engine: ScriptEngineFactory, ScriptEngineManager, or both? The short answer is that a ScriptEngineFactory is always responsible for creating instances of a script engine. The next question is "What is the role of a ScriptEngineManager?"

A ScriptEngineManager uses the service provider mechanism to locate all available script engine factories. The service provider mechanism has been covered in Chapter 7 of this book.

A ScriptEngineManager locates and instantiates all available ScriptEngineFactory classes. You can get a list of instances of all factory classes using the getEngineFactories() method of the ScriptEngineManager class. When you call

a method of the manager to get a script engine based on a criterion such as the
`getEngineByName(String shortName)` method to get an engine by name, the manager
searches all factories for that criterion and returns the matching script engine reference.
If no factories are able to provide a matching engine, the manager returns `null`. Refer
to Listing 10-3 for more details on listing all available factories and describing script
engines that they can create.

Now you know that a `ScriptEngineManager` does not create instances of a script
engine. Rather, it queries all available factories and passes the reference of a script
engine created by the factory back to the caller.

To make the discussion complete, let's add a twist to the ways a script engine can be
created. You can create an instance of a script engine in three ways:

- Instantiate the script engine class directly.

- Instantiate the script engine factory class directly and call its
  `getScriptEngine()` method.

- Use one of the `getEngineByXxx()` methods of the
  `ScriptEngineManager` class.

It is advised to use the `ScriptEngineManager` class to get instances of a script
engine. This method allows all engines created by the same manager to share a state
that is a set of key-value pairs stored as an instance of the `Bindings` interface. The
`ScriptEngineManager` instance stores this state. Using this method also makes your code
unaware of the actual script engine/factory implementation class.

Note   It is possible to have more than one instance of the
`ScriptEngineManager` class in an application. In that case, each
`ScriptEngineManager` instance maintains a state common to all engines that
it creates. That is, if two engines are obtained by two different instances of the
`ScriptEngineManager` class, those engines will not share a common state
maintained by their managers unless you make that happen programmatically.

Executing Scripts

A `ScriptEngine` can execute a script in a `String` and a `Reader`. Using a `Reader`, you can execute a script stored on the network or in a file. One of the following versions of the `eval()` method of the `ScriptEngine` is used to execute a script:

- `Object eval(String script)`
- `Object eval(Reader reader)`
- `Object eval(String script, Bindings bindings)`
- `Object eval(Reader reader, Bindings bindings)`
- `Object eval(String script, ScriptContext context)`
- `Object eval(Reader reader, ScriptContext context)`

The first argument of the `eval()` method is the source of the script. The second argument lets you pass information from the host application to the script engine that can be used during the execution of the script.

In Listing 10-2, you saw how to use a `String` to execute a script using the first version of the `eval()` method. In this section, you will store your script in a file and use a `Reader` object as the source of the script, which will use the second version of the `eval()` method. The next section discusses the other four versions of the `eval()` method. Typically, a script file is given a `.js` extension.

Listing 10-5 shows the contents of a file named `helloscript.groovy`. It contains only one statement in Groovy that prints a message on the standard output.

Listing 10-5. The Contents of the helloscript.groovy File

```
// Print a message
println('Hello from Groovy!')
```

Listing 10-6 has the Java program that executes the script stored in the `helloscript.groovy` file, which should be stored in the `scripts` sub-directory in the current directory. If the script file is not found, the program prints the full path of the `helloscript.js` file where it is expected. If you have trouble executing the script file, try using the absolute path in the `main()` method such as `C:\scripts\helloscript.js` on Windows, assuming that the `helloscript.js` file is saved in the `C:\scripts` directory. All scripts used in examples in this chapter are provided under the `Java9APIsAndModules\scripts` directory in the source code.

Listing 10-6. Executing a Script Stored in a File

```java
// ReaderAsSource.java
package com.jdojo.script;
import java.io.IOException;
import java.io.Reader;
import java.nio.file.Files;
import java.nio.file.Path;
import java.nio.file.Paths;
import javax.script.ScriptEngine;
import javax.script.ScriptEngineManager;
import javax.script.ScriptException;
public class ReaderAsSource {
    public static void main(String[] args) {
        // Construct the script file path
        String scriptFileName =
            "scripts/helloscript.groovy";
        Path scriptPath = Paths.get(scriptFileName);
        // Make sure the script file exists. If not,
        // print the full path of the script file and
        // terminate the program.
        if (!Files.exists(scriptPath)) {
            System.out.println(
                scriptPath.toAbsolutePath() +
                " does not exist.");
            return;
        }
        // Get the Groovy script engine
        ScriptEngineManager manager =
            new ScriptEngineManager();
        ScriptEngine engine = manager.getEngineByName(
            "Groovy");
```

```
    try {
        // Get a Reader for the script file
        Reader scriptReader = Files.newBufferedReader(
            scriptPath);
        // Execute the script in the file
        engine.eval(scriptReader);
    } catch (IOException | ScriptException e) {
        e.printStackTrace();
    }
    }
}
```

Hello from Groovy!

In a real-world application, you should store all scripts in files that allow modifying scripts without modifying and recompiling your Java code. You will not follow this rule in most of the examples in this chapter; you will store your scripts in String objects to keep the code short and simple.

Passing Parameters

The Java Scripting API allows you to pass parameters from the host environment (Java application) to the script engine and vice versa. In this section, you will see the technical details of parameter passing mechanisms between the host application and the script engine.

Passing Parameters from Java Code to Scripts

A Java program may pass parameters to scripts. A Java program may also access global variables declared in a script after the script is executed. Let's discuss a simple example of this kind where a Java program passes a parameter to a script. Consider the program in Listing 10-7 that passes a parameter to a script.

Listing 10-7. Passing Parameters from a Java Program to Scripts

```java
// PassingParam.java
package com.jdojo.script;
import javax.script.ScriptEngine;
import javax.script.ScriptEngineManager;
import javax.script.ScriptException;
public class PassingParam {
    public static void main(String[] args) {
        // Get the Groovy engine
        ScriptEngineManager manager =
            new ScriptEngineManager();
        ScriptEngine engine = manager.getEngineByName(
            "Groovy");
        // Store the script in a String. Here, msg is a
        // variable that we have not declared in the script
        String script = "println(msg)";
        try {
            // Store a parameter named msg in the engine
            engine.put("msg",
                "Hello from the Java program");
            // Execute the script
            engine.eval(script);
        } catch (ScriptException e) {
            e.printStackTrace();
        }
    }
}
```

```
Hello from the Java program
```

The program stores a script in a `String` as follows:

```java
// Store the script in a String
String script = "println(msg)";
```

In the statement, the script that will be executed by the script engine is

```
println(msg)
```

Note that `msg` is a variable used in the `println()` function call. The script does not declare the `msg` variable or assign it a value. If you try to execute this script without telling the engine what the `msg` variable is, the engine will throw an exception stating that it does not understand the meaning of the variable named `msg`. This is where the concept of passing parameters from a Java program to a script engine comes into play.

You can pass a parameter to a script engine in several ways. The simplest way is to use the `put(String paramName, Object paramValue)` method of the script engine, which accepts two arguments:

- The first argument is the name of the parameter, which needs to match the name of the variable in the script.

- The second argument is the value of the parameter.

In your case, you want to pass a parameter named `msg` to the script engine and its value is a `String`. The call to the `put()` method is

```
// Store the value of the msg parameter in the engine
engine.put("msg", "Hello from Java program");
```

Note that you must call the `put()` method of the engine before calling the `eval()` method. In your case, when the engine attempts to execute `print(msg)`, it will use the value of the `msg` parameter that you passed to the engine.

Most script engines let you use the parameter names that you pass to it as the variable name in the script. You saw this kind of example when you passed the value of the parameter named `msg` and used it as a variable name in the script in Listing 10-7. A script engine may have a requirement for declaring variables in scripts, for example, a variable name must start with a $ prefix in PHP and a global variable name contains a $ prefix in JRuby. If you want to pass a parameter named `msg` to a script in JRuby, your code would be as shown:

```
// Get the JRuby script engine
ScriptEngineManager manager = new ScriptEngineManager();
ScriptEngine engine = manager.getEngineByName("jruby");
// Must use the $ prefix in JRuby script
String script = "puts($msg)";
// No $ prefix used in passing the msg parameter to the
```

```
// JRuby engine
engine.put("msg", "Hello from Java");
// Execute the script
engine.eval(script);
```

Properties and methods of Java objects passed to scripts can be accessed in scripts, as they are accessed in Java code. Different scripting languages use different syntax to access Java objects in scripts. For example, you can use the expression msg.toString() in the example shown in Listing 10-7, and the output will be the same. In this case, you are calling the toString() method of the variable msg. Change the statement that assigns the value to the script variable in Listing 10-7 to the following and run the program, which will produce the same output:

```
String script = "println(msg.toString())";
```

Passing Parameters from Scripts to Java Code

A script engine may make variables in its global scope available to the Java code. The get(String variableName) method of a ScriptEngine is used to access those variables in Java code. It returns a Java Object. The declaration of a global variable is scripting language dependent. The following snippet of code declares a global variable and assigns it a value in Groovy:

```
// Declare a variable named year in Groovy
// Note the missing of the 'def' in front of it. If you
// don't prepend 'def', Groovy puts the variable in a
// script-wide global scope.
year = 1969;
```

Listing 10-8 contains a program that shows how to access a global variable in Groovy from Java code.

Listing 10-8. Accessing Script Global Variables in Java Code

```
// AccessingScriptVariable.java
package com.jdojo.script;
import javax.script.ScriptEngine;
import javax.script.ScriptEngineManager;
```

```java
import javax.script.ScriptException;
public class AccessingScriptVariable {
    public static void main(String[] args) {
        // Get the Groovy engine
        ScriptEngineManager manager =
            new ScriptEngineManager();
        ScriptEngine engine = manager.getEngineByName(
            "Groovy");
        // Write a script that declares a global variable
        // named year and assign it a value of 1969.
        String script = "year = 1969";
        try {
            // Execute the script
            engine.eval(script);
            // Get the year global variable from the
            // engine
            Object year = engine.get("year");
            // Print the class name and the value of the
            // variable year
            System.out.println("year's class: "  +
                year.getClass().getName());
            System.out.println("year's value: " +
                year);
        } catch (ScriptException e) {
            e.printStackTrace();
        }
    }
}
```

```
year's class: java.lang.Integer
year's value: 1969
```

The program declares a global variable year in the script and assigns it a value of 1969 as shown:

```java
String script = "year = 1969";
```

When the script is executed, the engine adds the year variable to its state. In Java code, the get() method of the engine is used to retrieve the value of the year variable as shown:

```
Object year = engine.get("year");
```

When the year variable was declared in the script, you did not specify its data type. The conversion of a script variable value to an appropriate Java object is automatically performed. In this case, the value 1969 was evaluated as an Integer.

Advanced Parameter Passing Techniques

To understand the details of the parameter passing mechanism, three terms must be understood clearly: bindings, scope, and context. These terms are confusing at first. This section explains the parameter passing mechanism using the following steps:

- First, it defines these terms.

- Second, it defines the relationship between these terms.

- Third, it explains how to use them in Java code.

Bindings

A Bindings is a set of key-value pairs where all keys must be non-empty, non-null strings. In Java code, a Bindings is an instance of the Bindings interface. The SimpleBindings class is an implementation of the Bindings interface. A script engine may provide its own implementation of the Bindings interface.

Note   If you are familiar with the java.util.Map interface, it is easy to understand Bindings. The Bindings interface inherits from the Map<String,Object> interface. Therefore, a Bindings is just a Map with a restriction that its keys must be non-empty, non-null strings.

Listing 10-9 shows how to use a Bindings. It creates an instance of SimpleBindings, adds some key-value pairs to it, retrieves the values of the keys, removes a key-value pair, etc. The get() method of the Bindings interface returns null if the key does not exist or the key exists and its value is null. If you want to test if a key exists, you need to call its contains() method.

Listing 10-9. Using Bindings Objects

```java
// BindingsTest.java
package com.jdojo.script;
import javax.script.Bindings;
import javax.script.SimpleBindings;
public class BindingsTest {
    public static void main(String[] args) {
        // Create a Bindings instance
        Bindings params = new SimpleBindings();
        // Add some key-value pairs
        params.put("msg", "Hello");
        params.put("year", 1969);
        // Get values
        Object msg = params.get("msg");
        Object year = params.get("year");
        System.out.println("msg = " + msg);
        System.out.println("year = " + year);
        // Remove year from Bindings
        params.remove("year");
        year = params.get("year");
        boolean containsYear = params.containsKey("year");
        System.out.println("year = " + year);
        System.out.println("params contains year = " +
            containsYear);
    }
}
```

```
msg = Hello
year = 1969
year = null
params contains year = false
```

You will not use a `Bindings` by itself. Often, you will use it to pass parameters from Java code to a script engine. The `ScriptEngine` interface contains a `createBindings()` method that returns an instance of the `Bindings` interface. This method gives a script engine a chance to return an instance of the specialized implementation of the `Bindings` interface. You can use this method as shown:

```
// Get the Groovy engine
ScriptEngineManager manager = new ScriptEngineManager();
ScriptEngine engine = manager.getEngineByName(
    "Groovy");
// Do not instantiate SimpleBindings class directly.
// Use the createBindings() method of the engine to create
// a Bindings.
Bindings params = engine.createBindings();
// Work with params as usual
```

Scope

Let's move to the next term, which is scope. A scope is used for a Bindings. The scope of a Bindings determines the visibility of its key-value pairs. You can have multiple Bindings occurring in multiple scopes. However, one Bindings may occur only in one scope. How do you specify the scope for a Bindings? I cover this shortly.

Using the scope for a `Bindings` lets you define parameter variables for script engines in a hierarchical order. If a variable name is searched in an engine state, the `Bindings` with a higher precedence is searched first, followed by `Bindings` with lower precedence. The first found value of the variable is returned. The Java Scripting API defines two scopes. They are defined as two `int` constants in the `ScriptContext` interface. They are

- `ScriptContext.ENGINE_SCOPE`

- `ScriptContext.GLOBAL_SCOPE`

The engine scope has higher precedence than the global scope. If you add two key-value pairs with the same key to two `Bindings`—one in the engine scope and one in the global scope—the key-value pair in the engine scope will be used whenever a variable with the same name as the key has to be resolved.

Understanding the role of the scope for a `Bindings` is so important that I run through another analogy to explain it. Think about a Java class that has two sets of variables: one set contains all instance variables in the class, and another contains all local variables in a method. These two sets of variables with their values are two `Bindings`. The type of variables in these `Bindings` defines the scope. Just for the sake of this discussion, I define two scopes: instance scope and local scope. When a method is executed, a variable name is looked up in the local scope `Bindings` first because the local variables take precedence over instance variables. If a variable name is not found in the local scope `Bindings`, it is looked up in the instance scope `Bindings`. When a script is executed, `Bindings` and their scopes play a similar role.

Defining the Script Context

A script engine executes a script in a context. You can think of the context as the environment in which a script is executed. A Java host application provides two things to a script engine: a script and the context in which the script needs to be executed. An instance of the `ScriptContext` interface represents the context for a script. The `SimpleScriptContext` class is an implementation of the `ScriptContext` interface. A script context consists of four components:

- A set of `Bindings`, where each `Bindings` is associated with a different scope

- A `Reader` that is used by the script engine to read inputs

- A `Writer` that is used by the script engine to write outputs

- An error `Writer` that is used by the script engine to write error outputs

The set of `Bindings` in a context is used to pass parameters to the script. The reader and writers in a context control input source and output destinations of the script, respectively. For example, by setting a file writer as a writer, you can send all outputs from a script to a file.

Each script engine maintains a default script context, which it uses to execute scripts. So far, you have executed several scripts without providing script contexts. In those cases, script engines were using their default script contexts to execute scripts. In this section, I cover how to use a `ScriptContext` by itself. In the next section, I cover how a `ScriptContext` is passed to a `ScriptEngine` during script execution.

You can create an instance of the ScriptContext interface using the SimpleScriptContext class:

```
// Create a script context
ScriptContext ctx = new SimpleScriptContext();
```

An instance of the SimpleScriptContext class maintains two instances of Bindings: one for the engine scope and one for the global scope. The Bindings in the engine scope is created when you create the instance of the SimpleScriptContext. To work with the global scope Bindings, you will need to create an instance of the Bindings interface.

By default, the SimpleScriptContext class initializes the input reader, the output writer, and the error writer for the context to the standard input System.in, the standard output System.out, and standard error output System.err, respectively. You can use the getReader(), getWriter(), and getErrorWriter() methods of the ScriptContext interface to get the references of the reader, writer, and the error writer from the ScriptContext, respectively. Setter methods are also provided to set a reader and writers. The following snippet of code shows how to obtain the reader and writers. It also shows how to set a writer to a FileWriter to write the script output to a file:

```
// Get the reader and writers from the script context
Reader inputReader = ctx.getReader();
Writer outputWriter = ctx.getWriter();
Writer errWriter = ctx.getErrorWriter();
// Write all script outputs to an out.txt file
Writer fileWriter = new FileWriter("out.txt");
ctx.setWriter(fileWriter);
```

After you create a SimpleScriptContext, you can start storing key-value pairs in the engine scope Bindings because an empty Bindings in the engine scope is created when you create the SimpleScriptContext object. The setAttribute() method is used to add a key-value pair to a Bindings. You must provide the key name, value, and the scope for the Bindings. The following snippet of code adds three key-value pairs:

```
// Add three key-value pairs to the engine scope bindings
ctx.setAttribute("year", 1969, ScriptContext.ENGINE_SCOPE);
ctx.setAttribute("month", 9, ScriptContext.ENGINE_SCOPE);
ctx.setAttribute("day", 19, ScriptContext.ENGINE_SCOPE);
```

If you want to add key-value pairs to a Bindings in a global scope, you will need to create and set the Bindings first, like so:

```
// Add a global scope Bindings to the context
Bindings globalBindings = new SimpleBindings();
ctx.setBindings(globalBindings,
    ScriptContext.GLOBAL_SCOPE);
```

Now you can add key-value pairs to the Bindings in the global scope using the setAttribute() method, like so:

```
// Add two key-value pairs to the global scope bindings
ctx.setAttribute("year", 1982,
    ScriptContext.GLOBAL_SCOPE);
ctx.setAttribute("name", "Boni",
    ScriptContext.GLOBAL_SCOPE);
```

At this point, you can visualize the state of the ScriptContext instance, as shown in Figure 10-1.

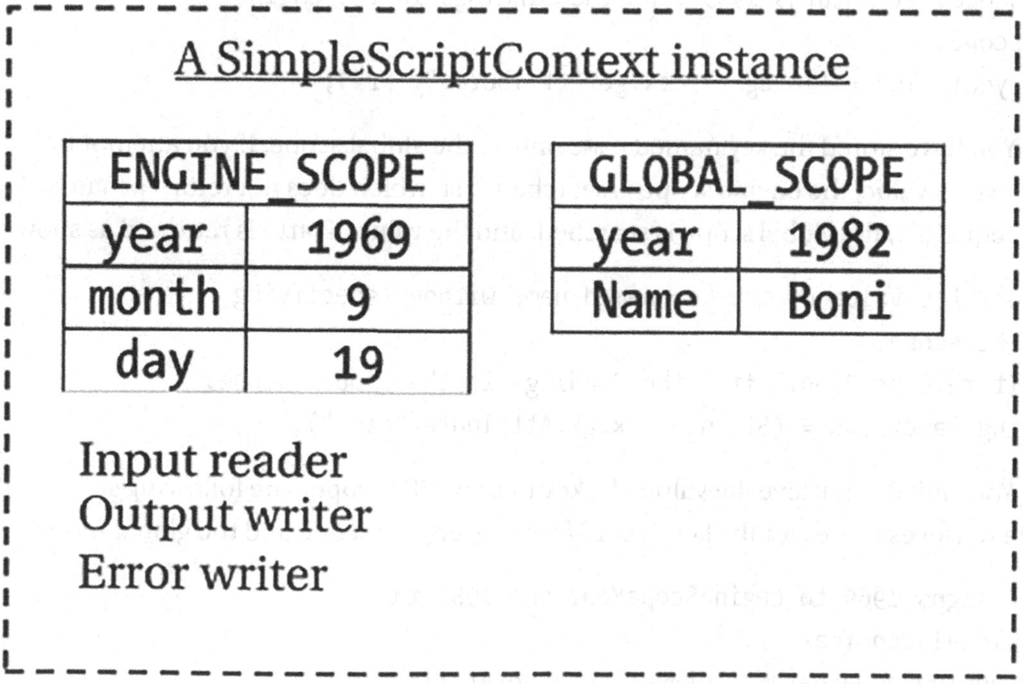

A SimpleScriptContext instance			
ENGINE_SCOPE		**GLOBAL_SCOPE**	
year	1969	year	1982
month	9	Name	Boni
day	19		

Input reader
Output writer
Error writer

Figure 10-1. *A pictorial view of an instance of the SimpleScriptContext class*

You can perform several operations on a `ScriptContext`. You can set a different value for an already stored key using the `setAttribute(String name, Object value, int scope)` method. You can remove a key-value pair using the `removeAttribute(String name, int scope)` method for a specified key and a scope. You can get the value of a key in the specified scope using the `getAttribute(String name, int scope)` method.

The most interesting thing that you can do with a `ScriptContext` is to retrieve a key-value without specifying its scope using its `getAttribute(String name)` method. A `ScriptContext` searches for the key in the engine scope `Bindings` first. If it is not found in the engine scope, the `Bindings` in the global scope is searched. If the key is found in these scopes, the corresponding value from the scope, in which it is found first, is returned. If neither scope contains the key, `null` is returned.

In your example, you have stored the key named `year` in the engine scope as well as in the global scope. The following snippet of code returns 1969 for the key `year` from the engine scope as the engine scope is searched first. The return type of the `getAttribute()` method is `Object`:

```
// Get the value of the key year without specifying the
// scope. It returns 1969 from the Bindings in the engine
// scope.
int yearValue = (Integer) ctx.getAttribute("year");
```

You have stored the key named `name` only in the global scope. If you attempt to retrieve its value, the engine scope is searched first, which does not return a match. Subsequently, the global scope is searched, and the value `"Boni"` is returned as shown:

```
// Get the value of the key named name without specifying
// the scope.
// It returns "Boni" from the Bindings in the global scope.
String nameValue = (String) ctx.getAttribute("name");
```

You can also retrieve the value of a key in a specific scope. The following snippet of code retrieves values for the key "year" from the engine scope and the global scope:

```
// Assigns 1969 to engineScopeYear and 1982 to
// globalScopeYear
int engineScopeYear = (Integer) ctx.getAttribute(
```

```
        "year", ScriptContext.ENGINE_SCOPE);
int globalScopeYear = (Integer) ctx.getAttribute(
        "year", ScriptContext.GLOBAL_SCOPE);
```

Note   The Java Scripting API defines only two scopes: engine and global. A subinterface of the `ScriptContext` interface may define additional scopes. The `getScopes()` method of the `ScriptContext` interface returns a list of supported scopes as a `List<Integer>`. Note that a scope is represented as an integer. The two constants in the `ScriptContext` interface—ENGINE_SCOPE and GLOBAL_SCOPE—are assigned values 100 and 200, respectively. When a key is searched in multiple `Bindings` occurring in multiple scopes, the scope with the lower integer value is searched first. Because the value 100 for the engine scope is lower than the value 200 for the global scope, the engine scope is searched for a key first when you do not specify the scope.

Listing 10-10 shows how to work with an instance of a class implementing the ScriptContext interface. Note that you do not use a ScriptContext in your application by itself. It is used by script engines during script execution. Most often, you manipulate a ScriptContext indirectly through a ScriptEngine and a ScriptEngineManager, which are discussed in detail in the next section.

Listing 10-10. Using an Instance of the ScriptContext Interface

```
// ScriptContextTest.java
package com.jdojo.script;
import java.util.List;
import javax.script.Bindings;
import javax.script.ScriptContext;
import javax.script.SimpleBindings;
import javax.script.SimpleScriptContext;
import static javax.script.ScriptContext.ENGINE_SCOPE;
import static javax.script.ScriptContext.GLOBAL_SCOPE;
public class ScriptContextTest {
    public static void main(String[] args) {
        // Create a script context
```

```
ScriptContext ctx = new SimpleScriptContext();
// Get the list of scopes supported by the script
// context
List<Integer> scopes = ctx.getScopes();
System.out.println("Supported Scopes: " + scopes);
// Add three key-value pairs to the engine scope
// bindings
ctx.setAttribute("year", 1969, ENGINE_SCOPE);
ctx.setAttribute("month", 9, ENGINE_SCOPE);
ctx.setAttribute("day", 19, ENGINE_SCOPE);
// Add a global scope Bindings to the context
Bindings globalBindings = new SimpleBindings();
ctx.setBindings(globalBindings, GLOBAL_SCOPE);
// Add two key-value pairs to the global scope
// bindings
ctx.setAttribute("year", 1982, GLOBAL_SCOPE);
ctx.setAttribute("name", "Boni", GLOBAL_SCOPE);
// Get the value of year without specifying the
// scope
int yearValue =
    (Integer) ctx.getAttribute("year");
System.out.println("yearValue = " + yearValue);
// Get the value of name
String nameValue =
    (String) ctx.getAttribute("name");
System.out.println("nameValue = " + nameValue);
// Get the value of year from engine  and global
// scopes
int engineScopeYear = (Integer) ctx.
    getAttribute("year", ENGINE_SCOPE);
int globalScopeYear = (Integer) ctx.
    getAttribute("year", GLOBAL_SCOPE);
System.out.println("engineScopeYear = " +
    engineScopeYear);
```

```
        System.out.println("globalScopeYear = " +
            globalScopeYear);
    }
}
```

```
Supported Scopes: [100, 200]
yearValue = 1969
nameValue = Boni
engineScopeYear = 1969
globalScopeYear = 1982
```

Putting Them Together

In this section, I show you how instances of Bindings and their scopes, ScriptContext, ScriptEngine, ScriptEngineManager, and the host application work together. The focus is on how to manipulate the key-value pairs stored in Bindings in different scopes using a ScriptEngine and a ScriptEngineManager.

A ScriptEngineManager maintains a set of key-value pairs in a Bindings. It lets you work with those key-value pairs using the following methods:

- void put(String key, Object value)
- Object get(String key)
- void setBindings(Bindings bindings)
- Bindings getBindings()

The put() method adds a key-value pair to the Bindings. The get() method returns the value for the specified key; it returns null if the key is not found. The Bindings for an engine manager can be replaced using the setBindings() method. The getBindings() method returns the reference of the Bindings of the ScriptEngineManager.

Every ScriptEngine, by default, has a ScriptContext known as its default context. Recall that, besides readers and writers, a ScriptContext has two Bindings: one in the engine scope and one in the global scope. When a ScriptEngine is created, its engine scope Bindings is empty, and its global scope Bindings refers to the Bindings of the ScriptEngineManager that created it.

By default, all instances of the ScriptEngine created by a ScriptEngineManager share the Bindings of the ScriptEngineManager. It is possible to have multiple instances of ScriptEngineManager in the same Java application. In that case, all instances of ScriptEngine created by the same ScriptEngineManager share the Bindings of the ScriptEngineManager as their global scope Bindings for their default contexts.

The following snippet of code creates a ScriptEngineManager, which is used to create three instances of ScriptEngine:

```
// Create a ScriptEngineManager
ScriptEngineManager manager = new ScriptEngineManager();
// Create three ScriptEngines using the same
// ScriptEngineManager
ScriptEngine engine1 = manager.getEngineByName(
    "Groovy");
ScriptEngine engine2 = manager.getEngineByName(
    "Groovy");
ScriptEngine engine3 = manager.getEngineByName(
    "Groovy");
```

Now, let's add three key-value pairs to the Bindings of the ScriptEngineManager and two key-value pairs to the engine scope Bindings of each ScriptEngine:

```
// Add three key-value pairs to the Bindings
// of the manager
manager.put("K1", "V1");
manager.put("K2", "V2");
manager.put("K3", "V3");
// Add two key-value pairs to each engine
engine1.put("KE11", "VE11");
engine1.put("KE12", "VE12");
engine2.put("KE21", "VE21");
engine2.put("KE22", "VE22");
engine3.put("KE31", "VE31");
engine3.put("KE32", "VE32");
```

Figure 10-2 shows a pictorial view of the state of the ScriptEngineManager and three ScriptEngines after the previous snippet of code is executed. It is evident from the figure that the default contexts of all ScriptEngines share the Bindings of the ScriptEngineManager as their global scope Bindings.

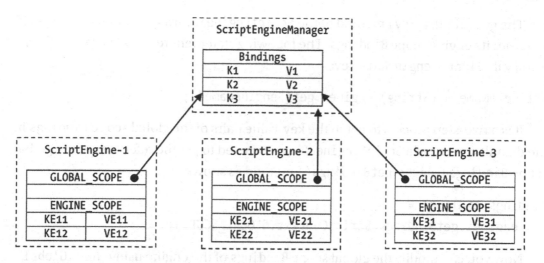

Figure 10-2. *A pictorial view of three ScriptEngines created by a ScriptEngineManager*

The Bindings in a ScriptEngineManager can be modified in the following ways:

- By using the put() method of the ScriptEngineManager

- By getting the reference of the Bindings using the getBindings() method of the ScriptEngineManager, and then using the put() and remove() methods on the Bindings

- By getting the reference of the Bindings in the global scope of the default context of a ScriptEngine using its getBindings() method, and then using the put() and remove() methods on the Bindings

When the Bindings in a ScriptEngineManager is modified, the global scope Bindings in the default context of all ScriptEngines created by this ScriptEngineManager are modified because they share the same Bindings.

The default context of each ScriptEngine maintains an engine scope Bindings separately. To add a key-value pair to the engine scope Bindings of a ScriptEngine, use its put() method as shown:

```
ScriptEngine engine1 = null; // get an engine
// Add an "engineName" key with its value as "Engine-1"
// to the engine scope Bindings of the default context
// of engine1
engine1.put("engineName", "Engine-1");
```

The get(String key) method of the ScriptEngine returns the value of the specified key from its engine scope Bindings. The following statement returns "Engine-1", which is the value for the engineName key:

```
String eName = (String) engine1.get("engineName");
```

It is a two-step process to get to the key-value pairs of the global scope Bindings in the default context of a ScriptEngine. First, you need to get the reference of the global scope Bindings using its getBindings() method as shown:

```
Bindings e1Global =
    engine1.getBindings(ScriptContext.GLOBAL_SCOPE);
```

Now you can modify the global scope Bindings of the engine using the e1Global reference. The following statement adds a key-value pair to the e1Global Bindings:

```
e1Global.put("id", 89999);
```

Because of the sharing of the global scope Bindings of a ScriptEngine by all ScriptEngines, this snippet of code will add the key "id" with its value to the global scope Bindings of the default context of all ScriptEngines created by the same ScriptEngineManager that created engine1. Modifying the Bindings in a ScriptEngineManager using the previous code is not recommended. You should modify the Bindings using the ScriptEngineManager reference instead, which makes the logic clearer to the readers of the code.

Listing 10-11 demonstrates the concepts discussed in this section.

Listing 10-11. Using Global and Engine Scope Bindings of Engines Created by the Same

```
ScriptEngineManager
// GlobalBindings.java
package com.jdojo.script;
import javax.script.ScriptEngine;
import javax.script.ScriptEngineManager;
import javax.script.ScriptException;
public class GlobalBindings {
    public static void main(String[] args) {
        ScriptEngineManager manager =
```

```
        new ScriptEngineManager();
    // Add two numbers to the Bindings of the
    // manager - shared by all its engines
    manager.put("n1", 100);
    manager.put("n2", 200);
    // Create two JavaScript engines and add the name
    // of the engine in the engine scope of the default
    // context of the engines
    ScriptEngine engine1 = manager.getEngineByName(
        "Groovy");
    engine1.put("engineName", "Engine-1");
    ScriptEngine engine2 = manager.getEngineByName(
        "Groovy");
    engine2.put("engineName", "Engine-2");
    // Execute a script that adds two numbers and
    // prints the result
    String script = """
        def sum = n1 + n2
        println(engineName + ' - Sum = ' + sum)
    """;
    try {
        // Execute the script in two engines
        engine1.eval(script);
        engine2.eval(script);
        // Now add a different value for n2 for each
        // engine
        engine1.put("n2", 1000);
        engine2.put("n2", 2000);
        // Execute the script in two engines again
        engine1.eval(script);
        engine2.eval(script);
    } catch (ScriptException e) {
        e.printStackTrace();
    }
    }
}
```

```
Engine-1 - Sum = 300
Engine-2 - Sum = 300
Engine-1 - Sum = 1100
Engine-2 - Sum = 2100
```

A ScriptEngineManager adds two key-value pairs with keys n1 and n2 to its Bindings. Two ScriptEngines are created; they add a key called engineName to their engine scope Bindings. When the script is executed, the value of the engineName variable in the script is used from the engine scope of the ScriptEngine. The values for variables n1 and n2 in the script are retrieved from the global scope Bindings of the ScriptEngine. After executing the script for the first time, each ScriptEngine adds a key called n2 with a different value to their engine scope Bindings. When you execute the script for the second time, the value for the n1 variable is retrieved from the global scope Bindings of the engine, whereas the value for the variable n2 is retrieved from the engine scope Bindings as shown in the output.

The story of the global scope Bindings shared by all ScriptEngines that are created by a ScriptEngineManager is not over yet. It is as complex, and confusing, as it can get! Now the focus will be on the effects of using the setBindings() method of the ScriptEngineManager class and the ScriptEngine interface. Consider the following snippet of code:

```
// Create a ScriptEngineManager and two ScriptEngines
ScriptEngineManager manager = new ScriptEngineManager();
ScriptEngine engine1 = manager.getEngineByName(
    "Groovy");
ScriptEngine engine2 = manager.getEngineByName(
    "Groovy");
// Add two key-value pairs to the manager
manager.put("n1", 100);
manager.put("n2", 200);
```

Figure 10-3 shows the state of the engine manager and its engines after this script is executed. At this point, there is only one Bindings stored in the ScriptEngineManager, and two ScriptEngines are referring to it as their global scope Bindings.

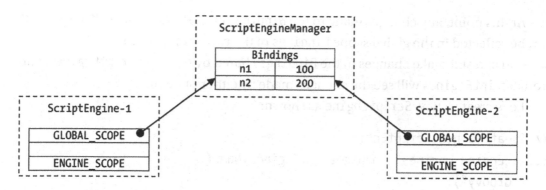

Figure 10-3. *Initial state of ScriptEngineManager and two ScriptEngines*

Let's create a new `Bindings` and set it as the `Bindings` for the `ScriptEngineManager` using its `setBindings()` method, like so:

```
// Create a Bindings, add two key-value pairs to it, and
// set it as the new Bindings for the manager
Bindings newGlobal = new SimpleBindings();
newGlobal.put("n3", 300);
newGlobal.put("n4", 400);
manager.setBindings(newGlobal);
```

Figure 10-4 shows the state of the `ScriptEngineManager` and two `ScriptEngines` after the previous snippet of code is executed. Notice that the `ScriptEngineManager` has a new `Bindings`, and the two `ScriptEngines` are still referring to the old `Bindings` as their global scope `Bindings`.

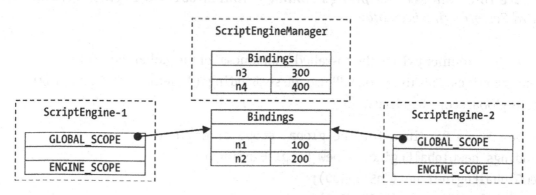

Figure 10-4. *State of ScriptEngineManager and two ScriptEngines after a new Bindings is set*

At this point, any changes made to the Bindings of the ScriptEngineManager will not be reflected in the global scope Bindings of the two ScriptEngines.

You can still make changes to the Bindings shared by the two ScriptEngines, and both ScriptEngines will see the changes made by either of them.

Let's create a new ScriptEngine as shown:

```
// Create a new ScriptEngine
ScriptEngine engine3 = manager.getEngineByName(
    "Groovy");
```

Recall that a ScriptEngine gets a global scope Bindings at the time it is created and that Bindings is the same as the Bindings of the ScriptEngineManager. The states of the ScriptEngineManager and three ScriptEngines, after the previous statement is executed, are shown in Figure 10-5.

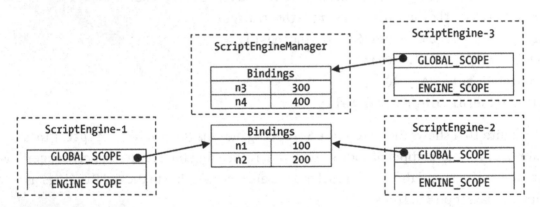

Figure 10-5. *States of ScriptEngineManager and three ScriptEngines after the third ScriptEngine is created*

Here is another twist to the so-called "globalness" of the global scope of ScriptEngines. This time, you will use the setBindings() method of a ScriptEngine to set its global scope Bindings:

```
// Set a new Bindings for the global scope of engine1
Bindings newGlobalEngine1 = new SimpleBindings();
newGlobalEngine1.put("n5", 500);
newGlobalEngine1.put("n6", 600);
engine1.setBindings(newGlobalEngine1,
    ScriptContext.GLOBAL_SCOPE);
```

Figure 10-6 shows the states of the ScriptEngineManager and three ScriptEngines after the previous snippet of code is executed.

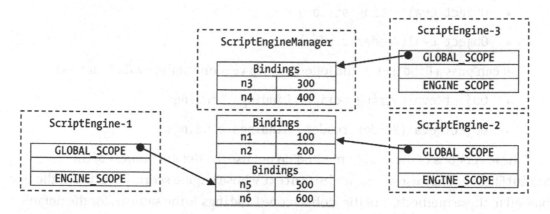

Figure 10-6. *States of ScriptEngineManager and three ScriptEngines after a new global scope bindings is set*

Note   By default, all ScriptEngines that a ScriptEngineManager creates share its Bindings as their global scope Bindings. If you use the setBindings() method of a ScriptEngine to set its global scope Bindings or if you use the setBindings() method of a ScriptEngineManager to set its Bindings, you break the "globalness" chain as discussed in this section. To keep the "globalness" chain intact, you should always use the put() method of the ScriptEngineManager to add key-value pairs to its Bindings. To remove a key-value pair from the global scope of all ScriptEngines created by a ScriptEngineManager, you need to get the reference of the Bindings using the getBindings() method of the ScriptEngineManager and use the remove() method on the Bindings.

Using a Custom ScriptContext

In the previous section, you saw that each ScriptEngine has a default script context. The get(), put(), getBindings(), and setBindings() methods of the ScriptEngine operate on its default ScriptContext. When no ScriptContext is specified to the eval() method of the ScriptEngine, the default context of the engine is used. The following two versions of the eval() method of the ScriptEngine use its default context to execute the script:

- `Object eval(String script)`

- `Object eval(Reader reader)`

You can pass a Bindings to the following two versions of the eval() method:

- `Object eval(String script, Bindings bindings)`

- `Object eval(Reader reader, Bindings bindings)`

These versions of the eval() method do not use the default context of the ScriptEngine. They use a new ScriptContext whose engine scope Bindings is the one passed to these methods, and the global scope Bindings is the same as for the default context of the engine. Note that these two versions of the eval() method keep the default context of the ScriptEngine untouched.

You can pass a ScriptContext to the following two versions of the eval() method:

- `Object eval(String script, ScriptContext context)`

- `Object eval(Reader reader, ScriptContext context)`

These versions of the eval() method use the specified context to execute the script. They keep the default context of the ScriptEngine untouched.

The three sets of the eval() method let you execute scripts using different isolation levels:

- The first set lets you share the default context by all scripts.

- The second set lets scripts use different engine scope Bindings and share the global scope Bindings.

- The third set lets scripts execute in an isolated ScriptContext.

Listing 10-12 shows how scripts are executed in different isolation levels using the different versions of the eval() method.

Listing 10-12. Using Different Isolation Levels for Executing Scripts

```java
// CustomContext.java
package com.jdojo.script;
import javax.script.Bindings;
import javax.script.ScriptContext;
import javax.script.ScriptEngine;
import javax.script.ScriptEngineManager;
import javax.script.ScriptException;
import javax.script.SimpleScriptContext;
import static javax.script.SimpleScriptContext.
    ENGINE_SCOPE;
import static javax.script.SimpleScriptContext.
    GLOBAL_SCOPE;
public class CustomContext {
    public static void
    main(String[] args) throws ScriptException {
        ScriptEngineManager manager =
            new ScriptEngineManager();
        ScriptEngine engine = manager.getEngineByName(
            "Groovy");
        // Add n1 to Bindings of the manager, which will
        // be shared by all engines as their global scope
        // Bindings
        manager.put("n1", 100);
        // Prepare the script
        String script = """
            def sum = n1 + n2
            println(msg + ' n1=' + n1 + ', n2=' + n2 +
                    ', sum=' + sum)
        """;
        // Add n2 to the engine scope of the default
        // context of the engine
        engine.put("n2", 200);
        engine.put("msg", "Using the default context:");
        engine.eval(script);
```

```
        // Use a Bindings to execute the script
        Bindings bindings = engine.createBindings();
        bindings.put("n2", 300);
        bindings.put("msg", "Using a Bindings:");
        engine.eval(script, bindings);
        // Use a ScriptContext to execute the script
        ScriptContext ctx = new SimpleScriptContext();
        Bindings ctxGlobalBindings =
            engine.createBindings();
        ctx.setBindings(ctxGlobalBindings, GLOBAL_SCOPE);
        ctx.setAttribute("n1", 400, GLOBAL_SCOPE);
        ctx.setAttribute("n2", 500, ENGINE_SCOPE);
        ctx.setAttribute("msg", "Using a ScriptContext:",
            ENGINE_SCOPE);
        engine.eval(script, ctx);
        // Execute the script again using the default
        // context to prove that the default context is
        // unaffected.
        engine.eval(script);
    }
}
```

```
Using the default context: n1=100, n2=200, sum=300
Using a Bindings: n1=100, n2=300, sum=400
Using a ScriptContext: n1=400, n2=500, sum=900
Using the default context: n1=100, n2=200, sum=300
```

The program uses three variables called msg, n1, and n2. It displays the value stored in the msg variable. The values of n1 and n2 are added, and the sum is displayed. The script prints what values of n1 and n2 were used in computing the sum. The value of n1 is stored in the Bindings of ScriptEngineManager that is shared by the default context of all ScriptEngines. The value of n2 is stored in the engine scope of the default context and the custom contexts. The script is executed twice using the default context of the engine, once in the beginning and once in the end, to prove that using a custom Bindings or a ScriptContext in the eval() method does not affect the Bindings in the default context of the ScriptEngine. The program declares a throws clause in its main() method to keep the code shorter.

Return Value of the eval( ) Method

The eval() method of the ScriptEngine returns an Object, which is the last value in the script. It returns null if there is no last value in the script. It is error-prone, and confusing at the same time, to depend on the last value in a script. The following snippet of code shows some examples of using the return value of the eval() method for Groovy. The comments in the code indicate the returned value from the eval() method:

```
Object result = null;
// Assigns 3 to result
result = engine.eval("1 + 2");
// Assigns 7 to result
result = engine.eval("1 + 2; 3 + 4");
// Assigns 6 to result
result = engine.eval("""1 + 2; 3 + 4;
    def v = 5; v = 6""");
// Assigns 5 to result
result = engine.eval("""1 + 2; 3 + 4;
    def v = 5""");
// Assigns null to result
result = engine.eval("println(1 + 2)");
```

It is better not to depend on the returned value from the eval() method. You should pass a Java object to the script as a parameter and let the script store the returned value of the script in that object. After the eval() method is executed, you can query that Java object for the returned value.

Listing 10-13 contains the code for a Result class that wraps an integer. You will pass an object of the Result class to the script that will store the returned value in it. After the script finishes, you can read the integer value stored in the Result object in your Java code. The Result needs to be declared public so it is accessible to the script engine.

Listing 10-13. A Result Class That Wraps an Integer

```
// Result.java
package com.jdojo.script;
public class Result {
    public int val = -1;
}
```

The program in Listing 10-14 shows how to pass a `Result` object to a script that populates the Result object with a value. The program contains a `throws` clause in the `main()` method's declaration to keep the code short.

Listing 10-14. Collecting the Return Value of a Script in a Result Object

```java
// ResultBearingScript.java
package com.jdojo.script;
import javax.script.ScriptEngine;
import javax.script.ScriptEngineManager;
import javax.script.ScriptException;
public class ResultBearingScript {
    public static void
    main(String[] args) throws ScriptException {
        // Get the Groovy engine
        ScriptEngineManager manager =
            new ScriptEngineManager();
        ScriptEngine engine = manager.getEngineByName(
            "Groovy");
        // Pass a Result object to the script. The script
        // will store the result of the script in the
        // result object
        Result result = new Result();
        engine.put("result", result);
        // Store the script in a String
        String script = "3 + 4; result.val = 101";
        // Execute the script, which uses the passed in
        // Result object to return a value
        engine.eval(script);
        // Use the result object to get the returned value
        // from the script
        int returnedValue = result.val; // -> 101
```

```
    System.out.println("Returned value is " +
        returnedValue);
    }
}
```

Returned value is 101

Reserved Keys for Engine Scope Bindings

Typically, a key in the engine scope Bindings represents a script variable. Some keys are reserved, and they have special meanings. Their values may be passed to the engine by the implementation of the engine. An implementation may define additional reserved keys.

Table 10-1 contains the list of all reserved keys. Those keys are also declared as constants in the ScriptEngine interface. An implementation of a script engine is not required to pass all these keys to the engine in the engine scope bindings. As a developer, you are not supposed to use these keys to pass parameters from a Java application to a script engine.

Table 10-1. *Reserved Keys for Engine Scope Bindings*

Key	Constant in ScriptEngine Interface	Meaning of the Value of the Key
"javax.script.argv"	ScriptEngine.ARGV	Used to pass an array of Object to pass a set of positional argument.
"javax.script.engine"	ScriptEngine.ENGINE	The name of the script engine.
"javax.script.engine_version"	ScriptEngine.ENGINE_VERSION	The version of the script engine.
"javax.script.filename"	ScriptEngine.FILENAME	Used to pass the name of the file or the resource that is the source of the script.

(*continued*)

Table 10-1. (*continued*)

Key	Constant in ScriptEngine Interface	Meaning of the Value of the Key
"javax.script.language"	ScriptEngine.LANGUAGE	The name of the language supported by the script engine.
"javax.script. language_version"	ScriptEngine.LANGUAGE_ VERSION	The version of the scripting language supported by the engine.
"javax.script.name"	ScriptEngine.NAME	The short name of the scripting language.

Changing the Default ScriptContext

You can get and set the default context of a ScriptEngine using its getContext() and setContext() methods, respectively, as shown:

```
ScriptEngineManager manager = new ScriptEngineManager();
ScriptEngine engine = manager.getEngineByName(
    "Groovy");
// Get the default context of the ScriptEngine
ScriptContext defaultCtx = engine.getContext();
// Work with defaultCtx here
// Create a new context
ScriptContext ctx = new SimpleScriptContext();
// Configure ctx here
// Set ctx as the new default context for the engine
engine.setContext(ctx);
```

Note that setting a new default context for a ScriptEngine will not use the Bindings of the ScriptEngineManager as its global scope Bindings. If you want the new default context to use the Bindings of the ScriptEngineManager, you need set it explicitly as shown:

```
// Create a new context
ScriptContext ctx = new SimpleScriptContext();
// Set the global scope Bindings for ctx the same as the
// Bindings for the manager
```

```
ctx.setBindings(manager.getBindings(),
    ScriptContext.GLOBAL_SCOPE);
// Set ctx as the new default context for the engine
engine.setContext(ctx);
```

Sending Script Output to a File

You can customize the input source, output destination, and error output destination of a script execution. You need to set appropriate reader and writers for the ScriptContext that is used to execute a script. The following snippet of code will write the script output to a file named output.txt in the current directory:

```
// Create a FileWriter
FileWriter writer = new FileWriter("output.txt");
// Get the default context of the engine
ScriptContext defaultCtx = engine.getContext();
// Set the output writer for the default context of the
// engine
defaultCtx.setWriter(writer);
```

The code sets a custom output writer for the default context of the ScriptEngine that will be used during the execution of scripts that use the default context. If you want to use a custom output writer for a specific execution of a script, you need to use a custom ScriptContext and set its writer.

Note   Setting a custom output writer for a ScriptContext does not affect the destination of the standard output of the Java application. To redirect the standard output of the Java application, you need to use the System.setOut() method.

Listing 10-15 shows you how to write output of a script execution to a file named output.txt. The program prints the full path of the output file on the standard output. You may get a different output when you run the program. You need to open the output file in a text editor to see the script's output.

Listing 10-15. Writing the Output of Scripts to a File

```java
// CustomScriptOutput.java
package com.jdojo.script;
import java.io.File;
import java.io.FileWriter;
import java.io.IOException;
import javax.script.ScriptContext;
import javax.script.ScriptEngine;
import javax.script.ScriptEngineManager;
import javax.script.ScriptException;
public class CustomScriptOutput {
    public static void main(String[] args) {
        // Get the Groovy engine
        ScriptEngineManager manager =
            new ScriptEngineManager();
        ScriptEngine engine = manager.getEngineByName(
            "Groovy");
        // Print the absolute path of the output file
        File outputFile = new File("output.txt");
        System.out.println(
            "Script output will be written to "
            + outputFile.getAbsolutePath());
        try (FileWriter writer =
                new FileWriter(outputFile)) {
            // Set a custom output writer for the engine
            ScriptContext defaultCtx =
                engine.getContext();
            defaultCtx.setWriter(writer);
            // Execute a script
            String script =
                "println('Hello custom output writer')";
            engine.eval(script);
```

```
    } catch (IOException | ScriptException e) {
        e.printStackTrace();
    }
  }
}
```

Script output will be written to file output.txt in the current working directory.

Invoking Procedures in Scripts

A scripting language may allow for creating procedures, functions, and methods. The Java Scripting API lets you invoke such procedures, functions, and methods from a Java application. I use the term "procedure" to mean procedure, function, and method in this section. I use the specific term when the context of the discussion requires it.

Not all script engines are required to support procedure invocation. The Groovy engine supports procedure invocation. If a script engine supports it, the implementation of the script engine class must implement the Invocable interface. It is the responsibility of the developer to check if a script engine implements the Invocable interface, before invoking a procedure. Invoking a procedure is a four-step process:

- Check if the script engine supports procedure invocation.

- Cast the engine reference to the Invocable type.

- Evaluate the script that contains the source code for the procedure.

- Use the invokeFunction() method of the Invocable interface to invoke procedures and functions. Use the invokeMethod() method to invoke methods of the objects created in a scripting language.

The following snippet of code performs the check that the script engine implementation class implements the Invocable interface:

```
// Get the Groovy engine
ScriptEngineManager manager = new ScriptEngineManager();
ScriptEngine engine = manager.getEngineByName(
    "Groovy");
// Make sure the script engine implements the Invocable
// interface
```

```
if (engine instanceof Invocable) {
    System.out.println(
        "Invoking procedures is supported.");
} else {
    System.out.println(
        "Invoking procedures is not supported.");
}
```

The second step is to cast the engine reference to the Invocable interface type:

```
Invocable inv = (Invocable) engine;
```

The third step is to evaluate the script, so the script engine compiles and stores the compiled form of the procedure for later invocation. The following snippet of code performs this step:

```
// Declare a function named add that adds two numbers
String script = "def add(n1, n2) { n1 + n2 }";
// Evaluate the function. Call to eval() does not invoke
// the function. It just compiles it.
engine.eval(script);
```

The last step is to invoke the procedure or function:

```
// Invoke the add function with 30 and 40 as the function's
// arguments. It is as if you called add(30, 40) in the
// script.
Object result = inv.invokeFunction("add", 30, 40);
```

The first argument to the invokeFunction() is the name of the procedure or function. The second argument is a varargs that is used to specify arguments to the procedure or function. The invokeFunction() method returns the value returned by the procedure or function.

Listing 10-16 shows how to invoke a function. It invokes a function written in Groovy.

Listing 10-16. Invoking a Function Written in Groovy

```java
// InvokeFunction.java
package com.jdojo.script;
import javax.script.Invocable;
import javax.script.ScriptEngine;
import javax.script.ScriptEngineManager;
import javax.script.ScriptException;
public class InvokeFunction {
    public static void main(String[] args) {
        ScriptEngineManager manager =
            new ScriptEngineManager();
        ScriptEngine engine = manager.getEngineByName(
            "Groovy");
        // Make sure the script engine implements the
        // Invocable interface
        if (!(engine instanceof Invocable)) {
            System.out.println(
                "Invoking procedures is not supported.");
            return;
        }
        // Cast the engine reference to the Invocable type
        Invocable inv = (Invocable) engine;
        try {
            String script =
              "def add(n1, n2) { n1 + n2 }";
            // Evaluate the script first
            engine.eval(script);
            // Invoke the add function twice
            Object result1 = inv.invokeFunction(
                "add", 30, 40);
            System.out.println("Result1 = " + result1);
            Object result2 = inv.invokeFunction(
                "add", 10, 20);
            System.out.println("Result2 = " + result2);
        } catch (ScriptException |
```

```
            NoSuchMethodException e) {
        e.printStackTrace();
    }
}
}
```

```
Result1 = 70
Result2 = 30
```

An object-oriented or object-based scripting language may let you define objects and their methods. You can invoke methods of such objects using the invokeMethod() method of the Invocable interface, which is declared as follows:

```
Object invokeMethod(Object objectRef, String name,
    Object... args)
```

The first argument is the reference of the object, the second argument is the name of the method that you want to invoke on the object, and the third argument is a varargs argument that is used to pass arguments to the method being invoked.

Listing 10-17 demonstrates the invocation of a method on an object that is created in Groovy. Note that the object is created inside the Groovy script. To invoke the method of the object from Java, you need to obtain the reference of the object through the script engine. The program evaluates the script that creates an object with an add() method and stores its reference in a variable named calculator. The engine.get("calculator") method returns the reference of the calculator object to the Java code.

Listing 10-17. Invoking a Method on an Object Created in Groovy JavaScript

```
// InvokeMethod.java
package com.jdojo.script;
import javax.script.Invocable;
import javax.script.ScriptEngine;
import javax.script.ScriptEngineManager;
import javax.script.ScriptException;
public class InvokeMethod {
    public static void main(String[] args) {
```

```
// Get the Groovy engine
ScriptEngineManager manager =
    new ScriptEngineManager();
ScriptEngine engine = manager.getEngineByName(
    "Groovy");
// Make sure the script engine implements the
// Invocable interface
if (!(engine instanceof Invocable)) {
    System.out.println(
        "Invoking methods is not supported.");
    return;
}
// Cast the engine reference to the Invocable type
Invocable inv = (Invocable) engine;
try {
    // Declare a global object with an add() method
    String script = """
        class Calculator {
          def add(int n1, int n2){n1 + n2}
        }
      calculator = new Calculator()
      """;
    // Evaluate the script first
    engine.eval(script);
    // Get the calculator object reference created
    // in the script
    Object calculator = engine.get("calculator");
    // Invoke the add() method on the calculator
    // object
    Object result = inv.invokeMethod(calculator,
        "add", 30, 40);
    System.out.println("Result = " + result);
} catch (ScriptException |
```

```
            NoSuchMethodException e) {
        e.printStackTrace();
    }
  }
}
```

Result = 70

Note   Use the Invocable interface to execute procedures, functions, and methods repeatedly. The evaluation of the script, having procedures, functions, and methods, stores the intermediate code in the engine that results in performance gain on their repeated execution.

Implementing Java Interfaces in Scripts

The Java Scripting API lets you implement Java interfaces in a scripting language. Methods of the Java interface may be implemented in scripts using top-level procedures or instance methods of an object. The advantage of implementing a Java interface in a scripting language is that you can use instances of the interface in Java code as if the interface was implemented in Java. You can pass instances of the interface as arguments to Java methods. The getInterface() method of the Invocable interface is used to obtain the instances of a Java interface that is implemented in scripts. The method has two versions:

- `<T> T getInterface(Class<T> cls)`

- `<T> T getInterface(Object obj, Class<T> cls)`

The first version is used to obtain an instance of a Java interface whose methods are implemented as top-level procedures in scripts. The interface type is passed to this method as its argument. Suppose you have a Calculator interface, as declared in Listing 10-18, that has two methods called add() and subtract().

Listing 10-18. A Calculator Interface

```
// Calculator.java
package com.jdojo.script;
public interface Calculator {
    int add (int n1, int n2);
    int subtract (int n1, int n2);
}
```

Consider the following two top-level functions written in Groovy:

```
def add(n1, n2) {
    n1 + n2
}
def subtract(n1, n2) {
    n1 -n2
}
```

These two functions provide the implementations for the two methods of the Calculator interface. After these functions are compiled by a Groovy scripting engine, you can obtain an instance of the Calculator interface as shown:

```
// Cast the engine reference to the Invocable type
Invocable inv = (Invocable) engine;
// Get the reference of the Calculator interface
Calculator calc = inv.getInterface(Calculator.class);
if (calc == null) {
    System.err.println(
        "Calculator interface implementation not found.");
} else {
    // Use calc to call add() and subtract() methods
}
```

You can add two numbers as shown:

```
int sum = calc.add(15, 10);
```

Listing 10-19 shows how to implement a Java interface using top-level procedures in Groovy. Consult the documentation of a scripting language to learn how it supports this functionality.

Listing 10-19. Implementing a Java Interface Using Top-Level Functions in a Script

```
// UsingInterfaces.java
package com.jdojo.script;
import javax.script.Invocable;
import javax.script.ScriptEngine;
import javax.script.ScriptEngineManager;
import javax.script.ScriptException;
public class UsingInterfaces {
    public static void main(String[] args) {
        // Get the Groovy engine
        ScriptEngineManager manager =
            new ScriptEngineManager();
        ScriptEngine engine = manager.getEngineByName(
            "Groovy");
        // Make sure the script engine implements
        // Invocable interface
        if (!(engine instanceof Invocable)) {
            System.out.println(
                """Interface implementation in script
                    is not supported.""");
            return;
        }
        // Cast the engine reference to the Invocable
        // type
        Invocable inv = (Invocable) engine;
        // Create the script for add() and subtract()
        // functions
        String script = """
            def add(n1, n2) { n1 + n2 }
            def subtract(n1, n2) { n1 - n2 }
        """;
```

```
    try {
        // Compile the script that will be stored in
        // the engine
        engine.eval(script);
        // Get the interface implementation
        Calculator calc = inv.getInterface(
            Calculator.class);
        if (calc == null) {
            System.err.println(
                """"Calculator interface implementation
                    not found.""");
            return;
        }
        int result1 = calc.add(15, 10);
        System.out.println(
            "add(15, 10) = " + result1);
        int result2 = calc.subtract(15, 10);
        System.out.println(
            "subtract(15, 10) = " + result2);
    } catch (ScriptException e) {
        e.printStackTrace();
    }
    }
}
```

```
add(15, 10) = 25
subtract(15, 10) = 5
```

The second version of the getInterface() method is used to obtain an instance of a Java interface whose methods are implemented as instance methods of an object. Its first argument is the reference of the object that is created in the scripting language. The instance methods of the object implement the interface type passed in as the second argument. The following code in Groovy creates an object whose instance methods implement the Calculator interface:

```
class GCalculator {
    def add(int n1, int n2){n1 + n2}
    def subtract(int n1, int n2){n1 + n2}
}
calculator = new GCalculator()
```

When instance methods of a script object implements methods of a Java interface, you need to perform an extra step. You need to get the reference of the script object before you can get the instance of the interface, as shown:

```
// Get the reference of the global script object calc
Object calc = engine.get("calculator");
// Get the implementation of the Calculator interface
Calculator calculator =
    inv.getInterface(calc, Calculator.class);
```

Listing 10-20 shows how to implement methods of a Java interface as instance methods of an object using Groovy.

Listing 10-20. Implementing Methods of a Java Interface As Instance Methods of an Object in a Script

```
// ScriptObjectImplInterface.java
package com.jdojo.script;
import javax.script.Invocable;
import javax.script.ScriptEngine;
import javax.script.ScriptEngineManager;
import javax.script.ScriptException;
public class ScriptObjectImplInterface {
    public static void main(String[] args) {
        // Get the Groovy engine
        ScriptEngineManager manager =
            new ScriptEngineManager();
        ScriptEngine engine = manager.getEngineByName(
            "Groovy");
```

```java
// Make sure the engine implements the Invocable
// interface
if (!(engine instanceof Invocable)) {
    System.out.println(
        """Interface implementation in script is
        not supported.""");
    return;
}
// Cast the engine reference to the Invocable type
Invocable inv = (Invocable) engine;
String script = """
  class GCalculator {
    def add(int n1, int n2){n1 + n2}
    def subtract(int n1, int n2){n1 + n2}
  }
  calculator = new GCalculator()
""";
try {
    // Compile and store the script in the engine
    engine.eval(script);
    // Get the reference of the global script
    // object calc
    Object calc = engine.get("calculator");
    // Get the implementation of the Calculator
    // interface
    Calculator calculator =
        inv.getInterface(calc, Calculator.class);
    if (calculator == null) {
        System.err.println(
            """Calculator interface implementation
            not found.""");
        return;
    }
    int result1 = calculator.add(15, 10);
    System.out.println(
```

```
                "add(15, 10) = " + result1);
            int result2 = calculator.subtract(15, 10);
            System.out.println(
                "subtract(15, 10) = " + result2);
        } catch (ScriptException e) {
            e.printStackTrace();
        }
    }
}
```

```
add(15, 10) = 25
subtract(15, 10) = 5
```

Using Compiled Scripts

A script engine may allow compiling a script and executing it repeatedly. Executing compiled scripts may increase the performance of an application. A script engine may compile and store scripts in the form of Java classes, Java class files, or in a language-specific form.

Not all script engines are required to support script compilation. Script engines that support script compilation must implement the Compilable interface. Groovy engine supports script compilation. The following snippet of code checks if a script engine implements the Compilable interface:

```
// Get the script engine reference
ScriptEngineManager manager = new ScriptEngineManager();
ScriptEngine engine = manager.getEngineByName(
    "YOUR_ENGINE_NAME");
if (engine instanceof Compilable) {
    System.out.println(
        "Script compilation is supported.");
} else {
    System.out.println(
        "Script compilation is not supported.");
}
```

Once you know that a script engine implements the Compilable interface, you can cast its reference to a Compilable type as

```
// Cast the engine reference to the Compilable type
Compilable comp = (Compilable) engine;
```

The Compilable interface contains two methods:

- CompiledScript compile(String script) throws ScriptException

- CompiledScript compile(Reader script) throws ScriptException

The two versions of the method differ only in the type of the source of the script. The first version accepts the script as a String and the second one as a Reader.

The compile() method returns an object of the CompiledScript class. CompiledScript is an abstract class. The provider of the script engine provides the concrete implementation of this class. A CompiledScript is associated with the ScriptEngine that creates it. The getEngine() method of the CompiledScript class returns the reference of the ScriptEngine to which it is associated.

To execute a compiled script, you need to call one of the following eval() methods of the CompiledScript class:

- Object eval() throws ScriptException

- Object eval(Bindings bindings) throws ScriptException

- Object eval(ScriptContext context) throws ScriptException

The eval() method without any arguments uses the default script context of the script engine to execute the compiled script. The other two versions work the same as the eval() method of the ScriptEngine interface when you pass a Bindings or a ScriptContext to them.

Listing 10-21 shows how to compile a script and execute it. It executes the same compiled script twice with different parameters.

Listing 10-21. Using Compiled Scripts

```java
// CompilableTest .java
package com.jdojo.script;
import javax.script.Bindings;
import javax.script.Compilable;
import javax.script.CompiledScript;
import javax.script.ScriptEngine;
import javax.script.ScriptEngineManager;
import javax.script.ScriptException;
public class CompilableTest {
    public static void main(String[] args) {
        // Get the Groovy engine
        ScriptEngineManager manager =
            new ScriptEngineManager();
        ScriptEngine engine = manager.getEngineByName(
            "Groovy");
        if (!(engine instanceof Compilable)) {
            System.out.println(
                "Script compilation not supported.");
            return;
        }
        // Cast the engine reference to the Compilable
        // type
        Compilable comp = (Compilable) engine;
        try {
            // Compile a script
            String script = "println(n1 + n2)";
            CompiledScript cScript = comp.compile(script);
            // Store n1 and n2 script variables in a
            // Bindings
            Bindings scriptParams =
                engine.createBindings();
            scriptParams.put("n1", 2);
            scriptParams.put("n2", 3);
            cScript.eval(scriptParams);
```

```
            // Execute the script again with different
            // values for n1 and n2
            scriptParams.put("n1", 9);
            scriptParams.put("n2", 7);
            cScript.eval(scriptParams);
        } catch (ScriptException e) {
            e.printStackTrace();
        }
    }
}
5
16
```

Using Java in Scripting Languages

Scripting languages allow using Java class libraries in scripts. Each scripting language has its own syntax for using Java classes. It is not possible, and is outside the scope of this book, to discuss the syntax of all scripting languages. In this section, I discuss the syntax of using some Java constructs in Groovy. For the complete coverage of the Groovy, refer to the website at www.groovy-lang.org/.

Declaring Variables

Declaring variables in a scripting language is not necessarily related to Java. Often, scripting languages let you assign values to variables without declaring them. The types of variables then are determined at runtime based on the types of the values they store.

In Groovy, the keyword def is used to declare a variable. If you decide to omit the keyword def in a variable declaration, the variable is accessible script-wide, although not in classes you declare inside the script, and the value is accessible from Java after the script is processed. The following snippet of code declares two variables and assigns them a value:

```
// Declare a variable named msg using the def keyword
def msg = "Hello";

// Declare a variable named greeting without using the
// keyword def. We can later use
```

```
//     Object greeting = engine.get("greeting");
// in Java to get the value.
greeting = "Hello";
```

Importing Java Classes

Groovy sits on top of a JVM, so you can just import Java classes from the standard library into a Groovy script the same way as if it was a Java class file. The same holds for classes provided by libraries included in the project and for classes defined in your project:

```
// A class from the standard library
import java.text.SimpleDateFormat

// A class defined elsewhere in the project
import java17.script.SomeJavaClass

// Some library class. Must be inside the classpath.
import com.foo.superlib.Foo

def obj = new SomeJavaClass(8)
def sdf = new SimpleDateFormat("yyyy-MM-dd")
def foo = new Foo()
...
```

Other scripting languages define, or do not define, their own ways to import Java classes. Consult their documentation for details.

Implementing a Script Engine

Implementing a full-blown script engine is no simple task, and it is out of scope of this book. This section is meant to give you a brief, but complete, overview of the setup needed to implement a script engine. In this section, you will implement a simple script engine called the JKScript engine. It will evaluate arithmetic expressions with the following rules:

- It will evaluate an arithmetic expression that consists of two operands and one operator.

- The expression may have two number literals, two variables, or one number literal and one variable as operands. The number literals

must be in decimal format. Hexadecimal, octal, and binary number
literals are not supported.

- The arithmetic operations in an expression are limited to add,
  subtract, multiply, and divide.

- It will recognize +, -, *, and / as arithmetic operators.

- The engine will return a `Double` object as the result of the expression.

- Operands in an expression may be passed to the engine using global
  scope or engine scope bindings of the engine.

- It should allow executing scripts from a `String` object and a
  `java.io.Reader` object. However, a `Reader` should have only one
  expression as its contents.

- It will not implement the `Invocable` and `Compilable` interfaces.

Using these rules, some valid expressions for your script engine are as follows:

- `10 + 90`

- `10.7 + 89.0`

- `+10 + +90`

- `num1 + num2`

- `num1 * num2`

- `78.0 / 7.5`

The Scripting API uses the service provider mechanism to discover script engines.
The service type is the `javax.script.ScriptEngineFactory` interface. Your script
engine must provide an implementation for this service type. You will package your
script engine in a separate module named `jdojo.jkscript`, as declared in Listing 10-22.

Listing 10-22. The Declaration of a jdojo.jkscript Module

```
// module-info.java
module jdojo.jkscript {
    requires java.scripting;
    provides javax.script.ScriptEngineFactory
        with com.jdojo.jkscript.JKScriptEngineFactory;
}
```

The module reads the `java.scripting` module because it needs to use types from this module. The module provides an implementation of the `javax.script.ScriptEngineFactory` service interface, which is the `com.jdojo.jkscript.JKScriptEngineFactory` class. You do not need to export any packages of your module because no other modules are supposed to access any types from this module directly.

As part of your implementation for the `JKScript` script engine, you will develop three classes as listed in Table 10-2. In the subsequent sections, you will develop these classes.

Table 10-2. *Classes to Be Developed for the JKScript Script Engine*

Class	Description
Expression	The `Expression` class is the heart of your script engine. It performs the work of parsing and evaluating an arithmetic expression. It is used inside the `eval()` methods of the `JKScriptEngine` class.
JKScriptEngine	An implementation of the `ScriptEngine` interface. It extends the `AbstractScriptEngine` class that implements the `ScriptEngine` interface. The `AbstractScriptEngine` class provides a standard implementation for several versions of the `eval()` methods of the `ScriptEngine` interface. You need to implement the following two versions of the `eval()` method: `Object eval(String, ScriptContext)` and `Object eval(Reader, ScriptContext)`
JKScriptEngineFactory	An implementation of the `ScriptEngineFactory` interface. This is the service provider for the `javax.script.ScriptEngineFactory` service interface.

The Expression Class

The `Expression` class contains the main logic for parsing and evaluating an arithmetic expression. Listing 10-23 contains the complete code for the `Expression` class.

Listing 10-23. The Expression Class That Parses and Evaluates an Arithmetic Expression

```java
// Expression.java
package com.jdojo.jkscript;
import java.util.regex.Matcher;
import java.util.regex.Pattern;
import javax.script.ScriptContext;
public class Expression {
    private String exp;
    private ScriptContext context;
    private String op1;
    private char op1Sign = '+';
    private String op2;
    private char op2Sign = '+';
    private char operation;
    private boolean parsed;
    public Expression(String exp, ScriptContext context) {
        if (exp == null || exp.trim().equals("")) {
            throw new IllegalArgumentException(
                this.getErrorString());
        }
        this.exp = exp.trim();
        if (context == null) {
            throw new IllegalArgumentException(
                "ScriptContext cannot be null.");
        }
        this.context = context;
    }
    public String getExpression() {
        return exp;
    }
    public ScriptContext getScriptContext() {
        return context;
    }
```

```java
public Double eval() {
    // Parse the expression
    if (!parsed) {
        this.parse();
        this.parsed = true;
    }
    // Extract the values for the operand
    double op1Value = getOperandValue(op1Sign, op1);
    double op2Value = getOperandValue(op2Sign, op2);
    // Evaluate the expression
    Double result = null;
    switch (operation) {
        case '+':
            result = op1Value + op2Value;
            break;
        case '-':
            result = op1Value - op2Value;
            break;
        case '*':
            result = op1Value * op2Value;
            break;
        case '/':
            result = op1Value / op2Value;
            break;
        default:
            throw new RuntimeException(
                "Invalid operation:" + operation);
    }
    return result;
}
private double
getOperandValue(char sign, String operand) {
    // Check if operand is a double
    double value;
    try {
```

```
        value = Double.parseDouble(operand);
        return sign == '-' ? -value : value;
    } catch (NumberFormatException e) {
        // Ignore it. Operand is not in a format that
        // can be converted to a double value.
    }
    // Check if operand is a bind variable
    Object bindValue = context.getAttribute(operand);
    if (bindValue == null) {
        throw new RuntimeException(operand +
            " is not found in the script context.");
    }
    if (bindValue instanceof Number) {
        value = ((Number) bindValue).doubleValue();
        return sign == '-' ? -value : value;
    } else {
        throw new RuntimeException(operand +
            " must be bound to a number.");
    }
}
public void parse() {
    // Supported expressions are of the form v1 op v2,
    // where v1 and v2 are variable names or numbers,
    // and op could be +, -, *, or /
    // Prepare the pattern for the expected expression
    String operandSignPattern = "([+-]?)";
    String operandPattern = "([\\p{Alnum}\\p{Sc}_.]+)";
    String whileSpacePattern = "([\\s]*)";
    String operationPattern = "([+*/-])";
    String pattern = "^" + operandSignPattern
            + operandPattern
            + whileSpacePattern + operationPattern
            + whileSpacePattern
            + operandSignPattern + operandPattern
            + "$";
```

```java
        Pattern p = Pattern.compile(pattern);
        Matcher m = p.matcher(exp);
        if (!m.matches()) {
            // The expression is not in the expected format
            throw new IllegalArgumentException(
                this.getErrorString());
        }
        // Get operand-1
        String temp = m.group(1);
        if (temp != null && !temp.equals("")) {
            this.op1Sign = temp.charAt(0);
        }
        this.op1 = m.group(2);
        // Get operation
        temp = m.group(4);
        if (temp != null && !temp.equals("")) {
            this.operation = temp.charAt(0);
        }
        // Get operand-2
        temp = m.group(6);
        if (temp != null && !temp.equals("")) {
            this.op2Sign = temp.charAt(0);
        }
        this.op2 = m.group(7);
    }
    private String getErrorString() {
        return "Invalid expression[" + exp + "]"
                + "\nSupported expression syntax is: "
                + "op1 operation op2"
                + "\n where op1 and op2 can be a number "
                + " or a bind variable"
                + " , and operation can be"
                + " +, -, *, and /.";
    }
    @Override
```

```java
    public String toString() {
        return "Expression: " + this.exp + ", op1 Sign = "
                + op1Sign + ", op1 = " + op1
                + ", op2 Sign = " + op2Sign
                + ", op2 = " + op2
                + ", operation = " + operation;
    }
}
```

The Expression class is designed to parse and evaluate an arithmetic expression of the form

```
op1 operation op2
```

Here, op1 and op2 are two operands that can be numbers in decimal format or variables, and operation can be +, -, *, or /.

The suggested use of the Expression class is

```
Expression exp = new Expression(expression, scriptContext);
Double value = exp.eval();
```

Let's discuss important components of the Expression class in detail. Instance variables exp and context are the expression and the ScriptContext to evaluate the expression, respectively. They are passed in to the constructor of this class.

The instance variables op1 and op2 represent the first and the second operands in the expression, respectively. The instance variables op1Sign and op2Sign represent signs, which could be + or -, for the first and the second operands in the expression, respectively. The operands and their signs are populated when the expression is parsed using the parse() method.

The instance variable operation represents an arithmetic operation (+, -, *, or /) to be performed on the operands.

The instance variable parsed is used to keep track of the fact whether the expression has been parsed or not. The parse() method sets it to true.

The constructor accepts an expression and a ScriptContext and makes sure that they are not null and stores them in the instance variables. It trims the leading and trailing whitespace from the expression before storing it in the instance variable exp.

The `parse()` method parses the expression into operands and operations. It uses a regular expression to parse the expression text. The regular expression expects the expression text in the following form:

- An optional sign + or - for the first operand

- The first operand that may consist of a combination of alphanumeric letters, currency signs, underscores, and decimal points

- Any amount of whitespace

- An operation sign that may be +, -, *, or /

- An optional sign + or - for the second operand

- The second operand that may consist of a combination of alphanumeric letters, currency signs, underscores, and decimal points

The regular expression (`[+-]?`) will match the optional sign for the operand. The regular expression (`[\\pAlnum\\pSc_.]+`) will match an operand, which may be a decimal number or a name. The regular expression (`[\\s]*`) will match any amount of whitespace. The regular expression (`[+*/-]`) will match an operation sign. All regular expressions are enclosed in parentheses to form groups, so you can capture the matched parts of the expression.

If an expression matches the regular expression, the `parse()` method stores the matches into respective instance variables.

Note that the regular expression to match the operand is not perfect. It will allow several invalid cases, such as an operand having multiple decimal points, etc. However, for this demonstration purpose, it will do.

The `getOperandValue()` method is used during an expression evaluation after the expression has been parsed. If the operand is a `double` number, it returns the value by applying the sign of the operand. Otherwise, it looks up the name of the operand in the `ScriptContext`. If the name of the operand is not found in the `ScriptContext`, it throws a `RuntimeException`. If the name of the operand is found in the `ScriptContext`, it checks if the value is a number. If the value is a number, it returns the value after applying the sign to the value; otherwise, it throws a `RuntimeException`.

The `getOperandValue()` method does not support operands in hexadecimal, octal, and binary formats. For example, an expression like "0x2A + 0b1011" will not be treated as an expression having two operands with `int` literals. It is left to readers to enhance this method to support numeric literals in hexadecimal, octal, and binary formats.

The eval() method evaluates the expression and returns a double value. First, it parses the expression if it has not already been parsed. Note that multiple calls to the eval() parses the expression only once. It obtains values for both operands, performs the operation, and returns the value of the expression.

The JKScriptEngine Class

Listing 10-24 contains the implementation for the JKScript script engine. Its eval(String, ScriptContext) method contains the main logic:

```
Expression exp = new Expression(script, context); Object result = exp.eval();
```

It creates an object of the Expression class. It calls the eval() method of the Expression object that evaluates the expression and returns the result.

The eval(Reader, ScriptContext) method reads all lines from the Reader, concatenates them, and passes the resulting String to the eval(String, ScriptContext) method to evaluate the expression. Note that a Reader must have only one expression. An expression may be split into multiple lines. Whitespace in the Reader is ignored.

Listing 10-24. An Implementation of the JKScript Script Engine

```java
// JKScriptEngine.java
package com.jdojo.jkscript;
import java.io.BufferedReader;
import java.io.IOException;
import java.io.Reader;
import javax.script.AbstractScriptEngine;
import javax.script.Bindings;
import javax.script.ScriptContext;
import javax.script.ScriptEngineFactory;
import javax.script.ScriptException;
import javax.script.SimpleBindings;

public class JKScriptEngine extends AbstractScriptEngine {
    private final ScriptEngineFactory factory;
    public JKScriptEngine(ScriptEngineFactory factory) {
        this.factory = factory;
    }
```

```java
@Override
public Object
eval(String script, ScriptContext context)
throws ScriptException {
    try {
        Expression exp =
            new Expression(script, context);
        Object result = exp.eval();
        return result;
    } catch (Exception e) {
        throw new ScriptException(e.getMessage());
    }
}
@Override
public Object
eval(Reader reader, ScriptContext context)
throws ScriptException {
    // Read all lines from the Reader
    BufferedReader br = new BufferedReader(reader);
    String script = "";
    try {
        String str;
        while ((str = br.readLine()) != null) {
            script = script + str;
        }
    } catch (IOException e) {
        throw new ScriptException(e);
    }
    // Use the String version of eval()
    return eval(script, context);
}
@Override
public Bindings createBindings() {
    return new SimpleBindings();
}
```

```
    @Override
    Public  ScriptEngineFactory getFactory() {
        return factory;
    }
}
```

The JKScriptEngineFactory Class

Listing 10-25 contains the implementation for the ScriptEngineFactory interface
for the JKScript engine. Some of its methods return a "Not Implemented" string
because you do not support features exposed by those methods. The code in the
JKScriptEngineFactory class is self-explanatory. An instance of the JKScript engine
may be obtained using ScriptEngineManager with a name of jks, JKScript, or jkscript
as coded in the getNames() method.

Listing 10-25. A ScriptEngineFactory Implementation for the JKScript Script
Engine

```
// JKScriptEngineFactory.java
package com.jdojo.jkscript;
import java.util.List;
import javax.script.ScriptEngine;
import javax.script.ScriptEngineFactory;
public class JKScriptEngineFactory
        implements ScriptEngineFactory {
    @Override
    public String getEngineName() {
        return "JKScript Engine";
    }
    @Override
    public String getEngineVersion() {
        return "1.0";
    }
    @Override
    public List<String> getExtensions() {
        return List.of("jks");
    }
```

```java
@Override
public List<String> getMimeTypes() {
    return List.of("text/jkscript");
}
@Override
public List<String> getNames() {
    return List.of("jks", "JKScript", "jkscript");
}
@Override
public String getLanguageName() {
    return "JKScript";
}
@Override
public String getLanguageVersion() {
    return "1.0";
}
@Override
public Object getParameter(String key) {
    switch (key) {
        case ScriptEngine.ENGINE:
            return getEngineName();
        case ScriptEngine.ENGINE_VERSION:
            return getEngineVersion();
        case ScriptEngine.NAME:
            return getEngineName();
        case ScriptEngine.LANGUAGE:
            return getLanguageName();
        case ScriptEngine.LANGUAGE_VERSION:
            return getLanguageVersion();
        case "THREADING":
            return "MULTITHREADED";
        default:
            return null;
    }
}
```

```
    @Override
    public String
    getMethodCallSyntax(String obj, String m, String[] p) {
        return "Not implemented";
    }
    @Override
    public String
    getOutputStatement(String toDisplay) {
        return "Not implemented";
    }
    @Override
    public String
    getProgram(String[] statements) {
        return "Not implemented";
    }
    @Override
    public ScriptEngine
    getScriptEngine() {
        return new JKScriptEngine(this);
    }
}
```

Packaging the JKScript Files

To let others use your JKScript engine, all you need to do is to supply the modular JAR for the jdojo.jkscript module.

Using the JKScript Script Engine

It is time to test your JKScript script engine. The first and most important step is to include the jdojo.jkscript.jar, which you created in the previous section, to the application's module path. After that, using the JKScript script engine is no different from using any other script engines.

The following snippet of code creates an instance of the JKScript script engine using JKScript as its name. You can also use its other names, jks and jkscript:

```
// Create the JKScript engine
ScriptEngineManager manager = new ScriptEngineManager();
ScriptEngine engine = manager.getEngineByName("JKScript");
if (engine == null) {
    System.out.println(
        "JKScript engine is not available. ");
    System.out.println(
        "Add jkscript.jar to CLASSPATH.");
else {
    // Evaluate your JKScript
}
```

Listing 10-26 contains a program that uses the JKScript script engine to evaluate different types of expressions. Expressions stored in String objects and files are executed. Some expressions use numeric literals and some bind variables whose values are passed in bindings in the engine scope and global scope of the default ScriptContext of the engine. Note that this program expects a file named jkscript.txt in the current directory that contains an arithmetic expression that can be understood by the JKScript script engine. If the script file does not exist, the program prints a message on the standard output with the path of the expected script file. You may get a different output in the last line.

Listing 10-26. Using the JKScript Script Engine

```
// JKScriptTest.java
package com.jdojo.script;
import java.io.FileNotFoundException;
import java.io.IOException;
import java.io.Reader;
import java.nio.file.Files;
import java.nio.file.Path;
import java.nio.file.Paths;
import javax.script.ScriptEngine;
import javax.script.ScriptEngineManager;
```

```java
import javax.script.ScriptException;
public class JKScriptTest {
    public static void
    main(String[] args)
    throws FileNotFoundException, IOException {
        // Create JKScript engine
        ScriptEngineManager manager =
            new ScriptEngineManager();
        ScriptEngine engine = manager.getEngineByName(
            "JKScript");
        if (engine == null) {
            System.out.println(
                "JKScript engine is not available. ");
            System.out.println(
                "Add jkscript.jar to CLASSPATH.");
            return;
        }
        // Test scripts as String
        testString(manager, engine);
        // Test scripts as a Reader
        testReader(manager, engine);
    }
    public static void
    testString(ScriptEngineManager manager,
            ScriptEngine engine) {
        try {
            // Use simple expressions with numeric literals
            String script = "12.8 + 15.2";
            Object result = engine.eval(script);
            System.out.println(script + " = " + result);
            script = "-90.0 - -10.5";
            result = engine.eval(script);
            System.out.println(script + " = " + result);
            script = "5 * 12";
            result = engine.eval(script);
```

```
            System.out.println(script + " = " + result);
            script = "56.0 / -7.0";
            result = engine.eval(script);
            System.out.println(script + " = " + result);
            // Use global scope bindings variables
            manager.put("num1", 10.0);
            manager.put("num2", 20.0);
            script = "num1 + num2";
            result = engine.eval(script);
            System.out.println(script + " = " + result);
            // Use global and engine scopes bindings.
            // num1 from engine scope and num2 from
            // global scope will be used.
            engine.put("num1", 70.0);
            script = "num1 + num2";
            result = engine.eval(script);
            System.out.println(script + " = " + result);
            // Try mixture of number literal and bindings.
            // num1 from the engine scope bindings will be
            // used
            script = "10 + num1";
            result = engine.eval(script);
            System.out.println(script + " = " + result);
        } catch (ScriptException e) {
            e.printStackTrace();
        }
    }
    public static void
    testReader(ScriptEngineManager manager,
            ScriptEngine engine) {
        try {
            Path scriptPath = Paths.get("jkscript.txt").
                toAbsolutePath();
            if (!Files.exists(scriptPath)) {
                System.out.println(scriptPath +
                    " script file does not exist.");
```

```
            return;
        }
        try (Reader reader = Files.
                newBufferedReader(scriptPath);) {
            Object result = engine.eval(reader);
            System.out.println("Result of " +
                scriptPath + " = " + result);
        }
    } catch (ScriptException | IOException e) {
        e.printStackTrace();
    }
  }
}
```

```
12.8 + 15.2 = 28.0
-90.0 - -10.5 = -79.5
5 * 12 = 60.0
56.0 / -7.0 = -8.0
num1 + num2 = 30.0
num1 + num2 = 90.0
10 + num1 = 80.0
Result of C:\Java9APIsAndModules\jkscript.txt = 88.0
```

JavaFX in Groovy

We can use scripting to speed up JavaFX development. In fact, mixing Java code and scripts helps to separate front-end and back-end logic, and because scripts are more concise compared to Java code, you can save some development time.

Listing 10-27 contains a simple HelloWorld-style JavaFX application.

Listing 10-27. A JavaFX Application Using a Groovy Script

```
package com.jdojo.groovyfx;

import javax.script.Invocable;
import javax.script.ScriptEngine;
import javax.script.ScriptEngineManager;
```

```java
import javax.script.ScriptException;
import javafx.application.Application;
import javafx.stage.Stage;

public class HelloGroovyFX extends Application {
    private Invocable inv;

    public static void main(String[] args) {
        launch(args);
    }

    @Override
    public void init() {
        // Create a script engine manager
        ScriptEngineManager manager =
            new ScriptEngineManager();
        // Obtain a Groovy script engine from the manager
        ScriptEngine engine =
            manager.getEngineByName("Groovy");
        // Store the Groovy script in a String
        String script = """
import javafx.scene.Scene
import javafx.scene.control.Button
import javafx.scene.layout.StackPane
import javafx.beans.property.SimpleStringProperty as SP

def go(def primaryStage) {
  primaryStage.setTitle "Hello World!"
  Button btn = new Button()
  btn.text = "Say 'Hello World'"
  btn.onAction = { def event ->
      println("Hello World!")
  }

  StackPane root = new StackPane()
  root.children.add(btn)
```

```java
            primaryStage.scene = new Scene(root, 300, 250)
            primaryStage.show()
        }

                """;
        try {
            // Execute the script
            engine.eval(script);
            inv = (Invocable) engine;
        } catch (ScriptException e) {
            e.printStackTrace();
        }
    }

    @Override
    public void start(Stage primaryStage) {
        try {
            inv.invokeFunction("go", primaryStage);
        } catch (Exception e) {
            e.printStackTrace();
        }
    }
}
```

For this to work, you must add the JavaFX libraries. For a Maven project, this is easy.
Just add

```xml
<dependency>
  <groupId>org.openjfx</groupId>
  <artifactId>javafx-base</artifactId>
  <version>16</version>
</dependency>
<dependency>
  <groupId>org.openjfx</groupId>
  <artifactId>javafx-graphics</artifactId>
  <version>16</version>
</dependency>
```

```
<dependency>
  <groupId>org.openjfx</groupId>
  <artifactId>javafx-controls</artifactId>
  <version>16</version>
</dependency>
<dependency>
  <groupId>org.openjfx</groupId>
  <artifactId>javafx-web</artifactId>
  <version>16</version>
</dependency>
```

inside the `<dependencies>` section of your `pom.xml` file.

The Groovy version of the front-end code is a little simpler to write compared to Java. In the script, you are able to call the methods of the Java classes using their properties. For example, instead of writing this in Java:

```
btn.setText("Say 'Hello World'");
```

you can write this in Groovy:

```
btn.text = "Say 'Hello World'"
```

An exception to this rule is

```
primaryStage.setTitle "Hello World!"
```

because in the `Stage` class, the `title` field has a type different from `String`.

Adding the event handler for buttons is easier, too. You can use a Groovy closure as the event handler for the buttons. Note that you are also able to use the `onAction` property to set the event handler rather than calling the `setOnAction()` method of the `Button` class. The following snippet of code shows how to set the `ActionEvent` handler for a button:

```
btn.onAction = { def event ->
    println("Hello World!")
}
```

Figure 10-7 shows the running JavaFX application.

Figure 10-7. *A JavaFX application with Groovy scripting*

Summary

A scripting language is a programming language that provides you the ability to write scripts that are evaluated (or interpreted) by a runtime environment called a script engine (or an interpreter). A script is a sequence of characters that is written using the syntax of a scripting language and used as the source for a program executed by an interpreter. The Java Scripting API allows you to execute scripts written in any scripting language that can be compiled to Java bytecode from the Java application.

Scripts are executed using a script engine that is an instance of the ScriptEngine interface. The implementer of the ScriptEngine interface also provides an implementation of the ScriptEngineFactory interface whose job is to create instances of the script engine and provide details about the script engine. The ScriptEngineManager class provides a discovery and instantiation mechanism for script engines. A ScriptManager maintains a mapping of key-value pairs as an instance of the Bindings interface that is shared by all script engines that it creates.

You can execute scripts contained in a String or a Reader. The eval() method of the ScriptEngine is used to execute the script. You can pass parameters to the script using the ScriptContext. Parameters passed can be local to a script engine, local to a script execution, or global to all script engines created by a ScriptManager. Using the Java Scripting API, you can also execute procedures and functions written in scripting languages. You can also precompile the scripts, if the script engine supports it, and execute the scripts repeated from Java to get a better performance.

You can implement your script engine using the Java Scripting API. You need to provide the implementation for the `ScriptEngine` and the `ScriptEngineFactory` interfaces. You need to package your script engine code in a certain way so the engine can be discovered by the `ScriptManager` at runtime.

Exercises

Exercise 1

What is a scripting language?

Exercise 2

What JDK module contains the Scripting API?

Exercise 3

Briefly describe the use of the following classes and interfaces: `ScriptEngineFactory`, `ScriptEngine`, `ScriptEngineManager`, `Compilable`, `Invocable`, `Bindings`, `ScriptContext`, and `ScriptException`.

Exercise 4

What is the use of the `eval()` method of a `ScriptEngine`?

Exercise 5

Write a program in which you create an instance of the `ScriptContext` interface using the `SimpleScriptContext` class. Store a few attributes in the engine scope and global scope, retrieve the same attributes, and print their values.

Exercise 6

How do you add attributes to the global scope and engine scope?

Exercise 7

How do you send the output of scripts executed by a `ScriptEngine` to a file?

Exercise 8

Write a snippet of code that checks if a `ScriptEngine` supports compiling scripts.

Exercise 9

Create an unmodifiable list of two strings using the `of()` method of the `java.util.List` interface and print the values in the list. Use Groovy scripting to write the code.

Exercise 10

If you want to roll out your own script engine, what is the name of the service interface whose implementation you must provide?

CHAPTER 11

Process API

In this chapter, you will learn:

- What the Process API is
- How to interact with the current process running the Java application
- How to create a native process
- How to get information about a new process
- How to get information about the current process
- How to get information about all system processes
- How to set permissions to create, query, and manage native processes

All example programs in this chapter are members of a jdojo.process module, as declared in Listing 11-1.

Listing 11-1. The Declaration of a jdojo.process Module

```java
// module-info.java
module jdojo.process {
    exports com.jdojo.process;
}
```

What Is the Process API?

The Process API consists of classes and interfaces that let you work with native processes in Java programs. Using the API, you can

- Create new native processes from Java code.
- Get process handles for native processes, whether they were created by Java code or by other means.

© Kishori Sharan, Peter Späth 2021
K. Sharan and P. Späth, *More Java 17*, https://doi.org/10.1007/978-1-4842-7135-3_11

- Destroy running native processes.

- Query processes for liveness and their other attributes.

- Get the list of child processes and the parent process of a process.

- Get the process ID (PID) of native processes.

- Get the input, output, and error streams of newly created processes.

- Wait for a process to terminate.

- Execute a task when a process terminates.

The Process API is small. It consists of the classes and interfaces listed in Table 11-1. I explain these classes and interfaces in detail with examples in the following sections.

Table 11-1. *Classes and Interfaces for the Process API*

Class/Interface	Description
Runtime	It is a singleton class whose sole instance represents the runtime environment of a Java application.
ProcessBuilder	An instance of the ProcessBuilder class holds a set of attributes for a process. Calling its start() method starts a native process and returns an instance of the Process class that represents the native process. You can call its start() method multiple times; each time, it starts a new process using the attributes held in the ProcessBuilder instance.
ProcessBuilder.Redirect	It is a static nested class that represents a source of process input or a destination of process output.
Process	It is an abstract class whose instances represent native processes started by the current Java program using the start() method of a ProcessBuilder or the exec() method of a Runtime.
ProcessHandle	It is an interface whose instances represent handles to native processes whether they were started by the current Java program or by any other means. You can control and query the state of the native process using this handle.
ProcessHandle.Info	An instance of the ProcessHandle.Info interface represents a snapshot of the attributes of a process.

In Java, you are able to start native processes and work with their input, output, and error streams. Also, it is possible to work with native processes that you did not start and to query the details of processes. For the latter, you use an interface named ProcessHandle, from inside the Process API. An instance of the ProcessHandle interface identifies a native process; it lets you query the process state and manage the process.

Compare the Process class and the ProcessHandle interface. An instance of the Process class represents a native process started by the current Java program, whereas an instance of the ProcessHandle interface represents a native process whether it was started by the current Java program or by other means. The Process class contains a toHandle() method that returns a ProcessHandle.

An instance of the ProcessHandle.Info interface represents a snapshot of the attributes of a process. Note that processes are implemented differently by different operating systems, so their attributes vary. The state of a process may change anytime, for example, the CPU time used by the process increases whenever the process gets more CPU time. To get the latest information on a process, you need to use the info() method of the ProcessHandle interface at the time you need it, which will return a new instance of the ProcessHandle.Info interface.

All examples in this chapter were run on Ubuntu Linux. You may get a different output when you run these programs on your machine using Windows or any other different operating system.

Note   The CLI code snippets can easily be converted to their Windows counterpart by adapting the executable and argument file paths.

Knowing the Runtime Environment

Every Java application has an instance of the Runtime class that lets you query and interact with the runtime environment in which the current Java application is running. The Runtime class is a singleton. You can get its sole instance using the getRuntime() static method of this class:

```
// Get the instance of the Runtime
Runtime runtime = Runtime.getRuntime();
```

Using the `Runtime`, you can know the maximum memory that the current JVM can use, the currently allocated memory in the JVM, and the free memory in the JVM. Here are the three methods that let you query the JVM's memory in bytes:

- `long maxMemory()`
- `long totalMemory()`
- `long freeMemory()`

JVM allocates memory lazily. The `maxMemory()` method returns the maximum amount of memory that the JVM can allocate. The method returns `Long.MAX_VALUE` if there is no maximum memory limit.

The `totalMemory()` method returns the currently allocated memory by the JVM out of the maximum memory it can allocate. When the JVM needs more memory, it allocates more memory, and the `totalMemory()` method will return the currently allocated memory. The JVM can allocate maximum memory up to the amount returned by the `maxMemory()` method.

The `freeMemory()` method returns the unused memory out of the currently allocated memory by the JVM. How do you know the memory used by the JVM? The following formula will give you the memory used by the JVM at a specific point in time:

```
Used Memory = Total Memory Free Memory
```

Use the `availableProcessors()` method to get the number of available processors to the JVM.

Use the `version()` method to get a `Runtime.Version` that represents the version of the Java runtime environment. Refer to the Javadoc for the `Runtime.Version` class for more details about the JDK/JRE versioning scheme. Listing 11-2 shows you a few applications of the `Runtime` class in querying the Java runtime environment. You may get a different output.

Listing 11-2. Querying the Java Runtime Environment

```
// QueryingRuntime.java
package com.jdojo.process;
public class QueryingRuntime {
    public static void main(String[] args) {
        // Get the Runtime instance
        Runtime rt = Runtime.getRuntime();
```

```
    // Get the JVM memory
    long maxMemory = rt.maxMemory();
    long totalMemory = rt.totalMemory();
    long freeMemory = rt.freeMemory();
    long usedMemory = totalMemory freeMemory;
    System.out.format(
        "Max memory = %d, Total memory = %d,"
        + "Free memory = %d, Used memory = %d.%n",
        maxMemory, totalMemory, freeMemory,
        usedMemory);
    // Print the number of processors available to
    // the JVM
    int processors = rt.availableProcessors();
    System.out.format("Number of processors = %d%n",
        processors);
    // Print the version of the Java runtime
    Runtime.Version version = rt.version();
    System.out.format("Version = %s%n",
        version);
  }
}
```

```
Max memory = 3126853632,
   Total memory = 201326592,
   Free memory = 198351728,
   Used memory = 2974864.
Number of processors = 8
Version = 17+01-123
```

You can invoke the garbage collection using the gc() method of the Runtime class. The System.gc() static method is the convenience method for the Runtime.getRuntime().gc().

Note   Method gc() is just a hint for the OS to start garbage collection at the next convenient time slot. You must not rely on the garbage collection to start immediately if gc() gets called.

You can terminate the JVM using the exit(int status) method of the Runtime class. The System.exit() static method is a convenience method for Runtime.getRuntime().exit(). By convention, a non-zero value for the status indicates an abnormal termination of the JVM. You can forcibly terminate the JVM using the halt() method of the Runtime class.

You can add and remove shutdown hooks to the JVM using the addShutdownHook(Thread hook) and removeShutdownHook(Thread hook) methods of the Runtime class. A shutdown hook is a thread, which is initialized, but not started. The JVM starts the thread registered as the shutdown hook when it is terminated.

Use one of its exec() overloaded methods to start a native process. You should use the ProcessBuilder class to start a native process. The exec() method of the Runtime class internally uses the ProcessBuilder class.

The Current Process

The current() static method of the ProcessHandle interface returns the handle of the current process. Note that the current process returned by this method is always the Java process that is executing the code:

```
// Get the handle of the current process
ProcessHandle current = ProcessHandle.current();
```

Once you get the handle of the current process, you can use methods of the ProcessHandle interface to get details about the process. Refer to the next section for an example on how to get information about the current process.

Note   You cannot kill the current process. Attempting to kill the current process by using the destroy() or destroyForcibly() method of the ProcessHandle interface results in an IllegalStateException.

Querying the Process State

You can use methods in the ProcessHandle interface to query the state of a process. Table 11-2 lists this interface's commonly used methods with brief descriptions. Note that many of these methods return the snapshot of the state of a process that was true when the snapshot was taken. There is no guarantee that the process will still be in the same state when you use its attributes later because processes are created, run, and destroyed asynchronously.

Table 11-2. *Methods in the ProcessHandle Interface*

Method	Description
`static Stream<ProcessHandle> allProcesses()`	Returns a snapshot of all processes in the OS that are visible to the current process.
`Stream<ProcessHandle> children()`	Returns a snapshot of the current direct children of the process. Use the `descendants()` method to get a list of children at all levels, for example, child processes, grandchild processes, great grandchild processes, etc.
`static ProcessHandle current()`	Returns a `ProcessHandle` for the current process, which is the Java process executing this method call.
`Stream<ProcessHandle> descendants()`	Returns a snapshot of the descendants of the process. Compare it to the `children()` method, which returns only direct descendants of the process.
`boolean destroy()`	Requests the process to be killed. Returns `true` if termination of the process was successfully requested, `false` otherwise. Whether you can kill a process depends on operating system access control.
`boolean destroyForcibly()`	Requests the process to be killed forcibly. Returns `true` if termination of the process was successfully requested, `false` otherwise. Killing a process forcibly terminates the process immediately, whereas a normal termination allows a process to shut down cleanly. Whether you can kill a process depends on operating system access control.
`ProcessHandle.Info info()`	Returns a snapshot of information about the process.

(continued)

Table 11-2. (*continued*)

Method	Description
boolean isAlive()	Returns true if the process represented by this ProcessHandle has not yet terminated, false otherwise. Note that this method may return true for some time after you have successfully requested to terminate the process because the process will be terminated asynchronously.
static Optional<ProcessHandle> of(long pid)	Returns an Optional<ProcessHandle> for an existing native process. Returns an empty Optional if a process with the specified pid does not exist.
CompletableFuture <ProcessHandle> onExit()	Returns a CompletableFuture <ProcessHandle> for the termination of the process. You can use the returned object to add a task that will be executed when the process terminates. Calling this method on the current process throws an IllegalStateException.
Optional<ProcessHandle> parent()	Returns an Optional<ProcessHandle>for the parent process.
long pid()	Returns the native process ID (PID) of the process, which is assigned by the operating system. Note that a PID may be reused by operating systems if a process terminates, so two process handles having the same PID may not represent the same process.
boolean supportsNormalTermination()	Returns true if the implementation of destroy() normally terminates the process.

Table 11-3 lists the methods and descriptions of the ProcessHandle.Info nested interface. An instance of this interface contains snapshot information about a process. You can obtain a ProcessHandle.Info using the info() method of the ProcessHandle interface or the Process class. All methods in the interface return an Optional.

Table 11-3. *Methods in the ProcessHandle.Info Interface*

Method	Description
`Optional<String[]> arguments()`	Returns arguments of the process. The process may change the original arguments passed to it after startup. This method returns the changed arguments in that case.
`Optional<String> command()`	Returns the executable pathname of the process.
`Optional<String> commandLine()`	It is a convenience method for combining the command and arguments of a process. It returns the command line of the process by combining the values returned from the `command()` and `arguments()` methods if both methods return non-empty optionals.
`Optional<Instant> startInstant()`	Returns the start time of the process. If the operating system does not return a start time, it returns an empty `Optional`.
`Optional<Duration> totalCpuDuration()`	Returns the total CPU time used by the process. Note that a process may run for a long time and may use very little CPU time.
`Optional<String> user()`	Returns the user of the process.

It is time to see the `ProcessHandle` and `ProcessHandle.Info` interfaces in action. Listing 11-3 contains the code for a class named `CurrentProcessInfo`. Its `printInfo()` method takes a `ProcessHandle` as an argument and prints the details of the process. We also use this method in other examples to print the details of a process. The `main()` method gets the handle of the current process running the process, which is a Java process, and prints its details. You may get a different output. The output was generated when the program ran on Linux.

Listing 11-3. A CurrentProcessInfo Class That Prints the Details of the Current Process

```java
// CurrentProcessInfo.java
package com.jdojo.process;
import java.time.Duration;
import java.time.Instant;
import java.time.ZoneId;
```

```java
import java.time.ZonedDateTime;
import java.util.Arrays;
public class CurrentProcessInfo {
    public static void main(String[] args) {
        // Get the handle of the current process
        ProcessHandle current = ProcessHandle.current();
        // Print the process details
        printInfo(current);
    }
    public static void printInfo(ProcessHandle handle) {
        // Get the process ID
        long pid = handle.pid();
        // Is the process still running
        boolean isAlive = handle.isAlive();
        // Get other process info
        ProcessHandle.Info info = handle.info();
        String command = info.command().orElse("");
        String[] args = info.arguments()
                            .orElse(new String[]{});
        String commandLine = info.commandLine()
            .orElse("");
        ZonedDateTime startTime = info.startInstant()
            .orElse(Instant.now())
            .atZone(ZoneId.systemDefault());
        Duration duration = info.totalCpuDuration()
            .orElse(Duration.ZERO);
        String owner = info.user().orElse("Unknown");
        long childrenCount = handle.children().count();
        // Print the process details
        System.out.printf("PID: %d%n", pid);
        System.out.printf("IsAlive: %b%n", isAlive);
        System.out.printf("Command: %s%n", command);
        System.out.printf("Arguments: %s%n",
            Arrays.toString(args));
        System.out.printf("CommandLine: %s%n",
```

```
            commandLine);
        System.out.printf("Start Time: %s%n", startTime);
        System.out.printf("CPU Time: %s%n", duration);
        System.out.printf("Owner: %s%n", owner);
        System.out.printf("Children Count: %d%n",
            childrenCount);
    }
}
```

```
PID: 4143
IsAlive: true
Command: /opt/jdk17/bin/java
Arguments: [-Dfile.encoding=UTF-8,
    -classpath,
    [<path-to-project>]/bin,
    -XX:+ShowCodeDetailsInExceptionMessages,
    com.jdojo.process.CurrentProcessInfo]
CommandLine: /opt/openjdk-16.36/bin/java
    -Dfile.encoding=UTF-8
    -classpath [<path-to-project>]/bin
    -XX:+ShowCodeDetailsInExceptionMessages
    com.jdojo.process.CurrentProcessInfo
Start Time: 2021-07-16T14:50:18.870+02:00
    [Europe/Berlin]
CPU Time: PT0.06S
Owner: peter
Children Count: 0
```

Comparing Processes

It is tricky to compare two processes for equality or order. You cannot rely on PIDs for equality of processes. Operating systems reuse PIDs after processes terminate. You may check the start time of processes along with the PIDs; if they are the same, the two processes may be the same. The equals() method of the default implementation of the

ProcessHandle interface checks for the following three pieces of information for two processes to be equal:

- The implementation class of the ProcessHandle interface must be the same for both processes.

- Processes must have the same PIDs.

- Processes must have been started at the same time.

Note   Using the default implementation of the compareTo() method in the ProcessHandle interface is not very useful for ordering. It compares the PIDs of two processes.

Creating a Process

You need to use an instance of the ProcessBuilder class to start a new native process. A ProcessBuilder manages a collection of native process attributes. Once you set all the attributes for the process, you can call its start() method to start a new native process. The attributes stored in the ProcessBuilder will be used to start the new process. You can call the start() method multiple times to start new processes using the attributes stored in the ProcessBuilder. The start() method returns an instance of the Process class that represents the new native process. You can use one of the following constructors to create an instance of the ProcessBuilder class:

- ProcessBuilder(String... command)

- ProcessBuilder(List<String> command)

The constructors let you specify the operating system program and arguments. Suppose you want to run the java program from inside /opt/jdk17/bin on Linux as follows:

```
/opt/jdk17/bin/java --version
```

You would create a ProcessBuilder to represent this command as follows:

```
ProcessBuilder pb = new ProcessBuilder(
    "/opt/jdk17/bin/java", "--version");
```

Using methods of the `ProcessBuilder` class, you can manage the following attributes of a process:

- A command

- An environment

- A working directory

- Standard I/O (`stdin`, `stdout`, and `stderr`)

- Redirection property for the standard error stream

A command is simply a list of strings representing the external program and its arguments. You can set the command in the constructor of the `ProcessBuilder` class. The following methods let you retrieve the command strings and set more command strings:

- `List<String> command()`

- `ProcessBuilder command(String... command)`

The `command()` method without any arguments returns the command strings already set in the `ProcessBuilder`. The `command()` method with a varargs argument lets you add more command strings. The following snippet of code creates a `ProcessBuilder` to launch JVM on Linux. It uses the `command()` method to set the command attribute:

```
ProcessBuilder pb = new ProcessBuilder()
    .command("/opt/jdk17/bin/java",
        "--module-path",
        "myModulePath",
        "--module",
        "myModule/className");
```

An environment is a list of system-dependent key-value pairs. It is initialized to a copy of the `Map<String,String>` returned from the `System.getEnv()` static method. You need to use the `environment()` method of the `ProcessBuilder` class to get the `Map<String,String>` and add key-value pairs to the map. The following snippet of code shows you how to set the environment attributes for a `ProcessBuilder`:

```
ProcessBuilder pb = new ProcessBuilder("mycommand");
Map<String,String> env = pb.environment();
env.put("arg1", "value1");
env.put("arg2", "value2");
```

By default, the working directory for the new process would be the working directory of the current Java process, which is usually the directory named by the system property `user.dir`. The following methods in the `ProcessBuilder` class let you get and set the working directory:

- `File directory()`
- `ProcessBuilder directory(File directory)`

The following snippet of code shows you how to set the working directory to `/home/USER/mydir` on Linux:

```
ProcessBuilder pb = new ProcessBuilder("myCommand")
   .directory(new File("/home/USER/mydir"));
```

The new process created by the `start()` method of a `ProcessBuilder` is created as a child process of the current process, which is the Java process running the code. In other words, the current Java process is the parent process of the newly created process. The new process does not own a terminal or console for standard I/O (`stdin`, `stdout`, and `stderr`). By default, the I/O of the new process is connected to the parent process over a pipe. You have an option to set the standard I/O of the new process to the same as its parent process by calling the `inheritIO()` method of a `ProcessBuilder`. There are several `redirectXxx()` methods in the `ProcessBuilder` class to customize the standard I/O for the new process, for example, setting the standard error stream to a file, so all errors are logged to a file.

Once you have configured all attributes of the process, you can call `start()` to start the process:

```
// Start a new process
Process newProcess = pb.start();
```

You can call the `start()` method of the `ProcessBuilder` class multiple times to start multiple processes with the same attributes previously stored in it. This has a performance benefit that you can create one `ProcessBuilder` instance and reuse it to launch the same process multiple times.

You can obtain the process handle of a process using the `toHandle()` method of the `Process` class:

```
// Get the process handle
ProcessHandle handle = newProcess.toHandle();
```

You can use the process handle to destroy the process, wait for the process to finish, or query the process for its state and attributes such as its children, descendants, parents, CPU time used, etc. The information you get about a process and the control you have on a process depend on the operating system access controls.

It is tricky to come up with examples to create processes that will run on all operating systems. If you can run other examples in this book, it means that you have JDK17 installed on your machine. You can use the `java` program on your machine to launch other processes in the examples. You can use the command attribute of the current process, which is the current running `java` program, to get the path of the Java program on your machine, so the examples will work on all platforms.

Let's look at a few examples of creating native processes using the Java program. You can print the Java product version information to the standard output and standard error using the `--version` and `-version` options, respectively, as follows:

```
/opt/jdk17/bin/java --version
openjdk 17 2021-05-16
OpenJDK Runtime Environment (build 17+1-123)
OpenJDK 64-Bit Server VM (build 17+1-123, mixed mode, sharing)

/opt/jdk17/bin/java -version
openjdk 17 2021-05-16
OpenJDK Runtime Environment (build 17+1-123)
OpenJDK 64-Bit Server VM (build 17+1-123, mixed mode, sharing)
```

In the previous outputs, you do not see any difference as to where the output was printed. Both outputs are printed to the same console because, by default, both standard output and standard error are mapped to the console. However, you will see the difference when you try capturing the outputs from these two commands in a program.

Listing 11-4 shows a program that runs the `java -version` command to print the Java product information to the standard output.

Listing 11-4. Capturing the Output of a Native Process

```java
// PipedIO.java
package com.jdojo.process;
import java.io.IOException;
public class PipedIO {
    public static void main(String[] args) {
```

```java
        // Get the path of the java program that started
        // this program
        String javaPath = ProcessHandle.current()
            .info()
            .command().orElse(null);
        if(javaPath == null) {
            System.out.println(
                "Could not get the java command's path.");
            return;
        }
        // Configure the ProcessBuilder
        ProcessBuilder pb =
            new ProcessBuilder(javaPath,  "--version");
        try {
            // Start a new java process
            Process p = pb.start();
        } catch (IOException e) {
            e.printStackTrace();
        }
    }
}
```

When you run the program ProcessIO class, it does not print anything. Where did the output go? The program created a new process, and the standard output of the process was connected to the parent process over a pipe. If you want to access the output, you need to read from the appropriate pipe. When the standard I/O of the new process is piped to the parent process, you can use the following methods of the Process to get the I/O streams of the new process:

- OutputStream getOutputStream()

- InputStream getInputStream()

- InputStream getErrorStream()

The OutputStream returned from the getOutputStream() method is connected to the standard input stream of the new process. Writing to this output stream will be piped to the standard input of the new process.

The InputStream returned from the getInputStream() is connected to the standard output of the new process. If you want to capture the standard output of the new process, you need to read from this input stream.

The InputStream returned from the getErrorStream() is connected to the standard error of the new process. If you want to capture the standard error of the new process, you need to read from this input stream. Sometimes, you want to merge the output to the standard output and standard error into one destination. It gives the exact sequence of output and the error for easier troubleshooting issues. You can call the redirectErrorStream(true) method of the ProcessBuilder to send the data written to the standard error to the standard output. I show examples of this kind shortly.

Note   You have options to redirect the standard I/O of a new process to other destinations such as a file, and in that case, the getOutputStream(), getInputStream(), and getErrorStream() methods return null.

The program in Listing 11-5 fixes the problem of not getting any output in the PipedIO class. It reads and prints the data written to the standard output stream in the pipe.

Listing 11-5. Capturing the Output of a Native Process

```
// CapturePipedIO.java
package com.jdojo.process;
import java.io.BufferedReader;
import java.io.IOException;
import java.io.InputStreamReader;
public class CapturePipedIO {
    public static void main(String[] args) {
        // Get the path of the java program that started
        // this program
        String javaPath = ProcessHandle.current()
                .info()
                .command().orElse(null);
        if (javaPath == null) {
            System.out.println(
```

```
                    "Could not get the java command's path.");
            return;
        }
        // Configure the ProcessBuilder
        ProcessBuilder pb =
            new ProcessBuilder(javaPath, "--version");
        try {
            // Start a new java process
            Process p = pb.start();
            // Read and print the standard output stream
            // of the process
            try (BufferedReader input =
                    new BufferedReader(
                        new InputStreamReader(
                            p.getInputStream()))) {
                String line;
                while ((line = input.readLine()) != null) {
                    System.out.println(line);
                }
            }
        } catch (IOException e) {
            e.printStackTrace();
        }
    }
}
```

```
openjdk 17 2021-05-16
OpenJDK Runtime Environment (build 17+1-123)
OpenJDK 64-Bit Server VM (build 17+1-123, mixed mode, sharing)
```

If you run the java command with a -version option, the output is written to the standard error. If you change the option from –version to -version in Listing 11-5, you will not get any output again because the output will be piped to the standard error stream. You have two ways to fix this:

- In the program, read from the InputStream returned from the getErrorStream() method of the Process instead of the InputStream from the getInputStream() method.

- Redirect the error stream to the standard output stream and keep reading from the standard output.

The following snippet of code creates a ProcessBuilder with the java -version command and redirects the error stream in the standard output:

```
// Configure the ProcessBuilder
ProcessBuilder pb =
    new ProcessBuilder(javaPath, "-version")
    .redirectErrorStream(true);
```

If you change the statement that creates the ProcessBuilder in Listing 11-5 to this statement, your program will work fine.

A new process can also inherit the standard I/O of the parent process. If you want to set all I/O destinations of the new process to the same as the current process, use the inheritIO() method of the ProcessBuilder, as shown:

```
// Configure the ProcessBuilder inheriting parent's I/O
ProcessBuilder pb =
    new ProcessBuilder(javaPath,  "--version")
    .inheritIO();
```

If you change the code in Listing 11-4 to match the previous snippet of code, you will see the output.

The ProcessBuilder.Redirect nested class represents the source of the input and destination of the outputs of the new process created by the ProcessBuilder. The class defined the following three constants of the ProcessBuilder.Redirect type:

- ProcessBuilder.Redirect DISCARD: Discards the outputs of the new process

- ProcessBuilder.Redirect.INHERIT: Indicates that the input source or output destination of the new process will be the same as that of the current process

- ProcessBuilder.Redirect.PIPE: Indicates that the new process will be connected to the current process over a pipe, which is the default

You can also redirect the input and outputs of the new process to a file using the following methods of the Process.Redirect class:

- ProcessBuilder.Redirect appendTo(File file)

- ProcessBuilder.Redirect from(File file)

- ProcessBuilder.Redirect to(File file)

In the previous snippet of code, you saw how to use the inheritIO() method of the ProcessBuilder class to let the new process have the same standard I/O as the current process. You can rewrite that code as follows:

```
// Configure the ProcessBuilder inheriting parent's I/O
ProcessBuilder pb =
    new ProcessBuilder(javaPath, "--version")
        .redirectInput(ProcessBuilder.Redirect.INHERIT)
        .redirectOutput(ProcessBuilder.Redirect.INHERIT)
        .redirectError(ProcessBuilder.Redirect.INHERIT);
```

The following snippet of code redirects the standard output of the new process to a file named java_product_details.txt in the current directory:

```
// Configure the ProcessBuilder
  ProcessBuilder pb =
      new ProcessBuilder(javaPath, "--version")
      .redirectOutput(
          ProcessBuilder.Redirect.to(
              new File("java_product_details.txt")));
```

Let's look at a little complex example that will explore more information about new native processes. Listing 11-6 contains the code for a class named Job. Its main() method expects two arguments: sleep interval and sleep duration in seconds. If they are not passed, the method uses 5 seconds and 60 seconds as the default values. In the first part, the method attempts to extract first and second arguments, if specified. In the second part, it gets the process handle of the current process executing this method using the ProcessHandle.current() method. It reads the PID of the current process and prints a message including the PID, sleep interval, and sleep duration. In the end, it starts a for loop and keeps sleeping for the sleep interval until the sleep duration is reached. In every iteration of the loop, it prints a message.

Listing 11-6. The Declaration of a Class Named Job

```java
// Job.java
package com.jdojo.process;
import java.io.IOException;
import java.util.ArrayList;
import java.util.List;
import java.util.concurrent.TimeUnit;
import java.util.stream.Collectors;
/**
 * An instance of this class is used as a job that sleeps
 * at a regular interval up to a maximum duration. The
 * sleep interval in seconds can be specified as the first
 * argument and the sleep duration as the second argument
 * while running this class. The default sleep interval
 * and sleep duration are 5 seconds and 60 seconds,
 * respectively. If these values are less than zero, zero
 * is used instead.
 */
public class Job {
    // The job sleep interval
    public static final long DEFAULT_SLEEP_INTERVAL = 5;
    // The job sleep duration
    public static final long DEFAULT_SLEEP_DURATION = 60;
    public static void main(String[] args) {
        long sleepInterval = DEFAULT_SLEEP_INTERVAL;
        long sleepDuration = DEFAULT_SLEEP_DURATION;
        // Get the passed in sleep interval
        if (args.length >= 1) {
            sleepInterval = parseArg(args[0],
                DEFAULT_SLEEP_INTERVAL);
            if (sleepInterval < 0) {
                sleepInterval = 0;
            }
        }
```

```
    // Get the passed in the sleep duration
    if (args.length >= 2) {
        sleepDuration = parseArg(args[1],
            DEFAULT_SLEEP_DURATION);
        if (sleepDuration < 0) {
            sleepDuration = 0;
        }
    }
    long pid = ProcessHandle.current().pid();
    System.out.printf(
        "Job (pid=%d) info: Sleep Interval"
        + "=%d seconds, Sleep Duration=%d "
        + "seconds.%n",
        pid, sleepInterval, sleepDuration);
    for (long sleptFor = 0; sleptFor < sleepDuration;
            sleptFor += sleepInterval) {
        try {
            System.out.printf(
                "Job (pid=%d) is going to"
                + " sleep for %d seconds.%n",
                pid, sleepInterval);
            // Sleep for the sleep interval
            TimeUnit.SECONDS.sleep(sleepInterval);
        } catch (InterruptedException ex) {
            System.out.printf("Job (pid=%d) was "
                    + "interrupted.%n", pid);
        }
    }
}
/**
 * Starts a new JVM to run the Job class.
 *
 * @param sleepInterval The sleep interval when the
 *   Job class is run. It is passed to the JVM as the
 *   first argument.
```

```
 * @param sleepDuration The sleep duration for the
 *    Job class. It is passed to the JVM as the
 *    second argument.
 * @return The new process reference of the newly
 * launched JVM or null if the JVM
 * cannot be launched.
 */
public static Process startProcess(long sleepInterval,
        long sleepDuration) {
    // Store the command to launch a new JVM in a
    // List<String>
    List<String> cmd = new ArrayList<>();
    // Add command components in order
    addJvmPath(cmd);
    addModulePath(cmd);
    addClassPath(cmd);
    addMainClass(cmd);
    // Add arguments to run the class
    cmd.add(String.valueOf(sleepInterval));
    cmd.add(String.valueOf(sleepDuration));
    // Build the process attributes
    ProcessBuilder pb = new ProcessBuilder()
            .command(cmd)
            .inheritIO();
    String commandLine = pb.command()
            .stream()
            .collect(Collectors.joining(" "));
    System.out.println(
        "Command used:\n" + commandLine);
    // Start the process
    Process p = null;
    try {
        p = pb.start();
    } catch (IOException e) {
        e.printStackTrace();
    }
```

```java
        return p;
    }
    /**
     * Used to parse the arguments passed to the JVM,
     * which in turn is passed to the main() method.
     *
     * @param valueStr The string value of the argument
     * @param defaultValue The default value of the
     *    argument if the valueStr is not an integer.
     * @return valueStr as a long or the defaultValue if
     * valueStr is not an integer.
     */
    private static long parseArg(String valueStr,
            long defaultValue) {
        long value = defaultValue;
        if (valueStr != null) {
            try {
                value = Long.parseLong(valueStr);
            } catch (NumberFormatException e) {
                // no action needed
            }
        }
        return value;
    }
    /**
     * Adds the JVM path to the command list. It first
     * attempts to use the command attribute of the
     * current process; failing that it relies on the
     * java.home system property.
     *
     * @param cmd The command list
     */
    private static void addJvmPath(List<String> cmd) {
        // First try getting the command to run the
        // current JVM
```

```
            String jvmPath = ProcessHandle.current()
                .info()
                .command().orElse("");
            if (jvmPath.length() > 0) {
                cmd.add(jvmPath);
            } else {
                // Try composing the JVM path using the
                // java.home system property
                final String FILE_SEPARATOR =
                    System.getProperty("file.separator");
                jvmPath = System.getProperty("java.home")
                        + FILE_SEPARATOR + "bin"
                        + FILE_SEPARATOR + "java";
                cmd.add(jvmPath);
            }
        }
        /**
         * Adds a module path to the command list.
         *
         * @param cmd The command list
         */
        private static void addModulePath(List<String> cmd) {
            String modulePath
                = System.getProperty("jdk.module.path");
            if (modulePath != null
                    && modulePath.trim().length() > 0) {
                cmd.add("--module-path");
                cmd.add(modulePath);
            }
        }
        /**
         * Adds class path to the command list.
         *
         * @param cmd The command list
         */
```

```java
private static void addClassPath(List<String> cmd) {
    String classPath =
        System.getProperty("java.class.path");
    if (classPath != null
            && classPath.trim().length() > 0) {
        cmd.add("--class-path");
        cmd.add(classPath);
    }
}
/**
 * Adds a main class to the command list. Adds
 * module/className or just className depending on
 * whether the Job class was loaded in a named
 * module or unnamed module
 *
 * @param cmd The command list
 */
private static void addMainClass(List<String> cmd) {
    Class<Job> cls = Job.class;
    String className = cls.getName();
    Module module = cls.getModule();
    if (module.isNamed()) {
        String moduleName = module.getName();
        cmd.add("--module");
        cmd.add(moduleName + "/" + className);
    } else {
        cmd.add(className);
    }
}
}
```

The Job class contains a startProcess(long sleepInterval, long sleepDuration) method that starts a new process. It launches a JVM with the Job class as the main class. It passes the sleep interval and duration to the JVM as arguments. The method attempts to build a command to launch the java command from the JDK_HOME\bin directory. If the Job class were loaded in a named module, it would build a command like this:

```
JDK_HOME/bin/java --module-path <module-path> \
--module jdojo.process/com.jdojo.process.Job \
<sleepInterval> <sleepDuration>
```

If the Job class were loaded in an unnamed module, it would attempt to build a command like this:

```
JDK_HOME/bin/java \
-class-path <class-path> \
com.jdojo.process.Job \
<sleepInterval> <sleepDuration>
```

The startProcess() method prints the command used to start a process, attempts to start the process, and returns the process reference.

The addJvmPath() method adds the JVM path to the command list. It attempts to get the command for the current JVM process to use as the JVM path for the new process. If it is not available, it attempts to build it from the java.home system property.

The Job class contains several utility methods that are used to compose parts of commands and parse the arguments passed to the main() method. Refer to their Javadoc for descriptions.

If you want to start a new process that should run for 15 seconds and wake up every 5 seconds, you can do so using the startProcess() method of the Job class:

```
// Start a process that runs for 15 seconds
Process p = Job.startProcess(5, 15);
```

You can print the process details using the printInfo() method of the CurrentProcessInfo class that you created in Listing 11-3:

```
// Get the handle of the current process
ProcessHandle handle = p.toHandle();
// Print the process details
CurrentProcessInfo.printInfo(handle);
```

You can use the returned value of the onExit() method of the ProcessHandle to run a task when the process terminates:

```
CompletableFuture<ProcessHandle> future = handle.onExit();
// Print a message when process terminates
future.thenAccept((ProcessHandle ph) -> {
    System.out.printf(
        "Job (pid=%d) terminated.%n", ph.pid());
});
```

You can wait for the new process to terminate like so:

```
// Wait for the process to terminate
future.get();
```

In this example, future.get() will return the ProcessHandle of the process. I did not use the return value, because I already had it in the handle variable.

Listing 11-7 contains the code for a StartProcessTest class that shows you how to create a new process using the Job class. In its main() method, it creates a new process, prints process details, adds a shutdown task to the process, waits for the process to terminate, and prints the process details again. Note that the process runs for 15 seconds, but it uses only 0.359375 seconds of CPU time because most of the time the main thread of the process was sleeping. You may get a different output. The output was generated when the program ran on Linux.

Listing 11-7. A StartProcessTest Class That Creates New Processes

```
// StartProcessTest.java
package com.jdojo.process;
import java.util.concurrent.CompletableFuture;
import java.util.concurrent.ExecutionException;
public class StartProcessTest {
    public static void main(String[] args) {
        // Start a process that runs for 15 seconds
        Process p = Job.startProcess(5, 15);
        if (p == null) {
            System.out.println(
                "Could not create a new process.");
```

```
            return;
        }
        // Get the handle of the current process
        ProcessHandle handle = p.toHandle();
        // Print the process details
        CurrentProcessInfo.printInfo(handle);
        CompletableFuture<ProcessHandle> future =
            handle.onExit();
        // Print a message when process terminates
        future.thenAccept((ProcessHandle ph) -> {
            System.out.printf(
                "Job (pid=%d) terminated.%n",
                ph.pid());
        });
        try {
            // Wait for the process to complete
            future.get();
        } catch (InterruptedException
                | ExecutionException e) {
            e.printStackTrace();
        }
        // Print process details again
        CurrentProcessInfo.printInfo(handle);
    }
}
```

Command used:
/opt/jdk17/bin/java
  --class-path /[<path-to-project>]/bin
  com.jdojo.process.Job 5 15
PID: 8701
IsAlive: true
Command: /opt/jdk17/bin/java
Arguments: [
  --class-path,

```
  /[<path-to-project>]/bin,
  com.jdojo.process.Job,
  5, 15 ]
CommandLine: /opt/jdk17/bin/java
  --class-path /[<path-to-project>]/bin
  com.jdojo.process.Job
  5 15
Start Time: 2021-07-16T18:11:42.510+02:00
  [Europe/Berlin]
CPU Time: PT0.01S
Owner: peter
Children Count: 0
Job (pid=8701) info:
  Sleep Interval=5 seconds, Sleep Duration=15 seconds.
Job (pid=8701) is going to sleep for 5 seconds.
Job (pid=8701) is going to sleep for 5 seconds.
Job (pid=8701) is going to sleep for 5 seconds.
Job (pid=8701) terminated.
PID: 8701
IsAlive: false
Command:
Arguments: []
CommandLine:
Start Time: 2021-07-16T18:11:58.489975569+02:00
  [Europe/Berlin]
CPU Time: PT0S
Owner: Unknown
Children Count: 0
```

Obtaining a Process Handle

There are several ways to get the handle of a native process. For a process created by the Java code, you can get a ProcessHandle using the toHandle() method of the Process class. Native processes can also be created from outside the JVM. The ProcessHandle interface contains the following methods to get the handle of a native process:

- static Optional<ProcessHandle> of(long pid)

- static ProcessHandle current()

- Optional<ProcessHandle> parent()

- Stream<ProcessHandle> children()

- Stream<ProcessHandle> descendants()

- static Stream<ProcessHandle> allProcesses()

The of() static method returns an Optional<ProcessHandle> for the specified pid. If there is no process with this pid, an empty Optional is returned. To use this method, you need to know the PID of the process:

```
// Get the process handle of the process with the pid
// of 1234
Optional<ProcessHandle> handle = ProcessHandle.of(1234L);
```

The current() static method returns the handle of the current process, which is always the Java process executing the code. You have already seen an example of this in Listing 11-3.

The parent() method returns the handle of the parent process. It returns an empty Optional if the process does not have a parent or parent cannot be retrieved.

The children() method returns a snapshot of all direct child processes of the process. There is no guarantee that a process returned by this method is still alive. Note that a process that's not alive does not have children.

The descendants() method returns a snapshot of all child processes of the process, direct or indirect.

The allProcesses() method returns a snapshot of all processes that are visible to this process. There is no guarantee that the stream contains all process in the operating system at the time the stream is processed. Processes may have been terminated or created after the snapshot was taken. The following snippet of code prints the PIDs of all processes sorted by their PIDs:

```
System.out.printf("All processes PIDs:%n");
ProcessHandle.allProcesses()
    .map(ph -> ph.pid())
    .sorted()
    .forEach(System.out::println);
```

You can compute different types of statistics for all running processes. You can also create a task manager in Java that displays a UI showing all running processes and their attributes. Listing 11-8 shows how to get the longest running process details and the process that used the CPU time the most. I compared the start time of the processes to get the longest running process and the total CPU duration to get the process that used the CPU time the most. You may get a different output. I got this output when I ran the program on Linux.

Listing 11-8. Computing Process Statistics

```
// ProcessStats.java
package com.jdojo.process;
import java.time.Duration;
import java.time.Instant;
public class ProcessStats {
    public static void main(String[] args) {
        System.out.printf("Longest CPU User Process:%n");
        ProcessHandle.allProcesses()
                .max(ProcessStats::compareCpuTime)
                .ifPresent(CurrentProcessInfo::printInfo);
        System.out.printf("%nLongest Running Process:%n");
        ProcessHandle.allProcesses()
                .max(ProcessStats::compareStartTime)
                .ifPresent(CurrentProcessInfo::printInfo);
    }
    public static int compareCpuTime(ProcessHandle ph1,
            ProcessHandle ph2) {
        return ph1.info()
```

```
                .totalCpuDuration()
                .orElse(Duration.ZERO)
                .compareTo(ph2.info()
                        .totalCpuDuration()
                        .orElse(Duration.ZERO));
    }
    public static int
    compareStartTime(ProcessHandle ph1,
            ProcessHandle ph2) {
        return ph1.info()
                .startInstant()
                .orElse(Instant.now())
                .compareTo(ph2.info()
                        .startInstant()
                        .orElse(Instant.now()));
    }
}
```

```
Longest CPU User Process:
PID: 2323
IsAlive: true
Command: /usr/lib/tracker/tracker-miner-fs
Arguments: []
CommandLine: /usr/lib/tracker/tracker-miner-fs
Start Time: 2021-07-16T13:43:03.590+02:00[Europe/Berlin]
CPU Time: PT14M35.72S
Owner: peter
Children Count: 0

Longest Running Process:
PID: 9019
IsAlive: true
Command: /opt/openjdk-16.36/bin/java
Arguments: [
  -Dfile.encoding=UTF-8,
  -classpath,
```

```
  [...],
  -XX:+ShowCodeDetailsInExceptionMessages,
  com.jdojo.process.ProcessStats]
CommandLine: /opt/jdk17/bin/java
  -Dfile.encoding=UTF-8
  -classpath [...]
  -XX:+ShowCodeDetailsInExceptionMessages
  com.jdojo.process.ProcessStats
Start Time: 2021-07-16T19:02:01.020+02:00[Europe/Berlin]
CPU Time: PT0.3S
Owner: peter
Children Count: 0
```

Terminating Processes

You can terminate a process using the destroy() or destroyForcibly() method of the ProcessHandle interface and the Process class. Both methods return true if the request to terminate the process was successful, false otherwise. The destroy() method requests a normal termination, whereas the destroyForcibly() method requests a forced termination. It is possible for the isAlive() method to return true for a brief period after a request to terminate the process has been made.

Note   You cannot terminate the current process. Calling the destroy() or the destroyForcibly() method on the current process throws an IllegalStateException. The operating system access controls may prevent a process from being terminated.

A normal termination of a process lets the process terminate cleanly. A forced termination of a process terminates the process immediately. Whether a process is normally terminated is implementation dependent. You can use the supportsNormalTermination() method of the ProcessHandle interface and the Process class to check if a process supports normal termination. The method returns true if the process supports normal termination, false otherwise.

Calling one of these methods to terminate a process that has already been terminated results in no action. The `CompletableFuture<Process>` returned from `onExit()` of the `Process` class and the `CompletableFuture<ProcessHandle>` returned from `onExit()` of the `ProcessHandle` interface are `completed` when the process terminates.

Managing Process Permissions

When you ran the examples in the previous sections, I assumed that there was no Java security manager installed. If a security manager is installed, appropriate permissions need to be granted to start, manage, and query native processes:

- If you are creating a new process, you need to have `FilePermission(cmd,"execute")` permission, where `cmd` is the absolute path of the command that will create the process. If `cmd` is not an absolute path, you need to have `FilePermission("<<ALL FILES>>","execute")` permission.

- To query the state of native processes and destroy the process using the methods in the `ProcessHandle` interface, the application needs to have `RuntimePermission("manageProcess")` permission.

Listing 11-9 contains a program that gets a process count and creates a new process. It repeats these two tasks without a security manager and with a security manager.

Listing 11-9. Managing Processes with a Security Manager

```
// ManageProcessPermission.java
package com.jdojo.process;
import java.util.concurrent.ExecutionException;
public class ManageProcessPermission {
    public static void main(String[] args) {
        // Get the process count
        long count = ProcessHandle.allProcesses().count();
        System.out.printf("Process Count: %d%n", count);
        // Start a new process
        Process p = Job.startProcess(1, 3);
        try {
            p.toHandle().onExit().get();
```

```
        } catch (InterruptedException
                | ExecutionException e) {
            System.out.println(e.getMessage());
        }
        // Install a security manager
        SecurityManager sm = System.getSecurityManager();
        if (sm == null) {
            System.setSecurityManager(
                new SecurityManager());
            System.out.println(
                "A security manager is installed.");
        }
        // Get the process count
        try {
            count = ProcessHandle.allProcesses().count();
            System.out.printf("Process Count: %d%n",
                count);
        } catch (RuntimeException e) {
            System.out.println(
                "Could not get a process count: " +
                e.getMessage());
        }
        // Start a new process
        try {
            p = Job.startProcess(1, 3);
            p.toHandle().onExit().get();
        } catch (InterruptedException
                | ExecutionException
                | RuntimeException e) {
            System.out.println(
                "Could not start a new process: " +
                e.getMessage());
        }
    }
}
```

Try running the ManageProcessPermission class using the following command assuming that you have not changed any Java policy files:

```
/opt/jdk17/bin/java \
-Dfile.encoding=UTF-8 \
-classpath /[<path-to-project>]/bin \
-XX:+ShowCodeDetailsInExceptionMessages \
com.jdojo.process.ManageProcessPermission
```

```
Process Count: 332
Command used:
/opt/jd17/bin/java
  --class-path [...] com.jdojo.process.Job 1 3
Job (pid=3858) info: Sleep Interval=1 seconds,
  Sleep Duration=3 seconds.
Job (pid=3858) is going to sleep for 1 seconds.
Job (pid=3858) is going to sleep for 1 seconds.
Job (pid=3858) is going to sleep for 1 seconds.
A security manager is installed.
Could not get a process count: access denied
    ("java.lang.RuntimePermission" "manageProcess")
Could not start a new process: access denied
    ("java.lang.RuntimePermission" "manageProcess")
```

You may get a different output. The output indicates that you were able to get the process count and create a new process before a security manager was installed. After the security manager was installed, the Java runtime threw exceptions while requesting the process count and creating a new process. To fix the problem, you need to grant the following permissions:

- The "manageProcess" RuntimePermission, which will allow the application to query the native process and create a new process

- The "execute" FilePermission on the Java command path, which will allow launching the JVM

- The "read" PropertyPermission on the "jdk.module.path" and "java.class.path" system properties, so the Job class can read these properties while building the command line to launch the JVM

Listing 11-10 contains a script to grant these four permissions to all code. You need to add this script to the JDK_HOME/conf/security/java.policy file on your machine. The path to the Java launcher is /opt/jdk17/bin/java, and it is valid on Linux only if you have installed JDK17 in the /opt/jdk17 directory. For all other platforms and JDK installations, modify this path to point to the correct Java launcher on your machine.

Listing 11-10. Addendum to the JDK_HOME/conf/security/java.policy File

```
grant {
    permission java.lang.RuntimePermission
        "manageProcess";
    permission java.io.FilePermission
        "/opt/jdk17/bin/java", "execute";
    permission java.util.PropertyPermission
        "jdk.module.path", "read";
    permission java.util.PropertyPermission
        "java.class.path", "read";
};
```

If you run the ManageProcessPermission class again using the same command, you should get output similar to the following:

```
/opt/jdk17/bin/java \
  -Dfile.encoding=UTF-8 \
  -classpath /[<path-to-project>]/bin \
  -XX:+ShowCodeDetailsInExceptionMessages \
  com.jdojo.process.ManageProcessPermission

Process Count: 330
Command used:
/opt/jdk17/bin/java
  --class-path [...]
  com.jdojo.process.Job 1 3
Job (pid=6093) info: Sleep Interval=1 seconds,
  Sleep Duration=3 seconds.
Job (pid=6093) is going to sleep for 1 seconds.
```

```
Job (pid=6093) is going to sleep for 1 seconds.
Job (pid=6093) is going to sleep for 1 seconds.

A security manager is installed.

Process Count: 330
Command used:
/opt/jdk17/bin/java
  --class-path [...]
  com.jdojo.process.Job 1 3
Job (pid=6114) info: Sleep Interval=1 seconds,
  Sleep Duration=3 seconds.
Job (pid=6114) is going to sleep for 1 seconds.
Job (pid=6114) is going to sleep for 1 seconds.
Job (pid=6114) is going to sleep for 1 seconds.
```

Summary

The Process API consists of classes and interfaces to work with native processes. Java SE has provided the Process API since version 1.0 through the Runtime and Process classes. It allowed you to create new native processes, manage their I/O streams, and destroy them. Later versions of Java SE improved the API, with an interface named ProcessHandle that represents a process handle. You can use the process handle to query and manage a native process.

The following classes and interfaces comprise the Process API: Runtime, ProcessBuilder, ProcessBuilder.Redirect, Process, ProcessHandle, and ProcessHandle.Info.

The exec() method of the Runtime class is used to start a native process. The start() method of the ProcessBuilder class is preferred over the exec() method of the Runtime class to start a process. An instance of the ProcessBuilder.Redirect class represents a source of input of a process or a destination output of a process.

By default, the standard I/O of the new process is connected to the current process over a pipe. You need to read and write the streams associated with the pipe to access the standard I/O of the new process. You have options to set the standard I/O of the new process to the same as that of the current process or redirect the I/O to other sources/ destinations such as a file.

An instance of the `Process` class represents a native process created by a Java program.

An instance of the `ProcessHandle` interface represents a process created by a Java program or by other means; it was added in Java 9 and provides several methods to query and manage processes. An instance of the `ProcessHandle.Info` interface represents snapshot information of a process; it can be obtained using the `info()` method of the `Process` class or `ProcessHandle` interface. If you have a `Process` instance, use its `toHandle()` method to get a `ProcessHandle`.

The `onExit()` method of the `ProcessHandle` interface returns a `CompletableFuture <ProcessHandle>` for the termination of the process. You can use the returned object to add a task that will be executed when the process terminates. Note that you cannot use this method on the current process.

If a security manager is installed, the application needs to have a `"manageProcess"` `RuntimePermission` to query and manage native processes and an `"execute"` `FilePermission` on the command file of the process that is started from the Java code.

Exercises

Exercise 1

What is the Process API?

Exercise 2

What does an instance of the `Runtime` class represent?

Exercise 3

How do you get an instance of the `Runtime` class?

Exercise 4

How do you use the `ProcessBuilder` class? What method of this class is used to start a new native process?

Exercise 5

What does an instance of the `Process` class represent?

Exercise 6

What does an instance of the `ProcessHandle` interface represent? How do you obtain a `ProcessHandle` from a `Process`?

Exercise 7

How do you get the handle of the current process representing the running Java program?

Exercise 8

What does an instance of the `ProcessHandle.Info` interface represent?

Exercise 9

What is the default standard I/O of the new process created by the `start()` method of the `ProcessBuilder` class?

Exercise 10

Can you terminate the current Java program using the Process API?

CHAPTER 12

Packaging Modules

In this chapter, you will learn:

- Different formats for packaging Java modules

- Enhancements to the JAR format

- What a multi-release JAR is

- How to create and use multi-release JARs

- What the JMOD format is

- How to use the `jmod` tool to work with JMOD files

- How to create, extract, and describe JMOD files

- How to list the contents of JMOD files

- How to record hashes of modules in JMOD files for dependency validation

A module can be packaged in different formats to be used in three phases: compile time, link time, and runtime. Not all formats are supported in all phases. Java supports the following formats to package modules:

- Exploded directory

- JAR format

- JMOD format

- JIMAGE format

Exploded directories and JAR format were supported before JDK9. The JAR format has been enhanced in JDK9 to support modular JARs and multi-release JARs. JDK9 introduced two new formats for packaging modules: JMOD format and JIMAGE format. I discuss the enhancements to the JAR format and the JMOD format in this chapter. Chapter 13 covers the JIMAGE format along with the `jlink` tool in detail.

© Kishori Sharan, Peter Späth 2021
K. Sharan and P. Späth, *More Java 17*, https://doi.org/10.1007/978-1-4842-7135-3_12

The JAR Format

We did not yet talk about non-modular and modular JARs in this book. However, both variants belong to a rather introductory style book, so we ask the reader to consult Oracle's Java documentation and the command help (entering `jar -h`) if more information about standard or modular JARs is needed.

In this chapter, I cover a new feature added to the JAR format, which is called a multi-release JAR.

What Is a Multi-release JAR?

As an experienced Java developer, you must have used a Java library/framework such as the Spring framework, Hibernate, etc. You may be using Java 17, but those libraries may be still using Java 8. Why can't the library developers use the latest version to take advantage of the JDK's new features? One of the reasons is that not all library users use the latest JDK. Updating a library to use the newer version of the JDK means forcing all library users to migrate to that newer JDK, which is not possible in practice. Maintaining and releasing a library targeting different JDKs is another pain when packaging the code. Typically, you will find a separate library JAR for different JDKs. Java solves this problem by offering library developers a particular way of packaging a library's code—using a single JAR containing the same release of a library for multiple JDKs. Such a JAR is called a *multi-release JAR*.

A multi-release JAR (MRJAR) contains the same release of a library (offering the same APIs) for multiple JDK versions. That is, you can have a library as a MRJAR that will work for JDK8 and JDK17. The code in the MRJAR will contain the class files compiled in JDK8 and JDK17. The classes compiled with JDK17 may take advantage of the APIs offered by JDK9 and later, whereas the classes compiled with JDK8 may offer the same library APIs written using JDK8.

A MRJAR extends the already existing directory structure for a JAR. A JAR contains a root directory where all its contents reside. It contains a `META-INF` directory that is used to store metadata about the JAR. Typically, a JAR contains a `META-INF/MANIFEST.MF` file containing its attributes. Entries in a typical JAR look like this:

```
- jar-root
  - C1.class
  - C2.class
```

```
    - C3.class
    - C4.class
  - META-INF
    - MANIFEST.MF
```

The JAR contains four class files and a MANIFEST.MF file. A MRJAR extends the META-INF directory to store classes that are specific to a JDK version. The META-INF directory contains a versions sub-directory, which may contain many sub-directories—each of them named the same as the JDK major version. For example, for classes specific to JDK17, there may be the META-INF/versions/17 directory, and for classes specific to JDK16, there may be a directory called META-INF/versions/16, etc. A typical MRJAR may have the following entries:

```
- jar-root
  - C1.class
  - C2.class
  - C3.class
  - C4.class
- META-INF
  - MANIFEST.MF
  - versions
    - 16
      - C2.class
      - C5.class
    - 17
      - C1.class
      - C2.class
      - C6.class
```

If this MRJAR is used in an environment that does not support MRJARs, it will be treated as a regular JAR—the contents in the root directory will be used, and all other contents in META-INF/versions/17 and META-INF/versions/16 will be ignored. So, if this MRJAR is used with JDK8, only four classes will be used: C1, C2, C3, and C4.

When this MRJAR is used in JDK16, five classes are in play: C1, C2, C3, C4, and C5. The C2 class in the META-INF/versions/9 directory will be used instead of the C2 class from the root directory. In this case, the MRJAR is saying that it has a newer version of the C2 class for JDK16 that overrides the version of C2 in the root directory that is for JDK8 or earlier. The JDK16 version also adds a new class named C5.

With a similar argument, the MRJAR overrides classes C1 and C2 and contains a new class named C6 for the JDK version 17.

Targeting multiple JDK versions in a single MRJAR, the search process in a MRJAR is different from a regular JAR. The search for a resource or class file in a MRJAR uses the following rules:

- The major version of the JDK is determined for the environment in which the MRJAR is being used. Suppose the major version of the JDK is N.

- To locate a resource or a class file named R, the platform-specific sub-directory under the META-INF/versions directory is searched starting at the directory for version N.

- If R is found in sub-directory N, it is returned. Otherwise, sub-directories for versions lower than N are searched. This process continues for all sub-directories under the META-INF/versions directory.

- When R is not found in the META-INF/versions/N sub-directories, the root directory of the MRJAR is searched for R.

Let's take an example using the previously shown structure of the MRJAR. Suppose the program is looking for C3.class and the current version of the JDK is 17. The search will start at META-INF/versions/17, where C3.class is not found. The search continues in META-INF/versions/16, where C3.class is not found. Now the search continues in the root directory, where C3.class is found.

As another example, suppose you want to find C2.class when the JDK version is 17. The search starts at META-INF/versions/17, where C2.class is found and returned.

As another example, suppose you want to find C2.class when the JDK version is 16. The search starts at META-INF/versions/16, where C2.class is found and returned.

As another example, suppose you want to find C2.class when the JDK version is 8. There is no JDK8-specific directory named META-INF/versions/8. So, the search starts at the root directory, where C2.class is found and returned.

Note All tools that process JARs—such as `java`, `javac`, and `javap`—are capable of working with multi-release JARs. APIs dealing with JARs also know how to deal with multi-release JARs.

Creating Multi-release JARs

Once you know the search order of the directories in a MRJAR when a resource or class file is searched on a specific JDK version, it is easy to understand how classes and resources are found. There are some rules on the contents of JDK version–specific directories. I describe those rules in subsequent sections. In this section, I focus on creating MRJARs.

To run this example, you need JDK8 and JDK17 installed on your machine.

I use a MRJAR to store the JDK8 and JDK17 versions of an application. The application consists of the following two classes:

- `com.jdojo.mrjar.Main`

- `com.jdojo.mrjar.TimeUtil`

The `Main` class creates an object of the `TimeUtil` class and calls a method in it. The `Main` class can be used as a `main` class to run the application. The `TimeUtil` class contains a `getLocalDate(Instant now)` method that takes an `Instant` as an argument and returns a `LocalDate` interpreting the instant in the current time zone. JDK17 has a method in the `LocalDate` class, which is named `ofInstant(Instant instant, ZoneId zone)`. We will update the application to use JDK17 to take advantage of this method and will keep the old application that used the JDK8 Time API for the same purpose.

The source code for this book contains two projects. The main project under the `jdk17book` directory contains a module named `jdojo.mrjar` for JDK17. The `jdk17book\jdojo.mrjar.jdk8` directory contains a project named `jdojo.mrjar.jdk8` that contains the JDK8 code.

Listings 12-1 and 12-2 contain the code for the `TimeUtil` and `Main` classes, respectively, for JDK8. The source code for these projects is simple, so I will not provide any explanation. I could have made the `getLocalDate()` method in the `TimeUtil` class a static method. I kept it as an instance method, so you can see in the output (discussed later) which version of the class is instantiated. When you run the `Main` class, it prints the current local date, which may be different when you run this example.

Listing 12-1. A TimeUtil Class for JDK8

```java
// TimeUtil.java
package com.jdojo.mrjar;
import java.time.Instant;
import java.time.LocalDate;
import java.time.ZoneId;
public class TimeUtil {
    public TimeUtil() {
        System.out.println(
            "Creating JDK 8 version of TimeUtil...");
    }
    public LocalDate getLocalDate(Instant now) {
        return now.atZone(ZoneId.systemDefault())
                .toLocalDate();
    }
}
```

Listing 12-2. A Main Class for JDK8

```java
// Main.java
package com.jdojo.mrjar;
import java.time.Instant;
import java.time.LocalDate;
public class Main {
    public static void main(String[] args) {
        System.out.println(
            "Inside JDK 8 version of Main.main()...");
        TimeUtil t = new TimeUtil();
        LocalDate ld = t.getLocalDate(Instant.now());
        System.out.println("Local Date: " + ld);
    }
}
```

```
Inside JDK 8 version of Main.main()...
Creating JDK 8 version of TimeUtil...
Local Date: 2021-09-22
```

872

We will put all the JDK17 classes in a module named jdojo.mrjar whose declaration is shown in Listing 12-3. Listings 12-4 and 12-5 contain the code for the TimeUtil and Main classes, respectively, for JDK17.

Listing 12-3. A Module Declaration for a Module Named com.jdojo.mrjar

```java
// module-info.java
module jdojo.mrjar {
    exports com.jdojo.mrjar;
}
```

Listing 12-4. A TimeUtil Class for JDK17

```java
// TimeUtil.java
package com.jdojo.mrjar;
import java.time.Instant;
import java.time.LocalDate;
import java.time.ZoneId;
public class TimeUtil {
    public TimeUtil() {
        System.out.println(
            "Creating JDK 17 version of TimeUtil...");
    }
    public LocalDate getLocalDate(Instant now) {
        return LocalDate.ofInstant(now,
            ZoneId.systemDefault());
    }
}
```

Listing 12-5. A Main Class for JDK17

```java
// Main.java
package com.jdojo.mrjar;
import java.time.Instant;
import java.time.LocalDate;
public class Main {
    public static void main(String[] args) {
        System.out.println(
            "Inside JDK 17 version of Main.main()...");
```

```
        TimeUtil t = new TimeUtil();
        LocalDate ld = t.getLocalDate(Instant.now());
        System.out.println("Local Date: " + ld);
    }
}
```

```
Inside JDK 17 version of Main.main()...
Creating JDK 17 version of TimeUtil...
Local Date: 2021-09-22
```

I have shown the output that you will get when you run the Main class on JDK8 and JDK17. However, the purpose of this example is not to run those two classes individually, but rather to package them all in a MRJAR and run them from that MRJAR, which I am going to show you shortly.

In order to handle MRJARs, the jar tool accepts an option called - release. Its syntax is as follows:

```
jar <options> --release N <other-options>
```

Here, N is a JDK major version such as 17 for JDK17. The value for N must be greater than or equal to 9. All files following the –release N option are added to the META-INF/versions/N directory in the MRJAR.

The following command creates a MRJAR named jdojo.mrjar.jar and places it in the C:\jdk17book\mrjars directory. Make sure that the output directory, mrjars in this case, exists before you run the following command:

```
C:\jdk17book>jar --create --file mrjars\jdojo.mrjar.jar ^
    -C jdojo.mrjar.jdk8\build\classes . ^
    --release 17 -C build\modules\jdojo.mrjar .
```

Notice the use of the –release 17 option in this command. All files from the build\modules\jdojo.mrjar directory will be added to the META-INF/versions/17 directory in the MRJAR. All files from the jdojo.mrjar.jdk8\build\classes directory will be added to the root of the MRJAR. The entries in the MRJAR will look like this:

```
- jar-root
  - com
    - jdojo
      - mrjar
```

```
      - Main.class
      - TimeUtil.class
- META-INF
  - MANIFEST.MF
  - versions
    - 17
      - module-info.class
      - com
        - jdojo
          - mrjar
            - Main.class
            - TimeUtil.class
```

It is very helpful to use the –verbose option with the jar tool while creating MRJARs. The option prints out many useful pieces of information that help diagnose errors. The following is the same command as before, but with the –verbose option. The output shows what files were copied and their locations:

```
C:\jdk17book>jar --create --verbose ^
    --file mrjars\jdojo.mrjar.jar ^
    -C jdojo.mrjar.jdk8\build\classes . ^
    --release 17 -C build\modules\jdojo.mrjar .

added manifest
added module-info: META-INF/versions/17/module-info.class
adding: com/(in = 0) (out= 0)(stored 0%)
adding: com/jdojo/(in = 0) (out= 0)(stored 0%)
adding: com/jdojo/mrjar/(in = 0) (out= 0)(stored 0%)
adding: com/jdojo/mrjar/Main.class(in = 1098)
    (out= 591)(deflated 46%)
adding: com/jdojo/mrjar/TimeUtil.class(in = 884)
    (out= 503)(deflated 43%)
adding: META-INF/versions/17/(in = 0)
    (out= 0)(stored 0%)
adding: META-INF/versions/17/com/(in = 0)
    (out= 0)(stored 0%)
adding: META-INF/versions/17/com/jdojo/(in = 0)
```

```
    (out= 0)(stored 0%)
adding: META-INF/versions/17/com/jdojo/mrjar/(in = 0)
    (out= 0)(stored 0%)
adding: META-INF/versions/17/com/jdojo/mrjar/Main.class
    (in = 1326) (out= 688)(deflated 48%)
adding: META-INF/versions/17/com/jdojo/mrjar/TimeUtil.class
    (in = 814) (out= 470)(deflated 42%)
```

Suppose you want to create a MRJAR for JDK versions 8, 16, and 17. The following command will do the job, assuming that the `jdojo.mrjar.jdk16\modules\jdojo.mrjar` directory contains classes that are specific to JDK16:

```
C:\jdk17book>jar --create --verbose ^
    --file mrjars\jdojo.mrjar.jar ^
    -C jdojo.mrjar.jdk8\build\classes . ^
--release 17 -C build\modules\jdojo.mrjar . ^
--release 16 -C jdojo.mrjar.jdk16\modules\jdojo.mrjar .
```

You can verify the entries in the MRJAR by using the `-list` option as follows:

```
C:\jdk17book>jar -list --file mrjars\jdojo.mrjar.jar

META-INF/
META-INF/MANIFEST.MF
META-INF/versions/17/module-info.class
com/
com/jdojo/
com/jdojo/mrjar/
com/jdojo/mrjar/Main.class
com/jdojo/mrjar/TimeUtil.class
META-INF/versions/17/
META-INF/versions/17/com/
META-INF/versions/17/com/jdojo/
META-INF/versions/17/com/jdojo/mrjar/
META-INF/versions/17/com/jdojo/mrjar/Main.class
META-INF/versions/17/com/jdojo/mrjar/TimeUtil.class
```

Suppose you have a JAR that contains resource and class files for JDK8, and you want to update the JAR to make it a MRJAR by adding resource and class files for JDK17. You can do so by updating the contents of the JAR using the -update option. The following command creates a JAR with only JDK8 files:

```
C:\jdk17book>jar --create --file mrjars\jdojo.mrjar.jar ^
    -C jdojo.mrjar.jdk8\build\classes .
```

The following command updates the JAR to make it a MRJAR:

```
C:\jdk17book>jar --update ^
    --file mrjars\com.jdojo.mrjar.jar ^
    --release 17 -C com.jdojo.mrjar.jdk17\build\classes .
C:\jdk17book>jar --update ^
    --file mrjars\jdojo.mrjar.jar ^
    --release 17 -C build\modules\jdojo.mrjar .
```

Take a look at this MRJAR in action. The following command runs the Main class in the com.jdojo.mrjar package, placing the MRJAR on the class path. JDK8 is used to run the class:

```
C:\jdk17book>C:\java8\bin\java ^
    -classpath mrjars\jdojo.mrjar.jar ^
    com.jdojo.mrjar.Main

Inside JDK 8 version of Main.main()...
Creating JDK 8 version of TimeUtil...
Local Date: 2021-09-22
```

The output shows that both classes, Main and TimeUtil, were used from the root directory of the MRJAR because JDK8 does not support MRJAR. The following command runs the same class using the module path. JDK17 was used to run the command:

```
C:\jdk17book>C:\java17\bin\java ^
    --module-path mrjars\jdojo.mrjar.jar ^
    --module jdojo.mrjar/com.jdojo.mrjar.Main

Inside JDK 17 version of Main.main()...
Creating JDK 17 version of TimeUtil...
Local Date: 2021-09-22
```

The output shows that both classes, Main and TimeUtil, were used from the META-INF/versions/17 directory of the MRJAR because JDK17 supports MRJAR and the MRJAR had versions of these classes specific to JDK17.

Let's give this MRJAR a little twist. Create a MRJAR having the same contents, but without the Main.class file in the META-INF/versions/17 directory. In a real-world scenario, only the TimeUtil class has changed in the JDK17 version of the application, so there is no need to package the Main class for JDK17. The Main class for JDK8 can also be used on JDK17. The following command packages everything we did last time, except the Main class for JDK17. The resulting MRJAR is named jdojo.mrjar2.jar.

```
C:\jdk17book>jar --create ^
    --file mrjars\jdojo.mrjar2.jar ^
    -C jdojo.mrjar.jdk8\build\classes . ^
    --release 17 ^
    -C build\modules\jdojo.mrjar ^
    module-info.class ^
    -C build\modules\jdojo.mrjar ^
    com\jdojo\mrjar\TimeUtil.class
```

You can verify the contents of the new MRJAR using the following command:

```
C:\jdk17book>jar --list --file mrjars\jdojo.mrjar2.jar
```

```
META-INF/
META-INF/MANIFEST.MF
META-INF/versions/17/module-info.class
com/
com/jdojo/
com/jdojo/mrjar/
com/jdojo/mrjar/Main.class
com/jdojo/mrjar/TimeUtil.class
META-INF/versions/17/com/jdojo/mrjar/TimeUtil.class
```

If you run the Main class on JDK8, you will get the same output as before. However, running it on JDK17 will give you a different output:

```
C:\jdk17book>C:\java17\bin\java ^
    --module-path mrjars\jdojo.mrjar2.jar ^
    --module jdojo.mrjar/com.jdojo.mrjar.Main
```

```
Inside JDK 8 version of Main.main()...
Creating JDK 17 version of TimeUtil...
Local Date: 2021-09-22
```

The output shows that the Main class was used from the JAR root directory, whereas the TimeUtil class was used from the META-INF/versions/17 directory. Note that you will get a different local date value. It prints the current date on your machine.

Rules for Multi-release JARs

You need to follow a few rules while creating multi-release JARs. If you make a mistake, the jar tool will print errors. Sometimes, error messages are not intuitive. As I have suggested, it's best to run the jar tool with the -verbose option to get more details on errors.

Most of the rules are based on one fact: a MRJAR contains an API for *one release* of a library (or an application) for multiple JDK platforms. For example, you have a MRJAR named jdojo-lib-1.0.jar that may contain version 1.0 of the APIs for the library named jdojo-lib, and that library may use APIs from JDK8 and JDK17. That means that this MRJAR should provide the same API (in terms of public types and their public members) when it is used on JDK8 on the class path, on JDK17 on the class path, or on JDK17 on the module path. If the MRJAR provides different APIs on JDK8 from JDK17, this is not a valid MRJAR. The following sections describe a few rules.

A MRJAR can be a modular JAR, and, in that case, it can contain a module descriptor, module-info.class, in the root directory, in one or more versioned directories, or a combination of both. The versioned descriptors must be identical to the root module descriptor, with a few exceptions:

- A versioned descriptor can have different non-transitive requires statements of java.* and jdk.* modules.

- Different module descriptors cannot have different non-transitive requires statements for non-JDK modules.

- A versioned descriptor can have different uses statements.

These rules are based on the fact that changes in implementation details are allowed, but not in the API itself. Allowing changes in the requires statement for non-JDK modules is considered a change in the API—it requires you to have different user-defined modules for different versions of the JDK. This is the reason why this is not allowed.

A modular MRJAR need not have a module descriptor in the root directory. This is what we had in our examples in the previous section. We had no module descriptor in the root directory, but had one in the META-INF/versions/17 directory. This arrangement makes it possible to have non-modular code for JDK8 and modular code for JDK17 in one MRJAR.

If you add a new public type in a versioned directory, which is not present in the root directory, you will receive an error while creating a MRJAR. Suppose, in our example, you add a public class named Test for JDK17. If the Test class is in the com.jdojo.mrjar package, it will be exported by the module and will be available to the code outside the MRJAR. Note that the root directory does not contain a Test class, so this MRJAR offers different public APIs for JDK8 and JDK17. In this case, adding a public Test class in the com.jdojo.mrjar package for JDK17 will generate an error when you create a MRJAR.

Continuing with the same example, suppose you add the Test class to a com.jdojo. test package for JDK17. Note that the module does not export this package. When you use this MRJAR on the module path, the Test class won't be accessible to the outside code. In this sense, this MRJAR offers the same public API for JDK8 and JDK17. However, there is a catch! You can also place this MRJAR on the class path in JDK17, and, in that case, the Test class is accessible to the outside code—a violation of the modular encapsulation and a violation of the rule that a MRJAR should offer the same public API across JDK releases. Therefore, adding a public type to a non-exported package for a module in a MRJAR is also not allowed. If you attempt to do so, you will receive an error message similar to the following:

```
entry: META-INF/versions/17/com/jdojo/test/Test.class,
    contains a new public class not found
    in base entries
invalid multi-release jar file mrjars\jdojo.mrjar.jar
    deleted
```

Sometimes, it is necessary to add more types for the same library to support a newer version of the JDK. These types must be added to support newer implementations. You can do this by adding package-private types to a versioned directory in a MRJAR. In this example, you can add the Test class for JDK17 if you make the class non-public.

The boot loader does not support multi-release JARs, for example, specifying MRJARs using the -Xbootclasspath/a option. Supporting this would have complicated the boot loader implementation for a rarely needed feature.

A MRJAR is supposed to contain different versions of the same file in a versioned directory. If a resource or class file is the same across different platform releases, such a file should be added once to the root directory. Currently, the jar tool issues a warning if it sees the same entry in a multiple versioned directory with the same contents.

Multi-release JARs and JAR URL

Before MRJARs, all resources in a JAR lived under the root directory. When you requested a resource from a class loader (ClassLoader.getResource("com/jdojo/mrjar/TimeUtil.class")), the URL returned was similar to the following:

```
jar:file:/C:/jdk17book/mrjars/jdojo.mrjar.jar!
com/jdojo/mrjar/TimeUtil.class
```

With MRJARs, a resource may be returned from the root directory or from a versioned directory. If you are looking for the TimeUtil.class file on JDK17, the URL will be as follows:

```
jar:file:/C:/jdk17book/mrjars/jdojo.mrjar.jar!
/META-INF/versions/17/com/jdojo/mrjar/TimeUtil.class
```

If your existing code expected the jar URL of a resource in a specific format or you hand-coded a jar URL likewise, you may get surprising results with MRJARs. You need to look at your code again and change it to work with MRJARs, if you are repacking your JARs with MRJARs.

Multi-release Manifest Attribute

A MRJAR contains a special attribute entry in its MANIFEST.MF file:

```
Multi-Release: true
```

The Multi-Release attribute is added by the jar tool for a MRJAR. If the value for this attribute is true, it means the JAR is a multi-release JAR. If its value is false or the attribute is missing, it is not a multi-release JAR. The attribute is added to the main section in the manifest file.

A constant named MULTI_RELEASE has been added to the Attributes.Name class, which is in the java.util.jar package, to represent the attribute Multi-Release in the manifest file. So, the `Attributes.Name.MULTI_RELEASE` constant represents the value for the `Multi-Release` attribute in Java code.

The JMOD Format

Java provides another format, called JMOD, to package modules. JMOD files are designed to handle more content types than JAR files can. JMOD files can package native code, configuration files, native commands, and other kinds of data. The JMOD format is based on the ZIP format, so you could use a standard ZIP tool to see their contents. The JDK modules are packaged in JMOD format for you to use at compile time and link time. JMOD format is not supported at runtime. You can find JDK modules in JMOD format in the `JDK_HOME\jmods` directory, where `JDK_HOME` is the directory in which you have installed the JDK. You can package your own modules in JMOD format. Files in the JMOD format have a `.jmod` extension. For example, the platform module named `java.base` has been packaged in the `java.base.jmod` file.

JMOD files can contain native code, which is a bit tricky to extract and link on the fly at runtime. This is the reason that JMOD files are supported at compile time and link time, but not at runtime.

Using the jmod Tool

Although you could use a ZIP tool to work with JMOD files, JDK ships with an especially tailored tool called `jmod`. It is located in the `JDK_HOME\bin` directory. It can be used to create a JMOD file, list the contents of a JMOD file, print the description of a module, and record hashes of the modules used. The general syntax to use the `jmod` tool is as follows:

```
jmod <subcommand> <options> <jmod-file>
```

You must use one of the following sub-commands with the `jmod` command:

- `create`
- `extract`
- `list`
- `describe`
- `hash`

The `list` and `describe` sub-commands do not accept any options. The `<jmod-file>` is the JMOD file you are creating or an existing JMOD file that you want to describe. Table 12-1 contains the list of options supported by the tool.

Table 12-1. *List of Options for the jmod Tool*

Option	Description
`-class-path <path>`	Specifies the class path where classes to be packaged can be found. `<path>` can be a list of paths to JAR files or directories containing application classes. Contents at `<path>` will be copied to the JMOD file.
`-cmds <path>`	Specifies a list of directories containing native commands, which need to be copied to the JMOD file.
`-config <path>`	Specifies a list of directories containing user-editable configuration files to be copied to the JMOD file.
`-dir <path>`	Specifies the target directory where the contents of the specified JMOD file will be extracted.
`-do-not-resolve-by-default`	If you create a JMOD file using this option, the module contained in the JMOD file will be excluded from the default set of root modules. To resolve such a module, you have to add it to the default set of root modules using the `-add-modules` command-line option.
`-dry-run`	Dry runs the hashing of modules. Using this option computes and prints the hashes, but does not record them in the JMOD file.
`-exclude <pattern-list>`	Excludes file matching the supplied comma-separated pattern list, each element using one of the following forms: `<glob-pattern>`, `glob:<glob-pattern>`, or `regex:<regex-pattern>`.
`-hash-modules <regex-pattern>`	Computes and records hashes to tie a packaged module with modules matching the given `<regex-pattern>` and depending on it directly or indirectly. The hashes are recorded in the JMOD file being created, or a JMOD file or modular JAR on the module path specified with the `jmod hash` command.

(continued)

Table 12-1. (*continued*)

Option	Description
-help, -h	Prints the usage description and the list of all options for the jmod command.
-header-files <path>	Specifies a list of path as <path> where header files for native code to be copied to the JMOD file are located.
-help-extra	Prints help on additional options supported by the jmod tool.
-legal-notices <path>	Specifies the location of the legal notices to be copied to the JMOD file.
-libs <path>	Specifies the list of directories containing native libraries to be copied to the JMOD file.
-main-class <class-name>	Specifies the main class name to be used to run the application.
-man-pages <path>	Specifies the location of the manual pages.
-module-version <version>	Specifies the module version to be recorded in the module-info.class file.
-module-path <path>, -p<path>	Specifies the module path to find the modules for hashing.
-target-platform<platform>	The <platform> is specified in the form of <os>-<arch>, for example, windows-amd64 and linux-amd64. The option specifies the target operating system and architecture, to be recorded in the ModuleTarget attribute of the module-info.class file.
-version	Prints the version of the jmod tool.
-warn-if-resolved <reason>	Specifies a hint to the jmod tool to issue a warning if a module is resolved, which has been deprecated, deprecated for removal, or incubating. The value for <reason> could be one of three: deprecated, deprecated-for-removal, or incubating.
@<filename>	Reads options from the specified file.

The following sections explain in detail how to use the `jmod` command. All commands used in this chapter should be entered into one line. Sometimes, I show them on multiple lines for clarity in the book.

You can create a JMOD file using the `create` sub-command with the `jmod` tool. The contents of a JMOD file are the contents of a module. Assume the following directories and files exist:

```
C:\jdk17book\jmods
C:\jdk17book\dist\jdojo.javafx.jar
```

The following command creates a `jdojo.javafx.jmod` file in the `C:\jdk17book\` jmods directory. The contents of the JMOD file come from the `jdojo.javafx.jar` file:

```
C:\jdk17book>jmod create ^
    --class-path dist\jdojo.javafx.jar ^
    jmods\jdojo.javafx.jmod
```

Typically, the contents of the JMOD file come from a set of directories containing the compiled code for a module. The following command creates a `jdojo.javafx.jmod` file. Its contents come from a `build\modules\jdojo.javafx` directory. The command uses the `–module-version` option to set the module version that will be recorded in the `module-info.class` file found in the `build\modules\jdojo.javafx` directory. Make sure to delete the JMOD file created in the previous step before you run the following command:

```
C:\jdk17book>jmod create --module-version 1.0 ^
    --class-path build\modules\jdojo.javafx ^
    jmods\jdojo.javafx.jmod
```

What can you do with this JMOD file? You can place it on the module path to use it at compile time. You can use it with the `jlink` tool to create a custom runtime image that you can use to run your application. Recall that you cannot use a JMOD file at runtime. If you try to use a JMOD file at runtime by placing it on a module path, you will receive the following error:

```
Error occurred during initialization of VM
java.lang.module.ResolutionException:
    JMOD files not supported: jmods\jdojo.javafx.jmod
...
```

Extracting JMOD File Contents

You can extract the contents of a JMOD file using the extract sub-command. The following command extracts the contents of the jmods\jdojo.javafx.jmod file into a directory named extracted:

```
C:\jdk17book>jmod extract --dir extracted ^
    jmods\jdojo.javafx.jmod
```

Without the -dir option, the JMOD file's contents are extracted into the current directory.

You can use the list sub-command with the jmod tool to print the names of all entries in a JMOD file. The following command lists the contents of the jdojo.javafx. jmod file, which you created in the previous section:

```
C:\jdk17book>jmod list jmods\jdojo.javafx.jmod

classes/module-info.class
classes/com/jdojo/javafx/BindingTest.class
...
classes/resources/fxml/sayhello.fxml
```

The following command lists the contents of the java.base module, which is shipped as a JMOD file named java.base.jmod. The command assumes that you have installed the JDK in the C:\java17 directory. The output is over 120 pages. A partial output is shown. Note that a JMOD file internally stores different types of content in different directories.

```
C:\jdk17book>jmod list C:\java17\jmods\java.base.jmod

classes/module-info.class
classes/java/nio/file/WatchEvent.class
classes/java/nio/file/WatchKey.class
bin/java.exe
bin/javaw.exe
native/amd64/jvm.cfg
native/java.dll
conf/net.properties
conf/security/java.policy
conf/security/java.security
...
```

You can use the `describe` sub-command with the `jmod` tool to describe the module contained in a JMOD file. The following command describes the module contained in the `jdojo.javafx.jmod` file:

```
C:\jdk17book>jmod describe jmods\jdojo.javafx.jmod
```

```
jdojo.javafx@1.0
exports com.jdojo.javafx
requires java.base mandated
requires javafx.controls
requires javafx.fxml
contains resources.fxml
```

You can describe the platform modules using this command. The following command describes the module contained in the `java.sql.jmod`, assuming that you installed the JDK in the `C:\java17` directory:

```
C:\jdk17book>jmod describe C:\java17\jmods\java.sql.jmod
```

```
java.sql@9.0.1
exports java.sql
exports javax.sql
exports javax.transaction.xa
requires java.base mandated
requires java.logging transitive
requires java.xml transitive
uses java.sql.Driver
platform windows-amd64
```

You can use the `hash` sub-command with the `jmod` tool to record hashes of other modules in the `module-info.class` file of a module contained in a JMOD file. The hashes will be used later for dependency validation. Suppose you have four modules in four JMOD files:

- `jdojo.prime`
- `jdojo.prime.faster`
- `jdojo.prime.probable`
- `jdojo.prime.client`

Suppose you want to ship these modules to your clients and ensure that the module code remains the same. You can achieve this by recording hashes for the jdojo.prime. faster, jdojo.prime.probable, and jdojo.prime.client modules in the jdojo.prime module. Let's see how to achieve this.

To compute the hashes for other modules, the jmod tool needs to find those modules. You will need to use the –module-path option to specify the module path where the other modules will be found. You also need to use the –hash-modules option to specify the list of patterns to be used for the modules whose hashes need to be recorded.

Note   You can also use the –hash-modules and –module-path options with the jar tool to record hashes for dependent modules when you are packaging a module as a module JAR.

Use the following four commands to create the JMOD files for the four modules. Note that I used the –main-class option when creating the com.jdojo.prime.client.jmod file. I use it again in Chapter 13 when I discuss the jlink tool. If you get a "file already exists" error while running these commands, delete the existing JMOD file from the jmods directory and rerun the command:

```
C:\jdk17book>jmod create --module-version 1.0 ^
    --class-path build\modules\jdojo.prime ^
    jmods\jdojo.prime.jmod
C:\jdk17book>jmod create --module-version 1.0 ^
    --class-path build\modules\jdojo.prime.faster ^
    jmods\jdojo.prime.faster.jmod
C:\jdk17book>jmod create --module-version 1.0 ^
    --class-path build\modules\jdojo.prime.probable ^
    jmods\jdojo.prime.probable.jmod
C:\jdk17book>jmod create --module-version 1.0 ^
    --class-path build\modules\jdojo.prime.client ^
    jmods\jdojo.prime.client.jmod
```

Now you are ready to record hashes for all modules whose names start with "jdojo. prime." in the jdojo.prime module using the following command:

```
C:\jdk17book>jmod hash ^
    --module-path jmods ^
    --hash-modules jdojo.prime.? jmods\jdojo.prime.jmod
```

Hashes are recorded in module jdojo.prime

Let's see the hashes that were recorded in the com.jdojo.prime module. The following command prints the module description along with the hashes recorded in the com.jdojo.prime module:

```
C:\jdk17book>jmod describe jmods\jdojo.prime.jmod
```

```
jdojo.prime@1.0
exports com.jdojo.prime
requires java.base mandated
uses com.jdojo.prime.PrimeChecker
provides com.jdojo.prime.PrimeChecker with
    com.jdojo.prime.impl.genericprimechecker
contains com.jdojo.prime.impl
hashes jdojo.prime.client SHA-256
5950...6ce95e9849f520f4b9f54bc520d7969c396dc4f93805121b
hashes jdojo.prime.faster SHA-256
5538...4e264cfa12848be32d3f0b9a5df506aa57ba4443dfcbdc6a
hashes jdojo.prime.probable SHA-256
a1b8...5d62313de97ee285ed845895c8ef3c52b53a16370dd3b2d5
```

You can also record hashes for other modules when you create a new JMOD file using the create sub-command. Assuming that the three modules jdojo.prime.faster, jdojo.prime.probable, and jdojo.prime.client exist on the module path, you can use the following command to create the jdojo.prime.jmod file that will also record the hashes for the three modules:

```
C:\jdk17book>jmod create --module-version 1.0 ^
    --module-path jmods ^
```

```
--hash-modules jdojo.prime.? ^
--class-path build\modules\jdojo.prime ^
jmods\jdojo.prime.jmod
```

You can dry run the hashing process for a JMOD file where the hashes will be printed, but not recorded. The dry run option is useful to make sure all the settings are correct without creating the JMOD file. The following sequence of commands steps you through the process. First, delete the jmods\jdojo.prime.jmod file, which you created in the previous step.

The following command creates the jmods\jdojo.prime.jmod file without recording hashes for any other modules:

```
C:\jdk17book>jmod create --module-version 1.0 ^
    --module-path jmods ^
    --class-path build\modules\jdojo.prime ^
    jmods\jdojo.prime.jmod
```

The following command dry runs the hash sub-command. It computes and prints the hashes for other modules, matching the regular expression specified in the –hash-modules option. No hashes will be recorded in the jmods\jdojo.javafx.jmod file:

```
C:\jdk17book>jmod hash --dry-run ^
    --module-path jmods ^
    --hash-modules jdojo.prime.? ^
    jmods\jdojo.prime.jmod
```

```
Dry run:
jdojo.prime
  hashes jdojo.prime.client SHA-256
5950...6ce95e9849f520f4b9f54bc520d7969c396dc4f93805121b
  hashes jdojo.prime.faster SHA-256
5538...4e264cfa12848be32d3f0b9a5df506aa57ba4443dfcbdc6a
  hashes jdojo.prime.probable SHA-256
a1b8...5d62313de97ee285ed845895c8ef3c52b53a16370dd3b2d5
```

The following command verifies that the previous command did not record any hashes in the JMOD file:

```
C:\jdk17book>jmod describe jmods\jdojo.prime.jmod

jdojo.prime@1.0
exports com.jdojo.prime
requires java.base mandated
uses com.jdojo.prime.PrimeChecker
provides com.jdojo.prime.PrimeChecker with
    com.jdojo.prime.impl.genericprimechecker
contains com.jdojo.prime.impl
```

You will see JMOD files in action again in Chapter 13 when you use the `jlink` tool to create custom runtime images.

Summary

Java supports four formats to package modules: exploded directories, JAR files, JMOD files, and JIMAGE files. The JAR format has been enhanced in JDK9 to support modular JARs and multi-release JARs. A multi-release JAR allows you to package the same version of a library or an application targeting different versions of the JDK. For example, a multi-release JAR may contain the code for a library version 1.2 that contains code for JDK8 and JDK17. When the multi-release JAR is used on JDK8, the JDK8 version of the library code will be used. When it is used on JDK17, the JDK17 version of the library code will be used. Files that are specific to a JDK version N are stored in the `META-INF\versions\N` directory of the multi-release JAR. Files that are common to all JDK versions are stored in the root directory. For environments not supporting multi-release JARs, such JARs are treated as regular JARs. The search order for a file is different in a multi-release JAR—all the versioned directories starting with the major version of the current platform are searched before the root directory is.

JMOD files are designed to handle more content types than JAR files can. They can package native code, configuration files, native commands, and other kinds of data. The JDK modules are packaged in JMOD format for you to use at compile time and link time. The JMOD format is not supported at runtime. You can use the `jmod` tool to work with JMOD files.

Exercises

Exercise 1

What formats can you use to package your modules?

Exercise 2

What is a multi-release JAR?

Exercise 3

Describe the structure of a multi-release JAR.

Exercise 4

What happens when a multi-release JAR is used on a JDK version (e.g., JDK8) that does not understand multi-release JARs?

Exercise 5

Describe the search order when a resource is looked up in a multi-release JAR.

Exercise 6

Describe the limitations of a multi-release JAR.

Exercise 7

What is the name of the attribute that is present in the `META-INF\MANIFEST.MF` file for a multi-release JAR?

Exercise 8

What is the `jmod` tool and where is it located?

Exercise 9

What is the JMOD format and how is it better than the JAR format?

Exercise 10

Java supports three phases: compile time, link time, and runtime. In what phases is the JMOD format supported?

Exercise 11

Suppose you have a JMOD file named `jdojo.test.jmod`. Write the command using the `jmod` tool to describe the module stored in this JMOD file.

Exercise 12

What is the location of the JDK modules in JMOD format?

CHAPTER 13

Custom Runtime Images

In this chapter, you will learn:

- What a custom runtime image and the JIMAGE format are
- How to create a custom runtime image using the `jlink` tool
- How to specify the command name to run the application stored in a custom image
- How to use plugins with the `jlink` tool

What Is a Custom Runtime Image?

Before JDK9, Java runtime image was available as a huge monolithic artifact—thus increasing the download time, startup time, and the memory footprint. The monolithic JRE made it impossible to use Java on devices with little memory. If you deploy your Java applications to a cloud, you pay for the memory you use; most often, the monolithic JRE uses more memory than required, thus making you pay more for the cloud service. With Java, it is now possible to reduce the JRE size—hence the runtime memory footprint—by allowing you to package a subset of the JRE in a custom runtime image called a *compact profile*.

The JDK is itself modularized, but you can also package your application code as modules and merge the required JDK modules and the application modules together. The way to accomplish this is to create a custom runtime that will contain your application modules and only those JDK modules that are used by your application. You can also package native commands in your runtime image. Another benefit of creating a runtime image is that you have to ship only one bundle—the runtime image—to your application users. They no longer need to download and install a separate bundle of JRE to run your application.

© Kishori Sharan, Peter Späth 2021
K. Sharan and P. Späth, *More Java 17*, https://doi.org/10.1007/978-1-4842-7135-3_13

The runtime image is stored in a special format called JIMAGE, which is optimized for space and speed. The JIMAGE format is supported only at runtime. It is a container format for storing and indexing modules, classes, and resources in the JDK. Searching and loading classes from a JIMAGE file is a lot faster than from JAR and JMOD files. The JIMAGE format is JDK internal, and developers will rarely need to interact with a JIMAGE file directly.

The JIMAGE format is expected to evolve significantly over time, and, therefore, its internals are not exposed to developers. The JDK ships with a tool called `jimage`, which can be used to explore JIMAGE files. I explain the tool in detail in a separate section in this chapter.

Note   You use the jlink tool to create a custom runtime image, which uses a new file format called JIMAGE to store modules. Java ships with the jimage tool to let you explore the contents of a JIMAGE file.

Creating Custom Runtime Images

You can create a custom platform-specific runtime image using the `jlink` tool. The runtime image will contain specified application modules with their dependencies and only the needed platform modules, thus reducing the size of the runtime image. This is useful for applications running on embedded devices that have a small amount of memory. The `jlink` tool is located in the `JDK_HOME\bin` directory. The general syntax for running the `jlink` tool is as follows:

```
jlink <options> --module-path <modulepath> ^
    --add-modules <mods> --output <path>
```

Here, `<options>` includes zero or more options for `jlink`, as listed in Table 13-1. The `<modulepath>` is the module path where the platform and application modules are located. Modules can be in modular JARs, exploded directories, and JMOD files. The `<mods>` is a list of modules to be added to the image, which may cause additional modules to be added because of transitive dependencies on other modules. `<path>` is the output directory where the generated runtime image will be stored.

Table 13-1. *List of Options for the jlink Tool*

Option	Description
-add-modules <mod>,<mod>...	Specifies the list of root modules to resolve. All resolved modules will be added to the runtime image.
–bind-services	Performs full service binding during the linking process. If the added modules contain uses statements, jlink will scan all modules on the module path to include all service provider modules in the runtime image for the service specified in the uses statement.
-c, –compress	Specifies the compression level of all resources in the output <0|1|2>[:filter=<pattern-list>] image. 0 means constant string sharing, 1 means ZIP, and 2 means both. An optional <pattern-list> filter can be specified to list the pattern of files to be included.
-disable-plugin <plugin-name>	Disables the specified plugIn.
-endian <little|big>	Specifies the byte order of the generated runtime image. The default is the byte order of the native platform.
-h, –help	Prints the usage description and a list of all options for the jlink tool.
-ignore-signing-information	Suppress a fatal error when signed modular JARs are linked in the image. The signatures of related files of the signed modular JARs are not copied to the runtime image.
-launcher <command>=<module>	Specifies the launcher command for the module. <command> is the name of the command you want to generate to launch your application, for example, runmyapp. The tool will create a script/batch file named <command> to run the main class recorded in <module>.

(continued)

Table 13-1. (*continued*)

Option	Description
-launcher <command>= <module>/<mainclass>	Specifies the launcher command for the module and the main class. <command> is the name of the command you want to generate to launch your application, for example, runmyapp. The tool will create a script/batch file named <command> to run the <main-class> in <module>.
-limit-modules <mod>,<mod>	Limits the observable modules to those in the transitive closure of the named modules plus the main module, if specified, as well as any further modules specified with the –add-modules option.
-list-plugins	Lists the available plugins.
-p, –module-path <modulepath>	Specifies the module path where the platform and application modules will be found to be added to the runtime image.
-no-header-files	Excludes the include header files for the native code.
-no-man-pages	Excludes the manual pages.
-output <path>	Specifies the location of the generated runtime image.
-save-opts <filename>	Saves the jlink options in the specified file.
-G, –strip-debug	Strips the debug information from the output image.
-suggest-providers [<service-name>,...]	If no service name is specified, it suggests the name of the providers of all services that would be linked for the added modules. If you specify one or more service names, it suggests providers of the specified service names. This option can be used before creating an image to know what services will be included when you use the –bind-services option.
-v, –verbose	Prints verbose output.
–version	Prints the version of the jlink tool.
@<filename>	Reads options from the specified file.

Let's create a runtime image that contains the four modules for the prime checker application and the required platform modules, which includes only the java.base module. The prime checker application was created in Chapter 7, in which I explained how to implement services. I included the source code for the prime checker application in the source code for this book. The modules are `jdojo.prime`, `jdojo.prime.faster`, `jdojo.prime.probable`, and `jdojo.prime.client`. You can choose any other modules to create a custom runtime image.

Note that the following command includes only three modules from the prime checker application. The fourth one, the `jdojo.prime` module, will be added because these three depend on the `jdojo.prime` module. The command assumes that you have packaged all four modules in JMOD format and stored them in the `jmods` directory. Packaging modules in JMOD format was covered in Chapter 12. The text following the command contains an explanation.

```
C:\jdk17book>jlink ^
    --module-path jmods;C:\java17\jmods ^
    --add-modules ^
    jdojo.prime.client,jdojo.prime.faster,
    jdojo.prime.probable ^
    --launcher runprimechecker=
    jdojo.prime.client/com.jdojo.prime.client.Main ^
    --output image\primechecker
```

(No line break and no spaces after "," and "=".)

Before I explain all the options for this command, let's verify that the runtime image was created successfully. The command is supposed to copy the runtime image to the `C:\jdk17book\image\primechecker` directory. Run the following command to verify that the runtime image contains the five modules:

```
C:\jdk17book>image\primechecker\bin\java ^
    --list-modules
```

```
java.base@9
jdojo.prime@1.0
jdojo.prime.client@1.0
jdojo.prime.faster@1.0
jdojo.prime.probable@1.0
```

If you get output similar to what is shown here, the runtime image was created correctly. The module version number, which is shown after the @ sign in the output, may be different for you.

The -module-path option specifies two directories: jmods and C:\java17\jmods. I saved the four JMOD files for the prime checker application in the C:\jdk17book\jmods directory. The first element in the module path lets the jlink tool find all application modules. I installed the JDK17 in the C:\java17 directory, so the second element in the module path lets the tool find the platform modules. If you do not specify the second part, you get an error:

```
Error: Module java.base not found,
    required by jdojo.prime.probable
```

The -add-modules option specifies three modules of the prime checker application. You might wonder why we did not specify the fourth module named jdojo.prime with this option. This list contains root modules, not just the modules to be included in the runtime image. The jlink tool will resolve all dependencies transitively for these root modules and include all the resolved dependent modules into the runtime image. The three modules depend on the jdojo.prime module, which will be resolved by locating it on the module path and, hence, will be included in the runtime image. The image will also contain the java.base module because all application modules implicitly depend on it.

The -output option specifies the directory where the runtime image will be copied. The command will copy the runtime image to the C:\jdk17book\image\primechecker directory. The output directory contains the sub-directories and a file named release. The release file contains the JDK version and a list of all JDK and user modules linked to this image. Table 13-2 contains the descriptions of the contents of each directory.

Table 13-2. *Sub-directories Inside the Output Directory*

Directory	Description
bin	Contains executable files. On Windows, it also contains dynamically linked native libraries (.dll files).
conf	Contains the editable configuration files such as .properties and .policy files.
include	Contains C/C++ header files.
legal	Contains legal notices.
lib	Contains, among other files, the modules added to the runtime image. On Mac, Linux, and Solaris, it will also contain the system's dynamically linked native libraries.

You used the -launcher option with the jlink command. You specified runprimechecker as the command name, jdojo.prime.client as the module name, and com.jdojo.prime.client.Main as the main class name in the module. The -launcher option makes jlink create a platform-specific executable, such as a runprimechecker.bat file on Windows in the bin directory. You can use this executable to run your application. The file contents are simply a wrapper for running the main class in this module. You can use this file to run the application:

```
C:\jdk17book>image\primechecker\bin\
    runprimechecker

Using default service provider:
3 is a prime.
4 is not a prime.
121 is not a prime.
977 is a prime.
Using faster service provider:
3 is a prime.
4 is not a prime.
121 is not a prime.
977 is a prime.
Using probable service provider:
3 is a prime.
4 is not a prime.
121 is not a prime.
977 is a prime.
```

(No line break and no spaces after "bin\".)

You can also use the java command, which is copied to the bin directory by the jlink tool, to launch your application:

```
C:\jdk17book>image\primechecker\bin\java ^
    --module jdojo.prime.client/com.jdojo.prime.client.Main
```

The output of this command will be the same as that of the previous command. Notice that you did not have to specify the module path. The linker, the jlink tool, took care of the module path when the runtime image was created. When you run the java command of the generated runtime image, it knows where to find the modules.

Binding Services

In the previous section, you created a runtime image for the prime service client application. You had to specify the names of all service provider modules with the –add-modules option that you wanted to include in the image. In this section, I show you how to bind services automatically using the –bind-services option with the jlink tool. This time, you need to add the module, which is the jdojo.prime.client module, to the module graph. The jlink tool will take care of the rest. The jdojo.prime.client module reads the jdojo.prime module, so adding the former into the module graph will also resolve the latter. The following command prints the list of suggested service providers for the runtime image. A partial output is shown:

```
C:\jdk17book>jlink ^
    --module-path jmods;C:\java17\jmods ^
    --add-modules jdojo.prime.client --suggest-providers

...
jdojo.prime file:///C:/jdk17book/jmods/
        jdojo.prime.jmod
    uses com.jdojo.prime.PrimeChecker
jdojo.prime.client file:///C:/jdk17book/
    jmods/jdojo.prime.client.jmod
jdojo.prime.faster file:///C:/jdk17book/
    jmods/jdojo.prime.faster.jmod
jdojo.prime.probable file:///C:/jdk17book/
    jmods/jdojo.prime.probable.jmod
...
Suggested providers:
  jdojo.prime provides com.jdojo.prime.
     PrimeChecker used by jdojo.prime
  jdojo.prime.faster provides com.jdojo.prime.
     PrimeChecker used by jdojo.prime
  jdojo.prime.probable provides com.jdojo.prime.
     PrimeChecker used by jdojo.prime
...
```

The command specifies only the jdojo.prime.client module to the -add-modules option. The jdojo.prime and java.base modules are resolved because the jdojo. prime.client module reads them. All resolved modules are scanned for the uses statement, and, subsequently, all modules in the module path are scanned for service providers for the services specified in the uses statement. All service providers that are found are printed.

Note   You may specify arguments to the -suggest-providers option. If you are using it without arguments, make sure you specify it at the end of the command. Otherwise, the option after the -suggest-providers option will be interpreted as its arguments, and you will receive an error.

The following command specifies com.jdojo.prime.PrimeChecker as the service name to the -suggest-providers option to print all service providers found for this service:

```
C:\jdk17book>jlink ^
    --module-path jmods;C:\java17\jmods ^
    --add-modules jdojo.prime.client ^
    --suggest-providers ^
    com.jdojo.prime.PrimeChecker
Suggested providers:
  jdojo.prime provides com.jdojo.prime.
     PrimeChecker used by jdojo.prime
  jdojo.prime.faster provides com.jdojo.prime.
     PrimeChecker used by jdojo.prime
  jdojo.prime.probable provides com.jdojo.prime.
     PrimeChecker used by jdojo.prime
```

Using the same logic as described before, all three service providers were found. Let's create a new runtime image that includes all three service providers. The following command does the job:

```
C:\jdk17book>jlink ^
    --module-path jmods;C:\java17\jmods ^
    --add-modules jdojo.prime.client ^
    --launcher runprimechecker=
        jdojo.prime.client/com.jdojo.prime.client.Main ^
    --bind-services
    --output image\primecheckerservice
```

(No line break and no spaces after "=".)

Compare this command with the command used in the previous section. This time, you specified only one module with the –add-modules option. That is, you did not have to specify the names of service provider modules. You used the –bind-services option, so all service provider references in the added modules are added automatically to the runtime image. You specified a new output directory named image\primecheckerservice. The following command runs the newly created runtime image:

```
C:\jdk17book>image\primecheckerservice\bin\
    runprimechecker
```

```
Using default service provider:
3 is a prime.
4 is not a prime.
121 is not a prime.
977 is a prime.
Using faster service provider:
3 is a prime.
4 is not a prime.
121 is not a prime.
977 is a prime.
Using probable service provider:
3 is a prime.
4 is not a prime.
121 is not a prime.
977 is a prime.
```

(No line break and no spaces after "bin\".)

The output proves that all three prime checker service providers, which were in the module path, were added automatically to the runtime image.

There is a catch when you used the `-bind-services` option in the previous command. Compare the sizes of the `image\primechecker` and `image\primecheckerservice` directories, which are 173MB and 36MB, respectively. You did use a shorter command. However, the size of the runtime image went up by 280. You do not want this. The problem is with using the `-bind-services` option that resolved all services, including the `java.base` module. You do not want to resolve any services other than the `com.jdojo.prime.PrimeChecker` service, which is defined in the `jdojo.prime` module. You can achieve this by using the `-limit-modules` option to limit the universe of observable modules to the following five modules:

- `java.base`

- `jdojo.prime`

- `jdojo.prime.faster`

- `jdojo.prime.probable`

- `jdojo.prime.client`

The following command is a revised copy of the previous command. This command uses the `-limit-modules`. Note that you have not included the `jdojo.prime.client` module in the `-list-modules` because this module is already in the `-add-modules`. Including it in the list of modules with `-list-modules` will not make any difference. This time, your runtime image will be 36MB as it was the first time.

```
C:\jdk17book>jlink ^
    --module-path jmods;C:\java17\jmods ^
    --add-modules jdojo.prime.client ^
    --compress 2 ^
    --strip-debug ^
    --launcher runprimechecker=
      jdojo.prime.client/com.jdojo.prime.client.Main ^
    --bind-services ^
    --limit-modules java.base,jdojo.prime,
      jdojo.prime.faster,jdojo.prime.probable ^
--output image\image\primecheckercompactservice
```

(No line break and no spaces after "=" or ",".)

Using Plugins with the jlink Tool

The jlink tool uses a plugin architecture to create runtime images. It collects all classes, native libraries, and configuration files into a set of resources. It builds a pipeline of transformers, which are plugins specified as command-line options. Resources are fed into the pipeline. Each transformer in the pipeline applies some kind of transformation to resources, and the transformed resources are fed to the next transformer. At the end, jlink feeds the transformed resources to an image builder.

The JDK ships the jlink tool with a few plugins. Those plugins define command-line options. To use a plugin, you need to use the command-line option for it. You can run the jlink tool with the --list-plugins options to print the list of all available plugins with their descriptions and command-line options:

```
C:\jdk17book>jlink --list-plugins
```

...

The following command uses the compress and strip-debug plugins. The compress plugin will compress the image, which will result in a smaller image size. I use the compression level 2 to have the maximum compression. The strip-debug plugin will remove the debugging information from the Java code, thus further reducing the size of the image.

```
C:\jdk17book>jlink ^
    --module-path jmods;C:\java17\jmods ^
    --add-modules jdojo.prime.client,
      jdojo.prime.faster,jdojo.prime.probable ^
    --compress 2 ^
    --strip-debug ^
    --launcher runprimechecker=
      jdojo.prime.client/com.jdojo.prime.client.Main ^
    --output image\primecheckercompact
```

(No line break and no spaces after "=" or ",".)

The output was copied to the image\primecheckercompact directory. The size of the new image is 33MB, whereas the size of the image created in the image\primechecker directory is 36MB. This is approximately 39% more compact image because of the two plugins you used.

The jimage Tool

The Java runtime ships the JDK runtime image in a JIMAGE file. The file is named modules, and it is located in JAVA_HOME\lib, where JAVA_HOME could be your JDK_HOME or JRE_HOME. JDK9 also ships with a jimage tool, which is used to explore the contents of JIMAGE files. The tool can

- Extract entries from the JIMAGE file

- Print the summary of the contents stored in the JIMAGE file

- Print the list of entries such as their name, size, offset, etc.

- Verify class files

The jimage tool is stored in the JDK_HOME\bin directory. The general format of the command is as follows:

jimage <subcommand> <options> <jimage-file-list>

Here, <subcommand> is one of the sub-commands listed in Table 13-3. <options> is one or more options listed in Table 13-4; <jimage-file-list> is a space-separated list of JIMAGE files to be explored.

Table 13-3. *List of Sub-commands Used with the jimage Tool*

Sub-command	Description
Extract	Extracts all entries from the specified JIMAGE files to the current directory. Use the -dir option to specify another directory for extracted entries.
Info	Prints the detailed information contained in the header of the specified JIMAGE file.
List	Prints the list of all modules and their entries in the specified JIMAGE file. Use the -verbose option to include the details of the entries such as its size, offset, and whether the entry is compressed.
verify	Prints a list of .class entries in the specified JIMAGE files that do not verify as classes.

Table 13-4. *List of Options Used with the jimage Tool*

Option	Description
-dir <dir-name>	Specifies the target directory for the extract sub-command where the entries in the JIMAGE files will be extracted.
-h, -help	Prints a usage message for the jimage tool.
-include <pattern-list>	Specifies a list of patterns for filtering entries. The value for the pattern list is a comma-separated list of elements, each using one of the following forms: • <glob-pattern> • glob:<glob-pattern> • regex:<regex-pattern>
-verbose	When used with the list sub-command, prints entry details such as size, offset, and compression level.
-version	Prints version information for the jimage tool.

I show a few examples of using the jimage command. Examples use the JDK runtime image that is stored at C:\java17\lib\modules on my computer. You will need to replace this image location with yours when you run these examples. You can also use any custom runtime image created by the jlink tool in these examples.

The following command extracts all entries from the runtime image and copies them to the extracted_jdk directory. The command takes a few seconds to complete:

```
C:\jdk17book>jimage extract ^
    --dir extracted_jdk C:\java17\lib\modules
```

The following command extracts all image entries with the .png extension from the JDK runtime image into an extracted_images directory:

```
C:\jdk17book>jimage extract ^
    --include regex:.+\.png ^
    --dir extracted_images ^
    C:\java17\lib\modules
```

The following command lists all entries in the runtime image. A partial output is shown:

```
C:\jdk17book>jimage list C:\java17\lib\modules

jimage: C:\java17\lib\modules
Module: java.activation
    META-INF/mailcap.default
    META-INF/mimetypes.default
...
Module: java.annotations.common
    javax/annotation/Generated.class
...
```

The following command lists all entries in the runtime image along with the entries' details. Notice the use of the –verbose option. A partial output is shown:

```
C:\jdk17book>jimage list ^
    --verbose ^
    C:\java17\lib\modules

jimage: C:\java17\lib\modules
Module: java.activation
Offset      Size    Compressed Entry
34214466    292              0 META-INF/mailcap.default
34214758    562              0 META-INF/mimetypes.default
...
Module: java.annotations.common
Offset      Size    Compressed Entry
34296622    678              0 javax/annotation/
                                              Generated.class
...
```

The following command prints the list of class files that are invalid. You may wonder how you make a class file invalid. Typically, you won't have an invalid class file—but hackers would! However, to run this example, I need to have an invalid class file. I used a simple idea—take a valid class file, open it in a text editor, and remove its contents partly and randomly to make it an invalid class file. I copied the contents of a compiled class file into the `Main2.class` file and removed some of its contents to make it an invalid class. I added the `Main2.class` file to the `jdojo.prime.client` module in the same directory as the `Main.class`. I recreated the runtime image using the previous command for the prime checker application for this example. If you use the Java runtime image that comes with the JDK, you will not see any output because all class files in the JDK runtime image are valid.

```
C:\jdk17book>jimage verify ^
    image\primechecker\lib\modules

jimage: primechecker\lib\modules
Error(s) in Class: /jdojo.prime.client/com/jdojo/prime/
    client/Main2.class
```

Summary

In Java, the runtime image is stored in a special format called JIMAGE, which is optimized for space and speed. The JIMAGE format is supported only at runtime. It is a container format for storing and indexing modules, classes, and resources in the JDK. Searching and loading classes from a JIMAGE file is a lot faster than from JAR and JMOD files. The JIMAGE format is JDK internal, and developers will rarely need to interact with a JIMAGE file directly.

The JDK ships with a tool called `jlink` that lets you create a runtime image in JIMAGE format for your application that will contain application modules and only those platform modules that are used by your application. The `jlink` tool can create runtime images from modules stored in module JARs, exploded directories, and JMOD files. The JDK ships with a tool called `jimage` that can be used to explore the contents of JIMAGE files.

Exercises

Exercise 1

What is a custom Java runtime image?

Exercise 2

What is the JIMAGE format?

Exercise 3

What is the `jlink` tool?

Exercise 4

Why do you use the `-launcher` option with the `jlink` tool?

Exercise 5

What is the effect of using or not using the `-bind-services` option with the `jlink` tool?

Exercise 6

What are the plugins for the `jlink` tool?

Exercise 7

How do you list the plugins available for `jlink`?

Exercise 8

Name two `jlink` plugins.

Exercise 9

Can you use a custom plugin with `jlink`?

Exercise 10

What is the `jimage` tool? Describe the use of the following four sub-commands for the `jimage` tool: `extract`, `info`, `list`, and `verify`.

CHAPTER 14

Miscellanea

In this chapter, you will learn:

- The selection of chapters, compared to the previous edition

- Various enhancements after JDK9

Deleted Chapters from Previous Editions

If you compare this book with previous editions, namely, *Java Language Features*, Second Edition, and *Java APIs, Extensions and Libraries*, Second Edition, you might miss some chapters that didn't make their way to the new edition. The main reason for that is that we didn't want the new book, which is a merger of the aforementioned books, to be too big.

The question is of course: how would you decide which chapters to omit? None of the chapters from the two second edition books is really outdated or one or the other way uninteresting. Decision points are not easy to find out, but the author decided to consider two aspects. First, if a topic too much belongs to a developer's standard know-how and information about it can easily be found in Oracle's documentation, including tutorials, a chapter was subjected to be removed from the third edition. Second, if a topic wouldn't show up too often in a developer's everyday work, and thus belongs to the corner-case type of possible topics, a chapter was subjected to be removed from the new edition as well.

In detail, the rationale for chapter selection is

- No inner classes: Pretty standard—the reader easily can find details in the Oracle documentation and elsewhere on the net.

- No input/output and no working with archive files: Not so important for server-side development. Standard stuff for applications and info can easily be found in the Oracle documentation and elsewhere on the net.

911

© Kishori Sharan, Peter Späth 2021
K. Sharan and P. Späth, *More Java 17*, https://doi.org/10.1007/978-1-4842-7135-3_14

- No garbage collection and no details about stack walking: Interesting, but to such detail not important for everyday work. Introductory texts can easily be found on the net.

- No collections: Important, but pretty standard stuff and subject of many introductory texts.

- No Module API: Developers rarely would have to use it.

- No reactive streams: While kind of "in," it is actually a Java library topic with just a few bolts in the Java standard. Best consult reactive streams library projects if you want to learn about it.

- No JDBC: A coherent topic and very well documented on the Web. Enterprise project developers almost never use JDBC directly.

- No Java Native Interface: Somewhat thwarts the Java philosophy (write once, run everywhere) and as such is a corner case.

- No Swing and no JavaFX: Front-end development is such a vast topic that it better gets handled in specialized books.

More JDK17 Novelties

In this section, I present a collection of helpful or interesting novelties, which entered the Java universe since the previous editions of the books this text is a successor of. Or, in version numbers, it describes what happened since JDK9. The list is not exhausting—some changes referring to internals or not so important in a developer's everyday work were left off.

Local Variables with Automatic Types

Scripting languages, including those that eventually run on a JVM, often allow for a simplified *undefined* type variable declaration, to simplify writing code. In Groovy, for example, this would be def, as in

```
// This is Groovy
def a = "Hello"
def b = 3
def c = 5.9
```

In JavaScript, you can write

```
// This is JavaScript
var a = "Hello";
var b = 3;
var c = 5.9;
```

The Java language developers for a long time insisted on precisely typed variable declaration for Java. Only with the later Java versions this was somehow relaxed, and it became possible to use var as a type placeholder for local variables. So you can write

```
// This is Java, inside a method
var a = "Hello";
var b = 3;
var c = 5.9;
```

You must initialize var variables, you cannot use var for class fields, and you cannot switch value types:

```
public class Car {
  private var a = "Hello";
  // <- Won't compile
}

...

var a;
a = 3;
// <- Won't compile

...

var b = 3;
b = 5.9;
// <-Won't compile
```

The var local variable syntax comes handy for longer types, and you can also use it for lambda parameters:

```
var x = new ArrayList<String>();
  // <-x has type ArrayList

  Function<String,Integer> fsi = (var s) -> s.length();
```

Caution   Do not overuse var local variable syntax. After all, a clean code programming state also is about expressiveness, and hiding type information makes complex code almost unreadable.

Launch Single-File Source Code Programs

For very short programs that consist just of a single class with a static void main(String[] args) method, you can bypass the compilation step and just write

```
java HelloTest.java
  # or, if we need args
  java HelloTest.java arg1 arg2 ...
```

This performs an in-memory compilation and then runs the main() method.

Enhanced switch Statements

The old venerable switch statement

```
int x = ...;
  switch(x) {
    case 1:
    case 2:
      System.out.println("1 or 2");
      break;
    case 3:
      System.out.println("3");
      fbreak;
```

```
    default:
      System.out.println("default");
  }
```

lacked a feature many other programming languages included: in Java, you could not use switch{ } as an expression. Besides, while useful in some scenarios, the fall-through mechanism (the missing break for case 1: in the preceding example) more often led to errors if a break was accidentally forgotten. For this reason, Java now has a new variant included with a slightly different syntax, replacing the : in the case sub-statements by ->:

```
var a = 5;
switch(a) {
    case 4 -> System.out.println("4");
    default -> System.out.println("default: " + a);
}
var b = switch(a) {
    case 4 -> -1;
    default -> a;
};
var c = switch(a) {
    case 4 -> -1;
    default-> {
        var x9 = a*2;
        yield x9; // goes to c
    }
};
```

So there no longer exists a fall-through if there is no break. In fact, breaks are obsolete and you cannot use them. Using this syntax, switch can have a value and thus be used as an expression. The new yield defines the outcome of switch in case you need { ... } blocks for more lengthy calculations.

Of course, you can still employ the old syntax if you don't need the new behavior.

Text Blocks

Multiline string literals always have been annoying in Java. Most developers used constructs like

```
String s = "This is the first line\n" +
    "This is the second line\n" +
    "This is the third line";
```

to enter multiline strings. A new feature allows for entering multiline strings more concisely:

```
String s = """
        This is the first line
        This is the second line
        This is the third line
    """;
```

One problem is left, however. If you write the last string to the console, you will see something like

```
This is the first line
This is the second line
This is the third line
```

with six spaces prepending each line.

Of course, you could write something like

```
String s = """
This is the first line
This is the second line
This is the third line
    """;
```

to avoid the unwanted indentation. This solution however breaks the indentation structure of your sources. As a remedy, the method `stripIndent()` was added to the String class:

```
String s = """
    This is the first line
    This is the second line
    This is the third line
""".stripIndent();
```

Output:

```
This is the first line
This is the second line
This is the third line
```

If you don't need the line breaks in the resulting string, you can escape the line endings using backslash characters:

```
String s = """
    This is the first line \
    Still inside the same line \
    Still inside the same line
""";
```

Just make sure each backslash is the last character of each input line.

Enhanced `instanceof` Operator

The usual `instanceof` operator has a new boilerplate code–avoiding variant that allows for immediately assigning the object in question to a correctly typed variable. So, instead of writing

```
Object s = "Hello";
...
if(s instanceof String) {
    String str = (String) s;
    if(str.equalsIgnoreCase("hello")) {
        System.out.println("Hello String!");
    }
}
```

you can more concisely write

```
Object s = "Hello";
...
if(s instanceof String str) {
    // use local variable 'str', which
    // is of type String
}
...
if(s instanceof String str &&
        str.equalsIgnoreCase("hello")) {
    System.out.println("Hello String!");
}
```

Value Classes: Records

Value objects are objects whose primary purpose is to hold a bunch of values. In traditional Java, you would write classes like

```
package jdk17;

import java.time.LocalDate;
import java.util.Objects;

public class Person {
    private String firstName;
    private String lastName;
    private LocalDate birthDay;
    private String socialSecurityNumber;

    @Override
    public int hashCode() {
        return Objects.hash(birthDay, firstName, lastName,
            socialSecurityNumber);
    }
```

```java
@Override
public boolean equals(Object obj) {
    if (this == obj)
        return true;
    if (obj == null)
        return false;
    if (getClass() != obj.getClass())
        return false;
    Person other = (Person) obj;
    return Objects.equals(birthDay, other.birthDay)
            && Objects.equals(firstName,
                    other.firstName)
            && Objects.equals(lastName, other.lastName)
            && Objects.equals(socialSecurityNumber,
                    other.socialSecurityNumber);
}

@Override
public String toString() {
    return "Person [firstName=" + firstName +
        ", lastName=" + lastName +
        ", birthDay=" + birthDay +
        ", socialSecurityNumber=" +
                socialSecurityNumber + "]";
}

public String getFirstName() {
    return firstName;
}

public void setFirstName(String firstName) {
    this.firstName = firstName;
}

public String getLastName() {
    return lastName;
}
```

```java
    public void setLastName(String lastName) {
        this.lastName = lastName;
    }

    public LocalDate getBirthDay() {
        return birthDay;
    }

    public void setBirthDay(LocalDate birthDay) {
        this.birthDay = birthDay;
    }

    public String getSocialSecurityNumber() {
        return socialSecurityNumber;
    }

    public void setSocialSecurityNumber(String
            socialSecurityNumber) {
        this.socialSecurityNumber =
            socialSecurityNumber;
    }
}
```

for a *person* value object. This class contains a lot of boilerplate code—actually, all information this class contains is given by its fields:

```java
private String firstName;
private String lastName;
private LocalDate birthDay;
private String socialSecurityNumber;
```

Everything else is derived (actually, I let my Eclipse IDE generate it).

To simplify using such value objects together with the restriction of immutability, in Java you can use *records*:

```java
// File Person.java
record Person(
    String firstName,
    String lastName,
```

```
    LocalDate birthDay,
    String socialSecurityNumber) {}
```

That is it! Everything else, getters, equals(), hashCode(), toString(), and a constructor, gets automatically provided. Setters are not defined, because records are immutable.

To use such records, you simply write

```
Person p1 = new Person(
    "John",
    "Smith",
    LocalDate.of(1997,Month.DECEMBER,30),
    "000-00-1234");
System.out.println("Name: " + p1.firstName + " " + p1.lastName);
```

Note that you just use the dot notation to access members; a getXXX() getter method is not provided.

The { } block in the record declaration can be used to impose constraints on parameters during construction. So you can write

```
// File Person.java
record Person(
    String firstName,
    String lastName,
    LocalDate birthDay,
    String socialSecurityNumber)
{
    public Person {
      if(lastName == null ||
            "".equals(lastName.trim()))
        throw new IllegalArgumentException(
          "lastName must not be empty");
    }
}
```

Sealed Classes

Sometimes, you want to limit the possible set of classes that can inherit from a given base class. You add the `sealed` keyword as a modifier and append `permits Class1, Class2, ...` to the class declaration, as in

```
// Circle.java
final class Circle extends Shape {
    ...
}

// Rectangle.java
final class Rectangle extends Shape {
    ...
}

// Shape.java
sealed class Shape
    permits Circle, Rectangle {
    // only Circle or Rectangle can
    // inherit from Shape
    ...
}
```

You usually use sealed classes if you need inheritance for classes inside a library, but you don't want user classes to inherit from library classes.

Summary

The rationale for chapters omitted if compared to the last editions, and a collection of useful or interesting novelties since JDK10, concluded the book.

APPENDIX

Solutions to the Exercises

This appendix contains solution hints to the exercises. Its intent is to provide some basic aid for working through the exercises and questions given at the end of each of the chapters, without going beyond the instruction level, and also no complete listings will be provided. This way, enough freedom will be given to you to extend the exercises to any depth suitable for your knowledge level and time schedule.

Exercises in Chapter 1

1. An annotation lets you associate (or annotate) metadata (or notes) to the program elements in a Java program. You declare annotations like

    ```
    [modifiers] @ interface <annotation-type-name> {
            // Annotation type body goes here
    }
    ```

2. Meta-annotation types are used to annotate other annotation type declarations.

3. Annotation types describe annotations, whereas annotation instances embody the annotation behavior of annotated elements.

4. No.

5. A marker annotation is used by annotation processing tools, which generate some kind of boilerplate code based on the marker annotation type. A marker annotation type does not declare any elements.

6. `@Override`

© Kishori Sharan, Peter Späth 2021
K. Sharan and P. Späth, *More Java 17*, https://doi.org/10.1007/978-1-4842-7135-3

7. Described in the text.

8. Proceed as described in the text.

9. No inheritance is allowed for annotations.

10. No void is allowed as a return type. No parameters are allowed. The meta-annotations `Target`, `Retention`, `Inherited`, `Documented`, `Repeatable`, and `Native` are described in the text.

11. Proceed as described in the text.

12. Proceed as described in the text.

13. Proceed as described in the text.

14. Gets described in the text.

15. Gets described in the text.

16. Proceed as described in the text.

17. Proceed as described in the text.

18. Try yourself.

19. Try yourself.

20. Proceed as described in the text.

Exercises in Chapter 2

1. Reflection is the ability of a program to inquire information about its own structure and execution state via introspection.

2. Consult the Java API documentation.

3. `Class` represents the structural information of any Java class.

4. Described in the text.

5. Described in the text.

6. Described in the text.

7. Described in the text and also present in the API documentation.

8. Described in the text and also present in the API documentation.

9. Described in the text and also present in the API documentation.

10. Described in the text and also present in the API documentation.

11. Try yourself (consult the module chapters in the documentation).

12. Described in the text and also present in the API documentation.

13. Described in the text and also present in the API documentation.

14. Try yourself.

15. Described in the text.

16. Make a guess, then try yourself.

17. Make a guess, then try yourself.

Exercises in Chapter 3

1. Described in the text.

2. Make a guess, then try yourself. (Described in the text, see section "Supertype-Subtype Relationship.")

3. Try yourself.

4. Described in the text.

5. Try yourself.

6. Try yourself.

7. Described in the text. Also, try yourself.

8. Type erasure.

Exercises in Chapter 4

1. Lambda expressions represent anonymous functions. They can be used as function literals for defining (instantiating) functional interfaces.

2. Described in the text.

3. Make a guess, then try yourself.

4. Make a guess, then try yourself (write *Function* = ... or *Operator*= ... to check).

5. Make a guess, then try yourself (write *Function* = ... or *Operator*= ... to check).

6. Described in the text.

7. Make a guess, then try yourself.

8. Make a guess, then try yourself.

9. Make a guess, then try yourself.

10. Make a guess, then try yourself.

11. Make a guess, then try yourself.

12. Try yourself.

13. Make a guess, then try yourself.

14. Make a guess, then try yourself.

15. Make a guess, then try yourself.

16. Make a guess, then try yourself.

17. Make a guess, then try yourself.

Exercises in Chapter 5

1. A thread is a unit of execution within a process. Threads can share memory, but they also have a non-shareable, local storage for variables.

2. Described in the text.

3. Described in the text.

4. Described in the text. Remember that new Thread() does *not* start a thread.

5.   Described in the text.

6.   Described in the text.

7.   Described in the text.

8.   Described in the text.

9.   Described in the text.

10. Described in the text.

11. Described in the text.

12. Described in the text.

13. Described in the text. Make a guess, then try yourself.

14. Described in the text.

15. Described in the text.

16. Described in the text.

17. Described in the text.

18. Described in the text.

19. Described in the text.

20. Described in the text.

21. Described in the text.

22. Described in the text. Also, consult the Java API documentation.

23. Described in the text.

24. Described in the text.

25. Described in the text.

26. Described in the text.

27. Described in the text.

28. Try yourself.

29. Try yourself.

30. Try yourself.

Exercises in Chapter 6

1. A stream is a sequence of data elements supporting sequential and parallel aggregate operations. An aggregate operation computes a single value from a collection of values.

2. In a collection, all items are present in memory, whereas in streams, items may be constructed or computed on the fly.

3. Answers: A: No. B: Internal. C: Functional. D: An infinite. E: Parallel. F: Terminal. G: May not.

4. Described in the text.

5. Try yourself.

6. Try yourself.

7. Try yourself.

8. Described in the text.

9. Described in the text.

10. Described in the text.

11. Described in the text.

12. Try yourself.

13. Described in the text.

14. Described in the text.

15. Described in the text. Try yourself.

16. Described in the text.

17. Try yourself.

18. Try yourself.

19. Try yourself.

20. Try yourself.

Exercises in Chapter 7

1. A service is a specific functionality provided by an application (or a library). Service interfaces are Java interfaces that describe services (without an implementation). Service providers implement and provision services.

2. Try yourself.

3. Try yourself.

4. Described in the text.

5. Described in the text.

6. Described in the text.

7. Described in the text.

8. Described in the text.

9. Described in the text.

10. Try yourself.

Exercises in Chapter 8

1. A network is a group of two or more computers or other types of electronic devices such as printers that are linked together with a goal to share information.

2. Described in the text.

3. A protocol is the set of rules to handle a specific network task.

4. Described in the text.

5. Described in the text.

6. Described in the text (first find out what the `0.0.0.0` address designates).

7. Described in the text.

8.   Described in the text.

9.   Described in the text.

10.   Proceed as described in the text.

11.   Described in the text.

12.   Described in the text.

13.   Described in the text.

14.   Described in the text.

15.   Described in the text.

16.   Described in the text.

Exercises in Chapter 9

1.   Java RMI enables a Java application to invoke a method on a Java object in a remote JVM.

2.   Described in the text.

3.   Try yourself.

4.   Described in the text.

5.   Described in the text.

6.   Try yourself. Proceed as described in the text.

7.   Described in the text.

8.   Described in the text.

9.   Described in the text.

10.   Described in the text.

11.   Described in the text.

12.   Described in the text.

13.   Described in the text.

Exercises in Chapter 10

1. A scripting language is a programming language that provides the ability to write scripts that are evaluated (or interpreted) by a runtime environment called a *script engine* (or an interpreter).

2. Described in the text.

3. Described in the text.

4. Described in the text.

5. Try yourself. Proceed as described in the text.

6. Try yourself. Proceed as described in the text.

7. Described in the text.

8. Try yourself. Proceed as described in the text.

9. Try yourself. Proceed as described in the text.

10. Described in the text.

Exercises in Chapter 11

1. The Process API consists of classes and interfaces that let you work with native processes in Java programs.

2. Described in the text.

3. Described in the text.

4. Described in the text.

5. Described in the text.

6. Described in the text.

7. Try yourself, as described in the text.

8. Described in the text.

9. Described in the text.

10. Try yourself.

Exercises in Chapter 12

1. JAR, JMOD, JIMAGE.

2. Described in the text.

3. Described in the text.

4. Described in the text.

5. Described in the text.

6. Described in the text.

7. Described in the text.

8. Described in the text.

9. Described in the text.

10. Described in the text.

11. Described in the text.

12. Make a guess, then try to find them yourself.

Exercises in Chapter 13

1. A custom runtime image consists of your application modules, bundled together with only those JDK modules that are actually needed to run the program.

2. Described in the text.

3. Described in the text.

4. Described in the text.

5. Described in the text.

6. Described in the text.

7. Described in the text.

8. Described in the text.

9. Described in the text.

10. Described in the text.

Index

A, B

Annotation
  array element, 24, 25
  class type, 19–21
  declaration, 6–10
  DefaultException class, 19
  definition, 1
  *e*mployee class, 2
  enum type, 21, 22
  error message, 4
  evolution, 66
  jdojo.annotation module, 1
  learning process, 1
  manager class, 2, 3
  marker elements, 28
  Merriam-Webster dictionary, 5
  meta types (*see* Meta-
    annotation types)
  module declarations, 58, 59
  monitoring tool, 28
  null reference, 25
  @Override annotation, 3
  package declaration, 58
  primitive data types, 17, 18
  process/source code level
    AbstractProcessor class, 68
    boilerplate code, 67
    command compiles, 67
    definition, 66
    getQualifiedName() method, 70
    jdojo.annotation.processor
     module, 72

    printMessage() method, 71
    process() method, 68, 69
    processors, 67
    source code, 68
    version processor, 68, 69, 72, 74, 75
  regular documentation, 5
  restrictions
    concatenate() method, 12
    default value, 14, 15
    getClass() method, 11
    method declarations, 11
    object class, 13
    return type, 12, 13
    throws clause, 12
    WrongVersion class, 10
  runtime access
    AccessAnnotation class, 62
    AccessAnnotationTest class, 63, 65
    AnnotatedElement interface, 59
    getAnnotationsByType()
     method, 65
    package-info.java file, 62
    program elements, 59
    repeatable type, 65
    test class, 60
    toString() method, 60
    version type, 61
  semantics, 6
  setSalary() method, 2, 4
  shorthand syntax, 25–28
  standard methods
    definition, 38

H

I

J, K

L

M

N, O

R

S

Printed in the United States
by Baker & Taylor Publisher Services